THE
DESIGN
OF
ADVERTISING

ROY PAUL
NELSON
University of Oregon
FIFTH
EDITION

THE
DESIGN
OF
ADVERTISING

wcb
Wm. C. Brown Publishers
Dubuque, Iowa

wcb group

Chairman of the Board/Wm. C. Brown
President and Chief Executive Officer/Mark C. Falb

wcb

Wm. C. Brown Publishers, College Division

President/Lawrence E. Cremer
Vice-President, Product Development/James L. Romig
Vice-President, Production and Design/David A. Corona
Vice-President, Cost Analyst/E. F. Jogerst
National Sales Manager/Bob McLaughlin
Marketing Manager/Marcia H. Stout
Director of Marketing Research/Craig S. Marty
Manager of Design/Marilyn A. Phelps
Production Editorial Manager/Eugenia M. Collins
Photo Research Manager/Mary M. Heller

Book Team
Senior Developmental Editor/Judith A. Clayton
Designer/Roy Paul Nelson
Production Editor/Kevin P. Campbell

By Roy Paul Nelson

The Design of Advertising
Publication Design
Editing the News
    (with Roy H. Copperud)
The Fourth Estate
    (with John L. Hulteng)
Articles and Features
Humorous Illustration and Cartooning
Comic Art and Caricature
Cartooning
Visits with 30 Magazine Art Directors
Fell's Guide to Commercial Art
    (with Byron Ferris)
Fell's Guide to the Art of Cartooning

To Willis L. Winter, Jr.

Contents

6
Applying the principles of design 124

7
Working with type 139

8
Working with art 166

9
What the designer should know about production 191

10
Working with color 212

16
Permanence in advertising design 336

17
Careers 360

Assignments 372

Glossary 383

Bibliography 392

Index 401

Preface

Like the previous editions of *The Design of Advertising,* this fifth edition serves journalism, business, art, and graphic design students interested in the creative side of advertising, especially its design aspects. It assumes that its student-readers have only modest backgrounds in art, typography, design, and production and so goes into these subjects in considerable detail. But it sets the stage, first, with information about advertising in general and with observations about the writing of copy. And while the book puts its emphasis on design, it reminds readers continually that what an ad says is what is really important and how good it looks is secondary to how well it sells.

This new edition retains the most useful illustrations from earlier editions and adds many more. It presents a chapter on careers for the first time and offers more examples of color printing. It updates, prunes, extends, rewrites, rearranges, and in some cases renames chapters in accordance with suggestions made by reviewers—users of the previous edition—picked by the publisher. For their helpful criticism, the author thanks especially Professors James L. Marra, Texas Tech, Lubbock; Keith F. Johnson, New Mexico State University, Las Cruces; and Michael W. Hataway, Hinds Junior College District, Raymond Campus, Raymond, Mississippi. He thanks, too, the hundreds of agency executives and art directors and clients from all over who gave permission to reproduce ads and supplied information about them. He also thanks Marie F. Nelson for her flawless typing and subtle editing; Professors Willis L. Winter, Jr., Willard Thompson, Jack Ewan, Steve Unwin, Bob Taber, Mary Stupp, Mary Fish, Bets Cole, Tom Rubick, Ted Schulte, John Crawford, Ken Metzler, and Max Wales, who teach or who have taught advertising and graphics courses at the University of Oregon, for their guidance and advice, and the editors and production people at Wm. C. Brown Publishers for their professionalism and patience.

THE
DESIGN
OF
ADVERTISING

1
The advertising world

"Without advertising, a terrible thing happens . . . ," says an institutional ad building a good name for the business. There is a pause in the script, and then this: "Nothing."

To those with something to sell, advertising can be that important. It can be that important, too, to those who only want to buy. A poster directs the traveler to a place to eat or spend the night. A direct-mail piece invites you to subscribe to a magazine. A classified ad announces a garage sale or a job opening.

But advertising can also set up false hopes and get people to buy things they don't need or shouldn't have. Like lawyers, ad makers can work for the unworthy as well as the worthy. Through advertising, every side gets a hearing. In the end, the reader or listener or viewer of the advertising renders the verdict.

Advertising sells not only products but also services and ideas. It can do a job for both profit and nonprofit organizations. Governmental agencies rank among the big users of advertising. In the words of *Time,* "Uncle Sam is becoming one of the greatest salesmen since P. T. Barnum."[1] *Advertising Age* reported that in 1981 the U.S. Government ranked twenty-sixth among all advertisers. Among government bodies doing advertising are the postal service, the armed forces, and Amtrak. One of the most widely recognized advertising symbols is the U.S. Forest Service's Smokey the Bear.

Advertising takes many forms and uses many approaches. People sometimes confuse advertising with publicity and public relations. Advertising differs from them in that it usually involves the *buying* of space or time. Publicity and public relations depend upon being noticed by the media and being incorporated into regular news and editorial columns or programs. The space and time they get, in that sense, is free.

Kinds of advertising

Looking at it from the standpoint of intended audiences, advertising falls into six categories:

1. *National advertising.* Another name for it is "brand-name advertising." The audience consists of potential customers for products sold in stores. The emphasis in the advertising is on the product rather than on where it may be purchased. Price usually is not mentioned. National advertising is found mostly in slick magazines and the broadcast media, although some of it appears in newspapers.

2. *Retail advertising.* Another name for it is "local advertising." Its purpose is to get potential customers into a particular store. Price is always mentioned. Retail advertising appears not only in newspapers but also on radio and television stations. Some retail advertising appears in regional editions of national magazines.

3. *Mail-order advertising.* Its practitioners prefer the term "direct-marketing advertising," but whatever it is called, it asks that the product be ordered by letter, coupon, or phone; the product arrives later by mail or some other carrier.

This kind of advertising combines elements of both national and retail

Ads can sell ideas and reactions as well as products. The Marists were not impressed with all the self-help books around in the early 1980s, especially those that promoted selfishness, and so took out a full-page ad in *Time* to protest—and to do a little recruiting. "Selfishness is not new; Jesus found it everywhere," starts out the copy. "What is new is the attempt to make it respectable, to celebrate it as a virtue, to package and sell it as a new-found cure-all." The Marists, according to this ad, follow "an older Book which is always new, which is never a fad."

Powerboat magazine, like other
magazines, promotes itself with T-shirts.
This one, designed by the magazine's
art director, John M. Whorrall, has a pop-
art feel with Superman-like lettering. The
lettering is a takeoff from the magazine's
regular logo, but it is close enough to be
recognized by readers.

advertising. It uses mostly magazines and direct mail, but it also makes use of radio and television. Orders are often taken on an 800 phone number, charged to credit cards, and sent out by United Parcel Service. *Time* estimates that UPS handles about 90 percent of "mail order" packages.

Mail-order advertising is sponsored by retailers not readily accessible to customers.

An appeal of mail order is that the customer has already paid for the item by the time it arrives. Getting it is like receiving a gift. And everybody, it seems, likes getting something through the mail. Some people do not like going out to shop.

Another appeal of mail order is that, because selling costs are low, prices listed in a catalog can be lower than prices at the store.

4. *Trade advertising.* The audience for this kind of advertising consists of retailers, wholesalers, or brokers. They are "customers," too—customers for products which they in turn sell to others. Instead of stressing

Yellow Pages advertising, despite its confined space, can take on a classy look, too. Deborah Kadas designed this all-centered ad for Ron Federspiel, D.D.S., Corvallis, Oregon. Linda Ahlers wrote the copy. The agency was Attenzione! (The exclamation mark is part of the agency title.)

This ad is designed to appeal to women who are heads of households. It appeared in *Black Enterprise*. The only color (red) appeared as the working part of the umbrella, a symbol of protection promoted by the Travelers Insurance Company. Mike Tesch art directed; Tom Messner wrote the copy. Ally & Gargano, New York, was the agency.

There are people more famous we insure. But none more important.

In this country, there are 7.7 million women who are sole heads of household. Their need for life insurance has always been obvious.

Of course, there are also millions of married working women who are joint heads of household. It's only been in recent years that the economic value of the housewife or the working mother has even been talked about.

The Travelers and its independent agents, though, have not been Jane-come-latelies in life insurance for women. As evidenced by the fact we were one of the first major companies to offer lower life insurance rates for women.

To get in touch with an independent Travelers agent, check your local Yellow Pages. They are there to help you; whether or not you even need insurance.

Women don't need any more help from insurance companies than men. Just the same help.

THE TRAVELERS

We offer life, health, auto, and homeowners insurance, and mutual funds and variable annuities for individuals, and virtually all forms of insurance for businesses. The Travelers Insurance Company, The Travelers Indemnity Company, Travelers Equities Sales Inc., and other Affiliated Companies of The Travelers Corporation, Hartford, Connecticut 06115.

The world is full of guarantees, no two alike. As a rule, the more words they contain, the more their protection is limited. The Lands' End guarantee has always been an unconditional one. It reads:

"If you are not completely satisfied with any item you buy from us, at any time during your use of it, return it and we will refund your full purchase price."

We mean every word of it. Whatever. Whenever. Always. But to make sure this is perfectly clear, we've decided to simplify it further.

GUARANTEED. PERIOD.

of fine wool and cotton sweaters, Oxford button-down shirts, traditional dress clothing, snow wear, deck wear, original Lands' End soft luggage and a multitude of other quality goods from around the world.

☐ **Please send free catalog.**
Lands' End   Dept. G-16
Dodgeville, WI 53533

Name _____

Address _____

City _____

State _____ Zip _____

Or call Toll-free:
800-356-4444
(Except Alaska and Hawaii call 608-935-2788)

A Lands' End ad puts the headline inside a box (making a certificate of it) and below the copy because the headline sums up rather than starts out the copy. This is a good way to dramatize the fact that the mail-order company offers an unconditional guarantee. Sam Fink was art director, Dick Anderson designer, Carl Volmer copywriter; the agency was Needham, Harper & Steers.

the benefits of the product, this kind of advertising stresses the profits that can be made from stocking and selling it.

A maker of lawn mowers and other power equipment runs this headline on a full-page, full-color ad showing various models: "Snapper. Engineered for Profit." The headline and copy are designed to convince retailers—readers of *Farm Store Merchandising,* where the ad appears—to stock the Snapper line. If anything, the ad, stressing "profit opportunities," is the antithesis of what an ad directed to ordinary customers would be.

5. *Industrial advertising.* In buying raw materials and machines to use in their manufacturing processes, manufacturers become customers, too.

Early ads tended to crowd a lot of type and art into limited space. But an occasional ad like the one for Nestor Cigarettes (a 1902 issue of *Puck*) was more posterlike.

The history of graphic design is the history of revivals. The 1980s popularity of big-opening and big-closing letters, for instance, traces itself back at least to the 1880s, when this retail ad appeared in the *Sporting News*. (Notice the handling of "Saddlery.")

HEIDEMAN - BENOIST
S-A-D-D-L-E-R-**Y**
COMPANY.
419 N. SIXTH ST.,
ST. LOUIS, MO.
TURF GOODS
OF EVERY DESCRIPTION.
Sweat Collars, Suits, Boots, Spurs, Etc.
IMPORTED and OUR OWN MAKE Saddles.
Have on hand a line of all the different makes in the country of Boots and other Goods.

In the 1930s and 1940s designers often relied on overlaps to bring various elements together. In this newspaper ad for Sunkist (1945), a pattern of oranges overlaps a grocer; a black rectangle overlaps the oranges; a white rectangle for copy overlaps the black rectangle; an orange slice and glass overlap the white rectangle; a small black rectangle overlaps the orange slice and glass.

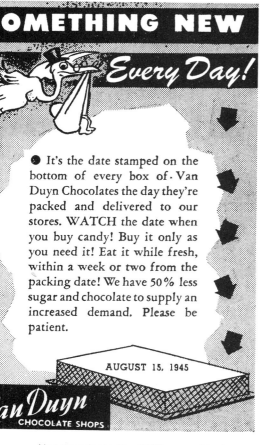

Also popular in the 1940s were black bars into which headlines could be reversed, lots of arrows, black dots in front of paragraphs, and mortises cut in irregular shapes.

Many early ads, and later ads, too, promised relief from symptoms if not recovery from diseases. An ad from the November 1942 issue of *The Boilermakers Journal* suggests that men with prostate problems could get "welcome relief" with vibrations from the rather formidable device that is pictured.

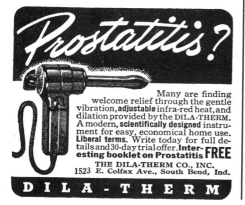

The audiences for both trade and industrial advertising are reached, in the main, through trade magazines and direct-mail advertising (not to be confused with mail-order advertising).

6. *Professional advertising.* This is advertising directed to physicians, architects, and others who advise people what to buy. Like national advertising, it stresses benefits to the user. Media used include professional or trade magazines and direct mail.

In recent years, professional people themselves, reluctantly in some cases, have engaged in advertising, if no more than to announce the opening of their offices. But a dentist in Portland, Philip J. Gross, used big type to announce that "Your Time Is Valuable Too! $10.00 Per Hour." The copy talked about the annoyance people feel in a waiting room and promised $10 an hour, "or any fraction thereof," when patients had to wait beyond their appointed time. The money was to be subtracted from the patients' bills. "Make your time even more worthwhile. Call for an appointment today."

More elaborate design ideas and expensive production techniques are employed in national, industrial, and professional advertising than in the other types. This is because audiences are larger (or more exclusive), space or time is more expensive, and, generally, stakes are higher.

Institutional advertising

The primary purpose of advertising is to sell products or services. But sometimes it is designed to do something else: to win an audience over to a point of view. We call such advertising *institutional* or *corporate advertising.* It can be national or local; it can address itself to any kind of audience; it can use any medium. In its design it often resembles editorial matter in the newspapers and magazines. An obvious example of institutional advertising is a full-page, mostly copy ad in the Sunday *New York Times* urging some political action or appealing for funds.

Institutional advertising often is prepared by public relations rather than advertising people. Advertising becomes but one of many tools available to public relations people. "The beauty of advertising [to do a PR job] is that it's the one form of communication which can't be edited [by outsiders]," says Richard Pruitt, executive creative director of Ogilvy & Mather, Hong Kong. "It can be as big as you can buy. You can run it as often as you can afford. You can tell your side of the story without interruptions. I believe that every corporation has a right—and in some cases a responsibility—to tell its side of the story."[2]

Companies or organizations that feel the sting of media criticism often turn to institutional advertising to tell their sides of stories. The tobacco industry has fought hard to discount reports of the connection between smoking and disease. Liquor companies take out ads to preach moderation. In an institutional ad, Seagram, the whiskey maker, shows through demonstration how drinking can affect one's handwriting. "I can drive when I drink" is written out five times, first before drinking, then after two drinks, four, five, and seven. The handwriting deteriorates more each time. The advertiser concludes: "When you drink too much you can't handle a car. You can't even handle a pen."

The Mormon Church recently spent $12 million on an advertising campaign in *Reader's Digest* to counter its critics and point out Mormon devotion to family and traditional values.[3]

Institutional advertising often is an exercise in self-praise. It attempts to build a favorable image for its sponsor.

When Wells Fargo Bank in California merged with American Trust Company, company officials were ready to go with the name American Trust, but designer Walter Landor convinced them that Wells Fargo would give them a more distinct image as the bank of the West. With an easily recognized symbol—a stage coach encased in a diamond shape—and some skillful advertising infused with an Old West flavor, the bank tends to appeal to newcomers, who pick it simply because it seems to come with the territory.

Image is particularly important among organizations whose products or services are relatively uniform.

If an attempt to sell a product creeps into institutional advertising, it does so noiselessly. A direct-mail piece McDonnell Douglas offers to travel agents to make available to their customers (there is a place on the back panel where agents can stamp their names) tells people how to tell one jetliner from another. *A Plane-Watcher's Guide to the World's Great Jetliners* shows them all, with "objective" descriptions under each. The DC–9 is described as "Simple and dependable, adaptable and comfortable . . . flown by more than forty airlines around the world." Descriptions of non-McDonnell Douglas planes in this folder tend to deal only with appearances. In a friendly gesture at the end, the folder says, after its listing of "Tips for Air Travelers," that "above all, [you should] talk with your travel agent. That's the best source of good advice on the whole world of flying!"

But there is no overt attempt to sell McDonnell Douglas planes to anyone (patrons of travel bureaus are not likely buyers) or even to convince people they should buy tickets on airlines using McDonnell Douglas planes.

Institutional advertising can use the same approaches and techniques that product-oriented advertising uses. ". . . Just as advertising disciplines and techniques are transferable in commercial practice, they are also transferable to social marketing activities," says William Weilbacher in a book called *Advertising*. "If the use of professional advertising counsel is inhibited in social marketing, it is often because the surface dissim-

Using what Dick Pruitt in Hong Kong calls a "classic Chinese editorial layout," Ogilvy & Mather created this institutional ad, one of a series, to tell China Light & Power's side of the story after consumer groups had circulated a petition saying, "If you want your electric bill to remain low, sign this." Note the box comparing electric rates in Asian countries. Both English and Chinese versions were designed, with the English format stemming from the Chinese. Clifford Shun-Wah art directed; Selina Kan was the Chinese copywriter. Pruitt was creative director and wrote the English copy.

The print media often allow similar advertisers to concentrate on special pages. The challenge, then, is for advertisers to make their ads stand out from others. Some do it with good design. For its ad on a newspaper church page, Faith Center uses a rounded-corner box that takes a turn at the bottom right into both Christian and peace symbolism. The logo falls outside the box. The material inside is set flush right against an axis that leads down to the symbols.

What's a fair price for electricity?

One of the problems in our business is that people don't really know how much electricity should cost.

You can't shop around your neighbourhood and compare electricity prices; but you can look around Asia and compare.

Here's what electricity costs in comparable Asian countries and cities.

Compared with all the Asian countries that answered our inquiry, China Light & Power's tariffs are among the lowest.

At China Light & Power we have worked hard to keep the cost of electricity down. We have invested in long-term projects such as coal-fired generating plant at Castle Peak. Coal costs about half as much as oil. Two

huge generators — using coal — are now in operation. Two more will go into operation during the next two years.

The record shows the new plant to be a wise decision. The two in operation are already saving millions of dollars everyday on fuel costs.

These fuel savings are passed directly and immediately back to our customers.

That's why the per unit cost of electricity for all of our customers has actually been coming down. Fuel savings have more than offset the increase in basic tariff of January, 1983.

Made fresh daily

Looking at prices around Asia, it almost makes us wish we could package electricity and export it. At our prices, we could certainly find many buyers. Of course that's impossible. No one has yet succeeded in storing and packaging electricity on a large scale. It must be generated continuously — and sold "fresh" everyday.

More importantly, our job is to serve Hong Kong. To make sure there is always plenty of fresh electricity when our customers need it.

At a fair price.

HOW MUCH DOES ELECTRICITY COST IN ASIA				
Tariff Comparison - Charge Per Unit* - May 31, 1983				
Place/ Category**	(1) Domestic HK¢/Unit	(2) Commercial HK¢/Unit	(3) Small Industrial HK¢/Unit	(4) Large Industrial HK¢/Unit
China Light & Power	58.5	55.9	50.2	41.0
Japan, Tokyo	72.6	102.9	65.4	60.3
Korea	75.2	144.2	63.3	50.7
Malaysia	65.9	78.5	72.2	57.8
Philippines, Manila	58.3	73.8	68.7	64.2
Singapore	64.6	73.2	55.1	48.6
Taiwan	45.6	80.1	41.6	35.2
Thailand	48.5	66.6	55.7	50.4

(1) Based on 150 units per month.
(2) Based on 5,000 units per month.
(3) Based on 120,000 units per month at a load factor of 300 units per kVA.
(4) Based on 4.6 million units per month at a load factor of 550 units per kVA.

* Charge per unit shown above incorporates fuel clause, if any, and exchange rates applicable are as at May 31, 1983.
** Information has not yet been received from Jakarta, Indonesia.

China Light & Power
Believing and Investing in Tomorrow

ilarities of social and commercial problems inhibit a recognition that marketing is marketing, no matter what its métier."[4]

When the Oregon legislature in 1983 voted against allowing Coors to sell its beer in the state, the company took out big newspaper ads to say, "We Lost. You Lost." The ad pointed out that Coors lost out in the voting not because it is unpasteurized (Oregon law demands that beer sold there be pasteurized) but because "The Senate has been under substantial pressure from a special interest group which stands to benefit from keeping our product off the market in Oregon." It was a hard-hitting ad, and it didn't mention that during the debate one legislator, speaking against Coors, a nonunion company, said it shouldn't be allowed to sell beer in the state because of the ultraconservative views of the owners.

Related to institutional advertising is *advocacy advertising*. The difference is that in advocacy advertising the sponsor pushes a point of view that may have nothing to do with selling the product or building an image. ". . . Corporations have taken to advocacy advertising because they feel they are not getting a fair shake from what they believe to be a generally hostile press; and because they are convinced that the business world can make significant contributions to public debate on issues of great importance—energy, nuclear power, conservation, environment, taxation, and free enterprise, among others," says Professor Robert Shayon of the University of Pennsylvania Annenberg School of Communications.[5]

Some state legislatures have drafted laws to restrict this kind of advertising. And the Internal Revenue Service does not regard the advertising as a necessary business expense, although there is some difficulty in distinguishing between advocacy advertising and institutional advertising, which *is* tax deductible.

Where advertising originates

Advertising can originate in the advertising department of the advertiser, in the advertising department of the medium that carries the advertising, or in an advertising agency.

An example of a government-sponsored ad. A two-pager, it features basically same-size silhouetted photographs. The ad is careful to show women as well as men, members of minority groups as well as nonminority people. That the several subheads vary in the number of lines does not hurt the design. It is better to say exactly what you want to say than to prune headline or subhead copy to fit some pattern.

A YEAR-BY-YEAR LOOK AT WHAT ARMY ROTC ADDS TO YOUR COLLEGE EDUCATION.

ARMY ROTC: A COLLEGE PROGRAM THAT TEACHES LEADERSHIP.

Army ROTC is a program that helps you earn a 2nd Lieutenant's commission at the same time you earn your regular college degree.

So regardless of your chosen major, add Army ROTC, and you'll add leadership and management training to your college education.

Training that develops you into a leader of people as well as a manager of money and resources.

Training that also provides you with up to $1,000 a year for your last two years of ROTC.

The Army ROTC Four-Year Program is divided into two two-year courses: the Basic Course and the Advanced Course.

What's more, during your first and second year, you incur no military obligation.

So if you're starting college soon (or if you're already enrolled), take a closer look at what Army ROTC will add to your college experience.

ARMY ROTC SCHOLARSHIPS.

Each year, Army ROTC awards hundreds of full-tuition, four-year scholarships, which can be used at 276 colleges and universities across the country. To win one, you must apply by December of your senior year of high school.

But even after you enroll in college, you can apply for either a three- or two-year Army ROTC scholarship. Just contact the Professor of Military Science on any campus hosting Army ROTC. (Another thing. All ROTC scholarships come with a four-year active duty obligation after graduation.)

YOUR FRESHMAN-SOPHOMORE YEARS: THE START OF TWO EDUCATIONS.

The Army ROTC Basic Course begins now. During the week, along with your other courses, you'll attend Army ROTC classes. Your ROTC subjects will include military history; management principles and leadership development; and military customs, courtesy, and discipline. Subjects that will lay the foundation for you to become an Army officer.

ONCE A SEMESTER, TRY SOMETHING CHALLENGING.

In Army ROTC, not all of your training takes place in the classroom. Some of it takes place in the field, too. Where you'll do something challenging. Like shooting the rapids. Or rappelling a cliff. Or finding your way through unfamiliar terrain, with nothing but a map and compass to guide you. These are just a few of the challenging field activities you'll enjoy doing in Army ROTC.

YOUR JUNIOR-SENIOR YEARS: EARN UP TO $1,000 A YEAR.

In the Advanced Course, which is usually taken in the last two years of college, your studies will include advanced management and leadership techniques. You'll earn while you learn, too. Up to $1,000 a year for your last two years of ROTC.

During the summer between your junior and senior years, you'll attend our six-week Advanced Camp. Here, you'll practice in the field the leadership principles you've learned in the classroom.

You'll be in command at least once during Advanced Camp. And you'll be responsible for leading other ROTC cadets through a number of challenging situations. The kind that will build your stamina and develop your self-confidence.

And attending our Advanced Camp doesn't cost you anything. In fact, you'll be paid for the six weeks you're away.

TAKE ARMY ROTC AND SERVE PART TIME WITH THE ARMY RESERVE OR ARMY NATIONAL GUARD.

Now you can choose to serve on part-time duty as a 2nd Lieutenant with your nearest Army Reserve or Army National Guard unit, wherever you plan to locate after college.

It's a good chance to get started on your civilian career while you also enjoy a nice extra income of over $1600 a year for the 16 hours a month (usually a weekend) and two weeks annual training that you serve with your unit.

GRADUATION: TWO BIG DAYS.

Army ROTC makes graduation day two big days in one. Because it's the day you receive your commission as a second lieutenant in today's Army—which also includes the Army Reserve and Army National Guard.

And it's the day you receive a college degree in your chosen major.

ARMY ROTC: IT'S WORTH A LOT TO YOU IN THE MILITARY. AND OUT.

More than one national leader or captain of industry started out as an Army ROTC lieutenant. So when we say your ROTC training can help with your career, we mean it. In the military. And out. Over 70% of the commissioned second lieutenants in the active Army are ROTC graduates.

On the other hand, if you choose a civilian career, your training will give you the edge over the competition, because it tells an employer you're bringing more than just enthusiasm to the job. You're bringing solid experience in managing people, money, and supplies. And this will make you a valuable commodity in today's job market.

That's a brief look at the Army ROTC Four-Year Program. Year by year. Step by step. From beginning to end.

If you'd like an even closer look at what Army ROTC adds to your college education, write: Army ROTC, P.O. Box 7000, Department F-C, Larchmont, New York 10538.

ARMY ROTC. LEARN WHAT IT TAKES TO LEAD.

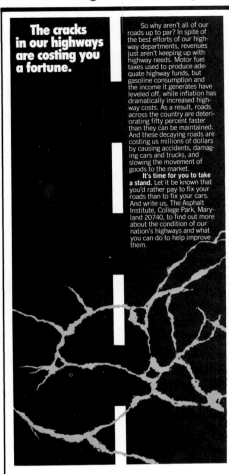

The cracks in our highways are costing you a fortune.

So why aren't all of our roads up to par? In spite of the best efforts of our highway departments, revenues just aren't keeping up with highway needs. Motor fuel taxes used to produce adequate highway funds, but gasoline consumption and the income it generates have leveled off, while inflation has dramatically increased highway costs. As a result, roads across the country are deteriorating fifty percent faster than they can be maintained. And these decaying roads are costing us millions of dollars by causing accidents, damaging cars and trucks, and slowing the movement of goods to the market.

It's time for you to take a stand. Let it be known that you'd rather pay to fix your roads than to fix your cars. And write us, The Asphalt Institute, College Park, Maryland 20740, to find out more about the condition of our nation's highways and what you can do to help improve them.

Announcing the breakup of our nation's highway system.

Our roads are deteriorating fifty percent faster than they can be maintained because we can't take proper care of them. Motor fuel tax revenues are down, and construction and maintenance costs continue to climb with inflation. The results are costing us millions of dollars in increased vehicle repairs, transportation slowdowns, energy waste, injuries . . . and deaths.

If we don't keep pace with our road maintenance problems today, we could face a major transportation breakdown tomorrow. Repairing our roads now would be far cheaper than waiting. This is not just because of inflationary pressures but because roads not properly maintained now will deteriorate to the point of needing replacement in the future. And replacement costs dramatically exceed repair costs.

It's time for you to take a stand. Our country needs to take a fresh look at highway funding to make sure our road system gets the money it desperately needs. This is also an important time for you to express your opinion on road upkeep. For all the facts and figures, write us at The Asphalt Institute, Dept. A, College Park, Maryland 20740.

These ads appeared in a series sponsored by The Asphalt Institute, College Park, Maryland. The basic design remained the same, with texture changes occurring at the bottoms. The strong, black, abstract art made an excellent field for use in reversing the sans serif headlines and body copy. Rhonda Serkes designed the ads; John Hyman wrote the copy. The agency was VanSant, Dugdale & Co.

In situations where numerous deadlines and copy changes take place, as with a large department store, a full advertising department is necessary. An outside agency may not be flexible enough or accessible enough. In situations where the advertiser is not big enough to support an advertising department, as with a small, locally owned specialty store, the medium—the newspaper or broadcast station—often will produce the advertising. The fee for such service may be built into the space or time rates.

National advertisers, of course, use advertising agencies, which not only create the advertising but also place it with the media. Even if a national advertiser has an agency, it may have a department, too, to handle some of the advertising, such as direct mail, and to coordinate the agency's efforts. A number of large national advertisers have established "in-house" agencies to create and place their advertising. An in-house agency would be more elaborate and offer more services than an advertising department.

Some small, local advertisers use agencies, too. Such advertisers are likely to pay a monthly fee for the agency's services. But typically an agency's compensation comes largely from commissions earned on advertising placed with various media. A medium charges the agency a rate that is 15 percent less than the stated rate for time or space; the agency in turn bills the client the full rate.

The commission system has its critics. There is the temptation for the agency to recommend expensive media simply because, with 15 percent of the cost going to the agency, the agency makes more money. A television commercial designed for repeated network showing brings more revenue to an agency than, say, an ad in a magazine. Ted Morgan, in a

Silva Compass of Binghamton, New York, goes to a stark and startling headline to get readers inside a broadside that discusses "Orienteering: The Sport with a Sense of Direction." This opening panel shows reverse letters on black; elsewhere the well-illustrated broadside features full-color art and photography. Dean Erickson designed; Pat Hanlon wrote the copy. The agency was Wm. L. Baxter Advertising, Inc.

New York Times Magazine article, imagines the following exchange taking place in an advertising agency:

Account supervisor: "Last year I raised my client's sales by 10 percent. I took them out of TV and put them into print at a saving of 50 percent in their ad budget."

Agency boss: "That's marvelous. You're fired."[6]

Not all advertising is commissionable. Direct mail, for instance, is not. No outside medium is involved. Some large national advertisers have worked out fee systems with their agencies to replace the commission system for all their advertising.

U.S. advertising agencies in 1982 achieved billings close to $40 billion. Young & Rubicam, Ted Bates Worldwide, J. Walter Thompson, Ogilvy & Mather, and McCann-Erickson rank among the biggest agencies in the country.

Agencies face much shifting of clients, as clients become restless and dissatisfied with how business is going. To name one client: Gallo, the winemaker, went through thirty agencies in thirty years.

Often an agency executive leaves to start a new agency, and some clients may go along. Sometimes an agency resigns an account because it is no longer profitable or because the agency finds the client's people hard to work with. Agencies develop personalities. Some become known as "creative shops." Others are known for the solid research that goes into their campaigns. By studying looks and content, people in the business often are able to tell which agency created an ad.

The images agencies develop for themselves—and the images are amplified in agency-sponsored ads in the advertising trade press asking for more business—are not necessarily deserved. And an agency known for its creativity might also be strong in research and marketing strategy. Good advertising results from both creative and research efforts.

Media of advertising

To reach their audiences, advertisers use a wide variety of media: newspapers (still the number-one medium in dollars spent), television, radio, magazines, outdoor and transportation posters, point-of-purchase materials (displays where customers do their buying), and direct-mail (leaflets, folders, booklets, brochures, and so on), and short films for showing in theaters. The package the product comes in is a form of advertising. When displayed, the product also is a form of advertising.

Advertisers write their names in smoke in the sky, paint them on blimps, sew them onto shirt and pants pockets and on the fronts or sides of swimming suits, spell them out in giant raised letters on the backs of pickups and on tires. An enterprising adman, Charles Bird, in Los Angeles in 1972 established Beetleboards of America, a medium consisting of Volkswagen owners willing to allow their cars to be covered completely with ads and slogans.

In the mid-1970s the lowly T-shirt and other items of clothing appeared to be America's most popular advertising medium. "Millions of young Americans—who love to parade as antibusiness snobs—are doing their parading dressed in Budweiser hats, Warner Bros. T-shirts, Olympia beer bikinis—and even *Jaws* underwear," observed an amused *Forbes* magazine. Some companies were in it for the money, but only some. Product makers like Coca-Cola and the cigarette companies just tried to break even; the profit came indirectly through all the free advertising they got from the walking, talking billboards.

Advertisers, unless restricted by law, place their messages anywhere they find blank space or an intermission in time.

The best advertising may be the showing of a product in the course of a regular movie or TV program. The showing often is neither innocent nor accidental; it is planned. It is planned by organizations—"product placers"—like Associated Film Promotions. In 1983 AFP was serving seventy clients with 450 brand names.

Fees paid by clients, who are guaranteed a certain number of showings, are said to be close to what regular commercials would cost, if you consider the audiences. Product placers succeed because they are quickly available to film directors to supply whatever props might be needed. The organizations often see scripts before filming begins and look for ways to work in their products.

It used to be that Hollywood hid brands or insisted on generic labels, but modern audiences apparently want more realism. It was inevitable that deals then would be made. "Today's movies don't just depict brand names," one writer has noted, "they tout them."[7]

Some media exist solely to serve narrow or specialized audiences. For instance, many radio stations and newspapers and about twenty magazines serve specifically the black population in this country. Another group of media serve the Spanish-speaking population. It is hard to think of any group that doesn't have its own media.

Hollywood released a series of films dealing with homosexuality in 1982 and launched separate advertising campaigns in specialized media to reach straight and homosexual audiences. One ad for *Making Love* showed the stars of the movie in a conventional pose; another ad (for homosexual media) showed a male star with his hand on the bare chest of a male co-star.

Advertisers have discovered that homosexuals form a well-educated, highly paid group that responds well to sales messages, especially for luxury items and leisure services. The publisher of *The Advocate,* a magazine for homosexuals, has called his readers a "recession-proof market."[8]

Although they see homosexuals as a good market, many advertisers would rather keep their advertisements in regular media than put them in magazines for homosexuals. The challenge often is to come up with an appeal to that specialized audience that does not turn off the straight audience. Some Calvin Klein jeans advertisements, for example, have been seen as "mainstream messages aimed at the homosexual male."[9]

Agencies tend to develop media mixes for their clients in order to reach the greatest number of good prospects at the lowest cost; but sometimes concentrating on one medium gives the advertiser the most for the money spent. Media tend to build specific audiences, and such audiences can be particularly responsive to the appeal of particular products. Some companies believe that, as a general rule, 80 percent of their output is consumed by 20 percent of their customers.[10]

Advertising's job

All the advertising textbooks tell us an ad has several jobs to do:

1. attract attention to itself;

2. enlist reader interest;

3. create desire—or capitalize on existing desire—for the product or service being advertised;

4. persuade readers to buy the products or services or accept the ideas being advanced;

5. show readers how and where they can buy the products or services or direct readers to specific courses of action.

Art and headline combine to attract attention to an ad. The headline generally states the ad's theme. Readers taking in only these two parts of the ad can at least get the gist of the message. If the art and headline combine to do their job properly, they lure readers into the copy.

It is not always necesary to go to drawings or paintings to portray the unreal. Photography often can do the job. And sometimes it can do the job better. Putting a sign like this into a scene before it is photographed is easy enough. Or it is possible to superimpose a sign like this over a photograph after it has been taken. This ad effectively brings home the point that the arts *do* need support over and above any admission fees that may be charged. Compton Advertising created it, one in a series, for the Business Committee for the Arts, Inc. Art director and designer: Rupert R. Witalis. Copywriter: John D. Burke.

The next great advance in school noise control.

Republic steel
Industrial Products

To sell school principals and college administrators on the quietness of its Low Decibel Lockers for school use, Republic Steel's Industrial Products Division offers to send out a cassette tape or a 45 rpm record containing "all the noise . . . [the] new locker doesn't make." All the official has to do is fill out the coupon. The full-color ad ran in *Nation's Schools & Colleges*. Art director: Jack Conyers. Copywriter: Robert Rosser. Agency: Meldrum & Fewsmith, Cleveland.

The lead sentence provides a bridge between the headline and the remainder of the copy. If the bridge spans too wide a gulf, the ad may need a second "deck" or "bank"—a headline between the main headline and the copy block.

The bulk of the copy elaborates on the promise of the theme and works to prove its case. In some cases the copy uses logic or rationalization. A good example of the latter is a slogan of used-car dealers: "Everybody drives a used car." That is pretty hard to refute.

The ending calls for action of some sort. In mail-order advertising, the ending often includes a coupon, to make the action as effortless as possible.

The call for action in an ad should be clear enough, but it need not be direct. Erwin Wasey, Ruthrauff & Ryan came up with an ad for Cheese of Holland showing a photograph of a cut-into ball of Edam cheese. The copy read:

> Pâté costs more than liverwurst.
> Bisque costs more than soup.
> Stroganoff costs more than stew.
> This cheese costs more than other Edam.
>
> Life is short.

Advertisers—at least those who are sure of their reputations—show increasing willingness to use understatement in their advertising. "For four generations we've been making medicines as if people's lives depended on them," says the Eli Lilly Company in its advertising.

Here is the entire copy block for a national newspaper ad for Mercedes-Benz showing a happy family riding in a car along a boulevard (there was no headline):

First paragraph: "It's been said that a house is the most important investment a man will ever make."

Second paragraph: "We're not so sure."

In each of these examples there is an implicit assumption that the reader gets the message and knows what to do about it.

The "new advertising"

In the 1960s a number of magazines (*Esquire* among them), a few newspapers, and the underground press allowed writers to put more of themselves into their writings. Objectivity, hardly obtainable in a pure state anyway, gave way to subjectivity, in which the writer expressed personal feelings rather than just those of the persons interviewed. Although the copy was journalism (nonfiction), it employed all the literary devices of fiction. In many cases the reader found it difficult to separate fact from fiction. Moreover, some writers were not content to merely write; they became *participants* in the news as well. The "new journalism" was born.

Just as we have a "new journalism," we also have a "new advertising." Not that the creators of advertising switched from an objective to a subjective approach. Advertising never did attempt to be objective. But advertising people became a little less obvious in their sales pitches. They became more sophisticated.

Robert Glatzer, an ex-advertising man, dates the "new advertising" from 1949 with the founding of Hewitt, Ogilvy, Benson & Mather (now Ogilvy & Mather International) and Doyle Dane Bernbach and to two men associated with these agencies: David Ogilvy and the late William Bernbach. "Realizing that a good advertisement must have some intrinsic value, some virtue of its own, they maintained that if an advertisement served as nothing more than a flack for the product, puffing it up rather than dealing with it, it would never be good at selling that product. . . . They removed the exclamation point from advertising."[11]

A newer "new advertising" agency is Ally & Gargano, which creates the admirable Federal Express commercials, among others. One of the Federal Express commercials starred the fast-talking John Moschitta. "I know it's perfect Peter that's why I picked Pittsburgh Pittsburgh's perfect Peter May I call you Pete." Amil Gargano, chief executive, says the agency has no fear of going over peoples' heads with its humorous and sophisticated approaches.

Unfortunately, not all of the users of "new advertising" approaches can match the originators either in their creativity or their believability. Imitation turns to caricature. A frantic hunt appears to be underway for new and shocking ways to present each advertising message.

Complaints against advertising

The complaints against advertising center not only on its manipulative powers but also on its tendency to build and perpetuate stereotypes. Every kind of pressure group seems concerned about its image as presented in the ads. Some of the demands made by pressure groups become excessive. Alka-Seltzer found it necessary to withdraw its amusing "Mamma Mia, That'sa Some Spicy Meatball" commercial because of complaints from the Italian Civil Rights League. Pressure from another group forced the "Frito Bandito" animated cartoon character out of his selling job.

Probably the most telling pressure comes from the feminist movement, which does not like the depiction of women as brainless housewives concerned only with the taste of the coffee they serve or the power of the laundry detergents they use. Nor do feminists approve of the depiction of women as mere sex objects.[12]

Feminist activities against advertising range from confrontations with the people who prepare advertising (and even revolts within agencies) to the defacing of subway ads with stickers saying "This ad insults women." Women Against Pornography gave a "Plastic Pig" award to Maidenform in 1982 for advertising that put a woman in lingerie playing the role of a doctor checking a patient's pulse. The company has since changed its advertising approach, putting its necessarily scantily clad women in more normal settings.

Women have been outraged, especially, by album cover art and album advertising. The *Jump on It* Montrose album, for instance, showed a closeup of a woman's covered crotch. The Rolling Stones' *Black and Blue* album was advertised with a bruised and bound woman saying, "I'm black and blue from Rolling Stones, and I love it." Advertising sometimes can't match a product in tastelessness. American Multiple Industries, Northridge, California, brought out an X-rated videogame called "Custer's Revenge" in 1982. It was a game in which the general rapes an Indian woman. The advertising said that "When you score, you score."

One group working against this kind of thing is Women Against Violence Against Women, which has, among other activities, organized boycotts against record companies.

To meet objections from militant feminists as well as nonmilitant people, agencies in the 1970s began showing women in previously unfamiliar roles. Barbara Lippert in *Adweek* traced the change to 1973 when Charlie fragrance in its ads began showing a "confident young model in a pantsuit, striding resolutely alone." Later women in commercials for other products began performing daring deeds previously assigned only to men.

This kind of advertising had two advantages. It met—or at least it appeared to meet—objections that had been raised. And it often carried an element of surprise. The race car driver removed a helmet, shook the head

MEN & WOMEN WITHOUT
FEAR OF DEATH TO
CRASH THEIR CAR IN
DELIBERATE HEAD-ON
COLLISIONS IN
THE WORLD'S LARGEST
DEMOLITION DERBY

Call Now 243-0090
Cuyahoga County Fair

Other critics question the purpose to which advertising is put. This appeared in a Cleveland newspaper.

Is it possible for an ad to be less attractive, less easy to follow than this one?

to allow some flowing curls to fall into place, and, by golly, it was a *woman* who was driving!

Often the advertising was able to establish the fact that the woman in an unfamiliar role could still maintain her identity as a woman. In a Pepsi commercial, "Sam" was unhappy over the fact that the boys would not let her play ball because she was a girl. The father trained her, and she then showed up the boys (all within the allotted thirty seconds); but when she returned to the bench to her Pepsi reward, she corrected an admiring boy teammate who called her "Sam," telling him that her name was Samantha.

What Lippert saw in the 1980s was a more traditional woman in many advertisements. She cited a study by Yankelovich, Skelly and White that found that women "now feel that it's O.K. to dress up and wear evening clothes. It's not seen as inconsistent." Women want the basic changes that have come about since the early 1970s, but they want romance, too.[13] Suzanne Gordon in *The Nation* has decried the turn the feminist movement has taken, from insistence on change to accommodation to an existing system: ". . . what has happened to reformist feminism in the past decade is perhaps the most dramatic example of capitalism's genius at defusing protest by winning the protesters over to the very values and institutions they once attacked."[14]

In the 1980s many women appearing in commercials everywhere were older—some in their mid-thirties—and holding down professional rather than menial jobs. No longer did women have to be empty-headed baby-doll types. In fact, there was some worry that the models were so successful, so self-confident that some women viewers would not be able to identify with them.

There is also the problem of male roles in commercials. Not many men would identify with, say, the crybaby with a cold who wakes up his wife to tell her he can't sleep.

Some complaints against advertising center on unintended misinformation. In 1983 Sears Roebuck & Co. had to revise a tire commercial that showed a newborn baby being driven home in its mother's arms instead of in a safety carrier as required by several states.

Subliminal advertising

The threat of subliminal advertising from time to time gets the attention of college instructors and their students. A few are sure that the people who write and design the ads are slipping in messages to influence the subconscious. Lightning messages flash on the screen, or sexual stimulation rests in the print ads. Perhaps a nude women lies camouflaged in a photograph, or a dirty word forms itself somewhere in the art.

The first subliminal scare occurred years ago with the coming of television. Some critics charged that films in the theaters carried quick unseen messages sending patrons rushing to the popcorn stands. And in the 1970s Wilson Bryan Key wrote a book that saw all kinds of manipulations and innuendos in advertising. No doubt a few sophomoric people in the creative end of advertising do sneak double meanings into the art and copy of some advertising in order to play the clown; but to argue that there is a conspiracy in advertising to actually sell products through subliminal devices is probably unwarranted.

"This [talk about subliminal advertising] is all pretty nutty, of course," Sid Bernstein concluded in his column in *Advertising Age,* "and no one seems able to explain why advertisers trying to sell shoes or sealing wax or telephone service would want to louse up their expensive ad messages with corny or dirty subliminal messages."[15]

Restraints upon advertising

Advertising previously had faced restrictions set up by government agencies, including the Federal Trade Commission, the Food and Drug Administration, the Federal Communications Commission, the U.S. Postal Service, the Securities and Exchange Commission, and the Alcohol and Tax Division of the Internal Revenue Service. And it had faced additional restrictions from state and local agencies as well as from the media running the ads. But in the 1970s these restrictions intensified, and the 1980s promised no letup.

As a protective measure, the industry itself in 1971 set up the National Advertising Review Board (NARB) to apply pressure against agencies and advertisers to get misleading ads out of circulation and off the air. The National Advertising Division (NAD) of the Council of Better Business Bureaus performed a similar function. On the positive side, the Advertising Council, in collaboration with advertising agencies, continued to produce free institutional advertising for selected public service organizations.

Professor Eric J. Zanot of Pennsylvania State University points out that the industry mechanism for curtailing deceptive advertising processed more cases during its first five years of combined operation than the FTC did. NARB and NAD dealt with more than one thousand complaints against national advertisers in that period. As a result, hundreds of ads were dropped or changed.[16]

Of course, by the time ads change, the damage may be done. The advertiser may have been ready to move on to another theme anyway. Some observers criticize self-regulation as nothing more than window dressing and image building. Still, the activity does show that the industry—at least some segments of it—is concerned about its responsibility to readers, listeners, and viewers.

The most blatant bad practices often come from fringe operators, more ambitious than sensitive—people who do not have much to lose when they resort to questionable tactics. And these people are harder to corner.

The trouble with this otherwise well-designed ad is that the plane with its "Curtain going up . . . up, up, up, up" is itself sinking down, down, down through the ad.

How layout fits in

A layout is an arrangement of headlines, copy blocks, photographs, works of art, logotypes, borders, and other typographic devices that serves as a preview for the client and a guide for the illustrator, the lettering artist, the engraver or offset cameraman, the typesetter, and the printer. To *lay out* (two words) an ad is to engage in activity that will produce a *layout* (one word).

When principles of design (described in chapter 6) are followed in doing the layout, the advertisement becomes a more than otherwise pleasing visual experience for the viewer. The advertisement then is said to be "designed," not merely "laid out." We associate the word "design," ordinarily, with the handsomest ads—those meant to stand for a period of months or years. A department store ad appearing in a newspaper might be merely "laid out"; a package or trademark almost surely would be "designed."

To paraphrase Matthew Arnold's definition of journalism, layout is design "in a hurry."

The word "advertising" used in the title of this book limits layouts to arrangements meant to help sell products, services, and ideas offered by *advertisers.* Kinds of layout activity *not* to be considered here include (1) *makeup,* the arrangement of news and editorial matter for newspapers and (2) *editorial design,* the arrangement of fiction and nonfiction and art for book and magazine publishers. Not that *advertising layout, makeup,* and *editorial design* do not have much in common. They do. But American journalism for admirable reasons draws a hard line between advertising and news-and-editorial; the workers in one field are segregated from the workers in the other. This book will not attempt to cross the line.

Who does the layout?

Everyone from the person in charge of a church bulletin to the head of a large corporation has tried doing rough layouts, and sometimes such layouts work well enough. But in most cases a layout needs the touch of someone with an art or design background. The people who do layouts professionally carry various titles.

Layout artist is a beginning title. Ideally a layout artist

1. sketches clearly enough for a client to see, before the ad appears in print, what kind of illustrations will be used;

2. letters well enough that the printer can tell, just by looking at the rough, what size and what style of type to set for the ad;

3. understands enough about the principles of design to produce an attractive arrangement of what may be inflexible elements in an assigned space;

4. knows enough about printing, platemaking, and typesetting to get the best possible effects with the least cost;

5. thinks as well as arranges;

6. shares the client's interest in selling.

A proficient layout artist begins taking on more elaborate and long-term projects and becomes a *graphic designer* (or just plain *designer*). A designer does much more than arrange elements and render them. A designer often plans the ads, chooses typefaces, and conceives the art and arranges for its execution. Eventually the designer becomes an *art director.*

The term causes some confusion. "For years," said art director Saul Bass, "[my mother] wondered what I do; that is, what I *really* do. She knew I did art work—and actually she was very happy about it despite some vagueness that surrounded the matter. Her only concern was that I should make a living, and I seemed to be doing all right. But finally her

Art directors tend to use the same basic design for each ad in a series in order to hold the ads together. But that does not mean that the ads have to look exactly alike. In this series, designer Terry Dwyer always puts a long headline at the top with double-line rules. He incorporates one piece of art with each headline and scatters other pieces in the body copy below. In two cases he uses square photographs with his headlines; in the third he uses cartoon art that stretches down low into the third column of copy. The logo does not always fall at the lower right-hand corner of the page. Two of the ads start their copy with boldface subheads or lead-ins. One starts with ordinary copy. These ads were directed to restaurants and schools in a position to order fish for their customers or students. Wattenmaker Advertising, Cleveland, was the agency; North Atlantic Seafood Association was the client. Linda Masterson wrote the copy.

curiosity overcame her timidity, and, I think with some prompting from the neighbors, she finally asked me what it was that I *really* did."

He continued: "I pulled out a proof of an ad that I had designed and I showed it to her and said, 'Mom, that's what I do.' She looked at this and said, 'Oh, I see . . .' and she pointed to a photograph in the ad and said, '*That's* what you do?' I said, 'Oh, no, you see, there are photographers—they are specialists—they know all about cameras and things of this kind, and they make the photographs.'

" 'Oh,' she said, disappointed, 'Then *this* is what you do?' I said, 'No, that's typography. You see there are special organizations who do nothing but set type—you know, Garamond, Caslon, etc. . . . these people do that.' Again she was a little disappointed. She pointed to the lettering and we went through this again. Finally she looked at me somewhat concerned, and said, 'Well, now, what do *you* do?' I said, 'Well, you see, I conceive the whole thing, and then I get all these people together and get them to carry out the process.' She looked at me very coyly, and said, 'Oh—you devil!' "[17]

What an art director does *is* hard to pin down, not only for the layman, but also for the people in advertising.

An art director in one agency may be mostly an executive, in another agency more a performer. If an executive, the art director supervises the work of assistant art directors, layout artists, pasteup artists, illustrators, photographers, lettering artists, typographers, platemakers, and printers. Some art directors are able to do finished work themselves—illustrations, lettering, pasteups. Other art directors don't even do rough layouts.

Jerry Fields, head of a placement agency in communications, has commented on "the increasing stature art directors have achieved in the eyes of management in the past several years." He said: "Being an art director is no longer a roadblock to the top job of agencies."[18]

"The same drive for control and autonomy that takes an art director from sketchman to creative director ultimately takes him to agency ownership," said Peter Adler, a partner in the Adler, Schwartz agency, Englewood Cliffs, New Jersey. "For me, it was never enough to be given a sheet of manuscript copy and a tentative layout. I had to be part of the creative process from its inception."[19]

Art directors who have become agency chiefs include George Lois of

People who buy BMWs like to read about the product before spending their money. This two-page magazine ad goes into plenty of detail as to why the car is not "boring." The giant headline, which balances off the copy, helps create a nonboring image for BMW. Clem McCarthy art directed; Martin Puris wrote the copy. The agency was Ammirati & Puris.

Lois Pitts Gershon; Tony Cappiello of Ries Cappiello Colwell; Bob Dolobowsky of Warren, Muller, Dolobowsky; Gene Federico of Lord, Geller, Federico, Einstein; Sam Scali of Scali, McCabe, Sloves; Arnold Arlow of Martin Landey, Arlow Advertising; and Ralph Ammirati of Ammirati & Puris. "A great agency can't be ruled by businessmen alone," says Lois, who has run four different agencies.

To simplify things, this book will refer to the person doing layouts as a *designer*. The term will remind readers that layout at its best is not just arranged, it is designed.

The designer can work for the advertiser (the manufacturer, wholesaler, retailer, service organization) if the advertiser has a large enough operation to merit an advertising department; for a medium (newspaper, magazine, television station, network, outdoor plant) doing work for smaller advertisers who do not have their own staffs or agencies; for an advertising agency; for an art or design studio; for a "creative" printer who does a job for small advertisers similar to what an agency does. Or the designer can freelance.

Nobody cares whether the designer is male or female, and that has almost always been true. In the field of design, women have not faced the discrimination they have faced in many other fields.

Style and taste

Design is largely a matter of style and taste.

The style of a layout distinguishes it from other layouts. Style may be formal or informal. It may be traditional or modern. Style preferences change, but any style can be dusted off and, if it fits the mood of an ad, used to good effect by a competent designer.

An understanding of style in layout and a highly developed sense of taste more naturally come from art training than from journalism and business training. For this reason, art students enter into a course dealing with advertising layout with considerably more poise and self-assurance than students from other disciplines. In addition, they already have some familiarity with the tools necessary to do the job.

But a layout is not an end in itself. It is a plan. The plan takes into account the nature of elements in the ad and how they can best be reproduced. It is the student from the journalism school or department, with training in production and an understanding of the media, who here comes on strong. Also, that student brings to the job of layout a deeper appreciation of the relationship of layout to the ad's copy.

Then there is the business or marketing major, who understands better than the art or journalism student, usually, the psychology of selling, and who sees the relationship of the ad to what the advertising textbooks call the "marketing mix."

Each of these students brings to a course in advertising layout peculiar abilities and interests. Each can contribute to class discussion. Each can benefit from class exchange, from the instructor's comments and criti-

Attenzione!, an advertising agency, designed its own Christmas card, a five-fold accordion-fold with the message all on one side. Writer Linda Ahlers used a "'Twas the night before Christmas" theme to tell the story of Santa trying to change his image, only to be dissuaded by Attenzione! "Since you've got a good thing now, why mess around?" Deborah Kadas designed the full-color piece.

cism—and, if the author has done what he set out to do, from a study of this book.

Sometimes, as a result of taking courses in advertising layout, students reorder their college programs. If the students are from outside the journalism school or department, if that is where the courses are being offered, they decide to take additional journalism courses, especially in writing and production. Journalism or business students taking the course may discover in themselves art and design talent they did not know they had. A few in this latter category may consider transferring to an art school or going to one upon graduation.[20]

1. John S. DeMott, "Pitchmen on the Potomac," *Time*, March 7, 1983, p. 68.

2. "Big Business Shuns Corporate Responsibilities," *Media: The Asian Marketing and Communications Magazine*, May 30, 1983, p. 10.

3. See front-page story in *Wall Street Journal*, November 8, 1983.

4. William Weilbacher, *Advertising* (New York: Macmillan, 1979), p. 454.

5. Robert L. Shayon, "Advocacy Advertising," *Pennsylvania Gazette*, May 1979, p. 9.

6. Restructured from an article by Ted Morgan, "New! Improved! Advertising!" *New York Times Magazine*, January 25, 1976, p. 52.

7. Joe Mancini, "Hollywood Hucksters," *United Airlines Magazine*, October 1983, p. 85.

8. Karen Stabiner, "Tapping the Homosexual Market," *New York Times Magazine*, May 2, 1982, p. 34.

9. Ibid., p. 82.

10. John S. Meskil, "The Media Mix," *Media Letter*, American Association of Advertising Agencies, January 1979, p. 2.

11. Robert Glatzer, *The New Advertising* (New York: Citadel Press, 1970), pp. 10, 11.

12. Judith Alder Hennessee and Joan Nicholson catalog offenses in "NOW Says: TV Commercials Insult Women," *New York Times Magazine*, May 28, 1972, pp. 12ff.

13. Barbara Lippert, "Agencies, Marketers Woo Postfeminist Woman," *Adweek*, March 7, 1983, pp. 17, 20.

14. Suzanne Gordon, "The New Corporate Feminism," *The Nation*, February 5, 1983, pp. 129, 143.

15. Sid Bernstein, "Subliminal Ads Attract Weirdos," *Advertising Age*, June 19, 1978, p. 16.

16. Eric J. Zanot, *The National Advertising Review Board, 1971–1976*, Journalism Monographs, Association for Education in Journalism, February 1976, p. 1.

17. Saul Bass, "Creativity in Visual Communication," *Creativity: An Examination of the Creative Process* (New York: Hastings House, 1959), pp. 122, 123. Quoted by permission.

18. Jerry Fields, "Art Directors' Salaries," *Art Direction*, January 1976, p. 46.

19. Peter Adler, "The Best of Both Worlds," *Advertising Age*, June 4, 1979, p. 60.

20. To aid such students in their choices, *American Artist* magazine in one issue each year publishes an Art School Directory. Reprints are available at a modest price from American Artist Reprints, 1515 Broadway, New York, N.Y. 10036.

Through its choice and handling of type, Metzdorf Advertising Agency, Houston, dramatizes its need for secretarial help. Art director, designer, and copywriter: Lyle Metzdorf.

We need two sharp secretaries, a classsey reception-est, and two accuratte clerk typists. Call Mr. Ivey for an appointment at Metzdorf Adv., 526-5361.

2
The creative process

Some years ago someone by mistake left out the display portion of an advertisement designed to bring in new subscribers to a magazine called *Commentary* and ran only a coupon under an area of framed-in white space. When that particular ad drew more response than others run in the *Commentary* series, creative people in advertising may have nudged one another and laughed nervously. They need not have despaired. Without the usual apparatus, this ad could not help standing out from others—a condition which of itself made the ad, innocently, "creative." Nor was leaving out an element or elements unique. To recruit copywriters, advertising agencies have run blank-space ads—on purpose—in *Advertising Age* with the headline: "We're at a Loss for Words."

A variation of the leave-it-out approach could be seen in an RCA ad featuring a turned-off set with this message on the screen: "Rather than simulate a ColorTrak picture, we urge you to see it for real. Up close, at your RCA dealer." Chivas Regal offered another example: a full-page pic-

AFTER 500 PLAYS OUR HIGH FIDELITY TAPE STILL DELIVERS HIGH FIDELITY.

If your old favorites don't sound as good as they used to, the problem could be your recording tape.

Some tapes show their age more than others. And when a tape ages prematurely, the music on it does too.

What can happen is, the oxide particles that are bound onto tape loosen and fall off, taking some of your music with them.

At Maxell, we've developed a binding process that helps to prevent this. When oxide particles are bound onto our tape, they stay put. And so does your music.

So even after a Maxell recording is 500 plays old, you'll swear it's not a play over five.

maxell

IT'S WORTH IT.

How do you show "high fidelity"? Maxell shows it by converting it to a high wind. The tipped lampshade and drink and blown hair and tie help establish the fact that the wind is coming with great force. And the slouched man is holding onto the chair almost in desperation. Lars Anderson designed the ad, and Peter Levathes wrote the copy. Scali, McCabe, Sloves, Inc., was the agency.

For a class project in Survey of Visual Design, Mary B. Gilbert, Corvallis, Oregon, hunted for various photographs of geometric patterns, organic textures, etc., (left column) and worked out transitions between them, using a stipple drawing technique for her in-between drawings. Her object here was to start and stop with a straight line. A good exercise in visual thinking. © Mary B. Gilbert.

ture of gray space with this headline at the bottom: "It's Hard to Keep a Bottle of Chivas Regal Around a Photographer's Studio."

The process of designing advertising involves a constant search for some new way—or, if not some new way, some proven way—to stop today's harried readers and listeners and interest them in the message. The stopping and interest-arousing get done, alas, through methods crude and loud. But they get done also through departure from the usual—as in leaving out the expected portion of the ad. And they get done through sensitive planning and arranging of necessary elements into aesthetically pleasing layouts.

No one will deny that undistinguished design (like the design in many of the examples shown in Julian Lewis Watkins's book *The 100 Greatest Advertisements*) can do a selling job. Nor will anyone argue that good design necessarily sells better than poor design. The product, if it is desirable enough, can sell itself. But designers will insist that design considerations cannot *hurt* an ad's chances and that the satisfactions of producing tasteful advertising far outweigh those of producing vulgar advertising.

Creativity: what it is

Like humor, creativity does not lend itself to dissection. Too much analysis of creativity by the creative person could dry up the source of new ideas. As Franz Schoenberner observed in *Confessions of a European Intellectual:* "The centipede, when asked with which foot he started to walk, became paralyzed." Hilaire Belloc made a similar observation about the water beetle: if it stopped to think, it would sink.

It is difficult even to define creativity. Adman John S. Straiton tried by telling what creativity is not. It is not showing off to other ad people, he observed. It is not amateurism. It is not "beads and beards." It is not being funny. It is not being "with it." "When someone else is dancing, the best way to be noticed is to stand still."[1]

"As far as I'm concerned, . . . [the] heart [of creativity] is *discipline*," said the late William Bernbach of Doyle Dane Bernbach. The discipline, as Bernbach saw it, breaks down into four activities:

1. Discipline to find the product's advantage.
2. Discipline to produce an ad that is sophisticated and aesthetic. "It's true that there's a twelve-year-old mentality in America," said Bernbach. "Every six-year-old has it."
3. Discipline to manage. It takes a creative person to encourage and guide other creative people and provide them with the right information. It takes creativity to be a good editor.
4. Discipline to develop social awareness and to be responsible to the public.[2]

Advertising Age made a similar observation in an editorial. "The essence of creativity, we submit, is working within a discipline. It's making those walls your canvas, not your cell. Advertising folks know this well. Working within the confines of a dull product, a duller marketing plan and a tough market, yet developing a winning ad campaign—now *that's* creative."[3]

Albert Szent-Gyorgyi said that discovery (which could be considered the same thing as creativity) is "seeing what everybody else has seen and thinking what nobody else has thought."

"The only truly creative being is God," observed Lois Ernst, creative director of Advertising to Women, New York. ". . . God, they say, created the world out of nothing." Mere mortals always start with *something*. Creativity as we know it, then, is "the ability to put two common things together that have never been paired before, forming a third thing by which the fusion becomes an original."[4]

"The creative person's responsibility is to collect all diverse components that make up a problem—the product facts, the product position, the media, the market research data, the media budget, the production budget—sort them out, weigh them, come to grips with what it is that should be said, then—finally—mold them into some form of theatrics," added Jack Badofsky, creative director of Marvin H. Frank & Co., Chicago.[5]

Shirley Polykoff, president of the agency bearing her name, said, "Creativity has always been just a knack or talent for expressing a single idea or simple concept in a fresh, arresting new way—what I call 'thinking it out square,' then saying it with flair."[6]

Edward A. McCabe, copy director at Scali, McCabe, Sloves, New York, agreed that simplicity is the key. You should put your propositions forward "with such utter simplicity that people are both astonished and moved. . . ."[7]

"What I think of as creativity is an intensity of awareness of the world around you, a heightened state of consciousness, a sense of being at one with the order of things," said Rollo May.[8]

Howard E. Gruber of Rutgers University, in a *New York Times* review of *The Courage to Create,* concluded that "there is no pleasure greater than wonder, and no wonder greater than human creativity. . . ."

Still, "creativity is not necessarily good. . . ," the late designer/illustrator Bill Tara said. "The Patent Office is full of examples of creative idiocy."

He also said: "In great numbers, the practitioners of advertising claim to possess this power [of creativity]. Mostly, this is conceit. They imply in their use of the word that they possess *great* creative abilities when, in actuality (and most of the advertising produced is evidence) they may have little more ability to *create new forms out of existing material* than the lady who knits antimacassers or the youth who paints decorative flames on his Chevrolet Impala. To paraphrase Fred Allen, some of the most vocal claimants to inventive and innovative abilities 'couldn't create a belch after a Hungarian dinner.' "[9]

Creative people: who they are

Studies show that creative people have an unusual capacity to record and report experiences; these people are discerning, alert, and deal easily with abstractions.

They are less likely than others to repress their impulses. They are less interested than others in what people think of them (so they are freer to be creative). They are not conformists, but they are not nonconformists, either. Rather, they are "independent."

But like their noncreative colleagues, creative people appreciate a little recognition. Creative people may have more than the usual share of ego and anxiety.

The chances are that creative people are not pleased with the way things are. Burt Prelutsky's description of the "master griper" in the defunct magazine *West* seems to fit the creative person: "A master griper is never put off by good news. A smile, he knows, is only a frown upside down. His motto is, 'Every silver lining has a cloud.' "

Creative people are not likely to be stimulated to creativity through psychological self-help books or movements. "Creativity does not emerge from a state of relaxation," said Rollo May, author of *The Courage to Create,* "but from a state of chaos. . . ."[10]

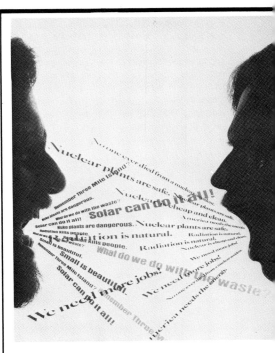

The Committee for Energy Awareness, sponsored by America's electric energy companies, took out a two-page ad in *Time* to point out that "There are two sides to the issue of nuclear power." One page consisted of the bleed photo you see here, with charges and claims coming from the mouths of the protagonists. Notice the faces chosen to represent the two sides. There is just enough stereotyping here to make the protagonists believable but not enough to cause offense. The antinuke man is, naturally, at the left, and bearded.

In one of its ads Saab uses a Rorschach-like device to "test" potential car buyers. "Do You See a Practical Car or a Performance Car?" asks the ad's headline. According to the ad's copy (not shown), Saab is both. "While our version [of the Rorschach test] may not reveal your personality traits, instinctual drives, or hidden neuroses, it should reduce any anxieties you might have about buying a Saab." The idea behind the ad and the copy approach take advantage of the car's slogan: "The most intelligent car ever built." Ron Arnold was art director; Peter Levathes wrote the copy. Ally & Gargano, Inc., was the agency.

There are extroverts among creative people, but the tendency is toward introversion.

Kingman Brewster, Jr., when president of Yale University, mentioned a correlation between "the creative and the screwball." "So we must suffer the screwball gladly," he declared. "The disclosure of subsurface truth is our highest accomplishment, no matter how unpleasant it may be to many of our most respectable friends."

Creative people delight in complexities, and when they find them, they look for unifying principles.

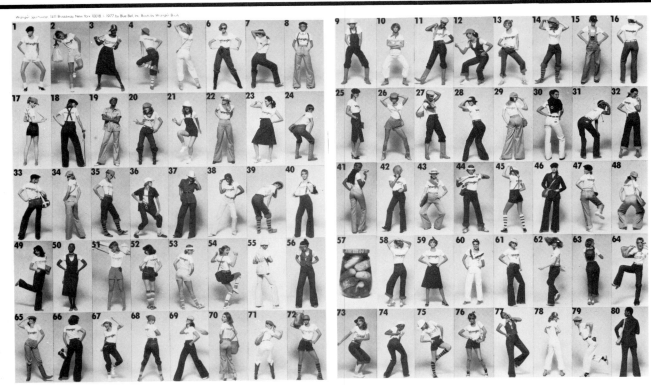

Wrangler
has more styles than Heinz has varieties.

Creative people have a wide range of information on hand. This is important. For creative people essentially engage in arranging items of information into combinations. The more creative people know, the more combinations they can come up with.

Designer Ivan Chermayeff saw the creative person in the field of design as "a borrower, co-ordinator, assimilator, juggler, and collector of material, knowledge, and thought from the past and present, from other designers, from technology, and from himself. His style and individuality come from the consistency of his own attitudes and approach to the expression and communication of a problem."[11]

Jack D. Ewan, former Fuller & Smith & Ross account executive now teaching at the University of Oregon, has observed, "He is most creative who borrows from the greatest number of sources."

Ron Hoff, creative director for Foote, Cone & Belding, thinks truly creative people have four qualities in common:

1. They are compulsive observers of the human condition.

2. They enjoy building a case. Creative people want to sway people. "There is a kind of arrogance in this desire—but it is a vital component if you want to succeed in advertising."

3. They see things differently from the way other people see things. "Creative people have the common touch, but they express it uncommonly."

4. They want the world to see what they have done.[12]

Creative people often become restless, looking for new challenges, moving from job to job. Advertising art directors often move from agencies to magazines. David Merrill, who art-directed *Time,* originally worked as an art director for Ogilvy & Mather. Since resigning as *Time's* art director in 1977, Merrill has run his own New York design studio to establish formats for new magazines or redesign old ones.

Many of today's important agencies were started when an employee

In this full-color, two-page ad designed for women's magazines, Wrangler Jeans uses a checkerboard of photographs to dramatize its many varieties and, in good fun, parodies a famous earlier campaign by a very different advertiser. Note item 57. Instead of only fifty-seven varieties, Wrangler has eighty, minus one. To make its point clear, Wrangler uses same-size photographs and basically same-size figures. Merv Shipenberg was art director, Austin Hamil writer. The agency: Altman, Stoller, Weiss.

left an older agency because it was too conservative in its approach to ad making. William Bernbach left Grey Advertising, he said, to start Doyle Dane Bernbach because Grey "didn't know how to make ads." "There is some evidence that, everything else being equal, if your agency achieves a reputation for high creativity, it will grow faster," said Paul Waddell, director of creative services at Evans Weinberg Advertising, Los Angeles.[13]

People who are creative in one area are usually creative in several. It was after a successful career as an illustrator that Milt Glaser turned to design—his main interest now. He continues to do illustrations for clients and causes he likes, and his designs often incorporate his own illustrations. He works in many styles. His design interests have expanded to include packages and even grocery store interiors, exteriors, fixtures, and advertising. The "I Love New York" insignia, with a heart in the place of "Love," now so widely imitated, was a Glaser idea.

The designer and redesigner of a number of magazines, Glaser sees a connection between publications and, say, store interiors. (The word *magazine* in French means "storehouse.")

His interest in package design, including food-package design, stems from his interest in gourmet food. He is an accomplished chef and, with the late art director Jerome Snyder *(Scientific American),* authored a book, *The Underground Gourmet,* and a column by the same name for the magazine *New York.*

After working with photographers, art directors often take up this activity themselves and do very well at it. Henry Wolfe is a case in point. His photography has appeared on magazine covers. Saul Bass went into filmmaking. Donald Spoto in *The Dark Side of Genius* (Little Brown, 1983), a biography of Alfred Hitchcock, reported that Bass, not Hitchcock, actually directed that famous shower scene in *Psycho.* Bass had done a storyboard of the sequence, and Hitchcock was impressed enough with Bass's work that he let him take over. (Bass was listed in the film credits as a consultant.)[14]

A correlation exists between high intelligence and creativity in some fields—nuclear physics, for example—but not necessarily in design. The good designer may have only an ordinary IQ. But the designer is able to make more than black-and-white distinctions: the dogmatist does not make a very good designer.

The designer's best work may come early. According to Jerry Fields, the director of a New York placement service quoted in the last chapter, agencies like to hire the young for creative jobs because, among other reasons, "the young art director or copywriter, or for that matter, the young

Art director Karen Mann uses a ransom-note approach to set the stage for a headline that talks about figures being ''released'' and copy that says ''Simmons gives us a stranglehold on Houston. At least 63% of newspaper readers in every crucial demo. So face the facts. Or pay the price. . . .'' The copy is set in a typewriter face, with strikeovers. The two-color ad (the clippings stand out from a field of tomato red) sells the *Houston Chronicle* as an advertising medium. Dick Sinreich wrote the copy. Rives Smith Baldwin & Carlberg/Y&R was the agency.

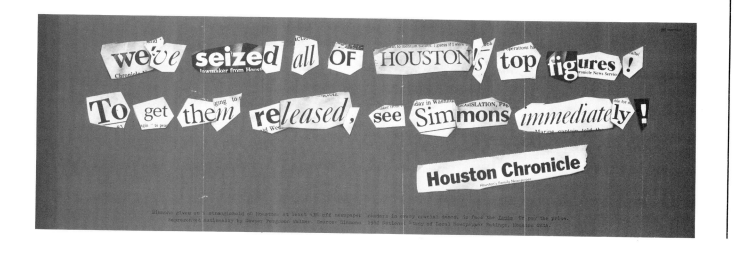

product, account, or ad manager . . . can take the risks involved in turning in new, exciting, innovating work." Also, "If he is shot down by his client or boss, the hell with it. He'll get a job someplace else or maybe hack around Europe for a couple of months before going to work again. But the older man can't afford to take risks with his job security because of all those obligations back in Darien. So he plays it safe and sticks to proven formula stuff that he knows worked in the past and that won't make any waves that might engulf him."[15] But Bob Gage, Doyle Dane Bernbach's first art director, thinks age has little to do with creativity. "If you keep on growing, if you know you haven't learned to do it as well as you'd like, and if you keep searching, if you remain a little unsure of yourself, you won't burn out. On the other hand, if you find a formula and stick to the formula, you can burn yourself out before you're thirty. . . ."[16]

The presidents of two West Coast agencies recognized as "creative" had differing ideas on how creative people should be treated. Do not let creative people near the client, said Dave Bascom of Guild, Bascom & Bonfigli, San Francisco (now part of Dancer Fitzgerald Sample). "Most

You can help. Send your contribution to the Muscular Dystrophy Association, 810 Seventh Avenue, New York, N.Y. 10019.

Al Hampel came up with the concept for this intriguing public-service ad for the Muscular Dystrophy Association; Sue Gelman wrote the copy; Jon Fisher art directed. The agency—the volunteer agency—was Benton & Bowles. Yousuf Karsh, as a member of MDA, contributes his photographic genius to the association each year by making camera portraits of its national poster children.

Influenced by the op art movement, the designer of this ad from several years past uses outside edges of letters in *"Life"* for a pattern idea. *"Now that we've got your attention . . ."* reads the headline. *". . . Use this coupon and get 27 weeks of Life for . . .,"* the copy continues.

creative people would be utterly shattered and destroyed if they had to work with the client." The late Ralph Carson of Carson/Roberts, Los Angeles (now part of Ogilvy & Mather International), held a contrary view. "They should be exposed to the problems of the market." Nor did the two agree on where to find creative people. Bascom liked to draw them from the ranks of musicians, writers, and artists who had proved their creativity, and he taught them to apply their talents to the special field of advertising. Carson felt these people were too often loners; hence they were out of place in an agency where people have to work together.

But Yousuf Karsh, the portrait photographer, thinks that "The loneliness of great men is part of their ability to create. Character, like a photograph, develops in darkness."[17]

In summary:

As a creative person, you do not readily accept rules and restrictions, including rules of design. You see how far you can go with unusual typefaces and untried combinations without hurting readability.

You see patterns where, to the average viewer, no patterns exist, and take advantage of them to better organize the elements you work with.

You find beauty in mundane things. Your role is to present these things from a different vantage point.

You sense a connection between items which, at first glance, seem unconnected, and you come up with an arrangement that connects them.

You are willing to take some chances with the printer and even the client in the interest of coming up with something new. And if accidents occur, you take advantage of them. Perhaps you can improve a piece of art through imaginative cropping or even patching. If necessary, to salvage the art, you may change your design. You remain flexible.

Although you work best in isolation, you do not necessarily shun brainstorming sessions with others or even conventions of like-minded artists. You always look for inspiration. You can never see enough good designs, go through enough printed pieces, or experience enough visual delights.

Creative people moving in on a new account often want to put their own mark on the advertising, even though it may be working well already. And the people close to a campaign tend to tire of it long before the public does. Changing a campaign, just for the sake of change, though, is a luxury creative people cannot afford. The secret of successful advertising often rests with its years of uninterrupted service.

Developing a style

Shortly after John F. Kennedy was assassinated, John Cogley, writing about style in politics—something Kennedy had—said that style "has something to do with taste, something to do with restraint and control, and something to do, finally, with grace and gallantry." Which is not a bad way for the designer to look at it: style *is* a matter of taste, restraint, control, grace. (We omit *gallantry* as being peculiar to nonartistic expression.)

Dwight Macdonald, considering style from the standpoint of the writer, observed that "style requires that certain effects be given up because they are incompatible with certain others." This suggests another word to add to the list: consistency. An effective style creates and maintains a single mood. It deals with a single theme.

All of this is applicable to advertising design. A layout has style when the person who does it is a person of taste—when the designer uses restraint in the choice of elements, controlling them for just the effects the client needs. The elements are arranged so that the ad, overall, appears graceful, even when the client is a grocery chain or a discount drugstore. Each element used appears related to other elements in the ad. Nothing

WHY IS THIS MAN SMILING?

Because he owns a Volvo. And in an age when many people are fed up with the quality of new cars, 9 out of 10 new Volvo owners are happy.

Why buy a car you'll have to grin and bear? When you can buy a car that will give you something to smile about?

VOLVO
A car you can believe in.

in the ad detracts from its theme. Nothing is used that does not advance the theme.

Of course, not every ad has to look like a perfume or quality automobile advertisement in the *New Yorker* magazine. A store with mainly *price* to sell, or variety in merchandise, must crowd its elements into the allotted space; but this can be done without doing violence to the concept here of style.

Some observers see a geographic influence on design. Alexis Gelber describes the peculiarities of graphic design originating in southern California. For one thing, artists there break all the rules of graphic design. That you break the rules becomes itself a rule. The southern California look includes "crazily angled italic typography, throbs of color, water imagery, a good deal of other-worldly light, and lots of skin. . . ." This compares to the New York look of "geometric forms, architectural backdrops, . . . [and] abstraction." Nor does the southern California look have much in common with the San Francisco look: "fine printing, classic typography, and elegant design. . . ."[18]

It is interesting, too, to compare design in the United States with design in other countries. Japanese graphic design, like Japanese fashion, greatly influenced America in the 1980s. Japanese advertising on the whole is less direct than U.S. advertising. So the design is more subtle. One observer points to a Japanese saying that explains the advertising there: "One thing is said, and ten things are understood." Says this observer: "If a company builds a strong, high-level image, the Japanese consumer assumes that it produces quality products. Advertising often minimizes the product and its benefits, and some graphics have nothing to do with the product being promoted."[19]

Esquire made famous the line, "Why is this man smiling?" in its "Dubious Achievements" issues, and Volvo capitalizes on the line in this excellent two-page full-color magazine ad. This man is smiling, as the copy explains, "Because he owns a Volvo." Volvo's agency—Scali, McCabe, Sloves—helps unite a series of ads for the car by featuring the same squared off headline face. The proportions in this particular ad are worth studying. The headline represents one area, a thin one; the grill represents another, a thicker one; and what is left over represents the final area, the thickest one. From top to bottom, then, you have thin, thick, and medium horizontal strips. The thick area gives designer Jim Perretti plenty of room to display the man's face, which is vital to the ad. Ed McCabe and Larry Cadman wrote the copy.

In Japan, graphic designers become celebrities, for design in advertising and business is a priority. Japanese business people are extremely image conscious. Designers in Japan work especially closely with management.

The changing face of style

A few highly talented designers and art directors bring a beauty and excitement to advertising design it would not otherwise have. They dictate taste for a season, then step aside to make room for a younger contingent. So much momentum does each new contingent of tastemakers generate that even the contingent it replaces adopts the new styles and mannerisms. Those who never were in the vanguard follow each trend as if by rote, often late—after the tastemakers themselves, bored by it all, have moved to some new level. Each style in type or art is defended, temporarily, with the same intransigence as the last.

But in recent years the styles have become shorter-lived. Newer ones come on before the old ones can be abandoned. And the styles from earlier eras—from the turn of the century (Art Nouveau) and pre-World War II days (Art Deco)—stage their comebacks. Movements in the fine arts, like op and pop art, exert their influence.

Massimo Vignelli, president of Vignelli Associates, a design studio, saw the 1960s as a decade of discipline, with Helvetica type and grids dominating the printed page. The 1970s were a decade of "appropriateness," with more experimentation and with complexity overriding the earlier simplicity. Where it used to be that "less is more," in the 1970s it was "less is a bore." The 1980s became a decade "intrigued by the pleasures of ambiguity. The fascinating possibility of conveying several interpretations, even contradictory ones, perfectly expresses the new romance with the significance of meanings, which we are now going through with renovated passion." Ornament, for years shunned by graphic designers, is back in the 1980s. In the words of Vignelli, it "comes back through the window like a bird."[20]

Where objectivity in design was the goal of 1960s designers, subjectivity appears to be the goal now. While this leads to design excitement, it brings with it the danger that designers will indulge themselves rather than serve readers.

But it should be pointed out that now almost every style has its proponents. The look of the 1930s and 1940s exists right next to the look of the 1980s. Almost anything goes, sometimes at the expense of readability.

All of which neutralizes to some extent the tyranny of the tastemakers in advertising. It also discourages the laying down of any rules by teachers of graphic design.

Advertising has always been more receptive to design experimentation than to copy experimentation and probably always will be. One reason is that the designer, often unlike the copywriter, works with a comparatively free hand. The designer does not have the problem the copywriter has of dealing with an area in which clients have, or believe they have, some proficiency.

The late Leo Burnett observed: "Any fool can write a bad ad—but it takes a real genius to keep his hands off a good one."

Determining the purpose of the ad

It is easy to denigrate the opinion of the client. The client has none of the training of the creative artist, none of the background. But it is the client's money, after all, that is being spent on the campaign.

"A creative person earns just as much while creating bad ideas which he himself discards, as he does while creating the one good idea which he submits as his best effort," argued James Maratta, a specialty sales consultant, writing some years ago in *Printers' Ink*. "An agency earns the same commission on an advertising campaign that fails as it does on the one that clicks. So the advertiser or employer who gambles and must foot the bill is not asking too much when he insists that his opinions be heard and his ideas used." Or at least considered.

What the client wants is maximum attention and response to the ads' invitation.

If the ads, however attractive, fail to bring this about, they do not count for much. Sometimes designers, intent on winning top awards at art directors' shows, forget this. So do their more amateur counterparts working on retail accounts who become caught up in cuteness and gimmickry.

Here is what Robert Pliskin, vice president in charge of art for Benton & Bowles, has to say about designers who forget their basic function: "Art directors who try to sell work because it's beautiful belong in some other business. Beauty is in the eye of the beholder, and there are few things more beautiful to a businessman than the upward curve of a sales chart. To sell his concept of beauty, the art director must be a salesman, and good salesmen communicate in clients' terms. Learn to sell, O chalk-dusted art director, or your great layouts will never find their place in media-land."

Speaking to delegates to an International Design Conference at Aspen, Colorado, William Bernbach said that designers must fight a tendency to worship technique and to become preoccupied with good looks. "The purpose of an ad," he observed, "is to persuade people to buy your product. The persuasion is in the idea and the words. And anything, however expert, that slickly detracts from that idea and those words is, for my money, bad design."

"Guess what this 'creative agency' loves most to create?" asked a Leo Burnett Co. ad in *Advertising Age*. The follow-up line answered succinctly: "Sales."

Facing the assignment

Beginning an assignment, the designer wrestles with a number of questions.

What is the purpose of the ad: to sell a product or a service or an idea? Does the advertiser want mostly to hold onto present customers or to attract new ones? Is the goal short or long range? Must the ad do the job alone, or will it be one in a series? What is the theme? The selling points? For what audience is the ad intended? What approaches are most likely to influence this audience? What medium will be used—newspapers? magazines? direct mail? What are the limitations and possibilities of this medium? What printing process is involved? Paper stock? What kind of art and type will reproduce best? How much can the client spend on production? Is color available? What size is specified? What format should be used? What time of the year will the ad run? Are some elements—photographs, stock art, sig cut—already picked for use? Is outside help available to do drawings, take pictures, handle the pasteup?

Sometimes the job calls simply for an announcement of the availability of a product and a statement of its price.

At other times the job is more complicated. The designer may be asked to dispel misinformation about the product; give the product a personality that will set it apart from others that really are quite similar; suggest to the public—or publics—additional uses for the product (as Scotch tape often does); or sell nonusers—purchasing agents, for instance, or retailers—on the merits of the product. Sometimes the ad means only to im-

Here is a dramatic way to show that "The shape our rivers and lakes are in today doesn't leave much to sing about." Trans Union Corporation ran the ad in *Business Week* to talk about its "complete range of services and processes in the water and waste treating industry." Designer: Howie Blum; agency: Earl Ludgin Company.

press the board of directors or the stockholders that the company *is* advertising.

The advertising designer who cannot deal with intangible things, with concepts, is likely to find fewer clients in the future. Advertising will deal more and more with ideas rather than with products. And there will be a narrowing of audiences for ads; a greater awareness by ad people of the merits of individual publications; an insistence by clients that advertising goals be stated and advertising effectiveness be measured. The designer who keeps abreast of developments in these areas obviously will be better prepared than other designers to meet the needs of clients.

The decisions the designer makes fall into two categories: those of content and those of form. On the former, the designer has the help of the copywriter (often the two work together) or, as is sometimes the case, the content decisions are already made. On the latter, the designer is almost always sovereign. The designer decides whether to use pictures or not. Sometimes pictures are superfluous. Copy—or a headline alone—may be enough to make the point. Copy becomes more important than art in a medium that readers consult frequently. A study conducted by Russell Marketing Research, Inc., for instance, showed that mostly-copy display ads in the Yellow Pages of telephone directories outpulled art-heavy ads by almost two to one among small-space ads and three to one among large ads.

If pictures need to be used, the designer must decide whether they should be photographs or drawings. Costs may be the determining factor. Other factors may be availability of models, the season of the year, or that most important of considerations, client preference.

Whatever kind of art is used, the designer must decide from which vantage point the subject will show up best.

Influencing choices will be the designer's knowledge of the kind of product (to be worn? consumed?), the kind of person likely to be interested in the product, the medium through which the ad will reach the reader.

Facing client stipulations

Helmut Krone, art director for Doyle Dane Bernbach, likes to work closely with the client, letting the client make some of the design decisions. Other art directors find client participation or direction frustrating. For instance, a poorly designed trademark must be included. Or a basic format and a set of colors, established earlier, must be followed.

Clients—and some advertising people and designers, too—have a great urge to unify all pieces of promotion, as if a single reader were to see all of them and in a single setting. There is some merit in this, of course; if the materials are promoted widely enough, familiarity with the firm and its program will likely be helped along by visual continuity. But the truth must be that much of this tying together of advertising pieces is nothing more than administrative tidiness, bringing great satisfaction to the perpetrators, perhaps, but having little actual effect on the sales curve.

So why, in an ad sponsored by a newspaper to get at media buyers in advertising agencies, should the designer be stuck with the Old English nameplate when the rest of the ad is in a modern typeface? Would a signature in the modern face, in place of a replica of the regular nameplate, hurt the ad's pulling power?

The designer will certainly try to convince the client to drop those elements which do not fit the new design. Failing that, the designer can at least minimize them in the design arrangement or update them slightly, retaining recognition while improving the appearance.

Visualization

In the late nineteenth century the few people called "visualizers" who attached themselves to fledgling advertising agencies enjoyed precious little prestige. Account people and copywriters worked up the copy, sketched a rough to show where it should go in the ad, and turned it over to the lowly visualizer, who did some lettering at the top, then carefully traced available stock art in the space left over. Visualizers usually knew a little more about typefaces than anyone in the agency, and they understood production; still, they were not much more than persons who traced things. Certainly they were not designers. The idea of *designing* an ad had not yet occurred to members of the fraternity.

As copywriters became more rushed, visualizers were allowed to sketch out the ads. The visualizers became "layout artists." As the visualizers' work increased, they asked for and got assistants, or they turned for help to freelancers in the area. They became *directors*—directors of art.

Their work took on added importance.

The earliest art directors functioned primarily as buyers, picking out paintings or drawings from submissions by artists, placing them on top of blocks of copy, and deciding on borders to fence off the ads. Appropriately, these directors worked anonymously; when the Art Directors Club of New York held its first exhibition of advertising art in 1921, the catalog named the artists who drew and painted the pictures but made no mention of the people who ordered the work, directed it, and laid out the ad in which it appeared. Not until 1934 did the club decide the director deserved a credit line on award-winning ads in the exhibition. Now, of course, the art director is recognized in the catalogs, right along with the artist or photographer, the client, and the agency.

To bring more prestige to the profession, the Art Directors Club of New York in 1971 started a Hall of Fame. Eight people were elected to the Hall of Fame in 1972, and several have been added each year since then. Some are—or were—advertising art directors, some magazine art directors, some both. Among members are M. F. Agha, Alexey Brodovitch, William Golden, Paul Rand, Cipe Pineles (the first woman member), Saul Bass, Herb Lubalin, Lou Dorfsman, Allen Hurlburt, and George Lois.

The best art directors appreciate the importance of copy in advertising, just as the best copy chiefs appreciate the importance of art and layout.

The student does not have to confine experimentation to the usual ad elements. These two examples by student Kim Frankel were produced through photochemistry: She exposed both sheets of sensitized printing paper to light. Before developing and fixing one, she fastened masking tape to the sheet; for the other, she dripped and splattered undiluted developer on the exposed sheet, then fixed it.

How do you dramatize the fact that, on some airlines (but not yours), the glamour has gone out of flying? Art director Craig Joslin and copywriter Jim Copacino dreamed up this idea of a flying bus. Note the use of parallel structure and a question-and-answer format in the headlines. The reader moves effortlessly from one page to the second. Overlapping small photos carry the reader to the slogan and the Alaska Airlines signature. The agency was Chiat/Day Advertising, Seattle (now Livingston & Co.).

Bay Area Rapid Transit (BART) system riders would recognize the base of this "phone" as the front of a BART train (note the windshield wiper). The six-column ad was prepared by Wilton, Coombs & Colnett, San Francisco, for a progress issue of the *Richmond* (California) *Independent.*

B-A-R-T makes it easy.

BART and its Information Center operate Monday through Friday from 6:00 am to 12 midnight. Call us about BART and local bus service. Chinese and Spanish speaking operators are on duty from 8:00 am to 5:00 pm. Just dial the prefix in your area and the letters B-A-R-T.

San Francisco/Daly City area 788-B-A-R-T
South San Francisco/San Bruno area 873-B-A-R-T

Oakland/Berkeley/Orinda area 465-B-A-R-T
Lafayette/Concord area 933-B-A-R-T
Fremont/Union City area 793-B-A-R-T
Hayward/San Leandro area 783-B-A-R-T
Richmond/El Cerrito area 236-B-A-R-T
Livermore/Pleasanton area 462-B-A-R-T
Antioch/Pittsburg area 754-B-A-R-T

One—the art director or the copy chief—has to have the final say, of course (a coeditorship is never a very effective arrangement in the communications field), but it need not always be the copy chief. Some ads—some campaigns even—are more appropriately directed by art- rather than copy-oriented executives.

Professor Max Wales told his classes in advertising at the University of Oregon: "Often advertisers choose to promote product benefits that are psychological, emotional, even silly. To explain these benefits in words proves embarrassing. Or ridiculous. So advertisers explain them indirectly—through art. The art director, then, rather than the copywriter, 'writes' the ad." Wales cited the many ads showing products being enjoyed by obviously upper-class or attractive people in luxurious or intriguing settings.

A few art directors *literally* write their ads. A memorable Volkswagen ad, "Don't Forget the Anti-freeze!" which was "presented by Volkswagen dealers as a public service to people who don't own cars with air-cooled engines," was both designed and written by a Doyle Dane Bernbach art director, Helmut Krone.

Around the agencies you do not hear the name "visualizer" used anymore. In today's advertising, anyone working on creative aspects is a visualizer. Someone has to "visualize" the ad before it gets sketched out. The process of "visualization" is surely the most important creative phase in advertising. If designers are creative in the broadest sense, they visualize the ad. If they are no more than craftsmen—albeit neat and wise in matters of production—someone else does the visualizing.

Sometimes the designer—or whoever does the visualizing—can best express the idea in literal terms. Perhaps a picture of the product will do, or a picture of a satisfied user. At other times, especially when the purpose of the ad is institutional, the designer will want to express the idea symbolically. One of the famous ads of an earlier decade showed a closeup of a baby's hand holding onto the index finger of a man's hand, dramatizing effectively the "implicit faith and confidence" users place in the product featured in the ad, in this case prescription chemicals bearing the Merck label. This is a visualization so natural, so appropriate, that it has, of course, been used many times.

To dramatize the ease and swiftness by which a passenger can get to Europe, TWA showed a map with only a narrow body of water separating

America and Europe. The headline said: "TWA Announces the Atlantic River."

At the very start—at the visualization stage—the designer wrestles with the problem of putting over a single idea.

For consumer product advertising, the idea may dwell on product quality, product uniqueness, package usefulness, product availability, price, or the service that goes with the product. Taking one of these—say, quality—the designer considers the various ways to illustrate such a concept. The process at this stage may be all mental; perhaps the designer has not yet picked up a pencil.

Choosing art and type styles and arranging elements within the ad follow the process of visualization.

Imitation

Why is advertising so susceptible to imitation? Seymour Luft in *Advertising Age* lists "the 10 most overdone and overdumb genres on TV." They include commercials that say, pompously, that the sponsor is "working for you"; that announce that the product has a new ingredient, making the earlier version worthless; that dig up old popular tunes and make jingles out of them; that go with fake ad libs by athletes; that show the All-American crew and correctly ethnic customers in a fast-food chain singing and dancing; that make you think someone in a commercial is a boy until she removes her hard hat and shakes out her hair; that have a succession of people taking turns singing off key; that move fast from young person to young person sweating attractively, gurgling soft drinks from glistening bottles; that show hard-working, hairy-chested men rewarding themselves with beer at the end of the day, with a sexy waitress moving through the group; that imitate the old Pete Smith movie shorts, with a voiceover explaining the humor, such as it is.[21]

Two photographs inset in a two-page bleed photograph, all in color, help tell the story of a change of shape and colors for Dial deodorant soap in a test market ad designed for Sunday newspaper supplements. All three photographs were necessary: one to show the new soap colors, one to show the soap in its wrappers so buyers could spot it on their store shelves, and one to show the product in use. An excellent example of coordination of large, middle size, and small photographs. The extra space between "looks" and "as" takes into account space likely to be lost in the binding. Art director: Bertram J. Hoddinott. Copywriter: James Dyer. Agency: Foote, Cone & Belding, Chicago.

CLEAR THE AIR
Solve air pollution problems.
Request Bulletin A.
OXY-CATALYST, INC.
Berwyn, Pa.

Some designers find it difficult to get any display in a small-space ad. But see what Oxy-Catalyst, Inc., was able to do with a column-inch several years ago in *Business Week* (the ad is shown here actual size). This ad stood out on a crowded page.

Mostly the duplication in advertising is inadvertent. Advertising people like to write off the duplication as great minds running in the same channels. Rival products have, essentially, the same selling points, and advertising people tend to think alike.

Sometimes the similarity is unmistakably deliberate, as when a store in a small city picks up a big-city store advertising theme or headline. The local advertising person is rushed and so gives in to plagiarism. Someone from out of town discovers it, and one of the trade magazines shows the two look-alike ads; the copycat ad maker loses face, if not a job.

It is possible to copyright an ad, and many sponsors do it now; but suits over copyright infringement are rare. What should discourage plagiarism is the healthy ego of ad people; why would they want to lean so heavily on others? Where's the fun in advertising then?

Anyway, it is the specific presentation that can be copyrighted, not the idea itself.

Designers should not be ashamed to study the patterns and arrangements and designs of other designers, and, when appropriate, to borrow parts of these, combine them with others, and apply them to their own layouts. Good designers maintain what they call, without apology, their "swipe files"—collections of clippings of ads and other works that are appealing (more about that later). They do not make the mistake of rushing to those files for help each time they face new assignments, but the very fact that they have noted the work and filed it has left impressions on their minds. A design solution that works once has a tendency to appear and reappear in the layouts of many designers, few of whom regard themselves as plagiarists.

Avoiding an advertising look

The designer should not feel that an ad has to *look* like an ad. "Adiness" is no universal virtue. The reason so many ads are look-alikes is that designers, like everyone else, are creatures of habit, prone to mimicry. With immunity to standard advertising formats well advanced among many readers, the designer should consider providing an *editorial* flavor to advertising, using the techniques the editor uses to involve readers in front-of-the-book features.

Some advertising designers play an interesting game with the media, trying to see how close they can approximate the format—the type, the style—of the publication in which the ad is to appear without having the magazine place that line of disavowal at the top, "An Advertisement," or reject the ad outright as too close to editorial handling.

The Christian Writers Guild, a La Canada, California, organization that trains writers, sponsors an ad that contains another "ad" above its ad, but the other "ad" is obscured by what looks like a bold, scribbled note: "Hon: Look!!" accompanied by a crudely drawn arrow pointing to the real ad. It looks as though a close friend or spouse has marked the page for whoever subscribes to the magazine. It is not a large ad, but it dominates the page because of the unusual graphic treatment.

Seeing the ad in context

In the fifteenth century, when typefaces for printing were first designed and cut, type designers were more concerned with the looks of individual letters than the overall impressions on the page. The second wave of designers rectified this. In advertising layout, the beginning designer often is most concerned with individual elements within the ad; the veteran designer rightly sees the overall design, the composition, and the design's effect as more important, knowing that the whole of an ad is greater than the sum of its parts.

Whatever the level of creativity, a designer will be influenced by what other designers are doing, if only to be different.

Furthermore, the veteran designer is more concerned with how the ad looks when it is in position than how it looks by itself, beautifully mounted and displayed for client approval. Its character may be considerably changed. Placement is as important in TV advertising as it is in print-medium advertising. After a scene in *Holocaust,* shown on NBC, in which Nazi victims are told that gas chambers are merely disinfecting areas, a Lysol commercial came on the screen.

The problem of juxtaposition extends to billboards. A sign outside of Burnet, Texas, showing several sizes of beer bottles of a particular brand, asked, "Which Bud's for You?" A sign next to it said, "Ask God." The second sign, which had a different sponsor, went on to say, "The Family That Prays Together Stays Together."

Is there a "right" approach?

Persons in the advertising business do not agree on the best approach to creativity. Some say the best approach is through brainstorming sessions. Brainstorming, said to have originated with Alex Osborn of Batten Barton Durstine & Osborn, brings a group of like-minded individuals together to stimulate each other into the production of ideas and solutions to problems. The group, in effect, pools its imagination. No matter how foolish the idea may be on the surface, it gets thrown onto the table for consideration. Theoretically, no participant is embarrassed; none worries about looking foolish. Comments and reactions flow unrestricted. One idea triggers another. Random associations are encouraged. What members of the group try to do is unloose the subconscious.

But brainstorming has its detractors. Saul Bass, for one. He says: "I fail to note the head-and-shoulders-above-the-crowd creative visual product of the agencies that have constantly utilized this technique."

Some say that despite protestations to the contrary, such sessions *restrict* rather than stimulate thought: participants are afraid they will embarrass themselves. Furthermore, such sessions release participants from responsibility should their ideas, after they are adopted, fail to work out. And it can be argued that fear of failure or an acute awareness of responsibility is a force for high-level performance. Artists no longer feeling stomach butterflies or damp palms may well wonder whether they are giving the work the attention and preparation they gave it in their earlier, more enthusiastic periods.

"Creativity, like any values, like moral or religious values, cannot be decided by a majority vote," Dr. Gregory Zilboorg told a Creativity Conference sponsored by the Art Directors Club of New York. "The worst type of sacrilege is making the artist a member of a committee." As a religious plaque says: "For God So Loved the World that He Didn't Send a Committee." Professor John E. Arnold of Stanford has said that the most daring idea a committee can adopt is the most daring idea the least-daring member of that committee can tolerate.

The antibrainstormers hold that a greater volume of usable ideas comes from persons operating independently: that the production of ideas is necessarily a lonely act.

It is clear that under neither system will ideas or solutions to problems present themselves until the participants engage in activities to stimulate their imaginations. The truly creative person is the one who reads and observes and listens and searches. In advertising, as in all fields of endeavor, the best ideas seldom come from the blue, they only *seem* to; the groundwork was laid hours or days before.

This small-space ad gets by nicely without any art. Christine O'Neal, wife of the president of the restaurant that sponsored the ad, designed it. The agency is Alan Brill Advertising.

Timing is important in an ad like this, sponsored by a tire store. It ran at election time.

William P. Lear, the late multimillionaire designer of the Learjet and inventor of some 150 patented items, thought the secret of creativity lies with the subconscious. "One of the unfortunate things about our educational system is that we do not teach our students how to avail themselves of subconscious capabilities," he said. "We don't teach them that they've got a computer, connected with the infinite, that has stored an unlimited number of relatively unimportant details which can be interrelated into the correct answer [to a problem]. You use your subconscious constantly without knowing it. It's like forgetting a name and remembering it later. What happened? You fed the information into your subconscious and then you thought of something else, but your subconscious said, 'I've got to work on this' and it came out with it. We don't teach students how to do that. We don't even tell them that they have a subconscious."

He added: "Feeding information to your subconscious is just putting the software into a computer. But your subconscious can't work on something that your conscious doesn't know anything about."[22]

Stimulating creativity

Jack Roberts of Ogilvy & Mather, imitating a 1960s writing and speaking style, said, "The truth is . . . , if you gotta ask [how to be creative]—you ain't never gonna know. It's all programmed, man, all locked-up in those mysterious genes. And the very best way to obtain a high creative potential is by careful selection of your mom and pop."[23]

But whether creativity is inherited or acquired, the spring from which it flows must constantly be fed—through reading and observation, through research, and through experimentation.

John Nazzaro, copy director for Chirurg & Cairns, Inc., Boston, has reminded his colleagues in advertising of the importance of reading. "Creative thinking depends upon a wide range of knowledge," he observed. "Since creativity is basically the perception of novel relationships, the general reader [the one who reads more than just the advertising magazines] is better equipped—has more knowledge to feed upon. Reading combined with experience is a winning creative combination."

And just plain observing what goes on around them helps give designers the necessary background to face assignments confidently. Designers are aware of fashions, fads, mannerisms, trends—and it shows in their work.

Rick Levine, who created an award-winning commercial for Burlington socks showing a man dancing hard to shake a sock off his foot, got his inspiration from seeing the film *Zorba the Greek,* which showed similar dancing. The idea in the commercial was to show that the socks were made to stay up.[24]

J. L. Marra, a lecturer at Texas Tech University, has pointed out that "advertising covers a wide and expansive area of various disciplines, and it is by exposure to these disciplines that advertising students benefit." Marra teaches advertising students to look for analogies in creating their ads. The students start with similes ("Hot coffee is as bracing as _____ "), then move on to more difficult, less direct analogies.[25]

Conducting research

Research is simply an attempt to uncover needed facts or prove what already may be suspected. The designer may conduct the research personally, asking questions of randomly selected persons; or, on a more scientific basis, colleagues who understand better than the designer the laws of sampling opinion and measuring behavior may do the job. Research does have its place in advertising. Rightly used, it is a help, not a threat, to the designer.

For instance, Landor Associates, a package-design firm, brings in potential customers and has its designers watch those customers from behind one-way glass. The designers learn things about type and color they never got at art school. And to see how a package looks in the real world, the design firm maintains a room with stocked supermarket shelves installed.

Trace, a service of Market Facts Inc., Chicago, using microprocessors, measures viewers' reactions to TV commercials second-by-second. Viewers punch buttons on five-button, hand-held devices while commercials run. The "1" button is for a very negative reaction, the "5" for a very positive reaction.

Phase One, Beverly Hills, California, uses computers with complex software to see if a planned commercial will say what its creators want it to say. Some 12,000 questions are asked of a typical commercial under study. For this service an advertiser pays $5,000.

Historically, creative people have tended to distrust the sciences—including the social sciences. Today creative persons—in advertising, at least—and science-minded persons appreciate and respect each other.

In his seminars for newspaper advertising people, Professor Fred Farrar of Temple University stresses the importance of research and the use of computers in conducting it. "Garbage in, garbage out," he reminds his listeners. "But if you don't have anything else, use garbage."

Experimentation

"No wonder some artists live such long lives, for there is so much to learn and discover in art!" observed Florence Margaret Daniels in her book *Why Art?*[26] There is much for graphic designers to discover, too.

No less an authority than Daniel Berkeley Updike (he was willing to call himself "a liberal conservative or a conservative liberal—whichever you like or dislike") has argued for typographic innovation. "To turn to another department of daily life," he wrote, "what would happen if no one had ever tried experiments with food? In the distant past there was the first human being who—as an experiment—ate an oyster, though perhaps first trying jellyfish with less comfortable results. Others died of eating toadstools before people learned that they could survive on mushrooms. Almost all our vegetable food we owe to gastronomic adventurers. Thus the most hide-bound conservative owes his sustenance to the fruits—and vegetables—of experiment." And quoting Goethe: "There is no past that we need long to return to, there is only the eternally new which is formed out of enlarged elements of the past; and our real endeavor must always be towards new and better creation."[27]

"To be satisfied is deadening and is excusable only in the aged," says art director William Miller. "Full and proper development can only come to those who dedicate their efforts and experiences toward constant improvement. As designers, we must evolve a continuing pattern of appraisal and self-criticism, based on an open conviction that we can do better. As designers with a strong tendency to think and create subjectively, we must train ourselves to review our creations objectively. We are not designing and creating to please ourselves, but to sell the products and services belonging to someone else."[28]

Using the "swipe file"

Samuel Butler in his *Notebooks* said, "The history of art is the history of revivals."

In Voltaire's view, originality was nothing more than judicious imitation. C. E. M. Joad thought it was little more than skill in concealing origins.

The trouble with the first ad is that the reader is not sure where to start the copy. Right after the three dots? Or over at the left? Both the headline and art lead to the second column. But logic tells you to start with the first column. A little rearrangement (the ad at right) solves the problem. The new ad also makes more interesting use of white space, brings the columns together to make a unit of them, and brings art and headline together, too. The vertical line, which serves no purpose, is eliminated. So are the dots, which are a design cliché. None of the type has to be reset in the new ad; nor is the art cropped any differently.

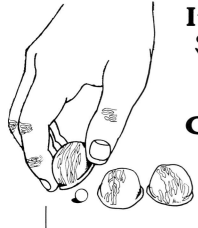

It's the Same Old Shell Game...

There's a bottom line to all this. Lane County is claiming it can't afford to meet the proposals of its employees for a salary increase that will help us keep up with the cost of living. But they can afford to meet them.

The facts show that the County Commissioners aren't telling the truth. A comprehensive budget study shows that without a doubt, there is several million in cash carry-over that they're not admitting to; millions extra in the contingency fund; more than a million in O and C revenues, and a discrepancy of many millions in the General Fund between what the County claims they can spend and what they've actually budgeted.

What this adds up to is that Lane County *can* afford to pay a decent salary increase to its employees, who have had only a 3.8% raise in the last 15 months, while the cost-of-living has soared into double digits.

The fact is Lane County can't afford *not* to treat its employees fairly. The rising demoralization and turnover in the county workforce that results from the shell game County management is playing on employees and taxpayers alike hurts us all.

Lane County employees don't want to be on strike. We want to be back on the job providing services to the public. But the County Commissioners broke off negotiations and walked out . . . even while AFSCME was willing and ready to bargain all night to reach a fair settlement.

The money's there. We have the facts to prove it. We can have a fair increase with no hike in taxes (only six percent of the operating budget comes from property taxes anyway) and no danger whatsoever of a fiscal shortfall. It's about time County management realized Lane County residents elected them to provide serious and stable government administration . . . not a carnival sideshow.

We want to be back on the job providing services to Lane County. The best way to get us there is to call the County Commissioners and tell them to stop playing games and get back to serious bargaining.

The old shell game has no place in a serious business-like negotiations. But it seems the County Commissioners haven't heard that yet.

It may be fine in a carnival, but when you pay taxes . . .or when you work for Lane County, you expect your elected officials to be honest and aboveboard about just how much money they really have and where it's actually going.

Not that Lane County's Commissioners are moving walnut shells around and trying to hide a pea. No; they're using a different kind of sleight of hand.

For example, in current negotiations with Lane County employees, the Commissioners are attempting to hide county money and shuffle it around with formidable names like 'cash carryover', 'Federal General Revenue Sharing', 'contingency fund', 'Building Expansion', 'Timber Revenues', and 'Oregon and California Railroad Revenues'.

Even by themselves, those are phrases designed to boggle all but a public administrator or an accountant. But to make it worse, in the budget, all expenses are combined into only three line items . . .personnel, materials and supplies, and capital outlay . . . making it impossible to follow the transfer of funds.

Paid for by **AFSCME** *in the public service*

It's the Same Old Shell Game

The old shell game has no place in a serious business-like negotiations. But it seems the County Commissioners haven't heard that yet.

It may be fine in a carnival, but when you pay taxes . . . or when you work for Lane County, you expect your elected officials to be honest and aboveboard about just how much money they really have and where it's actually going.

Not that Lane County's Commissioners are moving walnut shells around and trying to hide a pea. No; they're using a different kind of sleight of hand.

For example, in current negotiations with Lane County employees, the Commissioners are attempting to hide county money and shuffle it around with formidable names like 'cash carryover', 'Federal General Revenue Sharing', 'contingency fund', 'Building Expansion', 'Timber Revenues', and 'Oregon and California Railroad Revenues'.

Even by themselves, those are phrases designed to boggle all but a public administrator or an accountant. But to make it worse, in the budget, all expenses are combined into only three line items . . . personnel, materials and supplies, and capital outlay . . . making it impossible to follow the transfer of funds.

There's a bottom line to all this. Lane County is claiming it can't afford to meet the proposals of its employees for a salary increase that will help us keep up with the cost of living. But they can afford to meet them.

The facts show that the County Commissioners aren't telling the truth. A comprehensive budget study shows that without a doubt, there is several million in cash carry-over that they're not admitting to; millions extra in the contingency fund; more than a million in O and C revenues, and a discrepancy of many millions in the General Fund between what the County claims they can spend and what they've actually budgeted.

What this adds up to is that Lane County *can* afford to pay a decent salary increase to its employees, who have had only a 3.8% raise in the last 15 months, while the cost-of-living has soared into double digits.

The fact is Lane County can't afford *not* to treat its employees fairly. The rising demoralization and turnover in the county workforce that results from the shell game County management is playing on employees and taxpayers alike hurts us all.

Lane County employees don't want to be on strike. We want to be back on the job providing services to the public. But the County Commissioners broke off negotiations and walked out . . . even while AFSCME was willing and ready to bargain all night to reach a fair settlement.

The money's there. We have the facts to prove it. We can have a fair increase with no hike in taxes (only six percent of the operating budget comes from property taxes anyway) and no danger whatsoever of a fiscal shortfall. It's about time County management realized Lane County residents elected them to provide serious and stable government administration . . . not a carnival sideshow.

We want to be back on the job providing services to Lane County. The best way to get us there is to call the County Commissioners and tell them to stop playing games and get back to serious bargaining.

Paid for by **AFSCME** *in the public service*

Alexander Lindey summed it up this way: "Every work of art is, in the final analysis, a compromise between tradition and revolt. It cannot be otherwise. For a composition that is wholly devoid of newness is dead; one that is wholly unconventional is incomprehensible."[29] Some artists place their faith largely in traditional solutions to their design problems while others rely more on experimentation, but all artists are at least partially tradition oriented and partially experiment minded.

And all build, maintain, and use a "swipe file" of printed works that have impressed them.

Designer A copies from Designer B, who copied from Designer C.

"As a student at Cooper Union, I found that the best way for me to learn was to steal; to steal from the best until my ability and confidence made this nefarious activity unnecessary," admitted the late Herb Lubalin. "I think I 'borrowed' every design Paul Rand ever did. . . . And I was not alone."[30]

You could say that in graphic design there is nothing new under the studio fluorescent lamps. The novelist can only rework one of about three dozen basic plots that have been isolated in literature. Graphic designers have even fewer "plots" than novelists do (see chapter 5).

Yet designers can bring to a basic design pattern a touch, a character, that is theirs alone. Then they become creative.

"In art," observed George Bernard Shaw, "the highest success is to be the last of your race, not the first. Anybody, almost, can make a beginning: the difficulty is to make an end—to do what cannot be bettered."

Much of what we admire in graphic design—many of the ads that win prizes at the art directors' show—owe their excellence to earlier works. Designers stimulate the creative processes through these techniques:

1. *Adaptation.* Designers lift an art truth from a work in another field. The composition of a fine painting or the appeal of a well-designed building may suggest the pattern for elements in an advertisement. And nature provides an unending source of design ideas.

2. *Addition.* An austere arrangement for, say, an institutional advertiser or for the manufacturer of a quality product may provide the basis for a more complicated ad that combines several similar elements.

3. *Subtraction.* Designers lift part of an existing ad that appeals to them and build a new ad from it. Or they note the handling of type in an ad and, ignoring the rest of the ad, put together a new arrangement appropriate to the type. Perhaps a small part of a picture begs to be lifted away and blown up—magnified—in a new ad.

4. *Modification.* Designers see an appealing ad and, for another assignment, make only slight changes in the pattern. Four pictures are made into three, for instance, but the space they occupy may stay the same. The headline is moved from the top of the ad to a place near the bottom. And so on.

5. *Exaggeration.* One designer decides to push a headline out near the edge of the ad—to nearly bleed it. Another designer likes the effect, and comes even closer in another ad to bleeding the headline *and* the copy. Or the original designer resurrects one of the flamboyant types of the 1920s— a stenciled Bodoni known as Futura Black, for instance (a misnamed type, by the way, because it has no relationship to regular Futura). The next designer increases the same face to banner-head proportions.

Note what the product's background can do for it. The cars are the same. Their placement on the page is the same. But while the first car appears to be moving normally down a straight stretch of road, the second appears to be making a steep climb.

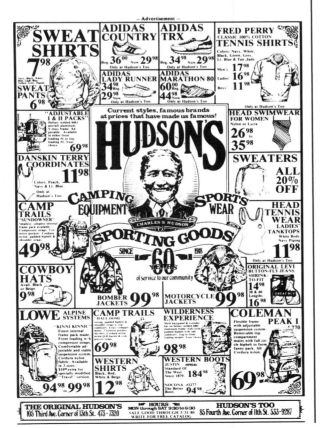

At first glance, you might get the impression that this is an ad from out of the past. The art and the handling of the headlines suggest it. What better way to put over the idea that prices are low and quality is good? And how better to make your retail ad stand out from all the others? This happens to be a retail ad for Hudson's stores from a magazine: *New York.* George Armstrong and Sid Paterson designed it under the art direction of Luis Baleiron. Carl Zimmermann wrote the copy. The agency was Paterson & Lawrence Inc.

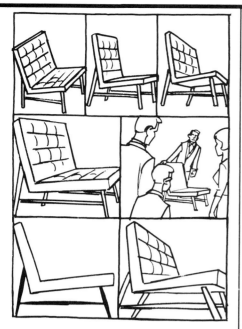

There are many ways of showing the product: bird's-eye view, normal view, worm's-eye view; the product close up, the product in panorama; the product in pattern or flat abstraction, the product foreshortened or in exaggerated perspective. Nor as a designer do you need to settle for a mere product portrait. You may emphasize some single feature of the product: its design or its durability. Or you may show the careful workmanship that goes into the product, or the company behind the product, or a satisfaction stemming from the product's use, or the class of people who buy the product.

6. *Opposition.* When the trend in retail advertising in town is toward blackness and reverses, the designer comes up with an ad that features lightface type and large masses of white space. When double borders and rounded corners are in, this designer drops borders altogether and squares off the elements. When everybody is using the Swiss-inspired gothics, the designer specifies Spartan or Futura.

As a student, you should not hesitate to lean on and borrow from the work of other designers. But, obviously, as you become more at home in graphic design, you should rely less and less on the crutches of adaptation, addition, subtraction, modification, exaggeration, and opposition—at least on their conscious use. At the lower levels of consciousness the borrowing process will, of course, continue.

Even as a beginning designer, though, you should appropriate for your own use only *ideas* from designs you admire. To what you borrow you should add some new twist, a touch of your own. Otherwise, quite apart from the ethics of the matter, you will realize little satisfaction from your work.

"It's no secret that there's a lot of borrowing of ideas practiced in our profession," observed designer Jerry Herring. "With the volume of work being produced, the similarity among products and services, and the fear of some clients to try the untried, an overlapping of marketing concepts, styles and phrases is probably unavoidable. Then, there's the proliferation of our trade publications and annuals, which regularly bring us the best work from around the rest of the country. If we see something we like, sooner or later most of us will allow some (or all) of it to find its way into our work."

Letting go

A well-muscled creativity can carry you far afield.

Gary Dahl resigned as creative director of Darien, Russell & Hill, a San Jose, California, advertising agency, when his tongue-in-cheek idea of considering rocks as pets resulted in a packaged product that became a favorite of the 1975 Christmas buying season. What Dahl did was to pack ordinary egg-shaped rocks and shredded newspapers in attractive boxes with holes to allow for "breathing."

What made the item enjoyable—and perhaps worth the $4 retail price—was the owner's manual which told of tricks you could teach your rock—tricks like rolling over and playing dead. The rolling over could best be taught on the side of a hill, the manual pointed out. As for teaching the rock to play dead: "Rocks enjoy this trick so much that often, when you're not even looking, they'll actually practice it on their own."

Dahl's name for the company he organized to market the product was Rock Bottom Productions. Publicity alone—the story was widely published—was enough to sell the rocks.

There followed the inevitable imitators and spin-offs.

After Christmas, a St. Louis company, Rock Group, promoted a Stud Rock with "instructions" on how to breed it with any other rock. The chairman of the company, Stan Leitner, admitted the idea grew out of the Pet Rock phenomenon. He realized the fad would soon be over, but he felt that there was still some time to cash in on it.

Still another firm, American Consumer, Inc., through The Crackerbarrel of Westport, Connecticut, offered a Pet Baby Boulder, which, according to an ad in the *Christian Science Monitor,* was "pretrained to obey sixteen commands," such as to "play dead," "sit," "stay," and "crack nuts." "Why Settle for a Piece of *That* Rock When You Can Have our PRETRAINED Pet Baby Boulder?" asked the ad's headline (question mark added). The price was $2.98, a dollar less than the original, plus $.40 "to partially cover postage and handling."

P.H. Sales in Bronxville, New York, in an ad in the *National Observer,* offered a Pedigree Rock. "Anyone can own a Pet Rock but only a select few deserve a Pedigree Rock." You could get a pair of them for $2.95.

For $1.99 a can, you could buy Pet Rock Food, "tasty tidbits of sand and small pebbles" marketed by the Center for Concept Development, New York. The label cautioned against overfeeding young rocks.

There was even a Pet Rock University at Glendale Heights, Illinois, that offered correspondence courses and degrees to Pet Rocks. And it was possible in California to arrange a burial at sea for your Pet Rock.

Milton Ribak, a New York PR man, published the bimonthly *Pet Rock News.*

At the tail end of the phenomenon King James Productions, Oak Park, Illinois, dreamed up a Trained Stick and sold it for $4.50. Stan Leitner, through his Rock Group, brought out an Invisible Piranha. The owner's manual listed some questions and answers about the fish. In answer to the question whether "a fish's age can be told," Leitner wrote: "Certainly. Mention it to anyone you think would be interested."

HDC Industries, Kokomo, Indiana, using the *National Observer,* "At Long Last" offered for $2.50 "the Add 'em Up Finger Machine that Helps You Count Up to Five." You stuck your fingers and thumb through the five numbered holes provided and you were ready to go. Tongue-in-Chic, Elmhurst, Illinois, offered a similar gadget.

Meanwhile, up in North Fayston, Vermont, John Bramblett was selling cans of "Vermont Green Mountain Air" at $2 each. Instructions on the can suggested: "Tilt can toward nose and inhale deeply. To simulate mountain air on a winter day, place in freezer for one hour prior to inhalation." John Bramblett had to go to Massachusetts to can his air. No one in Vermont could do it for him.

The marketing hit of the 1983 Christmas season was the ugly, but cute in its ugliness, Cabbage Patch Kids doll, which had to be "adopted," not just bought. Near riots occurred at stores where the dolls, scarce because of the demand, were sold. The phenomenon was something to delight the media, on the alert for Christmas stories. An editor of a newspaper reported that the doll he bought was kidnapped. He had no idea who could have taken the doll, but he knew it was not one of his reporters because, he said, there were no misspellings in the ransom note.

Facing "designer's block"

Stan Richards, president of The Richards Group, Dallas, noting the difficulties of unproductive days, thinks that during them designers may actually be producing: "It's on those black days when we feel very *uncreative* that we're really right in the middle of the creative process. Why? Because we're struggling, growing, developing. We're exploring new territory, places we have never been before. When we're feeling great, when everything is working, when we're at our 'most creative,' there's the very real danger that we're repeating ourselves—resolving problems we've solved many times before."

Still, the designer struggles from time to time with "designer's block." "If he accepts the fact that the seeds of the solution of any problem lie within the problem itself, he will be on the way to solving it," said British typographer John Lewis.

If, despite all your preparing and all your utilizing of the techniques for stimulating the creative process, "designer's block" happens to you, you may find these two suggestions helpful:

1. After some preliminary work on the project, forget it for a while. A coffee break, an errand run, some physical activity—or better yet, a break of several days' duration, when a deadline is not pressing—will give the

How is Bill Vanderdasson able to draw the vases and bowls in this J. K. Gill ad so that the right side of the drawing so perfectly matches the left? He does one vertical half first, then traces it, then flops the tracing, and retraces it onto the original drawing. To do these sketches he worked both from the art objects themselves and from photographs.

Art director Frank A. Mattucci of Frank J. Corbett, Inc., Communications, Chicago, did it all for this ad directed to doctors reading the journal *Diseases of the Colon.* He wrote and designed the ad and made the graceful, simple drawing inspired, perhaps, by a familiar Picasso drawing. This ad is a nice combination of halftone and line art, the line art predominating. The layout is formal.

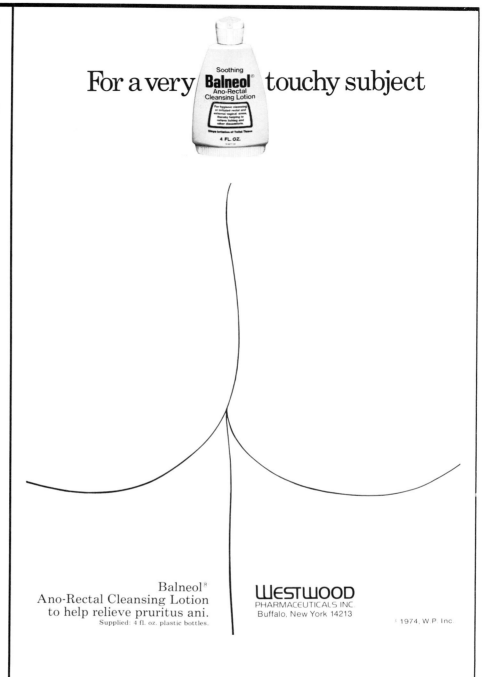

For a very **Balneol** touchy subject

Balneol®
Ano-Rectal Cleansing Lotion
to help relieve pruritus ani.
Supplied: 4 fl. oz. plastic bottles.

WESTWOOD
PHARMACEUTICALS INC.
Buffalo, New York 14213

© 1974, W.P. Inc

subconscious and even the unconscious a chance to work on the problem. The first temporary solution to the problem is likely to look quite different when you return to your drawing board.

2. Work on more than one project at a time. The moving from one job to another, from one activity to another, provides a change of pace that is almost as fruitful as a complete withdrawal from creative work. A solution to one problem can stimulate another solution to another problem. What can result is a kind of individual brainstorming session.

The great temptation is—procrastination.

In one of his essays Robert Benchley wrote, "I had decided to go to bed early and see how that would work, having tried everything else to catch up on my sleep." And so you might well, in the end, after taking part in a bull session, making some telephone calls, going out for coffee, plant yourself at your drawing table—having tried everything else to catch up on your assignments in Advertising Layout.

1. John S. Straiton, "The Fey Cult of Cutie-Pie Creativity," *Marketing/Communications,* November 1969, p. 64.

2. William Bernbach, "Bill Bernbach Defines the Four Disciplines of Creativity," *Advertising Age,* July 5, 1971, pp. 21–23.

3. "Creativity TV Style," *Advertising Age,* October 13, 1975, p. 14.

4. Quoted by Kathryn Sederberg, "Top Agency 'Creatives' Take a Closer Look at Creativity," *Advertising Age,* June 4, 1979, p. S–3.

5. *Ibid.,* p. S–3.

6. *Ibid.,* p. S–10.

7. *Ibid.,* p. S–10.

8. Quoted by John F. Baker in "Dr. Rollo May," *Publishers Weekly,* December 1, 1975, p. 12.

9. Originally in 1962. Reprinted in "Editor's Column," *Communication Arts,* January/February 1974, p. 10.

10. Quoted by Baker in "Dr. Rollo May," p. 13.

11. Quoted in "Design '64: Directions and Dilemmas," *CA: The Magazine of the Communications Arts,* September/October 1964, p. 81.

12. Ron Hoff, in Maxine Paetro, *How to Put Your Book Together and Get a Job in Advertising,* (New York: Executive Communications, 1979), pp. 77, 78.

13. Paul Waddell, "Try Creativity—It Sells," *Advertising Age,* December 13, 1982, p. M–36.

14. Sharon Churcher, "A Hitch in Hitchcock's Credits," *New York,* January 17, 1983, p. 12.

15. In a letter to the editor, *Advertising Age,* March 20, 1972, p. 88.

16. From "True Gage," a 1978 ad sponsored by *The Wall Street Journal.*

17. Quoted by *Time* in its "People" column, December 18, 1978, p. 85.

18. Alexis Gelber, "Play It as It L.A.'s,"*Art Direction,* May 1979, pp. 66, 67.

19. Mill Roseman, "Zen and the Art of Advertising," *United,* May 1983, pp. 76, 81.

20. Massimo Vignelli, "From Less Is More to Less Is a Bore. Is More the Better?" *U&lc.,* December 1982, p. 10.

21. Seymour Luft, "Imitation: The Highest Form of Blather-y," *Advertising Age,* November 15, 1982, p. M–30.

22. Quoted by Digby Diehl, "Q & A: Bill Lear," *West,* April 23, 1972, pp. 30–31.

23. Jack Roberts, "The Ten-Letter, X-Rated, Gold-Plated Word," *Art Direction,* July 1971, p. 78.

24. Bruce Kurtz, *Spots* (New York: Arts Communication, 1977), p. 70.

25. J. L. Marra, "Using Analogy to Teach Idea Generation in Advertising," *Communication: Journalism Education Today,* Fall 1978, pp. 2–5.

26. Florence Margaret Daniels, *Why Art?* (Chicago: Nelson-Hall, 1978).

27. Daniel Berkeley Updike, *Some Aspects of Printing, Old and New* (New Haven, Conn.: William Edwin Rudge, 1941), p. 48.

28. William Miller, *Outdoor Advertising Design* (Chicago: General Outdoor Advertising Co., 1958), p. 57.

29. Alexander Lindey, *Plagiarism and Originality* (New York: Harper & Brothers, 1952).

30. Herb Lubalin, "Herb Lubalin's Typography Issue," *Print,* May/June 1979, p. 43.

3
Putting it into words

"More than ever now, art directors and copywriters are working as a team," *Art Direction* reports. "In fact, many who are new to the business can't imagine working any other way. . . . Copywriters are learning to be more visual while art directors are learning to be more verbal."[1]

Where copy and art departments once operated independently at agencies, today they often work under a single banner. Art directors become interested and involved in the copy, and the copywriters help visualize the ads. Allen Rosenshine, president of Batten Barton Durstine and Osborn, thinks separate copy and art departments are "relics of the past."[2]

Whether they work as team members or independently, art directors and designers need to know something about copy. "Design, no matter how brilliant, can't bring success by itself. Design is only the relation between word and picture, and you've got to have the word first," observes William Cheney,[3] art director of *Sunset*. He has magazines in mind, but what he says applies to advertising as well.

The challenge of copy

The term *copy* originated in the early days of printing when the compositor received a manuscript with instructions to "copy it." Today, as a noun, *copy* refers to the nonvisual part of the ad: the text.

The writing of advertising copy is a demanding craft that few master. Even writers who do well in other literary endeavors do not always perform well in copywriting roles.

John W. Crawford in *Advertising* divided the copywriter's job into "two coequal and commingling" parts: one "a never-ending search for ideas"; the other "a never-ending search for new and different ways to express those ideas."[4]

Whatever the kind of advertising, the copywriter must choose each word carefully, making sure it carries just the right meaning. Naturally the copywriter wants to use those words that put the product, service, or idea in its best possible light. Some words do a better job of selling than others. Researchers at Yale University once drew up a list of words that aid most in the job of persuading. The words are these: *you, new, health, love, save, easy, proven, results, money, safety, discovery,* and *guarantee.* Not an inspiring list from a literary standpoint. But they are words worth considering for many kinds of advertising copy.

To this list most advertisers would add *free.* Advertisers know that getting something free appeals to the rich as well as the poor. A swanky condo in Manhattan in 1983 in a *New York Times* ad offered a free Rolls-Royce to people who would buy one of the units, priced from about $600,000.

Like most kinds of writing, advertising copy requires several revisions before it takes its final form. Rewriting is very much a part of the copywriter's craft. "Never be content with your first draft," Ogilvy & Mather tells its writers in its handbook *How to Write Better.* "Rewrite, with an eye toward simplifying and clarifying. Rearrange. Revise. Above all, cut."

A rewriting is best when it is delayed for a day or two or more. It is surprising how rough a piece of copy looks to a writer who allows it to cool for a time.

This Bay Area Rapid Transit poster invites reader participation by printing and overprinting, in various colors, answers to the question asked in the headline. Wilton, Coombs & Colnett, San Francisco, was the agency. Art director and designer: Nancy Bovee.

In the beginning, a multitude of voices rang out across the wires and rumbled: "Locations!" *A*nd out of the darkness sprang forth a land filled with cities great and small. Farms and forests. River towns. Southern settings. Urban lights. Industrial sites. Shores and harbors. All heavenly. *A*nd so the producers saw Illinois and said that it was good. *T*hen the voices sought casting directors. And talent begotten in the images and likenesses of the script. *A*nd lo, casting was fruitful. And extras multiplied. *Y*et the voices coveted crews of great strength. State of the art equipment. Post-Production. And were fearful of the cost. *B*ut Illinois calmed the voices. And the producers read the bottom line and saw that it was good. Very good. *C*aterers and hotel rooms were found. And the voices made a joyful noise. *S*till they desired a covenant with those most high. And it came to pass that city and state officials were perfect angels. *T*he sea of red tape parted. *A*nd the producers looked upon all that had gone before them in Illinois, gave thanks and said: "*L*et there be "Lights! Camera! Action!" *W*ord has it that Illinois is a divine place to shoot. Contact Lucy Salenger, Managing Director, Illinois Film Office. Department of Commerce and Community Affairs. 310 South Michigan Avenue, Chicago, Illinois 60604. (312) 793-3600. She'll make a believer out of you.

Illinois

An institutional ad sponsored by the Illinois Film Office to reach readers of *Variety* and *Hollywood Reporter* uses Biblical language to make the point that Illinois welcomes film makers. The copy ends on this note: "Word has it that Illinois is a divine place to shoot." Designer Robert Qually picked up on the slanting rays in the photograph to use bold italics for the opening words, the logo, and the caps that begin the sentences. The agency was Lee King & Partners, Inc., Chicago.

Often competing products possess a common characteristic, but one product becomes better known than the others for the characteristic because it is first to speak of it.

In a sense, the copywriter operates like an explorer, staking out a claim wherever possible. Claims in recent years have become both grandiose and tongue-in-cheek. Marlboro took title to open spaces with its "Marlboro Country" concept, while United Air Lines took over above with its "Friendly Skies of United." A beer company claimed that "weekends were made for Michelob." No matter how you felt about it, if you happened to be young, you were a member of "The Pepsi Generation," which jumps up and down a lot. You did not just drink Dr. Pepper, you became a "Pepper."

Levi Strauss & Co. uses a series of classy ads like this to explain its 501® ''Shrink-To-Fit™'' jeans. With good humor, the ad capitalizes on the fact that the product hasn't changed in 125 years. ''You keep buying original Levi's 501® blue denim jeans, and we'll do our best to keep adding no improvements.'' The jeans have a four-button fly. ''No need to go switching to something that might just be a temporary fad, like zippers.'' Bernie Vangrin art directed; Tim Price wrote the copy; Dugald Stermer did the illustrations. Foote, Cone & Belding/Honig, San Francisco, was the agency.

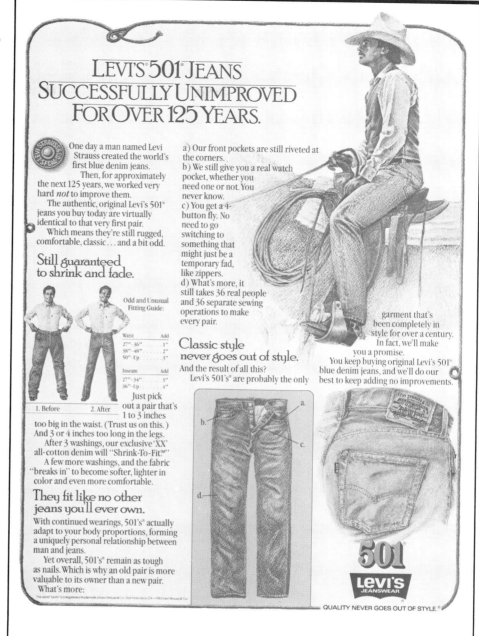

(Pages 50 and 51)
The copy and rough layout (both actual size) for an ad for The Benson, a quality hotel. The ad went through several changes before it was finally approved by the client. Art director: Rick McQuiston. Copywriter: Tom Wiecks. Agency: Cole & Weber, Portland.

Hanley Norins of Young & Rubicam quoted Aldous Huxley as saying, "The advertisement is one of the most interesting and difficult of modern literary forms." But Huxley did not go far enough, Norins said, for "copywriting is *the* most difficult and intense form of writing."[5] While Norins's thesis may be tinged with the hyperbole to be expected from an advertising person, he did build a strong case. In *The Compleat Copywriter* he pointed out that the copywriter should be able to handle all kinds of writing, for copy can take the form of a story, a piece of reporting, a poem, a play—any literary form. And whatever kind of literature the copywriter chooses to produce, it must be done with a limited number of words.

Not only that, the copywriter may write for an audience that does not necessarily want to read or hear what is said. If the audience is not hostile to what the copywriter says, it may at least be indifferent. Of course, the copywriter may write for a more receptive audience, too. The reader, listener, or viewer may be aware of needing the product. Or the ad may contain newsworthy information. Or the ad may deal with a product that is intrinsically interesting.

CLIENT: BENSON HOTEL

DATE:

TITLE:

JOB NO:

HEADLINE: Some of the unexpected extras you can expect at The Benson.

COPY: In an age of look-a-like hotel rooms and often less-than-helpful help, The Benson may take some getting used to. But it's an adjustment our guests love making.

Because at The Benson, the personal attention they receive is every bit as lavish as their surroundings. Which, considering the highly-polished Circassian walnut paneling, the cut-glass chandeliers, the gleaming silver, is saying a lot.

No wonder so many Portlanders cherish this hotel as something of a local landmark. And no wonder so many of those visiting Portland remember The Benson: we don't forget them.

The Benson Hotel, Broadway & Oak. Reservations, 228-9611.

SIG: THE BENSON:
One of the Few Remaining Classic Hotels.
Western International

CAPTIONS: With 24-hour room service, our guests' appetites can keep the kind of hours they like. We even guarantee drinks will be delivered within 12 minutes.

Guests can enjoy complimentary tea in the lobby each afternoon. And for early risers, there's piping hot coffee from 5:30 a.m. to 7:30 a.m.

Few American hotels have a concierge in their lobby, but The Benson does. His only job is helping guests feel at home.

In each room, there's an alarm clock, electric blankets--even a thermometer outside the window.

SOME UNEXPECTED EXTRAS YOU CAN EXPECT AT THE BENSON.

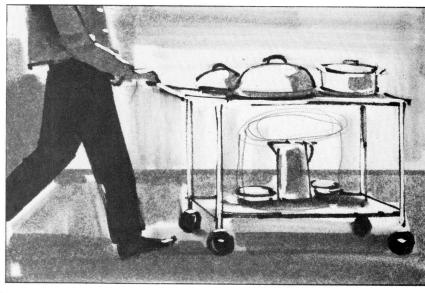

THE BENSON.
ONE OF THE FEW REMAINING GREAT HOTELS.

After a few years the copywriter may develop a product specialty, say in foods or automobiles. The copywriter may also specialize in writing for a single medium, like television or direct mail. But in the course of the job the copywriter writes for every class of reader. One ad may have to influence the youth market. Another ad, for the same product, may have to appeal to a minority group.

All of this is done without much recognition, for there are no bylines in advertising copy. The advertising copywriter remains anonymous. The only one who gains some recognition in an ad, if anyone does, is the artist who does the illustration. Under some circumstances—especially if the artist is well known—a signature is allowed, even encouraged. And on rare occasions the designer's name runs somewhere in the ad in small type. (Such a line is called a "credit line.")

If you do see a byline identifying the writer, it is a form of testimonial in which a famous person praises a product, as when golfer Lee Trevino's byline appears in a Dodge ad under the headline "How I Learned to Relax and Enjoy My Drives" (a little humor there). No one really believes Trevino wrote the ad, though—any more than anyone believes a president writes his own speeches.

"Any newscast can tell you what's happening. INSIGHT tells you why."

As Associate Editor of The New York Times, Clifton Daniel has a hot line to all the hot spots in the world.

Every night Mr. Daniel talks over the leading events of the day with Times authorities wherever they are. And you're invited to listen in.

Called INSIGHT, this unique series probes, analyzes and interprets what's *behind* the headlines. It lets you hear for yourself what distinguished Times correspondents, critics, columnists and editors have to say about important issues in this country and abroad.

Their eyewitness reports and opinions come to you completely unedited and unrehearsed, broadcast directly from phone booths, battlefronts, police headquarters, foreign embassies or wherever news is being made.

To be on top of the news, get behind it with Clifton Daniel and the unmatched worldwide resources of T] New York Times.

Get more insight into t. news from INSIGHT.

INSIGHT
7:30-8 PM/MON-FRI

WQXR/1560AM/96.3FM
RADIO STATIONS OF THE NEW YORK TIMES   STEREO

(Right)
A spread from a 7″ × 10″, 16-page, black-and-white campaign booklet used by Ivan Lebamoff in his successful run for mayor of Fort Wayne, Indiana. The "other mayor" referred to in the surprise headline is an honorary mayor to represent the real mayor at ceremonial functions, leaving the real mayor free to concentrate on his more important functions. Louis A. Centlivre, senior vice president and creative director of Bonsib Inc., wrote the copy (on a freelance basis) and Gil Franceschi did the designing. Although starting from behind, Lebamoff won the campaign and carried eight out of nine council members with him. His managers think the booklet with its straightforward approach played a major role. It had been mailed to every registered voter.

Designer Robert J. O'Dell crowds his type at the top, crops his grainy photograph close, and uses column rules to give this ad an urgency consistent with its news theme. The body copy in the right column does not wrap around the art; it is partially covered but still readable. The ad appeared in *New York*. The advertiser is WQXR AM and FM, radio stations of the *New York Times*. The agency is Kingen, Feleppa & O'Dell.

"All creative people have big egos," says Tom Little of McDonald & Little, Atlanta, Georgia, "but we are in the business to communicate the client's message, not to draw attention to ourselves." "I'd hate to see what could happen if names did appear," adds Arthur Taylor of Tracy-Locke, Dallas. "I'm sure it wouldn't end with listing just creative people." But Taylor does like the idea of running the name of the advertising agency in the ads, as the French do.

Art Spikol, advertising consultant and columnist for *Writer's Digest,* thinks signing ad copy might be a good idea. He says it might make copy more honest.[6]

The research phase

Advertising people get involved in three kinds of research: market research about the product itself and its buyers and potential buyers; copy testing involving the advertising both before and after it is run; and research on readers of the media carrying the advertising.

Copywriters engage in an informal kind of market research when they look for answers to questions like these: What does the product do? How does it benefit the buyer, and how will it hurt the person who does not use the product? Who is the potential buyer? Is the buyer necessarily the potential *user* of the product? What is the product made of? How well is it made? How much does it cost? Where do you find it? How does it compare with competing products?

When I become mayor the first thing I'll do is appoint another mayor.

A ribbon-cutting mayor you don't need. So when a ceremonial function comes up, like the opening of a new shopping center or another parking lot, I'll appoint an honorary mayor to represent me. I'll spend my time back at the office, wrestling with the bigger problems which confront us.

I plan to appoint a full-time ombudsman, a people's advocate. He'll have a listed telephone number. If you have a problem or complaint, call him and he'll get things done for you because he's going to have direct access to my office. Furthermore, he'll call you back to let you know what action to expect.

This won't be a nine-to-five administration. The city doesn't shut down at night, so why should the mayor's office? We're going to be available 24 hours a day, seven days a week, 52 weeks a year. When I'm not on duty, my appointed deputies will be and they'll know where to find me.

The press and broadcast media will know where to find me, too. At least once a week I'll hold a news conference. They'll be absolutely free to ask questions about the city government.

Then I'm going to reserve one day a week for you. On that day you can come to my office, sit across from me and we'll kick around ideas on how to make Fort Wayne a better city. If there's anything more effective than a face-to-face meeting, I don't know what it is.

So now you know how Ivan Lebamoff plans to function as mayor. Now let's examine some of the key issues in the campaign. Things you should give some serious thought to before you vote.

In hunting for facts, the copywriter cannot rely solely on information provided by the client. Being close to the subject, the client may not recognize what makes the product unique. What the client considers a selling point may be only vaguely of interest to the buyer.

A sample of users of the product yields valuable information the copywriter can use in the ad. Personal experience with the product may yield even more useful information, but the copywriter should be cautious about generalizing from that.

When the facts do not yield enough unique information, bright writing becomes all the more necessary. Good copy can make even the dullest of products interesting. It can make an advantage out of what seems to be a disadvantage. Said Pall Mall, a filterless cigarette in the days when filters were being played up in many other ads: "And you can light either end." (This ad caused Malcolm Bradbury in *Punch* to envision a cigarette with filters at both ends and a slogan: "And you can't light either end.") Jos. A. Bank Clothiers, which manufactures and retails traditional clothing, said in a headline for an ad selling polo shirts without insignias: "If You'd Rather Not Be Anybody's Billboard, We Can Save You as Much as $18.50." J. C. Penney made a similar appeal with its "Plain Pockets" jeans. Goodrich took advantage of the fact that it does not have blimps by referring to itself as "the other guys."

A soup company competing with Campbell's advertised on its can that "You don't need to add water," an effective way of saying that you get only half as much soup as from a can of condensed soup.

Williams-Sonoma, a mail-order house of San Francisco, described its Old Dutch Chocolate Bar like this: "For baking, candy making (and nibbling) its smooth texture and subtle, sweet light flavor know no equal. With any luck it will arrive already cracked, courtesy of the post office, and you can blissfully nibble on the shards. . . ."

The writer of a notice put up on a campus bulletin board understood the principle. "For Sale: Used Refrigerator," the heading said. Then: "Built like they used to build them." It was an advantageous if ungrammatical way of saying the refrigerator was old.

Sometimes an advertiser makes a virtue of big price. Farberware once showed a beautiful saucepan in full color with a $72 price tag leaning against it. "If The Price Doesn't Shock You," said the headline, "It Could Mean You're Either Very Rich or Very Serious about Cooking." The copy and some cutaway art went on to convince the person "serious about cooking" that the pan and other Farberware cookwear were worth the investment.

Another tactic is to publicize a failure, but this must be done with great subtlety. *Life* used to check the list of important advertisers, and when it found one not using the magazine, it took out a two-page spread in *Advertising Age* or even a general-circulation magazine like the *New York Times Magazine* and made its pitch. For instance, one posterlike ad used reverse letters on a solid red (*Life* red) background to yell the advertiser's name on an across-the-gutter diagonal: "Calvin Klein." In smaller reverse type, it advised: "Hey Calvin Klein, you belong in LIFE!"

No doubt such advertising startles the potential advertiser and, at the same time, alerts other advertisers that *Life* is a medium worth considering. The potential advertiser also enjoys some attention from potential customers.

Another technique is to pretend that your product has a problem when the problem is really an advantage. Rent-A-Wreck used this headline in one of its ads: "Rent-a-Wreck Apologizes to All of You Who Expected to Rent a Wreck." The copy admits that the cars available are "beauties from the seventies," fully restored on the inside.

The 1980s are a decade of individualism, when many people are not concerned anymore about what other people think of their dress and life-styles. This should affect the advertiser. What's "in" is not necessarily what sells, except perhaps among teenagers, a group particularly vulnerable to peer pressure.

Alvin Toffler has observed that we are becoming "demassified." The rise of special-interest groups shows this.[7]

To write effective copy, the copywriter must gather facts not only about the product but also about the potential user. Advertising copy must be slanted to a specific audience, taking into account its needs and even its background. The copywriter should know, if research can provide the information, the age level, income level, occupation, gender, and geographic location of the typical user. The copywriter should know, too, if someone other than the user influences the buying decision. For instance, how strong is the secretary's influence on the boss's decision concerning a typewriter for the office? Maybe the ad should be directed to the secretary.

Car makers have discovered that women now buy 40 percent of all new cars sold in the United States. This has resulted in a different approach to car advertising in recent years. To counteract the feeling of many peo-

Courtesy of the American Humane Education Society.

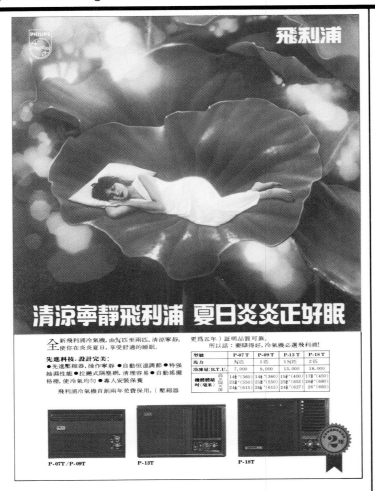

ple—especially older people—that long distance calls cost too much money and that often they mean bad news late in the night, AT&T launched its "Reach out, reach out and touch someone" campaign.[8]

Finding a theme

Advertising textbooks draw a distinction between selling points and benefits. Selling points in advertising copy, they say, are points as seen from the advertiser's position. Benefits are seen from the buyer's position. In most cases it is best to develop the copy around benefits.

The buyer is interested in the product not for its intrinsic worth but for the satisfaction it brings. Will it make the buyer happier? Healthier? More comfortable? More prosperous? More secure? More popular?

Will it make the buyer feel more important?

Will it make things easier for the buyer?

If the answer is "yes" to at least one of the questions, especially if the benefit is exclusive to the brand, the copywriter has a start toward developing a theme.

Whether the ad stands by itself or becomes part of a series, it should be single-minded in its approach. It is up to the copywriter to decide which of the several advantages a product offers should get principal play in the ad. The copywriter should have in mind one primary objective for the ad. It may be to get someone to ask for a particular brand of soap; to cut out and mail a coupon; to find God—something. And everything in the ad should point to that objective.

The copy may make several points, but one point must stand out. The late Rosser Reeves, as head of Ted Bates & Co., came up with an acrostic

Part of this ad's intrigue comes from the command to save the newspaper. Why save it? Because it will work as well as a drop cloth; the copy points out that the Power Painter ''is clean and easy to control.'' Ron Sackett wrote the copy; Dan Krumwiede art directed. The agency: Carmichael-Lynch Advertising, Minneapolis. The client: Wagner/Spray Tech.

for it: USP (for "Unique Selling Proposition"). Every product has one, he insisted. Once decided upon, the USP, in Reeves's view, had to be repeated in ad after ad, regardless of how much the repetition annoyed the critics. It has been reported that Reeves had the secretary at his agency answer the phone with "Good morning. Ted Bates, Ted Bates, Ted Bates." Other ad people have been less single-minded, but the one-point-per-ad idea is widely accepted.

In more recent years advertising people have talked about *positioning*—endowing a product with a personality that sets it apart from others in the minds of potential consumers. Sometimes a product is *re*positioned; Johnson's Baby Shampoo repositioned itself as a family shampoo, not merely a shampoo for babies.

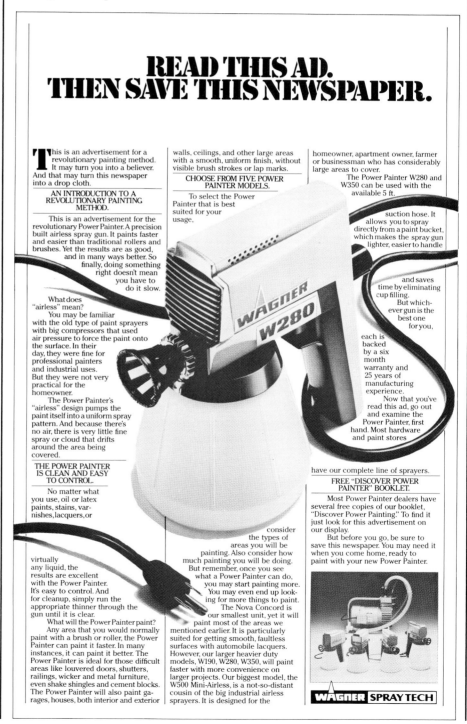

A company rides a theme until its usefulness wears thin or until the times change so that the theme is no longer valid. Sometimes an old theme is revived. For its fall 1976 advertising campaign, Maidenform once again used the "I dreamed . . ." theme first used in 1949. The earlier ads, which featured women who dreamed they appeared in public in their bras, were based on research that convinced company executives women had exhibitionist tendencies.

Sometimes the name of the firm suggests a theme. A restaurant—The Spagetti Warehouse ("spaghetti" apparently is purposely misspelled)—holds a "Warehouse Clearance Sale." "Every dinner on the menu is reduced 5 to 40%. . . . We've got new merchandise coming in every day and we've slashed prices. . . . Complete dinners . . . reduced for quick sale. . . . Our inventory won't last long at these prices, so come early."

Of course, the copywriter has to remember that advertising does not exist in a vacuum. How the competition might fight back becomes a consideration. The ad's theme should not invite a comeback. A Ford dealer in Traverse City, Michigan, once asked this question on a billboard: "This Is Ford Country. What Are You Driving?" A Plymouth dealer on another billboard came back with: "We ALL Drive PLYMOUTHS. What Country Are You From?"

A savings and loan association in southern California used the slogan "We won't give you any trouble." Another came back with: "You know, some businesses think it is enough not to give their customers any trouble. At _____ , we offer. . . ." And so on.

After three years of success with its "We Try Harder" campaign, Avis finally felt the sting of Hertz. "For years, Avis has been telling you Hertz is No. 1," an ad for Hertz said. "Now we're going to tell you why." (Carl Ally Inc. was the agency that prepared the ad.) "A magnificent retort," one writer in *Advertising Age* said. But another writer said it was free advertising for Avis.

Realizing that people do not like braggarts, many advertisers play down their dominance of a field. A few admit they have flaws. After its calamitous change to a discount operation, A & P in 1975 engaged in a humble-pie ad campaign to regain grocery store leadership it had lost to Safeway. The campaign, said to cost $10,000,000 just for television, admitted the mistake and said the chain was returning to a "price and pride" approach to retailing.[9]

Companies that do the best job of corporate or institutional advertising are those not afraid to admit they are not perfect, according to Richard S. Lessler, chairman of the board of Grey Advertising. And if companies have nothing to say, he adds, "they should not be afraid not to advertise."[10]

Developing an approach

In spite of all the health warnings and the growing militancy of non-smokers wanting to breathe unfouled air, an estimated 60 million Americans smoke. Each smokes an average of a pack and a half a day. Marlboro has captured about 20 percent of the market, thanks largely to its imaginative advertising. Winston, Salem, and Kool are pretty far behind, along with the other brands; but a mere 10 percent or even 5 percent share of the market still represents staggering profits for any brand. The advertising wars here are fascinating to watch.

For one thing, radio and TV are off-limits for the advertising, and the industry itself has eliminated celebrity endorsements. Magazines, newspapers, and billboards play a big role in the campaigns.

Lately the ads have directed their attention to women. Beige packages have been designed especially to attract this audience.

A nice house with the headline "Nightmare"? Why? The copy clears things up by pointing out that because of insulation and heating costs and sky-high mortgages (if you can get one), ". . . the dream house has become a nightmare. Suddenly, how to keep a roof over your head has become everybody's business." This nicely designed full-page ad appearing in the *New Yorker* makes a subtle pitch both for advertisers and subscribers for *Business Week*. Phil Gips designed the ad and Robert A. Fearon wrote the copy for Robert Fearon Associates, which was the agency.

Nightmare.

It's at the heart of the American tradition. Homesteaders heading west. A place to call our own. Just make up your mind on a colonial or a ranch, clapboard or brick. And where the roses might grow. But now it's how good is the insulation and how much will it cost to heat. Now it's mortgages that are sky-high and try to get one.

The prime rate is hitting home. And the dream house has become a nightmare. Suddenly, how to keep a roof over your head has become everybody's business.

And, everybody's business is also the price of gold, an OPEC decision, a new union contract. All are part of thinking America's daily conversation. *The fact is that more people are tuned in to business and economics than ever before.* In the office and at home. Why?

It's not that the importance of business has changed; it's always been part of everything in life. It's people's perception of business that has changed. They know that keeping ahead of the game is now an absolute necessity. *And they now know why serious business leaders have depended on Business Week for the past fifty years.*

Week after week, Business Week gets right to the heart of the artichoke. In bright, pithy style. Looking at the big and small events that make up the entire business picture. An early alert that the U.S. steel industry is in deep trouble. Art as an investment. How our wide ranging travel habits will be affected by a whole new set of airline industry problems. Coping with rising college costs. And hospital costs. And an analysis of the decline of the American standard of living.

Original reporting. Interpretation. That's what sets Business Week apart. *That's what makes Business Week more vital, more useful than any other business news source.* More than the dailies and TV with their reflex reporting. More than the leisurely fortnightlies. Week by week, Business Week gives meaning and perspective to the complex, ever changing world of business and finance.

What it all comes down to is this: *Business Week presents information that helps people do their jobs better.* And live their lives better.

BusinessWeek
The newsweekly of the '80s.

For advertising information: 212-997-4616   For circulation information: 800-523-7601.

The advertising takes one of two approaches: that either the cigarettes have only low harmful effects (the companies don't exactly come out and say cigarettes are good for you), or that they have a new and agreeable taste. Bright, a cigarette introduced in 1983, suggested that it could actually freshen your taste.[11]

Cigarette smokers tend to develop brand loyalties, so any new brand— or any existing brand, for that matter—is likely to try to get people to switch. A few years ago, one brand fought back by showing various people with black eyes who apparently would rather fight than switch.

What the competition does influences the approach copywriters take in the various product categories.

It's instructive to watch what advertising copywriters come up with each year for the new cars. To sell its 1984 Tempo, Ford reminded people that "form follows function." "First came completely new functional ideas. And then Tempo's pleasing form followed—naturally." Audi that same year in a headline said, "Audi's German Engineers Believe that Form Is Function. . . ." The copy said that "we at Audi don't believe that form follows function. Such conventional thinking builds conventional cars."

Vestiges of the "Me Decade" of the 1970s remain in the 1980s as one shampoo continues to tell women they're worth the high price of the product, and Jack Klugman talks about a copier "for the most important person in the world—me." People bring their copies of *Self* magazine up to the checkout counter apparently without any embarrassment.

Sometimes the copywriter ties the advertising to an event in the news. If the event has favorable connotations, and the product is somehow involved, the copywriter will mention that involvement in the copy. But even if the product is not involved, a propaganda device known as the "transfer" may be used. The copy first alludes to the event, then moves gracefully to the product. The secret is to find some comparison between the event and the product. Volkswagen did it nicely in 1969 with its full-page ad showing a picture of the Apollo 11 lunar module on the moon. The headline "It's Ugly, But It Gets You There" was followed simply by the Volkswagen insignia, the circle with its *V* and *W*. There was no copy block.

If it is hung on a news peg, copy must be written in a way to compensate for its lateness (advertising copy seldom can be as timely as news copy) and for the possibility of a change in the news.

Some copy approaches stretch credulity. Fujitsu, a computer maker, in one of its ads in in-flight magazines tells "How a Fujitsu Computer System Put Toru Okada to Sleep One Night." Little Toru is shown sound asleep, wearing a baseball cap and clutching his baseball mitt. A long copy block explains that Toru had been worried that a game he was to play in the next day would be rained out. Fortunately, a TV weather report reassured him the next day would be fine. The report had been made possible by Fujitsu. It is difficult to imagine U.S. airline passengers being moved enough by the contrived story to order Fujitsu equipment.

The French Company, a luggage maker, used the headline "The Attention Getter!" for one of its *New Yorker* ads. A piece of luggage was shown with copy that said, "You'll attract attention when you carry French luggage. . . . Face it, people are going to notice you." People may pick out luggage to enjoy its "beautiful fabrics, lush leathers, [and] . . . handcrafted high style," but do they pick it to draw attention to themselves?

An ad is effective when art, headline, and copy work together to make a single point. "The answer, the only answer, to neighborhoods like this is open housing in all communities," the copy for this ad points out. "To an extent, that will be reached through fair housing laws and complete enforcement of those laws. But more importantly, open housing depends on individual action. It depends on you. . . ." Art director and designer: Tom Gilday. Copywriter: Mike Faems. Client: Operation Equality, an affiliate of the Urban League of Cleveland. Agency: Griswold-Eshleman Co., Cleveland.

You're afraid to drive through a neighborhood like this.
Imagine what it's like to live there.

There are muggers in there. And rapists. And addicts. Not to mention fires, and filth, and rats. Yet people still live there.

In fact, there isn't even a problem filling those tenements. Because for many members of Cleveland minorities, it's the only housing they can get.

Prejudice built these slums. And it's keeping people in them.

The answer, the only answer, to neighborhoods like this is open housing in all communities.

To an extent, that will be reached through fair housing laws and complete enforcement of those laws.

But more importantly, open housing depends on individual action. It depends on you.

If you're a renter, or a landlord, or if you're buying or selling real estate, find out how you can help assure fair housing to every Clevelander.

Call Operation Equality at 295-1600.

You may be able to avoid that neighborhood.

But the person behind you may have to go in there. And stop.

Operation Equality, 4102 Lee Road; Joseph H. Battle, Director. An affiliate of the Urban League of Cleveland.

Even if they do, would they, as sophisticated *New Yorker* readers, be comfortable with this copy approach?

Putting yourself in the reader's place

Carl K. Hixon, executive vice president of Leo Burnett Co., Chicago, talks of "the singular ability of a good creative man or woman to step into almost anyone else's identity . . . [as though slipping into] a loose suit," able to feel what that person feels and what that person wants.

As a copywriter, you do not write primarily to fulfill or find yourself. You write to do a job for a client. To do that job, you must write with a knowledge of both the product and the target audience. You must look at the product not from the standpoint of the manufacturer or seller but from the standpoint of the user. You must put yourself in the reader's place. How best to phrase the message to convince readers that the product is for them? That is the question you must consider.

The background and needs of readers differ from publication to publication. Ideally, copy for an ad differs somewhat from publication to publication. A theme and style that work for the readers of the *New Yorker*, for instance, would not necessarily work for readers of *People*, or even for the readers of *New York*.

Involving the reader

An organization wanting advice or financial help from someone is not above appointing that person to an advisory or governing board or committee or giving away an honorary degree. Similarly, advertisers in recent years, to fight reader apathy, have involved the reader in their advertising. "How many mistakes can you find in this picture?" a greeting card manufacturer asks in an ad headline. Find enough of them and the company will send you a free ballpoint pen—and information on how you can make money in your spare time selling cards door-to-door. "Draw me," says an ad for a correspondence school, and if your drawing is good enough (it usually is), the school will invite you to take its art lessons.

But the involvement can be much more subtle than that. The copywriter can ask rhetorical questions, leaving the obvious unsaid. "One of America's two great beers," said a brewery in San Francisco. Never mind the name of the other "great" beer. Let readers supply a name. Just so they ponder the notion and identify as "great" the one that signs the ad.

A good example of a reader-participation ad was one by Del Monte showing a large, ripe tomato with the headline "If You Can See What's Wrong with This Tomato, Your Standards Are Up to Ours." It was a surprising headline, because the tomato was a beautiful specimen. A second headline, in much smaller type (so as not to give the answer away too quickly), read: "(High Shoulders Indicate a Large Stem End and Tough, Woody Core Material.)." A small inset photo at the bottom showing a Del Monte bottle of catsup and a can of tomato sauce was accompanied by the slogan "The more you know about tomatoes, the better for Del Monte." This seemed to justify the headline and at the same time praise the product.

Another example of a reader-participation ad was the one sponsored some years ago by "some citizens who think Congress made a mistake" when it killed a bill that would have given $40 million to cities and states for rat control. The ad showed a life-size rat, with a headline that read: "Cut This Out and Put It in Bed Next to Your Child."

On a less lofty level, Fort Howard Paper, to dramatize the fact that its rolls of toilet paper are larger than those of the competition, ran an industrial ad with a set of circles within circles (to represent various roll thicknesses) and invited readers (managers of industrial concerns) to "Put a Roll of Your Tissue Here and Find Out How Much Howard Can Save You in Maintenance Costs." Similarly, in a double-page full-color ad in the *New York Times Magazine,* Royal Doulton Bone China showed a place setting without a plate on the left page and a place setting with a Royal Doulton plate on the right page. The left-page headline: "Put Your China on This Page and Compare It to Ours." The right-hand page headline: "Honestly, Is There Any Comparison?"

Xerox, in one of its headlines, said, "Fool Your Copier Into Thinking It's Terrific." The ad contained the picture of a Xerox nameplate surrounded by dotted lines. The copy began: "First, cut out the Xerox nameplate on this page and paste it on your current small copier.

"Then, make believe it's giving you crisp, clear Xerox copies. . . ."

Pacific Northwest Bell in a direct-mail piece selling "Touch-Tone" service had the reader punch out a "Touch-Tone" keyboard from a photo of a phone and paste it over the dial of another photo of a phone.

Another way to involve the reader in the advertising is to use microfragrances, or scent-in-ink encapsulation. Research does not prove that this novelty results in increased sales, but no doubt it holds the reader to the ad longer.

"Unfortunately, there are some ads that smell without scratching," observes Al Hampel, president of D'Arcy-MacManus & Masius/New York.

Writing style

While art and design styles of other eras can serve advertisers today, copy style must be current. Rare is the advertiser who would be willing to put a sales message in the flossy, sentimental, overwritten language of advertising of the 1920s and 1930s. Take that classic ad sponsored by the New Haven Railroad in World War II, "The Kid in Upper 4." It was an appeal to civilian passengers, asking them to be patient during a time when first consideration had to be given to moving servicemen across the country. It told of the typical young soldier going to war:

"Tonight, he knows, he is leaving behind a lot of little things—and big ones.

"The taste of hamburgers and pop . . . the feel of driving a roadster over a six-lane highway . . . a dog named Shucks, or Spot, or Barnacle Bill. . . .

"There's a lump in his throat. And maybe—a tear fills his eye. *It doesn't matter, Kid.* Nobody will see . . . it's too dark."

As copy, it is inappropriate for today's sophisticated reader.

Even "The Penalty of Leadership" ad, sponsored by Cadillac in 1915, making its point that "In every field of human endeavor, he that is first must live in the white light of publicity," seems a little smug when read today.

Still, flair in writing can make the difference between copy that is remembered and copy that is tossed aside. Where flair gets its best chance is in narrative copy, which comes closest to imitating what you find in a short story, or in a script of the kind produced by playwrights or screenwriters.

Paco Rabanne, a cologne for men, in a two-page magazine ad shows a man in bed—he apparently is an artist, from the looks of the room—receiving a phone call. He's barely covered by a sheet. Empty glasses and a bottle rest on a tray at the foot of the bed. It is morning.

"Hello."

"You snore."

"And you steal all the covers. What time did you leave?"

And so on, with a number of double entendres of the kind to cause knowing winks and elbow jabs. She confesses that she took his bottle of Paco Rabanne with her when she left. Couldn't resist it. You get the idea that the woman is classy and well traveled; she's calling from San Francisco, of course.

". . . they're calling my flight."

She'll be back Tuesday.

It is an ad to be remembered by people who think a good-smelling cologne is the secret to a memorable night.

Another example:

Massage Pet, a roller device made for soothing back muscles, also helps the buyer make new friends, according to a tag attached to the device. (It takes a second person to roll it up and down the back.) "Let the good times roll!!!" says the tag, using more exclamation marks than necessary but, still, making its point effectively.

While the following examples happen to be headlines, the flair they exhibit is the flair body copy needs, too. Feel the rhythm. Appreciate the subtlety. Savor the word choice. See the pictures. "Good copywriters must always be conceptualizers before they are wordsmiths," says Carl K. Hixon.

"All Cadillacs Are the Same," says Tinney Cadillac of Buffalo, New York, in an ad in the *Buffalo Spree*. "All Cadillac Dealers Are Not."

"We Want to Lose You as a Customer as Soon as Possible," says the Weight Loss Clinic.

"Softens the Sidewalks," says an ad for Ripple Shoes. G. H. Bass & Co. calls its shoes "Personal Transportation."

"More Than Love Is Sweeping the Country" is the title Abbott Laboratories gives its booklet on venereal disease.

"Don't Lose Your Shape Trying to Keep It," says an ad for the Running Bra by Formfit Rogers.

"Why Lease a Car When You Can Lease a Legend?" the Porsche people ask.

"Let Us Put a Vacation in Your Backyard," implores a swimming pool company.

Olin uses a light touch to get its message across to industrial and governmental customers in this two-page, full-color magazine ad. The headline that goes with the cartoonlike painting brings to mind a reaction often expressed by the general in the *Beetle Bailey* comic strip. The copy handling is unusual in that it appears as a long quotation ending with a logo that reads, "says Olin." Art director and designer: Charles Piccirillo. Copywriter: Jane Talcott. Agency: Doyle Dane Bernbach, New York.

You can have "Specs Appeal," promises Buffalo Optical, Buffalo, New York.

"Pigments of the Imagination" is the way Colours by Alexander Julian describes the colors of its shirts and sweaters.

"The Lowest Price Cruise to Bermuda Is the Most Extravagant Way to Go," says Holland America, a cruise line.

"Take Me to Bed," invites Barnes & Nobel's ad for a small lamp that attaches itself to books. The light from the lamp "floods the entire page with a brilliant cool light guaranteed not to disturb anyone nearby."

"Jenson Introduces Goose Bumps," says a manufacturer of audio-video components.

"No Batteries Needed!" says William Morrow in an ad selling its children's books.

"A Desk for All Reasons," says The Door Store, New York, in an ad selling its furniture.

"McEnroe Swears by Them," says Nike in an ad mentioning that bad-tempered tennis player.

In its design, an ad often starts with a piece of art and repeats part of it at the bottom to tie things together. Copy often uses the same device. The final words make some reference to what was said at the beginning.

Stanley Musgrove, president of Friends of the USC Libraries, University of Southern California, started out a fund-raising letter with this heading: "Friends, Romans, Countrymen," with the "Romans" crossed out and "Trojans" printed in its place. (People at USC, of course, call themselves Trojans.) The copy began like this:

"Lend me your ears . . .

"I restate a well-known truth: the heart of a great university is its library system. . . ."

And after his appeal, Musgrove's last line was:

"Thanks for hearing me out."

An ad in *Newsweek* for the Freedom Phone Cordless Telephone talks about it as a device that "Makes Ordinary Phones Obsolete" in the headline, then winds down the copy with ". . . walk to your obsolete telephone, and call. . . ." It was an effective way of emphasizing the advanced nature of the product.

Guidelines for copywriters

Copy, like layout, is too much an art to be directed by a set of rules, but the beginning copywriter may find the following guidelines helpful.

1. *Write clearly.* While flair and even cleverness have a place in advertising copy, nothing is more important than clarity. That readers understand the copy is more important than that they be impressed by its style. Use plain language and concrete terms. Use uninvolved, short, subject-predicate sentences rather than long, complicated ones. Rely occasionally on sentence fragments. (But. Sentence fragments. Can be. Overdone.)

Robert O. Bach, senior vice president, creative services, N W Ayer, made this observation: "The simple truth is that too much advertising today is too complicated in manner, and complicated in matter. Complicated in manner with devious, intricate verbal and visual conceits; by oh-see-how-clever-I-am phrases and designs. And complicated in matter by that old bugaboo—trying to say too much in one advertisement. The advertisement that's not simple in matter, and not simple in manner, can evoke one of only two responses: no interest at all, or confusion. Either one costs just too much money to tolerate today."[12]

Parallel structure provides one good way to keep meaning clear. When you have several points of equal importance or you need to make com-

"Free" has always been an attention-getting word in advertising. In this newspaper ad from the early 1930s, a power and light company, using plenty of copy, announces a contest to win an electric ironer.

parisons, you should use the same basic phrasing for each. "Better tasting, faster acting, lasts longer" is clearer this way: "Better tasting, faster acting, longer lasting."

Do not allow sentences to carry two meanings if one of the meanings could be detrimental to your client. "We can't do enough for you" might be clear enough to most people, but the line carries the thought that "enough" is what people need and this advertiser cannot meet the need.

The Advertising Council, for the U.S. Forest Service, for years promoted the slogan, with the help of Smokey Bear, that "Only You Can Prevent Forest Fires." As a slogan it was vague, even misleading. People who heard it were not sure what it meant. Or people knew it was wrong because, after all, the other people could prevent forest fires, too. In later years the Advertising Council changed the slogan to "Only People Can Prevent Forest Fires." This was better.

Just making sure the copy covers all contingencies adds to the ad's clarity. An Anaheim, California, car dealer failed to put "One coupon to a buyer" or something similar on a $100-off coupon. A woman collected a pile of the coupons and demanded a car at a price minus the many hundreds of dollars on her coupons. When the dealer balked, the woman sued.

2. *Pick your words carefully.* Within the bounds of legal restrictions, good taste, and fair play, look for words that will do the best selling job for your client. This means weighing each word carefully for all its implications. "Sugar free," for instance, is, on balance, a better term than

"sugarless" because "free" has positive connotations where "less" has negative ones.

"Festival seating" is a rock concert promoter's euphemistic term for "general admission." "Installation available" means, of course, that the attractive sales price is not the whole price, unless the customer wants the muffler, or whatever, only to put on display somewhere. A rate of "$55 per night per person, double occupancy" eases the guests into a $110 room. "Some assembly required" warns the buyer of an hour or more of bruised knuckles and frustration. A car dealer saying "Not all cars sell for retail price" means, really, that "Few cars sell for retail price."

"We're Looking for People Who Love to Write" says the headline of an ad in *Writer's Digest* for Writers Institute, Inc., a correspondence school. That is more promising than "We're Looking for People Who Are Willing to Take Our Correspondence Course." The Institute of Children's Literature, another correspondence school (you'd never know by the name), uses a similar headline, but one that moves a little further from the real purpose of the ad: "We're Looking for People to Write Children's Books."

Using just the right words, you can impress one group of buyers without antagonizing another.

Toy manufacturers, coming out with their new boy dolls, complete with appendages, referred to them as "anatomically correct" dolls. Who could argue against dolls that are "anatomically correct"?

Current pressures make advertisers want to hedge in their copy. In a television commercial, Cascade showed women comparing recently washed glasses. "See the difference Cascade can make," one of them said. Notice the "can make." That is quite different from—and safer than—"makes."

3. *Write in active voice.* "You save up to 25 percent" is better than "Up to 25 percent can be saved." Textbook writers, including this one, too often lapse into passive voice to avoid attribution or to change the pace in long segments of prose. But copywriters, with their smaller segments, can avoid most passive voice. They make their copy more exciting when they do. They make it move along faster.

4. *Be concise.* As a general rule, the shorter the copy, the better—so long as it does the job. But not all advertising subjects lend themselves to short copy blocks. For a major purchase, for instance, a prospective buyer has the motivation to digest innumerable facts before making a decision. For most mail-order copy, where the prospective buyer does not have the chance to ask questions of the salesperson, copy can go on for several columns.

Even if, as for a Mercedes-Benz ad, a reader doesn't wade through long columns of copy, the impression is made that the car is good enough to merit all those words. Expensive items, especially, benefit from ads with lots of copy.

It is a simple matter to break up long columns typographically into short takes. With subheads, initial letters, small illustrations, small areas of white space, and other devices, a good art director easily can make long copy look short and inviting.

5. *Strive for easy transitions from one sentence to the next, from one paragraph to the next.* Copy should move smoothly, effortlessly. There should be no abrupt changes.

But avoid transitions that are artificial—sentence openers like "Fact is," "What's more," and "Yes." They become monotonous when used sentence after sentence.

Transitions do not always have to come at the beginnings of sentences, nor do they always have to be the obvious words of transition. The *content* of the sentence can be transition enough.

6. *Write vividly.* You should pick words that are vivid, precise, and

OUR GROSS NATIONAL PRODUCT.

Outdoor signs and billboards that are so grotesque, so poorly placed or spaced—so many miles of ugly. We've learned to live with it, even laugh about it. Until, one day, it's our oak tree they're chopping down. Our view that's being blocked.
America, the beautiful. Our America. The crisis isn't in our cities; the crisis is in our hearts. With a change of heart, we can change the picture. **AIA/American Institute of Architects**

Send this page to your local authority and ask him to support sign control laws.

One of a series of ads drawn up by The American Institute of Architects supporting housing for the poor, enforcement of air-pollution laws, control of water pollution, and sign-control laws. The series was united through ''picture window'' photography and bold, sans serif headline typography. The call for action consisted of a last line: ''Send this page to your local authority. . . .'' The agency was Doremus & Co., New York.

memorable, putting them together so they form a picture that will imbed itself in the reader's mind. Otto Kleppner, co-author of a textbook for beginning courses in advertising, reprints a Hendrik Van Loon quote to illustrate how vivid writing works, even though it doesn't happen to be a piece of advertising copy. The quote, meant to describe "eternity," goes like this: "High up in the North in the land called Svithjod there stands a rock. It is one hundred miles high and one hundred miles wide. Once every thousand years a little bird comes to this rock to sharpen its beak. When this rock has been worn away, then a single day of eternity will have gone by."[13]

One of the early teachers of advertising told a story of a beggar in Central Park who, with a routine "I am blind" sign, did a disappointing business. Then he changed his sign: "It is spring—and I am blind." Soon his hat overflowed.

You cannot deal with reality alone, a writer at McCann-Erickson has said. It would be like a man looking at a pretty woman through glasses that magnified the pores. "The girl you love may be 70.2 percent water, 25 percent oxygen, carbon, hydrogen, and nitrogen, and 4.8 percent mineral, but it would make a lousy love song."[14]

7. *Avoid the clichés of advertising copy.* They include these words and phrases, among others: *at last; now; full-bodied; amazing; fast-acting; fabulous; farm-fresh; improved; giant size; quick relief; hurry; while supplies last; passing the savings on to you; it's that simple; that's what . . . is all about; the . . . designed with you in mind; don't you dare miss it!; if you like to eat—and who doesn't?; just possibly the best . . . ; everything you ever wanted to know about . . . ; the bottom line;* and *getting it all together.*

These days everybody running a convention arranges at least one "hands-on" session. Another tiresome expression, used widely by advertisers now, is "state of the art." "People, quality, support and technology. That's state of the art service for state of the art products," said AT&T in an ad selling its information systems.

Copywriters put a lot of faith, too, in the word *creative.* They attach the word to inanimate objects as well as to people, as though inanimate objects in themselves hold the power to be creative. Conditions—even unpleasant conditions—also tend to be creative, in the minds of copywriters. A YMCA advertised classes in "Creative Unemployment."

Sometimes these words may be the best or the only way of expressing the idea. That they became clichés indicates that they did serve the advertiser well before they became shopworn. But the copywriter should search for other ways to make the point before resorting to a cliché. The reader has built up immunity to much of the language of advertising.

The clichés of advertising include nouns retrained to be self-conscious verbs and mid-length words stretched out to limousine size, like "sportcoatings" used by Southwick for its sportcoats. Ann Goodwillie of Omaha noticed a retail ad announcing a sale on handbags: "Come in and See Our Wide Variety of Stylings and Colorations." "Perhaps I will," she wrote in a letter to the editor of *Time* (whose magazine had just run an essay on English usage). "I'm sure they have large numerations of sizings and shapings. A new purse may just give me the right kind of liftation I need to carry me into the coming seasoning."

In one of its ads, Toshiba in a headline talks about "Auto-Reverse. At a Price You'll Fast Forward to."

Clichés also include words that somehow, to the copywriter, sound better than the normal words they replace. Like "plus." In advertising copy "plus" apparently means more than "and." So readers put up with sentences like this: "You get low price, plus we will. . . ."

8. *Avoid the obvious.* If a benefit is already generally known, it is a

How to write clearly

By Edward T. Thompson
Editor-in-Chief, Reader's Digest

International Paper asked Edward T. Thompson to share some of what he has learned in nineteen years with Reader's Digest, a magazine famous for making complicated subjects understandable to millions of readers.

If you are afraid to write, don't be.

If you think you've got to string together big fancy words and high-flying phrases, forget it.

To write well, unless you aspire to be a professional poet or novelist, you only need to get your ideas across simply and clearly.

It's not easy. But it *is* easier than you might imagine.

There are only three basic requirements:

First, you must *want* to write clearly. And I believe you really do, if you've stayed this far with me.

Second, you must be willing to *work hard*. Thinking means work—and that's what it takes to do anything well.

Third, you must know and follow some *basic guidelines*.

If, while you're writing for clarity, some lovely, dramatic or inspired phrases or sentences come to you, fine. Put them in.

But then with cold, objective eyes and mind ask yourself: "Do they detract from clarity?" If they do, grit your teeth and cut the frills.

Follow some basic guidelines

I can't give you a complete list of "dos and don'ts" for every writing problem you'll ever face.

But I can give you some fundamental guidelines that cover the most common problems.

1. Outline what you want to say.

I know that sounds grade-schoolish. But you can't write clearly until, *before you start*, you know where you will stop.

Ironically, that's even a problem in writing an outline (i.e., knowing the ending before you begin).

So try this method:

• On 3"x 5" cards, write—one point to a card—all the points you need to make.

• Divide the cards into piles—one pile for each group of points *closely related* to each other. (If you were describing an automobile, you'd put all the points about mileage in one pile, all the points about safety in another, and so on.)

• Arrange your piles of points in a sequence. Which are most important and should be given first or saved for last? Which must you present before others in order to make the others understandable?

• Now, *within* each pile, do the same thing—arrange the *points* in logical, understandable order.

There you have your outline, needing only an introduction and conclusion.

This is a practical way to outline. It's also flexible. You can add, delete or change the location of points easily.

2. Start where your readers are.

How much do they know about the subject? Don't write to a level higher than your readers' knowledge of it.

CAUTION: Forget that old—and wrong—advice about writing to a 12-year-old mentality. That's insulting. But do remember that your prime purpose is to *explain* something, not prove that you're smarter than your readers.

3. Avoid jargon.

Don't use words, expressions, phrases known only to people with specific knowledge or interests.

Example: A scientist, using scientific jargon, wrote, "The biota exhibited a one hundred percent mortality response." He could have written: "All the fish died."

4. Use familiar combinations of words.

A speech writer for President Franklin D. Roosevelt wrote, "We are endeavoring to construct a more inclusive society." F.D.R. changed it to, "We're going to make a country in which no one is left out."

CAUTION: By familiar combinations of words, I do *not* mean incorrect grammar. *That* can be *unclear*. Example: John's father says he can't go out Friday. (Who can't go out? John or his father?)

5. Use "first-degree" words.

These words immediately bring an image to your mind. Other words must be "translated" through the first-degree word before you see

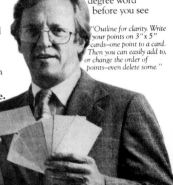

"Outline for clarity. Write your points on 3"x 5" cards—one point to a card. Then you can easily add to, or change the order of points—even delete some."

International Paper Company's ''How to Write Clearly'' ad, a good example of institutional advertising, contains some excellent advice for copywriters, although they are not the intended primary audience. The ad ran in *Newsweek* and similar magazines. Edward T. Thompson, editor-in-chief of *Reader's Digest,* wrote the copy; Herb Jager of Ogilvy & Mather designed the ad. Billings Fuess was the creative director.

---

good idea to stress an additional benefit, referring to the original benefit only tangentially. Sunsweet Prune Juice did that with an ad headlined "You Bought It for One Good Reason. Now We'll Give You Four More." The copy started out with the sentence "There are lots of good reasons for drinking Sunsweet Prune Juice, besides the obvious one." Other reasons listed were for nourishment, versatility (you can enhance other dishes with the product), energy, and flavor.

Copy often contains sentences or add-ons that are there probably on the advice of attorneys. "Use only as directed." Of course. "Void where prohibited." How could it be otherwise?

Necessary lines can be written in fresh and charming ways. Gump's in San Francisco doesn't settle for "No Smoking" signs in its store. It says instead, "Try Not to Smoke."

9. *Make comparisons.* Figures of speech can dramatize your point. Your product can be like something else; it can even *be* something else.

In a two-page ad in *Business Week,* IBM shows on the left page a huge

"Grit your teeth and cut the frills. That's one of the suggestions I offer here to help you write clearly. They cover the most common problems. And they're all easy to follow."

the image. Those are second/third-degree words.

First-degree words	Second/third-degree words
face	visage, countenance
stay	abide, remain, reside
book	volume, tome, publication

First-degree words are usually the most precise words, too.

6. Stick to the point.

Your outline– which was more work in the beginning–now saves you work. Because now you can ask about any sentence you write: "Does it relate to a point in the outline? If it doesn't, should I add it to the outline? If not, I'm getting off the track." Then, full steam ahead–on the main line.

7. Be as brief as possible.

Whatever you write, shortening–*condensing*–almost always makes it tighter, straighter, easier to read and understand.

Condensing, as *Reader's Digest* does it, is in large part artistry. But it involves techniques that anyone can learn and use.

• *Present your points in logical ABC order:* Here again, your outline should save you work because, if you did it right, your points already stand in logical ABC order–A makes B understandable, B makes C understandable and so on. To write in a straight line is to say something clearly in the fewest possible words.

• *Don't waste words telling people what they already know:* Notice how we edited this: "Have you ever

wondered how banks rate you as a credit risk? ~~You know, of course, that it's some combination of facts about your income, your job, and so on. But actually,~~ M̶any banks have a scoring system...."

• *Cut out excess evidence and unnecessary anecdotes:* Usually, one fact or example (at most, two) will support a point. More just belabor it. And while writing about some-

Writing clearly means avoiding jargon. Why didn't he just say: "All the fish died!"

thing may remind you of a good story, ask yourself: "Does it *really help* to tell the story, or does it slow me down?"

(Many people think *Reader's Digest* articles are filled with anecdotes. Actually, we use them sparingly and usually for one of two reasons: either the subject is so dry it needs some "humanity" to give it life; or the subject is so hard to grasp, it needs anecdotes to help readers understand. If the subject is both lively and easy to grasp, we move right along.)

• *Look for the most common word wasters:* windy phrases.

Windy phrases	Cut to...
at the present time	now
in the event of	if
in the majority of instances	usually

• *Look for passive verbs you can make active:* Invariably, this produces a shorter sentence. "The cherry tree *was* chopped down by George Washington." (Passive verb and nine words.) "George Washington *chopped* down the cherry tree." (Active verb and seven words.)

• *Look for positive/negative sections from which you can cut the negative:* See how we did it here: "The answer ~~does not rest with carelessness or incompetence. It lies largely in~~ hav-ing enough people to do the job."

• Finally, to write more clearly by saying it in fewer words: when you've finished, stop.

Edward T. Thompson

fingerprint. On the right a headline says, "No Two Businesses Are Alike Either." The copy points out that IBM offers a wide range of computers. "There's one that can be tailored to fit your unique needs and grow as your business grows." And, "Thousands of software programs are written for IBM."

"Designing great graphics is like hitting a home run," says Beckett Paper in an ad in *Art Direction* magazine directed to designers and art directors. "Printing them on anything but Beckett paper is like having no one on base."

10. *Tailor the copy to the audience.* As a copywriter you must "guard against intellectualizing."[15] You must both put yourself in the place of your reader and understand the medium your ad will appear in. What works for one medium does not necessarily work for another. Volkswagen's "Buy Low. Sell High." ad (as an example) was designed to be run in those magazines read primarily by the affluent. Persons other than stockholders would understand from the ad that the car does not depre-

ciate very fast, but they would miss some of the nuances of the copy: "The day you sell your car could very well be Black Tuesday . . . our tip . . . seasoned traders . . . you don't have to make a big investment . . . sealed underneath so the bottom won't suddenly fall out of your market . . . a lot of car makers did sell us short. . . ."

Right at the start your copy should pinpoint your audience. The Sponsors of San Francisco Performing Arts Center, Inc., in an ad in "Datebook," a section of the *San Francisco Sunday Examiner & Chronicle,* used this headline to single out ordinary citizens from the wealthy: "An Appeal to the Skinny Cats of San Francisco." "The fat cats have done their part," the copy began. "Over 5800 of them have already come up with $35 million to build the new Performing Arts Center.

"But it isn't quite enough, and rather than go back to them for the last $2 million, we turn to you and all the citizens of the San Francisco Bay Area. We want you to participate . . . .

"No one, fat or skinny, gets a button, a T-shirt, a card, a membership, or a favor. All you get is a good feeling, a feeling that will last a long time. You will have the special satisfaction of contributing to the health and well-being of this city."

11. *Write for the individual.* Although what you write is reproduced for multiple readership, write as if for a single reader. Attempt to maintain through mass communication the illusion of a salesman-to-buyer relationship. Your writing should be informal, conversational, and, where appropriate, intimate. A logical way of developing a one-reader feel in copy is by writing in second person. The word *you* is deservedly commonplace in advertising copy.

Reva Korda, creative head of Ogilvy & Mather, adds three "unfashionable opinions" about copywriting to the eleven guidelines presented here:

"The faster you write the copy, the better it will be." Korda says that a copywriter given too much time tends to get "too darn smart. . . . It's so easy to lose contact with your own natural, intuitive reactions to a product and what might make another human being want to buy it."

"If you can possibly manage to get away with it, work alone." Korda thinks a lot of advertising is bad because it is created by groups or by "what sometimes look like *mobs.*" She adds, ". . . you can always tell when an ad was written by one person—it will have a very special, very personal kind of rhythm."

"Write alone, write fast, and never, never write for test scores." She concludes: "*There is no method of pretesting that can hold a candle to good old-fashioned judgment.*"[16]

Naming names

It used to be that advertisers never named competitors. If they did, it was always "Brand X." That has changed. Although the self-regulatory organizations tend to discourage "comparative advertising," the Federal Trade Commission encourages it.

For years the makers of margarines have claimed for themselves the qualities of butter. The American Dairy Association is fighting back in its advertising, saying that there is nothing like the taste of real butter. Its slogan runs like this: "We'll never claim that butter tastes like margarine."

Xerox used appropriate wording in a headline to make its point against IBM. "Our New Typewriter Has More Memory Than What's Their Name's."

In promoting its fox-emblem polo shirts, J. C. Penney says, "See You

To dramatize and personalize its 24-hour-a-day access to savings accounts, Far West Federal Savings uses a Mr. Moneybags character: a tight cartoon drawing of a distinguished middle-aged man in a tux with spats, carrying a couple of money bags and a Far West Savings Card. Les Hopkins, with art direction coming from Dan Fast, designed it. Marketing Systems, Inc., is the agency.

Later, Alligator," referring to the better-known and more-expensive-emblem shirt by Izod.

The named product can be expected to fight back. After Scope began referring to Listerine as "medicine breath" mouthwash, Listerine in its advertising referred to Scope as a "sweet-tasting" mouthwash.

Some comparison advertising is friendly or tongue-in-cheek. And sometimes advertisers imitate or take off from familiar advertising campaigns. The Avis "We're Only Number 2" campaign, for instance, stimulated countless "We're Only Number 3" or "We're Only Number 24" advertisements by non-car-rental advertisers. The advertisements were executed in good fun, but they were never as effective as the original.

Ad talk

Advertising is pervasive enough that nearly everyone knows something about it. Occasionally an advertiser will quit pretending to be engaged in delivering a "message" and admit that what's presented is an *advertisement*. Kodak ended one of its ads to professional photographers with: "Thank you for taking the time to read this advertisement."

The advertiser may even let the reader in on how the ad was prepared. Sony did this effectively in a full-color "Picture Not Simulated" ad:

"Look at just about any TV ad in any magazine and somewhere on the page in tiny type you'll see three little words: 'TV Picture Simulated.'

"What these words mean is that the picture on the TV set isn't really a picture on a TV set. It's a still photograph. Which is superimposed over another photograph of a TV set.

"This ad is different, though."

The ad goes on to explain why Sony can do it, mentioning its "one-gun, one-lens" system.

The ad ended on this note:

"And if you think the picture looks good on this page, wait till you see it on the set."

Anthropomorphic selling

Advertising agencies still invent cartoon characters like Reddy Kilowatt and the Jolly Green Giant to help in the selling. And they dream up supposedly real-life characters like Mrs. Olson or Mr. Whipple, who get their kicks—their only kicks—from praising coffee, toilet paper, and other products.

A character does not necessarily have to work exclusively for one advertiser. King Features and other feature syndicates rent out their comic-strip characters to advertisers who think they can benefit from such association.

World-Wide Licensing & Merchandising Corp., New York, licenses "Mr. Magoo" as "the only sales force you need!"

For some advertisers, it is a recognizable style rather than a character that does the job. For several years one company has sold insurance through the full-page, full-color efforts of cartoonist Roland B. Wilson. Always there is a character about to be badly injured if not killed. Only a companion is aware of what is happening. The potential victim is always saying: "My insurance company? New England Life, of course. Why?" One of the longest-lived campaigns of this genre involved the cartoons of *New Yorker* cartoonist Richard Decker and the gagline/headline: "In Philadelphia, Nearly Everybody Reads the Bulletin." (Alas, the *Bulletin* is now gone.)

Sometimes the advertiser hires a well-known writer to step down from an editorial perch to produce advertising copy. For this kind of copy, a byline strikes the advertiser as appropriate. Perhaps the writer's good reputation will wear off onto the product. The same kind of thinking goes into the advertiser's request that the person who reads the news on radio or television also read the commercial.

The testimonial

Another advertising technique is to get official endorsement of a product from respected organizations, often by payment of a heavy premium for the honor. Forty-three companies spent millions of dollars for the privilege of using the 1984 Olympic Committee logo on wrappers and labels and in advertising. (One sponsor, Twinkies, earned the wrath of nutritionists, who felt that empty-calories food should not be linked with athletic prowess.)

A more common technique is to get famous people to say nice things about your product, again for a fee.

An advertising headline for an ad in *New York* reads: "Jill St. John Talks About Her First Time." The people drawn into the Q and A copy find out nothing about her sex life, of course, but learn that she had her first drink of Campari (the sponsor of the ad) at "an adorable sidewalk cafe in Rome." The smarmy copy is replete with double meaning and, after recounting her numerous experiences with the drink, ends with this St. John answer to "Well, you seem to have come a long way since your first time":

"What can I say? [The kind of trendy phrasing readers apparently can identify with.] It's hard to resist something when it just keeps getting better and better."

It seems to *Advertising Age* columnist Sid Bernstein that "there are currently more celebrities to the square inch plugging this or that product than has been the case for a long time, but most of them are trying to tell us things that . . . millions of . . . people simply do not believe; we believe . . . that they are simply lying for money."

Even Paul Samuelson, the distinguished economics professor, did a commercial—for Allied Van Lines in 1982. But later he felt some regret, saying his doing it was "a miscalculation."

When M*A*S*H stopped, Alan Alda spoke up for Atari home computers on TV under a million-dollar five-year contract. Many celebrities do commercials for more than one product. Bill Cosby has helped sell Jell-O, Coca-Cola, and Texas Instruments. Some celebrities seem ideally suited to sell certain products or services: Wilt Chamberlain, for instance, testifying to the roominess of TWA seats.[17]

Anacin used actress Patricia Neal for a time because, having recovered from a stroke, she was thought to be the ideal spokesperson for its "fight back and win against pain" campaign.

IBM used Charlie Chaplin's Tramp to introduce and sell its first mass-market computer. Potential buyers saw him in several commercials and many magazine ads. To use the character, IBM had to obtain rights from the Chaplin family company that licenses use of the late actor's image. Then it had to find an actor to imitate the Tramp. "The Tramp campaign has been so successful that it has created a new image for IBM," observed *Time*. The firm had a somewhat cold and aloof image previously. "The Tramp, with his ever present red rose, has given IBM a human face."[18]

If you do not have a celebrity to endorse your product, you can crown one of your own, as a hairspray manufacturer did when it came up with Rula Lenska, the British "movie actress." Russell Baker observed in one of his columns: "Unlike the usual 'celebrity,' whom Eric Sevareid once defined as a person who is 'famous for being famous,' Rula Lenska became famous for being unknown."

Testimonials have always been a part of advertising. In a newspaper ad in 1945, Diana Barrymore, "daughter of the great John Barrymore," appears as enough an authority to observe that "people today realize it is as necessary to use a deodorant as it is to use toothpaste." And the deodorant for Miss Barrymore was Arrid.

Clara Peller, the tiny elderly woman in the Wendy's commercial who growled "Where's the beef?" when shown a competitor's hamburger, became an overnight celebrity in 1984. The "Where's the beef?" line was picked up and used by Walter Mondale in his race against Gary Hart for the Democratic presidential nomination. It was also parodied in cartoons and talked about in sermons. All kinds of products, including T-shirts, came out bearing the slogan.

The FTC asks that celebrities who endorse a product actually use it. For those endorsements, celebrities' fees sometimes are more handsome than fees they can earn in their own fields. Celebrities on their way up— or down—are often the most willing to give testimonials.

But those at the top are often willing, too, especially when they are enthusiastic about the product. In the late 1970s when conservatism became chic, a number of important people were willing to go on record as readers of *U.S. News & World Report,* the most conservative of the three newsweeklies. The campaign stressed the idea that the magazine did not believe in frills, just important news. Cheryl Tiegs, Reggie Jackson, and Andy Warhol, among others, posed for full-page photos for the ads. For their appearances each received a token $1 fee.

One problem with testimonials is that the people who make them change. In the weeks when the commercials air, the person who made the commercial might make headlines in another—and unflattering—context. That person may not always be on good behavior. Or that person may die. When Jesse Owens died in 1980, Ogilvy & Mather quickly cancelled the American Express commercial featuring him, but unfortunately at least two stations did not get the word. "In the 1936 Olympics, I was the fastest man alive. But today I travel at a slower pace."

Humor in advertising

Parting with their money, for most people, is serious business. People do not buy from clowns: that is what advertisers have believed since advertising's beginnings. Many advertisers still believe it. Perhaps they are right. But some advertisers in recent years have relaxed a bit. They have allowed their copywriters to kid the customers along.

David Ogilvy of Ogilvy & Mather International, who for much of his career argued against humor in advertising, in 1979 came out *for* it. He said he used to envy Young & Rubicam, which had a reputation for funny commercials, but he did not allow his own staff to produce similar ones. "Thank God, now we can be funny, too. Our new research reveals that humor can be very effective if the humor is concentrated on the product."[19] The famous radio comedy writing team of Dick & Bert (Dick Orkin and Bert Berdis) never *made* fun of the product in their commercial; instead they *had* fun with it. "That's a big difference most copywriters fail to see," says Berdis.

Frank Beeson of Bend, Oregon, invents products that he sells largely through humorous promotion and advertising. His Fish 'n Wacker, a wooden club with a wooden ball on the end, designed to kill fish once you have them in a net, carries an attached card warning that the device is not for "whacking killer whales, man-eating sharks, enraged elephants or amorous bulls in pursuit of friendly cows." The card also warns that the device "shouldn't be used to swat flies on plate glass windows."

"If your shoes aren't becoming to you, they should be coming to us," says an ad for Joe the Shoe Doctor.

"Perform a death-defying act," says the American Heart Association. "Have your blood pressure checked."

"Eat while the iron is hot," says the announcer for a Cream of Wheat commercial that stresses the high iron content of that cereal.

A good deal of the humor is nothing more than punning. Kodel in its advertising plays around with the word *polyester*. It says that it puts the YES in polYESter, and announces that Joyce Sportswear for its summer clothes "says YES to Kodel."

Hartmann in advertising for its luggage makes "A Strong Case for the Proliferation of Paperwork." The "Strong Case" by implication applauds increase in business and also refers to the sturdy construction going into Hartmann briefcases that "carry a lot of paperwork."

Basin Harbor, a Vermont resort, says that "The Fun Never Sets!" there.

Sometimes it is the playfulness of the participants that gives the advertising its light touch. So successful has been Miller Lite's advertising campaign featuring good-natured ex-athletes that Penguin Books in 1984 brought out Frank Deford's *Lite Reading: The Miller Beer Commercial Scrapbook*.

"A woman's body should come with instructions," said an ad for a feminine hygiene product, Norforms. The sentence was accompanied by a line drawing of a demure woman wrapped in a towel. A tag labeled "Instructions" dangled from her wrist. A less imaginative copywriter would have come up with something like "Women's bodies are complicated. . . ."

"We're Trying to Change the Way America Sends Packages and a Lot of You Out There Aren't Cooperating," said Federal Express in a headline for an ad in the *Wall Street Journal*. The copy listed excuses a business person might make for not using Federal Express and then knocked the excuses over.

Advertisers today—some of them—are not afraid to make fun of the institution of advertising even as they advertise. United California Bank has a slogan that sounds like a typical advertising claim when first heard, but it soon becomes clear to the viewer or reader that the bank is having a little fun: "The best tellers in town. Or your money back." The beauty of the slogan is that it *can* be taken literally: a customer unimpressed with the tellers could close the account.

Few writers, though, can bring off humor successfully. Copywriters with doubts about their abilities as humorists should stick to straighter writing. David A. Schwartz of Lee Slurzberg Research, Inc., after one of his sur-

veys, concluded that "many of the cute, witty, or tricky slogans do not work well in the real world. Theoretically, they are great. In actuality the majority of them just don't make it. Advertisers frequently are just wasting their money."

Humor can differentiate a product from the competition, Frederick Sulcer, president of Needham, Harper & Steers, told a meeting of the Kansas City Advertising Club. But never resort to humor, he said, "if you have something more powerful to work with."

Because unrestrained humor could hurt rather than help sales, some of the best lines never see print. A lot of the humor in advertising circulates only among those who write it. Carl Ally has said he wishes he could have Preparation H as a client. He has a slogan ready: "Up yours with ours . . . and kiss your piles goodbye."

The logic of advertising

The copywriter should give reasons in the copy when possible. A store does not just have a sale. It has a sale because it is overstocked; or a holiday is coming up; or the manufacturer authorized a markdown; or (and here the mind rebels) the manager is out of town and the assistant manager has run amok; or something even more dreadful—a fire, maybe—has recently hit the store.

Here is Kodak in an ad telling about its grants to colleges: "No, we do not expect to sell Kodak Products on the strength of this. Buy them only because you are convinced they are good buys." That sounds reasonable enough.

"After a Point You're Not Buying Any More Car. You're Just Spending More Money," says a headline for a Ford LTD ad. That makes sense.

Contrast these to Schick Super-Chromium Blades' ridiculous assertion that its blades are "so comfortable you'll actually look forward to your next shave."

Roots, the natural footwear company, has used as a slogan or headline: "Be kind to your feet. They outnumber people two to one." It is a line that at first seems clever, but when you analyze it it becomes meaningless. If kindness is to be encouraged on the basis of numbers, you might just

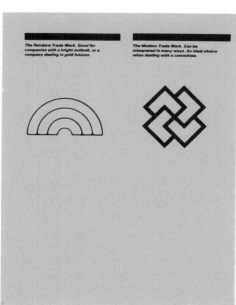

The cover says "Stock Trade Marks," and the inside pages of this booklet offer a number of them for sale. It is all deliciously tongue-in-cheek, a promotional piece for Herring Design, Houston, which turns out trademark design of a much higher order than displayed here. Although he meant the piece as a joke, Jerry Herring, the designer and writer, received a number of perfectly serious orders or inquiries about his "stock trade marks." Find a magnifying glass and read these pages carefully. The lesson is subtle and valuable.

as well preoccupy yourself with hands, eyes, ears, or breasts. And insects "outnumber people" by a margin far more impressive than two to one.

"Wake up to the sound of the surf in an unfurnished 2 bedroom Del Monte beach apartment," says an advertisement in the *Monterey* (California) *Peninsula Herald*. The trouble here is that the writer tries to do too much in once sentence, merging the future with the present, the imaginary with the practical. One hopes that by the time the fortunate renter has taken up residence at that surfside apartment, arrangements will have been made to furnish it.

"You know," said Arnold Palmer in a Pennzoil commercial, "this old tractor and I are a lot alike. We're both still running, and we're both still using Pennzoil." Is the viewer to assume that Palmer gulps down a quart every once in a while to keep moving?

"Ronald Reagan and Jerry Falwell would be happier if *The Nation* didn't exist at all," said the leftist magazine in a back page ad asking readers to buy subscriptions for their friends. It is unlikely that Reagan and Falwell, with all their other problems and concerns, give much thought to *The Nation*. The magazine has a small circulation, and what it says is confined largely to people in agreement with it.

"Spoil yourself with Satin," a slogan used by Satin cigarettes, may be more truthful than Lorillard intended, if you accept the surgeon general's warning that the product is dangerous to your health. There is more than one way to spoil yourself.

Another ad that unintentionally insults the reader or listener is the one saying that a store is conducting a sale as a thank-you for past patronage. "Because you've helped us through these hard times, we're offering you this merchandise at unheard-of prices." Nonsense. Readers and listeners surely didn't buy at the store to help it weather the economic storm; they bought there because the merchandise was what they wanted and the prices were right. Why can't the copywriter admit this?

Once the ad is written, it is a good idea to read it over specifically to weed out any fallacies. That is what the copywriter for American Airlines should have done back in the early 1960s when he wrote: "Fly American's Astrojets Nonstop to California and Back for $198 Plus Tax!" The *New Yorker* picked it up for a back-of-the-book filler and added the comment one would expect from a smug and amused Easterner: "Now you're making sense."

Another bit of copy that found itself memorialized in a *New Yorker* filler was this from a brochure for a cosmetics company: "Now you don't have to choose between a harsh, drying lipstick that doesn't smear, and a gentle, creamy formula. Because now Hazel Bishop gives you both." Think that one over.

Robert J. Gula attacked some of the logic of advertising in his *Non-sense: How to Overcome It* (New York: Stein & Day, 1980). As for "Everything's better with Blue Bonnet on it!" Gula asked, "Ever try it on your sherbet?"

"The leader in television is now a leader in television news," said ABC in 1980. Notice the switch from "the leader" to "a leader." It is one thing to be "the leader" among three commercial networks; it is something else to be "a leader." How many leaders can there be in a field of three?

"We not only cover the news, we *uncover* it," said an ABC affiliate. "Cover" and "uncover" in most people's minds have quite opposite meanings. How can the station do both? "We don't cover the news, we *uncover* it" would have made a better slogan.

As advertisers give up on appeals to logic they turn to emotion and sentiment, the last and perhaps best refuge for the copywriter. Advertisers, like all propagandists, have always preferred emotion to logic to sell their products and ideas. What we have witnessed in the 1980s is a sort

M. LaMont wine costs so much that only the very rich or very foolish drink it.

M. LaMont is smuggled in from Bordeaux by a bearded, hell-raising soldier of fortune named Big Stella.

M. LaMont is often compared to a Bon Jour '44.

The preceding three paragraphs are lies.

Yes, lies.

But lies that might come

in handy when you're serving M. LaMont wine to guests.

They think M. LaMont Chenin Blanc is a costly import.

It *tastes* expensive. Because it's an estate-bottled wine. And it's made the way expensive wines are made—with more premium grapes per bottle.

Yet it only costs about two dollars a bottle. And it's grown in California. And suddenly, almost secretly, it's become

one of the top five premi California table wines w it's available.

But you know how ma people are.

They don't think that a thing so economical and popular can really be th So lie a little.

Just to keep them happ

M. LaMont
The wine you tell lies a

A pack of lies.

Writer Ross Teel uses parallel structure and strong transitions to move the reader through the copy of this well-written and handsome ad, one in a series built on a "lies" theme. Mike Faulkner art directed. The agency: Ogilvy & Mather, Los Angeles.

of resurgence in it, brought about, some say, by the success of AT&T's "Reach Out and Touch Someone" campaign, which N W Ayer introduced in 1979.[20]

One reason for moving away from reason-why copy is that such copy needs to document its claims—not always easy to do. Emotion is less subject to challenge.

Truth in advertising

N. M. Ohrbach, the department store owner, many years ago gave this advice to Doyle Dane Bernbach, his agency: "I got a great gimmick. Let's tell the truth."

McCann-Erickson, in a symbol placed on its letterhead, expressed the ideal: "Truth Well Told."

The leaders in advertising have long advised their colleagues that truth, quite apart from moral considerations, makes good business sense. "In the first place," said an ad about advertising prepared by Doyle Dane Bernbach, "you go to heaven. In the second place, Ralph Nader can't lay a glove on you. And in the third place, telling the truth is the best known way there is of moving merchandise."

Later in the ad the copy said:

"We've got a confession to make; it's got nothing to do with heaven.

"People are as smart as we are.

"That's why we tell the truth."

But the truth is hard to pin down. Is it the truth, for instance, when Twinkies tells anxious mothers: "You can't scrimp when it comes to your children"? Are Twinkies the alternative to scrimping?

Truth involves not only what's said but what's left out. Public Citizen's Health Research Group complained to the Federal Trade Commission in 1983 that Playtex tampons' advertising campaign was "dangerous and misleading" because it failed to warn women that using the highly absorbent tampon might increase the risk of toxic shock syndrome.

Some say that advertising should tell both sides of the story. TV eliminated cigarette commercials in 1971, and there were pressures in the 1980s to eliminate commercials for alcoholic beverages. The increased media attention to the tragedies of drunk driving has contributed to the pressure. *The Booze Merchants,* published by the Center for Science in the Public Interest, Washington, D.C., suggested a ban on both radio and TV alcohol advertising. Candy Lightner, founder of Mothers Against Drunk Driving, thinks beer commercials make beer drinking seem romantic and even macho. The commercials should "show what really happens," she said.[21]

What is truth to one person may not be to another. What may be understandable to adults may be misleading to children. And an occupational hazard in advertising is that copywriters, after a period of time, begin to believe what they write where once they may have been skeptical.

Another problem concerns the distinction between facts and the truth. Novelists have long functioned under the assumption that truth lies somewhere beyond fact and that you can present the truth best through fantasy.

Dunlop, maker of sports equipment, in 1983 showed a photograph of John McEnroe holding a tennis racket and, stripped to the waist, looking remarkably muscular. "Max 200G Gives John More Muscle," read the headline. The body, spliced on and airbrushed in, was actually that of a body builder named Ted Martia. When a newspaper story appeared describing what had been done to the art, all kinds of complaints poured into J. Walter Thompson, the agency. A creative director there, annoyed, said the ad was merely an overstatement; "Anyone that follows tennis would know instantly that the body in the ad is not John's."[22]

If advertising copy is a kind of literature, the copywriter must be free to use fantasy. But the reader must *understand* that it is fantasy. In advertising, the test may well be: what is the *intent* of the advertising? If the intent is to deceive, then, in anybody's book, the advertising is not true.

To quote William Blake: "A truth that's told with bad intent/Beats all the lies you can invent."

Edward L. Bond, Jr., chairman of Young & Rubicam, told the National Industrial Conference Board: "We must ascertain and present the truth. But in the presentation of this truth, we must exercise all the imagery, imagination and artistry at our command."

"The more alike products are," said John Blumenthal, partner in Hawkins McCain & Blumenthal, New York, "the more creative advertising must be. If I want you to buy my peas versus their peas—both U.S. Government standard of identity items—give me the license to create a 'Jolly Green Giant' even though, to my knowledge, none actually exists."[23]

Edward L. Bond, Jr., added: "It is my opinion that we must not fall prey to the pressures that would have us turn every advertisement into a consumer report or a comparative rating sheet. We must not kill off the promise of a better tomorrow by bowing to the wishes of those who consider art and imagery to be falsehoods and the letter of the law to be the literature of the land.

"True, we must provide the information the consumer really needs to compare products. True, we must be informers as well as persuaders. But it's my contention that imagination, fantasy, hope and aspiration all have their place in advertising. Life is full of enough unhappiness for us to need a bit of levity, a dash of promise, and a soupçon of romance in our surroundings."

The mechanics of copy

Scali, McCabe, Sloves, New York, computerized its creative department in 1983. Using word processors, writers can call up information about a client's history, for instance, or about its personnel or marketing activities and work it into the copy. Once written, the copy can go immediately to the creative director's terminal, where it can be reviewed and changed, then sent back at once to the writer.

At most agencies, though, and in most advertising departments, the routine is a little more mundane. As a copywriter you would type your copy on 8½″ × 11″ sheets of paper, double- or even triple-spacing the lines. You would not attempt to type it in a width to match the width of the copy as it will appear in print, because typewriter type is quite different from the type that will be used in the ad. The copy in typed manuscript form usually occupies more area than the body type appearing in the ad.

For your final draft, you may want to find out how many characters each printed line will carry, set that number on your typewriter, and type to fit. Then you can tell quickly how many lines your manuscript will occupy in print.

On your original copy, do not hyphenate a word at the end of a line. This will save your typesetter from trying to figure out if it is a true hyphenated word or simply a word being carried over to the next line.

Copyediting and proofreading

William Safire, a syndicated columnist, offers annual awards—The Bloopies—to advertisers whose grammar and spelling annoy him. For instance, Safire is not happy with Campbell's Soup's headline "The Soup That Eats Like a Meal." He suggests additional possibilities to Camp-

tuesday
because of
inventory
m&f
eugene
will open
at noon

meier&frank

Unfortunately copywriters do not always use language precisely. What the copywriter of this ad meant to say was: ". . . M & F will not open until noon."

bell's copywriters: "The Meal That Eats Like a Soup" and "The Eats That Soup Like a Meal." He also gave an award to TWA for an ad that said that an earlier ad "contained an omission." An ad sponsored by the *New York Times* for Safire's column carried the line "Week after week he takes you behind the news for a hard look at why things sometimes turn out the way they do." Sometimes? Joseph Harriss of *Reader's Digest,* in response to the ad, noted: "The fact is, things always turn out the way they do."

Copywriters, like most writers, often fail to write with precision. "We couldn't care less" becomes "We could care less," which in reality means the opposite. Instead of allowing something to "center on," a copywriter might have it "center around," an impossibility. "All right" becomes "alright," a nonword in most dictionaries, and "a lot" becomes "alot," another nonword or a wrong spelling for "allot."

A clothing manufacturer featured this gag on one of its T-shirts: "If I said you had a beautiful body, would you promise to hold it against me?" The inclusion of "promise to" spoils the humor, such as it is. The double meaning is lost.

"Hopefully, your wardrobe will live up to it," said an ad for Targa, a fashionable pen by Sheaffer. What does the copywriter mean? That the buyer hopes it will be so? That Sheaffer hopes? That the buyer's wardrobe hopes? That the pen itself hopes? The line would be better like this: "We hope your wardrobe will live up to it." Or: "Just hope that your wardrobe will live up to it." Or maybe Sheaffer should drop the line.

Dangling construction has always been a problem for copywriters. "Originally intended for dairy cows, farmers use Bag Balm now for . . . ," a student wrote. The student meant, of course, that Bag Balm, not farmers, was originally intended for dairy cows.

"The reason leading roll-ons go on wet, and sticky, is because they're mostly water . . . ," said an ad for Dry Idea. It should have said, "The reason leading roll-ons go on wet, and sticky, is that. . . ." Or: "Leading roll-ons go on wet, and sticky, because. . . ."

When IBM in one of its ad headlines said, "Now You Can Get Everyone in the Company the Computer They Need," David A. Brukardt, manager of communications and public affairs for J. I. Case, Racine, Wisconsin, wrote to *Advertising Age* to complain about the grammar and to suggest that "they need" be changed to "he or she needs."

Some advertisers are so anxious to head off charges of "sexism" they will do anything to avoid the use of the generic "he." Going to "they" when the antecedent is singular is now common, and even sanctioned by some grammarians and linguists. Going to "he or she" and "him and her" is also common, but the double pronoun often ruins sentence rhythm and, overused, it becomes intrusive. Often the best answer is to recast the sentence so that both the noun and pronoun are plural.

Newspapers and other media have their full-time copyeditors and proofreaders, but advertising agencies, unfortunately, operate a little more informally. Copyreading, which goes on after the copy comes out of the typewriter, and proofreading, which goes on after the copy is set in type, are conducted much of the time by the copywriter, who may be too close to the copy to catch the errors. The ad may pass through several hands on its way to publication, with nobody giving priority to such mundane activities as copyediting and proofreading. So we continue to see in newspapers and even magazines such embarrassments as "it's" for "its" (as in "biggest in it's history") and "mens wear" (as though "mens" were a word). Of course, some errors are put there on purpose (". . . like a cigarette should") because, an agency person might argue, "That is the way people talk."

At any rate, the copywriter copyedits the manuscript while writing each draft, using a pencil with soft, dark lead to make corrections. When finally satisfied with the way the copy reads, the copywriter turns it over to a typist, who puts it into shape for client inspection. In a large agency the copy may get an additional working over by a copy chief before it goes to the typesetter.

When the copy comes back from the typesetter in galley form, it is ready for proofreading. At this stage, theoretically, the copywriter looks only for deviations from the original that may have been made by the typesetter, as when "a boxing exhibition" comes out as "a boring exhibition." Making changes—even necessary changes—on galleys is ticklish business because of the chance the typesetter may make additional mistakes in resetting lines. The copywriter, therefore, insists on seeing new proofs after any changes, to make sure the copy is at last free from errors.

If the change is the fault of the copywriter rather than the typesetter, it is charged to the client or agency as an "author's alteration." Excessive changes after type is set can be expensive.

The symbols used to indicate proofreading changes differ a little from those used to make copyediting changes because the typeset lines are closer together than the lines in the original manuscript. The marks must be put out in the margins rather than over or across the words to be corrected, as in copyediting.

The headline

On a newspaper or magazine, an editor or copyeditor writes the headline or title. In advertising, the copywriter does the job. The headline, although it gets unique graphic treatment to set it apart from other elements in the ad, can be considered as part of the copy—the most important part.

Its primary job is to arrest the reader. And, because it may be the only part of the copy that is read, it may have to do a selling job as well. If the message is dramatic enough, the copywriter may make one long headline out of the copy. A classic ad on air pollution prepared by Carl Ally Inc. for Citizens for Clean Air, Inc. really needed no copy block. It showed a man at the window of an apartment building overlooking an industrial complex. The headline said it all: "Tomorrow Morning When You Get Up, Take a Nice Deep Breath. It'll Make You Feel Rotten."[24] While it is best under normal circumstances for a headline to be short, there is no reason it cannot run on for several sentences.

The School of Visual Arts, New York, used one of those two-sentence, all-in-the-same-type headlines over an all-type ad: "What Our Teachers Do During the Day Is Their Own Business. Make It Yours." The implication in this ad appealing to potential night-school students was that the teachers there are professional artists.

The headline often dwells not on the product or service but on results that can be expected. Elaine Powers, a "fitness system" for women, in one ad showed a slim, well-built woman with the headline "Shapely Bodies for Sale." A coupon offered a special price on a three-month membership.

Nike in one of its ads expected you to take its headline two ways: "A New Shoe Will Never Fit Better Than the Last." But mostly Nike wanted you to think about the last that is used in the making of the shoe, and it showed art—a painting—that looked as much like human feet as like lasts. From the copy block: "From now on, when we use the word 'last,' we're talking about what comes first.

"We're talking about that rather strange looking device over which the shoe is initially formed. . . ."

B. Dalton's headline for an ad selling the book *Enjoy Old Age* was "Old Age for Beginners . . . a subject that will sooner or later be of interest

Repeating a slogan at the end of each ad is a good way of building recognition. But when the repetition is done mechanically, without considering the theme of a particular ad, it can create confusion, as in this copy for an ad asking for understanding during a difficult period for the sponsor, Continental Airlines. The illustration that accompanied this copy depicted a frustrated man phoning for a reservation. The headline and copy work well enough together, but the slogan at the bottom was obviously developed for ads that bragged about, not apologized for, the airline's performance.

merican has a plan for every saver

The copy for an American Federal Savings ad is not very well organized. The institution is a source for home loans. But at "high interest rates"? Will the reader understand that the high interest rates are for the *saver?*

to us all. If we're lucky." (B. Dalton's ads for newspapers are boxed in a unit that is in the shape of a book.)

Fulton Federal in the *Atlanta Journal* used the headline "Fiscal Fitness by the Numbers" followed not by a regular copy block but by an outline of 21 items, beginning with "(1) 5.25% Interest Earning Checking" and ending with "(21) 57 offices statewide."

The copywriter for a TWA ad moved into Biblical language (King James version) in a headline: "In Israel, Thou Shalt Not Just Sightsee." The copy suggested that a tourist should count on enjoying the sun and beaches as well as the "4,000 years of history" while visiting the "Miracle on the Mediterranean."

The headline can shock readers into thinking one thing with the copy soon telling them something else. "How I Get All the Men I Want," said a headline in *Advertising Age* for Times Mirror Network. With the headline was a photo of a woman. Small type told you she was a media planner. She was advising media buyers to buy space in *Popular Science, Outdoor Life, Golf,* and *Ski* to reach male readers.

"You're Wasting Your Time Reading this Newspaper," said the big-type headline in an Evelyn Wood ad. The copy explained:

"Not because it's not worth reading.

"You're wasting your time because you could be reading it three to ten times faster than you are right now.

"That's right—three to ten times faster. With better concentration, understanding, and recall."

The copy went on to make a pitch for the Evelyn Wood "reading improvement system."

A surprise is especially good when it traps the reader in a bias. "Don't Buy Life Insurance!" said a full-page ad in the newsmagazines. Great! Who wants to buy life insurance? But then, below a chunk of white space, in smaller type: "(. . . Until You Get the Facts.)." It was Northwestern Mutual Life's way of grabbing attention. "We feel confident that the more you know about life insurance, the more you'll appreciate our superiority."

The Quality Paperback Book Club, in a full-page magazine ad, asked: "Can You Afford to Support Your Reading Habit?" It was a good head because it suggested that book reading is a habit that *could* be expensive. The answer was to move from hardbacks to paperbacks.

"Down With Love!" said the headline for an ad sponsored by Continental Quilt, "The ultimate in down comfort." You saw a couple huddled beneath a down comforter. Read one way, the headline suggests that down and love go together. But read another way, the headline seems to work against the interests of the whole idea and so is somewhat flawed.

A headline for an advertisement differs from a headline for a news story in that the former adheres to no set of arbitrary rules. Its letters need not be counted out to fit a given column of space. Except in small space ads, it usually is written first and space is then assigned to it.

An advertising headline need not summarize the copy, as a news story headline does. Instead, it can be the first line of copy set in larger, bolder type. For instance, it can ask a question, with the answer coming in the first line of the smaller-type copy.

Like news headlines, the advertising headline often comes in two units: one in large type; one—probably with more words—in smaller type. Or the advertising headline, unlike the newspaper headline, can appear as two units of the same size type, the first unit separated from the second by a period and some extra space. And where newspaper headlines omit unimportant words like *and, an, a,* and *the,* advertising headlines use them. The rhythm of the headline sentence in advertising is more important than the amount of space the headline occupies.

Advertising headlines need not contain a subject and predicate. They can be mere tags or labels. They can take any literary form. Because they come in such infinite variety, they are more like magazine article titles than newspaper headlines.

Here are some classic headlines: "Do You Make These Mistakes in English?"; "They Laughed When I Sat Down to the Piano . . ."; "Often a Bridesmaid But Never a Bride"; "Blow Some My Way"; "The Kid in Upper 4"; "The Penalty of Leadership"; "At 60 Miles an Hour the Loudest Noise . . . Comes from the Electric Clock." Can you identify the advertisers?

The headline's relationship to the art in an ad is crucial.

In one kind of advertising, neither the art nor the headline is complete without the other. Half the basic ad idea is expressed in the art, the other half in the headline.

In another kind of advertising, the headline simply reiterates the art. The art says it one way, the headline another. But both say the same thing.

Either kind of advertising can be effective. What you should avoid is producing advertising in which the headline says something *different from* or *unrelated to* the art. In such a case, the two cancel out each other. They violate the rule that an ad should make but one central point. Professor Willis L. Winter, Jr., who teaches advertising at the University of Oregon, says, "The test of a headline/illustration combination is this: Does it, at a glance, convey the *essence* of the message the copywriter wishes to convey to the reader?"

The San Francisco Convention & Visitors Bureau, in an ad directed to potential visitors, used a photograph of one of its busy, hilly, cable-car streets. Taken with a telescopic lens, the photograph seemed to put cars and buildings right on top of cars in the foreground. The headline read, "San Francisco Isn't As Steep As It Looks." The copy listed several things one can do for nominal fees and concluded with this line: "Now, what's so steep about that?"

Functions of the headline

A headline can fulfill one of these functions:

1. It can report news about a product in the style of a newspaper headline. When Crest came out with a second flavor for its toothpaste, it ran an ad with this headline: "Crest Is Now Only 26 Flavors Behind Howard Johnson's."

2. It can offer advice, serving as a sort of one-sentence editorial. "Be Good at Being Bad," said a headline for My Sin perfume.

3. It can make a promise. "We Don't Take Off Until Everything Is Kosher," said a headline for EL AL Israel Airlines.

4. It can issue a command. Zero Population Growth did it with a pun: "Stop Heir Pollution."

5. It can arouse curiosity. A. B. Dick did it nicely in one of its ads: "If We Tell You Something About Yourself, Promise You Won't Get Mad?"

6. It can single out a segment of the audience. It may only pretend to do so, as in "Majorca Simulated Pearls . . . for Girls Who Prefer Real Ones." Or it may do it with deadly seriousness: "Arthritis Sufferers: Wake Up Tomorrow Without All That Stiffness!"

Clearasil singled out younger readers of women's magazines with this headline to go with a close-up of a young woman wringing out a sponge: "Wouldn't It Be Great If You Could Just Wring Out Your Oily Skin?" followed by the blurb: "That's the whole idea behind new Clearasil medicated cleanser." Older women with the opposite problem—dry skin—could turn to some other, more appropriate, page.

To some extent headlines take the place of slogans advertisers once ran

"I sold my violin with no fiddlin' around."

"Selling my calculator was easy as 1-2-3."

"Selling my mixer was easy-as-pie."

The *Seattle Times* uses puns in headlines for a series of ads promoting its classified section. "And no wonder!" reads the copy that follows the headlines. "500,000 people read *The Times* every day . . . more, probably, by thousands, than any other newspaper in Washington State. You can expect RESULTS—FASTER—from this great want ad value."

(some still run them) just below their signatures. One thing about the old slogans: they had a sense of rhythm about them. Headlines need that sense, too, especially if the advertisers mean them to be remembered and repeated. A headline should sound as though the copywriter tapped a foot while writing it. For instance, this headline for Monaco Shaver: "The Shaver That Went to the Moon."

A bit of rhyme ("Pollution Solution"—bicycle shop) and even a little alliteration ("Faith Is a Family Affair"—Institute of Life Insurance) can help make a headline remembered. But alliteration can be overdone. It works best when only a couple of words in the headline, preferably apart from each other, begin with the same letter.

Kinds of headlines

Headlines do not fit very easily into categories, but a few categories stand out because of the frequency of their use. They include the following.

1. *The takeoff.* Some of the best headlines are variations of popular expressions, song and book titles, and even other advertising headlines.

"Ladies, Please Squeeze the Chicken," said Frank Perdue in a headline for one of his Perdue Inc. chicken ads, an obvious takeoff from a line made famous by a grocer selling toilet paper on television. "Daddy, What Did You Do in the War Against Pollution?" asked a little girl in a Keep America Beautiful ad prepared by the Advertising Council. "We're Putting Our Money Where Your Mouth Is," said a headline for an ad for General Telephone & Electronics. "From Those Wonderful Folks Who Brought You Harper's Ferry," said a headline for a new magazine called *Black Sports*—a headline takeoff on Jerry Della Femina's book title, which itself was a takeoff on an old advertising claim.

Lone Star Beer, brewed in Texas, has called itself "The Beer That Made Milwaukee Nervous."

In an ad in *Selling Sporting Goods,* the Australian Trade Commissioner used the headline "Anyone for Profit?" The tennis racket art had a big dollar sign in the strings. A subhead read: "Australian Sporting Goods Net You Sales." The headline was a takeoff on a classic line about tennis, and the subhead used a pun that related to the sport. "Sport is big time Down Under," read the copy. "That's why you'll invariably find Aussies in the winning lists somewhere. A lot of it has to do with the gear and equipment they use. . . ."

A Gillette Techmatic ad took off from another medium when it ran an ad in *Esquire* with the headline: "We Interrupt This Magazine to Bring You a Techmatic Commercial." The art consisted of a storyboard of a series of shots of a man shaving.

The Israel Government Tourist Office in a *New York* ad declared: "If You Liked the Book, You'll Love the Country."

The takeoff appears sometimes in collaboration with the pun. "When News Breaks, We Pick Up the Pieces," said a headline for an all-news radio station in New York, WINS. "What Foods These Morsels Be!" said a headline for the Knife & Fork Inn, an Atlantic City seafood restaurant. "What a Way to Glow!" said a headline for Vanity Fair Mills, Inc., in an ad for a flashy hostess robe. "Palm Springs! It's a Nice Place to Visit, But You Wouldn't Want to Leave There," said an ad for the Palm Springs Convention and Visitors Bureau. "Are You Two Feet Away from Being Well Dressed?" asked Interwoven Satin Stripes ® Socks.

Sometimes the takeoff is in the form of a malapropism or a spoonerism. From an earlier era: "Chevrolet—the Smartest Make You'll Ever Move!"

2. *Double meaning.* "More Goes Into a Bra Than Most Men Dream of," read the headline for an ad for *Industry Week* in *Advertising Age.*

The ad told how bras are made and concluded: "[*Industry Week* is] the new way for managers in industry to keep up on all of industry."

A dog food provides another example of a double-meaning headline. "Alpo Gives It to You Straight." The headline implies that the product contains nothing but meat and that its advertising is truthful.

Safeway Stores provides still another example with its "Try a Little Tenderness" line directing readers to its meat counters.

In one of its ads, B. Dalton, the book seller, talked about opening "A 30,000 Story Building on West Broadway" in a West Coast city.

"We've packed all 30,000 stories into our new store on West Broadway. . . . Mystery stories. Children's stories. Reference books. Travel guides. And more. . . ."

With a double-meaning headline, it is important that both meanings have a favorable connotation. "Get the Full Saab Story" was clever in that "Saab" could be read as "sob," but is "sob story" a good term to use to sell an automobile? Another car maker's headline worked better: "Best of All . . . It's a Cadillac."

Tide employed double meaning—both meanings favorable—in "It's the Best Detergent on American Soil."

3. *The double take.* The term comes from comedy parts in the movies in which a character looks but does not see; the full impact hits him a few seconds after he turns away, and so he looks again in disbelief. Studio-type greeting cards make use of the device with their two-step gags: the routine-appearing line on the cover; the surprise twist inside.

Increasingly in advertising, headlines divide into two sections, but usually the surprise section comes first, followed by the explanation. "Be the Last on Your Block," said the large-type headline for an appliance store; then, in smaller type, "to Start Supper . . . with the New Litton Minutemaster Microwave Oven."

"El Producto Flavor Is Years Behind the Competition," said a cigar ad; then, "How's That for Progress!"

"Stamp Out Rock & Roll," said Brooks in one of its headlines. The copy for this ad, sponsored by a maker of running shoes, pointed out that the Brooks Chariot shoe helps control the problem of "excessive motion caused by heel strike. This slipping from side to side is often called lateral instability. We simply call it 'rock and roll.' " The shoe has a "rollbar" in the midsole area.

"Give Him Madame Rochas Perfume. A Few Drops at a Time," said the headline in a *New Yorker* ad. The art showed a woman applying the perfume to her body.

4. *Contrast.* Sometimes the point can be best dramatized by setting up contrast within the headline. Example from a De Beers Consolidated Mines ad for diamonds: "It's the Last Thing She'd Expect. The First Thing She'd Wish For." The headline for an ad for Saga Mink read: "Life Is Too Short and Winter's Too Long to Go Without Mink."

"Good News for Bad Knees," said Converse, maker of running shoes, in the headline of one of its ads. The copy pointed to two new shoes designed to reduce the risk of knee injuries. "The Price of Looking it Up Just Went Down," said Barnes & Noble on a catalog page selling reference books.

5. *Jargon.* Regional dialect or hip language does not do much for sales. The intended audience quickly recognizes a lack of authenticity or sincerity. But a little jargon appropriate to the subject, especially if used in a lighthearted way, can add dimension to a headline.

Example: For an NBC ad announcing a five-part series called "The Search for the Nile," a copywriter, remembering a famous encounter between a reporter and an explorer-missionary, came up with this headline: "You'll Be There When Stanley Meets Livingstone, We Presume."

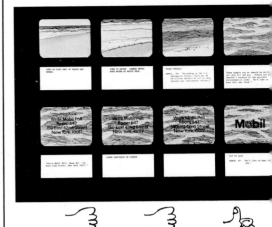

Why do two networks refuse to run this commercial?

When two out of the three television networks refused to accept a Mobil "idea" commercial, Mobil turned to print media to complain. What was involved, Mobil felt, was the First Amendment guarantee. The print media ad not only asked the question the commercial asked: Should there be offshore drilling for oil?; it also asked the question: Should the networks exercise such control over commercials? Was this commercial controversial enough to justify CBS's and ABC's turning it down? Art director/designer: Steve Graff. Copywriter: a Mobil public relations staff member. Agency: Doyle Dane Bernbach.

Slogans

Not only does an individual ad need a theme to unite each of its elements, a series of advertisements with the same sponsor—an advertising campaign—needs a theme to bring the ads together. Much of the value of advertising is cumulative.

The objectives of the advertising campaign help determine the umbrella theme, which may be expressed verbally in repeated headlines or phrasing. Or it may be expressed visually in familiar typography or art styles.

Sometimes the theme can be capsuled in a slogan. A slogan is a line of copy that appears usually at the close of the copy or with the signature or logotype, although it can serve also as the ad's headline. It differs from a headline in that it stays the same from ad to ad, and often it is in smaller type.

Because it is used over and over, the slogan better be good. Clairol used its "Does she or doesn't she?" slogan for fifteen years. The slogan started when coloring one's hair was considered not quite respectable.

It is refreshing to find a company willing in its slogan to speak in other than euphemistic terms. *Forbes* magazine decided to play up the fact that it is a business magazine proudly devoted to the free-enterprise system. It signed off its ads with the line "Forbes: capitalist tool."

When Stimorol, a Danish-made chewing gum, made its U.S. debut in 1982, it used the slogan "At last, a chewing gum for the rich." And the opening ad in the *New Yorker* mentioned not chewing itself but "The Stimorol experience." The company was not likely to make money selling its gum only to the rich, but the slogan was enough to appeal to the curious and—according to Michael Stone, acting as Stimorol's agent in the United States (the gum has long been sold in Europe)—to the insecure as well. Stimorol has a strange taste, a stronger taste than U.S.-made gum. "If you tell people they're supposed to like it, that people with cultivated palates do, then they're more likely to respond favorably," said Stone.[25]

Cunard, a cruise-ship line, uses "Getting there is half the fun," and sometimes the variant "Life is too short to get there too fast," a dig at the more popular mode of overseas travel. Club Med, which arranges vacations, uses the slogan "The antidote for civilization," suggesting to its young patrons the getting-away-from-it-all quality of its services.

The dentists have a good slogan in their "Teeth. Ignore them and they will go away."

Rhythm and rhyme help make a slogan memorable. Texaco provided an example: "You can trust your car to the man who wears the star."

A Boston store provides an example of a logo that nicely combines a slogan. Above the logo it says: "It Took." Then the name of the store appears in large type: "Lechmere." Then it goes back to the smaller type for the last line: "To Give Low Prices a Good Name."

Fred Meyer, a chain of stores in the Northwest, uses the slogan "Love 'em or leave 'em" for its photo finishing department. "You either love your pictures or leave them and we will remake them or gladly refund your money. You only pay for those prints you want to keep."

The slogan need not be confined to a single sentence. The Wool Institute uses two sentences, although admittedly they are short: "Wool. It's got life."

Slogans can be protected by registering them as trademarks. The Florist Association of Greater Cleveland discovered this in 1983 when Anheuser-Busch sued for trademark infringement. The association had used "This Bud's for you" in a flower ad.

Some slogans are sufficiently well known to inspire parody. *Magazine*

Age ran a "Fractured Slogan" contest and received entries like these:

"Smirnoff . . . it leaves you senseless."—Brian Hanley of Young & Rubicam.

"The Maidenform Woman . . . you never know where she'll pop out."—Rob Geiger of Durkee Foods.

"Fly the frenzied skies of United."—Karen Lane, Karen P.H. Lane Public Relations/Advertising.

Some famous slogans from the past: "It floats." "You're in good hands. . . ." "Good to the last drop." "LS/MFT." "Leave the driving to us." Some are still used.

One of the most successful of the car-makers' slogans was Packard's "Ask the man who owns one." It was first used in 1911, and it lasted until the car's demise after World War II. Ford's "There's a Ford in your future" was another durable slogan. It was revived briefly in the 1980s as "There's a Ford in America's future."

1. "Which Came First: Copy or Design?" *Art Direction,* September 1983, p. 79.

2. "Brand Image, Character Termed All-Important," *Advertising Age,* August 30, 1982, p. 14.

3. In a speech to the Association for Education in Journalism and Mass Communication, Corvallis, Oregon, August 8, 1983.

4. John W. Crawford, *Advertising,* 2d ed. (Boston: Allyn & Bacon, 1965), p. 173.

5. Hanley Norins, *The Compleat Copywriter* (New York: McGraw-Hill, 1966), p. 6.

6. "Hellbox," *Media People,* November 1979, p. 12.

7. "Lifestyle of the '80s," *U.S. News & World Report,* August 1, 1983, p. 45.

8. Michael J. Arlen in his *Thirty Seconds* (New York: Penguin Books, 1981) tells the story of how the N W Ayer advertising agency developed this theme and made the commercials.

9. Jeff Greenfield, "We're Sorry," *Columbia Journalism Review,* January/February 1976, pp. 14, 15.

10. Quoted by Jerry Walker, Jr., "Ad-ventures," *Editor & Publisher,* November 13, 1971, p. 16.

11. Bernice Kanner, "Tobacco Road," *New York,* January 17, 1983, p. 16.

12. Quoted in "Quotes," *Marketing/Communications,* January 1972, p. 54.

13. Otto Kleppner and Norman Govoni, *Advertising Procedure,* 7th ed. (Englewood Cliffs, N.J.: Prentice-Hall), 1979.

14. Quoted by Joseph Seldin in *The Golden Fleece* (New York: Macmillan, 1963), chap. 13.

15. Volney Palmer, "The Final Say," *Advertising Age,* January 28, 1980, p. 44.

16. Reva Korda, "How to Break the Rules," *Advertising Age,* March 5, 1979, pp. 47, 48.

17. Gail Bronson, "In Advertising, Big Names Mean Big Money," *U.S. News & World Report,* July 4, 1983, p. 60.

18. "Softening a Starchy Image," *Time,* July 11, 1983, p. 54.

19. "David Says O & M Ads Can Be Laughing Matter," *Advertising Age,* November 12, 1979, p. 110.

20. Bill Abrams, "If Logic in Ads Doesn't Sell, Try a Tug on the Heartstrings," *Wall Street Journal,* April 8, 1982, p. 27.

21. "MADD Leader Backs Ad Curbs," *Advertising Age,* July 18, 1983, p. 74.

22. "Mac the Bod Ads Lifts Eyebrows," *Advertising Age,* July 25, 1983, pp. 3, 86.

23. John Blumenthal, "Is Truth Bar to Creativity?" *Advertising Age,* October 9, 1978, p. 75.

24. To be consistent, the text for this chapter shows all advertising headlines in caps and lower case even though a large percentage of headlines these days are set in all lowercase. The chapter shows slogans in lowercase.

25. Quoted by Elaine F. Weiss, "King of the Chews," *Harper's Magazine,* October 1982, p. 23.

High style and creativity, in both copy and design, mark the ads of the John Wanamaker stores, Philadelphia.

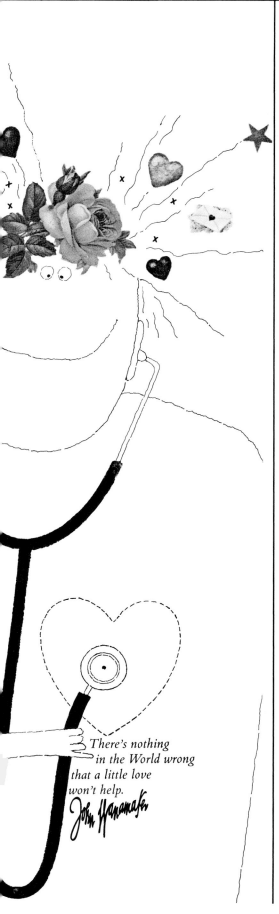

There's nothing in the World wrong that a little love won't help.

John Wanamaker

4
Layout tools and techniques

Armed with all the fancy tools available from Arthur Brown & Bro., Inc., A. I. Friedman, Inc., Dick Blick, Flax, or the other big art supply stores, you doubtless would be able to produce slicker layouts than without them. But the thought behind the layout and the dexterity with which you handle the tool—it could be a lowly ball-point pen used on a sheet of typing paper—really determine the quality of the layout.

Still, one of the functions of a course in advertising layout is to provide an introduction to the tools and supplies available. This chapter will discuss, first, the tools and supplies that are primary, then those that are helpful but not vital to your progress. The chapter ends with some advice on using the tools.

Primary tools and supplies

In a typical school situation, students are crowded into a classroom too small, really, to accommodate them comfortably. Lighting is inadequate; only a few can work near a window. And there are probably no lamps on the drawing tables, just overhead lights. Taborets—those handy little tables with drawers that hold the artists' tools and supplies—are not regarded by university administrators as vital to the program, so you may have to place what you need on nearby shelves or on the floor.

The drawing tables are adequate, but the stools are hard and provide no back support. If another class uses the room, the tables are filthy with pencil shavings, chalk dust, and smudges. Old newspaper and magazine clippings on the floor and in the corners of the room add to the clutter.

Some of this can be corrected, of course—with the instructor's admonitions and the students' cooperation—but the fact remains, working conditions in the typical layout classroom are far from ideal. You may be tempted to do the work at home, when the lecture part of the class is over. The trouble with this solution is that you will miss the counsel of your instructor and the inspiration and stimulation of other students working nearby. Furthermore, away from the "studio," you may put off doing the assignment.

Better to stick it out.

In the typical layout class a drawing table will be supplied. You will want to consider buying the following items:

1. *Layout pad*. If you plan to do a lot of tracing from a mat book or from alphabet cards, you should get a *tracing* pad—sheets of tissue-thin paper. Otherwise, a bond-paper *layout* pad will do. The bond paper should be thin enough, though, that some tracing is possible. The two most commonly used pad sizes are 14″ × 17″ and 19″ × 24″, each with fifty sheets. The instructor will probably ask that all students get the same size pad. The smaller one is big enough for most jobs and handy to carry back and forth to class (if pads cannot be stored at school); the larger one is better if you have full-page newspaper ads to do and if you cannot attach the pad high on the drawing table—if you have to let it lie against the bottom lip of the drawing table as you work.

If you are allowed to use thumbtacks on your drawing table, you should push the tacks through the inside back cover of the pad, at the top left and right corners, into the table. If tacks are not allowed (and that is understandable), you can fasten all four corners of the inside back cover to the table with strips of masking tape. Or you can simply let the pad rest against the lip of the tilted drawing table. But if you then have to work low on the board, you may be bothered with back strain.

Throw the cover sheet of the pad up and over the top of the drawing table, and there you have your exposed first sheet, ready to work on.

If your hands have a tendency to perspire as you work, put a sheet of paper underneath your drawing hand and keep it there as you work, moving it when necessary. Perspiration on the drawing paper not only will cause smudges but also will make areas of your paper incapable of receiving the pencil or other medium.

To protect underneath sheets from indentations made by the pressure of your drawing instrument, cut a sheet of heavy white paper to size and slip it in underneath the sheet you are working on.

You will appreciate the fact that layout-pad paper is semitransparent. Rip off the sheet you are working on when you feel you are ready to make an adjustment in the layout and slip that sheet underneath a new sheet. Move it around and trace those parts of the original rough you wish to retain.

2. *T-square.* T-squares come in 18″, 24″, 30″, 36″, 42″, and even larger sizes, in wood, in wood with transparent edges, in metal, and in plastic. Get one about the length of your layout pad's width.

The T-square must be kept true. Never use its top edge as a guide while cutting paper with a knife or razor blade. Keep the T-square hanging, T-style, from the top of the drawing table; there is less chance, then, that a passing student will get it hooked in a sleeve, dashing it to the floor. The top of the T must not be jarred.

In using the T-square, make sure it is pushed snugly against the left edge of the drawing table, drawing board, or layout pad. Hold it down firmly with your left hand as you rule your horizontal line.

It is possible to buy a "shifting head" T-square with one fixed head and one that adjusts to any angle. You can also buy a Rol-Ruler, which allows you to rule parallel lines at regular intervals.

3. *Triangle.* You could use both a 45-degree and a 30–60 degree triangle, but only the 30–60 is necessary. Get a 10″ transparent one.

An adjustable triangle that converts to any degree from 0 to 90 is also available. It also has a built-in protractor.

Like the T-square, the triangle must be protected against scratches and nicks at the edges.

The triangle, placed firmly against the T-square edge, is used to make vertical and also diagonal lines. Actually you *can* get along without one. Placing the pencil firmly against the edge of the T-square where you want the vertical line drawn, you can pull the T-square downward and the pencil with it. Some layout artists, pressed for time, do this even when a triangle is nearby. You can also rule vertical lines by hanging your T-square from the top.

For around $5 you can buy a hard aluminum triangle—the Fairgate—that can double as a straightedge along which you can draw a knife. One edge is calibrated in inches and sixteenths. This triangle comes with twenty-six different size circles cut into it, so it can be used also as a template.

4. *Pencils.* Drawing pencils range from 6B (very black and soft) to 9H (very light and hard). This is the lineup: 6B, 5B, 4B, 3B, 2B, B, HB, F, H, 2H, 3H, 4H, 5H, 6H, 7H, 8H, 9H. You should have two or three of these in the 4B to 2H range—perhaps a 4B, a 2B, and for tracing purposes a 2H.

The harder the lead, the longer the point will hold. But you will have to press harder to make your mark, and it will be lighter.

These abstractions of artists' and designers' tools appeared as art on a folder distributed by A. I. Friedman, Inc. You can see the folder in chapter 14.

In addition to ordinary drawing pencils, a number of other pencils await your selection. A chisel point, like Eberhard Faber's "Microtomic," makes single-stroke letters. Try it in a 2B hardness. A "General's Sketching Pencil," with its large, flat point, fills in large areas of gray. If you want an extra-black matte finish, try Eberhard Faber's "Ebony" pencil or "Wolff's Carbon Drawing Pencil."

You will also find a set of color pencils useful.

Whatever pencils you use, keep them sharp. You will want a knife or single-edge razor blade nearby to constantly whittle away the wood around the points. A sandpaper pad puts a finishing touch on a sharpened point. You can also buy a metal "sandpaper pad" called a "pencil pointer." Unlike a regular sandpaper pad, this is a permanent tool.

To get more mileage out of your pencils, you can buy a pencil lengthener, a sort of metal tube with lock that holds both round and hexagon pencils.

A mechanical or electric pencil sharpener can be used on all but the chisel points. These must be sharpened by hand to preserve the chisel features.

It is not a good idea to combine pencil with ink in a rough layout because of the difference in the strengths of the blacks. The combination might suggest a printing job in black and gray inks, not likely for an advertisement.

5. *Erasers.* The advantage of using a pencil to do a layout is that you can correct your mistakes. You are not likely then to leave the layout the way it first unfolds just because you find it is too much trouble to change it. But you will need an eraser or two: an art gum and a Pink Pearl. You will need a kneaded eraser if you work in pastels or charcoal. You might also want an eraser shield—an ultrathin piece of metal in which are cut a number of small shapes that can be fitted over areas to be erased.

6. *Pens.* Ballpoint pens and fibre- or acrylic-tip pens (like the Pentel and the Flair) are useful for drawing thumbnail sketches. For more advanced roughs these pens have the disadvantage of permanence. Put an experimental line down on paper with one of them and there is no turning back. You can appreciate Jean Ening's contention that for perfect control and accuracy—and for flexibility—nothing beats a well-sharpened pencil in doing rough layouts.

Still, Pentels and similar instruments make nice additions to your toolbox. They make marks that have an authority about them. They come in colors plus black; and the points are either rounded or chisel-shaped (your choice). Unfortunately, the points do not hold up for long.

Pentel introduced a new kind of pen in the mid-1970s: a Rolling Writer, which combines the firmness of the ballpoint with the flexibility of the fibre- or acrylic-tip pen. Unlike the ballpoint, the Rolling Writer can be used upside-down, in case you have funny writing and drawing habits.

Another instrument you might want to consider is a technical fountain pen, like the Rapidograph, which makes a line of uniform thickness. It can be equipped with points varying from very fine to medium thick. Unless you use your Rapidograph regularly, you may be plagued with clogging problems. A good, cheap substitute is the Stylist, which is a sort of throwaway technical fountain pen. The regular Stylist has a water-base ink; the Stylist 2 has an oil-base ink, extra dense and good for reproduction. The ink will not bleed under T-squares and triangles. Faber-Castell and Nikko make similar pens.

Unless you are doing finished drawings or very careful lettering for comprehensives, you will have little need for regular metal pen points, penholders, and india ink.

7. *Markers.* A few years ago most designers used nothing but pencils or chalks (pastels) for their rough layouts and comps. Today almost every-

body uses felt-tip markers—if not for all the elements in the layout, at least to indicate the art.

You have a choice of several shades of gray in either warm or cool tones. (If your roughs are to be reproduced, you would probably choose the warm grays, as they tend to reproduce a little better.) You also have a wide choice of colors. For instance, Magic Markers, one brand, offers 194 colors, including 18 grays.

Markers make transparent lines and areas that can be blended into other shades or colors. They come in fine or blunt points.

Letraset makes a LetraJet Air Marker that converts regular markers into a sort of airbrush.

8. *Ruler.* You can get by with a discount drugstore plastic ruler. Or you might want to buy one of those plastic combination T-square rulers. But if you get into serious work, and especially if you do mechanicals, you will want a good 18- or 24-inch metal ruler calibrated in both inches and picas. Some stores carry an 18-inch C-Thru Standard Graphic Arts Ruler, in laminated vinyl, calibrated in inches, picas, and agate lines and carrying proofreader's symbols, printer's rules, percentage screens, halftone screens, copy counters, and a copyfitting system.

You can also buy a Graham Centering Rule, a transparent plastic ruler that, through colors, allows you to quickly find the center of a layout, pasteup, or piece of artwork.

9. *Chalks and crayons.* The cost of a starter set of color or gray markers can soar to $20 or $30. So some designers continue to use pastel color chalks. Pastels require the use of a can of fixative spray to prevent smearing.

Ordinary crayons or a set of color pencils provide the cheapest answer to the problem of indicating color on a rough layout. The beginning designer might want to start with them.

10. *Tempera.* To indicate reverse type in a solid or tone area, the designer uses a fine brush dipped in a bottle of tempera, show-card color, or "designers' color." A small bottle of white would probably get the most use.

11. *Rubber cement.* You will need it for patching and pasting (unless you have access to a waxing machine). A four-ounce can or jar will do. For brand, it is hard to beat Best-Test, which has been around a long time.

12. *Masking tape.* For use when you trace. It keeps the original from moving around. It also affixes reference material temporarily to your drawing table. And it attaches protective flaps to your comps.

Because the advertising layout course does not require students to do their own finished art, the chapter will not discuss drawing papers, illustration board, and other illustrator's supplies.

If you do not have to furnish your own T-square and triangle, you may find it possible to get by for an expenditure of less than $10 for supplies for a semester-long course, provided you are willing to use pencils instead of markers.

An ordinary toolbox makes an excellent holder for supplies. If you do not want to make that expenditure, you will find a shoe box works almost as well.

Other layout supplies to consider

You can do a layout with almost any drawing, writing, or marking tool on almost any surface. You do not have to worry about how it will reproduce, because you are still far removed from the production stage. You simply want your idea to be read—by someone who presumably is already interested.

As the designer, you are better able to foresee how it will look in print than anyone else. That look is what you try to communicate.

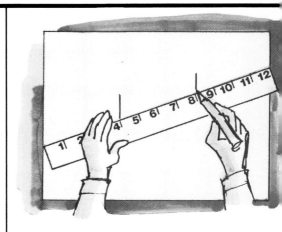

Your ruler can serve as more than a mere scale of distance. You can use it to quickly divide any distance shorter than the ruler into a given number of equal portions. Let us say you want to divide the long edge of an 8½″ × 11″ sheet of typing paper into three parts, as for a two-fold (three panels per side) direct-mail folder. Eleven does not divide very easily into three parts. But watch this: we place the low end of the ruler against one of the short (8½″) edges and swing the ruler in an arc until some number divisible by three hits the other short edge, in this case twelve itself. Three into twelve is four. Mark your paper at four and at eight (the mark at twelve takes care of itself), then draw lines perpendicular to the long edges. You then have your three equal panels.

Student Tracy Wong tries his hand with gray felt markers to produce a rough drawing of a pencil sharpener to be used in one of his ads. He does his outlining with a black fine-tip marker.

At the very rough stage you can use a tool that will leave a heavy, crude, even permanent mark. You are not interested in detail yet, or in polish. You are interested in spontaneity, even in graphic accidents. At the middle stages, you will want to use a tool that leaves a mark that can be adjusted. That is why a pencil is ideal for middle-stage layouts.

As you get into your assignments, you will find some need for a few tools you already have at home, such as a pair of scissors and a compass (the kind used for making circles).

As you become more proficient with the basic tools and materials, you may want to explore others. For instance: a pair of dividers—an instrument invaluable for making quick space comparisons and for marking equal space divisions.

You may want sheets of dry-transfer letters to make headlines on your comps look as though they are printed. And sheets of "Greeking" to simulate body copy. And transparent color sheets to indicate flat areas of color.

When you get into the designing of direct-mail pieces, you may want to work with colored paper.

Eventually, you will have to have some type-specimen sheets.

And maybe you will want a camera lucida or a commercial art projector/viewer for enlarging or reducing photographs and artwork onto your layouts so they can be traced in their printed sizes. You may also want a light table, a paper cutter, a taboret, and other pieces of equipment.

Pasteup supplies

The tools and supplies described above are for rough layouts and comprehensives. When you get into pasteups (camera-ready copy), you need to make additional acquisitions. Companies that sell pasteup supplies by mail include: Dot Pasteup Supply Company, 1612 California St., Omaha, Nebraska 68101; APA Institute Ltd., 1306 Washington Ave., St. Louis, Missouri 63103; and The Printers Shopper, 111 Press Lane, Chula Vista, California 92010. All issue catalogs.

The Studio, Box 6, Westport, Connecticut, offers Board-Mate, a template for quickly ruling any page size on a mechanical without any drafting equipment but a pen.

To do a pasteup, you need first to choose a base sheet. For many jobs you can use smooth book paper, preferably 70 pound or heavier. The piece you use should be bigger than the trim or final size of the ad you are doing the pasteup for. Make sure the paper can take pen and ink, for you may want to rule lines or make drawings directly on your pasteups. For more important jobs, you will want to use illustration board thick enough so it will not bend. Illustration board allows removal and repasting of the elements and offers a superior surface for inking.

Some pasteup artists, when doing booklets, do rough pasteups on tissue paper with galleys of type and proofs of art before attempting the finished pasteups. Where possible, they use a light table. This means their pasteups have to be done on paper that is thin enough for light to show through.

If you do pasteups for a house organ or some other regularly issued publication, you will want to use sheets printed with a grid showing page edges and copy areas. The printing will be in light-blue ink which the camera will not pick up. The lines are only for the pasteup artist's eyes.

Which bonding agent you use to fasten type and art to your pasteup sheet is also important. Today the preferred bonding agent is wax. Any piece of paper to be pasted down can be run quickly through a waxing machine. Then it is a matter of simply pressing the elements into place.

A table-top waxer costs several hundred dollars. Lectro-Stik, a small hand-held waxer, is available for around $40.

Rubber cement has one advantage over waxing in that a rubber-cemented piece will have less tendency to pop off, at least for a while. Some pasteup artists use rubber cement for putting down small pieces, but for larger pieces they prefer waxing. They see a big advantage to waxing: the piece can be moved around easily before it is burnished down. And it can easily be peeled off and repositioned.

Still, if you put a piece into position immediately after applying rubber cement, you can move it around a bit before the cement dries. But you have to be quick about it.

Make sure your rubber cement is thin enough, and apply it sparingly and evenly over the whole back surface. You need fresh sheets of paper—cheap paper—underneath to pick up the excess cement. One trick is to use an old copy of a magazine for this purpose, turning a page each time you have a new piece to rubber cement.

Using rubber cement, you are likely to encounter spots and small areas of excess cement that have seeped out from under the pieces and onto the pasteup sheet. You can pick these up with rubber-cement pickups, sold for this purpose, or chunks of old rubber cement that have dried out. They will still be slightly sticky.

A glue stick—like Faber-Castell's UHU Stic or Dennison's Glue Stic (some makers of this tool like the shortcut spelling) or Elmer's Glue Stick—is handy for bonding small pieces to a page. A pasteup is a temporary thing. After the pasteup has been photographed, you will not care if the bonding agent deteriorates and the elements fall off. If for some reason a permanent bond is desired, rubber cement should be applied to *both* the underside of the element and the surface of the base paper or board. When both have dried, put them together. Carefully.

When you are satisfied that the piece is exactly where it belongs, press it down firmly or burnish it with a bonelike tool or roller, trying not to smear the type. Sometimes just pressing down with the T-square is enough. The T-square must be kept clean. For pasteup work, a steel rather than a plastic-edge T-square works best, because you can draw a knife or razor blade against its edge to trim unwanted paper.

You can do some of your trimming with a pair of scissors. But you will also need a single-edge razor blade or an X-acto knife for finer work.

For about $20 you can buy a gridded 12″ × 18″ cutting board made of a special plastic that seals itself after a cut has been made. It also lubricates the cutting tool, prolonging its sharpness. You can use the board to trim and adjust pieces of type or art before pasting or pressing them into place.

To fit photographs or other art to the design, you need a proportion wheel or proportion slide rule. When you have the to-be-printed dimensions figured, mark them out in the margins of the art and put down your crop marks.

To take care of last-minute jobs, you should have on hand a selection of press-on or dry-transfer alphabets. With them you can set type right at your drawing board.

To produce lines or borders, some pasteup artists prefer using a ballpoint pen to a ruling pen or tape. But a ballpoint pen may blob or skip at the beginning of the line. And the artist using it may not start or end the line at exactly the right place. To solve this problem you can put small pieces of paper at both ends temporarily and keep blobs and skips off the mechanical. And you will not overshoot your dimensions.

When applying a correction patch to a pasteup, it is a good idea to cut a mortise for it, throwing away what would be underneath. That way, if the patch happens to pop off, you will not be embarrassed by a printing of the covered up error, although a blank space is embarrassing enough. The blank space will be easy to spot on the proof.

As a beginning exercise in an advertising layout class, Irene Ishikawa, using an ordinary pencil, nicely captures the feel (right) of a printed advertisement (left). What she produces here is really an after-the-fact comprehensive rough layout.

Care and treatment of tools

You can hardly expect to bring order to your advertisement if you do not have it in your working area. Your table should be wiped clean before you start, your materials arranged neatly nearby for easy accessibility. All pencils should be sharpened, their points long enough to provide necessary fine lines, short enough so they will not break when you press down on them.

Pick up any leftover scrap and clutter and get rid of it before you tackle your new assignment. Enough will accumulate as you go along.

Perhaps you will stop midway to restore order once again.

You will stop often to reshape your tools.

Each time you resharpen your pencil, head it into a small box or wastebasket. Do not allow shavings or lead scrapings to dirty your table or working area. Do not use pastels, chalks, or charcoal unless you have a wiping cloth or tissues at hand.

If you use a pen, wipe it off immediately after use; do not allow ink to cake at the point. If you use a brush, have a pan of water handy or use a nearby washroom immediately after painting. When ink or paint hardens at the hair roots, the point frays and spreads. Shape the point with your fingers as you wash it out with cold water and a little bit of soap.

Do not lay materials out on the tilted drawing board; they will surely roll off and break. If you have no other storage area, use masking tape to affix a small box at the top right (or left if you are left-handed) and place your materials there.

Except when you design direct-mail pieces, always leave white space all the way around each layout. This provides room for handling and, if necessary, for writing instructions or explanations to the instructor, client, or printer. The ad may bleed in the medium, but it never bleeds on the layout pad.

Experience will tell you how hard you can push the tools—how much pressure is needed. Beginners often fail to make their marks firmly enough. You should think of most of the marks you make as representing pure black ink. The thinness of the line will vary, but the pressure will remain fairly constant.

As you use your tools, act as though you, not they, are in charge.

Putting your tools to work

You can experiment with layout by cutting various shapes from black or gray or colored construction paper and arranging and rearranging them to see the great variety of arrangements that are possible. Work within some given field—say on an 8½″ × 11″ sheet of white paper.

Do not worry at the beginning about how nearly the elements approximate actual advertising elements.

From a program of working with cutouts you can move to a program of working with pencil (or marker) and paper, drawing basic elements within rectangles representing ad dimensions.

Line is the basic element you work with.

When you change the line's direction, you begin to define a shape. Shape is line with a second dimension. When you put the shape into perspective and add thickness, you give it form and create the illusion of a third dimension.

You can work with five kinds of lines: curved, spiral, meandering, zigzag, and straight.

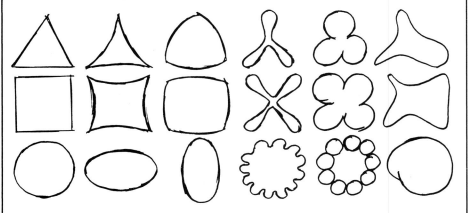

You can use lines to portray the three classic shapes in art: the triangle, the rectangle (or square), and the circle. Each of these suggests innumerable other shapes.

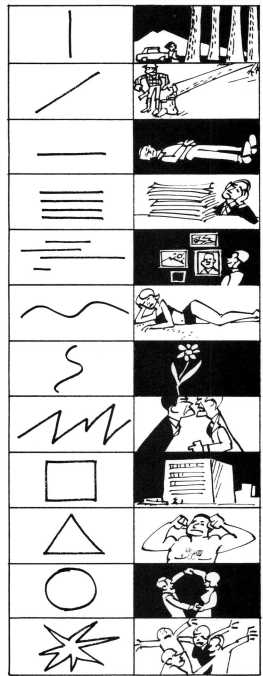

What lines can suggest, reading from top to bottom: dignity, action, rest, monotony, variety, grace, growth, dissension. When they begin to form shapes, they suggest: solidarity, strength, unity, excitement.

When you give each of the three classic shapes the illusion of a third dimension, you have a cone (or pyramid), a cube (or box), and a sphere (or tube) to work with—and all the elements they suggest.

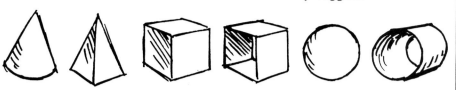

By combining classic shapes you come up with a great variety of other shapes.

And then there are the free, or less geometric, shapes.

Give these shapes the illusion of a third dimension and you are on your way to portraying products in advertising.

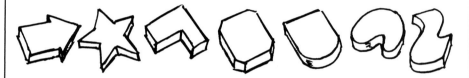

Let us see what happens, now, when you show classic shapes in combination.

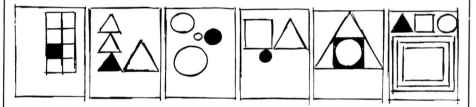

Now experiment with classic shapes and free shapes in association, add sets of lines, and you are coming close to designing complete advertisements.

Lines—or the *suggestion* of lines—in an advertisement in themselves contain meaning. Straight lines suggest strength, direction, opposition. Curved lines suggest grace, movement, growth. Lines convey the moods they do because they are abstractions of objects and figures that originate the moods.

Some drawing hints

You do not need much ability in drawing to do acceptable thumbnails and rough layouts. Even to do comprehensives, you can get by with ordinary tracing, copying, and even patching. Only for mechanicals do you need professionally produced artwork. So do not apologize that you "can't even draw a straight line." What you lack in drawing ability you can make up for with your sense of design. The best drawings and illustrations, anyway, are as much designed as they are drawn and painted.

For much of your work you can get by with stick figures for people and boxes for props. You can describe these items in the margins if you feel your viewer—instructor, boss, or client—cannot make them out. But even stick figures can be endowed with size, facing, direction, mass, and tone.

Maybe for your figures you should think in terms of logs rather than sticks. And instead of settling for boxes for your props, settle for shapes that are a bit more descriptive. Every object can be reduced to a basic shape.

And do not think only of side views. Consider head-on views, three-quarter views, back views, views from above, views from below.

You are a visualizer if not an artist. Leave the final drawing and rendering to a professional. You do the directing.

You do not need always to think of art as photographed or drawn from a normal viewing angle. Sometimes it is better to view your subject from above or, as in the example above, from low on the ground. (Courtesy of Print Media Service, produced by Dynamic Graphics, Peoria, Illinois.)

Perspective and foreshortening

To give objects a three-dimensional feel, you turn to *perspective*. Perspective allows you to show two or three sides of an object and makes the object look more realistic.

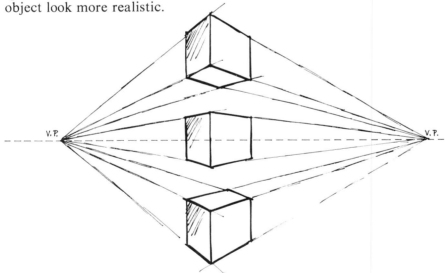

To put an object—say a box—into perspective you must draw its parallel lines in such a way that, were the lines extended, they would meet at a common point (called the "vanishing point") on the horizon. For each panel of art (drawing, painting, or photograph) in your ad you establish a horizon line that each object within the panel can relate to.

An object can be below, above, or on the horizon line. You create a "bird's-eye view" of items below the horizon line and a "worm's-eye view" of items above.

In presenting an object in an ad, you must decide which view shows off the object best and most clearly informs the viewer of its properties.

When you show more than one item in a panel, your perspective problems multiply. But if you remember that you have but one horizon line to a panel, and if you establish it in your mind, you will be making a good start.

Do not feel that the vanishing points—or even the horizon line (and it is usually an imaginary line)—need to be within the panel. The closer together you put the vanishing points, by the way, the closer your viewer is to the object pictured.

Each object in your panel can have its own set of vanishing points. For instance, there are one-point and three-point perspectives as well as two-point perspective, and there are also *elevated* vanishing points (as for houses with pitched roofs), but all of this is too complicated to go into here, and a knowledge of it is probably not necessary to do sketches for rough layouts.

When drawing objects that are not rectangular, fit them first into rectangles and work out the perspective. This will give you a better chance to portray the objects realistically.

Several books deal fully with the subject of perspective, and if you become serious about exploring its possibilities, you can get a set of sixteen large three-point perspective grids covering various angles. Kleidon & Associates, Medina, Ohio, offers this product, described by Dugald Stermer as "incredibly useful."

You can also show depth in a drawing by making objects in the background grayer or weaker than objects in the foreground. Objects in the foreground also have more detail.

Closely allied to perspective is *foreshortening,* which asks that objects close to the viewer be made to look larger than items farther back. It also asks that the part of an object closest to the viewer be made to look larger than a similar size part that is farther back. Hence, in a front view a person's extended hand looks larger than that person's other hand held down at his side.

You can help further to create the illusion of distance by overlapping objects in your panel. This also helps you to create a more interesting composition.

Optical illusions

Sometimes you may find that lines and shapes say things you do not mean them to say. Uncontrolled optical illusions may be at play. As a designer you need to understand how optical illusions affect your design.

1. A horizontal line is easier to see than a vertical line. This is because the eye moves naturally horizontally, recording what it sees easily. So a horizontal line will appear longer than its equivalent vertical line. And it will seem heavier. To compensate for this, an artist wanting a vertical to appear exactly as long and as heavy as a horizontal lengthens it slightly and makes it a bit heavier. Actually, then, the vertical is longer and heavier than the horizontal; optically they appear the same. (A good sans serif typeface that appears to be built of even strokes actually has vertical strokes slightly heavier than its horizontal strokes.)

Here is one of the better known optical illusions, used by a number of organizations to startle or make a point. *Mad* magazine calls it the "Piouyet." Daniels, Sullivan & Dillon, Nashville, once referred to it as a "triple-shafted dual fork used in an integro-differential computer." SmokEnders, an organization that conducts seminars to help people stop smoking, once used it as a big E in the middle of its logotype.

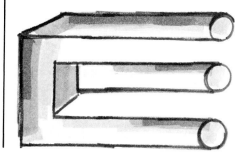

2. Lines or stripes running in a single direction tend to lengthen that direction. A chubby woman understands this; she avoids dresses with horizontal stripes but keeps in her wardrobe, perhaps, a dress or two with vertical stripes. A dress with vertical stripes would not interest the tall woman.

3. A filling-in of a shape with tone or color or with elements tends to reduce the size of the shape. A dark room, or a cluttered room, appears smaller than an equivalent room finished in a light shade or sparsely furnished.

4. What is nearby or what surrounds a figure influences its apparent size. This can best be shown through a diagram.

In the first example the thin lines pull back the eyes, keeping the heavy line short. In the second example the thin lines stretch the heavy line, making it appear longer than it really is. In reality, the heavy lines are of equal length.

In the examples that follow, the designer puts the optical illusion to work. The thin lines now have been converted to ad elements. Notice that in the example at the right the elements stretch the car, making it appear sleeker than the car at the left. Yet, in reality, the cars are the same length (and height).

A number of companies have used classic optical illusions as main art for their ads to make the point that readers should not jump to conclusions. "Quick, Your First Impression! A Rabbit or a Duck?" asks the *Detroit Free Press* in a media ad in *Advertising Age*. The art is a drawing from a New York Public Library collection that, seen one way, looks like a duck; seen another way, it looks like a rabbit. "Naturally," the copy block begins, "first impressions count. But, as you've probably seen from the picture above, first impressions can be deceiving. Like when you're buying the 5th largest market. . . ."

Advertising elements

Ogilvy & Mather can get away with an ad like this: a full-page, full-color photograph in the *New Yorker* showing a man in a good-looking shirt wearing an eye patch. Nothing else to the ad. No copy. No headline. No signature. Yet everyone knows the ad is for Hathaway.

But the usual ad needs more than a single unexplained picture. It needs essentially these:

1. *Headline* (or headlines). Often a headline in large type is followed by a headline, a longer headline, in smaller type. Probably the most important single element in the ad, the headline carries the theme of the ad. Seeing the headline, the reader gets everything the advertiser really has to say. Occasionally the ad is all headline, with only a signature added.

A good advertising headline brings news to the reader, gives advice, promises something, arouses curiosity, narrows the audience to people who

This is no way to talk to London, England.

In this phone company ad directed to the business community of Houston, the headline leans on the art, and the art leans on the headline. With either element missing, the initial impact would be lost. Another element, the coupon, is less intrusive than is usual because clipping and mailing it is only an alternative to making a phone call. The strong, textured art helps define the depth of the copy block, which, you will notice, is slightly rounded at the top to conform to the mailbox's contour. The designer is Jerry Herring.

are really interested or affected, makes a command. It does one or several of these things.

These are matters for copywriters, of course, but are also matters for designers, even if they do not do any of the writing. In headlines particularly, designers exercise considerable control over usage and clarity. Many headline errors can be traced to designer haste or ignorance. Designers must take care in what they letter in on the roughs; they must look for more than spacing problems when they check the proofs.

Two problem areas deserve mention: (1) the breaking up of a headline into lines or "takes," and (2) the use of punctuation.

If a headline must occupy more than one line, the lines should break at natural pauses. Consider this headline from an ad that appeared in major magazines:

Give him
Royal Oak
Scented Lotion
and kiss small
talk goodbye.

The lines "and kiss small" and "talk goodbye" confuse the reader. They would make more sense broken up like this:

and kiss small talk
goodbye.

Punctuation errors most often involve the use of the apostrophe and the question mark. With the apostrophe, it is often a matter of the copywriter or designer not knowing when it is needed. With the question mark, it is a matter of simply forgetting to draw it in. A left-out question mark can change the meaning of a sentence. Don't you agree.

2. *Copy block.* The copy block or column, in small type, amplifies the headline. It helps convince the reader. It closes the sale. The ad maker tries to keep it short, terse—but not for all ads, and certainly not for mail-order advertising.

Many advertising people will not buy the idea so prevalent today that pictures do more for advertising than copy does. One has written: "A picture worth a thousand words? You give me 1,000 words and I'll take the Lord's Prayer, the Twenty-Third Psalm, the Hippocratic Oath, a sonnet by Shakespeare, the Preamble to the Constitution, Lincoln's Gettysburg Address, and I'd still have enough words left over for just about all of the Boy Scout oath. And I wouldn't trade you for any picture on earth."[1]

When copy runs long, the designer breaks it up into short takes, using white space or white space with a subhead for an occasional optical oasis for the reader. The designer must not treat the copy block as though it were a neutral element occupying areas not preempted by more spectacular art elements. The designer's primary function should be to get people to read the copy block.

Too often, especially in retail advertising, the copy block is set too solid. Leading (pronounced "ledding") would make the copy more inviting. And the type should be set in the largest possible size that is appropriate to the column width.

3. *Art.* As used here, art is a panoramic term, including photographs, drawings, paintings, borders, rules, ornaments, blocks of color or gray tones, areas of white space. Furthermore, type by itself, skillfully arranged, can be considered a piece of art.

The art may merely arrest the viewer, or it may serve a higher purpose: cooperating with the headline and copy in telling the advertiser's story.

"One Alternative to Flossing Daily," says a headline for a Johnson & Johnson Dental Floss ad. An accompanying photograph shows false teeth in a water glass.

The experts have not settled the half-century-old argument: What does the best job for the advertiser, a photograph or an illustration? But a comparison of advertising today with advertising of a few years ago shows that photographs seem to be winning. In most circumstances, they are less expensive, and people seem more willing to believe them. But drawings and paintings still have their place. Just as a novel can carry more truth than a piece of nonfiction, a drawing can say more than a photograph. And drawings are not put off by seasons or weather. Neither do they require models' releases.

Borders are another art element to consider. Advertisers want borders on their ads when several even-sized announcements compete with one another on a page and there is danger that the reader cannot tell when he leaves one ad and reads another. The larger the ad or the fewer ads per page, the less need for borders. Even if they are not needed, borders are used by designers when they feel their decorative touch adds to the mood of the ad.

Borders are displayed in the printer's type-specimen book. Designers choose them as they choose types. Or they design their own.

Fine-line rules or thicker lines and bars are sometimes useful inside an ad to organize, emphasize, or segregate elements.

4. *The logotype.* Advertisers have to identify themselves. Sometimes they do it subtly, with a last line buried in the copy block. Usually they do it with a line in display-size type set apart from the body type, at the bottom of the ad. The identifying line—called a "logotype" or "logo" or (by retailers) "signature" or "sig cut"—may be accompanied by an insignia or trademark. A slogan may also be included.

Elliot Young, president of Perception Research Services, Inc., has reported one of his tests showing that readers fail to see the logotype almost half the time because of its location in an ad. His advice is to "make sure the logo or product name isn't too low on the page."[2]

Peripheral elements

Some kinds of advertising require additional elements peculiar to their functions. Retail advertising appearing in newspapers, for instance, needs strong price display. In most retail ads, prices are set in type that is larger and bolder than body copy or even headlines. Such price units can be treated as separate design elements.

Advertising in both newspapers and magazines often carries coupons, either to present to grocers or to fill out and mail. The designer not only has to decide on placement of these coupons but also must worry about the design of the coupon. An ad for a fashion seminar might include a coupon in the shape of a dress pattern. The reader would have to cut out the dress along the dotted line after filling in the blanks. Mistakes in design of a mail-in coupon are making it too small to fill out or too inconvenient to cut out or—worst of all—printing it in reverse letters on a black or dark-color background so that pencil or pen markings will not show up.

For some kinds of advertising the designer may want to consider as a peripheral element the "scratch and sniff" strips made by the 3-M Company, Minneapolis. Not only are these used in magazine and direct-mail advertising; they are used on containers as well. A potential customer can scratch the strip on, say, a can of shaving foam, smell it, and then decide whether he wants to buy. A "scratch and sniff" strip an inch long contains some 50,000,000 microscopic plastic bubbles impregnated with just about

Given: a vertical and a horizontal picture and eighteen lines of copy (the shaded areas represent pictures; the ruled lines represent copy). The problem: without changing the sizes, arrange these in an area about twice as big as the sum of the area of the elements to be arranged. With such limitations, is it possible to come up with more than one acceptable arrangement? The diagrams here suggest an affirmative answer. Turn them upside down and you have another set to consider.

The border that holds this black-and-white ad together and separates it from other ads on the page is pleasantly broken by headline and art. The ad is shown here actual size. Larry Lurin is the illustrator; Sussman & Sugar the agency.

any aroma needed. The bubbles burst when a fingernail is run across the strip.

The Northern Illinois Gas Company used "scratch and sniff" strips on direct mail to customers to help them recognize the smell that accompanies a gas leak.

Now it is no longer necessary for an advertiser to produce its own "scratch and sniff" insert for a magazine because 3-M has worked out a system with leading magazine printers so that the magazine itself can handle production. Nor is it necessary to use strips. The fragrance can be applied directly to the ad as part of the printing operation.

Arranging the elements

As an advertising designer, then, you work with these several elements as you lay out an ad. You may decide what they should be, making all the plans, assigning all the work. Or you may simply put them together as they are handed to you.

In either case, your knowledge of the principles of design helps you. You reduce the various elements to shapes—rectangles, triangles, circles, and irregular shapes—and then apply what you know of balance, proportion, sequence, unity, and emphasis. (See chapters 5 and 6.)

First you get enough items together so that the total elements area—the area covered by the headlines, copy, art, and logotype—adds up usually to *more than* half the area of the assigned space. (The rule of proportion suggests that an ad should not be *exactly* half message and half white space.) Then you try various arrangements of the elements. You could cut out pieces of paper to approximate the elements; or you could simply draw squares, triangles, circles, and other shapes directly on the paper to approximate the elements. As you work, you gradually increase the detail so that the elements *look* like the elements they are supposed to be.

Indicating the elements

What tools you choose and how you use them affect the fidelity of the elements you need to show. Here's how to proceed:

Headlines. Using your T-square, rule a set of guidelines for each line of display type (more about this in chapter 7) and, using an ordinary pencil or a chisel-point pencil, quickly sketch in the letters in approximately the height and width of the intended letters. With practice, you will take up just about the same amount of space the letters set in type will take up. For early-stage roughs, you should not be concerned about the width of the *strokes* of the letters or even the basic shape of the letters. You can mark the style and size in the margins of your layout. Or—poor practice—you can leave it to the printer to decide.

For finished roughs and comprehensives, you *are* concerned about the look of the typeface you letter. You want your lettering to be close to the finished type. The detail of each stroke does not concern you as much as the overall weight and tone of the letters. For heavy letters, you will "scrub" your strokes, adding blackness as you move from letter to letter. Or you may outline the letters with a fine point and then fill in the space between the outlines. Or you may use your chisel point and get the correct thickness with single, broad strokes.

When the headline is not yet written, you can use a series of jumbled letters (consonants, usually) or a series of *M*s and *W*s. Or just a zigzag line, with high "ups" occurring where the capitals would be.

How much space to leave between lines of the headline will be a problem at first. You will have to study headlines in several ads to get the feel of spacing. The usual error is to leave too much space between words, too much space between lines.

Approximating the tone of the headline may also be a problem. The firmness of the pencil strokes should remain constant; the tonal variations can be achieved through decreasing or increasing the widths of the strokes, not by varying the pressure of the drawing tool on the paper surface.

Copy. It is the *effect* of an area of type that you want; you are not concerned about what the copy actually says. And so a great variety of methods of indicating copy suggest themselves to you. You can draw ordinary boxes and write "copy" across the area. You can paste down a proof of the copy already set or cut out copy set for another job and paste it into place.

But here are four other, more acceptable, ways to handle copy indication for rough layouts.

Four ways of indicating body copy on a rough layout or comprehensive. Body-copy indication should be line for line.

1. Rule a series of thin parallel lines, *one for each line of type.* Your number of lines per column inch should equal approximately the number of lines of actual type you would get—that is, from 6 to 14, depending upon the size type you plan to use. Ordinarily, you would have 7, 8, or 9 lines per inch.

Before ruling the lines—and they should be firmly drawn with a sharp pencil or a ruling pen—draw, in *light* pencil strokes that barely can be seen, the outside measurements of the copy block. They will help you contain your ruled lines. Use your T-square to rule all lines.

2. Rule a series of thin parallel lines, *two for each line of type.* The top line represents the top of the x-height of the letters; the bottom line, the bottom of the x-height. (The x-height is the height of lowercase letters—not counting the ascending strokes, as in the *b* or *d,* or the descending strokes, as in the *g* or *j.*)

3. Rule a series of lines using a chisel-point pencil, with a lead width equal to the x-height. These lines, grayer than the fine solid lines of methods 1 and 2, are thicker, so the overall tone is about the same. You can keep them even, or you can vary the pressure as you rule, to give the effect of different-shaped letters and occasional capitals.

You would use one ruled line for each line of actual type.

4. Use a pen or sharp pencil and draw a series of zigzag or spiral lines, occasionally letting the zag or the spiral rise slightly above the normal alignment to simulate a capital.

Using any of these four methods, you will want paragraph indentation occasionally, unless the copy is to be set in block paragraphs; and you will want to simulate boldface letters and subheads, if these will be used.

You would *never* type the copy directly on the layout. The typeface on a typewriter is too different in character, size, and spacing to approximate printers' composition. In practice, the copy that will be set—the copy coming from the advertising copywriter—is typed on a separate sheet of paper and keyed to the layout by a slugline typed at the top, like "Copy A." You then write "Copy A" somewhere across the copy block in the rough layout and circle it.

Art. If art is already available—if pictures have been taken, drawings made, or the client has access to a proof book of mats—the indicating of the art is simply a matter of tracing. Perhaps "simply" makes it sound too easy.

There is such a thing as tracing creatively: proceeding, with a crude medium, to reproduce the art so the client can see what it really looks like. As a designer you should be particularly interested in capturing the *tone* and *style* of the art. Certainly you should be able to show whether the art is halftone or line.

If halftone, the art in the layout should be done with a soft pencil, gray chalks, or gray markers. Heavy outlines should be avoided. Tones should be blended—rubbed—with the fingers or with a piece of cloth or cotton. The tracing should show clearly whether the art is squared off or in silhouette form.

If line, the art should be sharp, crisp. If a screen pattern is part of the original, the tone, laid with a pencil, should be even.

You may decide that only a part of the original art should be included in the ad. You may decide further to increase the size of that part, or decrease it—or change the overall size of the artwork.

When artwork is not provided—when it is your job to visualize the art—you will have to do some original drawing. Stick-figure drawing under many circumstances is good enough, with description across the face of the drawing or in the margin. Even so, you should make some attempt to show whether what you have in mind is halftone or line art. Again, if halftone, lay an even tone of gray over the affected area first, using a blunt

To execute this rough art, a *Detroit Free Press* layout artist used gray pastel chalks and, for outlining, a Pentel.

For this quick drawing the artist used a chunk of lithographic crayon. The drawing is shown actual size.

When drawing figures for quick roughs or when laying an area of gray, use an ordinary pencil boldly, applying lead from the side of the point rather than from the tip.

pencil, blending the tone with your fingers. Or you can paste a piece of gray paper into position and work on that. If line, you can draw an amoeba-shaped outline and simply write inside the shape a description of what you have in mind.

The logotype. The advertiser uses a logotype or sig cut in a variety of sizes. You need to know what sizes are available. For a particular ad, you choose the size that is big enough to stand out, small enough not to over-shadow other elements in the ad. Indicating the logotype is usually a matter of tracing a proof or a printing of one. Or it is a matter of pasting one into place.

Too often you are stuck with a signature that needs updating. It does not fit today's advertising design. Sometimes you are allowed to modify it slightly to make it better fit the typography of the ad. If you cannot do that, you can at least run it smaller than you would if it were well designed.

If the advertiser as yet has no logotype, you can design one from available types as you would design the ad's headline. Here you have a beautiful chance of adding unity to the ad; the headline and the logotype can be set in the same style of type.

The look you are after

If two words could describe the look you are after in using your tools to do a layout, the words would be "crisp" and "juicy." The lettering should look crisp, the art juicy. To get crisp letters, work with sharp tools. If you use a pencil, stop after every few letters or words (depending upon the softness of the lead) and sharpen the point. For the art, think more in terms of tone than of outline. And make sure you get a wide range of tones, from solid or near-solid black to light gray.

1. Actually, the Chinese proverb has it that one picture is worth *more than* ten thousand words (see *Bartlett's Familiar Quotations*), which makes his point even stronger.

2. "Place Company Logo Higher in Ad . . . ," *Folio,* August 1982, p. 39.

5
Layout stages and formats

Layouts vary in quality from crude, less-than-actual-size doodles to carefully drawn and lettered exact-size works of art that, to the untrained eye, look as though they have already been printed. It is not so much the layout artist's ability or lack of it that explains this variance as the intended use to which the layout will be put. If it is to be used by the artist as a trial run, or by the copywriter as a guide to the amount of space to fill, or by the illustrator as a guide to composition in taking or drawing pictures, or by the printer as a guide in setting type and arranging design elements, the layout can be less than exact. If it is for the client, to help in decision making before money is spent on production, the layout will be carried to a more finished stage.

First roughs often are more spirited than later polishings, and the designer, in carrying the layout through the various stages, tries to hold onto any happy accidents that occur early in the process. But the designer cannot settle for a first try; considerations involving the nature of the product or service, attitude of the client, specifications of the medium, and the like, make the hunt for the ideal solution to a selling problem too involved for that. Besides, later compromises with the client certainly will force additional adjustments.

The ad in final form may be but a distant relative of the first rough layout.

Thumbnails

Because it takes less time to doodle in miniature than in actual size, the designer usually starts out by making thumbnail sketches, or *thumbnails,* using pencil, ballpoint pen, Pentel, crayon, or whatever tool may be handy.

The thumbnail should be in proportion to the ad as it is to appear in print. Quarter-size is normal.

Even at this first stage the designer thinks in terms of tones as well as outlines, suggesting halftones with areas of gray, line drawings with amoeba shapes, headlines with zigzag lines, copy with parallel lines. Dozens of sketches may precede the development of a final layout.

Rough layouts

The second stage is the *rough layout.*

Some designers skip the thumbnail stage altogether, because they feel whatever good effect they come up with loses too much in translation to the normal size. Their full-size layouts are as rough as thumbnails would be, maybe rougher.

An extremely crude rough layout is sometimes called a *shop rough,* meaning it is meant to serve simply as a hurried guide to the back shop. The heads may be lettered in, but type styles or weights are not approximated; instructions and descriptions are written on the outside margins. Or the compositor picks types to fit. Ads for retailers run in newspapers often are produced in this way.

A *finished layout* is a rough layout carried to a stage where headings are lettered in a style and weight clear enough to make marginal descriptions unnecessary, and artwork and photographs are drawn to look much like the finished product. Copy is indicated with carefully ruled parallel lines. Spacing is close to exact.

Most rough layouts fall somewhere in between "shop roughs" and "finished layouts." Students in advertising layout classes, especially those offered by journalism and business schools, work beyond the shop rough level but not quite up to the finished layout level.

In situations where several people must see a layout at one time—as in department store operations when department heads and members of the newspaper advertising staff both must check prices—more than one copy of the rough layout is needed. The artist works with carbon sheets, or the store makes copy prints of the layout.

At any rate, no retailer appearing regularly in newspapers, and certainly few direct-mail users, expect or need better than rough layouts. Even clients of advertising agencies accept layouts finished only to this level.

Comprehensives

But sometimes a layout gets further polish. Call it a *comprehensive* or *comp*. Important clients who pay thousands of dollars for single magazine insertions understandably demand comprehensives before they okay their ads.

A comprehensive is a layout that is perfect in every detail. Headings are hand-lettered in ink or tempera, artwork painted in acrylics or designers' colors or drawn in ink, photographs pasted into place or so carefully approximated in pastels or markers you would swear they *were* photographs. Copy may actually be set. If copy is only indicated, a ruling pen and certainly a T-square are used. Drawn and put together on illustration board, the comprehensive is matted and either covered with a flap or wrapped in cellophane.

A lot of work? Yes. But how else can the client check the mood, the effectiveness of the ad prior to plunging into costly production?

Sometimes the comp comes before rather than after the rough layout. The rough layout then merely defines some changes suggested by the client after seeing the comp.

Basic formats

Whether you start right off on a comprehensive or try some thumbnails and rough layouts first, you will be trying to put the elements of the ad into a pleasing and useful arrangement. The number of arrangements and patterns you can come up with as a designer are almost endless, but it is possible to fit most print-medium advertisements into ten basic categories or formats, if you interpret them loosely enough. A professional designer might balk at such categorizations, saying that the art is too lively, too full of surprises to pin down so abruptly. And some other writer on design might come up with a different set of categories. But a set like the one that follows may help the beginner see some new possibilities for design.

Mondrian layout

Let us start with one of the most widely recognized formats: Mondrian layout, named after the Dutch painter Piet Mondrian. Involved in a lifetime affair with proportion, Mondrian, using black bars and lines and solid areas of primary color, divided his canvases into vertical and horizontal rectangles and squares.

Mondrian reworked his designs many times before he was satisfied with

For this finished rough layout, Cheryl Frederickson, then art director of Swearingen Advertising Agency, Portland, used nothing but a nylon-tip marker. The display type is carried to a stage where, if you cannot recognize a specific face, you can at least get a feel for the size and weight of the face and the nature of the serifs.

the sizes and relationships of each of the rectangles to be painted. He carried this concern to the decor of his studio: an out-of-place ashtray greatly disturbed him. To Mondrian, beauty was exclusively geometric. He avoided the color green because it was too close to nature. "All in all," he is quoted as saying, "nature is a damned wretched affair. I can hardly stand it."

The advertising designer, while not sharing Mondrian's intensity, nevertheless freely applies Mondrian's principles to the printed page. The designer uses rectangles of type or art much as Mondrian used solid blocks of color. Sometimes the designer retains the lines or bars Mondrian used to separate elements; sometimes the designer leaves them out.

Mondrian ads appear everywhere for a few months, then die out, then come back again. And no wonder the style returns to popularity: a Mondrian arrangement is an easy, logical, workable, effective way to display type and art.

The designer of Mondrian ads, like the master himself, is more interested in proportion as a design principle than in eye-travel or emphasis or any of the other principles. There is nothing wrong with this. For some advertising, proportion deserves chief consideration, if for no other reason than to set the ad apart from other ads whose designers have stressed some other design principle.

Designers with newspaper backgrounds take naturally to Mondrian layout because of their experience with column rules and cut-off rules and boxes on the newspaper page. But Mondrian layout is considerably more subtle than newspaper makeup. The idea is to come up with a fitted set of vertical and horizontal rectangles (with perhaps a square thrown in)— all in different sizes. Lines separating the rectangles can be of even or varying widths; at their thinnest they are bolder than ordinary newspaper column rules. Sometimes the designer uses Ben Day or color rules in combination with solid black rules.

One or two of the rectangles may be filled with halftones; others may contain copy; others may be blank.

If the ruled lines are heavy, typefaces should be bolder than normal. Sans serifs or gothics are appropriate types to use.

Mondrian layouts are used more frequently in magazines than in newspapers, because the multiplicity of lines and resulting rectangles tend to break the ad into sections that may be scattered optically when smaller ads are placed alongside, as on a newspaper page. Large reverse-L-shape ads (or step ads) in newspapers sponsored by department stores or women's fashion stores, however, make use of the Mondrian principle with considerable success.

In arranging the rectangles, the designer lightly rules a series of horizontal and vertical lines, then eliminates some of them, either entirely or partially, and strengthens others, striving to leave rectangles of varying sizes and dimensions. The balance is almost always informal.

Swiss design, with its orderly approach, has some ties to Mondrian layout. But in Swiss design, lines or bars are not shown; they appear only in the mind of the designer. And the design is based often on a grid of squares instead of rectangles.

Although it was not his purpose, the Dutch painter Piet Mondrian, with his tightly organized canvases of straight lines and pure bright color, inspired a style of advertising layout known as Mondrian layout. While the painter left large areas of solid color, the advertiser fills in such areas with art or type. In this example, the designer, Larry Zink, lets one area remain blank. This was an 8½″ × 11″ full-color bleed advertisement appearing as an insert in the quarterly *DA*, showing art directors and others who buy paper how Beckett Brilliant Opaque vellum finish stock takes printing impressions. The agency: Brewer, Jones, Feldman.

Sun Life of Canada used a modified Mondrian approach in this ad, one of a series. The black band at the top and the deeper one at the bottom carry type in reverse; the widest band carries the photo, cropped to tie "Margaux Hemingway" to the type below. A bold ad that commands attention in the magazines it appears in. Ted Duquette was the art director, Betsy Duquette the copywriter. Ingalls Associates was the agency.

To Margaux Hemingway, security is living up to your name.

To many others, security is a high-yield Sun Lifemaster* universal life policy. A comprehensive insurance plan as well as a valuable investment tool, Sun Lifemaster effectively combines the protection of whole life with the low cost of term. Cash values build quickly at highly competitive, tax-deferred interest rates. Adjustable premiums and coverage are another reason why Sun Lifemaster could be the only insurance policy you'll ever need. Call or write Sun Life today for free information.

Picture-window layout

More popular than Mondrian and especially suited to magazines is the format known in the trade as "Ayer No. 1," after the agency that pioneered its use. We will call it "picture window." Doyle Dane Bernbach for Volkswagen has had particular success with this format, but probably theme and copy brilliance and wit have been more important than layout. The least you can say for picture-window layout is that it does not get in the way of the ad's message. No "art for art's sake" here, just generous display of picture and tight editing of copy so it will fit the small space remaining.

The designer often bleeds the picture and crops close, almost overpowering the reader. Below the picture is a one-line, centered headline; copy may be broken into two or three short columns. The sig cut may be worked into the last column of the copy, thereby saving some space.

To tie the picture with the copy, the designer may overprint or reverse some of the headline onto the picture. Or the designer may line up the copy with some axis within the picture. The picture is usually at the top, but nothing prevents the designer from pushing it down a bit, placing the headline and even the copy above. A smaller picture—or perhaps a line drawing for contrast—can be placed near the copy.

The nature of the picture will affect the designer's decision on placement and type style for the headline.

Leading the body copy from 2 to 6 points helps keep the copy from looking as if it is merely fill and also makes it more readable. (See chapter 7.)

In this picture-window ad, designer Thierry Da Rold of Lord, Geller, Federico, Einstein uses the same type for both headline and logo. His generous paragraph indentations and the single-column format give the ad, one of a series, some distinction from other picture-window ads.

Our simplest part.

We don't even make it ourselves.
It's so simple that we can entrust it to someone else.
This isn't anything unusual, especially when you consider the fact that there are over 12,000 parts in a single Steinway grand. Many of them standard enough that we can have them made for us, and still expect them to measure up.
But there are some things that no one but a Steinway craftsman can touch. Things like our intricate and patented Accelerated Action. Or the soundboard. Or just about anything that we consider critical to sound and tone.
Because when all is said and done, it's our name that goes on each piano.
For more information, please write John H. Steinway, 109 West 57th Street, New York, N.Y. 10019.

Steinway & Sons

Copy-heavy layout

The advertiser chooses a mostly-copy format for two reasons: (1) What is to be said is too involved, too important, too unique, too dignified to be put in pictures; (2) most other ads in the medium will be picture-window or at least heavily picture-oriented, so a gray, quiet, copy-heavy approach makes a good change of pace.

Because copy-heavy advertising takes itself rather more seriously than other advertising, it usually puts its elements into formal balance. Lines of the headlines, set in roman, are centered; copy begins with a large initial letter and is broken into two or more columns. The sig cut is centered underneath. But a more interesting arrangement can result from less formal balance, with the ad retaining the dignity it would have in a more formal arrangement.

The designer should plan for a blurb or secondary headline as well as a main headline.

Even though the copy is voluminous, there may be room for a few quiet illustrations.

When copy is long, it must be broken somehow into easy-to-take segments. The beginning designer often makes the mistake of marking such copy to be set solid, because it is so long. But long copy, even more than short copy, should be leaded, by at least a point or two. Furthermore, the copy at logical breaks should be refreshed with subheads of one kind or another. Subheads can be flush right, flush left, or centered, in a typeface slightly larger or bolder than the body type, or in all caps. Extra space should frame such subheads.

Subheads can also be formed from the first two or three words of a paragraph, set in boldface. Extra space should be provided to separate the bold beginning from the paragraph above.

These thumbnails show some approaches to copy-heavy layout.

Clarke Aronson Goward, a Boston advertising agency, introduces itself with this copy-heavy ad to the trade. All that copy is necessary to convince advertisers that this is an agency to consider. The small photo of the principals provides necessary graphic relief.

Frame layout

A photographer can get a pleasantly composed picture by taking the shot from one of nature's nooks, with foliage and a rock formation in the foreground, dark and out of focus, framing the heart of the picture. In advertising, the designer easily frames a layout with a border, doing it sometimes with artwork that is drawn to leave room in the middle for headline and copy.

Frame layout, used more in newspaper advertising than in magazine advertising, keeps elements within bounds, preventing their being associated with some other ad on the page.

There is something cozy about frame layout.

But it does tend to decrease the optical size of the ad. Furthermore, the ad, if placed at the edge of a page, loses additional white space between the edge of the ad and the edge of the page that an unframed ad would pick up.

A variation of the frame layout is the one in which kidney-shaped artwork is spread over a large portion of the layout, creating a cul-de-sac of white in which the headline and copy are placed. Another variation is the layout using a picture—a photograph, usually—that completely covers the area. Type is either surprinted or reversed in nonpatterned or plaintoned areas.

These thumbnails show some approaches to frame layout.

This simulated thumbnail, sketched in gray felt markers, might have preceded the full-size layout or comprehensive for the Olivetti ad shown at the right. This is about the right size for a thumbnail. Some designers do thumbnails larger, some smaller—but always in proportion to the final size of the ad. Ordinarily thumbnails are drawn in rougher form than this. They are not meant to impress anyone. The designer is only thinking out loud.

With the copy concentrated inside a light area of the ad, this one could qualify as an example of frame layout. The original is in full, but muted, colors. Henry Wolf designed it. The agency: Trahey/Wolf Advertising (later Trahey Advertising).

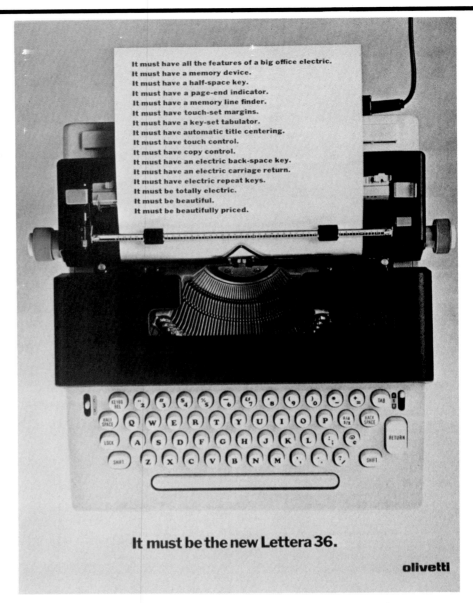

It must have all the features of a big office electric.
It must have a memory device.
It must have a half-space key.
It must have a page-end indicator.
It must have a memory line finder.
It must have touch-set margins.
It must have a key-set tabulator.
It must have automatic title centering.
It must have touch control.
It must have copy control.
It must have an electric back-space key.
It must have an electric carriage return.
It must have electric repeat keys.
It must be totally electric.
It must be beautiful.
It must be beautifully priced.

It must be the new Lettera 36.

olivetti

A frame for this formally balanced ad is formed by the crab's claws reaching around the body copy. The boldness of the headline matches the boldness of the art, which has a woodcut feel. Ray Dodge designed this newspaper ad; Candace McKinley wrote the copy. The agency was Thuemmel, Marx & Associates (now Marx, Knoll & Mangels), Portland.

These thumbnails show some
approaches to circus layout.

Circus layout

An orderly approach in design is probably more important to the editorial
than to the advertising side. The reader is already interested in editorial.
The purchase of the newspaper or magazine proves this. Advertising has
to work harder for attention. And to set itself apart from the staid editorial material, it takes more liberty with basic design principles. It does
not mind standing on its head or wearing a lampshade.

Moreover, there is something to be said for some disorder in an ad. It
slows down the reader, making things more difficult to take in. And in the
process of working through the disorder, the reader may remember more.

We can call design of this type "circus layout." Filled with reverse
blocks, oversize type, sunbursts, tilts, and assorted gimmicks, it may not
win prizes in art directors' competitions, but apparently it does sell merchandise—at least a certain kind of merchandise to a certain class of customers.

Its apparent disarray (actually, under a good designer its elements are
thoughtfully arranged) is sometimes found in advertising for lofty clients.
It was this kind of layout, in the capable hands of art director Otto Storch,
that helped bring *McCall's* out of its "Togetherness" rut to the number
one position among women's magazines in the late 1950s.

Circus layout takes in a wide range of layout approaches and deals
usually with a larger-than-average number of components.

The secret of good circus layout lies in the dedication of the designer
to basic principles of design. Elements are organized into units, which in
turn are organized into a unified pattern. Faced with many elements of
equal weight, the designer achieves a pleasing proportion by bunching
some into a particularly heavy unit, to contrast with other units in the ad.

Here's how!

This month, WCBS-TV, Channel 2 New York, launches the new television season with the most excitement-packed program lineup in its history.

You will, of course, be seeing the complete CBS Television Network schedule of entertainment and information programming.

But we're not stopping there. This season we're adding some special nighttime program surprises of our own. Seven new shows especially selected for the enjoyment of viewers in the New York area.

Doesn't it look like the good times will be *extra* good on WCBS-TV?

The David Frost Revue
Sundays 10:30 pm
A new and decidedly different comedy series. Britain's most exportable blessing since the founding fathers heads a guffaw of comedy greats in once-over-lightly looks at everything from love to money to food to doctors. Such guest stars as Lucille Ball, Flip Wilson, Art Carney and Dom DeLuise join David and Co. in blackouts and sketches devoted to a different topic each week.

Johnny Mann's Stand Up and Cheer
Mondays 7:30 pm
Youth has its melodious way. With songs from the roaring 20s right up to the rocking Now. The Johnny Mann Singers will have you chiming in as they swing through the Americana songbook. Great guests, too. Such as John Forsythe, Robert Morse, Jack Jones and John Davidson.

The Golddiggers
Tuesdays 10:30 pm
All-new! Tippy tap toe...and away we go! With the most beautiful, bouncy, talented bevy of pulchritude in show business. Want more? How about a guest list that includes Eddie Albert, Bob Newhart, Godfrey Cambridge, Lou Rawls and George Maharis? And comic turns from the likes of Charles Nelson Reilly and Larry Storch! Put it at the top of your not-to-be-missed list.

Doctor in the House
Wednesdays 7:30 pm
Diagnosis: an epidemic of belly laughs. In this riotous look at medical students, their professors and nurses—on duty and off.

Based on the hugely successful film series. Starring Barry Evans. Take as directed: once weekly. Without fail.

Kenny Rogers and The First Edition
Thursdays 7:30 pm
In "Rollin' on the River," an up-to-date, upbeat re-creation of the excitement and razzma-tazz of the riverboat jamborees. Already set to climb aboard this season are such special guests as Tommy Smothers, Karen Black, Barbara McNair, Kris Kristofferson and B. B. King. Smooth sailing? You betcha!

Circus!
Fridays 7:30 pm
The smell of the sawdust, the roar of the lions, the spectacle of the Big Top. They're all here and more. In on-location visits to the world's most famous circuses. Including Copenhagen's Circus Bennewein, the Hungarian State Circus and Japan's Circus Kinoshita. MC Bert Parks gets it all on.

Jerry Visits...
Saturdays 7:30 pm
Ever long to know what lies behind the gates of movie stars' homes? Who hasn't! And here's your chance to find out. As Jerry Dunphy goes calling on such Hollywood nabobs as Henry Fonda, Eva Gabor, Glenn Ford and Jerry Lewis. Wear something comfortable and come on along.

WCBS-TV 2 WHERE THE GOOD TIMES ARE

Variety is a main concern, and the designer gets it chiefly through size, shape, and tone changes within the ad.

Retail advertisers find circus layout especially useful. Because retail ads are often directed to bargain hunters, prices played up in large sizes become an important element, ranking with headlines and art units.

One of the contributions of the underground press of the late 1960s was the attention it gave to the circus approach in graphic design. Thanks to the flexibility of the offset printing process, circus layout became the predominant format. Often self-conscious and amateurish, it nevertheless influenced the design thinking of the establishment press. In the hands of designers who knew what they were doing, it resulted in some engaging, if complicated, advertising in the 1970s.

Multipanel layout

Breath-purifying toothpaste, body-building iron tablets, and pimple-restricting yeasts started multipanel layout a couple of generations ago with their ads in Sunday comic sections, made to look just like the regular fare. Today this "comic strip" layout technique is more useful than ever, although it has grown a bit more sophisticated, with photos replacing the drawings, in most cases, and with conversation set in type beneath the pictures rather than ballooned within.

The designer often plans for panels of equal size, feeling that the staccato effect keeps the reader moving effortlessly through the ad. A proportional difference is achieved by keeping the block of panels larger than

This two-page ad could be considered an example of circus layout. Lou Dorfsman designed it for WCBS-TV, New York. The unorthodox and lively use of photographs, some square-finish, some silhouette, seems appropriate to the "Good Times" theme. An early 1970s ad, with a logo (based on Broadway type) right out of the 1930s.

the block that remains to house the headline, explanatory body type, and signature.

The panels can be used to tell a story, or they can be used simply to display a series of products, pretty much in checkerboard fashion.

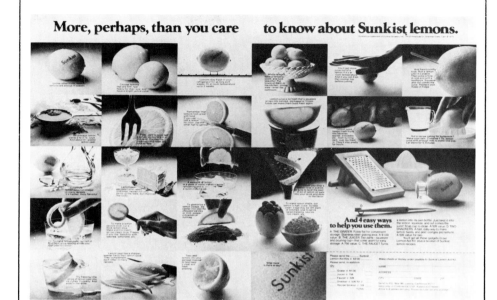

This two-page full-color magazine ad shows some of the many uses of the ordinary—correction: the *Sunkist*— lemon. The ad uses the multipanel format. Ralph Price was the art director, Jean Craig the creative supervisor, Jack Foster the creative director. The agency was Foote, Cone & Belding.

These thumbnails show some approaches to multipanel layout.

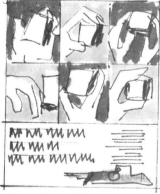

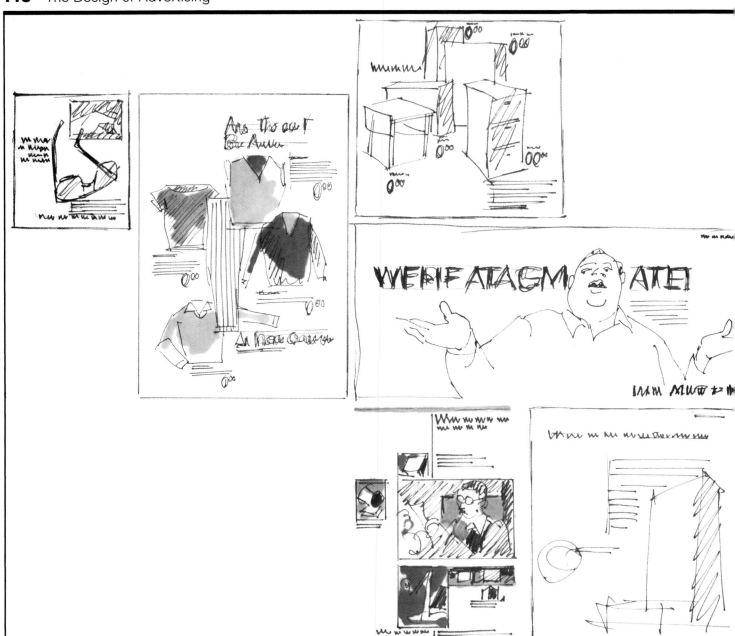

Silhouette layout

In another kind of layout the designer arranges elements in such a way as to form one imposing and interesting silhouette. As Professor Hallie J. Hamilton explains to students at Northern Illinois University, silhouette layout evolves from the unique shape created by the design of the ad, not by the shape of the elements used.

The more irregular the silhouette, the better. To test a silhouette, the designer tries to imagine the elements in the ad blacked in.

To illustrate the superiority of an irregular silhouette over a regular one, consider the ancient art of paper-cutting portraiture. The scissors artist always works from a side view, never a front view. Otherwise, no one would recognize the portrait. One portrait would look just like the next. The outline of a front view of a face is never as interesting as the outline of the side view. Silhouette layout is "side view" layout.

Just combining a silhouette photograph with some almost-touching copy will give you a silhouette ad. But you can use regular square or rectan-

These thumbnails show some approaches to silhouette layout.

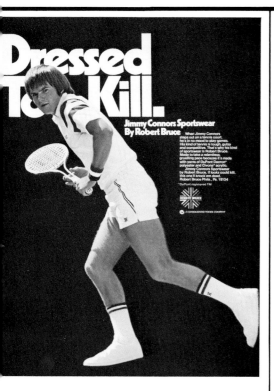

This is a full-page, full-color magazine ad for Robert Bruce apparel. The second and third words in the headline are separated to make room for the art. Each element in this ad comes close to touching another to form one massive reverse silhouette that stands out strongly against a dark background. Art director and designer: Lawrence L. Alten. Copywriters: Edmond F. Cohen and B. J. Kaplan. Agency: Alten, Cohen & Naish, Inc., Philadelphia.

This is one of a series of Magazine Publishers Association ads designed to sell magazines as an advertising medium. This one is a good example of the silhouette format: the ragged-edge type hugs the art and forms an irregular white frame. The ad holds together nicely as a single unit. Art director and designer: Richard R. Huebner. Copywriter: Alix Nelson. Agency: Shirley Polykoff Advertising, New York.

gular photographs, too. *The way they are put together*—staggered rather than stacked—gives the ad its silhouette look.

Too much white space separating elements within the silhouette destroys the unity of the ad; so the designer usually pushes white space to the outside, forming a sort of border.

In silhouette layout many designers arrange elements so that something in the ad touches each of the ad's edges, preferably at spots unrelated to each other. This accomplishes two things: (1) it prevents the white frame from turning into an even halo that could diminish, optically, the ad's size; and (2) it prevents the medium's encroaching on white space the client has paid for. Another way in a silhouette ad to guarantee that the client gets all the space purchased is for the designer to place dots at all four corners of the pasteup. Checking tear sheets of the ad and finding that both dots at the top, say, are missing, the advertiser is alerted to the possibility that the medium has taken away some of the space.

If your product needs a reflective audience, a selective audience PRINT IT!

If the purchase requires deliberation—or liberation from the accepted way of doing things, nothing performs like print.

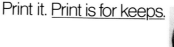

Print it. Print is for keeps.

Shirley Polykoff
Copywriter
and President

Shirley Polykoff
Advertising, Inc.

Magazine Publishers Association, Inc. 575 Lexington Avenue, New York, N.Y. 10022

Big-type layout

Type manufacturers, typesetting houses, printers, and periodicals all issue type-specimen sheets or books for their clients, so that the clients can look over the selection and marvel at it and pick those types that may be appropriate for a given job or use. In their largest sizes, types hold particular appeal to the artist and the designer, who derive an almost sensual pleasure through study of type's peculiar curves and corners and serifs and stroke variations. Suspecting that type beauty might also be appreciated by the layman, or knowing that big type commands greater attention than small type, designers sometimes turn to a type-specimen approach in their layouts. "Second coming" type pushes boldly through the ad, leading to a small amount of body copy; or the body copy itself is set in a type that is well beyond the normal 10- to 12-point sizes used in ordinary ads.

Type overpowers art in layouts like this. Art may not even be needed.

Ordinarily we associate big-type ads with hard-sell retailers; but well-designed or graceful types, used large size, perhaps screened to a percentage of black, serve image-conscious clients as well.

Some of the best big-type ads use lowercase letters rather than all caps because lower case is more interesting.

If only a few words are involved, the designer takes some liberties with readability. Lines may ride piggyback on each other; they may overlap; they may be doctored to intensify the mood of the ad.

This example of big-type layout uses lowercase letters. Lowercase letters are basically more interesting than all capitals, especially in type so large. Notice that in this ad all type, including the lines of body copy, are centered. The agency is Benton & Bowles. The client is Avis Rent A Car System, Inc.

Hello Avis, I'm lost.

Avis has a toll-free Hot Line so you can tell us off when we goof. But we'd like you to use our Hot Line for things other than gripes...like if you happen to get lost.

Now, no matter where you lose yourself, all you have to do is call the special Avis Hot Line...(800) 231-6000*...free of charge. You'll also find the number on your Avis rental agreement envelope when you rent a sparkling new Plymouth or other fine car. If we let our customers get lost, maybe that's what they'll tell us to do.

Avis is going to be No.1. We try harder.

*IN TEXAS CALL (800) 792-1961
© AVIS RENT A CAR SYSTEM INC A WORLDWIDE SERVICE OF ITT

These thumbnails show some approaches to big-type layout.

Another rebus ad—a small one—from the *New Yorker* does an institutional job for Spritzer & Fuhrmann, a New York jewelry store with branches in exotic places. You see the ad here actual size. Copywriter Dennis Webster with tongue in cheek talks about "simple" needs. John Nayduck of the John Nayduck Agency did the designing, using two weights of a modern sans serif (all caps) for the combination headline/body copy/signature. The address drops down in size.

Rebus layout

A rebus is a puzzle consisting of pictures that suggest words or syllables. A modified rebus is one in which an occasional word or phrase is omitted and a picture substituted. An advertiser will not make a puzzle of an ad—clarity is too important—but may want to amplify the copy by inserting a series of illustrations. They can be all the same size, for a staccato effect; or they can be in various sizes to add variety to the ad. The "copy" in some cases is nothing more than picture captions.

Alphabet-inspired layout

The beauty of letterform, established by scribes and type designers over a period of several centuries, provides one other source of inspiration for designers. The basic shape of letters, both capitals and lower case, can serve as the basic pattern for the arranging of elements within an ad.

An ad designed to approximate the shape of a letter of the alphabet—or a number, for that matter—usually is strong in both unity and eye-travel, two important design qualities. The designer, however, should avoid an arrangement that too closely suggests a particular letter. The letter should serve only as the starting point. The reader ordinarily would not be conscious that the ad took off from a letter or number.

It may be helpful to consider each of the ten basic formats described here before beginning your assignment. Choosing one, you will find innumerable variations occurring to you as you doodle. Combining two of them into a single format, you will find your explorations even more fruitful.

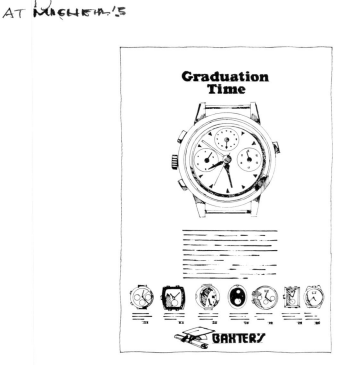

Turn the ad upside down and you have essentially a T shape. This rough layout is one of several produced by the Newspaper Advertising Bureau to stimulate newspaper display advertising departments to produce better designed advertising for their jewelry store clients.

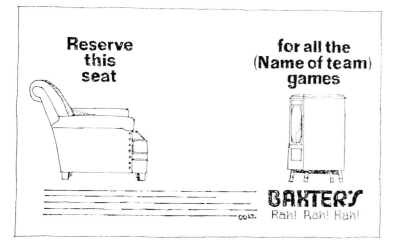

The letter X could be said to be the inspiration for this arrangement of headline, art, and body copy. At any rate, the two-page ad is dependent upon diagonals as a design pattern. This is one of a series, each ad showing users without tops partly for its quiet shock value and partly to show the product without other clothes distractions. The agency was Hicks & Greist, New York.

This U-shaped ad for an imaginary furniture store was roughed out by the Newspaper Advertising Bureau as a thought stimulator for display advertising staffs or newspapers. Note the concentration on one or two products, something a lot of retail stores cannot bring themselves to do in their newspaper advertising.

6
Applying the principles of design

The look that dominated advertising and just about every graphic arts form in the years after World War I was the Bauhaus look, with form following function. In the fourteen years of its existence, the Bauhaus in Germany moved three times, endured all kinds of criticism from both within and without, and graduated fewer than five hundred students.[1] Yet its influence was profound. Its teachers scattered to various parts of the world after the Nazis closed down the school in 1933. Several came to the United States to teach and design here. Much of what we understand about graphic design today and much of what we practice can be traced to the Bauhaus.

Despite the leftist nature of its politics, the Bauhaus brought fine arts and industry together. It recognized the needs of an industrial age.

The Bauhaus style asked for order, symmetry, and clarity in design, with grids playing an important part in the organization of material. Type lost its serifs. Heads sometimes appeared without any beginning caps. "Why should we write and print with two alphabets?" asked Herbert Bayer. "We do not speak with a capital 'A' and a small 'a.' " Decorative elements simplified themselves into geometric forms. Rules and bars appeared frequently. Sometimes elements in the design appeared on the diagonal. Overall, the look was one of precision.

In the years after World War II a sort of neo-Bauhaus look was born: it was clear, crisp, and beautifully organized. We called it "Swiss design." But by 1968 one designer had had enough: "The clean Swiss look is not the answer to every problem, no matter how much it has been embraced by designers," wrote Harvey Offenhartz. "This look is smart and extremely contemporary, but is not universally applicable as a layout solution. In its indiscriminate use as a style are the seeds of decreasing effectiveness and, therefore, eventual demise. It may well be the hallmark of the sixties, but it should never be the ultimate design style. There is no final solution in design. Searching for new expressions in communications is what good graphic design is all about."[2]

By that time a number of designers had already broken away. Their design could not have been further removed from the restrictions—and elegance—of Swiss design. The hippie culture, as much as anything, influenced type and art styles in the ads, just as it influenced dress styles. Then, as a reaction to the reaction, there arose among some designers an interest in the near past: in the 1930s and 1940s especially. The Bauhaus sans serif type faces, resurrected and slightly modified, replaced the Swiss gothic faces. At the same time ads became decorative and cluttered. It was all very camp to some designers, very "relevant" to others. Along with other affectations of the period there appeared again in ads the multiple stripes of yesteryear, the meandering lines, the pastel colors, the airbrushing, the cross-hatching, the swirls, the swashes and scripts, the ornate and heavy (in more ways than one) types. Just about everything was "in," including the durable Swiss look. And the juxtaposition did not matter much.

In a two-page ad in the *New York Times Magazine* in 1972, Lady

This is an example of Swiss design: highly ordered, based on a grid. Designer Michael Reid uses silver and black—camera colors—for this three-fold, all-on-one-side folder announcing a photography show at The Art Institute of Chicago. The irregular edge at the top right of the black area represents what a photographer feels for when working with cut film in the darkroom. The folder was designed to fit a no. 10 envelope, but when opened out it serves as a poster.

Manhattan showed a young woman in a blouse, tie, vest, and skirt in a variety of patterns and colors. The headline referred to "Our What-the-Hell Look." Not a bad term to describe the graphic design that seemed to prevail.

Experimentation would go on, of course. As one advertising art director put it: "For the last 1,000,000 years we have been searching for something new but it always turns out to be just another secret released by nature. We will continue searching. . . ."[3] But as advertisers demanded more performance from their advertising, there were signs, beginning in the 1970s, that design was returning to more traditional forms.

This fine Cabretta leather glove was worn for a four hour round of golf. It was soaked in a cloud burst. And left overnight in a locker to dry.

So was this one.

The parallel structure in the display of the two headlines and the two pieces of art help Foot-Joy make its point about its water-repellent glove. R. Stollerman art directed; Chester Gore designed; Chris Wigert wrote the copy. The agency was Chester Gore Co., Inc.

Sta-Sof is a remarkable, water-repellent glove by Foot-Joy. It resists absorbing perspiration or rain, thanks to a revolutionary tanning process created by Pittards of England for this superb Cabretta leather. It stays dry and grips better on the hottest days, or during the wettest weather. Best of all, it restores itself after you've played —so it's soft and supple and ready to play again. That's how it got its name: Sta-Sof.

"The Sta-Sof Glove" by **Foot-Joy** ®

Foot-Joy, Inc. Brockton, MA 02403. Member National Golf Foundation

The design process

"Design," like "creativity," is a virtue word, overused and not quite understood.

Design, the noun, is more than pattern. It is more than ornament or decoration. It is structure itself and the plan behind that structure.

It is the foundation of all the arts.

Design, the verb, applies to all human activity that attempts to organize.

Elizabeth Adams Hurwitz defined the word succinctly in the title of a book: *Design: A Search for Essentials.*

"Whenever we do something for a definite reason, we are designing," observed Professor Robert Gillam Scott of the Department of Design, Yale University. More formally: "Designing means creative action that fulfills its purpose."

Napier® 530 Fifth Avenue, NY 10036. At fine stores everywhere.

NAPIER IS GLEAMIER.

Cuff bracelet with golden and silvery finish, $15.

Diagonal thrusts in the art lead the reader from the product to the headline, which covers that part of the art least applicable to the product. The second and smaller headline nicely ties itself to the first, making a single unit out of the type. Ordinarily you would not combine a modern roman with a slab serif, but the two work together well here. The ad appeared originally in full color. Art director: Gene Federico. Agency: Lord, Geller, Federico, Einstein. The jewelry was designed by Eugene Bertolli.

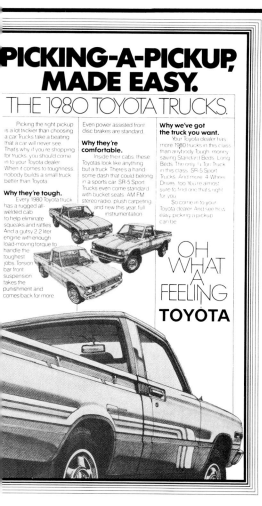

PICKING-A-PICKUP, MADE EASY.

THE 1980 TOYOTA TRUCKS.

Picking the right pickup is a lot trickier than choosing a car. Trucks take a beating that a car will never see. That's why, if you're shopping for trucks, you should come in to your Toyota dealer. When it comes to toughness, nobody builds a small truck better than Toyota.

Why they're tough.
Every 1980 Toyota truck has a rugged all-welded cab to help eliminate squeaks and rattles. And a gutsy 2.2 liter engine with enough load-moving torque to handle the toughest jobs. Torsion bar front suspension takes the punishment and comes back for more.

Even power assisted front disc brakes are standard.

Why they're comfortable.
Inside their cabs, these Toyotas look like anything but a truck. There's a handsome dash that could belong in a sports car. SR-5 Sport Trucks even come standard with bucket seats, AM-FM stereo radio, plush carpeting, and new this year, full instrumentation.

Why we've got the truck you want.
Your Toyota dealer has more 1980 trucks in this class than anybody. Tough money-saving Standard Beds, Long Beds. The only 1-Ton Truck in this class. SR-5 Sport Trucks. And more. 4-Wheel Drives, too. You're almost sure to find one that's right for you.

So come in to your Toyota dealer. And see how easy picking a pickup can be.

OH WHAT A FEELING

TOYOTA

This beautifully designed newspaper ad puts into effect most of the design principles discussed in this chapter. Ruled lines help segregate the ad (it is about 7″ × 12½″) from others on the page while uniting and organizing the various sections of the ad. The multiline border matches to some extent the striping on the bodies of the pickups. The entire ad is set in sans serif type, but in various sizes and weights. Note that the three subheads use parallel structure, each starting with "Why." The large illustration contrasts nicely with the smaller cluster of pickups above it, both in size and camera angle. The "Oh What a Feeling!" slogan was often repeated by Toyota for that model year. Bob Adams designed the ad; Chris Scheck wrote the copy. The agency: Dancer Fitzgerald Sample, Torrance, California.

"Design comes from a combination of intelligence and artistic ability," said Ivan Chermayeff of Chermayeff & Geismar Associates. "The designer in any area of activity is not primarily a creative artist. He is a creative person . . . [who] may even, by some rare coincidence, be an artist."

Art museum director Wallace S. Baldinger described the process of designing from an art standpoint: "When the artist designs, he practices no magic hocus-pocus. He simply performs on a more exacting and complicated level an act in which the rest of us engage every day. We design actually when we plan anything. We arrange and order it. We design when we set a table for dinner. Instead of tossing the silverware about haphazardly, we arrange it according to a scheme and we change the scheme every time we change the type of meal to be served. We design when we take notes in class, ordering every page much as the layout artist designs every page of a book to be published. The artist's job is simply more difficult, less conventional, more exploratory, less charted and familiar."[4]

Order and beauty: the relationship

In selecting and arranging elements, the advertising designer tries to achieve both order and beauty. The order which the designer creates out of a chaos of pictures, copy blocks, headlines, and white space makes it easy for the reader to read and understand the ad. The beauty makes the reader glad to be there.

Order is the overriding consideration. It simplifies the ad, even when it must carry innumerable items, as in a department store sales announcement. Ernest Dichter, the Viennese psychologist specializing in advertising research, believes that advertising can be too ordered, leaving little for the reader to do. The designer may want to allow for some *closure.*

"I am addicted to order," admits Chris Arvetis, art director and vice-president of Rand McNally. "To translate this addiction into something of value for this company, I have to listen to the ideas of many people, some [of the ideas] quite foreign to my own. I try to understand, evaluate, and then interpret them graphically."

The order of the ad has a lot to do with its beauty. Beauty is simplicity. But beauty is also variety.

The designer's whole function, as Philip C. Beam sees it, is "to create an arrangement of visual elements in any art work which will satisfy the human need for both order and variety in a world that is profuse and confusing on the one hand, and monotonous and boring on the other."[5]

Design and layout: the difference

The professionals in advertising tend to draw a distinction between design and layout as nouns.

A design differs from a layout in that a design is more studied, more finished, more lasting. The person creating a design starts from the beginning, making most of the decisions as to size, medium, typography, art, and so on. A design results from a truly creative effort.

A layout, on the other hand, makes use of what may already be available or what may be dictated by others. A layout involves a fitting together of elements, but a fitting together in the best possible combination and in the best possible order. A layout, considering the limitations, can represent a challenge every bit as invigorating as a design can.

Whether *designing* an ad or simply *doing a layout,* the artist follows basic principles of design, principles that, in one way or another, are applicable to all the arts.

Ingredients of design

The following raw materials go into the making of graphic design:

1. *Line.* Lines can be straight or curved, heavy or light, smooth or rough, continuous or broken, actual or merely suggested. Two items separated in a design can cause the reader to draw, optically, a line between them. Line conveys its own mood: if horizontal, calm; if vertical, dignity; if diagonal, vitality; if curved, grace.

2. *Tone.* Solid blacks or grays often fill much of the surface area in graphic design. The grays may be in the form of halftone reproductions. Tones provide contrast to lines in the design.

3. *Color.* Perhaps more than any other ingredient, color affects the mood of the ad. From a production standpoint, color is an expensive ingredient. There is such a thing, though, as "black-and-white color," which is simply another way of describing "tone."

4. *Texture.* When the tonal area has a discernible pattern, either even or rough, the design has texture. The paper the ad is printed on, itself, provides texture: it can be hard and smooth, hard and rough, soft and smooth, soft and rough. Texture involves the reader's sense of feel, optical or physical.

5. *Shape.* Several lines placed together, a single line that bends or curves, the area of tone—all these provide shape for the design. So do the overall dimensions of the ad.

6. *Direction.* Lines and the forms they make have a tendency to point, even to move. A main job of the designer is to control the direction.

7. *Size.* An ad usually has elements of varying sizes. The largest elements usually have the biggest impact.

The size of the ad itself also makes a difference. Bleeding a photograph or allowing a design element to extend out of a box suggests that the message of the ad is too big to be contained. Display type can run off the page, as when it lists the good qualities of a product. The reader gets the impression that there is much more to the story. This works in commercials, too, as when an announcer recites the states where a particular automobile is the best seller. It may be that the announcer, cut off in the middle of a name, is actually at the end of the list, but the viewer/listener does not know this. What the public assumes is as important to the advertiser as what the public knows.

A grid of twenty squares (top left) can stimulate thumbnails like those that follow. The first ad uses twelve of the squares for art, four for copy, and four for headline and white space. Many other combinations are possible, of course. A grid could also be constructed with a different number of squares, or with squares and rectangles, or with rectangles only. Rather than restricting design, a grid can expand its possibilities, even though it does bring order to advertising.

Advertising for a cause often calls for formal balance in design. This beautifully designed ad gets it, although the flush-left headline at the start of the first column adds an informal touch. White space concentrated at the bottom gives the ad pleasing proportions. The agency: John Zeigler Inc., which specializes in environment and cause advertising. John Zeigler himself designed the ad. Its purpose was to help victims of a disastrous cyclone and flood. This was before the war that broke out in late 1971 between India and Pakistan and before East Pakistan became Bangladesh.

Principles of design

What the architect's blueprint is to the potential homeowner and the builder, the designer's layout is to the advertising client and to the printer. And the skills necessary to produce a first-class advertising layout are related to the skills necessary to design an aesthetically pleasing and useful building, an appliance, even a painting.

Certain principles govern how advertising should be designed. These principles affect all art forms. The number of principles varies, depending upon how you phrase them. Their users may not even be conscious of them as principles. Asked to name them, many users doubtless would fail the examination, yet their designs may be highly effective, even academically appropriate. They design instinctively.

Not all persons called on to produce designs or layouts are so fortunate. They need the help a statement of principles can bring. They can improve their designs by making a conscientious effort to apply these principles to their assignments.

The principles of design apply (1) to each element within the ad and (2) to the collection or arrangement of the elements as a whole. An understanding of the principles can help designers better manage the order and variety they bring to advertising.

The principles of design are to the layout artist what rules of grammar are to the writer. And just as the grammarians do not agree entirely on what is right and what is wrong (can *like* ever be used as a conjunction? can you end a sentence with a preposition?), designers do not agree wholly on what is effective and what is not.

Nor do all writers on design offer the same set of principles to follow. But the following list, from an advertising standpoint, can be considered reasonably universal and inclusive:

1. The design must be in balance.
2. The space within the ad should be broken up into pleasing proportions.
3. A directional pattern should be evident.
4. A unifying force should hold the ad together.
5. One element, or one part of the ad, should dominate all others.

Reduced to single words, the list might read: balance, proportion, sequence, unity, and emphasis.

A well-designed ad is likely to incorporate all these principles, but it may be stronger in one than in the others.

Balance

When an ad is "in balance" it is at rest, at peace with itself. The student might well question this. Doesn't an ad need action? It does, of course, but not necessarily in its basic framework. The action comes in the liveliness of the art or photography and the copy and headlines. The design does not intrude.

The designer experiments with two kinds of balance: formal (symmetrical) and informal (asymmetrical). Under formal balance, every item that goes on one side of the ad is repeated, in size or shape, on the other. Items on an imaginary vertical center line spill over in equal portions on the left and on the right.

When does formal balance work best? The easy answer is: for institutional advertising and other serious-minded advertising. But the truth is, it can work well for any kind of advertising. One of its strengths is that it discourages trickery and gimmickry. It presents material in an easy to follow order. And, in contrast to informal balance, it often comes off well enough even when a rank amateur is doing the designing.

In informal balance, optical weight is still considered; but decisions affecting it are more complicated. The grown man gets on the teeter-totter with his young son: if the one moves in far enough toward the fulcrum, the other out far enough from it, their weights will be balanced.

The beginning designer should be willing to try informal balance at the very start. Formal balance is a too-easy, too-pat solution to a layout problem. And it is often inappropriate to the mood of the ad.

Laying out an ad, the designer may place one large picture on one side, probably allowing it to overlap the center line, a smaller picture on the other—out to the edge—and some type near but not on the center line. Squinting to study the ad-in-progress, the designer tries to determine whether or not the elements, reduced to optical weights, are balanced. Holding the ad up to a mirror, to check it in "mirror-reverse," or holding it upside down helps the designer make balance decisions.

Nor should the designer forget the relationship of the top of the ad to the bottom. All units of the ad should form a composition that appears to be balanced, with the optical center of the ad, a point just above the center and slightly to the left, acting as the ad's pivot.

Tell a student that an ad has to be "in balance"—that when you draw a line down the center, from top to bottom, half of the optical "weight" of the ad must fall on one side, half on the other—and watch that student bring to class a visually effective ad with elements arranged in an upside-down L shape. Isn't *that* ad off-balance?

Well, yes and no.

The fact that an unusual amount of white space is concentrated in one part of the ad in itself provides "weight," bringing the ad into balance. For optical weight is more than a matter of size and blackness. Of course, big elements and black elements "weigh" more than little elements and gray elements. But unusual-shaped elements "weigh" more than usual-shaped elements. And color "weighs" more than black and white.

So an ad that at first glance appears to be out of balance may, on closer inspection, actually be in balance.

Furthermore, *placement* of the ad in the magazine can affect its balance. An ad with material running across the top and down the right side, placed on a right-hand page, will, when seen with a filled editorial page on its left, appear to be perfectly balanced.

In a few cases, a lack of balance, bringing with it an optical tension, may actually be desirable in an ad. Such an ad may intrigue a reader. Certainly it will catch the reader's attention, unless there happens to be a rash of such ads.

The point is this: balance, as a design principle, need not—should not—straitjacket the advertising designer. More than any of the design principles, this one deserves occasional violation, even among students. Beginners are often *too* much concerned about balance. They seem to think design is *only* balance.

Proportion

When you put two or more elements together, you get proportion, whether you want it or not.

To the advertising designer, proportion is the relationship of sizes: the width of the ad to the depth; the width of an element within the ad to the depth of that element; the size of one area within an element to the size of another area within the element; the size of one element to the size of another element; the amount of space between two elements to the amount of space between one of those elements and a third element. Proportion

A beautiful study in proportion by designer Blanche Simkin for The Viking Press, and in the confines of small space. The ad is shown actual size. Agency: Waterman, Getz, Niedelman.

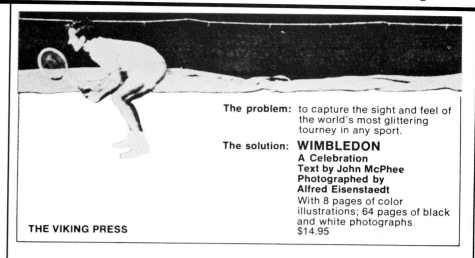

The problem: to capture the sight and feel of the world's most glittering tourney in any sport.

The solution: **WIMBLEDON**
A Celebration
Text by John McPhee
Photographed by
Alfred Eisenstaedt
With 8 pages of color illustrations; 64 pages of black and white photographs
$14.95

THE VIKING PRESS

also involves the tone of the ad: the amount of light area as opposed to the amount of dark area; the amount of color as opposed to noncolor.

Ideally these relationships vary. When they are the same—when widths equal depths, when distances between elements equal one another, when exactly half the ad is color and half noncolor—the ad becomes monotonous. This is not to say there should not be some consistency in proportion. For the sake of parallel structure, for instance, the distances between one size of subhead and the paragraphs below should all be the same.

For inspiration in matters of proportion, the designer turns to nature, where relationships are subtle. Looking at a hand, for instance, the designer sees that the distance between the top of a finger to the first knuckle is different from the distance between the first knuckle and the second. That second distance is different from the distance between the second knuckle and the third. Looking at a tree, the designer sees that the trunk does not have the same diameter as the branch. Nor is the trunk diameter *exactly twice* the branch's diameter.

As a man-made model of pleasing proportions, we have the Parthenon, said to be, in its original state, the most perfectly proportioned building in the world.

The "golden oblong,"[6] adopted by the ancient Greeks after much experimentation, remains as a model of space division for the advertising designer. That ratio of width to depth boils down, roughly, to 3:2 or, better, 5:3.

To achieve pleasing proportions in an ad, then, the designer arranges spaces so that the eye does not perceive obvious mathematical relationships. In most circumstances the designer avoids dividing the ad in halves, quarters, or thirds. It would not be a good idea to allow the design to be half art and half everything else (headline, copy, logo, and white space). Better to divide the ad into fifths. The top three-fifths of such an ad could be devoted to art—say a large photograph. The bottom two-fifths could go to the headline, copy, logo, and white space.

All of which suggests that a square, with its four even sides, in most circumstances is not as good a design element as a rectangle, with its two different dimensions. But the square came into its own as a useful shape for some ads in the 1960s and 1970s. Some magazines have even forsaken the traditional golden oblong—the 8½″ × 11″ page—for a square format. Some advertising designers have chosen the square as the shape for annual reports and other direct-mail pieces. Designers have also shown that beautiful design is possible on the square fields of record album covers.

In some cases, designers have not only worked successfully within the square format but also have divided that square into a grid of smaller squares, and they have placed the ad's elements into position in concert with the smaller squares. They have even used square rather than rectangular photographs. Ads built upon a grid of squares are part of the Swiss look in graphic design.

As a general rule, however, unequal dimensions and distances make for the best—or at least the most lively—design in advertising.

Sequence

The ad *may* do its job if the reader is allowed to wander aimlessly through the items on display, stopping here, stopping there. And it may not. So the designer prefers to set up a correct order for the reader's taking in of the items. The designer leads the reader by the hand through the maze to the climax of the ad.

To control sequence, the designer can do either of these:

Place the items in the path of what would be considered normal eye movement.

Blaze new trails, marking them clearly enough so the reader will not wander off and get lost.

Through habit, the eye moves from left to right and from top to bottom. Realizing this, the designer can arrange the elements so they start at the upper left, move across to the upper right, down to the lower left, then across to the lower right. A **Z** pattern is the obvious way of controlling eye travel.

But if all ads were arranged in this way, they would indeed be monotonous.

The eye moves naturally, too, from big elements to little elements, from black elements to lighter elements, from color to noncolor, from unusual

It's The Village of Rainbow Springs, located just 20 miles west of Ocala.

Here on many a morning, the sun barely beats the first foursome to the tee. And when the folks that live here aren't playing golf, you can often find them talking over their game in the pro shop or the country club restaurant.

For those who want a daily involvement with the golfing life style, The Village of Rainbow Springs has new Golf View Villas available.

Their rough-sawn cedar exteriors allow these villas to blend perfectly with the natural wooded surroundings. And each villa overlooks a lush fairway on our new championship golf course. (Introductory prices for the Golf View Villas start in the $60's.)

If this kind of life appeals to you, for retirement or a vacation home, you owe it to yourself to send for more information. We'll also be glad to send you complete details on how you can spend a few days with us on a Rainbow Days Tour.

Simply send in the coupon or call 489-2472. Or if you'd rather, just drive on over. The Village of Rainbow Springs is 2 miles north of Dunnellon on U.S. 41.

There's a place in Florida where golf isn't just a sport.
It's a way of life.

Golf View Villas Condominium, Inc.
Context Development Co.
Rt. 4, Box 600
Dunnellon, FL 32630
(904) 489-2472

☐ Please send me more information about the Golf View Villas in The Village of Rainbow Springs.

☐ Please send me more information about your Rainbow Days Tours. I understand I am under no obligation to buy.

Name
Address
City _____ State
Zip _____ Phone

THE VILLAGE OF
RAINBOW SPRINGS
The natural setting for the good life.
A joint venture of Holiday Inns, and Context Industries, Inc.

An example of three-point design where the visual units—the two-sentence boldface headline, the silhouette halftone, and the heavy-bordered coupon—organize into a triangle. The unjustified body copy fits into blank spaces created by the headline. The headline utilizes a sans serif with character—a face with slight differences in stroke thicknesses and with a *j* and *i* that have curved tops to accommodate the dots. Glen Ivie designed the ad; Bill Brown wrote the copy. The client: Context Development Co., Florida. The agency: Denton & French.

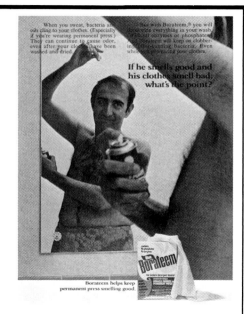

A series of diagonals in the art unites the copy, headline, art, and logo for this full-color ad for Borateem, a detergent booster. Note how the designer, Dennis Kuhr, gets the reader to move from the headline to the top-left of the ad and the copy block. The ad appeared in women's and home magazines. The agency is McCann-Erickson, Los Angeles.

shapes to usual shapes. Bearing this in mind, the designer actually can start the eye travel *anywhere* in the ad and then direct it to the left, the right, down, even up.

Sometimes the designer controls eye travel by providing a solid or dotted line—a sort of track—along which the eye can move effortlessly. But this is too obvious. A more subtle approach is to repeat shapes and sizes; the eye recognizes the related items and moves easily from one to another—jumping across the space in between—because the territory is familiar. You could say a line—an implied line—is there to act as a track.

Or the designer can get sequence through graduation of the size of elements. The eye moves as if up or down a series of steps.

Sequence at its best involves a sort of optical rhythm. The rhythm may be staccatolike, with several even-sized elements serving to hold the reader in line. It may take a crescendo form, each element building in intensity. It may take a diminuendo form, the elements letting readers down easily as they move away from the ad's main thrust. Or it may be more complicated, with "long beats" and "short beats" and "pauses" arranged in no easily described pattern.

If you want to find out where the eye does *not* travel in a design, study the cigarette ads. You can know that the box with the surgeon general's warning, whether it appears at the top or bottom of the ad, has been placed well away from the ad's visual thrust.

Unity

Perhaps the most important of the design principles, unity sees to it that elements within the ad tie together, that they appear to be related. Unity keeps the ad from falling apart. It is the ad's bonding agent.

Another word for unity is harmony. The designer creates harmony by selecting elements that go together and arranging them so that they "get along" with each other.

The elements going into the ad can best be unified when they have the same basic shape, size, texture, color, and mood. The type in a unified ad has the same character as the art.

The problem of unity becomes more acute when the designer works with unusually shaped ads: ads that are long and narrow or L shaped or ads that spill across two pages.

Where the ad is to go in a publication is always a concern. For a magazine, the designer should know whether the ad will receive a left-hand or right-hand placement. You can see that this would be important if the ad is to feature a coupon because it should be easily accessible to the reader and a pair of scissors.

The border. A border surrounding the ad provides one easy solution to the problem of unity. At least it keeps elements from becoming part of other ads on the page.

Sets of borders or boxes *within* the ad, provided they are alike in thickness and tone, can also help the ad's unity. The reader sees the relationship among them and so mentally ties the elements together.

White space. Wise use of white space can do wonders in unifying the ad. The secret is to keep the white space at the outside edges of the ad. Such white space plays the same role an ordinary border plays. When the designer allows white space to gather inside the ad, separating the units, the ad may fall apart.

The white space at the edges of the ad should take irregular shaping. It should be more than a mere band with the same thickness on all four sides. Remember the law of proportion?

The axis. To keep the elements in an ad fully related, no single device can help the designer more than an axis, real or imagined, preferably

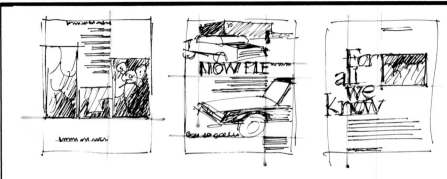

imagined. An ad could well make use of two or three or more axes, running vertically and horizontally.

The axis—the line running through the ad—forms a sort of base from which elements in the ad flare outward. The edge of a picture may suggest the edge of a headline. Or the edge of a strong element within the picture may suggest the edge of the headline. Obviously, it would not be a good idea to allow elements to move *alternately* out to the left and right. That would be monotonous. Nor is it necessary to have *every* element attach to an axis. An occasional element, or even most of the elements, can run across the axis, ignoring it. But the fact that two or more elements use a common axis helps hold all elements together. A relationship is set up.

Three-point layout. The designer can also unify the ad by using a three-point layout approach. Three units (uneven number) make for better proportion than two or four units (even numbers).

Moreover, when the eye sees three different items in a given area, it tends to make a triangle of them, drawing a line to connect each point.

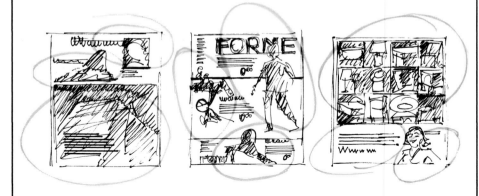

The ad may actually consist of more than three elements, but the elements would be organized into three basic groups. Or three intrusive pieces of art would be used, probably of unequal sizes, probably unequally separated.

Parallel structure. Showing art on the left and repeating it at the right brings unity to an ad, too, even when the ad crosses the gutter in a magazine. Celanese Fortrel Polyester in a two-page ad in the *New York Times Magazine* showed a full-page figure of a man at the left in an obnoxious polyester suit, the pattern dated, lapels too wide, stitching too obvious. At the right was a full figure in a dark suit that hung nicely, the fabric looking thin and rich like fine wool. The headline read: "We're About to Change the Way You Look at Polyester."

The copy talked about the the change in polyester ("Look what polyester is doing now"): ". . . people equate polyester with the artificial look of early fabrics. Well, those fabrics haven't been around for years. Advanced technology and constant developments have produced fibres that achieve the aesthetics of their natural counterparts but without sacrificing their great ease of care performance."

An ad that appeared in the *New York Times Magazine* for The Colonnade, a quality Boston hotel that features not only live chamber music but also a multilingual staff, a wine cellar, 24-hour room service, and an art collection. This ad celebrates the chamber music; four other ads in the series celebrated the other attractions. Note the correlation between the slant of the headline type and the slant of the harp strings, a nice way of uniting headline and art. The formal balance of the ad keeps its appearance appropriate to the subject matter. The agency: Clarke Aronson Goward, Boston.

Live chamber music is commonplace at grand hotels throughout Europe. And in Boston, at The Colonnade.

Only the Atlantic separates us from the other grand hotels.

For reservations call (617) 261-2800 or Loew's Reservations, Inc. A Distinguished Hotel represented by Robert F. Warner, Inc.

The use of parallel structure in the ad's design clearly dramatized the change in looks between early polyester suits and current ones. To make the comparison easy, it was necessary for the designer to keep the side-by-side figures in the same large size and to keep them at the same level on the pages.

Unity for spreads. When an ad stretches across two pages, the designer has a harder time than usual unifying the elements. Some methods for solving the problem:

1. With eyes, a hand, a crooked elbow, let the subject on the left-hand page point to the type matter on the right-hand page.

2. Use the same color on the two pages, the same typeface, the same art style.

3. Pick up an axis from the left-hand page and use it on the right-hand page.

4. Allow headline type to go across the gutter to the second page, but be sure you break the headline between words, not between letters. Or let the body copy start on one page and continue on the next, lining up the columns to form an axis. Or allow a picture to go across the gutter. Be sure you break the picture at a spot that is not crucial to its composition. Do not allow an important face, for instance, to be caught in the magazine fold, where it will become distorted. Across-the-gutter pictures work best at the center folds of magazines.

5. As for any advertising, push the white space to the outside edges, allowing the ad elements to congregate around the gutter.

6. Run a border all the way around the two-page spread, as if there were no gutter there.

There should be a word for people who take up hospital space they don't really need.

Outpatients.

It's expensive enough being in the hospital for a good reason. What a waste of money and facilities to be there for no good reason at all. Especially with the cost of health care spiraling at more than twice the rate of inflation.

It concerns us, because private health insurance now covers 177,000,000 Americans. 147,000,000 of these are protected against even catastrophic expenses.

Though we've accomplished this through healthy competition, we realize that no one, including us, has done enough about containing health care costs.

That's why, though the system is basically sound, we wholeheartedly back this idea: greater stress on alternate means of treatment, such as ambulatory care centers and Health Maintenance Organizations, for less costly care outside the hospital. (And insurance companies are paying for more and more types of outpatient services.)

There's a booklet called Cutting Hospital Stays. We'll send you one free if you'll write to us at the Health Insurance Institute, Dept. 14, 1850 K Street, N.W., Washington, D.C. 20006.

The rising cost of health care is one epidemic that definitely can be arrested.

THE HEALTH INSURANCE COMPANIES IN AMERICA
Let's keep health care healthy

You read the headline first in this well designed ad, see the photograph, and move directly to the followup headline, the one that answers the first one. The small silhouette art at the far right helps establish the "Outpatients" concept. Charles DeSimone art directed, George Allen wrote the copy. Grey Advertising was the agency.

Emphasis

Someone must make an early decision on what one item to emphasize in the ad: the art, the headline, the copy block. If the art, which *one* item of art?

That decision made, the designer looks for ways of focusing on that item of emphasis. One way is to single it out—move it away from the clutter of other elements. Another is to change its shape—making it different from all the others. Another is to make it bigger, bolder, more colorful.

How *much* emphasis it should get is another problem. Its basic importance, the attitude of the advertiser, the class of reader to be reached—this all is taken into account. The size of the ad—the room the designer has available—this makes a difference, too.

And the designer must decide where in the ad the item of emphasis should be placed. A first decision might involve the optical center of the ad. Placing the emphasized element there will assure its being seen.

The designer must keep in mind one important rule of emphasis: *all emphasis is no emphasis.* Only one item in the ad should get primary attention. No item should upstage the chosen item. Where several items get equal billing, emphasis is canceled.

Working with many small, similar-sized items in, say, a crowded retail ad or catalog page, the designer gathers several items together in a mass, maybe even puts a border around it, and that one mass becomes the element of emphasis in the ad.

You get emphasis primarily through a contrast between what needs to be emphasized and what can be subordinated.

A sudden change in direction will give emphasis. So will a change in size, in shape, in texture, in color, in tone, in line.

Beyond the principles

George Giusti, the widely admired illustrator, tells how he puts design principles to work: "By eliminating details, I achieve impact. By using fewer colors, I attain more contrast. By simplifying shapes, I make them bolder."[7]

In this 1-col. X 3½" ad (a 50-line ad, in newspaper parlance), Gumout proves you can observe all the principles of good design even in a small-space format. The eye-travel is well defined, the emphasis is provided by the name itself, unity is achieved through border and type consistency, proportions are made pleasant by the contrasting shapes of the two areas of white space; and the ad seems strongly, if informally, balanced. One of a series of national newspaper ads produced by Aitkin-Kynett Co., Philadelphia. Art director: James F. Scharnberg.

Cars start faster with GUMOUT Carburetor Cleaner.

The plane itself has wide horizontal lines, and so does the ad. The headline at the top and the plane below work together to bring the two pages together. The thin vertical rules between columns are interrupted occasionally by silhouette art. A nicely unified ad despite all the elements. Jay Morales art directed for Doyle Dane Bernbach; Giff Crosby wrote the copy.

We can't promise you faster airplanes.
Just faster airports.

The irony of it is, after you've done all that walking, you haven't gotten a single step closer to your destination.

American's SABRE computer system eliminates some of that legwork. With SABRE, any of our agents at any of our ticket counters—and even at our departure gates, at most airports—can check you in completely, in one simple operation, at the location that's best for you.

Round-trip boarding passes: our way of handing you one less line.

Or maybe even two less lines.

You see, American, unlike some other airlines, can give you all your boarding passes ahead of time, for all parts of your trip. That includes connections as well as your flight back home.

With passenger jets flying at just under the speed of sound, getting from one end of the country to the other is a fast, simple process.

But getting from one end of an airport to the other is a different story. Here's what American is doing about it:

On American, you do all your checking-in at one place. (Whichever place is easiest for you.)

There are some airlines that actually make you go to one place to pick up your tickets, and still another place to get your boarding passes and seat assignments.

RESERVED

Pre-reserved seating: you don't have to stand in line to find out where you sit.

Ever stand in a long line at a departure gate and watch the people ahead of you take all the window seats? And all the aisle seats? On American, you don't have to stand for that.

When you call us to reserve a flight, don't just tell us which flight. Tell us which seat. We can

And if you don't think that's so important, remember: holding on to all those boarding passes can save you from waiting in all those lines.

hold that seat for you, for as long as eleven months ahead of time, right up until 15 minutes before take-off.

All of us are committed to giving all of you the best service in the industry.

At American Airlines, we're working hard to make sure we give you the kind of service you deserve. After all, great service is what helped us earn our reputation.

And great service is what will help us keep it.

We're American Airlines. Doing what we do best.

American

The advertising designer follows the principles of design on each assignment either consciously or unconsciously. But it is impossible to apply these principles equally, because one may be more important than another, depending on the mood and purpose of the ad. Furthermore, the principles in some respects contradict one another. For instance, how can you have contrast if your ad is perfectly unified?

The designer tries to work as many of the principles—as much of each principle—as possible into each ad. Becoming more confident, the designer may want to deliberately violate one or more of the principles to give the ad an edge over its competitors.

Into each ad goes a bit of the designer's personality, which cannot be distilled as a "principle." Without this touch, the ad may be well designed, but it could be lifeless, sterile, dull.

"Beauty and style are qualities I count as secondary," says Helmut Krone, art director for Doyle Dane Bernbach. "If they are in the work, they come along for the ride. The only quality I really appreciate is *newness*, to see something no one has ever seen before."

The test of a good layout

When you have arranged your elements into a good layout—when you have designed your ad—see whether you can remove any one of the elements without hurting the ad's balance, its proportion, its unity. If you

J. C. Penney used this illustration in a newsletter to make the point to advertising managers at its various stores that "White space, like art, has a shape." When the art is centered, the space around it is relatively uninteresting. When the art is moved to the side and slightly cropped, the white space becomes a shape. When the art is enlarged, cropped even more, and lowered, the shape of the white space becomes dramatic.

find your ad does not suffer from having lost an element, you might well question its basic structure.

The removing of any one element should necessitate a complete redesigning of the ad. The relationship of the elements should be that strong.

1. Gillian Naylor, *The Bauhaus* (London: Studio Vista/Dutton Pictureback, 1968), p. 7.

2. Harvey Offenhartz, *Point-of-Purchase Design* (New York: Reinhold, 1968), p. 195.

3. James Miho of Needham, Harper & Steers in the foreword to the catalog of the 1970/1971 Communication Graphic Show sponsored by The American Institute of Graphic Arts.

4. Wallace S. Baldinger, *The Visual Arts* (New York: Holt, Rinehart & Winston, 1960), p. 28.

5. Philip C. Beam, *The Language of Art* (New York: The Ronald Press, 1958).

6. Called the "divine proportion" by Fra Luca Pacioli in 1509 and the "golden mean" by nineteenth-century artists, it figures out mathematically at exactly 1.618 to 1.

7. Quoted in Mary Anne Guitar's *22 Famous Illustrators Tell How They Work* (New York: David McKay, 1964), p. 108.

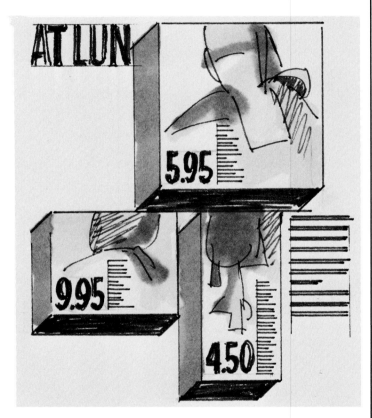

This rough layout for a retail ad attempts to put all the design principles to work. The balance is informal. The proportions set up by box sizes and areas of white space are unequal. Eye travel is controlled by butting items against each other. Unity is achieved by pushing white space to the outside edges. Emphasis comes from having one box bigger than the others and using giant type for prices.

Logo and art move off into a thin-line box that houses this mostly-copy ad for a resort at Cle Elum, Washington. The logo-and-art interruption is of the two-level variety—the line starting high at the top and dropping down a notch before continuing. The unjustified body copy picks up on an axis created by "RANCH & COUNTRY INN." Nancy G. Kimmick, a principal of Country Inn Enterprises, Inc., designed the ad. Norma Howard of Seattle did the logo.

Hidden Valley
RANCH & COUNTRY INN

90 scenic miles and minutes east of the Sound is a perfect little valley, nurtured by a wandering creek and protected by towering Ponderosa pine in the heart of the Cascade mountains.

A working ranch of 700 privately-owned acres that raises and trains quarter horses to take you over 40 miles of mountain and meadowland trails.

A Country Inn that can accommodate only 35 individuals in comfortable, private cabins and offer you cuisine that is a pleasure to serve.

A very special place to share with family and friends, enlighten citied senses, refresh, renew and stop all forward motion.

Hidden Valley. A Valley, a ranch, and a Country Inn. A unique alternative to the usual for dinner, overnight or a week.

By reservation only.   1-509-674-2422
Cle Elum, Washington 98922

An uncommon way to relate lines in a headline is to pick up an axis formed by the slant of one of the letters, in this case the *A*. The face is Avant Garde Gothic or one of its imitators, with *A*s that lend themselves particularly well to this kind of treatment. The headline appeared originally in an ad sponsored by Nordstrom, a fashion store.

7

Working with type

Don't be misled by David Ogilvy's satire on the agony of designers in selecting just the right face: "Once upon a time I was riding on the top of a Fifth Avenue bus," he wrote, "when I heard a . . . housewife say to another, 'Molly, my dear, I would have bought that new brand of toilet soap if only they hadn't set the body copy in ten-point Garamond.' "[1]

Ogilvy himself takes his typography seriously: do not use type "self-consciously"; do not print it in reverse or over a tint block; do not use more than one face in a headline; do not use sans serifs for body type; do not go wider than forty characters; break up long columns with subheadings; indent at the beginnings of paragraphs—these are among his famous twenty "precepts for the production of a good layout."

Where our letters came from

To appreciate the uses and abuses of type, a designer should know something of how type came into being. The Egyptians first worked out an alphabet, but theirs was a mixed affair: partly alphabet and partly picture writing. The Phoenicians, those businessmen-traders on the east shore of the Mediterranean Sea, borrowing from the Egyptians, developed an alphabet that had trade rather than literary purposes. It was made up of what we today call consonants. The literary-minded Greeks, adding vowels, improved the Phoenician alphabet (and gave the alphabet its name), and the Romans modified the Greek alphabet. Scholars count some two hundred alphabets, fifty of them in use today. Our own alphabet of twenty-six letters, derived from the Roman, is the world's most widely used.

Form of the letters

The history of letterform is largely the history of writing tools. The nature and shape of the writing instrument affected the character, the flow of the letters. The reeds, either sharpened to a point to make a pen or frayed at the end to make a brush, gave character to Egyptian writing on papyrus; the stylus used on wax tablets helped shape the rather angular Greek alphabet. Putting important Roman inscriptions on columns of stone affected roman letters (but differently from what one would suppose; the letters were apparently drawn first with an instrument that made thick and thin lines).

Letters of the alphabet were first drawn or written and only lately in world history cut and punched in metal. The tool used in most writing hands was the broad-nibbed pen. Turned at a slight angle, with the angle kept constant, the pen made its thick and thin markings on the writing surface—markings that became the inspiration for our roman typefaces.

The Greek alphabet, completed by the sixth century B.C., was an alphabet without serifs (serifs are tiny cross strokes at the terminals of main strokes). By the time typefaces were cut for printing, some twenty centuries later, serifs had been added to the alphabet. One explanation of the coming of serifs is this: When letters were carved in the columns of Rome, the up-and-down strokes, straight as they were, seemed to bulge in the center. An optical illusion, to be sure, but maddening, nevertheless. So the lapidary artists swelled the ends of the strokes slightly to compensate for this. The swellings evolved into serifs.

The body copy you are reading has serifs.

It was not until 1816, when type cutting was well established, that the idea of a serifless type occurred to the type designers and punch cutters. The design of letters had come full circle.

Sans serif types, popular for a time, then forgotten, came back strong in 1916, when Edward Johnston designed a beautifully balanced version for the London Underground Railway, and then in the 1920s, when a group of typographers and artists at the Bauhaus in Germany began giving their attention to type design, which in Germany and elsewhere had degenerated as an art. Widely acclaimed then, the types coming out of the Bauhaus were probably too impersonal, too much stripped down (an overreaction to decoration that had perverted so many of the faces at the turn of the century). But at least one of the faces—Futura—is still highly regarded by many typographers.

Meanwhile, in England, Eric Gill developed a sans serif with a personality. There was the slightest hint in the Gill face of variety in the thickness of the strokes. Some said his sans serif had some of the character of the Trajan caps.

In the 1950s European type designers brought out several new sans serifs that differed from earlier sans serifs in that vertical and horizontal strokes varied slightly in thickness, the rounds of the letters were slightly squared, and the terminals were cut on a constant horizontal. We refer to these sans serifs—there are several of them—as "Swiss gothics." Three of the best known are Helvetica, Univers, and Folio. So popular did they become that they nearly eclipsed the earlier sans serifs. But a reaction set in among some designers, and in the 1970s Futura, Spartan, Kabel, and others of the earlier sans serifs were back to compete with the Swiss gothics. The subheads in this book are set in modern sans serifs related to the Swiss gothics.

At the beginning of the sixteenth century, Aldus Manutius of Venice cut a new type called "Cancelleresca" or "Chancery," a face we have come to know as italic. A roman face that slanted slightly, it earned wide popularity because it not only was a beautiful face, it also saved space. Italic letters can be designed narrower than upright letters without impairing their readability.

Most typefaces today come in both upright and slanted—or italic—versions. The slanted version differs considerably in character from its upright relative; italic's job, after all, is to provide emphasis within a block of copy. But the sans serif faces and at least one roman face—W. A. Dwiggins's Electra—come with italics (sometimes called "obliques") patterned on the upright letters of the face, the listing to the right being the only difference. (Electra also comes with a more normal cursive italic.)

This line is set in italics.

Some roman italics come with a special set of capital letters—and lowercase letters, too—called "swash caps" or "swash letters." Terminal lines on these letters curve gracefully and maybe a little self-consciously beyond their ordinary boundaries. Out of favor for a time, swash caps enjoyed a revival among graphic designers when the first edition of this book was written. It was in the 1960s that the swash feature extended to some lowercase letters as well. By 1970 type designers had even come up with swash letters for some sans serifs. Swashes seemed to be everywhere.

Bookman Italic was among the earliest faces to adopt the swash treatment. It is still a popular face.

Menagerie Mime Theatre

Typography is a subtle art. The headline accompanying the nicely framed line-conversion art at the left suffers somewhat from poor optical spacing between lines. There seems to be more space between "Menagerie" and "Mime" than between "Mime" and "Theatre." The handling at the right shows one way of solving the problem. In the new handling note the diagonal formed by the *i, i,* and *t.*

Bookman Italic

Menagerie Mime Theatre

From Gutenberg's day until the eighteenth century, type designs were calligraphic, or based on handwriting of the period. Two styles of handwriting predominated: humanistic (rounded), found mostly in Italy and favored by Renaissance artists, and gothic (angular). From the humanistic hand came the types we today know as roman; from the gothic hand came the types we today know as black letter or text—or "Old English," although the hand belongs to Germany and the Low Countries. The blackness of the gothic hand—and the letters based on it—struck the Italians as crude; hence the term of derision, "gothic," a nickname that stuck until another "vulgar" type came along, this one without serifs. Today "gothic" no longer refers to Old English but instead to the modern form of sans serif type.

The eighteenth century saw the appearance of what we today call the modern roman faces: faces with a more precise look, with greater contrast in main strokes, the serifs thin and flat, looking as though they were tacked on as an afterthought. Bodoni, the most famous of these, remains a respected and much used face today in fine book text matter and (in bolder versions) newspaper headlines as well. Modern roman faces marked a departure from the practice of patterning types from handwriting and lettering. These were letters designed specifically for the printing process. The mark of mechanization, of industry, was upon them.

And then came the avalanche of new faces in the nineteenth century: the fat faces, the antiques and Egyptians, the sans serifs. They came to answer a need for boldness and blackness, for advertisers especially, who needed attention-getting types.

The English, in the main, designed them. Fat faces were wide versions of romans, bearing the blackness of the early gothics. Egyptian types were composed of strokes of uniform thickness, and at their terminals lay unbracketed, slablike serifs. Sans serif types—first cut by William Caslon IV—had strokes of uniform thickness; serifs were missing. Caslon called his letters "Egyptian," too (things Egyptian were "in" at the time), but the term did not stick. "Sans serif" did—and then an old standby, "gothic," and later "grotesque" (descriptive term!) served as names, and still do.

The point system

We must concern ourselves not only with type style but also with type size.

The typographer has a unique system for measuring types. The key word is "point." There are 72 points to the inch; a half inch is 36 points; a quarter inch, 18 points.

Types vary in size—in the heights of their capitals—from 5½ points to 72 points; and, in some styles, they go even larger, and even smaller. The letters never are quite as high as their point size. The measurement is taken from the slug on which the type is cast; there has to be a little room left over for the descending strokes that go below the base line.

Standard sizes are, for body types, 5½, 6, 7, 8, 9, 10, 11, and 12; for display types, 14, 18, 24, 30, 36, 42, 48, 60, and 72. These sizes all used to have proper names: agate (5½) and pica (12) remain useful.

Until recently, most newspapers sold space in agate lines—fourteen of them to the column inch.

"Pica" is particularly useful as a unit of measurement. Worth 12 points, it divides an inch into handy units of six. Points are used mainly to measure type sizes, picas to measure column and picture widths and depths. A column of copy 3 inches wide would be, using printers' terminology, 18 picas wide. The designer finds it easier to work in pica units than in sixteenths. Picas and half picas provide 12 units to the inch. Twelve is more dividable than 16.

Categories of type

We can classify types broadly into four basic categories (sometimes called "races"):

1. *Romans.* Roman letters make use of both thick and thin strokes, which bring some variety to the letters. Hooked on at the terminal points of the strokes are short cross-strokes, called "serifs." It is possible to put the romans into three subcategories: old style, modern, and transitional. In the old-style romans the difference between the thick strokes and the thin strokes is not great, and the serifs seem to merge into the main strokes; they are triangular in shape, sometimes somewhat cupped.

The thickest part of the strokes in the rounds of the letters—as in *C, G,* and *O*—fall at points that are on a diagonal. The axis of the old-style romans, in other words, is tipped—as it happens, to the left.

Often the old-style romans have a hand-cut look about them; slight imperfections add to their charm. The left top serif on the *T* may slant in one direction, the right top serif may be just slightly off that angle. There is a subtlety to these letters that other letters do not have.

The letters are based on early roman letters, especially those carved in that majestic column in Rome honoring the Emperor Trajan. Many typographers consider them even today the most beautiful of all our letters—and the most readable.

Two of many families that fall under the old-style roman heading are Caslon and Garamond.[2]

In modern romans the difference between the thick strokes and the thin strokes is more pronounced, and the serifs are stiff and straight. There is a T-square, triangle, and compass look about the letters. The thickest parts of the rounds are on a horizontal line. Not quite as readable as the old-style letters, they still are useful and actually preferred by some typographers.

They look best on slick paper.

The best known of the modern romans is Bodoni, which comes in a great variety of sizes, weights, even styles. Today's Bodonis are somewhat removed in character from the original Bodoni types.

Some of the roman types just do not fit in the two main subcategories. They have some of the old-style character, some of the modern. That beautiful face called Baskerville, one of the roman families, is lighter than the usual old style, but less mechanical than the modern. Ditto Times Roman, a form of which you are now reading. We call such romans "transitional."

Art directors love the standard old-style, modern, and transitional romans—the Caslons, the Garamonds, the Bodonis, the Baskervilles, the Times Romans—but occasionally they look for a more relaxed roman, one with an oddity of character. Such a face is ITC (for International Typeface Corporation) Souvenir, a face widely used by advertisers in the 1970s and 1980s. The example below shows you some of the face's characteristics: the bowed look of the *v,* for instance, and the unfinished lower loop of the *g.*

ITC Souvenir Light

2. *Sans serifs.* These are faces with strokes of even thickness. No serifs terminate the lines. Without the horizontalizing offered by serifs, the eye, some typographers say, has trouble getting from letter to letter. Readability is impaired. And the even thickness of the strokes makes for monotony.

ABCDEFGHIJKL
MNOPQRSTUV
WXYZ

abcdefghijklmnopq
rstuvwxyz

1234567890

In the opinion of many art directors, one of the most beautiful roman faces ever designed was Baskerville, shown here in an 18-point size. Baskerville is used mostly as body type.

ABCDEFGHIJK
LMNOPQRSTU
VWXYZ

abcdefghijklmno
pqrstuvwxyz

1234567890

One of the most useful of the new-wave, Swiss-inspired gothics is Helvetica, shown here in an 18-point size, medium weight. The captions in this book are set in Helvetica light.

Meier & Frank, a department store, for its 122nd anniversary sale logo uses Supermanlike letters: letters with three dimensions, shaded, drawn in perspective. Notice how the artist puts the units together. They wrap around a corner. At the same time they seem nicely tucked into a cove, with some of the letters (the *ND*) nestled in among the others. The result is a comfortable compactness, and a logo with a style both distinctive and contemporary.

But some of the sans serifs are designed to overcome this. If readability is a problem with sans serifs, it is basically a problem brought about by uniqueness. We are not used to columns set in sans serif types. Perhaps in the future sans serifs will be seen more often in body types. And we will find them every bit as readable as the romans.

Right now sans serifs appeal to almost everyone as headline faces.

Sans serif faces come in three distinct varieties: the Bauhaus-inspired sans serifs with their T-square, triangle, and compass look, like Futura and Spartan; the Swiss-inspired gothics and the grotesques with their less geometric, more sophisticated look, like Helvetica and Univers; and the types that have the thicks and thins of romans but not the serifs, like the beautiful Optima, the not-so-beautiful Radiant, and the funky Broadway type.

3. *Slab serifs.* Call them "square serifs" if you like. These letters have much the character of the sans serifs (some students of type put them with the sans serifs), but they *do* have serifs, rather strong ones, in strokes that match the main strokes of the letters in thickness. In the past these letters have been known as "antiques" and "Egyptians." Some of the family names reflect the Egyptian influences: Cairo, Karnak, Stymie, Memphis. Another family name reflects the buildinglike quality of the letters: Girder.

Most slab serifs are quite unreadable in large doses of body copy. But for special kinds of advertising, slab serifs make good headlines. When the serifs are bracketed (when they merge gradually into the main strokes), and when some difference in stroke thickness is evident, as in the Clarendon faces, the type has considerably more grace and beauty than otherwise. Some type scholars put the Clarendons in a category by themselves, because from both an historical and design standpoint, they have little in common with the basic slab serifs. Others class the Clarendons with the romans.

4. *Miscellaneous.* You may have seen other lists of faces that give Old English, Latins, scripts, even italics, separate headings. It is best for our purpose to combine all these under one heading, keeping them with the ornamental families that do not seem to fit any other category: faces like P. T. Barnum (with oversize serifs), Dom Casual (looks as if it were done with a brush), Umbra (shadow letters), Balloon (looks as if a cartoonist did it), Cooper Black (a grocery handbill type that made something of a comeback in the 1960s), Peignot (with its French look), and other types with only occasional uses.

Old English, sometimes called "text," sometimes "black letter," sometimes (wrongfully now) "gothic," has little value to advertisers. A lumber company manager might think it a dandy type for his letterhead, but the

designer with any integrity will soon talk him out of it. If the company must have "dignity" in its printing, it will get it more easily with an old-style roman. Even a church will find old-style romans more fitting, and certainly more readable.

The *Latin letters* are characterized by oversize triangular serifs. The letters of some Latin families are wider than normal letters.

The *scripts* have never been very successful as types. One word describes most of them: phony. They are supposed to look like handwriting. Trouble is, they have little of the grace, little of the irregularity of handwriting. When a handwritten look is needed, the designer should turn to a lettering person or a calligrapher. National advertisers make little use of script types these days. But local advertisers who cannot afford original art and plates do use them. Old standbys are the Brush and Kaufmann families.

One thing the designer soon learns when working with a script or Old English face: never order it in all caps. In the Brush letters that follow, "TEACHING" is almost unreadable.

TEACHING JOB FOR YOU?

When script letters do not join, they should be called *cursive,* but the assigned family names in the cursives and scripts ignore the distinction. Some students have trouble distinguishing between cursives and roman italics, even though cursives seldom have the grace of italics.

Italics, from a historical standpoint, could be considered a separate type category, as could "Old English," but in the case of the italics, the slanting feature has been applied to all the other races—we have roman italic, sans serif italic, and so on. So the designer today thinks of italics as a *form* of any of the main categories.

The categories to stick with for most ads are the romans, the sans serifs, and, to a limited extent, the slab serifs—and their italics. The other categories contain too many faces that are affected, too cute, unreadable. Type should not upstage the message.

Once in a while one of the decorative faces gets rediscovered by an eager young designer, who uses it. A few others use it. And until everyone jumps on the bandwagon and spoils the party, the type is hot for awhile. But it soon crawls back into its hole, where it belongs.

UNIVERS Univers 45
UNIVERS Univers 46
UNIVERS Univers 47
UNIVERS Univers 48
UNIVERS Univers 55
UNIVERS Univers 56
UNIVERS Univers 57
UNIVERS Univers 58
UNIVERS Univers 63
UNIVERS Univers 65
UNIVERS Univers 66
UNIVERS Univers 67
UNIVERS Univers 68
UNIVERS Univers 75
UNIVERS Univers 76

Ultra Bodoni Italic Optima **BROADWAY** *Garamond Italic* **Lydian**

Stymie Light **Eurostile Bold Extended** *Palatino Italic* **P. T. Barnum**

Franklin Gothic Condensed **Franklin Gothic Wide** *Kaufmann Script* **Brush**

Century Schoolbook *Century Schoolbook Italic* **Spartan Black** *Mistral*

BALLOON EXTRABOLD Caslon No. 540 **Caslon Bold Condensed** Engravers Old English

COPPERPLATE GOTHIC HEAVY *Commercial Script* Cheltenham Medium

A Swiss-designed sans serif (or gothic), Univers comes in twenty varieties of weights and widths, each ranging in size from 6 to 48 points. The designer found it necessary and logical to give each series a number rather than a name like "medium" or "ultra" or "condensed." Here you see some—not all—of the variety in the 18-point size. Studying this chart you can see that odd-numbered faces are roman, even-numbered italic. In each group of ten numbers, the faces become more condensed as the numbers increase. And at each jump of ten, they become bolder.

Families, series, and fonts

Fitting into the several categories are the many "families" of types. The families are divided into series, and the series are divided into fonts. Modern roman, for instance, would be a category, Bodoni would be a family in that category, Ultra Bodoni would be a series within that family (it is a fat letter with unusual stroke contrast), and 24-point Ultra Bodoni would be a font in that series.

A typeface family often gets its name from the person who designed the face. Caslon came from William Caslon, an English engraver. Baskerville came from John Baskerville, an English writing master. Bodoni came from Giambattista Bodoni, an Italian printer. People like these are now called type designers. They may be responsible for a number of faces, not just faces that bear their names, and they are likely to design typefaces full-time.

Type designers

A few type designers in England at the turn of the century—William Morris among them—revolted against the garish faces then so popular and brought out revivals of the earlier faces of Nicolas Jenson, Aldus Manutius, and others of the fifteenth-century Venetian school. Morris, the medievalist, interested in a heavy-textured type page, also designed an "Old English" that was readable—unusual for such a face.

Among type designers in America, Thomas Maitland Cleland, Daniel B. Updike, Bruce Rogers, Frederic W. Goudy, William A. Dwiggins, and Will Bradley stand out. Cleland styled *Fortune* magazine and later the experimental newspaper of the 1940s, *PM*. Updike became the nation's foremost typographic historian. Rogers became famous for the Bibles he designed and for several typefaces, primarily Centaur. Goudy designed several faces, including an old-style roman that bears his name. Dwiggins designed fine books for Alfred A. Knopf and designed several faces for Linotype, including Caledonia, the face used for the first edition of this book. Bradley designed faces for the American Type Founders.

Hermann Zapf stands out as a contemporary type designer. Among the many faces he has designed are Palatino, Optima, and Melior, examples of which you see here. The faces come in a variety of weights, of course, and, like most faces, their true beauty comes through better in the regular rather than the bolder versions. But advertisers tend to prefer bold weights, at least for their headlines.

Palatino Semi-Bold

Optima Semi-Bold

Melior Semi-Bold

These representative display or headline faces are broken down into series. Some of these faces come in body-type sizes, too. Each of the italic faces is available in an upright version. Most of the faces are available in other weights. Ultra Bodoni italic is a modern roman. Optima is a sans serif, but one that looks a little like a roman because of its classic design. Can you put each of the others in its proper "race"?

Newer Zapf faces include Zapf Book, Zapf Chancery, and Zapf International, all developed for the International Typeface Corporation.

Zapf believes that type designers should not adapt classic designs to the present but should, instead, come up with new designs appropriate to today's printing technology. "We should show our respect for the typography of the past by not using it as a cheap source of ideas."[3]

Tom Carnase is another contemporary type designer. He was involved in the designing of logos for *New York* and *Esquire* and L'eggs pantyhose. But he is best known for the typefaces he has designed: more than fifty of them, including Avant Garde Gothic, which he created in collaboration with the late Herb Lubalin.

Today's type designers must create faces that fit computer-generated letterforms. Their letters must accept the digitizing required. Zapf has found that his Optima, for instance, does not take to digitized storage.[4]

Through the efforts of people like Zapf and Carnase and the several type houses, hundreds of new typefaces come out each year to intrigue advertisers. New Aster is a text and display typeface introduced in 1983 by Mergenthaler Linotype Company. Its thick and thin strokes put it in the roman category, but it is a roman with slab serifs that, on some letters, become a bit unusual (note the r). The bold stroke in the N and the bold strokes in the w look as though they overextend themselves. New Aster is available in four weights. In all, a strong roman.

New Aster

One of the most respected of the modern type designing firms is International Typeface Corporation. One of its many faces, available from a number of suppliers, is ITC Benguiat, shown here in a medium weight. Another roman, it is a face with a good deal of character. Some might classify it as an eccentric face. Note the pulled out look at the bottom of the C; the small, triangular upper loop on the B; and the cramped, squatty look of the g.

ITC Benguiat

The variety of faces

The typical printer's type-specimen book displays a bewildering number of faces. But with two or three standard faces in all their various sizes and weights the designer often has all that's needed.

When asked to design a good book typeface, Edward Johnston replied: "There is one already." The implication was that one good face was enough.

Kurt Weidemann, the German typographer, has said that "three thousand typefaces are no progress, but a declaration of bankruptcy. In order to communicate a message effectively, ten typefaces and ten times ten ways of typographic arrangement are more than enough."

See the variety you can get in a single font—a single face in a single size:

ALL CAPS
SMALL CAPS
CAPS AND SMALL CAPS
Caps and Lower Case
all lower case
ALL CAPS ITALICS
Caps and Lowercase Italics
all lowercase italics

Then, staying in the same face and size, but adding boldface, you get eight more varieties. Many faces come not only in regular and bold but also in several other weights, from extra light to ultra bold. Further, you can get some faces in expanded (wide) and condensed (narrow) versions.

Finally, you can l e t t e r s p a c e.

Multiply these by the hundreds of *different* typefaces, then by the sev-

Soft
love
PASSION
Elegance
OLD
Responsible
BRIGHT
reliable
abnormal
Graciousness
silver
Mechanics
COLORFUL
Nostalgia
fantastic
IMAGE
DIMINISH
PRESTIGE
WINTER

Choice of type can have almost as much of an effect on communication as choice of words. Here are some type choices made by art directors for words in their advertising headlines. In most cases, the entire headlines were set in these faces.

eral sizes in each face, and you get some idea of the great variety of typefaces available.

Still, the type-design houses keep introducing new faces.

Much can be said in defense of them, even though their design violates much of what many of us learned from earlier typographers and type designers. True, these new faces—many of them—*are* eccentric. In place, line after line, they present a pattern that is busy. Yet, in small takes the faces can be lively and useful. They *are* a change of pace. And in short headlines they are readable enough and so full of character as to nicely amplify what the words themselves are saying.

Although some type-design houses have been pressing for it for years, typefaces do not enjoy copyright protection. Hence new faces, once introduced, are soon duplicated by other houses that give the faces different but similar names. Paladium, for instance, is almost a dead ringer for the classical, calligraphic Palatino. Oracle duplicates the handsome, serifless roman Optima. Helios has the modern look of Helvetica. Century Textbook looks like Century Schoolbook, California looks like Caledonia, English Times and Press Roman look like Times Roman.

Type preferences

Graphic designers using the faces often develop strong preferences for one over the others. Their preferences change as times change and new faces become available. That everyone else uses a face can be a discouraging factor. Helvetica, possibly the most popular sans serif face ever designed, has recently come in for some criticism.

Peter Rauch, art director of *Money*, says he would "never specify Helvetica outside the borders of Switzerland." He contends that roman faces are more believable than sans serif faces. They are also "more humanistic." For a poster announcing the availability of International Typeface Corporation's version of Garamond at Typographics, a typesetting firm, Jack Summerford featured a big "Helvetica"—set, of course, in Garamond.

The choice of a typeface should depend not on a designer's personal preference but instead on the appropriateness of the type to the ad's message and readers. Typefaces do carry moods. A mood can be important in the choice of a face for an ad's headline.

Type moods

Type can be graceful, powerful, quiet, loud, beautiful, ugly, old fashioned, modern, simple, decorative. The roman faces suggest a classic mood, the sans serifs a contemporary mood, but this should not prevent your using, say, Baskerville for young professionals or, say, Futura for retirees. And if you want a mood to be obvious, you can turn to one of the offbeat faces.

For instance, Hobo, designed in 1910, has an art nouveau feel. Not a graceful face, it still would be an appropriate face to go with art from that period.

Hobo

One of Photo-Lettering's more recent faces is Moore Digital Upright, shown below. If you were looking for a headline face to sell one of those digital clocks, this might be the one to use.

DIGITAL

Art directors increasingly rely on photolettering for advertising headlines. Photo-Lettering, Inc., New York, in business since 1936, is a leading source. A recent catalog shows samples of nearly ten thousand type styles. Available are all the standard faces plus a great variety of exotic and contemporary faces not available elsewhere. Many of the faces are designed exclusively for Photo-Lettering by leading letterform artists and calligraphers. Each of the faces can be condensed, expanded, slanted, tightly fit, or otherwise adjusted, making the possibilities for headline display almost endless. Shown here are one-line specimens of some of the more unusual faces. These include, reading from the top:

Lisson Extempora 1
Gonzales Jeanette
Swinger 10
American Uncial
Futura Maxi 000
Stan-Fu-Tendrils 1
Deutsch Black
Bauhaus Geometric 9
Papirtis Pink Mouse
Bernstein M. Orbit
Calendar Black
Parisian
Rubens Condensed Outline
Pacella Clarendon Oblique Swash 10
Manifold 3
Barclay Engravers Expanded Bold
Caruso Roxy
Windsor Outline
West Espana Contour
Davison Bolero
Push Pin Myopic Open
Compass

Mierop Inline
Peter Max Riverside Drive
Neon
Glaser Filmsense
Bifur Graphic
Prisma Bauhaus
Glaser Babyfat Outline
Cenotaph
Delacroce Beta #1
Allen Sculpture
Chwast Art Tone
Obese
Bordanaro Grumpy Open
Rosenblum Razzamataz
Jefferson Aeroplane
Tension
Chwast Blimp
Calypso
Magnetic Ink
Julino Paperclip
Benquiat Chrisma Contour
Hobo Outline

And if you want to suggest that something is changing to better fit its environment, you could turn to Photo-Lettering's Allen Chameleon.

CHAMELEON

When you decide to run a headline in color ink, you choose a typeface a little larger, a little fatter than you would choose for black ink. This will compensate for the lack of darkness.

When you decide to run a headline in reverse, you choose a face that does not have small, weak serifs. The sans serifs are best for reversing. Bodoni among the romans would be a poor choice.

On mixing types

Ideally, you would stick to the same type family for any one job, getting your variety through changes in both size and blackness, and by turning to condensed and expanded versions and to italics. But often a single face is not versatile enough. Or the printer does not have a full range in any one family. And so you mix types.

The mixing of one *body* face with another *headline* face is not so vital a matter as the mixing of one *headline* face with another *headline* face.

For most ads you should confine your mixing to two faces—or three, at the most. Four or more faces in headlines create a hodgepodge.

You should be less concerned with historical factors—types designed at the same period do not necessarily go together—than with the character of the letters. Caslon and Bodoni faces, for instance, both designed in the eighteenth century, do not go together; one is an old-style roman, the other a modern roman. Common sense tells you that an old-style and a modern type do not go together. This is true especially for the romans.

Sans serifs are another matter. A good sans serif can be used with almost any other type. In mixing, it is considered a neutral type. Types that should not be mixed with sans serif are the slab serifs (they are too much like the sans serifs in basic structure) or Old English (which should be combined only with romans).

To lay down a set of rules on type mixing is impossible. Type mixing is so much a matter of taste. And in the right hands, almost any combination, for certain effects, is workable.

Perhaps this rule will help: The types you mix should be either very similar or very dissimilar. If one of the types is almost-but-not-quite like the other type, the reader will sense that something is amiss.

The case for readability

It should not be necessary to argue for so obvious an ideal as readability. But the new crop of student designers each year (if this teacher-author's experience is typical) continues to insist on making headline letters and copy blocks "different"—understandable in light of the hush that comes over teachers in the elementary and secondary schools as their young charges engage in their acts of creativity.

The typical student has to learn that, when working with type, being different is seldom a virtue.

The reader has no time to learn a new alphabet or variation; familiar type design and arrangement do the best jobs for advertisers.

What is the reader used to?
1. Capitals and lower case, not all capitals.
2. Letters reading from left to right, not up and down.

The Carolyn Davis Story

Swash caps and even swash lowercase letters made a comeback in the 1960s and found continued wide acceptance afterwards, especially for book titles and magazine advertising. Swashes seem best suited to heavy roman letters like Bookman, but they are also available in other roman and even sans serif typefaces. This example is from a direct-mail piece published by *Reader's Digest* to promote its monthly signed advertising column.

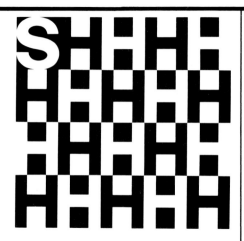

U.S. News & World Report plays around with an *S* and some *H*s to create a headline-art piece for its back cover ad in the *1980 Librarians' Guide,* a publication of F. W. Faxon Company, Inc., Westwood, Massachusetts. The purpose of the ad was to encourage librarians' ordering of the magazine, because it offers "No noise . . . just news." Notice the pattern that is formed by alternating the black-on-white and white-on-black *H*s.

3. Lines of type running horizontally, not on a diagonal.

4. Letters and words with even spacing.

So avoid all-cap headlines, headlines with letters arranged stepladder fashion, tilted display lines, and peculiar spacing. Make it easy for the reader. Do not let the type upstage the advertiser's message.

Professor David A. Wesson of Marquette University's College of Journalism questions some of the arguments that roman faces are more readable than sans serif faces. "Because differences are slight . . . the decision to use a face will remain largely aesthetic and situational."

He says that "if there is an edge for romans, it may be that the added strokes to many letters may assist readability by providing additional information—in the classic Information Theory sense—to ambiguous letter combinations. A case in point is the word 'Illinois,' which, set in a monotonal sans serif, is a real eye-stopper."

He cites Univers as a nonambiguous sans serif because it mimics the thick and thin strokes of the roman faces, adding information that makes it close to roman in readability. Optima, less subtle in its thick and thin strokes, is another example. Even so, Wesson advises romans for long columns of body copy.[5]

Body type

Chapter 4 covered methods of indicating body type on the layout.

Body type is sectioned into paragraphs, and this should be indicated on the layout. Paragraph beginnings (you are only estimating where they fall, of course) should be noted with indentations or extra spacing—or both. Some designers forego both indentations and extra spacing, leaving each new paragraph marked only by space that may occur at the end of the last line of the preceding paragraph.

An initial letter—the first letter of the first paragraph writ large—enables the reader to make the adjustment from the large headline type to the small body type, but some designers consider initials as dated. There are many possibilities: initials rising higher than the other letters in the first line, or sticking out at the left, or buried in the block. The remainder of the first word can be set in caps or small caps to further ease the reader into the copy block.

The size of the type affects the width of the column. The bigger the type, the wider the column can be. Some designers believe the copy block should be about as wide as an alphabet-and-a-half—thirty-nine characters—of lowercase letters. When they want copy to spread over a wider area, they break it into two or more columns.

The copy in this book is set in columns almost twice as wide as they should be, according to the thirty-nine-characters rule, but the numerous subheads and art pieces and the generous gutter margins help overcome readability problems. A two-column-per-page format would complicate the handling of art in the book.

Your copy block or column can take these forms:

1. *Fully justified.* Left and right edges are perpendicular. Stated differently, the copy is flush left, flush right. This is the normal way of setting copy.

2. *Flush left, ragged right.* The right edge is ragged as on a manuscript produced by a typist. This is seldom used in long blocks. But actually, because we are accustomed to typewriter copy, and because ragged right means more uniform word spacing, such copy possibly is easier to read than justified copy. A few newspapers are experimenting with such composition for their news columns. And many book publishers are using it for art books. Specialty magazines, including company magazines, seem to prefer it. And, to suggest warmth and informality, annual reports increasingly are using it.

Flush left, ragged right setting results in less hyphenation at ends of lines as well as more even spacing between words. If you do not mind an extra-ragged looking right edge on your copy block, you can order a flush-left setting that eliminates all hyphenation.

3. *Flush right, ragged left.* In this kind of setting, the left edge rather than the right edge is ragged. Now this is a different matter. The eye has to hunt its place after each line, and the reader is slowed. But in short takes, flush right, ragged left typography can be effective, as for a fashion advertisement. Use it sparingly.

4. *Ragged left and right.* This setting is better for multiline headlines than for copy. Sometimes it works for small sections of body type. The silhouette the copy makes certainly has character. Sometimes the silhouette takes a recognizable shape—geographic, facial, or whatever. It is easy to be too cute with this form of typography.

5. *Each line centered.* In short takes, this setting works well enough, especially if the ad needs a classical or formal look. Such setting, though, is still a novelty.

Picture captions

Picture captions—newspaper people call them cutlines—should be near enough to their pictures so the reader will see at once the connection. They appear most often in italic or in type smaller or bolder than the body type. The caption ordinarily goes below the picture, but it can go at the top, side, even inside in a hollowed-out box (called a mortise), as a surprint (black type over a gray area), or as a reverse (white type in a gray or black area). But in most ads, the headline and the copy do what picture describing is necessary; a caption is not necessary. If a picture has to be explained, it probably is not pulling its fair share of the advertising load.

The designer should not forget to indicate any planned captions on the layout.

Display type

The rules for typography—the rules for readability—break down a bit when you get to display types, especially when you have only a few words to contend with. In display types, you can crowd, tip, fit in and under, screen down—and still not hurt readability much. "I would think that any typographic trick is justified . . . ," British typographer John Lewis has said. "Ugliness is a perfectly permissible feature of such typography. Anyhow, who is to say what ugliness is?"

Almost anything goes. The Lady Carpenter Institute of Building & Home Improvement Inc., New York, used this headline on an ad for "creative survival classes."

DON'T DO THINGS BACKWARDS

(headline shown in mirror-reversed type)

Swissair ended the headline for an ad with the word *sleep* and, to dramatize it, laid the letters on their backs. The period after the word makes the arrangement obvious.

sleep.

(word shown rotated/reversed)

If this copy seems more obscure than some of the other copy in this book, it is because it is not copy at all but "Greeking," a dry-transfer material used on finished layouts and comps (but not mechanicals) to simulate copy. You would rub it onto your layout in the same way you would rub on dry-transfer letters.

Ordinary typographic tricks are best performed by a lettering artist or a pasteup artist using reproduction proofs.

If the type is to be set photographically, certain basic tricks, such as tight fitting or overlapping, can be done as the type is set.

The Fotomaster camera, operated by some composition houses, offers additional possibilities. This camera can change one dimension of hand-drawn letters or reproduction proofs of type (expanding or condensing the type) while holding another dimension. It can slant the letters either to the left or right, put them in perspective, put them in an arc or circle, convert them to outline letters, twist them, or otherwise distort them. The camera can do the same thing with ordinary artwork. Obviously the designer should ask for such service only occasionally.

When you want a headline with more than one line, avoid arranging the lines—squeezing and expanding them—to fit a geometric shape. This is an old-time newspaper headline practice that has been largely abandoned. Certainly "inverted pyramids" and flush-left–flush-right headlines have little to recommend them to advertising designers.

You should avoid changing type as you move from line to line in a single headline. You want your headline to appear as a unit.

Allen Q. Wong, professor of art at Oregon State University, demonstrates the beauty of calligraphy in this two-language inscription. He skillfully combines three different letterforms into a single unifying design. Part of the beauty of the piece of art (and that's what it is) comes from the dry-brush texture in the Old English letterform. Note the condensed nature of the Old English and the closeness of its fit.

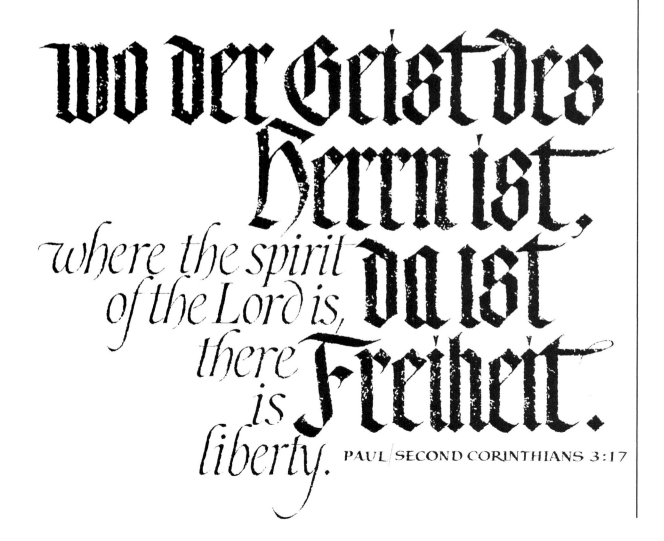

Wo der Geist des Herrn ist, where the spirit of the Lord is, there is da ist liberty. Freiheit. PAUL/SECOND CORINTHIANS 3:17

Calligraphy

Hand-drawn letters and handwriting do a job for advertisers that machine-set type can never do. For headlines on institutional ads, formal ads, ads with headlines more prominently displayed than usual, designers turn to the calligrapher rather than the typographer.

"Calligraphy" means, simply, "elegant handwriting." Calligraphic letters combine a certain freedom with a certain order. For some jobs they stand separately, as type does; for others, they merge into each other in a sort of advanced stage of penmanship.

The father of modern calligraphy is Ludovico Degli Arrighi, a sixteenth-century scribe, whose *La Operina,* perhaps the world's first handwriting manual, still merits scrutiny. His particular style—there are a number of styles—became known as "chancery cursive." His tool was the broad-nib pen. His slightly slanting strokes were quick, sometimes connected, sometimes not. The style is neither restrictive nor precise. Some of the beauty of chancery cursive lies in the imperfections of the strokes.

Since World War II we have seen a renaissance in the use of chancery cursive—or "italic handwriting," as some call it.

Punctuation in display type

"Don't worry too much about punctuation. We know an editor who agonized so much over a colon that he got colitis and ended up with a semicolon," wrote Alden S. Wood in *Reporting,* a defunct magazine for industrial editors. But *someone* has to worry about punctuation. Nowhere is correct punctuation more important than in display type, where errors are so harsh, so noticeable. Designers, in their haste, often are responsible for them.

Misused quotation marks can be more a problem than omitted ones. Consider this headline for an ad for Scott Tissues:

Don't let this
"SO-CALLED BARGAIN"
fool you!

The writer meant, of course, SO-CALLED "BARGAIN." The people who are fooled by so-called "bargains" do not go around calling them "so-called bargains"; they call them, simply, "bargains." The "so-called" is the copywriter's editorializing; as a matter of fact, when quote marks are used with "bargain," editorializing is already accomplished; the "so-called" is not even needed.

Newspaper headline writers use single rather than double quote marks in headlines, but advertisers need not follow so silly a rule. (No problem for the British: they wisely use single quote marks throughout, except, of course, when they have a quote within a quote.)

Newspaper headline writers never use periods in headlines, but advertisers often do. Using periods, you are able to show two complete sentences in a headline. You do not have to go to a new typeface for the second sentence. You are able to present two parallel thoughts. You are able to deliver a one-two punch.

Maybe you will use a little white space to separate the two sentences, and maybe not.

Sometimes you need two pieces of punctuation after a line, because no one piece will do the job. Some typefaces provide interabangs—question marks merged with exclamation marks—but readers are not used to them.

This book jacket was designed in 1949 by Oscar Ogg for William Sloan Associates, the publisher. The beautiful calligraphy is not only appropriate but also timeless. In the original, the large lettering is black, the smaller lettering and border red, the decorations green.

?
!

When you have a combination question-exclamation, you are better off doing what the *Christian Science Monitor* did in this heading for a subscription renewal notice: use both a question mark and an exclamation mark.

But ordinarily you would avoid exclamation marks—they are an admission you could not bring enough excitement to the headline through legitimate design innovations. Nor should you rely on that much-overused device the ellipsis (a series of dots at the end of a headline), unless it is necessary to carry the reader across a page or panel to a connecting headline.

Word emphasis

It is easy to fall into the trap of emphasizing a word in the headline by making it bigger or by setting it in another face. Designers who do this are unsure of themselves. They are like writers who overuse exclamation marks or italics.

Ordinarily a headline does not need internal graphic change of pace. When it does need it, the change of pace should involve a single word or phrase. If two different sections of the headline get the treatment, the two will cancel out each other.

In the following headline, Lady Madonna Maternity Boutique, New York, emphasized "PRETTY" by giving it its own line, but the real reason for the second line is to make the headline clear. If "PRETTY" had stayed up there with the other words, the headline would not have worked very well.

WE MAKE PREGNANT PRETTY

Copyfitting

For display type, copyfitting involves tracing letters from a type-specimen book or lettering them freehand in their approximate sizes. The experienced typographer, working for the typesetting house, can take a quick look at the rough and pick out the face in the size closest to the designer's rendering. Of course, designers who do not want to be disappointed in the resulting impact should take their guidelines from an existing size and do a reasonably close approximation of the widths of the letters and the thicknesses of the strokes. Some designers not only specify the type's name in the margin of the rough; they also specify the size, even when their roughs are rather finished. And they include instructions on how the headline should be set. For instance, the instruction may read: "Set extra tight" (possible in photocomposition).

For body type the process is a little more complicated.

Either you will be given an amount of copy and asked to figure how much space it will take, or you will decide on the amount of space you wish to devote to copy in your layout and then ask the copywriter to write to fit.

You should learn copyfitting, then, literally backward and forward.

If copy is too long, you can (1) adjust the layout to fit it, (2) select a smaller typeface, (3) remove the leading between the lines, or (4) ask the writer to prune the copy. If it is too short, you can (1) adjust the layout, (2) select a larger typeface, (3) use more leading, or (4) ask the writer to add words.

Let us try a problem: You have a couple of pages of typed copy. How much space will it take?

The procedure for solution is as follows.

1. Count the characters in the manuscript. (Determining the average number of characters in a line and multiplying that average by the number of lines is good enough for most jobs, although there are more accurate ways of determining the number of characters. Do not worry about the short lines at the ends of paragraphs; the material in type will have short lines, too. An instrument that can help you count characters is the Copi-Counter, which rolls along your manuscript or galley of type and registers distances in inches, picas, and agate lines.) Let us say your manuscript has 1,856 characters.

2. Decide what width you want the copy block to be; for example, 16 picas.

3. Select the typeface and size, perhaps 10-point Bodoni Book.

4. Find out how many characters you can get in the line width you have chosen. (You will have to consult a copyfitting chart found in your printer's type-specimen book or use an A/D Copyfitter, a Lee Streamlined Visual Control Copyfitter, or a Haberule Visual Copy Caster.) The number of characters in a 16-pica line of 10-point Bodoni Book, it turns out, is 44. (Baskerville, to compare, would give you 41; Garamond, 46.)

5. Divide the total number of characters in the manuscript by the number of characters you get in a line of type. This will give you the number of lines of type you can expect. In our example, 1,856 divided by 44 is 42, with just a little left over. Let us say we will have 42 lines of type.

6. Multiply the number of lines by the point size of the type. If you want any leading, add that amount to the point size, before you multiply. In our example, let us put the 10-point Bodoni Book on a 12-point slug—two points of leading per line. So: 42 (number of lines) times 12 (point size plus leading) gives us 504. This means the copy block will be 504 points in depth.

7. Convert the points into picas: 504 divided by 12 (12 points in a pica) gives us 42. Our copy block, then, is 16 picas wide by 42 picas deep. (It could also be two 16-pica columns by 21 picas, or three 16-pica columns by 14 picas.)

Ideally you should go through this process for every paragraph of the body copy. In common practice, designers, especially for rush jobs, estimate the copy block in toto.

An easier but less accurate way to fit copy is through the square-inch method. Draw several 1-inch squares (three are enough) over random parts

VOGUE
HOUSE & GARDEN
GLAMOUR
MADEMOISELLE

This is an example of nestled typography with letters and lines fitted snugly into each other. The face is a sophisticated adaptation—a hand-drawn version—of Ultra Bodoni, with oversize caps. This handling is ideal for a logo—especially one that says ''Group''—but it would not work well for a headline with many words. Designer: Bob O'Dell; agency: Kingen, Feleppa & O'Dell.

SITE SEEKING
IN THE
SOUTHWEST?

let us
do your
spadework

Texas Electric Service Company, Fort Worth, places the main part of its headline for this *Business Week* ad inside a bold abstraction of the instrument suggested by the headline. The "let us do your spadework" is "reversed" in the black area. Such reversing usually calls for a sans serif type. The thin strokes of a face like Bodoni would fill in, and disappear, making the type unreadable.

of copy already set in the type style and size you want and count the numbers of words in each. Take an average. Then count the words in your typed manuscript, and divide by your average number. This will give you the number of square inches of type matter you can expect. Say it is 12. That means your copy block can be 2″ × 6″; or 3″ × 4″; or 2½″ × almost 5″.

In his classes at the University of Georgia, Professor Robert Anservitz distributes a table that tells roughly how many words you can expect to get in a square inch of typical body type.

6 point solid	47	10 point solid	21
6 point leaded	34	10 point leaded	16
8 point solid	32	12 point solid	14
8 point leaded	23	12 point leaded	11

You can use this table in three ways.

To figure the size of a copy block for a given amount of copy:
1. Count the words in your copy.
2. Pick a type size and setting (solid or leaded).
3. Divide the number of words in your copy by the number taken from the chart.
4. Decide on a width (or depth) for your copy block.
5. Divide the answer you got in step 3 by the width (or depth) you decided on in step 4. This will give you your other dimension.

To figure the number of words needed to fill a given space:
1. Multiply the width of the space by the length, in inches.
2. Pick a type size and setting (solid or leaded).
3. Multiply the number taken from the chart by the answer you got in step 1.

To figure the size of type necessary to fit a given amount of copy in a given amount of space:
1. Divide the number of words in your copy by the number of square inches in your available space.
2. Consult the table for the number closest to the answer you got in step 1.

A variation of the square-inch method is the *column*-inch method. For this method, find copy that is set exactly as you want your copy set—in the right width—and simply measure a block an inch deep and then count the words. Do the same thing in two more places and take an average. Divide the average into the number of words in your typed manuscript, and you have the number of column inches of type that the copy will fill.

Using either the square-inch or column-inch method, if you count out characters rather than words, you will get a more accurate reading.

Spacing

Spacing becomes a prime consideration in composition. You could say spacing is more important than type style or size.

The designer, not the printer or typesetter, must make most spacing decisions. The rule of good proportion comes up again; the designer tries to provide unequal space divisions between sections of typography (the space between the headline and the start of the copy will be different from the space between the end of the copy and the logotype), but not, of course, within a section, such as between lines within a block of body copy or lines within a headline. And if several copy blocks are preceded by same-size headlines, the space between the headline and the block of copy in each case would be the same. Consistency here is more important than variety.

Type is designed by the manufacturer so that the space between letters is constant. This is all right for smaller sizes, but in display sizes the equal spacing becomes unequal *optically*. The space between two As (AA), for

instance, appears larger than the space between two Ms (MM). Advertising designers can see to it that some adjustment is made by the typesetter; in the layout too they will compensate for the spacing irregularity.

The beginning advertising designer soon tries the trick of adding uniform spaces between letters—letterspacing. It is best to avoid letterspacing because it inhibits readability. A more durable trend among designers is to take space away, to somewhat crowd the letters, especially in the sans serifs and gothics. (This requires a pasteup of proofs of the letters, or it requires photocomposition.)

And it will take beginning designers a while to catch on to the fact that the spacing between *words* in type is really less than they think (about the width of an average-width lowercase letter). Too much space between words detracts from the unity of the headline and makes it hard to read.

Almost any type in its smaller, body sizes is made more readable, however, if a little extra spacing is provided between *lines*. Type can be leaded automatically as it is set, whether it is "hot type" (metal) or "cold type" (photocomposition), and metal type can be leaded by hand afterward. Leading, of course, increases the depth of the copy block. It is possible to lead too much. This is the test for a copy block: Squint and look at it. If it appears as a rectangle of gray, fine. If it appears as a series of horizontal stripes, you have too much leading; if it appears as a solid, cramped pattern, you have too little. A good rule of thumb: For advertising copy, always lead two points. The type you are now reading is leaded one point.

Lettering headlines

Here is how you go about lettering-in your headlines: Scribble them quickly at first on an odd-size sheet, trying to take up as much room as you know they will take up in type. Check the sheet then with an alphabet of about the right face and size and mark your guidelines. Rule the guidelines on another sheet, then place the original sheet under the new sheet and begin to trace the letters somewhat more carefully than before, filling in the strokes where needed to give the headline the weight it needs. Use pencil; and do not be afraid to erase when you need to. Too often students who find lettering a tedious job get caught up in a wrong size and refuse to make an adjustment because they have already invested too much time on the original.

Making a hasty first sketch will help you avoid this impasse.

Use a 2B or a 4B pencil for large display letters; something a little harder—as hard as an HB—for smaller letters. Hard-lead pencils hold their point better; and you need a sharp point for small letters.

You should not attempt to letter sizes any smaller than 14 points. Twelve points and below can be considered body type; this you can indicate with ruled lines.

Even for rough layouts, try to imitate real letters. Do not make up your

A quick way of indicating a reverse is to scribble your "letters" in first, using *M*s and *W*s, then scrub strokes up to and around them.

Here are the six basic strokes and some rough lettering made with them. For roman letters, use a chisel-point pencil for the basic strokes, then go back and, with a sharp-point pencil, draw the serifs. Making sans serif letters with single strokes is a little more difficult; you must constantly change the pencil angle. As you move to more finished roughs, you will want to use the outline and fill-in method, drawing letters freehand or tracing them. Letters for the last two lines here were traced from 60-point Caslon and Futura Demibold alphabets.

own alphabets. Get the right stroke thicknesses. Put serifs where they belong. When lettering sans serif headlines, some students put serifs on the capital *I*. This is usually wrong. Typewriter typefaces may use serifs to give width to the *I*, and license-plate letters use serifs to help the police distinguish between *1* and *I*, but few sans serif typefaces come with serifs on any of the letters.

You should rule three guidelines for every line in the headline: a line for the top and for the bottom of the capitals and a line for the top of the x-height. You skip some space before ruling the next set; that skipped space is the interlinear channel. It can be a little bit less than the x-height if the type is to be set solid, or it can be considerably more if the type is leaded. But you must leave at least enough space for descending lowercase strokes. The x-height is usually a little more than half the cap-height space; but this depends, of course, upon the design of the face.

Rule your guidelines with a finely sharpened pencil. Rule them dark enough so you can see them without hunting for them but light enough so the reviewer of your work will not be conscious of them.

After you have arranged the spacing for the three guidelines and established the space for the interlinear channel, mark them on a small slip of paper and use that slip as your guide in marking the remaining lines in the headline.

You might want to rule a series of vertical lines to help keep your letters perfectly upright—or a series of slightly diagonal lines for italics. The beginning designer tends to make italics slant too drastically. The slant is minimal.

Six 36-point alphabets illustrating main type categories: (left page) old-style roman, transitional roman, modern roman; (right page) sans serif, slab serif, miscellaneous. Families represented: Garamond, Times Roman, Bodoni; News Gothic, Clarendon, Cooper Black. Notice that some 36-point faces look bigger than others (because of differences in boldness and in x-heights). Notice the differences in alphabet widths. Clarendon, classed here as slab serif, has some of the characteristics of a modern roman; Cooper Black (the grocery store type), classed here as miscellaneous, has some characteristics of old-style roman.

ABCDEFGHIJKLMNOPQRSTUVWXYZ
abcdefghijklmnopqrstuvwxyz
$1234567890 .,-:;!?"&

ABCDEFGHIJKLMNOPQRSTU
VWXYZ
abcdefghijklmnopqrstuvwxyz
$1234567890 .,-:;!?"&

ABCDEFGHIJKLMNOPQRSTUVWXYZ
abcdefghijklmnopqrstuvwxyz
$1234567890 .,-:;!?"&

ABCDEFGHIJKLMNOPQRSTUVWXYZ
abcdefghijklmnopqrstuvwxyz
$1234567890 .,-:;!?"&

ABCDEFGHIJKLMNOPQ
RSTUVWXYZ
abcdefghijklmnopqrstuvw
xyz
$1234567890 .,-:;!?'""&

ABCDEFGHIJKLMNOPQRS
TUVWXYZ
abcdefghijklmnopqrstuv
wxyz
$1234567890 .,-:;!?"'&

When you work with large letters—and you are not tracing—you can use a strip of heavy paper cut to the width of your letter strokes as a constant check on stroke width.

Optical spacing

In lettering large-size types you should be concerned more about optical than mechanical spacing. Allowances have to be made when parallel strokes fall next to each other and also when diagonal strokes running in opposite directions fall next to each other. Furthermore, certain letters should extend slightly over top and below bottom guidelines. The top of the *A,* for instance, and both the top and bottom of the *O.* Triangles and rounds of letters, in other words, should extend slightly beyond the guidelines.

And when aligning headlines vertically—when lines are flush left—you make some allowance for optical illusion. The left leg of the *A,* for instance, can protrude slightly from the vertical alignment of lines. Some designers like to let quote marks fall outside the vertical alignment, feeling that the true edge of the line begins with the letters themselves.

For quick newspaper jobs, you would not bother making adjustments; but for magazine ads you would ask for some handwork in setting headlines. Or you would ask for photolettering. Perhaps you would have the headlines hand lettered.

Observing letters

To understand where the thick and thin strokes fall in roman letters, you should try this exercise. Using a chisel-point pencil or, better, a Speedball pen in the "C" series, sketch out an alphabet of both capital and lowercase letters, first with the pen held at an angle, for old-style roman letters, then with the point held straight up, for modern roman letters. Remember, the angle is held constant, regardless of the stroke. (You may have to relax the angle somewhat when you make your M, N, U, and Z.)

The standard height of the capitals can be from five to ten times the width of the broad pen stroke (the boldness of the typeface would determine this).

When you have drawn the two roman alphabets in both upper and lower case, try a sans serif alphabet. This time, you will have to change the pen angle with each stroke, twisting the wrist to give each stroke the full width of the point.

In doing these exercises, be sure your pencil or pen rests firmly on the paper before you begin each stroke. Otherwise you will get only part of the instrument's point width.

When you get away from tracing the letters—when you draw them freehand—watch particularly the relationship of the stroke width to the height of the letters. And watch the width of each letter—widths vary a great deal from letter to letter and from face to face. (One notable exception is Century Schoolbook, with its near sameness in letter width—a little like the type on the typewriter.)

Watch, too, the counters (enclosed spaces in lowercase letters). It is too easy for the amateur to increase or decrease counter space, greatly altering the character of the letter.

In lettering italics, notice that italic caps are very much like the upright caps, only sloped, while lowercase italics are quite different from lowercase uprights.

Perhaps the best rule for the beginning letterer would be this: master two or three faces—no more at first. Learn these well. An old-style roman, a modern roman, a good medium-weight sans serif. They can meet almost

AT FIRST NATIONAL YOU DON'T HAVE TO BE A BIG SAVER TO EARN BIG INTEREST.

To make a word or name or phrase stand out in a headline, you do not need to underline it or set it in bigger type. You can simply push it out from the flush-left set of lines, as First National Bank of Oregon does here.

How long has it been since you said, "Let me speak to someone in charge," and she said, "Speaking"?

Because punctuation does not have the weight of regular letters, many designers leave it outside any axis they set up in arranging lines in a headline. See how it works in this flush-left headline for a Research Information Center ad.

WHEN SPORTS NEWS IS HOT, CALL A HOT REPORTER.

When you have a multiline headline, each line centered, it is a good idea to arrange words so that each line takes a different length; and the lengths should not grow progressively wider or narrower. Irregular lengths like these make for a more pleasing silhouette. Pacific Northwest Bell, in this all-caps headline for an ad promoting its Sportsphone, uses tight spacing not only between letters and words but also between lines. If each line carried more words, tight spacing like this might result in decreased readability.

all your needs. After you know them well, it will be time to add a face or two to your repertoire: like a condensed and an expanded sans serif.

You may be surprised as you compare faces in the same point size. They will not appear to be in the same size. One may have a small x-height, the other a large x-height; the baselines may even be on different levels, making for differences in the length of the descenders. Some faces come in what is called "titling" form: that is, only in caps, with the caps occupying nearly all of the available letter height. Such caps would be considerably larger than ordinary caps in the same point size.

A single face, in its various sizes—certainly in its various weights—changes character. For instance, as the size of the type gets smaller, the counter area increases in proportion to the size of the letter. Otherwise, in the very small sizes, it might be so small heavy inking would fill it in.

Some faces are designed to be wider than others. When you want to pad your copy block, you might well choose such a type—a much better practice than adding unnecessary words. Baskerville is a wider than average typeface. Some faces—the extended faces—carry width to an extreme. Others—the condensed faces—carry it to the other extreme.

For the love of letters

Try to imagine this:

Ed McMahon is sitting next to Johnny Carson, and Carson is showing off some of the ten thousand typefaces available from Photo-Lettering Inc., a New York typesetting house. There is Push Pin Myopic C, with letters vibrating before your eyes; Chwast Blimp, looking balloonlike; Neon, looking as though a fluorescent tube is running through it; Obese, with bottom-heavy letters; Jefferson Aeroplane, looking psychedelic. There are typefaces designed to look like paperclips, stars, flames, computer printouts, needlepoints, and so on. McMahon, as usual in this kind of skit, is overly impressed. "In that one type-specimen book you have *every single typeface* anybody ever thought of!"

"You are wrong, Newsprintbreath," Carson responds. "I have some typefaces here you can't find in that book."

And if he really had additional oddball faces to show, they might well have been conceived by Jeanine Holly, an advertising copywriter and sometimes artist. Holly is the typophile who discovered that Campbell's Condensed Alphabet Soup has only seventeen letters.

She wrote: "Several evenings ago, whilst entertaining myself with my favorite book, *The Design of Advertising,* I noted a few [typeface] omissions which your postperson and I humbly bring to your attention.

"I realize the ridiculousness of even attempting to include all types of types in your chapter, 'Working with Type.' One can only scratch the surface. . . .

"However, my recent dealings . . . have given me great insight into . . . all useful, if not essential, types. Most of these appear in your book. But I have enclosed a dozen . . . *not* in your text which I have found liturgically indispensable in my day-to-day contact[s]. . . ."

Some of Holly's types follow.

The first is Garabaldie. Its tie to Garamond is not pronounced. But if you are after a virile look in an advertising headline. . . .

The second is Pencilsharpener Electra, a typeface not likely to gain the wide acceptance as a body face that the original Electra enjoys. Even as a display face, some letters in Holly's version appear unplugged.

The third face, Noose Gothic, is not to be confused with News Gothic. The new face might fit well over an ad depicting the Wild West. Unfortunately the sample submitted does not show the treatment Holly has in mind for such hard-to-hang letters as *I, J, L, U, V,* and *Y.*

The fourth face is Five O'Clock Shadow Xtra Heavy. It is too bad that the face was not available to newspapers and magazines during the Nixon presidency.

Nor is Holly alone in her experimentation with typefaces and letterform. Dover Publications, New York, offers *Fantastic Alphabets,* twenty-four ready-to-use faces created by Jean Larcher, a good-humored French artist and designer. The example you see here is Crayon (French for "Pencil"), a face you might want to consider for the headline for an ad for office supplies.

When you do tire of the more normal faces, or when you find that phototypesetting systems cannot give you the distortion you want in those faces, you can turn to faces like those shown here. And to occupy yourself in those lonely hours after your Advertising Layout assignment has been turned in to your instructor, you might want to try to design a playful alphabet of your own.[6]

Letters have a fascination for many people in advertising and related businesses.

In a playful mood, Joshua Faigen of Downtown Type, Pittsburgh, worked up a "menu" of "type dinners." (All dinners included alphabet soup.) Among entrées:

Crunchy Caslon Cakes .... 12½ picas
   Delectibly kerned and served on a bed of tender boiled semicolons.
Stymie Stew .... 8 picas
   Delicious diphthongs and dot-leaders in a rich, justified broth.

You ought to have a good reason for arranging type in unnatural formations. In this case, the playfulness works, because the rounded corner of the headline imitates the rounded corner of the bus. Both the bus and the figures are abstracted, to give this ad a poster-feel. It ran in *Airtides,* the unofficial newspaper for personnel at McGuire Air Force Base, Pemberton, New Jersey. The headline might have worked better with punctuation or some other separation between "GAS" and "TRY."

The letters shown here were either drawn or doctored to make them say more than they normally would say. Taken from several advertisements.

A piece of art forms one of the letters for this ad for the Swiss National Tourist Office, Zurich, Switzerland. To emphasize height, the designer uses a condensed version of a typeface much like Cooper Black. The copy inside the map of Switzerland extends the theme: "There's a mountain of wonderful reasons why so many experienced travelers in Europe vacation in Switzerland."

Helvetica Cutlets with Asterisks .... 15½ picas
We'll gladly substitute Century Schoolbook Steaks for those who prefer serifs.

Supergraphics

The 1960s brought an interesting application of typography to interior and exterior building design. Partly to decorate and dramatize walls and partly to point people in the right direction, designers and letterform artists produced "supergraphics": huge letters and numbers, sometimes much larger than people-high. Supergraphics could be used to change completely the scale and form of hallways or staircases. And cheaply. All one needed was paint.

Vivid, pulsating, sometimes clashing colors formed words or individual letters and numbers. Viewed up close, supergraphics appeared to be nothing more than flat, geometric design. Farther away, they showed up as beautiful typography, usually of the Swiss gothic variety. Advertising had found another medium.

1. David Ogilvy, *Confessions of an Advertising Man* (New York: Atheneum, 1963).

2. Type scholars distinguish between the "newer" old-style letters of Caslon (English) and Garamond (French) and the older letters of the incunabula (Venetian), but such distinction is not necessary for our purposes.

3. Quoted in "Zapf on Tomorrow's Type," *Communication World,* November 1983, p. 20.

4. Ibid., p. 21.

5. Letter to the author from David A. Wesson, Milwaukee, Wisconsin, undated. Quoted by permission.

6. This segment appeared earlier in a slightly different form in the author's "The Look of the Book" column in *IABC News,* a publication of the International Association of Business Communicators. Reprinted by permission.

The Alleycats, a disco group in Hong Kong, uses the letters of its name to build an appropriate symbol.

8
Working with art

Creating an ad, you often plan the art before all else. What art you decide upon determines the content of the headline, the style of the type, the placement of the headline, what the body copy says, perhaps the size and shape of the ad.

In deciding an ad "picture first," you hunt for an existing picture and

build your ad around it. Or, better, you conceive a picture and then make arrangements to have it made.

Whether the art provides the ad's pivot or simply emphasizes a point made by the copy, its nature is crucial to the ad's effectiveness.

The illustration should have an obvious tie to the headline. And the headline should have an obvious tie to the copy. A single theme should unite all three.

". . . You are not right if, in your ad, you stand a man on his head just to get attention," said William Bernbach of Doyle Dane Bernbach. "But you are right if you have him on his head to show how your product keeps things from falling out of his pockets."

Often the best way to express an advertising idea is through visual analogy. The VW ad shown in this chapter sees a connection between a gas pump nozzle and a gun. Another ad example elsewhere in this book sees

(Left)
How to illustrate the headline, "Over-Regulation Could Cost You the Shirt Off Your Back"? The National Cotton Council, Memphis, used this nicely staged photograph. The unlikely combination of formal dress with bare arms and chests gives the photograph its impact. It occupied most of the space in full-page ads appearing in the *Atlantic, Saturday Review, Dun's Review,* and similar magazines. "You might never get to wear cotton again," the copy began. "Not if the government has its way. Because federal regulations are demanding that the air in cotton processing plants be cleaner than is technologically possible. . . ." The copy ended on this note: "We, in the cotton industry, think it's time to get more reason into regulation. For more information. . . ." The agency: Ward Archer & Associates.

Here a cartoon drawing by Charles Piccirillo of Doyle Dane Bernbach tells the story, helped along by a single line at the bottom. Robert Levenson was the copywriter. The ad captured the frustration a typical driver felt as gas became scarce in 1979. The value of the illustration lies in its ambiguity. Is it a gun? No, it is only a nozzle. Still. . . .

Or buy a Volkswagen.

an ink blot as an automobile. Another sees a phone as a rapid transit vehicle. A mountain in another ad becomes the letter A. A lowercase g in a logotype becomes a pair of scissors.

Most designers find it easier to present tangibles rather than intangibles. They can think of ways to show the product itself, the product in use, the procedure for using the product, a benefit resulting from use of the product, harm that comes from not using the product; but how can one show, in a picture, "Sincerity"? "Integrity"? "Economy"?

Symbolism may be the answer. For instance, to illustrate stress you can show an executive type (cropped, maybe, so a face doesn't have to show) sitting at a desk after having snapped a pencil in two (each hand holds half of the pencil). If you don't want to show a snapped pencil, you can show one that's been chewed on.

It is a mistake sometimes to exaggerate a condition to make a point. It may be better to understate. Gravity Guiding System, a product to control sagging bodies, in a magazine ad with the headline "Your Chest Doesn't Belong on Your Stomach," shows a man with a bulging stomach. But the stomach is barely bulging. The picture of an excessively bulging stomach might cause a reader to think: "I'm not that bad. This product is not for me." A slightly bulging stomach, on the other hand, would tend to make the reader think: "Gee. Mine is worse than that. If that one is bad, I'd better do something about mine."

The art for an ad can stand in for a headline—or part of a headline. In a full-page ad in *People,* Johnson & Johnson Dental Floss used this big-type headline: "One Alternative to Flossing Daily." The expected second sentence was missing. In its place was a photograph of false teeth in a glass of water.

The logic of art

As an art director you must be careful that you do not settle for a scene or camera angle just because it is convenient. It should be logical, too. Solarcaine antiseptic spray, in an ad headlined "The Sunday Sunburn," showed a family coming home from the beach obviously suffering from sunburn. As a bird's-eye view into an open convertible, the art showed clearly the suffering of the parents and the two children. But the reader might well have asked, "Why not put the top up to make some shade?"

Columbia Record & Tape Club under the headline "Imagine . . . One Boring Day When You Have Nothing to Do . . . 11 Great Tapes *or* Records Arrive in the Mail . . ." showed a photograph of a mailman at the door holding the records—and they were unwrapped so that all the covers showed. As if we do not have enough trouble these days with the Postal Service without putting up with nosey mailmen opening our packages for us.

Of course, artistic license sometimes takes precedence over logic in the art of advertising. In the record-club case, the headline spoke of an arrival. Maybe the unwrapped delivery better made the point than a wrapped delivery or a scene showing the recipient (should it have been a man or woman? and how old?) sitting in the living room admiring the albums.

The value of surprise

To make the point quickly and clearly, the art may combine elements that ordinarily don't go together, as when a store selling electric adjusting beds shows people sleeping or relaxing on bare mattresses. The store—and the manufacturer supplying the art—are more eager to show the thickness of the mattress and its texture and ticking than to show a more realistic scene.

To illustrate the headline "The New Blaupunkt ARI Car Stereo Gives

As an art-buyer would you have spotted the error in this drawing used in an ad sponsored by KRON-TV, San Francisco? Look closely. The postman, sitting where he is, cannot possibly see the screen on the TV set placed in the mailbox. The artist should have moved him to the left.

"... if all printers were determined not to print anything till they were sure it would offend nobody, there would be very little printed."
—Ben Franklin

COOPERATION

LABOR MANAGEMENT

THE NEXT
50
YEARS

Congratulations
PHILADELPHIA DAILY NEWS
on your **50**th **Anniversary**
**THIS MESSAGE SPONSORED BY THE
FOLLOWING PARTICIPATING TRADE UNIONS
AFL - CIO**

Laborer's Int'l. Union of North America
Int'l Union of Electrical, Radio & Machine Workers
Seafarers' Int'l Union
Int'l Brotherhood of Electrical Workers, Local 98
Amalgamated Clothing Workers of America Joint Board
United Brotherhood of Carpenters & Joiners of America District Council
United Transportation Union, Local 300
Transport Workers Union of America, Local 234
Graphic Arts Int'l Union, Local 3-C
Int'l Association of Machinists & Aerospace Workers, Lodge 1
Int'l Ladies Garment Workers Union Joint Board
Amalgamated Meat Cutters and Butcher Workmen of North America, Local 195
American Federation of State, County and Municipal Employees District Council 33
American Federation of Teachers, Local 3
Service Employees Int'l Union, Local 252
Hotel and Restaurant Employees' and Bartenders' Int'l Union, Local 301
Bakery and Confectionery Workers Int'l Union of America, Local 6
Retail Clerks Int'l Association, Local 1357
American Postal Workers Union, Phila. Branch

Advertising people are not noted for their mechanical ability or their sense of how machinery works. This three-gears ad probably seemed like a good idea to the creators at the time. But despite what the ad suggests, no amount of "COOPERATION" could possibly make these gears turn. The *Wall Street Journal* ran a similar piece of art for one of its media ads in the 1960s, receiving a number of letters as a result explaining that a set of gears like this was a mechanical impossibility. The next time the ad ran the gears were correctly assembled.

You a Slight Edge in Traffic," art director Rich Adkins of Ogilvy & Mather showed a car floating in the air over a traffic jam. To better show the jam, he directed the stripping in of some additional cars into an already crowded lineup.

In a trade magazine ad directed to restaurant owners, 3M showed a place setting and a dish with an inviting serving of a vegetable, a roll, and—a clump of used, rusty steel wool. The headline read: "One of the Ingredients in This Chef's Surprise Even Surprised the Chef." The copy began like this:

"Maybe it's happened in your kitchen.

"A wayward chunk from a metal pad clogs a drain, damages a garbage disposal, cuts your hand.

"Or startles a diner at table four. . . ."

The copy went on to discuss the merits of Scotch-Brite No. 88 nylon scouring pads.

The value of vagueness

Sometimes the client needs art that can be read in more than one way, with detail minimized or even hidden.

An example is the retailer conducting a clearance of, say, women's coats. The clearance involves various styles. The retailer does not want the customer coming in looking specifically for a coat that is pictured. In this situation an illustrator can overlap a group of coats, showing them at angles that do not highlight the cut of the collar or the slant of the pockets. The illustration can avoid showing coats in their entirety. It can overlap figures and allow accessories to obscure some of the details of the coats.

When the Advertising Council in 1976 came up with a raised-hand "Fair Campaign Pledge" symbol for the Fair Campaign Practices Committee, feminists complained that the boxlike hand was too masculine looking, and the Council redesigned it, slimming it and making the fingers longer. It became a hand that could belong to either sex.

In one of its ads, New Balance, a running shoe, shows only the ankles and shoes of a runner (why face the problem of deciding whether to show a man or woman runner and deciding what ethnic group the runner is to belong to?). The art is a painting rather than a photograph to show fists jutting up from the pavement to pound at the soles of the shoes. The headline reads: "When You Hit the Road, Does the Road Hit Back?" The shoes in this art are generic; detailed New Balances are shown below along with copy saying, at the end, that if you buy this brand "You'll hit your stride. Without getting hit back."

Pictures and the truth

Chapter 3 mentioned the ethical problems faced by the copywriter wrestling with word choices to sell the client's products. The art director working with pictures faces similar ethical problems, and in some respects they are more subtle and more persistent.

Because pictures can communicate more readily than words, they can also lie more effectively. And their lies are the more insidious because people tend to believe pictures where they would distrust words.

Picture lies seem more blatant in mail order than in other kinds of advertising. In their enthusiasm for their objective, the art director and the illustrator for a mail-order ad sometimes show the product with more glamour, more gloss than it actually has. The proof is in the customer's unwrapping.

More than ethics is involved in using pictures that lie either directly or indirectly. Increasingly it is a matter of legality. Advertisers who use de-

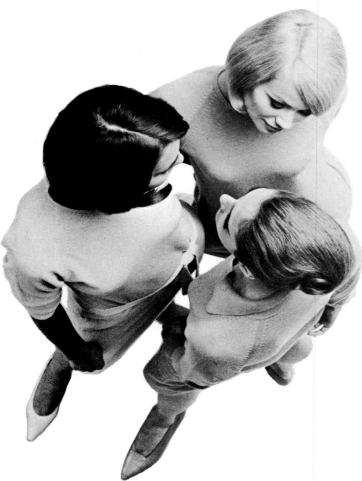

What IBM wanted to show in this ad prepared by Ogilvy, Benson & Mather (now Ogilvy & Mather) was Speed! The accompanying copy discussed the rapidity with which the company's computer systems worked, especially the one employed at the scene of the 1964 Olympics competition at Tokyo.

To emphasize the fact that the blondes, brunettes, and redheads who read *TV Guide* were younger than the women who read the general-circulation magazines (you will find "fewer heads tinged with silver among *TV Guide* readers"), the art director, for an ad meant to reach advertising media buyers, used this photo with its unusual vantage point. That women in this ad were classified by hair color made concentrating on the hair by photographer Harold Krieger entirely reasonable.

"Has the toast of Chicago had too much marmalade?" asked *a Chicago Sun-Times/Chicago Daily News* full-page ad in the advertising trade press when both papers were still alive. "Sad about that old star. She used to be such a paper doll. Now she puffs a lot. Performs mostly for older audiences—who remember her when. Times have changed. You've got to see the new talent in town. The Sun Times and Daily News combination." The media buyers for agencies, readers of the ad, understood full well the *Sun-Times/Daily News* was making a case against the competition, a Chicago institution called the *Chicago Tribune*.

ceptive pictures are finding themselves challenged by consumers and consumer groups. Retailers with art only closely resembling merchandise for sale are careful to include the line "Similar to Illustration."

What to watch for in pictures

Photograph or drawing or painting, the picture you choose to use is subject to the same principles of design the ad itself is. The good advertising picture is the well-designed picture. Composition of the picture is much more important than the medium the artist used.

Photographer Barry O'Rourke used a special lens to dramatize the perspective, and he shot from a worm's-eye angle to make these books look like massive Greek columns. Cropping at the sides and bottom added to the illusion. The art was part of a "Let These 3 Wise Men Into Your Home" ad of The Classics Club, Roslyn, N.Y. The agency was Schwab, Beatty & Porter.

Hertz used this art to dramatize its "pay-nothing-per-mile" rates for persons who want to do long-distance driving. Put together from two separate photographs and retouched at the center where the photographs meet, the art said "distance" in a most unusual way. The agency was Carl Ally Inc. (© Hertz System, Inc., 1972).

Sometimes the designer purposely plans a picture with a composition defect: too much neutral foreground or background. But the designer has a purpose: to use this area for surprinting or reversing some type. With tone all around, the ad holds together remarkably well.

Always important is the size of the art. Obviously, the larger a photograph or illustration, the more impact it will have.

Sometimes important is scale within the picture. If you want to show size, you will have to include in your picture something the reader can use to measure your primary subject, something to compare it with. A picture of rolling hills and a picture of something under a microscope can look the same in photography.

This illustration accompanied a headline that said: ''Is Small-Town America Really Disappearing? Not if 59,360 of Us Can Help It.'' The point of the ad, an institutional one, was to show that International Telephone and Telegraph Corporation was interested in small towns; a large percentage of its employees lived and worked in them. To get the effect of a small town ''disappearing,'' art director Laurance Waxberg first had a black-and-white print made from a 35-mm. color transparency, then had the print airbrushed around the edges, then had a line-conversion made of the art (with a circular-line screen). Photographer: Ward Allen Howe. Agency: Needham, Harper & Steers.

The variety of renderings

The beginning designer has a tendency to think of only two kinds of art in advertising: photographs and simple line drawings. You should realize that the variety of forms is much broader than that.

Among the kinds of art for halftone reproduction are photographs, oil or acrylic paintings, paintings in tempera or designers' colors, watercolor paintings, wash drawings, pastel or pencil drawings. Among the kinds of art for line reproduction are simple black-and-white line drawings, cross-hatch drawings, line drawings with Ben Day, scratchboard drawings, grease-crayon drawings, dry-brush drawings, line prints made from continuous-tone artwork.

Even the artist forgets about some of these. The designer then occasionally suggests to the artist a desired new treatment.

Most art is submitted to the printer larger than it will appear in print. But try this sometime: Ask your artist to do the drawing much smaller

A photograph could not possibly offer everything this painting by Carl R. Lauersen offers. The detail of the ships or barges off there in the distance is as clear as the detail of the buildings in the foreground. Such a wide range of detail was necessary because there was a complicated story to tell, and words alone could not do it. The art was one of two Lauersen full-color paintings (he used designers' colors) carried in a brochure published by the Portland Portable Port Company.

For minute detail, it is hard to beat scratchboard art. This piece was done for Phaelzer Brothers, Inc., Chicago, for use in advertising its prime filets.

than it is to appear. When it is blown up by the cameraman, it will look massive, crude, and really quite imposing. Or encourage your artist to use a makeshift tool, like a match stick dipped in ink and drawn across a sheet of blotter paper.

For her full-color fashion illustrations, Jean Ening has resorted to collages made from colored tissue paper. And when she cannot find paper with subtle enough colors, she "dyes" her paper by mixing watercolors and dipping the paper into the solutions.

A good way to show a newspaper clipping in an ad is to run a gray tint block over it. The clipping can be tilted, to make it look more natural, and its edge can be torn rather than neatly clipped. Make sure the tint block is light enough so that the small type can be easily read.

Do not attempt to construct such art by putting a piece of Zipatone over a clipping. That might result in a patched look. And the screen may not be fine enough. Instead, give the printer a separate piece of art, all black, and let him screen it as he photographs it and combines it with the negative of the type in making the plate.

The advertising medium affects your choice of art rendering. Designing an ad for the Yellow Pages, for instance, you would stick to line art. If you use a Ben Day screen, it would be rather coarse because printing of the Yellow Pages is high speed and the paper is lightweight. The medium asks you to avoid black areas because of show-through.

You should collect as many examples of renderings as you can and refer to them as you work on the picture phase of your advertisement. Learn

Lars Bourne, an artist in the advertising department of the *San Jose Mercury-News,* uses brush and ink for the outlines and grease crayon on rough-textured paper for the shading in this drawing done for a poster advertising bluegrass music (a sideline interest of Bourne's).

With pen shading of fine lines and crosshatching, line art can give the effect of tone. Union Pacific Railroad used this art for an institutional newspaper ad telling readers that the line is ''a vital link in speeding . . . perishables to distant markets. . . . These fruits are delivered to consumers in 'Orchard Fresh' condition.''

to imitate them on your layout pad. Experiment with your various tools to see which comes closest to approximating the kind of art you will use in your ad.

Art styles

The history of art records many movements in which groups of artists rebelled against current practices. The Postimpressionists rebelled against the objectivity and the "moment in time" nature of the Impressionists. The Expressionists brought emotion and strong personal responses into painting. The Fauves ("wild beasts"), who came along at the beginning of this century (see the work of Henri Matisse, André Derain, Maurice de Vlaminck, and Raoull Dufy), produced hectic but decorative canvases with vigorous color and broad, free strokes.

The following list of currently used art styles is offered to alert you to

A line drawing like this, made by the author with a fountain pen, takes line reproduction and prints well on any kind of paper from any printing process.

the existence of one or two you may not be aware of or have forgotten. It deals more with illustration than photography, because illustration is easier to categorize. It does not pretend to be exhaustive. Some styles simply defy categorization. Please bear in mind, too, that it is impossible for a list like this to avoid overlapping.

1. *Tight art.* Art that is smooth, polished, precise. It is carefully executed. There are no imperfections, but the artist may distort certain art truths, such as perspective. At worst, the art may seem painfully contrived. Often it has a flat, patterned quality.

2. *Loose art.* It moves along effortlessly. It may be crude and imperfect. Lines are probably done with brush rather than pen; solid areas are put there with broad strokes. If color is there, it is not in register. The art looks as though it may have been executed hastily, though in truth it may have taken as much time as a piece of tight art.

3. *Abstract art.* Simplified art, reduced to fundamental forms. If it has meaning, the meaning is subtle. It may carry different meanings to different viewers. The viewer's reaction to it is likely to be more emotional than intellectual, although it is defended and presumably appreciated more by intellectuals than nonintellectuals. Its opposite is realistic art.

4. *Realistic art.* Also called "representational art." Highly detailed, it leaves little to the imagination. It shows all the pores. It comes in a number of forms: sentimental-realistic (as in the early Norman Rockwell paintings), starkly realistic (to shock or disgust), surrealistic (to intrigue). There are many degrees of realism, including the recent superrealism that magnifies to the point of distortion.

5. *Cartoon art.* Art that exaggerates or that amuses. Cartoons can be executed in any medium, including oils, but they are most often produced in pen and ink or in washes (black watercolor). Comic-strip artists and gag cartoonists who have built reputations on the news/editorial side of publications are often enlisted to do cartoons for advertisers. We could come up with a list-within-a-list of cartoon styles.

6. *Painterly art.* Art that makes no attempt to hide its technique. The brush strokes are there for all to see and appreciate. The appreciation is likely to come from other artists rather than the general public. In watercolor paintings, the painting is done on smooth paper not meant to take the medium, causing a sort of water-on-oilcloth look. In line art, the rough pencil lines under the inked lines are not removed. This category would also include the kind of sketches done for rough layouts or comps and deemed good enough to use as finished art.

7. *Calligraphic art.* Line drawings executed in carefully controlled thick and thin lines.

8. *Shadow art.* Bold drawings with areas expressed by shadows, not outlines. Some edges are not defined. Milton Caniff provides an example of the style in *Steve Canyon*.

The photoengraver or offset cameraman has almost put the shadow artist out of business. The cameraman can get a strong shadow effect by

These two illustrations taken from *Enterprise,* the journal of the National Association of Manufacturers, show the difference between realism and abstraction. The art at the left is a carefully done pen-and-ink drawing, faithful to detail. The art at the right, also carefully done, eliminates most detail, concentrates on the most dramatic part of the building, and takes on a single tone and geometric proportions. Yet both pieces of art say "Capitol" or, as NAM uses them, "Washington."

An artist for Dynamics, Inc., uses brush and ink to execute this stock cartoon art, meant to be used to illustrate a sidewalk sale. The cartoon style allows for an interesting lineup of characters. Solid blacks and some strong drawn pattern add strength to the drawing.

Mexicana Airlines uses bold, stylized, almost abstract art in this newspaper ad to show that exotic cities in Mexico are "just a few steps away." The horizontal look of the ad is achieved through the art, the stretched out two-line headline, the wide subheadline, and the four shallow columns of type. All of which matches the horizontal logo drawn in unique all caps. The art director was John Coll. Designers were John Scott MacDaniels and John Coll. MacDaniels also wrote the copy. The agency was Dailey & Associates, San Francisco.

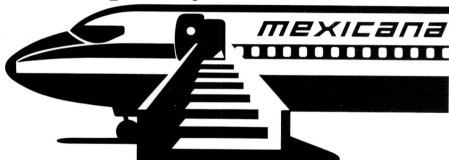

This is not an ad from the 1930s. It is an ad from the 1970s, showing how a style can be revived to do a selling job forty years after it dies out. The style is Art Deco. The medium used for the illustration is airbrush. Client: TWTF Restaurant Group. Agency: Warwick, Welsh & Miller. Art director: Ken Barre. Illustrator: Peter Palombi. Copywriter: Bob Skollar.

handling a photograph as though it were a piece of line art, photographing it without a screen and dropping all the middle tones.

9. *Silhouette art*. The artist reduces figures, faces, or props to solid, usually black, shapes. Silhouettes are in reality filled-in outlines that stand out against a light or white background; although the light and dark can be reversed.

A photograph of a figure or object with the background opaqued out would qualify as a silhouette.

10. *Op art*. Geometric art that capitalizes on optical illusions. It causes eye vibrations. It is a good attention getter, but its message is limited. It was popular for a time in the 1960s, but it is used only rarely now.

11. *Pop art*. Another has-been, although vestiges of it appear in some of the "now" art. It created quite a stir in the 1960s both as a fine arts movement and a style for advertising illustration. Essentially it is an application of the comic-strip style (adventure strip division) to the higher arts. Lots of blown-up Ben Day pattern. Balloons with conversation in them are big in pop art. It professes to see beauty in the mundane and banal. Or is it critical of them? Pop art is part of the "camp" picture.

12. *Psychedelic art*. Art said to be inspired by the drug culture. Containing swirls of improbable colors, it is decorative and contorted, a precursor of funky art.

13. *Art nouveau*. Art made from sinuous, graceful, decorative, curving lines in the manner of Aubrey Beardsley. Sometimes the lines are combined with areas of solid black or color. Pattern is important.

Art nouveau appeared originally in the late 1800s in the architecture of a building erected in Brussels. Beardsley was not the only artist to embrace art nouveau. Edvard Munch, the pessimistic Norwegian painter and lithographer, used it, for instance, in his *The Cry* (1893), and so did Paul Gauguin in his paintings.

14. *Art deco*. The look of the 1920s and 1930s has recently been revived. It offers sets of lines or stripes, rounded corners, geometric shapes, pastel colors, and rainbow motifs. The "deco" stands for "decoration." It is related to "camp" art.

Much of the work that comes out of the influential and prestigious Push Pin Studios in New York is art deco. A leading art deco illustrator (although the term does not adequately cover his versatility) is Milton Glaser.

His widely imitated style is flat, decorative; everything is done in consistent and persistent outline, even the shadows. Design seems more important than draftsmanship.

15. *"Camp" art.* It is so bad, corny, or low-brow that it is good. It takes on charm of its own. Rather than fight popular culture, it embraces it. It finds beauty in ugliness. It is part of the nostalgia kick we seem to be on. In an extreme form, it is "high camp."

16. *"Funky" art.* Inspired by the underground press and underground comic books (comix), funky art is characterized by much detail, rendered in fine line and crosshatching or, at the opposite extreme, airbrushing. A leading figure in the movement is Robert Crumb, a cartoonist.

Funky art is often vulgar, eclectic, and amateurish. Its practitioners say its lack of slickness attests to its "honesty."

17. *The montage.* A set of separate sketches are drawn or put together in a single unit. Or a set of photographs can be used. The pieces can butt up against each other, they can merge into each other, or they can overlap. Techniques involved in producing the various pieces can be the same or they can be wildly dissimilar. When the resulting art moves from the representational to the abstract, it is usually called a "collage."

Commercial art versus fine art

Commercial art smarts under unfair attacks by purists. The line these attackers like to draw between commercial and fine art looks very thin indeed as one studies closely the fine paintings and drawings that go into many of our advertisements.

"In this day and age," said Tomi Ungerer, a painter and widely admired offbeat cartoonist for advertisers, "it's ridiculous to make any differentiation between commercial and fine art. But if it has to be made, I

In this *New York Times Magazine* ad, the Dupont Plaza hotel in Washington, D.C., uses a *New Yorker* cartoonist, Robert Weber, to illustrate the point that people at other hotels have trouble checking out. At the Dupont Plaza you "Just drop your key at the desk" and you are "on your way. No tears. We'll bill you later." The various types of people in this other hotel's checkout line are worth studying. The cartoon approach is an ideal one to use in this kind of a presentation. Len Zimmelman art directed this ad; Carolanne Ely wrote the copy. The agency was Keye/Donna/Pearlstein.

Does your hotel have a hard time saying goodbye?

Not us. Just drop your key at the desk and be on your way. No tears. We'll bill you later.

And, if you need extra attention, or extra privacy, you've got it.

Come to the Dupont Plaza. We're right on Dupont Circle. Near the embassies, near the Phillips Collection and Georgetown. Near all the Washington you came to see.

If you'd like a little extra Washington the next time you come to town, come to the Dupont Plaza.

DUPONT PLAZA
Washington

Connecticut & Massachusetts Avenues,
N.W., Washington, D.C. 20036 • Tel. (202) 483-6000,
Toll Free (800) 421-6662

A Hotel Systems **hsi**
International Service

Pop art exercised an influence on advertising in the 1960s and 1970s. Robert Hagel was the art director for this ad prepared by McCann-Erickson for the Association of American Railroads. Barry Geller was the illustrator.

One of the best sources of stock art for advertising is Dover Publications, New York, with its *Pictorial Archives* series of books. The art in these books is in the public domain. Here are some pieces from *Chinese Cut-Paper Designs,* selected by Theodore Menten, published by Dover in 1975.

would put myself on the side of commercial art. Fine art has no function in society any longer. It lacks social meaning and is limited to museums and rich collectors. Stylistically, it is further limited. . . ."[1]

Perhaps Ungerer overstated it. But this much is certain: the challenge commercial artists face, as they set out to create an agreed-upon effect, is every bit as great as the challenge easel artists face as they pick up paints and brushes and wonder what wonderful accidents will happen to the canvas this time.

Stock art

When clients cannot afford original art or when it is not available, they have access to the work of the clip-sheet services. Clip-sheet art, consisting of drawings of every imaginable product and situation, comes on slick-paper stock ready to cut out and paste into place for the printer's cameraman. Volk and Dynamic Graphics are among the better-known clip-sheet houses.

In recent years clip art has gotten away from cuteness and predictability and has become more sophisticated and useful. All kinds of drawing and rendering techniques are used. All kinds of subjects are treated.

Lots of the art comes as prescreened halftones (shot with a 120-line screen). You paste this art down directly onto the mechanical, and the printer treats it as though it were line art (which it is). You can also find prescreened separations for four-color art.

Stock drawings are also available from a number of sources that have gathered together art in the public domain (no longer protected by copyright) and made it available in books which can be used as clip books. The only cost is the cost of the books themselves, which is minimal. A designer with a talent for drawing can add to or subtract from these drawings and combine them to make new drawings. Dover Publications, New York, is probably the biggest source. Its "Pictorial Archives Catalogue" lists scores of books, including the two-volume *Handbook of Early Advertising Art* and *293 Renaissance Woodcuts for Artists and Illustrators.* Art Direction Book Company, New York, offers a series of four looseleaf *Ron Yablon Graphic Archives* books.

One of the suppliers of dry-transfer letters, Letraset, also supplies dry-transfer stock art: small pieces, useful especially in direct-mail advertising.

THIS MAN IS WEARING GREY FLANNEL.
GREY FLANNEL.
GEOFFREY BEENE'S COLOGNE FOR MEN.
IT'S GOT STYLE.

This is a full-frame print showing the negative edge. Grey Flannel reverses its message in one corner of the print and reverses the name of a store on the frame. It is an unusual ad in several respects. There is no headline (unless you count the all-caps copy block as a headline). And you do not see the product. You only sense that the handsome man is wearing it. (The copy tells you so.) The ad occupied a full black-and-white page in the *New Yorker*.

"We believe that the sensuous texture of our fine kid suede with its rich smoky color, lizard trim, and the peerless Italian crafting we bring to all our designs, allows this beautiful duo to speak for itself," says the copy for this headlineless ad which appeared in *Harper's Bazaar* and *Vogue*. Creating the how-was-it-done? art was easy enough: the merchandise was laid against a flat surface and photographed from above. The agency: Trahey/Rogers, New York. Designer: Peter Rogers.

Stock photographs and old prints are available on a one-time-use basis from dozens of organizations, located principally in New York. R. R. Bowker Company lists these organizations in each year's issue of *Literary Market Place*. The annual *Writer's Market* carries a list, too. Charges for stock photographs are based on size of the advertiser and use to which the picture is put. A disadvantage, as with all stock art, is that other advertisers may use the same illustration.

The coming of photography

It was the talk of Paris in 1839. Louis Jacques Mandé Daguerre had found a way to record and fix an image on a silver plate. An early application to advertising can be found in an 1853 *New York Daily Tribune* ad, signed by a hatter, offering to every hat purchaser a free daguerrotype that, placed in the hat liner, would be "a great convenience in indicating one's own hat."[2]

What was to revolutionize advertising was the application of the principle of photography to the art of engraving. No more woodcuts or hand-cuttings on steel. In 1880 the *New York Graphic* ran its first crude halftone. Advertisers were quick to appropriate the new picture-reproduction process.

To come later was the use of the photograph itself to advertise. The

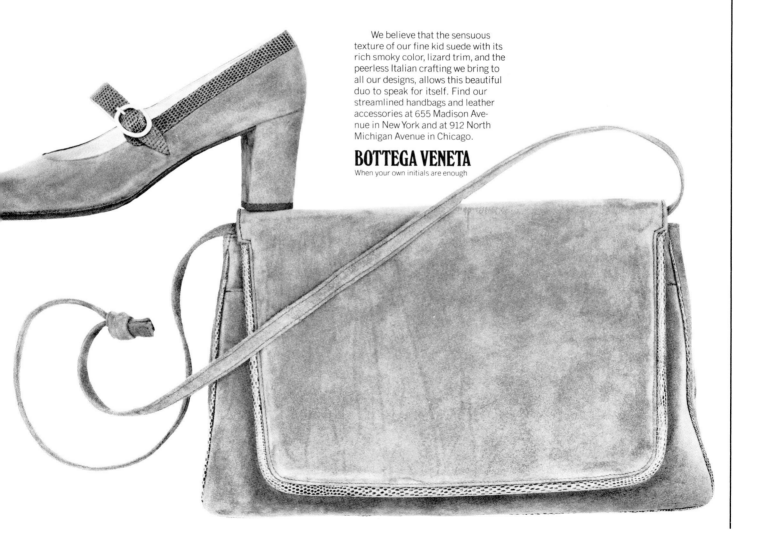

We believe that the sensuous texture of our fine kid suede with its rich smoky color, lizard trim, and the peerless Italian crafting we bring to all our designs, allows this beautiful duo to speak for itself. Find our streamlined handbags and leather accessories at 655 Madison Avenue in New York and at 912 North Michigan Avenue in Chicago.

BOTTEGA VENETA
When your own initials are enough

ARE YOU IN THE MARKET FOR A HARDTOP?

Every Volvo has six steel pillars holding up the roof. Each one is strong enough to support the weight of the entire car.

Of course, this kind of strength isn't built into a Volvo just so it will hold up a lot of cars.

Volvos are built strong so they'll hold up a lot of years. Exactly how many we can't guarantee. But we do know that in Sweden Volvos are driven an average of eleven years.

Are you sure you're in the market for a hardtop? Or is what you really want a hard top?

In Paris, the Givenchy mannequins are wearing his latest

To make everything go together, he designed Plus One, a sunlit summer lipstick to wear with his new colors in fashion. And what Givenchy calls fashion, the world does too. Now. Try it with a melon chiffon embroidered with pearls, a yellow gown with a shoulder bared, a peach dress belted, a buttonless green coat, a sandy silk wrap and a smile on your face. In the golden bamboo case $5 or the lipstick egg $6. Nail Gloss Plus One is the first new lipstick color of the year from the Givenchy Collection of Cosmetics.

Skillful camera work by Melvin Sokolsky for Givenchy Cosmetics emphasizes four sets of lips without showing other facial features not important to the ad. Note the interesting space divisions. This is truly a designed photograph. Art director was Peter Hirsch for Delehanty, Kurnit & Geller, Inc., Advertising.

Volvo in this ad follows a good advertising principle: don't just say it, *show* it. The reader quickly gets the impression that if the Volvo hardtop on the bottom can stand the weight of all those other Volvo hardtops, the car does indeed have a sturdy roof. This is a real photograph, not a composite. There was no retouching. The picture was taken by a camera in a sling held by an eighty-foot derrick. The agency was Scali, McCabe, Sloves.

drawn or painted illustration now reproduced through the marvel of photochemistry remained king until well into the twentieth century.

The development of the 35mm camera in 1925 made picturetaking, anywhere, easy and informal. And in the twenties the Bauhaus in Germany began its experiments with abstract photography. Then came color in the 1930s.

Photography gradually moved in on advertising. As it became more realistic, painters and illustrators, beaten at their own game, veered in an opposite direction. Nowadays, with photographers doing abstractions and

The private trains are ready.

Come aboard. Take a Four Winds 16 to 23-day Private Train Tour around the U.S.A., Mexico and Canada. You travel in your own air-conditioned Pullman streamliner, with private deluxe lounge cars. You stop over and stay at luxury hotels and resorts en route. And your private train is always there, spruced up and ready for the next exciting leg of your journey. Sightseeing everywhere. Fiestas. Parties. Fully-escorted. Great meals. Depart New York, Newark or Philadelphia. From $685, including most everything.

16 days through Mexico and the Southwest. Depart from New York, see Washington, New Orleans, San Antonio, Mexico City, Acapulco, Cuernavaca, Taxco, Monterrey, Laredo, Houston, Chicago, and return to New York. Includes 8 nights in luxury hotels. From $685, all inclusive. Departures June 12, July 10, Aug. 7, Sept. 11, Sept. 25, Dec. 18. 1966—Jan. 15, Jan. 29, Feb. 12, Feb. 26, Mar. 12.

17 days of the best of the Far West. Depart from New York, see Chicago, Zion National Park, Bryce Canyon National Park, Las Vegas, Boulder Dam, Los Angeles, Hollywood, Beverly Hills, Disneyland, Yosemite, San Francisco, Carmel, Monterey, Denver, Colorado Springs, Chicago, and return to New York. Includes 7 nights in luxury hotels. From $875, all inclusive. Departures June 18, July 2, July 16, July 30, Aug. 13, Aug. 27, Sept. 10.

23 days through Pacific Far West and Canadian Rockies. Depart from New York, see Chicago, Yellowstone National Park, Grand Teton, Glacier Park, Portland, Seattle, Victoria, Vancouver, Lake Louise, Banff, Calgary, Winnipeg, Great Lakes, Toronto, Niagara Falls, Buffalo, and return to New York. Includes 13 nights in luxury hotels. From $1095, all inclusive. Departures June 12, June 26, July 10, July 24, Aug. 7, Aug. 21.

23 days around the U.S.A. and Mexico. Depart from New York, see Washington, New Orleans, San Antonio, The Alamo, Mexico City, Cuernavaca, Taxco, Juarez, El Paso, Phoenix, Grand Canyon, Los Angeles, Hollywood, Disneyland, Yosemite, Carmel, Monterey, San Francisco, Denver, Colorado Springs, Chicago, and return to New York. Includes 11 nights in luxury hotels. From $1095, all inclusive. Departures June 12, July 10, Aug. 7, Sept. 11, Sept. 25, Oct. 9, Nov. 20, Dec. 18. 1966—Jan. 15, Jan. 29, Feb. 12, Feb. 26, Mar. 12.

17 days through the Far West and Canadian Rockies. Depart from New York, see Chicago, Glacier National Park, Seattle, Victoria, Vancouver, Puget Sound, Banff, Columbia Icefields, Lake Louise, Emerald Lake, Winnipeg, Great Lakes, Toronto, Niagara Falls, and return to New York. Includes 8 nights in luxury hotels. From $875, all inclusive. Departures June 18, July 2, July 16, July 30, Aug. 13, Aug. 27.

For reservations and additional information about Four Winds Private Train Tours, see your travel agent or call or write:

Four Winds Travel, Inc., Dept. 00
175 Fifth Avenue
New York N.Y. 10010
Phone: SP 7-0260

Please send me my free copy of your Americana Rail Cruise brochure fully describing the Private Train Tours.

Name_____

Address_____

City_____State_____

Phone_____

FOUR WINDS/PRIVATE TRAIN TOURS OF AMERICA

Art director Steve Kambanis for De Garmo Inc., got a lot of mileage out of a single piece of artwork for this good-looking Four Winds ad (which appeared in 1965 in the *New York Times*). For size variety, he simply used different cropping for each print. Lee Martin was the Four Winds advertising director.

signing their work, no wonder the poor advertising illustrators feel frustrated!

The big advantage of photography, of course, lies in its *believability*. The camera can lie as much as—more than—words, but the consumer will not believe that.

Speed provides a further advantage. A photographer in a single day can deliver to the advertising designer a couple of dozen shots, in contact form; the client can pick a favorite and have an 8″ × 10″ glossy print in a matter of hours.

In a media ad in *Advertising Age*, *Forbes* magazine, which likes to call itself a "Capitalist Tool," used this worm's-eye-view photograph to illustrate the headline, "The Action Doesn't Begin Until the Quarterback Calls the Play." "The men who call the plays are the men who start the action," the ad copy begins. "In boardrooms just as on gridirons. So if your advertising hasn't been getting the yardage you want, it may not be reaching the executives who are in charge of the ballgame." The copy goes on to discuss *Forbes* readers and their prominence in the business world. "More officers in the headquarters of the 500 largest industrial companies read FORBES regularly than any other magazine." Jon Foraste is the photographer, Robert Fearon the art director. Doremus & Co. is the agency.

American Telephone and Telegraph Company uses a full-page photograph of a crowded city street, shot from a high building, to dramatize the fact that "Right now, nearly half your salesmen's time is spent just getting to appointments." The solution, says a two-page ad in magazines read by businessmen: a new AT&T program called "Phone Power," whose purpose is to train salesmen in the art of selling by telephone. The agency was N W Ayer & Son, Inc.

Then there is the *flexibility* of pictures. They can be cropped to any size or shape and retouched with brush or airbrush or otherwise doctored to create a desired effect.

Finally, *price* must be considered. Although a good photographer might charge anywhere from $100 to $3,000 for an assignment, some photographers come cheaper; and for routine jobs, when you compare the rates for photographs with rates for artwork, artwork often suffers.

Some photographers need a lot of guidance; others are more creative. But you should have an idea in mind before you turn to any photographer.

Lou Dorfsman, creative director at CBS, says that if, as art director, you cannot explain your idea over the phone to your photographer, your idea is not thought out well enough. You are not ready for photography.

It is not necessary to appear on location passing out suggestions. "Allow photographers the opportunity to use their talented eyes, their good taste, their design and color sense as well as their technical skills," said David Deutsch, president of David Deutsch Associates, New York.

And do not stop there, Deutsch advises. Be willing to accept the ideas photographers offer. One of Deutsch's most successful ads for a client, Oneida stainless and giftware, showed a just-hatched chick alongside a spoon and bowl of eggs. The chick was the idea of photographer George Ratkai.[3]

Model releases

An illustration has an advantage over a photograph in that the illustrator or advertising agency does not need a model's release. When a photograph is used and it shows clearly a real person, that person's permission must be solicited before the photograph is published. A release does not have to be secured if the photograph is to be used for news purposes, but permission is always required in advertising. Without it, the agency or client faces the possibility of a suit for invasion of privacy. And the permission must spell out the specific use to which the photo will be put.

An agency in a small town learned this the hard way. One picture of a woman taken for a store catering to "queen size" women turned out to be just what the agency wanted for a reducing-academy client. The woman, looking well fed, was trying to get into a pair of pants. The ad carried the headline, " 'I Must Lose Weight.' " The model promptly sued the agency, charging that such publication damaged her reputation and caused her embarrassment and humiliation.

You can bet that the toast-of-Chicago dancer shown in this chapter had the uses of her picture spelled out to her before the paper went ahead with its ad. The *Hustler* man, shown in a later chapter, knew what was going on, too.

Advertising agencies have their own forms for model releases. The photographer takes the responsibility for having them signed. Standard model release forms are also available from camera stores. A fee for the model, real or token, is involved.

When an agency buys a photograph from a photographer, it usually buys one-time rights. Prices vary, but generally photographers expect to get more for advertising photography than for editorial photography. Photographers base their rates on time spent on the jobs, uses to be made of the photos, and their own reputations.

Amateurism in art

An advantage photography has over illustration is that in photography amateurism is harder to detect. We have cameras now that are virtually foolproof. Not that everything they produce is art. It still takes a great artist to be a great photographer. But from the standpoint of clarity and polish, you are more likely to get a usable piece of art from an amateur photographer than from an amateur illustrator.

One of the unfortunate aftermaths of the creative revolution of the 1960s was the feeling, still somewhat prevalent, that anybody can do it. We have long suffered retailers appearing on the TV screen doing their own extolling of the "preowned" cars or other merchandise they are selling. Now we have clients doing their own artwork. A dreadful example is Joan Baez's lettering and art for her "David's Album." The anti-intellectualism of the 1960s and 1970s has made an impact on graphic arts just as it has on the political, educational, and publishing establishments.

We can thank the underground press for a lot of this. The impact it has made on advertising typography and art is considerable. Not all the influence has been bad. Much of the art has been refreshing. But "funky" art is good only when it is executed by persons of talent. Amateurism is still amateurism. It is almost a sure bet that an art style that looks easy is actually very difficult to emulate.

Small, local advertisers without access to professional or stock art should explore the many possibilities of art-free advertising before settling for work prepared by amateurs.

Editing pictures

This is the day of magnified detail. Designers prefer photographs cropped close. They eliminate detail that does not contribute to the ad's message. Failing to get exactly what they want from the photographer, designers doctor photographs—crop, retouch, or otherwise alter them.

For pictures, like copy, can be edited.

Not liking its direction, a designer can decide to "flop" a picture (if the head is facing to the right, have it face left) simply by marking it "flop" in instructions to the printer. (The printer has merely to turn the negative over from its usual position when making the plate.) But the designer, before requesting this, should make sure the subject does not have a part in his hair (which would come out on the wrong side), or is not wearing a double-breasted suit (the buttons would be on the wrong side), or is not standing in front of a sign (the letters would be backward). The designer

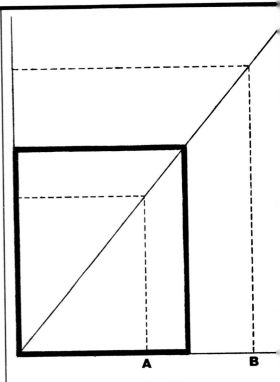

The diagonal method of changing a picture size on your layout involves putting a transparent sheet over the art (represented here by the heavy box) and, being careful not to press into the art, drawing a vertical line at its left edge and a horizontal line at its bottom and a diagonal line from the left bottom corner to the right top corner and beyond. Measure off the width you want along that bottom line and send up a new vertical. You can create a size for a narrow version of the art (say at *A*) or a wider version (at *B*). Either will be in correct proportion to the original.

should turn the picture over and look at it through a light table or up against a window to check such details.

But saying that editing of pictures is possible is not saying that editing is always or even frequently necessary.

Sometimes a piece of *line* art needs retouching. Maybe it is a piece that has already been reproduced; you want to reprint it in an ad, and you do not have access to the original. Part of the reproduction is faint. Some of the lines must be strengthened. But the piece is small, leaving you little room to maneuver in. The thing to do is to make a blowup copy, do your touching up on that, and then have the printer reduce it to the right size.

Cropping

Sometimes you can give a photograph more impact by "cropping" it— trimming away some of the detail. Perhaps you feel you can improve its composition. Perhaps you feel you can make it clearer.

Sometimes you would crop part of a figure out of a photograph in order to focus attention on an item of apparel. To sell a dress, for instance, you do not want the reader to squander attention on shoes, or the hairdo. When the art is a drawing rather than a photograph, the illustrator can render the garment in detail and tone, and permit the remainder of the drawing to fade or to appear in rough, weak outline.

In changing the dimensions of a picture you must settle arbitrarily on three different measurements, then figure out what the fourth will be. The four measurements are the width and depth of the original art and the width and depth of the art in its printed version.

You may start by picking a width and depth on the original. Then you will decide on either the width or the depth of the printed version. It can be anything you want. The part of the original area you want, let us say, is 25 picas by 33 picas. The printed width you want is 16 picas. Now, what will the printed depth be?

25 is to 33 as 16 is to x.

You can figure it mathematically; you can use a specially made slide rule or a "wheel" (a circular proportional scale calibrated in numbers that could represent picas or inches or anything you choose). Or you can use the diagonal method.

Your answer will be 21 picas. Your printed picture will be 16×21 picas.

To figure dimension change when working with silhouette art, you will have to enclose the silhouette in a tight-fitting rectangle.

Here is another problem you might face. You have a space for a picture that measures, say, 18 by 50 picas, a deep vertical. Your original is a regular $8'' \times 10''$ glossy photograph. The original picture is horizontal. You are going to have to take as much of the depth of that picture as possible. About the most depth you can take from a picture like that is 46 picas. So that is your third dimension. Now, how much width can you take from that original so that area will, in this case, *blow up* to fit the allotted space?

To use a proportion wheel, you turn the inside disk, which represents the size of the original art, to where an original measurement lines up with a printed measurement (outside disk). Let's say your original is 17 × 20 inches (width first) and you want the width of the printed art to be 7½ inches. As this portion of a wheel shows, 17 inches (below on the wheel) is to 7½ inches (above) as 20 inches is to 8⅞ inches. Proportion wheels are available from a number of sources, including Vip Engineering Services, Stanfordville, N.Y., and most have a built-in "percentage of original size" indicator. In the example used here, the percentage is just short of 45.

Figure that x is to 46 (the original area) as 18 is to 50 (the printed area). (Your equation is always "original width is to original depth as printed width is to printed depth.") So x equals 16½ picas.

Some designers like to work with square originals, as from a Rolleiflex camera, because it is easier to move to either a vertical or a horizontal from a square than it is to move from a horizontal to a vertical.

Arranging pictures

Back in the 1920s and 1930s, some designers thought it chic to tear the edges of photographs, order them in vignette forms, put them in montages, round their corners, put straight-line or decorative borders around them, or otherwise mutilate them. Although these methods of displaying art enjoy short revivals, they die out again, and designers let the art itself, not its accessories, do the talking.

For most advertising, it is a good rule to present pictures honestly and simply, without quirks, and in a size that can be easily read. So far as a photograph is concerned, nothing serves it quite so well as an ordinary rectangle.

At times its effect can be intensified by exaggerating the rectangle into a severe horizontal or vertical. The late Allen Hurlburt, an editorial art director (of the old *Look*), was a prime mover here. His magazine beautifully displayed deep vertical and wide horizontal photographs along with the more traditional rectangles and squares. But they were seldom tipped in at angles, nor were their edges tampered with.

Look was often able to pick up a subject, a line, or a direction from inside one photograph and match it with a visual thrust in a nearby photograph, thereby unifying a page or spread. Advertising designers do that, too. They also try to relate edges of pictures. They set up an imaginary axis—or several of them—within an ad and use them to line up pieces of art or copy.

When an ad calls for a bleed picture, you should plan for enough extra picture area at the bleed so that when the paper is trimmed, the composition of the picture will not suffer. But designers are not quite as enthusiastic about bleeding pictures as they once were. What is wrong with a slim margin of white around the picture?

With several pictures in the same ad, you might want to butt one edge against the other. Or you may want to arrange the pictures so that, from a distance, they blend into a single irregular shape. You would seldom run a headline across the face of a picture, and you would never run the headline partly over the picture, partly over the white space. The headline's background should be even textured.

As always, you would arrange the pictures so they "point" into the ad, not away from it. Using several pictures, you would try hard to make one picture lead into the other. And one of the pictures should always overshadow the others. Either that, or the mass of several pictures should overshadow other elements in the ad.

Handling pictures

Pictures must be protected from the ravages of wear and harsh treatment so they will be at their best when they finally are put up in front of the printer's camera.

If it is a photograph, you must not write on its back, unless you use a soft grease crayon. Nor can you attach a note to the picture with a paper clip. Any kind of an indentation will pick up a shadow, which will reproduce in the final printing. Crop marks, made with a grease crayon, must

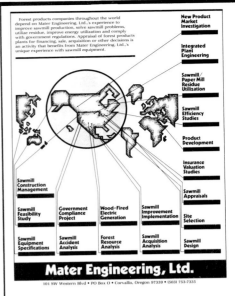

Mater Engineering, Ltd., Corvallis, Oregon, makes the point through a marked map in a two-color promotional piece that "Forest products companies throughout the world depend on . . . [our] experience to improve sawmill production, solve sawmill problems, utilize residue, improve energy utilization and comply with government regulations." Deborah Kadas art directed; Linda Ahlers wrote the copy. The agency was Attenzione!

be put out in the margins. Ordinarily four are enough: two at the bottom showing width extremities, two at the right side showing depth.

You don't want to get fingerprints on the photograph. You should handle it much as you would handle a stereo record.

No picture should be folded or rolled, not even a line drawing.

Indicating art on your layout

As a nonartist student taking a course in advertising layout, you may stand back in awe at that part of the work that requires some drawing. That you cannot draw well may keep you perpetually tense in class.

But the instructor does not expect fine draftsmanship. After all, it is not a "Freehand Drawing" or "Drawing and Sketching" course.

What the layout needs is simply the *feel* of the planned-for art. The details of the art are not important.

That is why you should learn to work in broad strokes.

If the drawing is supposed to be in line, a sharp pencil should be used, or a Pentel. Where blacks are desired, the areas should be blackened in. They should not be *grayed* in.

For halftones, a blunter pencil, a chisel-point pencil, a lithographic stick, a piece of charcoal or charcoal pencil, a set of gray pastel chalks, a set of gray markers, gray watercolor or opaque paints—any of these can be used to do the job. Then make your drawing on top of the tone. Or you may want to paste down a piece of gray bond or construction paper in the size of the halftone and draw on that. Or you can leave the gray paper as is.

Tone is what is important. Squinting at the drawing or viewing it from a distance, the onlooker should get the general idea of technique and medium and subject matter.

How better to illustrate the longevity of print than to show a photograph of one of forty-seven copies of the Gutenberg Bible still in existence? The purpose of this two-page ad by the Print Advertising Association was to sell print media to advertisers in face of competition from TV. The Bible was placed in the spread so that the fold occurs where the magazine itself folds. Designer: Tony Cappiello. Agency: Ries Cappiello Colwell.

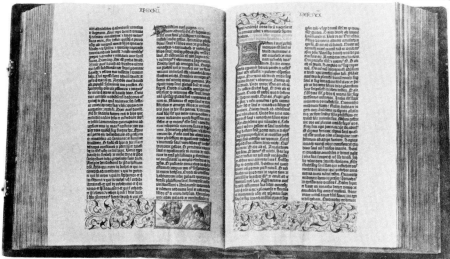

The printed page   can live forever.

This is a spread from the Gutenberg bible, the world's first book printed from movable type.

The Gutenberg bible came off the press in 1455. Some 47 copies are still in existence today.

A message in print is not like a message in time.

A message in time will last for 10, 20, 30 or 60 seconds. Like a stroke of lightning, a message in time lives gloriously for a moment and then dies.

A message in print can die just as fast. On the other hand, a message in print can be read for 10 minutes, can be taken to the store a week later or perhaps saved for several lifetimes.

If you have something important to say,

your message will last longer if you put it in print.

Your message in print will live as long as it is relevant to the needs and interests of your marketplace.

Your message in print can live forever.

To save time on some rough layouts, you should be willing to patch pieces together. If you have an extra copy of the art-service proof book, you can cut items out and paste them down rather than trace them. As a professional you no doubt would use a camera lucida or art projector, which permits you to draw art on the rough in a reduced or blown-up size. Or you would order photoprints, photostats, photomechanical transfers, or Velox prints from outside.

If a tracing is involved, and you cannot fit the original under the sheet on your layout pad, you can do the tracing separately and paste it into place. Or you can make your tracing, rub the back with graphite, then with a sharp, hard pencil redraw the tracing over the layout, transferring it. You can strengthen the lines when you remove the master copy.

You can, of course, paste down printed columns of type for your body copy, even though those columns are not the intended columns. They will *look* like the intended columns. You can also use simulated copy blocks available on sheets of transparent paper or plastic.

If you are doing a newspaper ad and you do not want a border around it, write "No border" in the margin. Otherwise the printer may interpret the guidelines defining the edges of the ad as a border. A nice way of making the ad stand out from the layout paper without drawing a border around it is to rub a tone up to its edges. Taking a squared sheet of paper, place it up against the border, from inside the ad, then, picking up some lead rubbings from the sandpaper pad, rub a tone across the edge of the overlaid sheet and onto the layout proper. Pulling the overlay sheet away, you will have a crisp edge in gray that feathers out away from the ad, like this:

Depending upon how finished your ad roughs are, you will want to prepare them for viewing by someone: instructor, client, printer, overseer, or just an admirer. In a classroom situation, the instructor may want the layouts kept attached in the layout pad. In this case, you will merely keep them unsmudged; and you will print a description of the assignment at some spot, say at the bottom, away from the ad proper. Otherwise, you can rubbercement the layout to a heavier sheet and flap it with a protective cover. Or you can cut a cardboard frame for it. Or you can cover it with cellophane after first cementing it to a stiff backing board.

The technique for preparing the work for presentation or viewing can be an art in itself.

1. Quoted by Art Schlosser, "Fine Art vs. Commercial Art: Will the Twain Ever Meet?" *Print,* September-October 1964, pp. 52–61.

2. Reported by Roy Pinney in *Advertising Photography* (New York: Hastings House, 1962).

3. David Deutsch, "When Do Suggestions Interfere with Job Creativity?" *Advertising Age,* January 28, 1980, pp. 43, 44.

9

What the designer should know about production

"What goes wrong between the designer's concept as represented by the comp and the final printed work is frequently born in the process of mechanical and photographic preparation," said Norman Sanders in the Introduction to his useful *Graphic Designer's Production Handbook.* "It results from a failure of communication between the graphic designer and the people involved in the constantly changing, highly technical lithographic industry."[1]

James Craig recognized the problem when he dedicated his book *Production for the Graphic Designer,* now a classic, "to every graphic designer whose printed piece did not quite measure up to his expectations!" In the Introduction to the book he said, "The designer should know enough about production to understand: (1) what the possibilities are in terms of typesetting, printing, paper, etc., (2) what factors to consider when choosing between systems, methods, processes, etc., and (3) how to *communicate* specifications to the people responsible for translating the designer's ideas into a printed piece."[2] Some aspects of production have changed dramatically since Craig wrote his book—putting more demands on designers but also expanding the possibilities for innovation. Edward M. Gottschall explored these in *Graphic Communications '80s.*[3]

Production is the process whereby the idea for an ad becomes a reality. It is what happens to the ad after the copy has been written and the ad designed.

Production includes the setting of the type, the making of the plates, and the printing and binding. It also includes the pasteup of the elements that go into the ad. Sometimes this is left to the printer, but increasingly it is done by the designer or an assistant called a *pasteup artist.*

Chapter 5 discussed the three stages an advertising design can go through: the thumbnail, the rough layout, and the comprehensive. The

To dress up this line graph and this bar chart, used in an annual report of Bucknell University, Newton Art/Advertising, Selingsgrove, Pennsylvania, added real chartmaking tools to the art and pasteups, then photographed the result. Each photo was run as a regular black-and-white halftone. The tools shown include a technical fountain pen, a template, an X-acto knife, and a ruler.

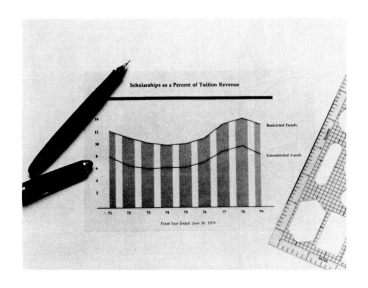

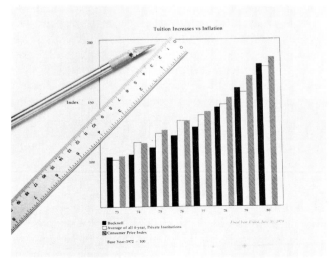

pasteup is actually a fourth stage in the process. It is also called *the mechanical* or *camera-ready copy*. What is produced at this stage is exactly what will show up in the final printing.

A person just starting out in advertising, especially with an advertising agency, may be assigned to the production department to take care of the many details involved and to see what happens to an ad when it leaves the creative department. Much of the work in the department involves contact with outside suppliers and service organizations.

A knowledge of production is especially important in direct-mail advertising, where every detail of design, typography, art, paper, and printing must be worked out. Ads going into newspapers and magazines require fewer production decisions, because the printing process, for instance, has already been determined, and paper choice has already been made. But many production problems must be solved there, too.

This chapter starts with a section on pasteups, then moves to typesetting, art reproduction, and printing.

Pasteups

Even though the pasteup is more important than the comprehensive, it is not so easy to read or so attractive. The pasteup artist is concerned only with what the camera can and cannot record, and works accordingly. A finished pasteup is photographed directly; the negative obtained is used to make the printing plate.

Some designers assign the job of doing finished pasteups to pasteup artists. A professional pasteup artist is a highly skilled, eminently patient sort of person who may have less creative flair than the art director or designer but more devotion to detail.

Doing a pasteup is a tedious and exacting job. What is put into place in the ad stays there, as is. A line of type pasted down just a fraction of an inch away from where it belongs will call attention to itself when the printing is done. Fingerprints, smudges, too-heavy guidelines—all hang on until they find their ill-won places on the printed sheet.

If you draw the job of doing the finished pasteup, you'll do it actual size—or you'll do it larger, to take a reduction. Increasing the size at the platemaking stage would accentuate any imperfections in the type you use.

Often the pasteup is done in two parts—one for line reproduction, one for halftone. Sometimes all or part of the rough layout is so successful from an artistic standpoint that it is incorporated "as is" into the pasteup. If determination of the size of the ad must be made, the designer will want to refer to the appropriate *Standard Rate & Data Service* publication or to the rate card of the medium in which the ad will appear. Periodicals sell their space in standard-size units. If the ad is for a newspaper, the designer will do the ad in a size that is a multiple of a column inch (1 column wide by 1″ deep). If the ad is for a magazine, the designer will do it in column-inch multiples or perhaps in a quarter-, half-, or full-page size. The medium may have some special restriction the designer will have to know about. Most newspapers, for instance, will not accept an ad that is wider in number of columns than it is deep in inches—an ad, say, that is 8-col. × 1″. But a 1-col. × 22″ ad may be okay. Some papers restrict the use of reverses (white set inside black blocks) and typefaces that are the same as typefaces used in the editorial section.

Handling type and art

You have to be careful in handling the pieces of headlines and the chunks of body copy. You might smear the type or put smudges around it. Some pasteup artists use a fixative spray on type and headlines if they are in

This keyline drawing was used as art for the three color circles reproduced in chapter 10. That the circles are not completely filled in allows the printer, with some hand work, to make three different negatives from one piece of art.

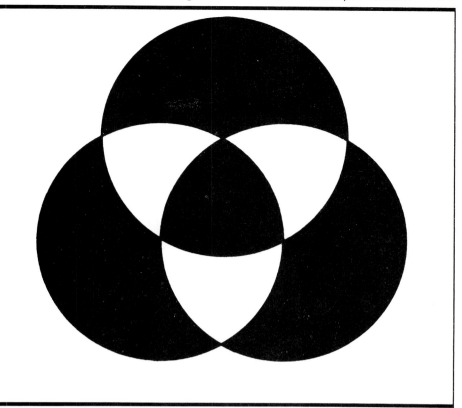

the form of reproduction proofs or if they have been produced through strike-on composition. And they use tweezers to pick up the pieces.

When chunks of body copy are fitted together, it becomes difficult to maintain consistent spacing between lines. The eye of the pasteup artist is easily confused by shadow lines formed by the patches. The inconsistencies do not show up until a printed copy is made either from the negative or the plate. To avoid inconsistencies, you must continually check spacing with a pair of dividers or a finely calibrated ruler.

That the pasteup will be photographed as line art means that you can do all kinds of patching. For instance, you can cover mistakes or smudges with white tape. One thing you cannot do is put Zipatone pattern over a patch. When you do that, the Zipatone acts as sort of a halftone screen; the shadow made by the patch will show up in the printing as a line.

Assuming that no color is involved, all line material—type proofs and drawings—to be run actual size is put on the same master sheet. Line art that has to be reduced or enlarged is simply noted on the sheet and turned in as separate pieces to be photographed in another operation and stripped into place on the negative flats by the production workers.

Photographs can be pasted into place, actual size, but in the plate-making process they will have to be shot separately from the pasteup itself. It is better to submit the photographs as separate units. In their place on the pasteup you can either draw black blocks to represent them or affix pieces of red thin-plastic sheets (art stores have sheets specially made for this purpose, with one side waxed so it will stick). On the cameraman's negative the black or red blocks will appear as transparent areas into which he can easily strip the halftone negatives he has made through screening.

Sometimes it is desirable to have prescreened prints made of the photographs; these are pasted into place; then the whole pasteup can be shot as line. A further advantage is that you can rework the dots, touch up the "reproduction," apply some highlights, add some solid blacks. And for line artwork, especially when a change of size from the original is needed, photocopy prints to size can be ordered and these pasted into place. Then there is no question about where and how they will fit.

One of the biggest jobs of the pasteup artist involves the scaling of photographs and other pieces of art. You may want to reduce or enlarge the art, or you may want to use only a part of it. Maybe you will want to change its composition from a vertical to a horizontal—or vice versa.

You have the width and the depth of the original art to consider and the width and depth of the printed art. In most cases you choose three of these four measurements—any three—and then, using a proportion wheel or slide rule or doing it mathematically or with a calculator, you figure out the fourth measurement. For instance, the width of the original is to the depth of the original as the width of the printed piece is to x. What must x be? That is what you must figure out.

When colors are involved, you may have to provide thin plastic or acetate overlays, with separate art for each color. This calls for register marks (tiny crosses) on the original and the overlays so that the printer can correctly line up the negatives and plates.

For simple two-color jobs, you can mark on a tissue overlay those pieces that are to run in color. The printer then shoots the original pasteup twice, once for the black and once for the color.

Pasteup procedure

The supplies and equipment you need to do pasteups were discussed in chapter 4. This chapter is concerned with techniques.

To do a pasteup, you should follow these steps.

1. Using a T-square, line up your pasteup sheet or board on your drawing table and anchor it at the top and bottom with small pieces of masking tape.

2. Using a blue pencil, rule in the outside dimensions of your printed piece. Then rule in the inside dimensions or copy areas. If you are to use bleeds, rule an extra line on the outside that gives your ad an eighth- or quarter-inch extension.

3. Using a ruling pen or a fine-line marker, rule in crop marks in black ink at all four corners.

4. Using a pair of scissors, trim your reproduction proofs or pieces of copy so that about an eighth-inch of white paper surrounds each of them. Be careful that you do not trim off any parts of the printed type.

5. Place the various elements on the layout sheet and move them around until you have them exactly where you want them. Then trace their corners lightly with a blue pencil so that you will know their places later.

6. One by one turn the pieces upside down on sheets of clean paper and apply your rubber cement, sparingly. Keep it thinned.

7. While the rubber cement is still wet, place the piece in its correct position, sliding it slightly as necessary, checking its placement with your T-square and triangle. You have to work fast. The piece will soon anchor itself. You will have to help it along by applying a slight pressure to it.

8. Clean up any excess rubber cement at the edges of the pieces (rub with a clean cloth or a piece of dried rubber cement), then rule or tape any lines or borders. Or, do your inking *before* pasting down the elements.

9. Using transfer letters, you can set headlines directly onto the pasteup. But you might be better off setting the headlines on separate sheets of paper, trimming them, then pasting them down as units.

It is vital during the pasting down phase that each line or block be perfectly parallel, perfectly lined up vertically, perfectly spaced where pieces butt together. You should check spacing constantly with T-square, triangle, and dividers. The patching that you engage in will result in optical illusions that make it difficult to spot errors in spacing. You may not

A pasteup artist demonstrates how to use transfer letters. The next letter to be "set" here is *E*. In the top picture, the artist lifts the sheet of letters to the mechanical. Second, he positions the *E*. Third, using a blunt stylus, he rubs the letter from the top so it will transfer from below onto the mechanical. Fourth, using the flat end of the stylus and the backing sheet of the transfer letters, he smooths down the letter. (Photos courtesy of Chartpak.)

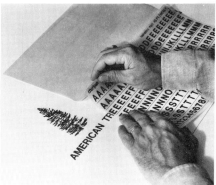

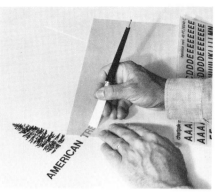

see the errors until the Van Dyke (or proof) stage, when changes can be expensive.

Eventually you can train your eye to spot spacing inequalities early in the process. You will have to depend less and less on your T-square. Of course, if you use a light table, with light coming through from below, and gridded layout sheets, you can avoid T-squares, too.

Using a waxer instead of rubber cement also simplifies the procedure.

The camera will pick up smudges, scratches, and dents as well as the pasteup image. It is necessary, then, to protect the finished pasteup with a flap of paper hooked to swing out from the top. The pieces of art that are to be photographed separately should be flapped, too.

If the client must see the pasteup, show a photocopy of it rather than the real thing. This will protect the original from smudges and markings and fall-offs. The less handling the better.

Goodbye to pasteup?

Pasteup may eventually become obsolete—it already is in some plants—as direct-to-plate technology becomes more readily available. The designing is done on a video screen. This is called pagination in the newspaper industry.

A number of systems are now available. Scitex Corp. of Israel has designed a Vista system especially for *Time* magazine. This system allows an art director to move copy, headlines, and scanned art around on a screen to produce a complete page proof. The art director can call up any available picture and crop it or change its size and even silhouette it. No waxing, no X-acto knives necessary. Actually, there are two screens: one presents the "menu" of stories and pictures, the other acts as the layout area. A cursor controls it all.

Setting type

It is important that as a designer choosing typefaces you know a little bit about how type is set.

Printers call the setting of type "composing" and the type itself "composition." They work with two basic kinds of composition: *cold type,* by far the most common, and *hot type,* the older form.

Cold type

No question about it: no matter which typesetting system is used, the product costs dearly. In the years since the systems were invented, printers have been able to perfect precious few changes. One exception is the linecasting machine that can be activated with tapes typed by lowly typists, thus doing away with the high-salaried operators. Another exception is computerized justification of the right-hand margin when tape is used. The notable progress in typesetting technology has come through the experimentation and innovation accompanying the rapid rise of offset lithography: through cold type.

"Cold type composition," as a term, sometimes gets confused with "photocomposition." The first term is the broad heading; the second term is a form of cold type composition.

You can count five different methods of cold type composition. The first three produce large-size letters, the last two small letters, or body copy.

1. *Hand lettering.* In the hands of a professional, hand lettering surpasses types for beauty and effectiveness. In the hands of an amateur, nothing could be worse aesthetically.

2. *Hand setting of letters printed on sheets.* Two kinds are common:

cut-and-press-on letters, and the more popular dry-transfer letters. The press-on letters (they are a little hard to find now) come on sheets that are lightly waxed on one side for adhesive purposes. The user cuts the letters out with a knife or razor blade and presses them into place one by one on the pasteup. Transfer letters are printed on the underside of their transparent carrying sheets, their faces rather than their backs against the sheets. The user moves the whole sheet until a letter is in the right place and then literally rubs it off the back of the sheet onto the pasteup.

Dry-transfer letters require a little more skill to use than press-on letters. They are better on comps because they leave no trace of patching, as press-on letters do. And you can "surprint" them over continuous-tone art. But for the pasteups themselves, press-on letters reproduce as well as transfer letters do. Both kinds of letters come in countless varieties and sizes from several manufacturers, and in opaque white as well as black inks. Prestype, which claims to have invented dry-transfer letters, offers some alphabets in opaque colors: red, yellow, blue, and gold.

Waxing machines have eliminated the need for rubber cement and other adhesives in some design studios. This is the Artwaxer, one brand. When the photoset headline has been waxed on its reverse side, it is trimmed and then pressed into place on the mechanical.

Zipatone offers a Cook's Circle series of letters that are put into a sort of perspective to make them fit circles, as when the designer is creating a seal.

Some of the manufacturers, including Prestype, offer a service whereby you can design your own type or logos or make pasteups of type or art you use frequently and then order special dry-transfer sheets of the material.

For from less than $1 to $5 or more, depending upon the brand, you can buy a sheet of letters of a particular face and size—a sheet that will last through several jobs. When you run short on one letter, you can build it by combining parts of other letters. For instance, making some adjustments you can build an *h* with an *l* and an *n*. And when you make a mistake with dry-transfer letters, you can lift it away with tape.

To use these letters correctly, you have to understand letterform and spacing. Beginners often space the letters unevenly and too generously. And beginners have trouble lining up lowercase letters that have ascenders or descenders. The *g,* because of its two loops, often ends up out of alignment. Beginners also fail to realize that some letters are designed so that their angles and rounds extend above and below the guidelines.

Among punctuation marks, the colon most often is wrongly placed. The beginner fails to locate the bottom period of the colon on the baseline.

You would not want to get stuck with the job of setting very *many* lines of type, especially in a small size, but for the small agency and ad department up against a deadline, press-on and dry-transfer letters are a godsend. Certainly they are preferable to most hand lettering.

You have access to one other handset system. This one involves type printed on individual pieces of heavy paper and a "stick" that holds the pieces until they can be taped together. Fototype introduced the system in 1935. You can get details from Fototype Incorporated, 1414 Roscoe St., Chicago, Illinois 60657.

3. *Photolettering.* Machines from several manufacturers make use of negatives of complete alphabets that are dialed or otherwise put into proper position for light to shine through the desired letter onto sensitized paper. Such machines release strips of paper which carry photographically produced headlines.

4. *Strike-on composition.* This kind of composition can be produced on anything ranging from the lowly portable typewriter to a sophisticated tape-operated machine with proportional spacing (letters of various widths). If a typewriter is used, though, it should be an electric one. For crisp impression of letters, it should also be equipped with a use-once carbon ribbon. One of the best is the IBM Selectric. Both it and the Varityper are made to permit quick changes of faces, even in the middle of a line.

Most strike-on machines require two typings in order to achieve justification of the right-hand margin. The Justowriter and the Flexowriter, however, produce a tape that is fed into a second unit, which in turn produces automatically justified composition.

5. *Phototypesetting.* In the early 1950s linecasting machines were made available in versions equipped with individual negatives in place of the familiar mats. When the operator hit the keyboard keys, the negatives moved into position and, line-by-line, allowed light through to sensitized galley paper. Here we had columns of type produced photographically—type as good as though it were produced by conventional hot type machines.

But phototypesetters making use of linecasting machine principles are not used much anymore. "Harnessing photography to metal-casting procedures was as inefficient as putting a jet airplane engine into the canvas fuselage of Snoopy's Sopwith Camel," Edmund C. Arnold observed.[4]

Newer phototypesetting machines operate photoelectronically. They use master disks or grids containing all necessary characters in negative form. Even more sophisticated phototypesetting machines make use of cathode ray tubes. In the process, pictures of type characters on the tube are projected onto photographic paper.

The purpose of these innovations, of course, has been to speed up typesetting. The phototypesetting machines of today can be activated with

When art directors order display typography from Paul O. Giesey/ Adcrafters, Portland, they refer to this chart (shown here in reduced size) and accordingly mark their copy for extra-tight, tight, or regular spacing.

EXTRA TIGHT SPACING—SANS-SERIF

Visually Spaced on Photo Typositor

TIGHT SPACING—SANS-SERIF

Visually Spaced on Photo Typositor

REGULAR SPACING—SANS-SERIF

Visually Spaced on Photo Typositor

EXTRA TIGHT SPACING—SERIF

Visually Spaced on Photo Typositor

TIGHT SPACING—SERIF

Visually Spaced on Photo Typositor

REGULAR SPACING—SERIF

Visually Spaced on Photo Typositor

prepunched tape; and justification, hyphenation, and other time-consuming decisions can be programmed into the computer. And the composition can be elegant enough to please the most demanding of typographers.

Cold type is designed primarily for offset printing; its product can *only* be photographed. But now the printer can use phototypesetting negatives to make exposures directly onto plates, thus bypassing the photographing of prints.

Hot type was designed for letterpress. But by getting a perfect proof—a reproduction proof—from the type, the offset lithographer can easily adapt it to offset printing. By taking a picture of it, the printer treats it as though it were a piece of line art.

Hot type

Somewhere in the manufacturing process, the type we call "hot type" makes use of molten metal poured into molds, or mats (matrices), as type is cast. Old-school printers refer to such type simply as "type"—as though there were no other. They bring in the adjective "cold" when they refer to the other and newer kind of type, to distinguish it from the metal.

The first method of setting type—hand setting—dates back more than five hundred years to Johann Gutenberg, who perfected it. And the system hasn't changed much. To set such already-manufactured pieces of type—called "foundry type"—the printer or compositor picks up each letter or symbol one by one and places it in a composing stick, which may be adjusted for the line-length desired.

The second method of setting type (we are still dealing with hot type) is by linecasting machines. You know it as Linotype composition; but Linotype is a trade name and, technically, should not be used as the generic name for this process. At least one other brand name is involved here: Intertype.

Printers call this process for setting type the "linecasting system" because the product of the Linotype or Intertype machine is a line o' type cast as one unit on a metal slug. Such composition is cast line by line; the lines, or slugs, are gathered in a tray or galley and then "proofed" for client inspection. (Proofing of all hot-type composition involves making a first printing from the type on long, narrow sheets of paper on a proof press that is usually hand operated.)

In machine composition, what is assembled are not pieces of type but the mats (molds) of the individual letters and symbols from which the lines are cast. The type is then manufactured right on the scene from molten lead.

Essentially, the Linotype and the Intertype machines have four basic sections: the magazine, which houses the mats; the keyboard, which releases the mats from the magazine and causes them to assemble in lines; the casting mechanism, which does the manufacturing; and the distribution system, which, in Rube Goldberg-like style, causes each mat to return to its compartment in the magazine.

Linecasting machine composition is used for small sizes of type—for columns of copy; but it can also produce type as large as half an inch high.

The third method of setting hot type involves the Ludlow process. Ludlow composition is in one way related to the foundry operation, in another way related to linecasting composition. The letters assembled in Ludlow are assembled by hand. But they are not individual pieces of type; they are matrices, or mats, from which the type will be cast in lines, or slugs.

The Ludlow mats are kept in cases or drawers, as type is kept for the foundry operation. After the mats are assembled in the compositor's stick, they are put into the casting device and the line of type emerges almost at once. Like type in the foundry operation, the mats have to be redistrib-

The 3-M Brand Promat Model 100 "Letter Compositor" produces instant letters with "no messy chemicals, processing time or warm-up. It's a dry system. . . . Negative and positive letters are instantly imaged and simultaneously dispensed on tear-resistant film." 3-M says this machine, which can produce a variety of typefaces in sizes ranging from 14 to 72 points, can be used in normal room light. No special training is necessary for the operator.

The Photo Typositor, made by Visual Graphics Corporation, New York, has an "ingenious photographic optical viewing system" that permits the operator to see every letter as he composes a headline photographically. The machine as shown here rests on a table; the operator uses it sitting down—in a fully lighted room. The headline is completely processed within the machine and comes out (at the left) ready to trim and paste into place. More than 1,000 fonts of type are available. The letters in each font can be reduced or enlarged to 175 sizes. Any spacing between letters and words is possible. The machine is equipped with modification lenses that can slant, expand, contract, elongate, or otherwise change the letters. And letters can be overlapped, staggered, screened, or put into perspective—all within the machine.

The ACM 9000, described by Compugraphic Corporation as an "all-purpose phototypesetter," can set complete ads "in position." Types of various sizes and design can be freely mixed, even within a line. Shown here are both the keyboard unit and the tape-operated phototypesetting unit.

A compositor sets a headline using Ludlow matrices.

Mergenthaler's "Elektron" Linotype. Tape-operated, this linecasting machine sets fifteen standard newspaper lines a minute. The machine can also be operated manually. The magazines of matrices are at the upper right, the keyboard below, the casting mechanism at the left. The matrices go up and across the back for redistribution to the magazines.

Shown here is Monotype's Monomatic II: the keyboard and (at right) the caster.

uted by hand for further use. Ludlow, its slugs T-shaped, is useful for setting large-size types, especially types for headlines in newspaper ads.

The fourth method of setting hot type involves the Monotype process, an English invention. Monotype consists of two machines, one with a keyboard to punch a tape or ribbon, the other with a casting mechanism that receives the tape and automatically casts type from each matrix case. The final product is more like the product of the foundry operation than Linotype setting in that individual pieces of type are produced.

The Monotype system makes possible careful fitting of type and easy corrections, and is especially useful in tabular and scientific work.

Each of these hot type composition systems was developed for letterpress printing, where they are still used. But they can be used for offset printing, too. What you would need would be reproduction proof, made on a special press, which you would use for your pasteup. But in most instances cold type composition would serve your needs just as well, and probably at much lower cost.

Computer typography

Today much advertising type of the cold type variety is set by computerized electronic systems involving keyboard entry devices, computers, and output devices. Digital information originated by the first of these components is stored by the second and manipulated by the third. The verbal output is in the form of printed pages which are the equivalent of reproduction proofs.

The typesetting process starts when an operator punches a keyboard and the video display terminal (VDT), a cathode ray tube which looks like a TV screen, shows what is being typed or has been typed. The material typed can be stored and called up later for editing and correcting.

The computer to which the VDT is attached can be programmed to spell and hyphenate correctly and to make other decisions in connection with the typesetting.

The output device typically involves a phototypesetter.

Justification and the accompanying hyphenation at the ends of the lines actually were easier and less expensive in the days of hot type and letterpress; today, with computer typesetting and offset lithography, unjustified lines are cheaper. In unjustified setting, the computer does not have to check its word-bank memory to see where the hyphenation is permissible on words that are to be carried over. Besides, you can get two or three percent more words set in the same amount of space when you go to unjustified setting. And when you find a mistake in the middle of a paragraph, there is less need for all the rest of the paragraph to be rerun because there is space to play with.[5]

In-house typesetting

With typesetting costs soaring, a number of agencies have set up in-house typesetting departments. In-house typesetting can result in both lower costs and greater flexibility. The agency can get type set whenever it wants it. Last-minute changes present no problem.

It used to be that in-house typesetting meant a minimum of available faces. But today plenty of faces can be stocked at modest expense.

A disadvantage of in-house typesetting is the scarcity of trained people to operate the machinery. An in-house typesetter needs typing skill, an appreciation of good typography, and mastery of machinery. You do not often find people who have all these qualities.[6]

The typesetting machines or systems cost anywhere from a few thousand dollars to $100,000. One system involves *direct-input* typesetting (the keyboard is connected to the typesetter). Another system involves *off-line* typesetting (keyboarding is separated from typesetting). *Off-line* typesetting can result in much speedier production. And with an off-line system, an agency can do the keyboarding in house and have the typesetting done outside.

An in-house system provided the type for the book you are reading.

This kind of drawing, strong, rough, done with a brush on a rough-textured paper, calls for line reproduction. Part of an ad sponsored by *Printing Production* magazine; used by permission.

Reproducing pictures

Cartoons. Paintings. Wash drawings. Scratchboard drawings. Photographs. The list of kinds of art the advertising designer works with is a long one. But from the printer's standpoint, the list boils down to two items: line drawings and halftones.

Put another way, the printer can reproduce art (including photographs) in one of two ways. This chapter offers additional background to the discussion in chapter 8 about these two ways.

Line reproduction

Artwork done in black ink on white paper in lines and solid areas of black calls for line reproduction. In making the plate, the printer (more correctly, the *engraver* or *offset cameraman*) takes a picture of the art, using high-contrast film. He uses the film then to expose a sensitized plate, as a photographer in a darkroom exposes a sensitized sheet of paper. For letterpress printing, the plate goes through the etching process, by which parts that are not to print are, in effect, eaten away and parts that are to print are left standing. This is photoengraving. For offset lithography, a

A silhouette halftone of the Model A. The original print was improved through airbrushing.

This printed halftone is blown up to show the relationship of dot size to tonal scale. A print like this can be used ''as is'' for an unusual effect, as designer Doug Lynch used this one on his jacket design for *New Deal Mosaic,* a book published by University of Oregon Books.

different kind of a plate—thinner, for one thing—is used; it does not have to be etched. The term "photoengraving" does not apply.

Artists and printers work constantly to devise ways of adding tone to line drawings to give them the effect of halftones or more pattern and texture. The original system for adding tone to line drawings was developed by Benjamin Day in the nineteenth century. Still in use today, it involves the affixing of a pattern in certain areas of either the negative or the plate by the printer or engraver. The artist directs placement by shading in those areas with a light-blue pencil or watercolor tone (the engraver's camera does not pick up the light blue). More recent developments allow the artist to place the tone directly onto the drawing. There are several methods: use of sheets of transparent paper or plastic on which a pattern is printed; use of drawing paper with built-in patterns that can be brought out with chemicals or pencils, and use of sheets from which shading patterns can be rubbed off onto the original artwork.

The tone, of course, is an optical illusion; it is formed by closely placed black dots or lines that merge into middle values as the eye recedes from them. Under a magnifying glass, they show up for what they are: line art, ready for camera.

Line art can be patched, scratched, and retouched; the printer has no trouble keeping resulting shadows and slight differences in tone from registering on the plate. Often line art is reduced in order to remove slight imperfections in the drawing. If reproduction proofs of type are to be used, they would be shot as line art.

Halftone reproduction

A designer wanting to use a photograph or piece of artwork that has a continuous tone moving subtly up and down the tonal value scale (a wash drawing, fine pencil drawing, or painting) will ordinarily order halftone reproduction. ("Halftone" is not a very good term, because many continuous tones are involved: light, middle, and dark. It is more than a matter of having tones that are halfway between white and black. But "halftone" is the term we are stuck with.)

Photographs with a good tonal range give you the best reproduction. With the new technology, glossy prints are no longer necessary, and in some cases they are actually less useful than matte-finish or luster-finish prints. The luster-finish print is less subject to cracks and scratches, and it is easier to retouch.

To hold onto the many tones of the original, the engraver (or offset cameraman) inserts a screen between the lens and the film. The standard screen is a two-ply piece of glass; one ply has opaque lines cut in one di-

A photograph shown first as a regular halftone and then as halftones made from other than dot screens. (Photo by the author.)

rection, the other has lines cut perpendicular to the first lines, forming a crosshatching. The resulting small squares act as individual lenses, breaking up the light into dots of various sizes, depending upon how much is reflected from the subject being photographed.

From then on the negative is used the same way as for a line reproduction.

A halftone, then, has small dots over the entire area of the print, even if some of the area is meant to be white. With special handling, the printer's cameraman can work some blank areas—pure white—into the artwork where it is needed. Such halftones are called "highlight" or "dropout" halftones.

The student must understand that, whatever system of printing is used, where continuous-tone artwork must be reproduced, screening is necessary. Printers do not print ordinarily in shades of gray. They print in black. The effect of gray must be achieved through optical illusion. Stepping back from a halftone printed in a publication, you see it as tones of gray, from light to dark. Looking at it closely (perhaps with a magnifying glass), you see the dots—and nothing but black ink. Pinpoint dots cover and define the lighter areas, larger dots the darker areas.

For pictures in color, separate plates and printings must be made for each color used. Through judicious use of the plates for black, yellow, red, and blue inks, the printer is able to achieve the illusion of full color. If the color picture is a halftone, each of the plates will be made up of dots.

As artists and printers work to make line art look like halftone art, they also work to make halftone art look like line art. Eastman Kodak Company in 1953 introduced the Tone-Line process by which continuous-tone art—photographs, primarily—is changed into line art with unusual texture. Several different textures are available. A photograph thus con-

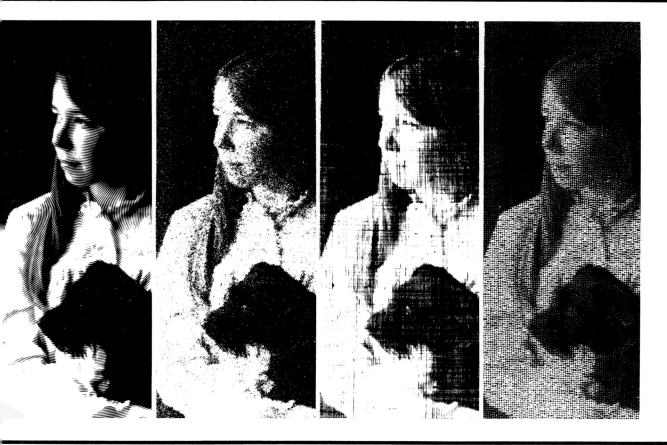

verted is ready for line reproduction. Looking at the reproduction, the reader might conclude it was a drawing of some kind.

A similar effect can be had simply by ordering line reproduction for a continuous-tone original. What happens is this: the tones darker than 50 percent fill in as solids; the tones lighter than 50 percent drop out altogether. It is as though an artist had drawn a picture using no lines, only shadows.

Plates for printing pictures continue to demand large expenditures from advertisers. It was to alleviate some of these costs that offset lithography was developed.

Paper stock

All graphic designers consider paper in their planning. Some types reproduce well only on smooth stocks; other types seem designed for rough stocks. Halftones, depending on their screens, need certain papers in order to show up well. The designer always makes adjustments to fit the paper used by the medium carrying the ad—except in direct mail. Here, as a representative of the "publisher," the designer can choose paper stock to fit the design. Faced with hundreds of different papers from scores of manufacturers, and aware that paper represents from one-quarter to one-half the cost of the job, the designer of direct mail quickly becomes something of a paper expert.

Paper, priced by the pound, is sold in rolls or in reams of 500 sheets. If the sheet size is 24″ × 36″ and 500 such sheets weigh 70 pounds, it will be designated: 24 × 36—70. The last number indicates the thickness of the paper. A "70-pound" sheet is thicker than a "60-pound" sheet in its class (more about classes in a minute). But a 60-pound sheet in one class might be thicker than a 70-pound sheet in another class. Likewise, 70-pound book paper is much thinner than 70-pound cover stock because the basic size for cover stock on which ream weight is based is smaller.

The classes of paper used in printing are these:

1. *Newsprint*. Used almost exclusively by newspapers.
2. *Book stock*. This is an important class. We break it down into:
    (a) Antique. Soft, bulky, rough. The *texts*, used in fine printing, have some rag content. The *vellums* are smoother. Often off-white or cream-colored.
    (b) Offset. Smooth, uncoated. Usually seen in harsh white.
    (c) Gravure. Absorbent, to take the large amount of ink applied in rotogravure printing.
    (d) English finish. Clay-content paper, smooth but not glossy and without much bulk. Used extensively by major magazines.
    (e) Super. Clay-content paper that is polished (although English-finish paper is sometimes polished, too). The clay acts as a starch.
    (f) Coated. Coating substance is attached to the surface, not built it. The paper then is supercalendered, resulting in high gloss.
    (g) Bible paper. Tissue-thin but opaque.
3. *Writing stock*. It comes in flat varieties (calendered to smooth finish), bonds (crisp, permanent, sometimes with rag content), and ledger (with good folding properties because it is made from long-fiber pulp).
4. *Cover stock*. Heavier paper than book paper, but with many of the same qualities and in the same varieties.
5. *Cardboards*. Sheets are bonded to one another, like plywood veneers. This class includes the Bristols and coated blanks, usually with smooth, English finishes.

Printing processes

Advertising designers have to know something about printing when doing an ad for a newspaper or magazine and a lot about the subject when doing a direct-mail piece. Working with other media, the designer adapts to a printing process. Working with direct mail, the designer may have to pick the process and, beyond that, the printer who offers the best quality at the lowest price. Then the designer works closely with the printer to make the job go smoothly.

One reason for checking with a printer before beginning a design job is to determine the ink flow for the piece. If a booklet has a number of full-color photos, for instance, it might be necessary to arrange them so that the printer can adjust the inking to better maintain their quality.

You should plan your mechanical, as well as the design itself, so that you do not ask the impossible of the printer. "When you design a piece that requires a 'perfect' anything in the production sequence, you are paving the way for disappointment," observed Norman Sanders, president of Sanders Printing Corporation, New York. "This is especially true when the design requires perfection in the final trimming."[7] For instance, you would not line up a series of small geometric shapes right next to the edge of a page.

Offset lithography

By far the most popular printing process—for direct-mail pieces as well as for newspapers and magazines—is offset lithography. Even a small town is likely to have several printing houses with offset presses.

A folded-down 16-page signature ready for trimming at the top, right, and bottom.

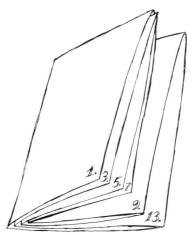

This book was printed by offset lithography.

No other process for short and medium pressruns, and even long pressruns, can so inexpensively reproduce photographs and artwork and so evenly lay on large areas of color. No other process can use as copy blocks the product of so many different typesetting machines. Even typewriter "composition" can be used. Graphic designers like offset because (1) it is more flexible than other processes, offering unlimited design possibilities, and (2) the designer can do all the makeready work, bypassing the composing room. The designer can exercise exact control over placement of elements.

Offset lithography, as a printing process, is based on an art form: stone lithography. In offset lithography, the printing impression is made from the plate to an intermediary rubber-covered roller, then to the paper. The impression, in other words, is "offset" on the way to the paper.

The image on the plate is smooth; you cannot feel it as you rub your hand over it. How, then, can it print?

Chemistry provides the answer: oil or grease and water do not mix. The image is grease-based; in the printing, both a water with glycerin and an ink are applied to the plate. The water stays away from the impression areas; the ink stays away from the damp or watered areas and sticks to the impression areas.

In regular stone lithography, the artist draws on a flat plate with a grease-base crayon; the artist applies the water and ink, then places the paper down on the plate. What results is an impression in mirror-reverse; a head facing right, for instance, would be facing left in the printing. In offset lithography, the "wrong facing" takes place on the rubber-covered cylinder; when the impression is then made on the paper, the facing is right again.

The following diagram shows how offset lithography works.

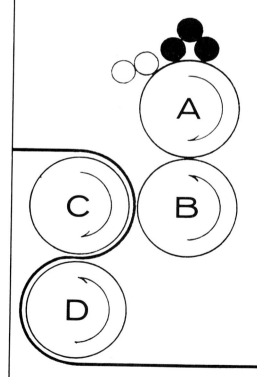

The plate wraps around cylinder A and picks up the dampening agent from the small rollers at the top left and ink from the small black rollers. The plate transfers its image to the rubber blanket wrapped around cylinder B, which retransfers to the sheet of paper coming around the impression cylinder, C. The sheet-transfer cylinder, D, delivers the paper from the press.

To make a plate for the press somebody has to make a pasteup. Line artwork and reproduction proofs of type are pasted in position exactly as they are to appear in the final printed version of the job. Photographs and other continuous-tone art are usually submitted separately to the cameraman, who photographs them through a screen and then "strips" the negatives into position with the line negatives. If original line artwork is oversize (or undersize) it is shot separately and reduced (or enlarged) to the correct size and stripped into place. The composites of stripped-in negatives—they are called "flats"—are used then to make the plates.

Because everything on the pasteup page has to be photographed anyway, you can use all the line artwork you want (provided it is done to size) for no extra cost.

Offset lithography is not always cheaper than letterpress, even for printing lavishly illustrated, short-run direct-mail pieces. If particularly high standards are needed, offset lithography can cost every bit as much as letterpress. And business conditions might prompt a letterpress house to underbid an offset house on a job that, on the surface, would seem like a natural for offset. Obviously, consultation with more than one printer is advisable.

Letterpress

In the letterpress operation, a *raised surface* makes the impression. The material that will do the printing (it usually is unyielding, tough metal) is "type-high" (something slightly under an inch); anything not meant to print must be less than "type-high."

Letterpress can make immediate use of type set by hand or machine. No photographing is necessary. Many advertising people and printers agree that all-type jobs of quality call for letterpress printing.

But letterpress, with its sharpness and harshness of impression, does an excellent job of printing pictures, too. No process does better for line drawings. And halftones, provided the screen is fine enough and the paper smooth enough, are at their best in letterpress impression. They should be square or rectangular, however. The hard edges of letterpress have a tendency to "fill in" on vignettes and highlight halftones.

The cost-conscious designer should understand that, good as pictures can look in letterpress, they do cost more in this process than in offset lithography.

The printer if not the designer regards letterpress as the flexible process. Last-minute changes can be made easily, even to the point of stopping the presses. More readily than other printers, the letterpress printer makes proofs available at any stage for checking by the designer and client.

For long runs in letterpress and for all runs on letterpress rotary presses (not all letterpress presses are rotary), the printer makes mats (molds) of the pages, from which durable plates are cast. Plates used for rotary presses have to be rounded to fit the cylinder. For short runs (a few thousand) on nonrotary presses, the printer uses the type and engravings as provided.

Gravure

In gravure, everything that is to print is incised on the printing plate, making tiny wells of varying depths. That includes the type. The ink is deposited in these wells (excess ink is wiped from the plate by the "doctor blade") and moves from them to the paper in the printing.

Everything that is to print, then, has been screened. You do not notice the screen because it is 150-line or finer; and the small dots are further

You are looking at the *reproduction* of a *photograph* of a *mat* of a *line drawing* offered by Crown Zellerbach to grocers wanting to feature a picture of Tuf 'n Ready Towels in newspaper ads (when the newspapers are letterpress). The newspaper backshop would use the mat to make a casting in metal. The words "Tuf 'n Ready" and "Towels," the outlines, and the screened tones below "Towels" are recessed in the mat to receive the molten metal.

minimized as the ink is sucked out of the wells and onto the slightly absorbent paper. The type, though, even to the naked eye, is often fuzzy. Obviously, this is no process for reproducing column after column of type.

It is an ideal process, however, for reproducing photographs or any continuous-tone art. The gradations of tone in gravure, thanks to the fine screen, are almost as complete as in the continuous-tone original. Great tone subtlety is possible in this process.

Gravure is called "rotogravure" when the presses take paper on rolls rather than in sheets. Rotogravure is reserved for extra long pressruns— runs in the millions. The setting up of the original plates, whether for sheet-fed gravure or rotogravure, is costly.

Stencil printing

Of only limited use in advertising, stencil printing does not make use of a plate to hold and transfer ink. Instead, the ink passes through a cloth, called a "stencil."

In silk-screen printing, the cloth is stretched over a frame, and areas that are not to print are covered with a frisket made of paper or some similar material. The ink is literally pushed through onto waiting paper below; it hangs up in areas that are covered. Silk-screen printing is useful for posters with small pressruns. Transit-advertising cards often are silk-screened. Recent developments make possible the printing of coarse-screen halftones.

In-house printing

An increasing number of advertisers are doing their own printing.

As in commercial printing, in-plant printing makes wider use of offset than any other printing process, but a number of substitute printing processes are gaining in popularity.

Duplicating machines, all needing some kind of stencil or master from which to print, can be used for letters and uncomplicated leaflets and folders. These machines include the following:

1. *Mimeograph.* In mimeographing, a form of stencil printing, a cloth comes covered with a layer of wax. When you type or draw on the stencil, in effect you push to one side some of the wax and expose the cloth, which is porous; it allows ink, then, to pass through. It is possible to reproduce halftones, which can be scratched onto stencils in dot form electronically.

2. *Spirit duplicator.* Typing or drawing with an ordinary hard pencil or ballpoint pen makes the master, which is the reverse side of the work sheet. In operation, moistened paper comes in contact with the carbon, picking up some of the carbon for the impression.

3. *Multilith.* This baby offset machine prints with either a flexible metal or a paper plate. A pasteup must be photographed to make the metal plate; you can draw and type directly onto the paper plate.

4. *Multigraph.* This is a baby letterpress process, with type, looking like typewriter type, set by hand and slipped into grooves on a drum, which is covered with an inked ribbon to make impressions. Once popular, the process is now infrequently used.

5. *Automatic typewriter.* An activating device on the typewriter is controlled by a perforated tape (the master). A secretary types in the name, address, and salutation; then the machines types automatically, shutting off for a name insertion occasionally, if desired.

Then there are the office copiers or photocopiers. They have an advantage over duplicators in that anyone can operate them.

The first of them—by the Xerox Corporation—went on the market in 1960. Suddenly carbon paper and stencils were unnecessary in some offices. Ralph Keyes wrote in *New Times:* "Besides replacing water coolers as a good place to meet people, Xerox machines have altered our social fabric in fundamental ways. They've revolutionized how politicians campaign, journalists report and bosses treat secretaries. . . . Xerography has all but repealed parts of our copyright law and made possible a new one for Freedom of Information. It's also created new art forms, become a people's printing press and seduced us generally with its glowing green light."[8]

Marshall McLuhan added: "Whereas Caxton and Gutenberg enabled all men to become readers, Xerox has enabled all men to become publishers."[9]

At one time it was not economical to use a copying machine to make more than a dozen copies of an original. If several hundred copies were involved, the job called for a duplicating machine. But copiers have their per-copy cost set low enough now that for many jobs it is a toss-up which process is more economical. And the copiers are getting more sophisticated. Some print on both sides at once. Some reproduce color. Some collate.

Copiers can also aid in the rough-layout stage of design. Students find that they can reduce full-color reproductions from magazines to black-and-white prints when their instructors have specified "no color." They can also copy, if crudely, three-dimensional objects. If they want the printing to be on a color stock and they've done their roughs on white paper, they can use tinted paper to make copies on a copier. The roughs, then, will look like the final printed pieces.

A trade magazine, *In-Plant Reproductions,* devotes itself exclusively to the challenges of in-plant printing. Some in-plant printing departments employ two hundred people or more and keep several presses and photocopiers busy turning out folders, brochures, labels, and other pieces.

The reproduction doesn't show it, but the trolley car punches out from this thick-paper reproduction and folds into a three-dimensional toy. The restaurant has a real car like this inside, and patrons can be seated in it. This printed unit is distributed free to kids and others who want it. Byron Ferris did the designing.

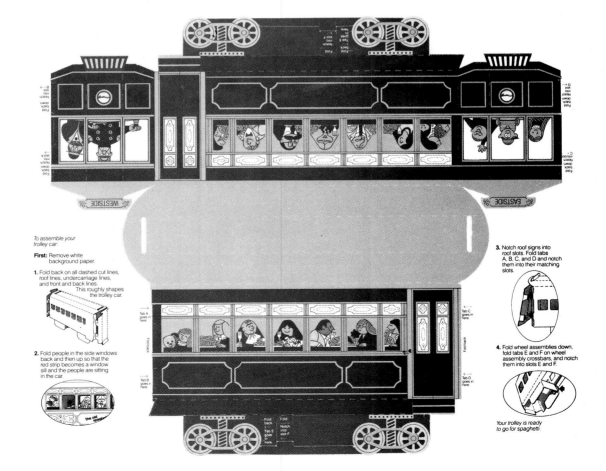

To assemble your trolley car:

First: Remove white background paper.

1. Fold back on all dashed cut lines, roof lines, undercarriage lines, and front and back lines. This roughly shapes the trolley car.

2. Fold people in the side windows back and then up so that the red strip becomes a window sill and the people are sitting in the car.

3. Notch roof signs into roof slots. Fold tabs A, B, C, and D and notch them into their matching slots.

4. Fold wheel assemblies down, fold tabs E and F on wheel assembly crossbars, and notch them into slots E and F.

Your trolley is ready to go for spaghetti.

A computer terminal showing copy being written (and type being set). Photo courtesy *Register-Guard*, Eugene, Oregon.

Production accessories

Among production tricks and devices available to advertising designers, especially to designers of direct-mail pieces, are these:

1. *Die-cutting*. Provided the paper stock is heavy enough, the designer can ask for the "printing" of holes or cutouts of various shapes. These should be kept well away from the edges so they will not weaken the folder and cause it to tear. The designer can get the effect of a die-cut by asking the printer simply to cut one end of the mailer at a diagonal. No special plates are required for this.

2. *Embossing*. This is achieved through use of a relief die (below) and an engraved die (above). The resulting insignia or design can be blind (without ink) or printed. If printed, the ink is applied before the embossing. Embossing can add the look and feel of luxury to letterheads, annual reports, and brochures.

3. *Automatic numbering*. For letterpress jobs, the printer can lock up with type and engravings a little mechanical device that prints numbers and changes automatically to a higher number with each impression.

4. *Perforating*. For pages or coupons that are to be torn from the mailer, the printer can "print" a higher-than-type-high dotted knife edge wherever the designer wants it. Like die-cutting, perforating requires a special pressrun.

1. Norman Sanders, *Graphic Designer's Production Handbook* (New York: Hastings House, 1982), p. 189.

2. James Craig, *Production for the Graphic Designer* (New York: Watson-Guptill, 1974).

3. Edward M. Gottschall, *Graphic Communication '80s* (Englewood Cliffs, N.J.: Prentice-Hall, 1981).

4. Edmund C. Arnold, *Ink on Paper 2* (New York: Harper & Row, Publishers, 1972), p. 61.

5. Leonard Shatzkin makes a strong case for unjustified lines in "No Justification for Hyphenation. . . ," *Publishers Weekly,* April 11, 1980, pp. 33, 34.

6. Jaclyn Fierman, "Dearth of Quality Operators Causes In-House Headaches," *Advertising Age,* May 28, 1979, pp. 5–12.

7. Sanders, p. 189.

8. Ralph Keyes, "America's Favorite Reproduction System," *New Times,* January 9, 1976, p. 34.

9. Quoted by Donald M. Morrison, "What Hath Xerox Wrought?" *Time,* March 1, 1976, p. 69.

10

Working with color

Henry Ford offered his Model T in any color the customer wanted, so long as it was black. Printers of the day operated basically under the same arrangement. To advertisers then, black was quite enough.

Even today advertisers appreciate the value of black. Black does the best job of clearly reproducing ordinary photographs, artwork, and type. Black ink on white paper gives the advertiser a greater range of tone than any single color on white.

And using a single ink—it should be black—to reproduce an ad is cheaper than using the several inks necessary to create color.

Why use color?

Black by itself has a place in advertising, but if luring readers to your ad is a primary concern, you should consider color. In 1979 a Cahners Advertising Research study showed that advertising readership in specialized business magazines increased 38 percent when ads ran in four colors, 20 percent when they ran in two (black plus a color).[1] A recent Starch INRA Hooper survey found that a full-page ad in color attracts 50 percent more readers than the same ad in black and white. Better than black alone, color represents with high fidelity the product, its setting, the people using it. It creates the right atmosphere, the right mood for the ad. It can emphasize easily what needs to be emphasized.

"Black-and-white is for budgets," Eastman Kodak Company said in an ad in *Advertising Age*. "Color is for results." It is the Kodak company's contention that "many products are bought for function, but are sold on appearances. Such as fine tools. To show them in black-and-white can indicate ho-hum work. Color can say pride and craftsmanship."

Food and fashion advertising, especially, benefit from full color. "But the acid test involves the product or situation which is essentially colorless," says the booklet *Color Is for Results* published by Eastman. "The budget-minded advertiser can show a glass of milk, a tuxedo, or a ski slope in black-and-white and get away with it. But if he uses four-color printing. . . ." What followed was a series of "white"-product ads showing that white carries some beautiful built-in colors. You have to look hard for colors in four-color printing of white. But colors are there.

". . . [White] carries with it a reflection not only of other colors, but of texture and tone variation that needs the warmth of four-color reproduction": Phil Gleeson, director of advertising for Paris Accessories for Men. "The interplay of metallic highlights, shadows, and reflections is too subtle to be captured in black-and-white": S. G. Force, vice president of marketing, Hardware Division, Emhart Corporation.

Full color in a consumer magazine costs the advertiser about a third more than black-and-white. But where advertisers have checked effectiveness of full color, as in a split run, results from the color version of the ad have run as high as fifteen times better than those for the black-and-white version.

There are other reasons for using color. College athletic departments use full color for the tickets they sell to football games—partly to make

Taking off from the color thrust of a full-color photograph, a maroon frame ties things together for this International Gold Corporation ad. The color in the art is subdued, and the art itself is severely cropped to better display the gold jewelry. Note how the man's face relates visually to the headline and how the woman's hand relates to the "14K" unit shown on the same diagonal. The agency was Doyle Dane Bernbach; the art director was Lou Byke; the copywriter was Howard Brookstein.

Real gold.
Slip it on her fingers and she'll know what's in your heart.

FOR A FREE BROCHURE ON BUILDING A KARAT GOLD JEWELRY WARDROBE WRITE: INTERNATIONAL GOLD CORPORATION, LTD., 900 THIRD AVENUE, NEW YORK, N.Y. 10022.

14K KARAT GOLD

Nothing else feels like real gold.

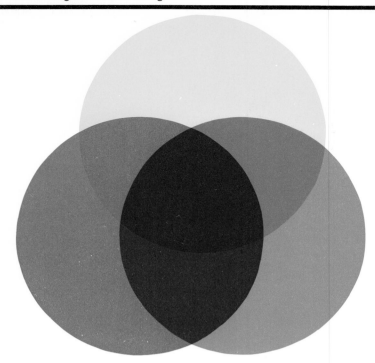

These three color balls show how additional colors are made in printing when one color is printed over another.

them appear to be worth the $10 or more they cost the patron, but mostly to discourage outsiders from duplicating the tickets and selling them.

Color is a main ingredient in package design. Color identifies. People look for a red box or a green bottle or a yellow tube. Ask a student what book was used in a course in Principles of Advertising last year, and chances are you will hear "a red one" or "one with a brown cover." Faber Birren has observed that where people in tests are exposed to various shapes in various colors, they recall the colors more readily than the forms.

Time and *National Geographic,* among the magazines, gain recognition through persistent use of color borders on their covers: *Time* with red, *National Geographic* with yellow. A *Redbook* is on the newsstands; and there used to be a *Bluebook.* Think of all the products or companies that incorporate color in their names: Green Giant, Blue Bonnet, Blue Ice, Yellow Cab, Red Zinger among them. In most cases the packages show the colors.

Some ads build their themes around the color used. For a two-page spread in a *New York Times* special travel magazine, *Life* went with a single color: maroon. The bold color covered both pages, with only a floating bottle on the left page and a small amount of copy on the right page, both of them reversed in the color. The bottle had a note in it, as though someone marooned on an island was summoning help. The ad, directed to media buyers in advertising agencies, compared *Life* to *Travel & Leisure.* "Has *Travel & Leisure* Been Marooned?" read the headline. "Not really," the copy began. "But though no one's leaving them behind, the latest Simmons shows that *Life* has made impressive gains." *Life* was selling itself to advertisers wanting to reach travelers and others with high incomes.

If extroverts dominate your audience, you would be more likely to use color than otherwise. Hermann Rorschach, the Swiss psychiatrist, found the cheerful person more responsive to color, the melancholy person more responsive to shape. (In any circumstances, the color lover is more easily influenced than the person who is not much interested in color. The person

Milton Glaser (note the signature) did the illustration for this "Earth's First Soft Drink" Perrier ad. That the bottle seems to be bursting forth from the earth helps the copy line make its point that the product is "Not manufactured, but created by the earth when it was new." The green of the bottle matches the green of the earth to tie the two together. The merging-colors background nicely sets off the art and the reversed and surprinted type lines. The agency was Waring & La Rosa, Inc., New York; the art director and copywriter was Joe La Rosa.

Tom Rubick's photograph of the pier at Huntington Beach, California, is shown here separated into four colors for printing. The full-color reproduction results from combining the four plates made from the separations.

interested more in shape than in color tends to be introverted and pedantic while exercising strong control over impulses.)

When depending on shape alone—no color—the designer forces the respondent to do more of the work, to *participate* in the ad. Color allows the reader to be more passive. Color comes to the reader. It follows that to weed out lukewarm prospects, an advertiser might want to avoid color.

But, in general, color these days is almost mandatory in advertising. On long-run ads especially, where so much is invested, the additional cost for color in proportion to the complete cost for the job is minimal in most media. Even in newspaper advertising, color is taking hold.

It is almost impossible to get away from this ad, your eye moving from the Movado watch up the hand, down through the cat, and onto the watch again, ready to read the small amount of copy. A truly beautiful piece of work designed by Vincent J. Schifano, using a photograph by Barry Seidman. The copywriter was Carol Corwen. Tolson & Company Advertising, New York, was the agency; Wilbar Company, Inc., did the color process work.

Magically slim. Small, sleek and
very beautiful. Quartz, in 14 karat gold.
The 5½ Ligne, by Movado.

MOVADO
Swiss watchcraft at its most bewitching

What color can do

Robert Weber in a *New Yorker* cartoon shows a clerk in a menswear store trying to sell a shirt to a customer. The clerk says, "It comes in five important colors."

People attach remarkable—even healing—qualities to color.

The Impressionist painters helped us develop a love of color and an appreciation of what it can do. No longer do ad makers shy away from unusual combinations of colors. Ad people try all kinds of colors and combinations, using them for their psychological and emotional possibilities. Advertisers pay attention to the cultural and social application of colors as they create their ads for various groups.

Sometimes an advertiser picks a color for its shock value rather than for its appropriateness. Poster colors tend to be primary colors: bright, even fluorescent, and generously applied. Sophisticated advertisers tend to use more subtle colors. Often a color ad, even though printed in four (or full) colors, has the look of a single color, with the other colors severely restricted to create a near monochrome. An RCA album featuring The Judds in 1984 showed the mother-daughter duo in what appeared to be shades of violet only, but the printing was actually in full color. This is not a new idea. Pable Picasso created monochrome paintings during his blue and rose periods.

The mid-1980s saw a trend toward muted, pastel colors. One writer traced the trend to an architect, Michael Graves, who had created a stir with his unorthodox buildings with chalky facades. Bloomingdale's in New York commissioned Graves to design one of its shopping bags: "a lovely pastel bag featuring a light blue column with delicate yellow curls," as *Art Direction* put it.[2]

Many advertisers rely on advice and findings of the Color Association of the United States. For instance, they have learned to put bright-colored letters on white packages because such colors suggest strength and purity. Soft-drink manufacturers use white on cans to suggest that the product is low in calories.

Color preference often stems from public events. A rush to golds, browns, and earth tones followed the 1978 King Tutankhamen traveling exhibit. When times are bad, grays seem to be preferred. When times get better, colors become more lively.

The love of change also influences the choice of color. Faber Birren, a color researcher, thinks an "in" color has a life of about three years.[3]

Dimensions of color

You can think of color in terms of both light and pigment. The color is in the light, as Sir Isaac Newton proved in 1667 when he subjected light to a prism. But it takes pigment to show it. All items in nature and on paper that have "color" really have pigments which soak up some of light's color waves while reflecting others. What is reflected is the color you see. The skin of a banana, for instance, soaks up all waves but yellow.

Inks used in printing are made, basically, of pigment concentrates derived from plants, animals, and minerals. Printers can use these as they come from tube or jar or mix them for additional colors.

Like any of nature's wonders, color has its three dimensions: the "width" is the *hue,* the "depth" is the *value,* the "thickness" is the *intensity.*

The hue is the name of the color: red, blue, or whatever.

Value has to do with the lightness of the hue. The lighter the hue, the greater its value. Adding white—lightness—to the hue, you get a *tint*; adding black—darkness—you get a *shade.*

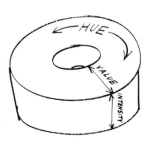

Intensity has to do with the brightness of the color. High-intensity colors are bright colors. A color which has faded through exposure to the elements—maroon is particularly vulnerable—is said to have lost its intensity or "chroma," another word for intensity.

An object shown in a bright color looks larger than the same object shown in a dark color. The bright color radiates—draws the eye outward, expands the object. So if size is what you are selling, you would show a bright-color version of your merchandise.

Any hue can be high-value or low-value, and any can be high-intensity or low-intensity. A hue with high value (light yellow) can still have low intensity (it can be grayed down).

When you realize there is more to color than hue, you can see why colors that ordinarily you would not put together (green and blue? red and brown?) *do* go together very well, provided you choose the right values and intensities. As a matter of fact, you can combine *any* colors (as nature does) if you give them some thought. Even, let us say, a green and a pink.

Convince yourself there is no such thing as an ugly color. There are only wrong combinations. Or the right color in the wrong setting.

Let us say your school colors are green and yellow and you are asked to use them on a direct-mail piece. If you choose a middle kelly green and put it next to canary yellow, you may well be disappointed. But darken and gray the green (lower its value and its intensity) and push the yellow to an umber or an ocher or a beige, and you may change your mind.

White or black or the gray they make in mixing have value—gray can range from light to dark—and you could say they have hue, but they have no intensity.

Of the three dimensions of color, value is the most important. Otherwise, black-and-white advertising would be *infinitely* inferior to color advertising. And that just is not so.

The importance of value can be seen in most of the illustrations in this book. Many of them appeared originally in color. They show up as well as they do because of the values of the color used. The hues and intensities make little difference. Color-blind people[4] get along in life as well as they do because the values of the colors are different enough to establish solid contrasts.

So when using color in advertising, give plenty of attention to the values of the colors you choose.

Primary and secondary colors

From the printer's and artist's standpoint there are three *primary* colors (or hues): red, yellow, and blue.[5] Mixing these, the printer or artist can get additional colors. Any two primary colors mixed in equal amounts make a *secondary* color. Secondary colors are violet[6] (red and blue), green (blue and yellow), and orange (red and yellow).

The primary and secondary colors make up what are known as "standard colors."

Additional mixing of the standards provides any number of other colors, including the so-called earth colors—the browns—and colors subtle and subdued. The S. D. Scott Printing Co., Inc., New York, has published a *Process Color Guide* that shows five thousand colors that can be made by mixing the three primary colors and black.

You can sharpen your appreciation of color by studying *New Yorker* covers. You may not always like the art, you may miss the irony or the nuance, but you will see, each time, a subtle combination of colors that can only be described as satisfying. Watch especially for the covers painted by Gretchen Dow Simpson.

Full color helps this strong, beautiful ad make the point that "Jamaica is a rainbow of people." The one-word headline is set in a typeface large enough to appear in reverse letters in a patterned area of the photograph and to even bleed at the top. Note how the headline settles down in back of one of the bodies, as a logo for a magazine might do. The ad has a kind of magazine cover look. Arlene K. Hoffman, president of Hoffman Mann Inc., New York, designed the ad. Robert Freson took the photograph.

The color itself may not be so important as what surrounds it. Here one color, represented by the cups, is seen in three settings, from light to dark. Notice how the cup color seems to change as the background changes.

JAMAICA

Jamaica is a rainbow of people. People who came from all parts of the world and brought with them the rich heritage and culture that is Jamaica today. A very special part of this heritage is Jamaican friendship. Jamaicans go out of their way to share their country with you and make you love it as much as they do. Any place in the Caribbean can offer you the warmth of the sun. But only in Jamaica can you bask in the special warmth of our people. **Because we're more than a beach. We're a country.**

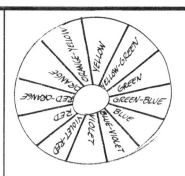

The color wheel

To help students understand color, teachers introduce a color wheel containing six standard colors—yellow, green, blue, violet, red, and orange—and six colors in between them.

The closer colors are on the wheel the more harmonious they are. Colors opposite each other on the wheel have nothing in common; different as they are, they "complement" each other. Mixed together, they turn a neutral gray.

Staring at one color for a while, then moving away and looking at a white sheet, you see a hint of its complement. And when one color is featured in a sunlit setting, its shadow will show evidence of the complement.

When you use more than one color in a job, you may want color harmony. You will use mostly colors adjacent on the color wheel then. But if you want color contrast, you will use colors widely separated on the wheel.

Designers do not shrink from combining harmonious *and* complementary colors in a single job. Nor do they avoid always the mixing of warm and cool colors. But colors should be *mostly* harmonious or *mostly* complementary; similarly, they should be *mostly* cool or *mostly* warm.

Appropriate colors

Color is one area in design (along with type) that can be researched. Falstaff Brewing Company, for instance, through studies made by Lee Research, St. Louis, found that reds, oranges, and yellows worked best for its products in its direct-mail, point-of-purchase, and packaging programs.

People develop—maybe they are born with—individual preferences in color. An R. H. Bruskin Associates survey found that, among adults, blue is the favorite color—and by a wide margin; red was the second favorite color; green was third. Other studies show that men like blues, women reds. For ads meant to be read by one or the other sex, you might capitalize on this. But you must not indulge yourself, from a color standpoint, by playing your favorite just because it is your favorite. For instance, while you may prefer subdued colors, you should remember that in an ad directed toward teenagers, harsher, brighter colors might be a better choice.

Not only should you have an awareness of color preferences among various publics; you should know the moods certain colors create. Take the matter of warmth and coolness in colors. Certain products, certain services deserve a cool setting; others a warm setting. Cool colors are the greens and blues. Warms are the reds and yellows. A blue with some red in it—a blue tending toward the violet—would be less cool than a blue without any red. Even neutral colors—grays—can be either warm or cool, depending on the mixture of pigment.

Warm colors cheer readers, stimulate them; cool colors calm them, make them feel rested. When a color is too cool, it becomes depressing. When it is too warm, it is too stimulating.

Warm colors seem to advance—move out from the sheet. Yellow is the most advancing color of all. Cool colors recede. When you want a hand jutting out from a poster in an "Uncle Sam Needs You" pose, you will see to it the hand gets painted in warm tones, the area around it in cool tones. Working warm colors in at the edges of the ad you will, in effect, give it a border and unify it.

A single hue, though basically warm *or* cool, comes in *both* warm and cool versions. For instance: red, a warm color, when blued a bit becomes cooler than normal.

In working out details for a Schmid Brothers campaign to sell its fine giftware, art director Harry Kirker of Marvin & Leonard Advertising Company, Boston, decided to show, through full-color photography, a contrast of textures. "Each piece is delicate," he said, "and we wanted to put it against something rough." Kirker hired Phil Marco, New York, as his photographer. Each of the photographs used in the series, including this one, took about three hours to produce, not counting preparation. Kirker and Marco looked long for models—men on the street—with just the right hands to provide the contrasts. For this photo, Marco used a glazier who had been installing windows in a nearby building. A mixture of fine clay and water was rubbed on the glazier's hands before the photograph was taken.

Only Karl Gulrich can turn earth, water and fire into Schmid.

Schmid. Beautiful things that say, beyond words, who you are.
Crystal • Porcelain • Figurines • Music Boxes • Collectibles • Randolph, Mass.

Consider how reference to color has entered the language to help it cover mood and attitude: *green* with envy, true *blue, yellow* in battle, *red*-faced, do it up *brown, purple* prose, *white* knuckles, *black* mood.

Nobody knows how all these references to colors got started, but some of them seem logical enough. When some people are embarrassed, their faces *do* turn red. When you hold onto a steering wheel too hard, you *do* stop the flow of blood to your knuckles.

It is certainly true that some colors stimulate people more than others. Knute Rockne, the football coach at Notre Dame, had his team's dressing room painted red, the visitors' dressing room blue, because he was convinced the red would keep his team fired up. Blue, he thought, would relax the visitors, causing them to let their guard down.

Interior decorators know that warm colors tend to make rooms smaller, while cool colors make them larger. It has even been suggested that rooms where temperatures must be kept low *feel* warmer to people if the rooms are decorated in warm colors like browns, oranges, and reds.

Blue Nun shows that you do not need copy or even a headline to sell a product. In this case, a photograph alone—but a beautiful full-color photograph—does the job. The ad (it ran in the *New Yorker*) was the idea of W. J. Schieffelin III, chairman of Schieffelin & Co., wine and spirit importers. Mark Yustein and Jerry Della Femina produced it at the agency: Della Femina, Travisano & Partners, New York.

The author's black-and-white photograph of Alice Chan at work on a layout is shown (1) in black and white, (2) in duotone, (3) in black on a tint block, and (4) as posterized art.

1

2

3

4

Symbolism of color

Colors not only carry moods; they also carry symbolism. The symbolism and the mood may be related, but a good bit of the symbolism results from mere usage. Interestingly, a single color may say opposite things.

For instance, *yellow* is a sacred color in the Orient and in Europe, especially as it approximates the color in gold. In the West it can mean "treachery" or a lack of courage.

We associate yellow with madness. It is, after all, the color van Gogh was at home with.

With a small amount of green, yellow becomes especially unpleasant to most people.

Popular in America in the nineties, when it said "elegance," yellow later lost favor. But if the color you use must be luminous, what better choice (sticking with standard inks) than yellow!

It is the warning color.

Red symbolizes passion. Some say it raises the blood pressure, speeds the pulse. The American Automobile Association is convinced that people who drive red cars cause more accidents than people who drive cars painted other colors. Red-car drivers appear to have a more carefree spirit.

But red is also a color appropriate to the religious. It is zealous.

Red also suggests happiness.

Orange represents knowledge and civilization. And it is the color of warmth, energy, force, and gaiety.

Violet, combining blue (spirituality) with red (courage), is the logical color for royalty. It also stands for loneliness.

More on the blue side, violet stands for depression.

Blue, a cool, passive color, stands for both aloofness (the blue blood) and fidelity (true blue). It also stands for sobriety and fear. It suggests sky, water, ice. It says "transparent."

Green, the most restful of colors, says "fresh." It is a fruitful color. But it can also convey a feeling of guilt, disease, and even terror.

White is for purity, of course, and truth. In some Oriental countries, white is used for mourning.

Black symbolizes depression, sorrow, gloom, death. But it also carries with it a degree of sensuality and even elegance.

The unusual in color

Do not be afraid to move away from ordinary use of color. For instance, try overlapping colors, letting a new color form in the area of overlap. The transparent ink will do this for you automatically. For dramatic treatment of a short headline, you can allow a large letter in one color to overlap a large letter in a second color.

Or run part—only part—of an illustration in color, the rest in black and white. Or run a tint block behind the part you want emphasized.

Or use color blocks alternately with black-and-white blocks, placing items and prices in each block.

Or run artwork in a medium-to-light color as a pattern or decorative element, leaving the type, in black, in full command.

Or underneath a copy block run some art in a weak color, not so it will be seen clearly but so it will provide atmosphere for the ad. An old device, admittedly, but one that can be dusted off and used occasionally.

Or use off-register color. The color plate is prepared without much regard for how it fits, so that one color will spill over into another's area. The resultant art has a refreshing looseness.

Or have the art for the color plate prepared with a crayon after the

Black-and-white photography would have told about the shape and workings of this hardware, but it took full color to bring out its beauty and to capture the attention of persons making important decisions about building design and construction. With the right photographer on the job, there is color to be found in every object, no matter how gray it may appear to the uninitiated. The client: Russwin. Agency: Horton, Church & Goff, Rhode Island. Art director: Bob Saabye. Copywriter: Ted Albert. Photographer: Clint Clemens.

Soften the look of security.

For the mechanical for the two-color folder shown below, the designer had to prepare the original art (in black) and three overlays: one for the outside color (a tint of black plus yellow), one for the pure yellow inside the sun, and one for the tint of black in the clouds. The client: Midgley's Glass; the art studio: Rubick & Funk.

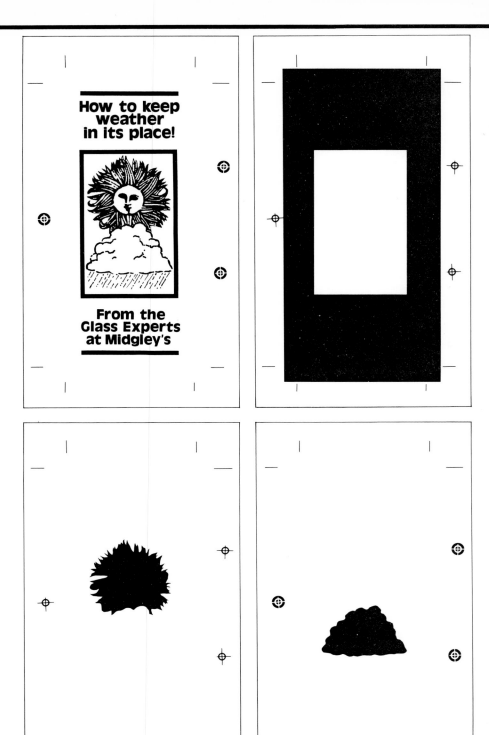

fashion of the elementary school artist. The primitive look has a charm all its own.

Or run only one tiny spot of color in the ad, but in a bright ink. You could, for instance, design your ad so all type is reversed in a black block. Then you would choose one of the reversed lines or words and fill it with color.

Or run a line reproduction of a photograph over a solid color block. You will be surprised at the strength, the power of such treatment.

Or surround your color areas with bold, black lines and boxes.

Or try fluorescent or metallic inks and papers made from offbeat materials and in nondescribable colors.

The production of color

When you settle for black-and-white, you get a one-color printing job. Adding a color, say blue, you get a two-color job. Blue would be called, then, a "second color."

You can get two-color, three-color, four-color printing—or more. *Look* magazine, before it died, made noise about offering advertisers a fifth color: white. That does not sound like much, but when you compare a pure white ink with the off-white you have in most magazine paper stock, you see that a little added white might be worth the extra expense. Some auto manufacturers, when they introduce their new models, buy a fifth color in the magazines. The fifth color often is silver.

But for most ads, four colors will give you all the color range you need: besides the primary colors, you get green, orange, brown, purple, and the others. Primary colors are either printed side by side, and the reader's eye mixes them, or, transparent, they are printed on top of each other and so change in the printing.

The graphic designer works basically with two kinds of color in printing: *spot* (or flat) and *process.*

In process color work (four-color) the photoengraver or cameraman, using filters, separates the primary colors in the color original (color transparency, color print, or painting) and records the separation on film. The resultant negatives help produce positive prints, which are rephotographed, through a screen, to make new negatives. The new now-screened negatives help make plates—one for each primary and for black. The combination of colors provides a full-color effect. "Full color" is possible with just three plates (omitting the black), but such short-cutting produces inferior reproductions.

In spot color, an artist can separate the colors for the printer, offering artwork for each color on its own sheet. This can be done by making the principal part of the drawing, usually the black part, on a sheet of drawing paper or a piece of illustration board, then making a drawing of each of the other main colors on a sheet of frosted acetate, which is fastened over the original. Even though the overlays are for other colors, the artist works in black or red, colors that will be picked up easily by the camera. When the plates are ready, the printer will use the correct inks.

In making the overlay for the printer, the artist puts down a series of "register marks" to help the printer line up the plates in printing.

If the colors are rather simply used with no overlapping, the artist can make a single drawing—called a "keyline drawing." On a tracing paper overlay—a guide to the printer—the artist marks with color pencils where the color is to go. The printer simply makes more than one copy of the line negative—three if the job is three-color—and then paints out on each negative the part that is not to print.

While advertisers like color in their ads to make the product realistic or the package recognizable, there are problems. For instance, it is difficult to match exactly a color on a package with a color in a periodical. Different inks are used. And color on one kind of stock—on the carton—looks different when it is printed on magazine stock or newsprint.

Where you place the color in designing a direct-mail piece can make a difference in the quality of the color, especially if it involves both process and spot color pieces. Check with your printer at the design stage to determine the most advantageous placement.

For letterpress reproduction on cheap newsprint, McCann-Erickson, San Francisco, agency for Ortho Lawn Food, decided the best way to show a lush lawn was through black-and-white pen-and-ink shading. The artist creates the illusion of shadow by short white lines in a black area. He shows "color" on the sacks by using the Ben Day process. For gravure publications and publications using a better-quality paper stock, the agency showed the same scene through full-color photography.

Cutting the cost of color

Whenever you use color in advertising you can count on an earlier deadline—to take care of color separations, additional presswork, and the like—and more expense. For a short-run job, the expense and trouble may not be worth it.

As a designer, you have a number of ways of keeping color costs down. For instance, when you would like to use color photography but cannot afford it, you might consider one of three possible handlings of black-and-white photographs which, although more expensive than regular handlings, still keep the budget manageable.

One is the *duotone*. In this case, a single photograph submitted to the printer is used to make two negatives (the screen is turned slightly for the second) and two plates. One plate prints a color, the other prints black. (In some advertising, where high quality is needed, one plate prints black, the other a gray.) With a duotone you get the feel of color while holding onto the strength, the tone variation, offered by black.

Another handling is the *halftone over a tint*. The student may not be able to tell this from a duotone, but the trained observer sees a big difference. The color under the halftone remains constant; the picture has less depth, but there is a satisfying, a restful quality there you cannot get

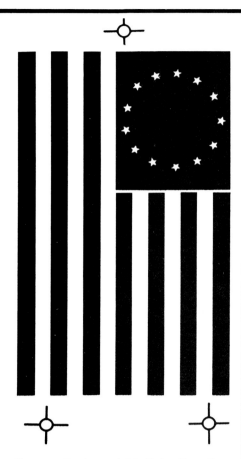

Because the bars of this Betsy Ross flag do not quite touch where they run into the field containing the stars, this art—a "keyline drawing"—can easily be used for two-color printing. It is all the printer needs to make one plate for printing the red stripes and another for printing the blue field. Metro Newspaper Service offers art like this as part of its monthly package. Those are register marks at the top and bottom. In the final printing neither those nor the identifying code would show.

any other way. It is like printing in black on a pastel stock, but with pure white at the edges of the picture.

A third handling involves a *silhouette halftone in a field of color*. The color goes only up to the edge of the black-ink silhouette, so the halftone itself is printed on the white paper stock. A special piece of artwork has to be made for the color plate.

All three of these require two printings. You would use any one of them when you plan to use a second color anyway.

You might also try "posterizing" the colors. You will get "full color" without resorting to process color. And you will get an unusual effect.

Here is how it works:

Submitting a regular photograph to the printer, ask for two, three, or four line negatives (depending upon how many colors you want), each negative getting more exposure than the one before. One negative, for instance, might pick up all tone 80 percent and above, another all tone 60 percent and above, another all tone 30 percent and above. Use the negative that picked up the most tone—30 percent and above—for the *lightest* color—yellow. Use the one next in line for red. Use the third for blue.

The colors are printed on top of one another (the lightest color being printed first) so that one color does not obscure the others.

And now consider the ways of getting color without paying anything for it:

1. Use tints of a single color. In black—or in any color—you can use Ben Day-like blocks of various strengths. The same inking, the same presswork takes care of it all. The tints range from 10 percent of the solid tone up to 90 percent of the solid tone. Taking one of them, say 60 percent, you can ask for it in any of several screens, from 50- to 133-line and beyond. In other words, a single tint is available in various degrees of coarseness.

To get a tint of the second color, you shouldn't go darker than a 70 percent screen. Higher-percentage screens result in a closing up of the dots. Nor should you often go finer than a 100-line screen. Finer screens (120-line, 133-line, 150-line) need a lot of attention in printing, and the stock should be smooth, preferably coated.

Printing a tint block over another color, you get a brand new color—a third color. A tint of black over yellow will give you a green. The same tint over red will give you a maroon.

2. Print in a colored ink, skipping the black. This will work only if the color you choose is dark, near a black. Otherwise your halftones will be washed out, faded. And your type will be hard to read. You can print the color on a stock other than white, say dark green on gray.

3. Print in black, but on a colored stock.

4. Confine your color to one side of the sheet—or one side of the signature, if a booklet is involved. You will get a second color on fewer pages but at a lower printing cost.

5. Rely on "black-and-white color." This simply means combining generous blocks of blacks with ruled rectangles and Ben Day tints; putting reverses in some of the blocks, surprints in others; using a variety of types. The effect is circusy, perhaps a little cheap; but the job will be "colorful."

Choosing a second color

An advertiser talking about color in a magazine—especially in a general-circulation magazine—means, usually, *full* color. Talking about color in newspapers or direct mail, the advertiser means, usually, black plus one color—a second color.

As an imaginative designer, you can do a lot with a second color. You can almost create the illusion of a full-color job, and at a considerable savings over full-color costs. All in one ad you can run black on white, color on white, white surrounded by color, white surrounded by black, and color surrounded by black. Screening the color to a tint or tints and using further surprints and reverses and tints of black over the color, you can get even more variety.

So the second color to choose, usually, would be in the medium range— light enough to contrast with the black areas, dark enough to contrast with the white of the paper.

As second colors, medium greens and blues are also good. Yellow is poor. If yellow is the second color, it should be used in large blocks with no reverses; it should not be used by itself to print the type.

At least for direct mail, no two-color combination works better than red and black. One group of tests over a fourteen-year period showed red and black outpulled every other combination. Writing to circulation directors of magazines, Eliot Schein, president of Schein/Blattstein Advertising, said, "If the graphics people you use are getting tired of red and black, it would be better to change graphics people rather than to allow them to change your colors. No—mint green and purple will not pull better than red and black."[7]

That is a pretty black-and-white observation, and obviously there are some clients—and some audiences—who deserve different color combinations in two-color printings. But at least you should give some initial consideration to red and black. One big advantage of red as a second color is that it gives you such good contrast to the black, and yet it is bold enough to stand out nicely from the white of the paper. Furthermore, the color is dark enough to take reverses, light enough to take surprints.

It is not a good idea to cover the *entire* area of the ad with the color. When you do that, you throw away your white. Actually you are back to a one-color job again: black on a colored stock.

Indicating color on your layout

Color pencils, crayons, pastel sticks, color felt markers, color ink, colored paper, tempera paint, designers' colors, and watercolors all can be used to indicate color on the layout. Because it is impossible with these tools to depict exactly the color you have in mind, as a guide to the printer you would submit with the layout a color swatch clipped from some other printing or a code number from an ink-specimen book.

The ideal tool is the marker, available in a generous variety of colors and in blunt and fine tips. If you cannot afford all the colors you need to do a layout, you can come close by applying available colors over each other on the layout.

If you use a color pencil, use it "side fashion" to cover large areas.

Crayon or pastel sticks are useful for covering large areas, too. Break off a less-than-one-inch chunk and scrub on the color, like this:

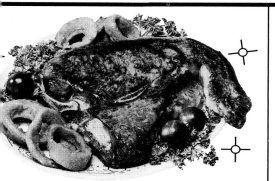

RED PLATE

BLUE PLATE

YELLOW PLATE

Proofs in black of each of the plates used in three-color process printing of halftone art. (Courtesy Metro Newspaper Service.)

In covering large areas, work in broad sweeps. Do not be concerned about filling in perfectly to every edge. What you want is a basic tone. In some cases you may be able to use pieces of colored paper.

You may find it necessary to use more than one tool to indicate a single color: something blunt for the solid areas, something fine for the lettering. It is not always easy to match the colors. One of the advantages of markers is that blunt and fine tips are color-coordinated.

To show type in reverse you can either outline the letters and fill in around them or lay down a solid area of color and do your letters in white paint. If you use pastels for the solid areas, you will have to apply a fixative before you paint the letters.

Keep the principles of design in mind as you work. Proportion is particularly important. Do not allow your ad to become half black and white in area, half color. Either let color dominate, or use it for accent purposes. A spot of color in two or three places in the ad will give you more color impact than color scattered indiscriminately throughout.

1. "Readership Jumps 38% When Ads Are in 4-Color," *Folio,* November 1979, p. 29.
2. "The "Post-Modern Palette," *Art Direction,* October 1983, p. 39.
3. "The Bluing of America," *Time,* July 18, 1983, p. 62.
4. Color blindness seems to be mostly a male phenomenon. John Adkins Richardson in *Art: The Way It Is* (New York: Harry N. Abrams, 1973) reported that 8 percent of men and only 0.5 percent of women are color-blind.
5. Some scholars consider green as a fourth primary.
6. Violet is called "purple" when on the bluish side.
7. Eliot DeY. Schein, "Twenty Tips," *Folio,* February 1980, p. 78.

11
Newspaper advertising

In the 1980s newspapers continue to hold onto their title as the number one medium for advertising. About 30 percent of all money U.S. advertisers spend on the media goes to newspapers—to the 1,750 dailies and the 7,600 weeklies or semiweeklies. Close to 700 of the dailies publish Sunday issues.

Most of the dailies are evening papers, although in large cities with both morning and evening papers the morning paper usually is larger.

The advertisers' needs play a big part in a newspaper's decision about when to publish. The switch from afternoon to morning publication among the dailies came about largely because advertisers wanted readers to have the whole day to consider items on sale in the stores. One weekly in a resort area—the *News Guard* of Lincoln City, Oregon—does not publish on Thursdays, when weeklies traditionally are published, but on Wednesdays, to give local residents a chance at sale items before tourists roll into town.[1]

Advertising accounts for close to two-thirds of the contents of daily and Sunday newspapers. What is left is called the "news hole," and into that

Juster's, a quality men's store in Minneapolis, decided to let its customers try writing ads, and so conducted a contest which drew 148 entries. The winning ad was published, along with copy (extreme right) describing the contest and naming other winners. Bruce Bildstein wrote the prize-winning copy. Joe Duffy designed the ad. Duffy, Bringgold, Knutson & Oberprillers, Inc. was the agency.

This is the overall winner in the Juster's "Write an Ad" contest. The First Prize of a $500 wardrobe from Juster's goes to **Mr. Bruce Bildstein** *of 1909 Emerson Avenue South, Minneapolis.*

Introducing the perfect shirt for the hopelessly indecisive.

Of all the decisions you have to make, none is harder than choosing between two favorites. And all too often that decision is between your favorite oxford cloth dress shirt and your favorite knit polo shirt.

Which gave us a wonderful idea. Why not make a shirt that combines the best features of both? (Actually the idea belongs to a master shirtmaker. We simply had the vision to seek him out.)

We call the combination of these two staples of tradition the Juster's Oxford Sport Shirt. And in this case, the sum is just as great as its parts.

The fabric is pure cotton oxford cloth. It gives the shirt its crisp drape and everlasting comfort. And with it you get all those important oxford cloth shirt details.

For example, a generous box pleat in back (with traditional hanger loop, of course) to let the shirt move with you, instead of against you. There's also a full buttoned placket and double felled stitching at the shoulders and sides.

The men's version even has a secure button front pocket with an opening for your pen or pencil.

And since this is a sport shirt, above all, we added the best features of a knit polo shirt. The sleeves are short and feature rib knit cuffs. The collar is also rib knit, in pure cotton, so it stands up to years of use and abuse.

The result is a shirt that can be very casual, but yet can be almost formal, too. Which means you may decide to wear it quite often.

You'll find the Juster's Oxford Sport Shirt in five colors: yellow, melon, pink, blue or helio. (All have a white collar and cuffs.) You'll also find that it comes in the wide Juster's range of sizes for both men and women.

Because after all, we can't make all your decisions for you.

Juster's

Nicollet Mall • Southdale • Brookdale • Ridgedale
Maplewood • Rosedale • Highland Village

There are a lot of good writers out there.

When we ran our "Write an Ad" contest, we expected perhaps 50 or 60 entries at most.

But we were, frankly, overwhelmed. First, by the sheer number. We received 148 entries, with some people sending as many as four separate efforts.

Second, by the quality. The majority of the ads were well thought out and well-written. (Those who lament the passing of literacy in our society would be exhilarated by the quality of our entries.)

And finally, by the depth of research done. Entrants commandeered our salesmen for details, studied at the library, and in general immersed themselves in the subject.

Ultimately, we made our decisions based on quality of copy, incisiveness of headlines, and strategic thinking (i.e., creating a selling story particular to the shirt, versus a generic all-cotton story, an anti-designer-shirt approach, and the like).

The Second Prize ($250 in clothing) goes to **Mr. Tom G. Evans III** *of 742 North Pascal in St. Paul. (Headline: "By the time the collar of most oxford cloth shirts is broken in, the shirt has broken down.")*

Our two Third Prizes of $100 in clothing from Juster's go to **Mr. Alan S. Jaffee** *of 2508 Lyndale Avenue South, Minneapolis (Headline: "Juster's Rules of Fashion: Once you know all the rules, you can break them"), and* **Mr. Bill Hampton** *of 307 West 15th Street, Minneapolis. (Headline: "Not to exaggerate, but we just reinvented the shirt".)*

It was exceedingly difficult to make the final choices. We only wish we had another twenty or fifty prizes to award.

But for all of you who entered, we thank you for your efforts and obvious dedication to the task. If nothing else, you've become more astute customers through your research.

Do you think we should run a contest like this again? Let us know.

A full-color, full-page newspaper ad, designed as a sampler, sells Lloyd Center, Portland, as a place to go Christmas shopping. Joe Erceg designed; Art Farm did the illustration.

go news, editorials, and features of various kinds. In the mid-1940s advertising occupied a little more than half the total space.

A newspaper's readership always exceeds its circulation. Professor Fred Farrar of Temple University says that the long-accepted premise that 2.3 readers see a single copy of a newspaper is being adjusted upward. The new thinking has it that 2.7 readers see each copy. Where advertising rates remain constant, this makes newspapers a better buy for advertisers than in the past.

What a newspaper charges for various size ads is covered on a rate card made available to all advertisers. The cards not only spell out space rates; they also outline special requirements. For instance, the *News Times and Lincoln County Leader* at Newport, Oregon, charges extra "for layouts requiring extra camera work, such as reverses, screening, extra negatives or more than five photographs per ad."

One of *Standard Rate & Data Service*'s regularly issued publications covers newspapers and their rates and requirements.

Like other media, newspapers do some policing of ads, refusing to accept those that violate rules set up by management.

Except for the smallest papers, the news/editorial side operates completely independently of the advertising side. But a series of exposés on the news side caused the advertising staff of the *St. Petersburg Times and Evening Independent* to adjust its policy on accepting ads from home repair people. A large percentage of them had been operating without proper licenses. Now a license number has to be included in ads these people place with the newspaper.

Leading newspapers

A 1983 *Advertising Age* survey of journalism professors' preferences for daily newspapers resulted in the following first-ten ranking: *New York Times, Washington Post, Los Angeles Times, Wall Street Journal, Boston Globe, Chicago Tribune, Miami Herald, Philadelphia Inquirer, Louisville Courier-Journal*, and *Christian Science Monitor.* A similar survey among advertising agency media executives, conducted a little more informally, brought out essentially the same ranking, with the *Chicago Tribune* going up a little higher on the list. The agency executives, of course, were looking at papers from the standpoint of their effectiveness as advertising media.

Two of the papers on the list, the *Wall Street Journal* and *Christian Science Monitor,* are national dailies. That category expanded in late 1982 when *USA Today* appeared. Unlike the other two, *USA Today* is designed for the average reader rather than for just the businessperson or the intellectual.

"Without modern market research satellite date transmission and facsimile printing, *USA Today* could not exist," observed Everette Dennis, dean of the University of Oregon School of Journalism. "It is the product of a new information society made possible by computers and satellites. It is also the result of human effort, the work of a gifted staff. . . ."

The paper draws on writing from the staffs of Gannett's chain of eighty-eight local dailies. With its mostly short news items, the paper is marked by flashy graphics and excellent full-color printing. It directs itself especially to the television generation. Its well-designed weather maps have influenced weather coverage in other dailies.

Another full-color newspaper ad for Lloyd Center, doing an institutional job to attract back-to-school trade. Part of the promotion involved the distribution of free apples. Art director and designer: Joe Erceg.

Robin Rickabaugh designed this unusual restaurant ad and did the calligraphy. Marilyn Musick wrote the copy. The studio responsible for the design is Rickabaugh Design, Portland.

Delicious!

We're filled with fresh ideas to take you back to school. In style. We're Lloyd Center. And we have all the crisp new looks that are going places this fall. All the shapes and colors you want to take with you on campus. And off. We're 113 great stores brimming over with everything you need for fall. With cool-weather values that won't take too big a bite out of your budget. Visit us Monday through Friday 9:30 to 9, Saturday 9:30 to 5:30, Sunday, noon to 5. We'll send you back to classes stylishly. Wrap you up wonderfully. And make it all a delicious shopping experience!

Come to Shop and Stay for Fun! Parking is free and easy. Bus routes are a breeze.

Take a Big Bite.

We have free apples for you! One thousand apples given away daily. August 14 through August 21, 1 pm.

Off and Rolling.

Lloyd Center and KPAM free roller disco party. Featuring Disco Delivery, refreshments, prizes. Friday, August 15, 7 to 10 pm, Ninth and Halsey Street parking lot.

All-American Auto Show.

A great display of cars from the Sandy Boulevard Auto Dealers Association. August 14 through 21.

Ups and Downs.

The D'Air Devils Trampoline Team gets a jump on back-to-school. Friday and Saturday, August 15 and 16, noon and 2 pm. Lloyd Center Central Mall.

What's Cooking?

Tasty recipes at the Oregon Pork Cook-Out King Contest. Friday, August 15, 10 am to 4 pm; Saturday, August 16, 11 am to 3 pm. Lloyd Center Central Mall.

"Funtasia."

Magic under the big top. Carnival rides, too. For the benefit of the National Federation of the Blind, August 22 to 31, Thirteenth and Multnomah Street parking lot. For ticket prices and performance times, phone 774-2828.

Music to Your Ears. The All-American Boys Chorus from Orange County, California performs for you. Sunday, August 17, 3 pm. Central Mall.

Family Fun Run. Lloyd Center and KOIN-TV present the first annual Summer's End Run for the benefit of the American Diabetes Association. Sunday, August 24, 10 am. Register now in Lloyd Center Mall. For further information phone 282-2511.

LLOYD the Original ... and still original

It thinks of itself as "a second read" in the cities where it has news-stands, but clearly the dailies in the big cities served by *USA Today* look upon the newspaper as serious competition.

The newspaper image

Like other publications, newspapers strive to keep their images up. Aware that some critics think it is superficial, *USA Today* used front cover space on *Editor & Publisher* (the magazine carries ads there) to say that "if *USA Today* is lightweight, call it Boom-Boom Mancini!" The ad quoted an *Adweek* writer to say that the features are written to be understood, that people quote from them at cocktail parties, that the sports section is "a sports fan's dream," and that the lively and colorful graphics in the paper inspire better graphics in other papers. "Like the championship boxer, [*USA Today*] 'packs a wallop'—for readers and advertisers."[2]

Some image-making campaigns for newspapers are designed to attract subscribers, others to attract advertisers. The campaigns to attract advertisers are the more persistent. Such advertising sells the community as one that is receptive to brand-name as well as local advertising. It sells the paper as a vital force in the community, respected for its news and editorial coverage. It also tells of its advantages over other media, including competing newspapers.

The bigger dailies have been upgrading their locally edited magazine sections to woo local advertisers who lean toward the city and regional magazines and magazines with regional editions. To give advertisers better production, newspapers sometimes print these sections away from their home bases in rotogravure. Or they make use of "heatset" offset presses that offer better quality printing than that available from regular offset presses.

National advertising

Two kinds of advertising get into the newspapers: national and local.

National ads for newspapers, prepared by advertising agencies, are much like magazine ads. Local ads, prepared by local advertisers, local agencies, or by the newspapers' advertising departments, are something else again. This chapter is concerned mostly with these ads.[3] But first, some observations about national advertising.

National advertising arrives at the newspaper in proof, mat, or plate form, ready for insertion. The creative work has already been done. The newspaper does little more than make sure the advertising gets published on the appointed date.

For the national advertiser, the newspaper offers a chance to go into detail about advertising first placed on TV or in the magazines. There is more space. But the newspaper ad can introduce products as well.

Publishers' representatives call on agencies and advertisers to convince them that the papers can deliver the kinds of audiences the advertisers need to reach.

To help national advertisers decide when to buy newspaper space, the Newspaper Advertising Bureau programs information about news/editorial content in 1,350 of the daily newspapers. Using the NAB service, an advertiser can schedule ads for days when appropriate stories or features appear and even request that the ads appear nearby.

Various combinations of independently owned newspapers exist to better serve the national advertiser. For instance, the advertiser can buy the "Golden Gate Suburban Group" of four newspapers in the Bay Area outside of San Francisco, involving one insertion order and one bill.

Like all media, newspapers suffer as well as profit from trends in ad-

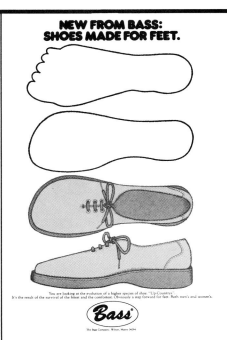

NEW FROM BASS: SHOES MADE FOR FEET.

You are looking at the evolution of a higher species of shoe. "Up-Country." It's the result of the survival of the fittest and the comfortest. Obviously a step forward for feet. Both men's and women's.

Bass

The Bass Company, Wilton, Maine 04294

An example of national advertising designed for newspaper insertion. Art director Peter Paris uses art to dramatize the idea that these Bass shoes are, as the headline says, "made for feet," and that the shoes are, as the copy points out, "the evolution of a higher species. . . ." The species is "the result of the survival of the fittest and the comfortest. Obviously a step forward for feet." George Castleman wrote the copy. Chirurg & Cairns, Inc. was the agency.

vertising. An advertiser—or a class of advertisers—will become disillusioned with one basic medium and move to another. Mercedes-Benz for a time discontinued its newspaper advertising in favor of spot advertising on television because of the "irresponsibility" of some newspapers. The company felt that it was getting poor reproduction. And some papers would not even send tear sheets. Another reason given by the company was that the price of the car kept it out of the reach of most newspaper readers.

Local advertising
Local advertising breaks down into two categories: classified and display. Classified advertising makes little use of design. For most newspapers it is nothing more than column after column of small-type listings.

Display advertising, on the other hand, *does* require designing, and often it is the newspaper that does the job. On a small newspaper it may be the ad manager or a salesperson who does the designing. A large daily may offer the advertiser the services of a staff of designers, layout artists, illustrators, pasteup artists, and copywriters, in some cases without additional charge.

Unfortunately, a lot of the design looks its price. Kenneth R. Kinney explained why: "This medium of ours [newspapers] is so powerful, it gets so overwhelmingly to each cranny of the retailer's market, *any* advertising that's legible can produce satisfactory results. That, of course, is why so much retail newspaper advertising is so bad at worst, so bland at best; it doesn't *have* to be good to win."[4]

But it does not have to be bad, either. Many designers, working with

Amway uses vertical alignments for the elements in this large newspaper ad but puts everything on a slant for a sense of urgency and to make the large amount of copy inviting. It also breaks up the copy with subheads reversed in black bars along with some small abstract drawings which dramatize the listing of products offered by the organization. The logo and the horizon line in the photo of the yacht are the only horizontal elements, and they are there to provide a bit of contrast, some change of pace. Amway is unable to show all one million of the distributors mentioned in the headline, of course, but the cropped crowd-scene photograph helps make the point. The ad was designed by Ward Veldman; the agency was Stevens Inc. of Grand Rapids, Michigan.

the advertiser or with the medium, are trying to upgrade the design in local newspaper ads.

All must be done with an eye on the clock. The people in the display advertising department tend to live by Wallace Wood's Rules of Drawing:

1. Never draw what you can copy.
2. Never copy what you can trace.
3. Never trace what you can cut out and paste down.[5]

Hurried printing on thin, pulpy newsprint makes even the most carefully designed ad often a disappointment. What the designer must do, then, is learn to design around the limitations, which "no more prevent good design being done for newspapers than the limitations of the sonnet form prevent the creation of good poetry. . . . In fact, the talented designer, like the talented poet, takes advantage of such limitations."[6] For instance, the designer uses bold, nonregistered colors and large art executed in heavy ink or crayon line. This is not to say that ordinary halftones can't be used when necessary. In many letterpress papers and most offset papers, continuous-tone art, provided it is big enough, reproduces quite well.

The newspaper medium has the advantage, important to designers as well as copywriters, of serving readers who are actually hunting for ads. It also gives designers a giant format to work with.

Years ago newspapers claimed just about all of the advertising placed by retail establishments. Now other media, including regional editions of national magazines and, of course, the new city magazines, run retail ads. Each year television—and radio—make further inroads into this market. And direct mail continues to appeal to many retailers as a useful advertising medium. Outdoor posters are part of the retail picture, too.

Although the switch to offset has improved reproduction quality in newspapers, production deficiencies continue to annoy many advertisers. Hy Leder, advertising manager of Ohrbach's, which does most of its advertising in newspapers, is not convinced that ROP (run of paper) color has attained "sufficient fidelity to convey Ohrbach's fashion visuals to best advantage."[7] J. Warren McClure, a marketing consultant, registered the additional complaint that "today's display advertising deadlines are often more stringent than in the old hot metal days."

Local advertisers, including retail advertisers, make more use of classified advertising than they did in the past. Texas Tech University offers a seminar in effective use of the classifieds.

Retail advertising

A few stores take out full-page newspaper ads, especially at holiday time, to polish their images, but primarily the stores take out ads, large or small, to sell merchandise, and often merchandise that has been marked down. Stores constantly search for new ways to say "sale" and new excuses to

Kathleen Gordon-Burke of KGB Graphics, Eureka, California, faced with the job of promoting panda bear premiums offered by one of her clients, Coast Central Credit Union, dreamed up a connection between "panacea" and a word she made up, "pandacea." This newspaper ad was the result. She cropped "panacea" to help the reader focus on "pandacea."

A shallow newspaper ad running across the bottom of a page can dominate the page, especially if it is designed to work like a poster, as this Coast Central Credit Union ad does in *The Union* of Arcada, California. Kathleen Gordon-Burke of KGB Graphics, Eureka, designed and wrote the ad.

pana-cca, 1 pana-sia;
1. a pretended remedy for all ills.

pan̆da-céa, 2 pan̆da-céa, *n.*
2. Coast's <u>comfort</u> from financial ills.

give your money and a Panda Family a good home

[ie, *deposit* $500 • 18 month certificate • earn 8% — *take home* Papa Panda or Brother Pickwick • earn 8½% with a checking account

deposit $250 • 18 month certificate • earn 7½% (available only to members *under 18*) — *make a home for* Mama & Baby Panda]

All certificates are compounded mon over a year. They carry a 180-day for of interest. Passbook each day theres *Rates may raise. Call Coastline for a update — 443-CASH or 800-851-9727 will not be less than advertised. This ends September 30, 1983.

EUREKA
ARCATA
FORTUNA
CRESCENT Cr
WEAVERVILLE

**COAST CENTRAL
CREDIT UNION**

COAST IS A FINANCIAL CO-OPERATIVE FOR QUALIFIED INDIVIDUALS.
AND YOU MAY BE MORE ELIGIBLE THAN YOU THINK.

Each member account insured $100,000
Administrator, National Credit Union

COAST IS LENDING MONEY!

11·75%
AUTO LOANS

**COAST CENTR.
CREDIT UNIO**

48 MONTHS
13% DOWN
PLUS TAX & LICENSE

443-CASH
800 851-9727

Each member account insure
Administrator, National Credit Union

conduct one. A sale becomes a "celebration" (or a "sell-a-bration"), a "riot," or, if the store has class, an "event." And the reason for the sale turns out to be that somebody goofed and ordered too many of the items, a new shipment is coming in, the tax season is at hand, a holiday is ahead, or it just happens to be the end of the month.

A New York grocery chain, D'Agostino, during the 1983 one hundredth birthday celebration of the Brooklyn Bridge, offered "50 cheers for the Brooklyn Bridge"—50 sale items in a *New York Times* full-page ad. The bridge was "twice the age of D'Agostino, yet she makes us feel so young!" said the opening copy. This store's slogan is "If there's not one near you . . . move!"

The Newspaper Advertising Bureau says retail advertising should clearly identify the store and narrow in on potential customers, make one element in the ad stand out from the others, leave out any unessential elements, organize elements as the store itself is organized, and stress benefits of shopping at that particular store.

Sometimes retail advertising does more. The ads for Swensen's Market, Twin Falls, Idaho, contain short editorials written by the store's owner, Jerry Swensen. Some are humorous, some argumentative and even controversial. Subject matter varies. One editorial criticized Evel Knievel's daredevil jump over Idaho's Snake River Canyon. Swensen tries to tie his comments to what's being advertised. He ran his anti-Knievel editorial in an ad selling bologna. He says he produces his unusual ads to make them stand out from the big ads sponsored by chain groceries.

The purpose of the advertising may be to educate rather than sell. Kal Ruttenstein of Bloomingdale's says that his advertising often promotes avant-garde merchandise just to get curious shoppers into the store. ". . . not every woman wants to wear . . . [unusual clothes]. So for her, we have the classics, the clothing she's comfortable wearing. But she feels good knowing it comes from the store that features the latest. And by displaying the new looks, we're educating her. Next year, or the year after that, maybe today's far-out design will be modified a bit, and . . . she'll be more likely to try it on. . . ."[8]

Even when it's for a department store, the advertising may narrow in on a specific audience. Bloomingdale's went after young buyers and apartment dwellers who could shop only on Saturdays with a "Saturday's Generation" series of newspaper advertisement in Saturday morning papers. This resulted in a special "Saturday's Generation" shop within the store featuring contemporary furniture, molded plastic goods, and play clothes.

That the advertising department of a store must satisfy the various merchandise department heads and buyers does complicate things. The job becomes even more complicated when departments within a store are franchise operations.

Then there is the matter of co-op money. When a manufacturer offers to pay for part of the cost of the advertising, the store advertising usually has to incorporate certain items into the ad and run them at agreed-upon sizes.

A retail ad can do something a national ad cannot very well do. It can bring competing brands together and not only compare them but give each of them a good sales pitch and then allow the reader to make up his own mind. A Father's Day ad in the *New York Times* by B. Altman & Co. is instructive here. The nearly full-page ad carried this headline: "Find Your Father's Favorite Quote and We'll Tell You His Favorite Fragrance." Photographs of seven shave lotions/colognes followed, along with quotations. For instance, Yves St. Laurent brand carried a line from Ralph Waldo Emerson: "Who so would be a man must be a non-conformist," while Givenchy Gentleman brand carried a line from Voltaire: "Change everything, except your loves."

a warm invitation to a hot coffee-tasting

Come quaff a convivial cup, or a couple, or more. Sip from a special sampling of our gourmet coffee: "Supremo Colombian", "Costa Rican—Superior", "Venezuelan Tachiras", "Escondido Mexican." Your taste buds will be tantalized with sensations surging from mellow to bracingly bright. Toothsome tidbits accompany.

Our special coffee-tasting takes place each day, Monday, May 1, through Friday, May 5, 9 a.m. to 4:30 p.m., as we celebrate the GRAND OPENING of the new Red Wagon Store at 197th and Sandy.

Our gracious greeter Laura Buck is here to make you warmly welcome as she did at the former 2nd and Jefferson location. We've also brought along the same nostalgic atmosphere and the satisfying scents of teas, spices and seasonings from all over the world, with more spacious surroundings to view them in.

the Red Wagon has moved

To reach the new Red Wagon Store from Downtown or Vancouver, take 80 N (Banfield) freeway to the 181st Avenue exit, then to Sandy Blvd. and on east to the new Boyd Coffee building and the Red Wagon Store at 197th and Sandy. (Gresham gourmets, you're practically here.)

The Red Wagon Store also mails fine coffees. If you'd like to conduct your own coffee-tasting cozily in your home, send for our Coffee Sampler. It contains half-pound bags of Colombian, Costa Rican, Kenyan, Guatemalan, Mocha-Java Blend and Red Wagon Blend — 6 coffees in all, 3 lbs. roasted and mailed the day we receive your order, and we pay postage.
Address: Red Wagon Store, P.O. Box 20547, Portland, Oregon 97220
Send _____ Coffee Samplers @ $4.95 each postpaid.
Specify: ☐ Reg. grind   ☐ Drip grind
☐ Whole bean
Enclosed is my check for $ _____
Name _____
Address _____
City/State/Zip _____   RW1

RED WAGON STORE

It must have been an interesting exercise for the copywriter, searching for just the right quotations and matching them with the products. The manufacturers did not supply the quotations. And their attachment to the products was purely arbitrary and possibly tongue-in-cheek. But you can just see readers browsing through the ad, looking for a quotation that might be appropriate to their fathers, and then settling for brands that otherwise might have been overlooked. It did not matter that the quotations were never passed along to the fathers, although in some cases perhaps they were.

Not all retail advertisers take themselves seriously. In an ad selling winter clothes, Macy's of New York uses this headline: "Ralph Lauren: His Clothes Make City Survival a Real Possibility." As though survival in the city without such clothes were impossible. And even with them, you could not be sure. The copy started out like this:

"It took a native New Yorker like Ralph to come up with clothes suited to a habitat this unpredictable. He knows as well as anyone that life in The Big City is tough. And that's why his Polo Westernwear has the built-in flexibility to handle it all. Without sacrificing an ounce of style."

Headlines can make a big difference in retail advertising. An effective automobile-dealer ad for Harry Hollywood Cadillac, Miami Beach, used a question headline: "What Makes a Cadillac a Harry Hollywood Cadillac?" Three subheads, each followed by a paragraph of copy, attempted an answer. The first read: "It Isn't the Price." The second: "It Isn't the Location." The third: "It Must Be the People." The reader could take in only the headline and subheads and still get the message. The subheads were parallel in structure—a plus. And they had a rhythm to them— another plus.

Sometimes you may want to make your ad look like anything but an

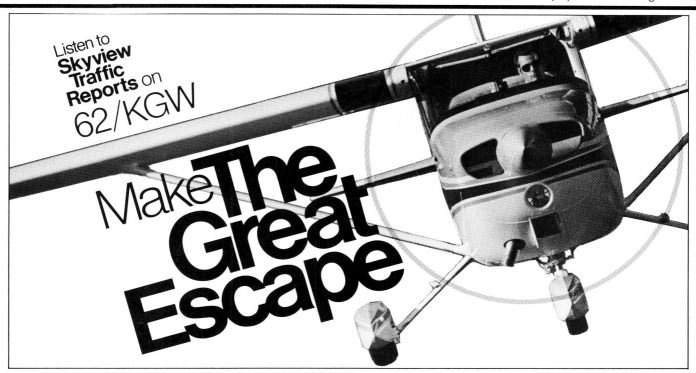

This multicolumn newspaper ad says "action" because its elements are designed on a diagonal. The diagonal also helps create the feeling of a plane making its turn above a city's rush-hour traffic. Designer Rick Campbell uses an axis on the left to line up most—but not all—of the lines of sans serif type. The photograph, by Maryanne Akin, is silhouetted, and a circle of Ben Day is added to create the illusion of a propeller going around. The copy is by Joan Teel, the station's promotion director. The advertiser is KGW, a Portland, Oregon, radio station.

ad. Some retailers have made their ads look like newspaper front pages, with lots of "stories" and flush-left headlines, along with a "Sale" logo.

One way of dramatizing the fact that one-only items in a sale are going fast is to print a "SOLD" across the description of items that sell during an ad's production. Car dealers and furniture stores use this technique.

Sometimes it pays to make the art, border, or background of an ad appropriate to the season. A store selling school supplies, for instance, might want to show the supplies on a notepaper or ruled-tablet background.

Most department stores, discount stores, chain drugstores, grocery stores, furniture stores, and building supply stores produce omnibus ads, with many items pictured and described. The better stores engage occasionally in one-item advertising, and when that happens the ads look more like magazine ads. One-item ads often dwell on quality, but sometimes they feature low price.

It is vital that a store develop a graphic style that will immediately identify the store for regular customers. Perhaps the store will always use the same typeface for its headlines and the same style of art for its illustrations. It will surely develop a logo or sig cut that has a character of its own. Ohrbach's changed its logo to include an exclamation mark after the "Oh" and in front of the "rbach's." The "Oh!" helps lend excitement to all the ads. Ohrbach's, long a leader in retail advertising, is one store that combines price advertising with institutional advertising. The idea is to appeal to *customers,* not just *shoppers.*

Because telling readers where to buy is a chief function of retail advertising, the logo or signature should show up large in the ad and maybe in more than one place. The address, hours of business, and phone number should be included. Realizing that people have trouble remembering numbers, some advertisers study their phone numbers on the dial and discover combinations of letters that spell out appropriate words. Low Q, Box 937, Sag Harbor, N.Y. 11963 for a fee offers a computer printout of "up to 2,187 letter combinations inherent in your . . . phone number."

Hog Wild!, a Boston store that sells, among other items, an Oinkolator alarm that attaches to a refrigerator to sing out "Oink! Oink! Oink! when you open the door, uses this phone number: 523–PIGS.

Word phone numbers are not confined to retailers or local advertisers. United Air Express advertises this number: 800–PACKAGE. But Allan Provost, Longan-Provost Advertising, Miami, is not impressed. He wrote to *Advertising Age* that he can dial 722–5243 much faster. "Phone numbers like . . . [PACKAGE] are too much 8768253."[9]

Arlan Koehler, creative director for Norman, Craig & Kummel, New York, described the "Seven Deadly C's of Retail Newspaper Ads." They are *color,* poorly used; *co-op* money that forces a store to bend its image to fit the manufacturer; *contracts* with the media that lure retailers into running ads when they have nothing to say; *consistency,* whereby a store's style does not change with the times; *cuteness* that produces such empty phrasing as "Where quality and economy walk hand in hand"; *competition* that prompts stores to copy each other; and *cost* that causes a store to settle for less than the best advertising and most qualified advertising personnel.[10]

The size of the ad

Standard-size newspapers (as opposed to tabloids) offer advertisers a size impact they can beat only by going to outdoor advertising. A double-truck ad, or even a full-page ad, especially with color, can be overwhelming. These are used for both institutional and retail advertising.

But advertisers can go to smaller ads and still get the impact they need.

Professor Fred Farrar of Temple University advises people attending his newspaper advertising seminars to consider vertical half pages with one color. Such ads, he says, dominate not only the page but also a double truck. Two full columns—a quarter of a page in most newspapers—can also dominate a page, and such an ad "is impossible to bury." It will not get lost among the other ads. Farrar also points out that small units repeated frequently in a single issue can dominate a newspaper.

The technical revolution that came to newspapers in the 1960s and 1970s gave advertisers better reproduction of art and color and more flexible typography.[11] But it also added to the confusion of sizes. Dailies and weeklies adopted all kinds of new formats and column widths. One agency executive counted 320 distinct formats among dailies in 1979. Any one of these could work well enough for advertisers in a local area, but consider the frustration of a national agency trying to place an ad in papers across the country.

In 1984 most newspapers adopted the expanded Standard Advertising Unit system of ad measurements built on a six-column page. The new measurements cover a page size that is 55 to 56 inches wide. A single column is 2½″ wide.

Up until recently, newspapers—at least the big ones—and their advertisers measured space in agate lines: 14 to the inch. The trend is away from agate lines to plain inches.

Who does the ads?

The *News Times and Lincoln County Leader,* an 11,000-circulation weekly at Newport, Oregon, employs three full-time advertising people, who, along with advertising director Betty Giles, sell advertising as well as write and design it. With, say, one additional employee, the paper would consider making one employee strictly a creator of ads, leaving the selling to the other employees.

An occasional ad is prepared for speculative sale to a nonadvertiser.

Many retail concerns have used the whale-of-a-sale theme but few with the freshness of Macy's New York. In this two-page newspaper ad, we do not even see the whale. The high-impact art nicely dominates the spread and carries the reader to the right-hand page where all the bargains are listed. A five-line blurb elaborates on the headline, urging customers to "Come early, don't let the big buys get away." The sale items are conveniently grouped under no-nonsense headings.

No custom art is offered. Only about 20 percent of the ads "travel" to advertisers as proofs. But a surprisingly large percentage of the ads appear in color.[12]

The *Times-Standard* of Eureka, California, is a 21,500-circulation letterpress daily. Like a number of the remaining letterpress dailies, it uses cold-type composition as though it were an offset paper. Its display advertising department employs six "account executives" and an advertising manager who "do it all," according to staffer Bob Smith. Because the paper is unable to offer all the creative services local advertisers want, several small agencies and art studios have sprung up to provide copy, design, and art services. Agencies came to town, too, to handle local advertising because the advertisers didn't want to be bothered by the many media reps, including those from radio and TV stations, Smith reports.

Like many cities and towns, Eureka has a shopper—an aggressive one—to compete with the daily.

The *Times-Standard* bothers to make proofs only for advertisers whose ads take up 30 inches of space or more.[13]

In many cities the newspapers' display advertising departments are not as active as they once were. Economic conditions have forced some of the cutbacks. And increasingly, at least among the bigger advertisers, creative help from the medium is no longer needed. Retailers have their own supply of art and ready-made ads from the home office, from specialized mat services, or from manufacturers. Many stores maintain ad departments of their own big enough to do all the work in-house. Macy's San Francisco operation, for instance, includes photographers as well as illustrators, photographic studios as well as art studios, typographers as well as copywriters, typesetting equipment as well as typewriters.

Many stores, members of a chain, leave the preparation of ads to company headquarters. Under this arrangement, the advertising departments of the local stores make minor adjustments in the ads so that they will conform to availability of the merchandise. Unfortunately, those "minor adjustments" can ruin an ad's design.

Some stores, like Ohrbach's, hire agencies to do most of the creative work. Or, as in the case of Penney's, the store does the ads for newspapers "in-house" and hires an agency to do the national ads for TV and magazines. Some papers do not offer commissions to local agencies unless the ads are submitted camera-ready.[14]

Offset lithography and cold-type systems, when they came along, revolutionized the way local ads were prepared by newspapers. There was no more backshop cutting and sawing of spacing materials and borders. All this work could be done by artists at their drawing boards, using proofs, paper, film, and printed tapes. Lower costs and greater flexibility of design were the results.

Next to come—it is already here in some plants—is the elimination of the pasteup process. The goal of many newspapers is to do the designing on video terminals and send printouts directly to the printer.

Whoever does the advertising finds any number of aids offered by outside organizations. For instance, the Advertising Checking Bureau, Inc., studies the advertising content of most daily and Sunday newspapers and offers information to advertisers, for a price, on what the competition is doing.

Those special sections

In recent years newspapers have undergone vast technological changes, giving advertisers better service and reproduction quality. Many newspapers run special advertising sections or tabloids built around themes or product classes. Back-to-school sections and annual car-care sections are common. This is one area where editorial and advertising departments sometimes work together. Feature material on the theme helps separate the ads. Some newspapers take their features from outside organizations. The features come camera- or scanner-ready. These are called "advertorial packages."

Organizations like Champion Spark Plug Co. and National Home Improvement Council provide newspapers with free advertorial packages.[15]

Increasingly, advertisers are preparing their own newspaper sections, in tabloid form, to be inserted into copies after they come off the presses.

The reliance on preprinted tabloids makes early deadlines for advertisers a necessity, and this means that stores have a harder time stocking the items advertised. This is especially true of branch stores, whose advertising is prepared out of town. Hence, in many newspapers, you find small-space disclaimer ads in the regular sections of the paper, pointing out that certain items did not arrive on time. Such ads often contain corrections, too, to merchandise descriptions and sometimes to prices listed.

A Sears, Roebuck & Co. executive has suggested that newspapers carry a single "retraction page" to cover all the errors in all the inserts for a single day.

Illustrations versus photographs

When display advertising began, in the last century, the illustrator was king. Then along came photography, and the illustrator lost out in the scramble for believability, which the photographer, with so little effort, seemed able to deliver. But photography never did dominate retail advertising as it did advertising in the magazines. The retail advertiser found that, in newspapers, line or wash drawings worked best. They were easier to reproduce.

With the change by most newspapers to offset and the resultant improvement in the reproduction of photographs, retailers turned more and more to photography. Some stores, to get away from the pack, switched back.

The Perfect Gift

Whether the one you will buy for this Mother's Day is the stay-at-home type who would love a patchwork-patterned Snug Sack® for cozy reading or a lady executive who would really appreciate an all-leather attache case with her initials embossed in gold, we can help you make the right choice. And we'll gift wrap your perfect gift selection free of charge.

Leeds

ELMWOOD: 3211 N. CENTRAL AVE,
DAILY 10 to 9 SAT. till 5:30 SUN. 12 to 5

For this black-and-white ad, a Print Media Service artist takes a drawing of a rose from the PMS clip book, blows it up, screens it, crops it, and runs it underneath some boldface copy. The headline done in calligraphy echoes the pattern of the rose. The art and the type would be submitted separately to the printer, who would combine two negatives to make the plate.

At left, a piece of montage art from Print Media Service, a monthly stock-art service supplied by Dynamic Graphics, Peoria, Illinois. Below, the start of an ad that makes use of only a couple of parts of the montage. The woman has been cropped, and vertical lines of shading are painted out. The man has been cropped and retouched, too, but the retoucher has not bothered painting out remains of the woman's arm as it crosses his back. But nobody notices.

Fashions for the SPORTING CROWDS...

An artist at Saks Fifth Avenue said, "You can really fake it with a drawing. With a photo there's no way to help a bad outfit." A B. Altman artist pointed out that "A woman can more closely associate with the way she would look in a sketch. In a photo, she sees another woman's face."[16]

Another advantage of illustration over photography is that, typically, it costs about a third of what photography, including model's fees and retouching, would cost. This does not mean that in the major markets art comes cheap. Some artists charge more than $300 per figure.

Such prices are beyond the reach of retailers in the smaller cities, of course, but does this mean these retailers have to settle for art of inferior quality? Not necessarily. The art schools turn out hundreds of eager young

illustrators each year, and most of them will have trouble locating in the major markets. Illustration can come cheap. And Alan Koehler reports that "big stores have been known to make their costly art and photography available to smaller out-of-town stores for entirely reasonable fees. Write the stores you admire, to see. If you don't happen to have similar merchandise, the visuals can be used in an institutional or thematic way."

The art services

Newspapers and their retail-advertising accounts can always use the art services, which are convenient, economical sources of ready-made illustrations. An art service consists of a proof book of illustrations, issued periodically, along with mats of each of the illustrations for the few letterpress papers still published. A mat is a thick-paper mold into which the stereotyper pours molten metal, thus duplicating the original engraving from which the mat was made.

Metro Associated Services, with headquarters in New York, and SCW, Inc. (Stamps-Conhaim), Chatsworth, California, the two best-known art services, offer general monthly services to daily newspapers and junior services to weeklies. The cost varies according to the newspaper's size. The newspaper utilizes the art in ads it prepares for advertisers who do not have their own advertising departments or agencies.

Most newspapers get two or more copies of each book, one to file, the others to cut up. For rough layouts, the designer either traces or clips and pastes the art into place. The printing and paper stock are of a quality that allows the art to be used in finished pasteups, too.

Artists can get more out of art services than nonartists can. Artists see any number of possibilities for combining pieces or parts of pieces to make new art. And artists can retouch stock art and add to it.

Naturally critical of existing works, artists find compelling need to improve them by making various adjustments. In the hands of artists, stock art almost becomes exclusive art.

But nonartists can get a lot out of the services, too. Deciding which pieces are appropriate is more of an editing than an artistic exercise. And some art pieces come in parts separated with thin white lines. They are designed to be cut apart and refitted.

Some of the art each month comes as color separations. And much of the black-and-white art separates easily enough into two parts for two-color printing. A given piece of art also comes in several sizes.

Among art services designed for the advertiser rather than the medium are those provided by Tobias, Meyer & Nebenzahl, New York, although TM&N has some newspaper subscribers. Stores value these services for their exclusivity and speciality. Separate services are available for men's and young men's clothing stores, jewelry stores, and shoe stores.

Editor & Publisher International Year Book, in its "Newspaper Art

Constructing his figures pretty much out of geometric shapes for a highly stylized, flat, abstract look, a Print Media Service artist manages to create enough types (above) to give the advertising designer a good cross section of people to work into an ad that is to appeal to everybody. But suppose you do not want a horizontal lineup. You cut the figures apart, make prints of varying sizes, and overlap them, as in the PMS-prepared ad below. Same art, different effect.

You Work Hard for Your Money. It's Time Your Money Worked Hard for You.

Money in a Citizen's savings account earns the highest interest rate allowed by law, compounded daily. That's a hard-working savings account! Start yours today.

CITIZENS' BANK
204 Central Avenue
Mon Thurs 9 a m 5 p m Fri 9 a m 7 p m

and Mat Services Directory," lists more than forty companies offering mat and art services to newspapers and advertisers. One of the newer art services is Print Media Service (PMS), offered monthly by Dynamic Graphics, Inc., Peoria, Illinois. Some newspaper ad managers think the art is more sophisticated than what is offered by the other services. Dynamic Graphics also sells its more generalized Clipper service to newspapers.[17]

Stores that are part of a chain have their own art and advertising services. A central office coordinates the ads, giving them a design relationship.

Art from manufacturers

Local advertisers also have access to art supplied by manufacturers of products they sell.

A problem arises when mats from several manufacturers are combined in a single ad. The various pieces of art may be executed in different, incompatible styles. Or one piece of art may come in the wrong size; it may have to be reduced or enlarged. If the art is a halftone, this will affect the dot pattern. The ad may appear with one item in coarse screen with other items in regular screen.

These are problems facing the user of the regular art services, too, but the designer has enough choices there to design a multi-item ad with pieces of art in related art styles and screens.

As do the general art services, advertisers' art services sometimes offer complete ads. All the retailer has to do is run a logo at the bottom. Such advertising does not contribute much to a unique image for a store, though.

Borders for the ads

For ads carrying listings unrelieved by illustrations, borders become the only decorative element. "Newspapers can't seem to get enough of them," observed Hazel L. Kraus of Metro, whose organization, like the other art services, always includes a number of borders in each new proof book.

Borders may surround the ad or fence off certain of its sections or simply appear and reappear in places in the ad to provide continuity or typographic relief.

The border may be made up of tiny illustrations taken from the art service and run in a line. It can build atmosphere for the ad: a lineup of holly leaves for Christmas, a set of stars between two flowing stripes for the Fourth of July, and so on. But it should be in character with the headline face.

Some advertisers develop borders of their own and use them ad after ad to tie their series together.

The printer has a stock of borders on which the advertiser can draw. Some of these are made on linecasting machines.

A warning about borders: they make ads look smaller than they would look without borders. Furthermore, when the border is too imposing, it acts as an optical fence, discouraging entry. Some advertisers solve this by running borders on only two of four sides—usually at the top and bottom.

The border need not be the usual ruled line or line-pattern. It can be a full drawing "hollowed out," with room in the center for the type. The border in this case is more of a frame. (See chapter 5.)

Color in newspapers

Color in newspapers has increased since the launching in 1982 of *USA Today,* the national paper with all the full-color photographs and maps. "Has *USA Today* ushered in the era of the four-color daily newspaper?"

You can also take part of the regular lineup and reverse the figures into a black block.

asked a writer in *Editor & Publisher,* who then answered his own question: "Quite possibly so."[18]

The South has been a leader in the move to full-color newspapers, with the *St. Petersburg Times, Dallas Times-Herald, Atlanta Journal and Constitution,* and the *Dallas News* leading all papers in 1982 in ROP color. Some papers, including the *San Antonio Light* and the *Orlando Sentinel,* are even running their daily comics in color. The *St. Louis Post-Dispatch* was doing this as far back as the late 1940s.

Newspapers have been criticized for using color as a graphic device rather than a communication tool. Richard Curtis, managing editor of *USA Today,* says that "if color can't be done properly with quality, then it should not be used."

To some editors, "properly" means confining color—full color—to food and fashion sections and soft news. There is some feeling that full color gives glamor to photographs of killings and other tragedies. Black and white handling, they feel, works better here.[19]

It could be argued that papers using little color on the news/editorial side provide a more receptive background for color in advertising. The advertising stands out more. Probably the first firm to use color in a newspaper was Mandel Brothers, Chicago, adding red to the black in a full-page ad. That was in 1903. For some years color in newspaper advertising remained a rarity. Now it is common—even in small and medium-size papers.

And restrictions on its use have died.

It used to be that an advertiser, to get newspaper color, would have to agree to run the ad at a spot where it was convenient for the printer to apply color. Now the advertiser enjoys ROP—run of paper—color.

A "major technical breakthrough in the reproduction of ROP newspaper color" was announced by the American Newspaper Publishers Association in 1971 with the introduction of a color line-conversion process for "a richer, cleaner, posterlike reproduction at lower cost."[20] The *Nashville Banner* and *Tennessean* pioneered its use.

Offset presses and color scanners in recent years have greatly improved the quality of newspaper color. Scanners "automatically provide separations that meet specifications for highlights, densities, dot gain or loss, etc. The specifications are programmed into a computer that operates the scanner," a writer in *Presstime* observed. It takes less than a half hour to get a set of separations.[21]

The advertiser also has access to color for advertising in the Sunday comics section. Some comics sections are printed by the newspapers that run them, some by organizations removed from the papers.

Sunday comic strips may look like the result of process color work, but the color is strictly flat or spot. Four plates are made—yellow, red, blue, and black—and all are in line. The tone is accomplished with Ben Days and juxtaposition of dots.

As in magazines, color in newspaper advertising raises the cost of the space to the advertiser. The more colors, the higher the space cost, naturally. And in some cases the advertiser has to buy a given amount of space—say more than half a page—before being able to buy color for the ad. Some newspapers charge a flat additional fee for color, no matter how big the ad is. Using color means observing a deadline hours earlier than the regular deadline.

Although a *Milwaukee Journal* study has shown that full-page, full-color newspaper ads get up to 60 percent more readership than similar ads in black-and-white, a full-page ad or a well-designed smaller ad does not get quite the lift from color that a poorly designed ad gets, because the big and good ads do not need color as much. Color becomes a crutch to some designers.

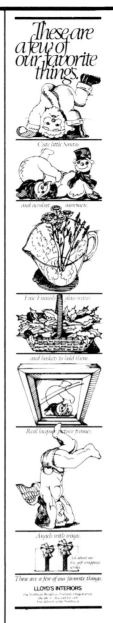

This well designed ad runs the full depth of a newspaper page, each cartoon panel illustrating one of the "favorite things" available at Christmastime at Lloyd's Interiors, Portland. No prices are necessary here. Ed Thjon did the art directing; Mike Hindman wrote the copy. The agency was Borders, Perrin & Norrander.

FARMERS MARKET

DID you know a ripe banana contains 75% water and has more sugar than any other fruit? Just another bit of trivia to add to your fruit and vegetable lore about **FARMERS MARKET**, 3rd & Fairfax, which has the freshest, tastiest produce in town at any of our nine (count 'em) stalls.

MORE than 20,000,000 operations are performed annually. This leaves you with about a one-in-eleven chance for some stitchwork. Get to know yourself better while you're still in one piece.

THE GUINNESS Book of Records claims the greatest height from which fresh eggs landed without breaking was 6000 feet from a helicopter manned by David Donaghue and John Cartwright, Feb. 8, 1974. We (Dick Kidson) ordered "over easy!," remember?

SPEAKING of eggs, try Bill Daniel's Poultry and Puritan Poultry here for the finest and freshest in town (don't drop 'em, for heavens' sakes). You'll find all double A's—Medium Grade AA, Large Grade AA, Extra Large Grade AA and Jumbo Grade AA. They're eggscellent.

TUSQUELLAS MEATS has a special going today and tomorrow on Point Cut Briskets, $1.79 lb., and First Cut Briskets, $2.79 lb., from his own, specially-aged meat. Also on sale is his ground center chuck (less than 14% fat content and prepared on the half-hour) at $2.29 lb.

SOME agriculturists apparently feel the easiest thing to raise is prices. There's always something special at **FARMERS MARKET**, 3rd & Fairfax.

Some newspaper advertisers adopt a standard format and use it day after day. Farmers Market in Los Angeles runs a sort of column with a regular column heading. The reader finds no illustrations below—just paragraphs calling attention to various stores, stalls, and restaurants, each paragraph beginning with some boldface type.

The Hitchcock Chair Co., Riverton, Connecticut, uses an old "hand carved" roman for headlines in this nearly full-page newspaper ad in order to convey the quality built into its product. The typeface—and the slightly wavy border—appear in most of its ads to help readers immediately recognize them. Art director Sue White achieves an informality of balance here without sacrificing the feel of quality. A sale ad does not have to look cheap, even though prices are.

Roughing in the ad

The typical local newspaper ad contains (1) a feature illustration, larger than any other in the ad; (2) a related headline; (3) a blurb or supplemental headline, longer than the first and in smaller type, that takes off logically from where the main headline leaves off; (4) a main copy block, short, amplifying the headline; (5) additional illustrations with their own headlines and copy blocks; and (6) the store name (logotype) shown at least once, perhaps twice. Prices are usually played prominently, in bold or display types, inside or alongside the copy blocks. Borders are optional.

For an extra large ad covering a wide range of items, you should plan on one main unit, a couple of secondary units, a few smaller—spot—units, and a listing. Each of the units can have its own illustration, the size often but not necessarily decreasing with the size of the unit.

It is best even for a multimerchandise store to concentrate, in a single ad, on one class of merchandise or on one department. If a hodgepodge is ordered, you should organize it at least into logical sections, with garden supplies in one place, auto supplies in another, and so on. Of course, one item should dominate. It would be an item specially priced or new to the store. You would have a good reason for playing it up.

Like any ad, a retail ad needs a theme. That the store has launched a sale is not really enough of a theme. The reader likes to have a reason. "Good Riddance," says a headline over a sale ad sponsored by Director's, a furniture store. Perhaps that is reason enough.

You do not have to force the theme. You do not have to mention it several times in the ad. But you should include a short block of copy after the headline to elaborate on the theme. The reader may not bother with it. But it is there, just in case.

To make your product or products look inexpensive, use heavy borders and boxes, reverse blocks, large illustrations, graphic gimmicks—and *crowd* your ad. To do the opposite—to stress quality rather than price—

lighten the typeface, use white space liberally. Choose roman for your headlines.

Do not bother with thumbnails when doing newspaper ads. Start with an actual-size ad, roughing in quickly the areas you plan to cover with illustration and type. Be concerned at first with sizes and relationships of areas, not with the looks and placement of the illustrations. With areas roughly established, look for illustrations in the proof book. Slide your layout sheet around over the illustrations until you find good placement for them, then trace them quickly. Do not be afraid to leave out parts of the illustrations. Use only what you need. That is one way of proceeding.

Another is to look for the illustrations first. What you find will determine the arrangement areas. Make quick tracings, then place them under your working sheet. You can rough in the headlines and establish unit areas while you retrace your drawings, moving from one to the other and back again. Work loosely, changing as you go, erasing, even throwing away a working sheet halfway along (you have not invested much time on it) and starting fresh. It is just a matter of retracing your tracings. Save those parts of the ad that look promising. When you have things pretty much as you want them, go back over your working sheet, tracing and marking more firmly than before.

If your client can afford original art—or if you cannot find what you want among the stock art files—the making of the ad rough becomes a more demanding job. You create the ad much as you would an ad for a national magazine. You are then less the layout artist, more the designer.

As for any advertising, layout and typed copy are kept separate. The headlines, even though lettered in carefully on the layout, should appear in typed form with the copy, with sizes clearly marked. When a discrepancy occurs between the layout and the typed copy, the compositor follows the typed copy.

You will not often have time to duplicate exactly the type you have in mind, so you should mark its name and series in the margins of the ad. Such indications will be repeated on the typed copy. You can leave unsettled the type size if the compositor is better able to determine that than you are.

Next to each illustration you trace you should place the art service code number.

What is being sold in an ad should influence its size and shape. The test is not so much how the ad looks in rough or even proof form. The test lies in how it looks on the page in competition with other ads. It is not a bad idea to place the proof on a page with other ads to see how it stands out.

Not only do newspapers offer advertisers deep verticals and wide horizontals; some of them offer L-, reverse L-, and T- shapes. Many newspapers have experimented with FlexForm, a system pioneered by the *Peoria* (Illinois) *Journal Star,* in which the advertiser can design an ad in *any* shape, zigzagging among news columns on a page for up to 65 percent of the space.

Odd shapes require extra designer attention. What you do to unify the ad is particularly important. You can use art that curves naturally into each area of the ad. Or you can use borders or illustrations that repeat themselves. On the other hand, you can divide the space into rectangles and treat each rectangle as a near-separate ad, repeating the logo each time.

Retailers like the idea of ads-within-ads, even in regular-shaped ads. The advantage of this format is that the readers are able to pick out and stay with sections that particularly interest them.

Small-space ads offer an even greater challenge to the designer. What can you possibly do in a 1-col. $\times$ 1″ ad? With reverses, borders, type in two or three sizes, compact illustrations, you can do quite a bit.

This is the rough layout for a manufacturer's ready-made ad supplied to stores selling the manufacturer's product: White Stag apparel. Jean Ening was the artist/designer.

Student Tracy Wong uses nylon-tip and felt markers to produce this rough layout for a full-page ad announcing that "Prices Have Fallen" at Tracy's department store. In this ad, the sale items are like leaves falling from the tree, but the gimmick is kept well within bounds. Note the pileup of leaves around the logo at the bottom.

Here is a rough layout for a J. C. Penney ad. Note that the three-line headline is all in one type size. There are no typographic tricks. The headline, captions, and art combine to make one massive unit.

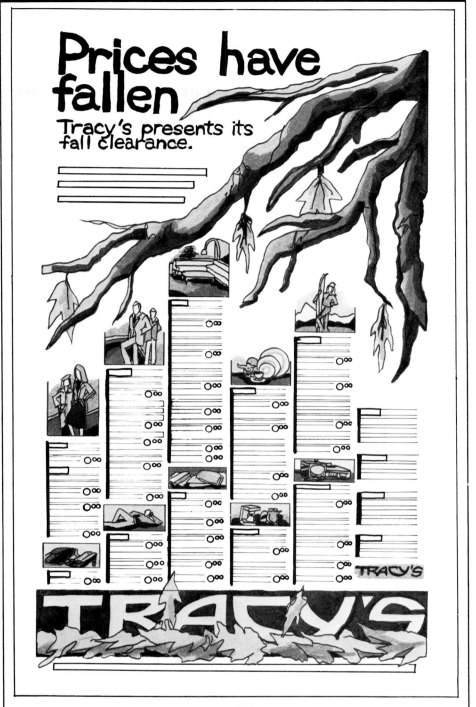

Using art in small-space ads, you should crop even closer than usual, using just a hint of the scene or product you want to exhibit. The reader, seeing this art, has a tendency to complete the drawing mentally, in effect increasing the dimensions of your ad.

For their own staff members and for their accounts, the newspaper provides specially printed semitransparent layout sheets, in full-, half- and quarter-page sizes, with columns ruled in and a scale of inches or picas marked at the side. You can use any part of a sheet, working usually at the top left so that you can keep track of measurements. Employed by the client, you will have a tendency to use as little space as possible; by the newspaper, as much as the client will buy.

Know the score and a lot more.

Sport is more than who beat whom. It's people, money, luck, strategy, politics. And it's all in Sports Weekender, every Saturday in The New News-Sentinel. Interviews, injuries, coaching philosophies—not just the highlights, but the sidelines as well.

Sports Weekender is just one of 11 new sections appearing each week in The New News-Sentinel. Covering subjects like Health & Science, Food, Religion, Lifestyles, Homes, People, Entertainment, T.V. Children and Weekend Fun.

To make The New News-Sentinel what today's newspaper should be, we can't just cover the stories everybody else does.

We have to tackle subjects some people consider out of bounds.

The New News-Sentinel

Thought for food.

The staff of our paper now devotes an entire section to the staff of life. It's called Food/Consumer. And it's full of mouthwatering recipes, lipsmacking photography, nutritional tips, price advice, coupons and buying hints.

All packaged in a smart, new, easy-to-read format you'll really eat up.

Food/Consumer is just one of 11 new sections appearing each week in The New News-Sentinel. Covering subjects like Health & Science, Lifestyles, Religion, Home, People, Entertainment, T.V. Children, Sports and Weekend Fun.

Making The New News-Sentinel what today's newspaper should be hasn't been easy.

But then, we've got an appetite for hard work.

The New News-Sentinel

Where to read the last word in fashion.

Pleated pants are still in. Culottes are back in. Sweaters will always be in. And longer hemlines are down but not out (yet).

Whether fashion is your hobby or your obsession, you'll find plenty to cheer about in Home/Style, a brand new feature in The New News-Sentinel.

Every Friday you can zip through articles on work clothes, play clothes, high fashion, low prices, styles, trends, re-births, colors, designers and more.

Home/Style is just one of 11 new sections appearing each week in The New News-Sentinel. Covering subjects like Health & Science, Food, People, Lifestyles, Religion, T.V. Entertainment, Children, Sports and Weekend Fun.

Making The New News-Sentinel what today's newspaper should be is serious business.

(It could even alter the fabric of our society.)

The New News-Sentinel

You'll read this section religiously.

The City of Churches has always deserved a newspaper of its own. Now it has one. Pathways. A whole new section devoted entirely to the religious trends and activities of Fort Wayne. Published each Saturday in The New News-Sentinel—the timely articles will still be fresh in your mind come Sunday.

In addition to Church news, interviews and history, there's a complete listing of who's giving sermons on what, where.

Pathways is just one of 11 new sections appearing each week in The New News-Sentinel. Covering subjects like Health & Science, Food, Lifestyles, Homes, People, Entertainment, T.V. Children, Sports and Weekend Fun.

Making The New News-Sentinel what today's newspaper should be takes a lot of hard work.

But on the seventh day we rest.

The New News-Sentinel

Told to design an ad of so many column inches, you can take up space either vertically or horizontally. "Around 60 column inches," for instance, would make an ad 3 columns by 20 inches, 4 columns by 15 inches, 5 columns by 12 inches, 6 columns by 10 inches, 7 columns by 8 inches, or 8 columns by 7 inches.

Working with these "grid" sheets, you will have little need for a T-square and triangle. Your roughs will be kept at the "shop rough" stage for most jobs. You may find a pair of scissors and a jar of rubber cement your most valuable tools. To indicate art, you may, for rush jobs, simply make a "rubbing" over a mat. Or clip it from the extra proof book.

You will become thoroughly familiar with the newspaper's type-specimen book, but much of your lettering will be stick figure, with notations about type written out in the margin.

Somewhere on the layout sheet, outside the ad itself, you should print the (1) name of the advertiser, (2) name of the publication (if it is not already printed), (3) date the ad is to appear, (4) size of the ad, and (5) preferred position, if any. (An advertiser who wants special placement usually pays a little more for the ad.)

Many retail advertisers are convinced that right-page placement is better than left-page placement and that ads high on the page get better readership than ads low on the page. Further, they insist that their ads be placed next to regular reading matter.

Newspapers often arrange the ads in a half-pyramid, with the low point at the left; small ads go at the top, larger ads at the bottom of the pyramid. Under this system, every ad has a fighting chance of getting next to editorial and news columns. No ads are "buried."

Some designers convince themselves that several small ads get better exposure than one large ad. Not only does the ad reach readers on several pages; it is sure to get placed at the top of the pyramid in each case. Other designers argue that one large ad has greater total impact than several smaller ads.

These are four of a series of full-page newspaper ads sponsored by the *News-Sentinel* of Fort Wayne, Indiana, to gain reader appreciation for the paper's various sections. Body copy placement varied from ad to ad, but the large headline and gridded background held the series together. The pictured reader was always dressed appropriately. That's a manikin reading the fashion section. Bonsib, Inc., was the agency.

1. Interview with Wayne R. Philips, *News Guard,* Lincoln City, Oregon, August 24, 1983.
2. *Editor & Publisher,* December 3, 1983.
3. Local advertising in other media will be considered in later chapters.
4. Kenneth R. Kinney, *Advertiser's Copy Service Newsletter,* December 1970, p. 1.
5. As specified in Arthur Bloch's *Murphy's Law Book Two* (Los Angeles: Price/Stern/Sloan Publishers, 1980), p. 23.
6. Tom Clements, "Newspapers as an Advertising Medium," *Print,* September-October 1971, p. 38.
7. Quoted by Daniel Lionel, "Ohrbach's Finds Newspaper Advertising Oh!-So-Good," *Editor & Publisher,* October 11, 1975, p. 26.
8. Maxine Brady, *Bloomingdale's* (New York: Harcourt Brace Jovanovich, 1980), p. 125.
9. Letter to the Editor, *Advertising Age,* March 7, 1983, p. 48.
10. Detailed in a talk given at an advertising workshop sponsored by the Federation Publicitaria de Puerto Rico in San Juan.
11. Of the total 1,772 daily newspapers published in the United States, about 80 percent are printed by the offset lithography process. Letterpress papers include mostly big dailies.
12. Interview with Betty Giles, *New Times,* Newport, Oregon, August 23, 1983.
13. Interview with Bob Smith, *Times-Standard,* Eureka, California, September 7, 1983.
14. Interview with Wayne R. Philips, *News Guard,* Lincoln City, Oregon, August 24, 1983.
15. Elise Burroughs, "Array of Vendors Feeds Appetite for 'Advertorials,'" *Presstime,* July 1983, pp. 36, 37.
16. "Grand Illusion," *Newsweek,* October 6, 1975, p. 96.
17. Schools that can't afford to subscribe to art services for instructional purposes find that they can get castaway copies, if a bit dated, from newspapers in town.
18. Bill Gloede, "What's Black & White and Red All Over?" *Editor & Publisher,* September 24, 1983, p. 15.
19. Wayne Kelly, "Newspapers Can Use Color Inappropriately," *Editor & Publisher,* October 22, 1983, p. 24.
20. *ANPA Newspaper Information Service Newsletter,* August 31, 1971, p. 2.
21. Tom Walker, "Newspapers Strive to Improve Color," *Presstime,* September 1982, p. 40.

12

Magazine advertising

The proliferation of magazines in the nineteenth century paved the way for national—or brand-name—advertising and created the need for advertising agencies to keep track of the many periodicals. It was only natural that these agencies eventually would produce the advertising going into the periodicals. Moreover, in their decisions on which magazines to buy space in, advertising agencies largely determine which magazines will survive, which will fail.

Magazines continually adjust their editorial formulas to hold onto and build audiences. When the record industry began its decline in 1979, *Rolling Stone,* which had been a bible to rock 'n' roll enthusiasts, began to make changes—to reposition itself in the market. New advertisers had to be recruited. Many nonrecord advertisers saw the audience as too narrow. Other advertisers were not impressed by the newsprint stock. So *Rolling Stone* began running more political articles and other articles likely to appeal to a slightly older audience. And it went to a slicker stock.

Any major trend, any switch in attitudes among Americans gives rise to a whole new collection of magazines. The computer age has inspired at least seventy new magazines, including many aimed at owners of specific makes of computers. *PC,* for instance, serves people who own IBM Personal Computers. It has at least one competitor: *PC World.* One 750-page issue of *PC* in 1983 carried 500 advertisements.

James K. Glassman, publisher of the *New Republic,* contemplated the phenomenon in a column in his magazine. Maybe the magazine had missed the boat on new magazines, he wrote. In a frivolous mood, he wondered if the magazine should launch a sister publication: *New Republic World: The Magazine for New Republic Readers.*[1]

Rivendell Marketing Company, New York, represents 125 "significant gay magazines, newspapers, and entertainment guides," many of them of recent vintage. The company estimates that homosexuals comprise 10 percent of the population and control 19 percent of the spendable income. Among other services, Rivendell offers advertisers "creative design and execution" to appeal to this audience.

The 1980s have seen the proliferation, too, of women's magazines, all vying for advertisers' dollars. But Carolyn Carter, president of Women in Communications, thinks that "even though there [are] more women's magazines on the market, it [is] hard to tell one from the other."[2]

Most of the new magazines—and the old ones, too—go after a youthful audience of big spenders. The writing on the editorial side reflects this. In *New York,* for instance, folk and rock star Richard Thompson (*New York* calls him folk-rocker Richard Thompson) doesn't become suddenly popular: instead, he makes "a megaleap into the public consciousness."

Consumer magazines

Professor Theodore Peterson of the Department of Journalism, University of Illinois, traces the modern magazine to 1893 and the cutting of the price of *Munsey's* to a mere dime. It was Frank Munsey's way of rescuing his failing magazine—to build a large circulation to offer to advertisers,

Wherever you want to go in Vermont, you'll find lots of offerings in the arts, and everything else from fiddling contests to country fairs – all at reasonable country prices. For a free vacation planning kit, write: State of Vermont, Dept. CD, Montpelier, VT 05602.

I plan to come: _____
        # of days   month
To: ☐ Inn ☐ Full Resort ☐ Hotel/Motel ☐ Camping

Name_____
        (please print)
Address_____
_____ Zip_____

A ticket-like box encloses a small-space ad that carries the headline "Write Your Own Ticket to VT." The entire ad is a coupon, which, when filled out, will bring a vacation planning ticket to the reader. To emphasize the fact that Vermont is more than beautiful scenery, the ad shows a violin. "Wherever you want to go in Vermont, you'll find lots of offerings in the arts. . . ." William Clark designed the ad; Bruce Patteson wrote the copy. Kenyon & Eckhardt was the agency.

**Arabian desert dwellers
engaged in traditional game**

Right, golf.
To people who work for us, a round of golf is an ordinary part of life in Saudi Arabia. There's no grass, so each player carries a portable "fairway" of artificial turf.
We're Aramco, the Arabian American Oil Company. There are 13,000 North Americans in Saudi Arabia with us. And some things about our lives there might surprise you.
1. We're doing something important. Aramco produces more oil than

any other company. Badly needed oil. Including about 15 percent of the oil America imports.
2. The Saudi Government and Aramco are working together on some *incredibly* large energy projects, communications networks, electric utilities, and more.
3. Our people are glad to be in Saudi Arabia with Aramco. They came for excellent pay and professional challenge.
4. After 46 years, in Saudi Arabia,

Aramco is still growing fast. So is the number of rewarding jobs we offer.
5. Jim Burchett, center, birdied the 16th to beat Mike Ehlers and "Sib" Sibley.

ARAMCO
SERVICES COMPANY
1100 Milam Building, F.S.G.A.,
Houston, TX 77002
(713) 750-6965

In a job market where recruits were scarce, direct-response ads, which ran in *Oil & Gas Journal,* weren't drawing as well as Aramco wanted, and so the company turned to a different kind of advertising (above) to supplement the direct-response ads. These new institutional ads were more subtle, more involving; and the art ran in full color. After the new campaign began running, the cost per response dropped from $97 to $65. The agency was Ogilvy & Mather, Houston.

who would pay his costs and give him his profits. "It was a daring, revolutionary move, and it worked. . . . [Munsey] outlined the basic pattern that magazine publishers have traced ever since."[3]

Munsey's magazine and others like it appealed to the broad middle class, a good target for the emerging brand-name advertisers.

When television came onto the scene after World War II and threatened magazines—and the other media—with its ability to deliver mass audiences to advertisers, magazines decided to join the numbers game in earnest. They tried to prove that they could deliver audiences of the kind TV could. Never mind how the magazines got their subscribers; just marvel at how many signed up. And never mind how much loss each subscriber represented; advertising revenue would make up the difference between what it cost to produce the magazine and what the subscriber was asked to pay.

Well, it turned out that you could not beat television when it came to delivering large numbers of persons to advertisers, and when a magazine was able to point to a large audience, not many people were aboard because they really wanted to be. This meant they were not very good prospects for the advertisers.

When *Woman's Home Companion, Collier's,* and the original *Saturday Evening Post, Look,* and *Life* died, it was not because they did not have large audiences—each of the magazines had a circulation in the millions; it was because their audiences were unfocused. Agencies were not impressed with the buying potential of these audiences. The magazines died because they could not get enough advertising.

To stay alive, magazines began to specialize. Each magazine brought together a group—a class—of readers who had much in common, who shared an enthusiasm for a way of living or a point of view. And the magazines began to let the reader pay for more of the costs of producing magazines. Previously what the reader paid was only token; advertisers covered most of the costs.

Even magazines that remain in the general-interest category are not so general-interest when you analyze them. Joe Cumming, professor of journalism at West Georgia College, observes that "the grand old general-interest magazines such as [the revived] *Life* and the *Saturday Evening Post* are out there posing as themselves when they really are special-interest magazines targeted to the older, sentimental groups."[4]

A magazine with a broad base enters into a specialty when it provides advertisers with only a portion of its audience, if that is what the advertiser wants. That portion can be geographic or demographic. The advertiser pays less for an ad, then, and reaches only one section of the country, say, or one class of reader: business people, for instance, or educators.

Newsweek has a demographic edition that goes to women subscribers and another that goes to executives (women and men, of course). *Time* has a business edition (the B edition) as well as editions going to people living in high-income areas (the Z edition) and to professional and managerial high-income households (the A edition). The business edition is further broken down to cover only company presidents, owners, partners, and directors (the T edition).

Specialized magazines

When people think of magazines, they think mostly of general-circulation magazines ("consumer magazines," or "consumer books" as the advertising fraternity calls them)—magazines found readily on the newsstands. But those account for only a few hundred of the tens of thousands of magazines published. Most magazines fall into the "specialized" category.

TLC, for example, is a magazine going to 250,000 hospital patients in

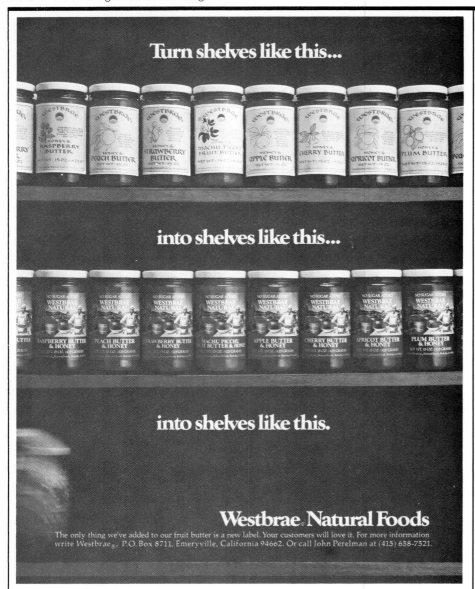

Turn shelves like this...

into shelves like this...

into shelves like this.

Westbrae Natural Foods

The only thing we've added to our fruit butter is a new label. Your customers will love it. For more information write Westbrae₈, P.O. Box 8711, Emeryville, California 94662. Or call John Perelman at (415) 658-7521.

Parallel structure helps Westbrae Natural Foods show dealers that its packaging has changed and, as a result, sales are likely to increase. The reader of this ad moves effortlessly down through the shelves to get the point. The full-page trade magazine ad is in full color, with solid black occupying most of the background to make things stand out. The agency: Gauger Sparks Silva, San Francisco. David Gauger wrote and designed the ad.

hospitals "in wealthy suburban communities." "100% of Our Readers Read or Have Breakfast in Bed," reads the headline of an ad sponsored by the magazine. They are people making changes in their living habits because of "doctors' orders." They belong to a previously "untapped and receptive market—people who need your products now," the magazine tells advertisers.

Like general-circulation magazines, specialized magazines thrive mainly on advertising revenue. An exception would be the opinion magazines—*National Review, New Republic, The Nation, The Progressive,* and the like—whose editorial policies are too controversial and circulation figures too miniscule to appeal much to advertisers. For these magazines, subscription rates—or endowments—must cover most of the costs. Only an occasional book publisher seems willing to invest advertising dollars here.

Another category of specialized magazines carrying little or no advertising are the company magazines, sometimes called "house organs." They contain no advertising because they are published to do a public relations job for the publisher, not to make money. In a sense, a company magazine is nothing but one big institutional advertisement.

Mattel's full-color, full-page magazine ad dramatizes the fact that its new doll line is "much like a real baby" by showing real babies large in the ad arranged to face the photo insert showing a "little girl [who] feel[s] like a real mommy" fussing over a doll. Art director: Vonnie Brenno. Copywriter: Vel Rankin. Agency: Ogilvy & Mather, Los Angeles.

People sometimes confuse company magazines with trade journals, which do contain advertising, plenty of it. Thumbing through a typical trade journal, fat with advertising directed to executives in the trades and professions, you get the impression the magazines exist solely to carry advertising. As a matter of fact, the advertising—for new products and equipment needed in industry—may interest readers more than the editorial matter, which in some trade journals is nothing more than puffery for the products and equipment advertised. Some trade journals do not charge for subscriptions, but they carefully control circulation to reach only those persons qualified to receive the magazine.

Statistics on magazines

Overall statistics on magazines as an advertising medium are a little hard to pin down because magazines appear in so many formats and frequencies, serving so many different audiences, fulfilling such a variety of purposes. Some exist primarily to make money, some to spread ideas, some to serve members of an organization, some to do a public relations job.

Advertising Age in its annual listing of media groups and their shares of advertising dollars spent, makes separate categories of "magazines" (weeklies, monthlies, women's), "farm publications," and "business publications."

Serving as clearinghouses of information about magazines as advertising media are the Magazine Publishers Association, 575 Lexington Ave., New York, N.Y. 10022 (general magazines) and the American Business Press, 205 E. 42nd St., New York, N.Y. 10017 (trade journals). In Canada information is available from the Magazine Association of Canada, 1240 Bay St., Suite 300, Toronto, Ontario M5R 2A7.

Industrial advertisers, even when they are advertising in trade magazines, require good design, too. This Stanley Hydraulic Tools ad uses a solid black background to display a full-color photograph of its HP-2 Hydraulic Power Unit. To better illustrate the "Double Destruction" possible, the designer uses two headlines and puts them side by side.

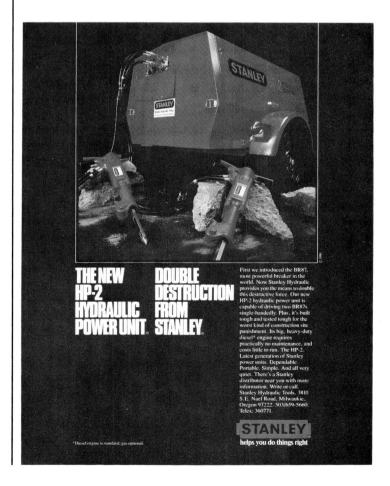

Looking for a new look?
Look for Encron® Strialine® It puts
a little texture in your line for a change.

Suit by Rona.

This fabric is knit of Encron® Strialine® polyester. That's why it has a lot going for it. The out-of-the-ordinary look of total texture. Plus the kind of performance you can depend on. If you're on the look-out for interesting new looks to spice up your new line of fabrics, contact us: American Enka, 530 Fifth Avenue, N.Y., N.Y. 10036. (212) 730-5360. And we'll show and tell you what the look of total texture can do for you.

Encron
Strialine
by

ENKA

The first
slub-filament
polyester.

American Enka uses a photograph within a photograph to show a fabric both in its for-sale state and in a converted state. This is a trade rather than a consumer ad, designed for insertion in *Textile World*. (Note the headline: ". . . a little texture in your line. . . .") The designer treats the three-sentence headline as he would a segment of copy: the first words are capitalized; sentences end with periods. The ad is especially strong in its proportions. Placement of the headline, body copy, inset photograph, and logotype divides the page into pleasing, uneven areas. Art director: Joe Suplina. Copywriter: Norma Stevens. Agency: DKG Advertising, New York.

If an ad too closely approximates editorial style of design, a magazine may label it "Advertisement," as the *Columbia Journalism Review* does this handsome ad for The National Right to Work Legal Defense Foundation. Two editorial touches: (1) the use of an initial letter to bridge the gap between headline and copy start, and (2) the use of column rules, which in this case, are interrupted by silhouette art. The logo is kept in the same type as the body copy to make the ad look less like an ad. Lee Edwards & Associates was the agency.

Advertisement

It's Pay Up Or Quit.

r Ollie Robinson and 6 co-workers for the lousing Authority of .ansas City, Mo., the f justice rolled, but

ut the help of a na-,al foundation they t have rolled at all. Ollie Robinson first .vork for the Housing y in 1960, there was no obinson voluntarily e union in 1966, when n, because he believed needed the protection labor unions. .v employees hired by ing Authority after 5, for maintenance jobs ed to join the union lues to keep their jobs. have any idea," says . that "the requirement as illegal." He didn't t Missouri state law public officials and om requiring public es to join a union to their own government. e day Ollie Robinson o-workers started pay- attention to "their" ficials doubled their thout asking them. on and his co-workers esign from the union told they couldn't.

They had no money for a lawyer. Many were afraid of losing their jobs.
Finally, one of them contacted the National Right to Work Legal Defense Foundation and the wheels of justice started moving. A law suit was filed. The Housing Authority quickly agreed to a consent decree—permanently preventing it from requiring employees to maintain union membership to keep their jobs.
The union, however, did not join in the decree. Five years of litigation were necessary to force the union to heed the law. Finally, in 1979 the Housing Authority employees received refunds of their union dues illegally taken from them.
Ollie Robinson was fortunate. He found help. But how many other Ollie Robinsons are there in America who don't know where to go for help?
The National Right to Work Legal Defense Foundation is helping everyone it can. It is currently assisting individual workers in more than 100 cases involving academic freedom, political

freedom, freedom from union violence, and the right to work for government without paying a private organization for that privilege.
For more information on how you can help workers like Ollie Robinson write:

The National Right to Work Legal Defense Foundation
Suite 600
8316 Arlington Boulevard
Fairfax, Va. 22038

Magazines are almost impossible to count. There are well over 1,000 general-circulation or consumer magazines, most of them available on the newsstands, and around 2,000 trade, technical, and professional journals, few of them on newsstands. Almost all of these carry advertising. In addition there are well over 10,000 company magazines.

Reader's Digest with a circulation of more than 18 million, *TV Guide* with around 17.5 million, and *National Geographic* with more than 10 million are among the nation's biggest magazines. Right up there, perhaps surprisingly, is *Modern Maturity* with more than 8 million, close to the circulation of *Better Homes & Gardens*. If you count *Parade* as a magazine, it leads the others with a circulation of more than 22 million coming from the 133 papers that distribute it.

Smithsonian is one of the recent success stories in magazine publishing. Classified as a "quality magazine," it made it to the ranks of big-circulation magazines in 1983 when it hit the 2,000,000 mark. In circulation it now ranks with the newsmagazines, although the biggest of those, *Time,* has a circulation of about 4,500,000. Even with its large circulation, *Smithsonian* boasts of a "household income" of its average reader of $52,000. The implication is that the magazine is a good place for advertisers—certain kinds of advertisers—to make their appeals.

A few other consumer magazines have circulations in the millions, but most, because of their specialized nature, stay under 1,000,000, and in many cases well under 1,000,000.

An advertising agency, in evaluating its magazine buy, is careful to distinguish between circulation figures and readership. Typically, a magazine claims two or three times more readers than subscribers and newsstand buyers. Only the subscribers and newsstand buyers can be accurately measured, though—through the Audit Bureau of Circulations.

Not all magazines can fairly claim that readership exceeds circulation. "A magazine distributed only to members of an association or institute may have fewer readers than its circulation because not all members will spend time reading something they receive as part of a membership," wrote Norman Hart in *Industrial Advertising and Publicity*. "Furthermore they probably do not bother to take it to the office and circulate it. Against this, many publications exist which can fairly claim a readership of eight or more people per copy."[5]

If a high percentage of a magazine's circulation came from newsstand sales, advertising agencies are likely to be impressed. Newsstand sales are a good indication of reader interest. Newsstand buyers read their magazines right away. They do not leave them lying around, their pages unturned. Two of the women's magazines, *Family Circle* and *Woman's Day,* claim total sales at the newsstand. You cannot subscribe to either magazine.

Magazines have learned that advertising agencies are interested not only in numbers but also in quality. They are interested in the editorial content of the magazines and in their design. Agencies want the right climate for their advertisements. This is why magazines occasionally, if not frequently, redesign themselves. They do it largely to impress advertising agencies.

The Big Three among business magazines, to name one group, pay a lot of attention to their design. *Business Week* went through a redesign in early 1983, with Martin Pederson in charge. Pederson designs the handsome *Nautical Quarterly*. *Fortune* was also redesigned in 1983, with Walter Bernard in charge. He has helped redesign *Time* and *The Atlantic*. *Forbes,* too, is a design-conscious magazine; also it is a bit irreverent compared to *Business Week* and *Fortune*.

The *New Yorker* is unusual among consumer magazines in that it is not designed in the ordinary sense. No one, not even an admirer of Baskerville body type and that unique display face designed by a cartoonist, opens up the magazine and goes into ecstasy about the graphics. And yet advertising agencies greatly appreciate the magazine's looks. In the *New Yorker* it is the beauty of the advertising that provides the visual treat. That and the gag cartoons, an art form the *New Yorker* practically invented. What a marvelous showcase for full-color, full-page advertisements! Nothing to detract the browser from the advertisers' messages on each slick-paper page. The *New Yorker* even rejects advertising it decides is not well designed.

A surprising number of magazine art directors have come from the ranks of advertising agencies. Art directors on small magazines occasionally volunteer to design ads for advertisers who do not have agencies (Dugald Stermer did this when he was art director at *Ramparts*), but this kind of service is far less common on magazines than on newspapers. And magazines, unlike newspapers, ordinarily do not have their own production facilities. Typesetting, platemaking, and printing all are farmed out.

Restrictions on magazine advertising

Magazines have worked out clearly defined guidelines of what their advertising departments will accept. Several magazines, the *New Yorker* and *Saturday Review* among them, said no to cigarette advertisers after the surgeon general's report. The old *Saturday Evening Post* up until its last decade would not accept liquor advertising. *Ms.* said no to anything smacking of sexism. *Reader's Digest* for its first three decades would not accept *any* advertising.

Some magazines—*Good Housekeeping, Parents,* and *Weight Watchers*—offer seals of approval for advertising appearing on their pages. Many magazines insist on testing products before accepting the advertising.

This full-page, full-color consumer-magazine ad is designed to show some "neat ways" to organize items in the kitchen using Rubbermaid products. No white lines or bars separate the twelve panels. Except for the copyright line, all type is reversed. Michael Feldman designed the ad; Walter Burek wrote the copy. The agency was Ketchum MacLeod & Grove, Pittsburgh. Used with permission of and © by Rubbermaid Incorporated.

The run-on typography complements the overlapping, motion-picture art to nicely unify this two-page full-color ad to retailers. That is Don Meredith in every pose, aided at the end by a second player. The little aside at the bottom right asks retailers to "See your Munsingwear Salesman for the details of the Spring 'Have A Great Weekend' Promotion." Art director: Jerry Robertson. Copywriters: Wolly Wohl and Mike Jay. Agency: Ogilvy & Mather, Los Angeles.

Bikingwear, hikingwear, tenniswear, racingwear, bowlingwear, brunchingwear, partyingwear, joggingwear, fishingwear, golfingwear, barbequeingwear, sailingwear, dancingwear, diningwear, travelingwear, Munsingwear. "Have a great weekend." Don Meredith

munsingwear

See your Munsingwear Salesman for the details of the Spring "Have A Great Weekend" Promotion.

RUBBERMAID BRINGS YOU SOME NEAT WAYS TO ORGANIZE.

Turn. Turn. Turn. Our Turntable saves space in cabinets.

You can stack twice as much on our Twin Turntable.

Mount your Paper Towel Holder near the action. Decorator colors.

Drawer Organizers keep everything in its place.

Knives here. Forks here. Spoons here.

A neat place for your place settings.

Hang your clean-up committee on any convenient door.

Keep it all together on your inside closet door.

Wrap and Bag Organizer. Another convenient hang-up.

Bottle Rack stores beverages in unused refrigerator space.

Can Dispenser really saves space in the fridge.

Rubbermaid ®

IT'S A HOUSEHOLD WORD

"What Sort of a Man Reads *Hustler?*" asks an ad addressed to media buyers in agencies. After listing some products the typical *Hustler* reader uses, like Blue Ribbon beer and Mennen's after-shave lotion, the ad warns: "When you talk to him in HUSTLER, you had better give it to him straight. . . . Otherwise he'll tell you to shove it." The ad ends on this note: "Playboy had him. . . . Penthouse wants him. . . . HUSTLER'S got him." You see here the art for the ad. Marbro Advertising, Columbus, is the agency. Quicksilver Photography took the photograph.

Sometimes a magazine accepts an ad reluctantly—and then runs an editorial disavowing it. *Commonweal* did this for a book, *Living with Sex: The Student's Dilemma,* which the editors felt contained "a number of moral judgments and recommendations . . . difficult, and in some cases impossible perhaps, to reconcile with Catholic teaching."[6]

Prevention magazine can claim it "spends many hours each month screening companies for reputability and financial responsibility, checking advertising copy and examining products and services submitted for advertising." A twenty-five-page manual for advertisers sets standards for, among other things, advertising copy and selling methods. "We expect copy to be preventative rather than curative in nature and we reserve the right to refuse any advertising without even giving a reason."[7] From a design standpoint, however, much of the advertising in *Prevention,* coming from small firms selling vitamins and similar products, is of a low order.

In a note above its "Personal" classified advertisement department, where men and women seek out each other's companionship, *National Review* has said this: "NR extends maximum freedom in this column, but

NR's maximum freedom may be another man's straightjacket. NR reserves the right to reject any copy deemed unsuitable."

Not that all this watchdogging is peculiar to the magazine medium. The other media set up standards of what is acceptable, too. But magazines, because of their tendency to cater to select audiences, set up a greater variety of restrictions and in many cases adhere to them more rigidly.

The economics of magazine publishing

High paper and postage costs at the beginning of the 1980s forced several adless magazines to begin accepting ads. Those magazines include *Changing Times, Modern Maturity, Dynamic Years,* and *NRTA Journal. Ms.* magazine found a way of partially circumventing the high postal rates in 1979 by affiliating with the Ms. Foundation for Education & Communication and gaining nonprofit status. Publisher Pat Carbine estimated that the move would cut postal costs in half. Other magazines have made similar arrangements. They include *Mother Jones, National Geographic, Audubon,* and *Natural History.* Under IRS arrangements, such magazines must be published primarily for "educational" reasons.

Paper supplies remain a problem for many magazines in the 1980s. Some major consumer magazines using coated stock have begun running ad sections on uncoated but supercalendered (polished) stock, and giving affected advertisers a discount.

Magazines have become more flexible with their advertising rates. *People,* with 85 percent of its circulation coming from newsstand sales, in 1979 began adjusting its ad rates on an issue-by-issue basis. On weeks when circulation is down, advertisers get cash credit for the difference between actual and published circulation figures.

Eight opinion or thought magazines got together to sell their combined circulation to advertisers wanting an intelligent audience but not wanting to deal individually with small-circulation magazines to get it. To dramatize their importance, each of the magazines picked a famous reader to feature in the two-page ad which ran in media likely to be seen by media buyers in agencies and by advertisers. Bill Nelson did the continuous-tone caricatures. Art director: Jack Anesh. Copywriter: Ned Viseltear. The agency was Anesh, Viseltear, Gumbinner.

In its attempt to lure advertisers onto its pages in 1980, *Esquire* offered a no-clutter guarantee. If any full-page ad faced another full-page ad, the advertiser could refuse to pay for the space. Furthermore, editorial material would occupy at least 57 percent of every issue. The magazine was also making an effort to sell a bigger percentage of copies on the newsstand. Other magazines have lowered rates during summer months, when circulation is down. Adjusting rates to better match audiences seems closer to the TV concept. *Advertising Age* noted that "advertisers of the not-too-distant future will be able to quite precisely match their print and television advertising goals to enable much more of an interaction between the two media. . . ."[8]

Magazines make reprints of ads available to advertisers and provide a number of merchandising services. When *Newsweek* decided for its June 6, 1983, issue to run a major article on "Showdown Over Smoking," it notified its cigarette advertisers, and all pulled out of the issue. They were back the next week. *Newsweek* runs from six to eleven pages of cigarette advertising every issue.

Magazines engage in extensive campaigns to convince advertisers that there is where their advertising belongs. *Seventeen* claims that its August back-to-school issue is read by one out of every two teenage girls and that *Seventeen* readers develop long-lasting loyalties to products. So it is important to get to girls while they are young. A Yankelovich study, *Seventeen* says, shows that 41 percent of adult women still buy the same brand of mascara they chose as a teenager and 29 percent use the same perfume. Twenty-six percent wear the same brand of bra.

What readers think of the magazine affects how they respond to advertisers. *Seventeen* tells advertisers that "Because she believes in us, she'll believe in you."

Serving the advertiser

In their attempt to win and hold advertisers, magazines court media buyers in agencies through personal contact, direct-mail advertising, and ads in the advertising trade press. A magazine's typical sales pitch contains information on the buying power and habits of the audience the magazine can deliver. Often the magazine is able to cite a price advantage.

But how can the media buyer compare advertising rates of magazines with different circulation figures? Of course, a magazine with a large circulation will charge more per page than a magazine with a smaller circulation. But how *much* more is reasonable? Is a $13,000 black-and-white page in *The American Rifleman* (1,400,000 circulation) about right when you compare it to a $40,000 black-and-white page in *Sports Illustrated* (2,504,000 circulation)? To help the media buyer make decisions, magazines compute their CPMs. A CPM represents the cost to reach one thousand subscribers and newsstand buyers with a full-page black-and-white ad. Magazine CPMs range from a dollar or two to fifty dollars or more. A small, specialized magazine is likely to have a higher CPM than a large, general-circulation magazine has. CPMs are not quite as useful as they once were because, in their attempt to fight TV statistics, some magazines are figuring in passalong readerships. This causes some confusion.

Most magazines base their page rates on the "live-copy area": the trim size of the page minus a border of white all around. If an advertiser wants the ad to bleed off the page, there is often an extra charge of from 10 to 20 percent. Advertisers feel that the extra charge is not justified now that most magazines are printed by offset or gravure. In the days of letterpress, bleed ads did cause extra trouble for magazines. Advertisers like to bleed their ads because, some feel, the ads look more contemporary. More important, bleeds on 8½″ × 11″ pages mean about 25 percent more space.

One of a series, this playful magazine ad crowds a remarkable amount of abstract art and many words into a small space. The ads run sometimes with two lines of copy underneath inviting readers to send for a catalog to Flents, 14 Orchard St., Norwalk, Connecticut. The designer: John Voytko. The agency: Shailer Davidoff Rogers, Fairfield, Connecticut.

This small lively ad for Finis Jhung Ballet, Inc., New York, appeared in *Dance Magazine*. It features good art, intentionally repetitious; good proportions; and the illusion of many typefaces (but actually the type is all a condensed sans serif). Art director: Howard Schiff. Designer: Joyce Tagliabue, Joyce Designs, Inc.

FINIS JHUNG BALLET, INC.
NEW SPACIOUS STUDIO
2182 BROADWAY at 77th ST., N.Y. 877-4740

FINIS JHUNG: PROF./INT./MEN/POINT
MATT TURNEY: SPECIAL EXERCISE for DANCERS
LIANE PLANE: BALLET FOR BEGINNERS
HECTOR MERCADO: JAZZ

Any number of loosely knit organizations exist to make it easier—and cheaper—for an advertiser to appear in several different magazines. For instance, in 1976 *Atlas, Columbia Journalism Review, Commentary, Foreign Affairs, National Review, The New Republic,* and *The New York Review of Books* formed The Leadership Network, a group of unrelated magazines edited for affluent intellectuals. The network could claim a combined circulation of 550,000. The divergent editorial policies, ranging from far left to far right, meant little audience duplication. Putting the same ad in all seven magazines, the advertiser could save twenty percent from what was needed when approaching each magazine separately. That same year *The Progressive, Change, Environment,* and *Bulletin of the Atomic Scientists* announced a similar alliance.

To help advertisers get additional mileage out of their ads, many magazines offer special marketing services, such as reprints wrapped in the magazines' covers and "As Advertised in _____" display cards. Magazines also send out calendars showing special issues planned so that advertising can be tied to editorial content.

Mediamatic Calendar of Special Editorial Issues (423 W. 55th St., New York, N.Y. 10019) lists editorial and special issue plans of about five hundred publications, mostly trade journals. It is up to the creative as well as the media departments in the advertising agencies to take advantage of the available information about the magazines' readers, plans, and merchandising aids.

The local advertiser and magazines

National advertisers make the most use of magazines, but local advertisers make some use of magazines, too. National magazines offer regional editions to such advertisers. Daily newspapers establish locally edited magazine sections. City magazines, set up partly to compete with the newspapers, represent one of the fastest growing segments of the magazine industry.

"Magazines are selective," says *Newsweek,* which publishes many regional editions. "The heaviest magazine readers are in the top brackets of buyers of products such as air travel, insurance, radial tires, business equipment, toiletries, cameras, watches . . . [*Newsweek*'s ellipsis].

"Some media are more equal than others. . . . Because they watch television themselves, a lot of retailers think television . . . [directs messages to people most able to act on them]. Not so. Even though television can vividly get a product recognized, the heaviest TV viewers, collectively, are in the lower income brackets. Because the local newspaper rep calls on them regularly, retailers think newspapers are also pretty good. Not necessarily. Newspapers sell 'price' or 'bargain,' but they too cut across all levels of customer affluence—or non-affluence."[9]

Magazine formats

Magazines come in a variety of formats, from pocket-size (*Reader's Digest*) to near-tabloid size (*Advertising Age*). Most magazines come in an 8½" × 11" size—or something close to that.

Magazines in a similar field tend to adopt the same page size so that an advertiser, producing an ad for one, can use the same ad for the others. But often an ad has to be designed so that it can be enlarged or reduced to fit magazines with different page sizes. Sometimes the ad will appear as a one-pager in one magazine, a two-pager in another. The designer's job is to take the original and redesign it, holding onto the same elements but resizing and perhaps reshaping.

A two-page ad poses a problem for the designer, who has to figure out ways to overcome the gutter that tends to keep the two pages separate. A two-page spread in a side stitched magazine (like *Esquire*) is more difficult to manage than a two-page spread in a saddle stitched magazine (like *Playboy*).

Some magazines accept inserts of a size different from the magazine proper. Some offer gatefolds—covers that open out to three or more pages.

Some magazines, like *Redbook,* accept advertising designed in an irregular shape, place it in the middle of a page, and fit editorial material around it.

The appropriate volume in the *Standard Rate & Data Service* series gives you all the information you need about a given magazine. A listing tells you, among other things, what the space rates are, what editions (geographic or demographic) are available, whether the magazine offers split runs (to test the relative effectiveness of two different ads), whether the magazine accepts ads that bleed off the page, and what the mechanical requirements are. Another *SRDS* volume that will prove useful is *Print Media Production Data,* which brings production information together from several *SRDS* publications.[10]

In considering a magazine's rate card and the information in *SRDS,* the agency creative department will have to decide, for instance, whether bleeding the ad is worth an extra 15 percent charge and whether specifying position in the magazine is worth *that* extra charge. (Advertisers seem to feel that being up front in a magazine and on a right-hand page gives them better readership.)

The most expensive page, because it is a page likely to be seen often, is the back cover. So revered is this page that a magazine would rather plant the address stickers over front-cover art than over any part of the back cover. A few magazines—*Editor & Publisher* is one—sell space on their front covers.

Up until the mid- to late-1970s you could stand out in a magazine if you used full color. Since then, more than half the ads in magazines have appeared in full color. Advertisers have looked for new ways to stand out, and magazine publishers—some of them—think they have the answer: Try checkerboard, staircase, or other offbeat sizes and shapes.

A checkerboard ad occupies the top half of a left-hand page and the bottom half of a right-hand page—or the top-left quarter and bottom right-hand quarter of a single page or succession of pages. A staircase ad takes one full column and then flattens out and spreads across two or three more columns. Another approach is for the ad to start on one page and finish on the other with room for editorial matter on both pages.

Other ways to get unusual impact in magazine advertising are to buy

This Fancy Fingers full-page, full-color ad appeared in *Essence.* Rounded corners help coordinate the photographs with the boxes that hold the body copy. A similar version, but with the fingers of a white woman, appeared in other magazines. This small reproduction does not show it well, but the lower loop of the *g* in the logo encloses a shiny fingernail. Reeds & Farris art directed; Chuck Lewis wrote the copy. The agency was Lee & Lee of South El Monte, California.

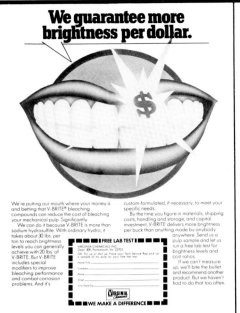

We guarantee more brightness per dollar.

We're putting our mouth where your money is and betting that V-BRITE® bleaching compounds can reduce the cost of bleaching your mechanical pulp. Significantly.

We can do it because V-BRITE is more than sodium hydrosulfite. With ordinary hydro, it takes about 30 lbs. per ton to reach brightness levels you can generally achieve with 20 lbs. of V-BRITE. But V-BRITE includes special modifiers to improve bleaching performance and combat corrosion problems. And it's

custom-formulated, if necessary, to meet your specific needs.

By the time you figure in materials, shipping costs, handling and storage, and capital investment, V-BRITE delivers more brightness per buck than anything made by anybody anywhere. Send us a pulp sample and let us run a free lab test for brightness levels and cost ratios.

If we can't measure up, we'll bite the bullet and recommend another product. But we haven't had to do that too often.

■■■ FREE LAB TEST ■■■
VIRGINIA CHEMICALS INC.
Dept 309, Portsmouth, Va. 23703.
OK. Put up or shut up. Have your Tech Service Rep pick up a sample of my pulp for your free lab test.

Name/Title _____

Company _____

Address _____

Phone _____

Email _____

City/State/Zip _____

VIRGINIA Chemicals

■■■ WE MAKE A DIFFERENCE ■■■

The coupon for this ad, when filled in, will bring a Virginia Chemicals representative to the pulp plant to pick up a pulp sample for a free lab test. "We're putting our mouth where your money is and betting that V-BRITE® bleaching compounds can reduce the cost of bleaching your mechanical pulp," the copy begins. The airbrushed art for this trade-magazine ad (it ran in *Pulp and Paper* and *TAPPI*) is inspired by pop art. The "balloon" holding the headline is styled to match the sharp angles of the brightness symbol. The coupon border is enboldened to make that element relate in blackness to the art above. Art director: Lewis F. Waggaman. Designer: William Borroughs. Copywriter: Thomas S. Mallonee. Agency: VanSant, Dugdale & Co., Washington, D.C.

the three- or four-page spreads offered by cover gatefolds, to buy a succession of magazine pages, to use a fifth color like silver, and to pay for inserts of various kinds.

You can also buy a scattering of space in magazines, allowing a series of ads to build momentum in a single issue.

Advantages of magazines

The big advantage magazines have over other media—an advantage shared by direct mail—is that magazines can really pinpoint an audience. It is hard to think of an interest group that does not have its own magazine. In 1980, for instance, cigar smokers got a new one called *Cigar*. Since 1974 comic book collectors have had *The Comic Buyer's Guide* to read each week. Each year sees the introduction of other narrow-audience magazines. A principal job of the designer of a magazine ad is to understand the interest group and control its attention.

Magazines have other advantages. With some exceptions, they tend to devote less of their total space to advertising than newspapers do. One study of fifty-two leading magazines showed a 51 to 49 ratio of advertising to editorial.

Magazines like to compare themselves to TV for advertising clutter, claiming that viewers are growing increasingly intolerant of the amount of broadcast time given over to commercials. The Magazine Publishers Association especially likes to cite the medium's advantages over television, which gets a much bigger share of the advertiser's dollar. True, commercials take up only a fraction of TV time, but you cannot escape them quite as easily as you can escape the ads in magazines.

Readers find magazine advertising less irritating. A majority of readers, Opinion Research Corporation finds, prefer magazines with advertising to magazines without.[11] And magazines can claim that some readers want the advertising as much as they want editorial content.

An ad in a magazine has longer life than an ad on TV and even in a newspaper. The reader can refer to it later. And copy can be longer. Using an 8½″ × 11″ (full-page) all-copy magazine ad sponsored by the Magazine Publishers Association, Al Hampel, then director of creative services for Benton & Bowles, demonstrated the fact that, as his headline phrased it, "It Would Take Eighteen 30-Second TV Commercials to Tell You What's on This Page."

In spite of the magazine industry's jealousy over TV, the advertising in magazines often ties itself to TV advertising. One reason is for the advertising to provide arguments in detail based on a theme only barely touched on by the commercial. The magazine ad puts the original ad in perspective. Or the magazine ad capitalizes on a popular TV commercial by simply restating its theme, giving it a little more mileage. The most memorable frame in the commercial is frozen for print. The magazine ad becomes reminder advertising.

When Jell-O used real housewives on television to demonstrate how easy it was to prepare a new gelatin dessert, the announcer, at the end of each commercial, referred the viewer to the women's magazines, where, in ads, the recipe could be found.

Occasionally a magazine ad shows the TV commercial in storyboard or photoboard form. The most important frames form into a "multipanel" ad (a kind of ad described in chapter 5).

The big advantage that magazines hold over newspapers as an advertising medium centers on production. All three of the major printing processes—offset lithography, letterpress, and gravure—are used for magazines. Sometimes a single magazine uses more than one process. Paper quality in magazines allows for crisper impressions, less showthrough, finer screening for halftones, and better color fidelity.

Nine associations covering media, advertising agencies, and production firms got together in 1976 to set color standards for advertising placed in publications printed on web offset presses. The new standards, updating a 1964 letterpress set and a 1966 business publications set, were spelled out in a fourteen-page booklet, now available from the American Association of Advertising Agencies, the Associated Business Press, and the Magazine Publishers Association. The standards were designed to assure advertisers the same color in magazines that they see and okay on progressive proofs.

The challenge of magazine ad design

Because the space it occupies is expensive, because it is meant to be seen several times, because it is produced by highly creative people in advertising agencies, a magazine ad often represents the best in current design thinking. Design quality remains at a rather consistent level in consumer

A coupon offering additional information dominates this trade-magazine ad directed to beauty-shop operators. The scissors are especially appropriate as art because they direct the reader to the coupon, and they represent a tool very familiar to the persons who will be reading this ad. The balance here is essentially formal; yet the ad has the vitality of one informally arranged. The inset art at the bottom right shows a poster offered free to those who fill out the coupon. The ad's sponsor is National Beauty Service of Chicago.

Unisex salon owners tell us,

Please send me more information and my promotional sign.
☐ I am currently a member of HSM.

My Name

Salon Name

Salon Address

City   State   Zip

MAIL TO: NATIONAL BEAUTY SERVICE
114 WEST ILLINOIS STREET, CHICAGO, ILL. 60610

MB105

"YOU'RE ONLY DOING HALF THE BUSINESS IF YOU'RE NOT DOING UNISEX"

Unisex is the rage today. More men than ever want their hair styled, not simply cut. And that can mean big business for the salon that decides to capitalize on it.

We have put together a new and unprecedented program designed to help you take advantage of this rapidly growing, new trend.

When you become a member of HAIRSTYLE-OF-THE-MONTH you will receive detailed 16"x 20" sketches of the latest unisex hairstyles and men's promotional signs.

Write today for more information about our revolutionary new program and we will send you, ABSOLUTELY FREE, a handsome 11"x 14" promotional sign to let people know you know how to style men's hair.

DON'T DELAY
MAIL THIS COUPON TODAY

MALE CALL! our cuts are today and terrific

Another well-designed small-space magazine ad with plenty of art. It says a lot, and most of what it says is hand lettered.

magazines. In trade and professional journals it rises to high levels—and sinks to low. Because trade-journal ads often deal with technical matters, most creative people prefer to work on ads for consumer magazines, where the imagination often is allowed greater play. But, in view of the numerous trade magazines published, much of the creative activity must center on ads done for the less familiar magazines.

Magazine ads, unlike newspaper ads, seldom make use of borders. The magazines' smaller pages give dominance to each ad. There is less need to fence out competing ads.

Often a coupon is involved. If it is a coupon to be filled out and mailed in, chances are it will contain a key: an agency-assigned "Dept." number, different for each magazine, that allows the agency or advertiser to measure the pulling power of one magazine against the other or one ad against the other. The designer should avoid tone in the area where the key number is to go. Otherwise a small rectangle will have to be cut out to accommodate changes in the number, and the number each time will stand out awkwardly.

If an ad is to bleed, the designer must remember to bleed only the art, not the headline or copy. Where bleeding is to occur, the final pasteup will carry art that extends slightly *beyond* the trim edge.

A magazine may set up any number of regulations as to what a designer can do. For instance, it may not be willing to let the designer adopt an editorial format that makes the ad look like part of the magazine itself. It may insist that the designer avoid using the magazine's headline/title face and body face. But, in general, the creative potential on magazine advertising design is boundless.

"Think of print as a brand-new medium," said Al Hampel to copywriters brought up in the TV age, "and the possibilities become astounding. Imagine a new form of advertising that lets you stretch out and sell your product in ways that no thirty- or sixty-second time span could possibly handle."

He concluded: "I could guarantee you this: If somehow print could be viewed as a new medium, you'd see a wave of jaded TV writers and art directors clamoring for print assignments as they once fought for the chance to get into show business via the TV commercial. Print needs that kind of reawakening."

1. J. K. G., "Man's Best Friend," *New Republic,* November 28, 1983, p. 43.

2. Quoted in "Best & Worst," *Adweek,* March 7, 1983, p. M.R. 32.

3. Theodore Peterson, "The Modern Magazine at Age 90," speech delivered at the University of Illinois, Urbana, October 18, 1983.

4. Quoted in "Best & Worst," *Adweek,* March 1983, p. M.R. 35.

5. Norman Hart, *Industrial Advertising and Publicity* (London: Halsted Press, 1978), pp. 148, 149.

6. "On Accepting Ads," *Commonweal,* October 1966, p. 7.

7. "What *Prevention* Advertising Means to You," *Prevention,* May 1976, p. 21.

8. "TV and Magazines: A Coming Together," *Advertising Age.* September 17, 1979, p. 16.

9. *Newsweek* advertisement in *Advertising Age,* January 12, 1976, p. 5.

10. Still another *SRDS* volume deals with college newspapers.

11. "Magazines versus Television," *Folio,* November 1979, pp. 77–79.

13

Broadcast advertising

A generation raised on television finds it difficult to imagine people planning their evenings so as not to miss the latest episode of "Amos 'n' Andy," "Fibber McGee and Molly," or one of the other popular radio programs of the 1930s or 1940s. The members of that earlier generation gathered in front of their radio sets and actually watched the dials as they listened to the words and music. What pictures they saw had to be pictures in their heads. In those days the commercials as well as the programs did their job without benefit of visual stimulation.

When TV came along after World War II, advertising agencies used techniques they understood: they simply made more radio commercials, adding pictures as one adds frosting on a cake. A lot of experimentation had to go on before TV commercials could attain the degree of sophistication and integration they now have.

Television not only added a visual dimension to commercials; it also added motion. When color came along later, television as an advertising medium was complete.

Ad makers in agencies who made the switch from radio and the print media to television discovered staggering staging possibilities, although the first TV commercials were not much more than radio commercials with speakers shown on the screen. The first experimental commercials were the ones that used simple animation.

Like most forms of advertising, TV commercials have gone through phases. The 1960s saw a creative explosion, with all kinds of techniques tried, some at the expense of the message. In the 1970s commercial makers depended more on research. Creativity seemed to move to Europe, where some of the best commercials were being made. In the early 1980s TV commercials relied largely on "new wave" graphics. What was shown was impressive but cold. As the decade unfolded, the commercials seemed to take on a new warmth. They were people oriented rather than machine oriented.[1] There was also a preoccupation with special effects.

TV commercials make wide use of computers to get their special effects. For instance, for a 1984 Olympics commercial, Robert Abel Associates fed the ABC and the Olympics logos into a terminal and manipulated them to get unusual combinations and angles. One commercial combined live-action footage of a fire (shot at half speed) with a computer-graphics torch.

Filmmaking and commercial making

The same kinds of talents that go into the making of motion pictures go into the making of TV commercials. But there are some important differences.

In the first place, commercials are short, usually no longer than thirty seconds. So the director can show only a few details. Mood becomes all important. The director must establish it instantly. And every action counts.

Second, the screen size is much smaller than theater screen size. This calls for more closeups. The commercial, then, achieves a sense of intimacy.

```
VISUAL: CU Capt. w/ telescope

AUDIO: VO
"Come join the captain on
his ship
with his Hershey's treat,"

VIDEO: Cut to ECU
```

Like any advertisement, a storyboard can start out as a thumbnail sketch, crudely drawn, with just enough detail to show, in-house, where the action is headed. This is a sample panel from student Pru Baird's charming animated sixty-second spot for Hershey's chocolate bars, a commercial meant to be seen by children. It features a jingle that starts out like this: "I saw a ship a-sailing, a-sailing on the sea/ And oh! it was all laden with tasty things for thee./ There were almonds in the cabin, and chocolate in the hold. . . ."

This is the original storyboard for a thirty-second commercial for a car agency. The nondescript fellow who emerges has become a sort of symbol for customers of Damerow-Beaverton Ford, which advertises ''the only price,'' a no-dickering discount on its cars. The beauty of this character, a sort of grown-up Charley Brown, is that almost anybody can identify with him. As in most original storyboards produced by agencies (in this case, Swearingen Advertising Agency, Portland), a box below each panel carries, first, the description (labeled ''VIDEO'') and, second, the words and sound effects (labeled ''AUDIO''). Copywriter Dan Cox developed the ad; Robin Atherly did the animation and developed the character.

Third, commercials on television, because they evolved from radio, depend more on audio impressions than theater films do. The idea for a commercial usually comes from a copywriter's script; the art director does the storyboard, with its visual impressions, later. Some of the time the TV viewer may not be watching the screen at all, just listening.

Fourth, commercials tend to intrude while theater films serve an audience that has paid to see them. Commercials must work to get the viewer's attention. They must dazzle. No wonder they sometimes appear to be more elaborate, more compelling than the programs themselves.

Fifth, commercials run again and again. The people who make them must try, somehow, to take the sting out of the redundancy.

Sixth, commercials direct themselves to selected audiences. The media buyers in agencies, then, in the time-slots and stations they buy, play a big role in making commercials successful.[2]

Considering the audience

To be effective, TV commercials must overcome two major handicaps. Both have to do with the audience. One concerns the hostility members

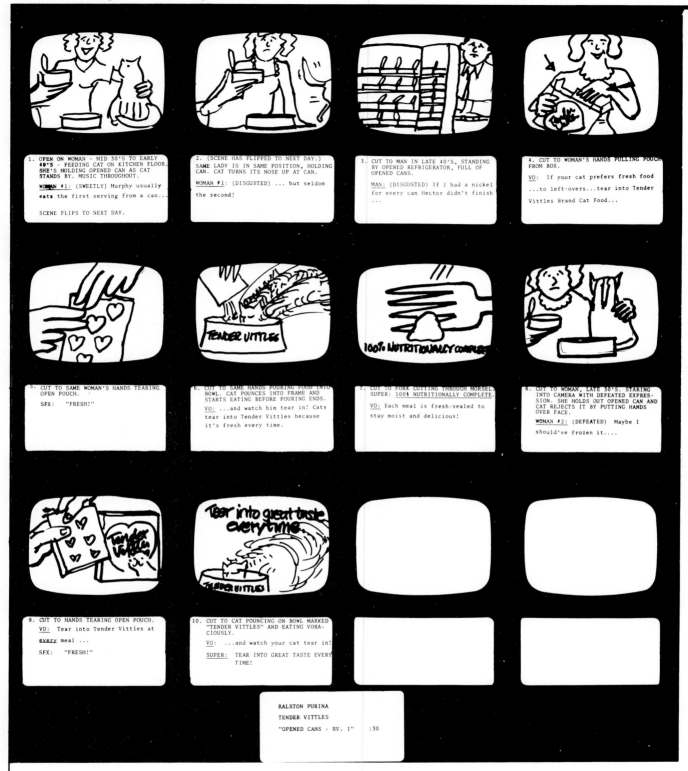

1. OPEN ON WOMAN - MID 30'S TO EARLY 40'S - FEEDING CAT ON KITCHEN FLOOR. SHE'S HOLDING OPENED CAN AS CAT STANDS BY. MUSIC THROUGHOUT.

WOMAN #1: (SWEETLY) Murphy usually eats the first serving from a can...

SCENE FLIPS TO NEXT DAY.

2. (SCENE HAS FLIPPED TO NEXT DAY.) SAME LADY IS IN SAME POSITION, HOLDING CAN. CAT TURNS ITS NOSE UP AT CAN.

WOMAN #1: (DISGUSTED) ... but seldom the second!

3. CUT TO MAN IN LATE 40'S, STANDING BY OPENED REFRIGERATOR, FULL OF OPENED CANS.

MAN: (DISGUSTED) If I had a nickel for every can Hector didn't finish ...

4. CUT TO WOMAN'S HANDS PULLING POUCH FROM BOX.

VO: If your cat prefers fresh food ...to left-overs...tear into Tender Vittles Brand Cat Food...

5. CUT TO SAME WOMAN'S HANDS TEARING OPEN POUCH.

SFX: "FRESH!"

6. CUT TO SAME HANDS POURING FOOD INTO BOWL. CAT POUNCES INTO FRAME AND STARTS EATING BEFORE POURING ENDS.

VO: ...and watch him tear in! Cats tear into Tender Vittles because it's fresh every time.

7. CUT TO FORK CUTTING THROUGH MORSEL. SUPER: 100% NUTRITIONALLY COMPLETE.

VO: Each meal is fresh-sealed to stay moist and delicious!

8. CUT TO WOMAN, LATE 30'S. STARING INTO CAMERA WITH DEFEATED EXPRESSION. SHE HOLDS OUT OPENED CAN AND CAT REJECTS IT BY PUTTING HANDS OVER FACE.

WOMAN #2: (DEFEATED) Maybe I should've frozen it....

9. CUT TO HANDS TEARING OPEN POUCH.

VO: Tear into Tender Vittles at every meal ...

SFX: "FRESH!"

10. CUT TO CAT POUNCING ON BOWL MARKED "TENDER VITTLES" AND EATING VORACIOUSLY.

VO: ...and watch your cat tear in!

SUPER: TEAR INTO GREAT TASTE EVERY TIME!

RALSTON PURINA
TENDER VITTLES
"OPENED CANS - RV. 1" :30

of the audience harbor for this kind of advertising. Commercials intrude on their entertainment.

The other problem concerns the welter of commercials seen each day by the typical viewer. In the average home, a TV set sends out programs—and commercials—for just about seven hours a day. While this statistic does not identify who watches what and for how long, it does suggest that, with present practices of stacking commercials, the typical viewer sees scores of them every day. They parade before the viewer in rapid succession, in no particular order, each with the same degree of urgency.

The rough storyboard at the left was the start of a Tender Vittles commercial, shown at the right as a photoboard. A photoboard is created by lifting key outtakes of a finished commercial. Jim Aaby, senior vice president of Wells, Rich, Greene, Inc., New York, wrote the commercial; Bill Mullen art directed. (Reproduced with permission of Ralston Purina Company.)

(MUSIC UNDER)
WOMAN 1: (SWEETLY) Murphy usually eats the first serving from a can. . .

(DISGUSTED). . .but seldom the second.

MAN: (DISGUSTED) If I had a nickel for every can Hector didn't finish. . .

VO: If your cat prefers fresh food to left-overs, tear into Tender Vittles Brand cat food. . .

SINGER: "FRESH"

VO:. . .and watch him tear in. Cat's love Tender Vittles, it's fresh every time.

100% NUTRITIONALLY COMPLETE

Each meal sealed to stay moist and delicious.

WOMAN 2: (DEFEATED) No? Maybe I should've frozen it.

VO: Tear into Tender Vittles at every meal. . .
SINGER: "FRESH"

TEAR INTO FRESH TASTE EVERY TIME.

VO:. . .and watch your cat tear in.

Under such circumstances, how much of what's seen can the viewer possibly retain? Not much—or at least not much *accurately*. One survey found that about 25 percent of commercials are attributed by viewers to competitors rather than to actual sponsors.

Ideally, then, a TV commercial makes restitution for the irritation it causes: it entertains the viewer. At the same time, it does something out of the ordinary to gain attention. And it makes sure that the viewer correctly associates the message with the specific product.

MMM Carpets in California has run snide comments in type at the bottom of the screen, comments that have little or nothing to do with the routine hard sell going on in the commercial. This is a daring practice, perhaps even questionable; but it does show that the firm wants to somehow relieve the tedium of commercials that might have to be seen again and again.

To some people, TV commercials have become an art form, with special showings arranged for audiences willing to give an evening over to watching them. Johnny Carson on "The Tonight Show" occasionally shows award-winning commercials as part of the entertainment. The humorous Federal Express commercials devised by the Ally & Gargano agency appeal to many as among the best of the commercials originating in the United States in the early 1980s.[3]

Who uses TV?

Manufacturers of food products, grooming aids, cleaning agents, home remedies, appliances, and automobiles continue to rely heavily on TV as an advertising medium, but some previously print-oriented advertisers are moving into TV, too, especially at the local level.

Among the department stores turning to TV is Penney's, whose no-nononsense, one-item-per-spot commercials reflect the clean, crisp design thinking evident in its newspaper ads. The store's New York headquarters has advised local store advertising managers to concentrate spots in one program rather than scatter them over several days. The store feels it can get more impact that way.

Even magazines use TV to sell their product. *People* and the three newsmagazines often use spots to call attention to features in current issues. The *National Enquirer* uses TV to congratulate its readers for having "enquiring minds." The *Wall Street Journal* uses TV to line up new subscribers. Book publishers, too, are showing an interest in TV advertising—for both their hardback and paperback editions. Peter Ognibene, who has written many TV commercials, explains why: "TV's potential for hardcover books is so enormous that titles selling 30,000 to 150,000 copies could, with TV advertising behind them, sell as much as ten times that number. And for paperback publishers the opportunities are equally dramatic."[4]

While many advertisers develop media mixes, some advertisers do it all on TV. Their products seem eminently suited to use by TV viewers.

Where advertisers have moved away from TV and back to print, it has been for reasons of cost and clutter. The most frequently heard complaint these days is that stations crowd too many commercials together at program or station breaks. The switch by advertisers from sixty-second to thirty- and ten-second commercials explains some of the crowding. Some stations are adding an 80 percent premium to the cost of ten-second spots in order to discourage their use and help eliminate the clutter.

The idea is to sell

In his *Hi and Lois* comic strip, Dik Brown in one episode has a kid talking about how funny a TV commercial is. A man interrupts to ask what the commercial is selling. The kid looks puzzled. "Selling?"

Too often the idea of selling gets lost in the attempt to be entertaining. Whatever techniques are used to involve the reader must lead, and quickly, to a pitch. Many ad people think that the pitch should come on right away.

And whatever is said must be repeated, not only within the ad but from ad to ad. Typically in a series, the related stories all lead to the same conclusion. The detergent *does* wash better, the margarine *does* taste like butter, the car *does* go farther on a tankful of gas.

The problem was to dramatize in a commercial the growth of savings and loan organizations. It could best be done by comparing the number of persons who own stock in all the stock exchanges, with the number who have savings in savings and loan organizations. Art director John Baeder with producer Eileen Rogers did it by simulating the animated light signs on Broadway, using a grid pattern of "light bulbs" that also looked like the board of a stockbrokerage house. The programmed effect of people walking was created by placing a sheet of acetate with dots (painted in white) between the actors and the camera lens. The client: The Savings & Loan Foundation. The agency: McCann-Erickson, New York.

Photoboard of a thirty-second animated spot making use of Far West's Mr. Moneybags symbol. The frame at the end brings up a special offer.

Young Man: Oh, man! I'm out of cash. Now what'll I do?

SFX: (Sproing!)

Moneybags: I'd be delighted to help you.

YM: Wha . . . ? Who are you?

MB: Mr. Moneybags, at your service.

I'll give you cash from your savings, take your deposit . . .

. . . or even cash a check. Why, I can help you in nearly as many ways as our tellers inside.

YM: And you're always open?
MB: Always.

YM: Wow, Mr. Moneybags, you're terrific!

MB: It's the Far West . . .

. . . way.

ANNCR: Make a transaction and get a coupon good for a Free Egg McMuffin or Big Mac at McDonald's.

A variation of the repetition idea involves a single script with different actors and settings for each commercial in the series. In the Brim coffee commercial, one person who makes coffee offers it to a colleague, who asks for only half a cup, saying the flavor is good but "It's the caffeine I can do without."

Like other advertisements, TV commercials can build images as well as sell products. To sell their new light beers, breweries were careful to show he-men calling for it in commercials. The companies did not want the beer burdened with an effeminate image, figuring the bulk of the buyers were men and that, further, women drinkers would not be turned off by a manly image.

And like other advertisements, TV commercials can address themselves to specific audiences in time slots when the best prospects can be reached. Consider how TV was used to sell 800,000 copies of a long-playing record by Roger Whittaker, a middle-aged British singer of sweet ballads (". . . the man who has thrilled millions around the world now brings his exciting music and pleasing manner to American audiences"). Tee Vee Records filmed Whittaker before a large and receptive Canadian audience and spliced the footage into the commercial to prove that he could draw an audience. The company also filmed Whittaker talking with great sincerity—the nice guy image. The commercial ran over and over again on selected stations in the United States.

Tee Vee Records explained its success with the observation that people who bought the record are the kind ill at ease in a record store, with its heavy beat and its smoking paraphernalia.[5]

1. EISENSTAEDT: I've been photographing life for most of my life.

2. And I've always set high standards
   for my prints.

3. So, when Fotomat asked to print
   a roll of my 35mm film...

4. ...with their Series 35 process...

5. ...I was skeptical.

6. I was also surprised. I must say
   Fotomat...

7. ...you do good work.
   ANNCR (VO): Bigger prints...
   custom quality. Series 35.

8. FOTOMAT MNEMONIC AS LOGO BUILDS.
   ANNCR: Only from Fotomat.

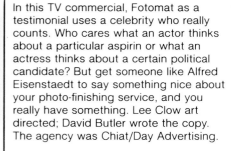

In this TV commercial, Fotomat as a testimonial uses a celebrity who really counts. Who cares what an actor thinks about a particular aspirin or what an actress thinks about a certain political candidate? But get someone like Alfred Eisenstaedt to say something nice about your photo-finishing service, and you really have something. Lee Clow art directed; David Butler wrote the copy. The agency was Chiat/Day Advertising.

Many advertisers use their commercials to make the point that their products have *two* redeeming values. A mint has both taste and breath-sweetening qualities. A toothpaste has both flouride and breath-sweetening qualities. A toilet paper has both softness and color. A beer has good taste and is less filling. In each case two silly people argue about the qualities, each adamant about one quality, each blind to the other. The poor viewer gets the point.

Emotion and sentiment in commercials

AT&T's "Reach out and touch someone" campaign, which started in 1979, prompted a rush by other advertisers to sentiment and emotion as selling tools in the 1980s. "Many advertisers have turned to sentiment because they've run out of compelling appeals to logic," a *Wall Street Journal* writer observed; ". . . for the increasing number of products that don't differ markedly from their competitors, new arguments are hard to find."

Advertising agencies have found that sentimental or emotional commercials need to be seen several times in order to register on viewers. Commercials based on logic score better on first-time-seen tests.[6]

Japanese commercials, especially, rely on emotion. The population density in Japan means less need for verbalizing, more need for intuition. For instance, body language means more there.

The Japanese don't want reasons. Any fast talking or hard or persuasive sell turns off the viewer. Repetition is not a problem, because the viewer feels that if a commercial is popular, the product must be selling well.[7]

Kinds of TV commercials

Advertisers use commercials in three ways: as *network advertisements,* shown on national shows; as *spot advertisements,* prepared nationally and shipped to various stations for local showings; and as *local advertisements,* prepared locally and shown locally. In each case the advertisement is called a "commercial" or a "spot."

Commercials tend to fall into these categories:

1. *The narrative.* Like a feature-length motion picture, this kind of commercial has a plot. Typically the story introduces a problem, then shows how the use of a particular product solves the problem.

The story can be told in live-action photography or in animation. Often a little exaggeration, a little humor moves the story along. IBM, to sell one of its sophisticated typewriters, showed a typist with several arms doing several things at her desk while her typewriter was automatically centering, underlining, and so on. At the end of the commercial a man came up with several gloves and asked: "Are these your gloves?"

Federal Express in one of its humorous commercials in 1982 portrayed the Postal Service, its competitor, as run by lazy, incompetent people. The angered Postal Service demanded that the commercial be taken off the air. *New York* magazine, noting this, offered the Postal Service its "If the Shoe Fits Wear It" Award.

2. *The slice-of-life.* Admen in a less enlightened age referred to it as "the two broads in the kitchen" commercial. More believable, theoretically, than a story, this commercial does not have a traditional hero or heroine. Instead it features people who are very, very ordinary—people who could well live next door to the viewer.

While the story commercial leans heavily on fiction techniques, the slice-of-life commercial creates the impression it is a piece of nonfiction. Viewers are supposed to have a sort of "Ain't it the truth!" reaction to the commercial.

Slice-of-life commercials often show an ordinary person burdened by some everyday problem—bad breath, cavities, constipation, clothes that do not come clean—only to be advised by some other ordinary person who has the word about a miracle product.

In slice-of-life commercials people like to pull the bill of someone's cap down over his forehead, or they like to wink. Another favorite device is to have ordinary people in commercials singing off-key. Apparently agencies and advertisers feel that we can listen to "Sometimes I feel like a nut, sometimes I don't" singing without losing our lunches.

Closely allied to slice-of-life commercials are "continuing character" commercials that feature a presumably believable character who seems to spend his every waking moment praising a certain product: a soft toilet tissue, a tasty coffee, an altered coffee that does not cause jangled nerves.

3. *The testimonial.* Famous people—or unknowns—caught by a can-

did camera tell what they like about a product and urge, directly or indirectly, others to try it. These people are not acting a part; they are believers—or so it appears.

Viewers are supposed to react like this: "If it's good enough for her, it's good enough for me."

The testimonial can also be used to *unsell* a product or do an institutional job. One of the most moving TV commercials ever made had William Talman, the TV actor, in a starring role some six weeks before he died of lung cancer. He was a cigarette smoker. He knew he was dying, but he wanted to expend what energy he had to dissuade others from smoking.

In the commercial, which was produced by the American Cancer Society, the Talman family was shown in various settings, then Talman was shown with fellow actor Raymond Burr, and then Talman was shown in a closeup. "You know," he said, "I didn't really mind losing those courtroom battles [on TV]. But I'm in a battle right now I don't want to lose at all because, if I lose it, it means losing my wife and those kids you just met.

"I've got lung cancer.

"So take some advice about smoking and losing from someone who's been doing both for years. If you haven't smoked, don't start. If you do smoke, quit. Don't be a loser."

4. *The announcer commercial.* Many commercials make use of an announcer who makes comments while a story unfolds. But some commercials are simpler than that. They show *only* an announcer, a no-nonsense type, often, who looks straight into the camera, telling viewers why they should try a product or order a service. If the announcer is well known, the commercial takes on some of the qualities of a testimonial.

The announcer commercial has less flair than the testimonial, and the viewer understands that a professional pitchman is on the screen, however sincere the pitchman may appear to be.

The announcer commercial, like the testimonial, is relatively inexpensive to produce.

In one announcer commercial for Stay-Dry antiperspirant, the agency president himself, Bob Dolobowsky, of Warren, Muller, Dolobowsky, appeared on the screen, holding up the product, telling viewers how sincere his agency was in preparing advertising for it. Dolobowsky wrote his own copy.

5. *The demonstration.* The best way to sell some products is to show how they are made, how they compare with others, or how they are used. A demonstration commercial may call for rather elaborate graphics and casting. Or it may show just the product and one announcer to do the demonstration.

Television is remarkably suited to this kind of selling—better suited, even, than face-to-face contact. In television, the camera can move in close to focus on detail, then move out again to give an overall view. And live action can be combined with drawings and diagrams.

An effective commercial of this genre was one sponsored by Contac showing its colorful "tiny time pills" bouncing in slow motion as a capsule is taken apart to show the viewer what is inside.

Another was a Doyle Dane Bernbach commercial for Heinz. It started by focusing on two bottles. One was labeled, simply, "Catsup" (the word has two spellings). The other was "Heinz Ketchup." The audio went like this: "Announcing the first televised/ketchup race./On the right . . . the world's leading ketchup . . ./on the left . . ./a well-known challenger./On your mark . . ./Get set. . . ." Then there were several frames showing the bottles turned upside down. Catsup poured out of the challenger, but it barely oozed out of the Heinz bottle. Then: "Heinz loses./Heinz is too thick . . ./too rich . . ./to win a ketchup race." It worked because it had an element of surprise in it. It pretended to show the product in an unfavorable light, but of course the viewer was not to be fooled.

One of the most persistent users of the demonstration is Polaroid. The demonstration is a natural for this advertiser. During its first years, Polaroid was sure enough of its product to do its demonstrations live.

6. *The song-and-dance.* In this kind of commercial, the advertiser tries to get the gaiety and flavor of a musical extravaganza into a sixty-seconds-or-less format.

Radio long ago proved the value of songs to sell products. The person living in the 1930s and 1940s found it almost impossible to escape the advertising jingles of the period or to keep from humming them. Coca-Cola showed that in the 1970s a jingle can still work. Its "Buy the World

This durable thirty-second Doyle Dane Bernbach-created commercial so impressed Quaker Oats Company officials when they first saw it that they put it on the air (in 1972) without pretesting. Sales for the previously slow selling Life cereal increased dramatically. The three kids in the commercial are brothers in real life, too.

1ST BOY: What's this stuff?
2ND BOY: Some cereal. Supposed to be good for you.

1ST BOY: D'you try it?
2ND BOY: I'm not gonna' try it, you try it.

1ST BOY: I'm not gonna' try it.

2ND BOY: Let's get Mikey!
1ST BOY: Yeah!

2ND BOY: He won't eat it. He hates everything.

2ND BOY: He likes it!

Hey Mikey!
ANNCR: (VO) When you bring Life home, don't tell the kids it's one of those

nutritional cereals you've been trying to get them to eat. You're the only one who has to know.

a Coke" commercial even fostered a pop record. Other advertisers have enjoyed similar success. "We've Only Just Begun," made popular by The Carpenters, was originally part of a series of commercials for Crocker Bank, San Francisco, when that bank was trying to appeal to youthful patrons.

But the full-fledged TV song-and-dance commercial we saw in the 1960s is a bit rare now because of the expense involved.

7. *The special-effects commercial.* The television commercial producer has access to all kinds of equipment and skills to bring about special effects. Camera tricks include unusual angles, fades, frozen action, and interruption in time so doors can close by themselves and people or props can change position, disappear, or appear as if by magic. Goldsholl Associates of Chicago, one of the leading studios for special effects, often uses the "stop motion" technique where the object is moved slightly by hand before each frame is shot. A technique for filming a drawing in progress is to show the drawing first, erase a bit before each frame is shot, and then show the film backward. Nytol uses a modest special effect when it films two of its tablets upright, the *N*s showing, then allows them to roll slightly so that the *N*s become *Z*s, appropriate letters for a product that brings sleep to the user.

Toppling dominoes became a popular special effect for commercials in the late 1970s. Someone pushes off the lead domino and down they go, one after the other, some thirty of them each second, spelling out a name or leading the viewer to some final visual treat or message. A Penn State student, Bob Speca, made a fine living for himself setting up dominoes for advertisers and then toppling them as a camera recorded the effect. National Bank of Dallas, Northern California Savings Bank, Purolator Air Freight, and other advertisers signed him up at fees ranging from $1,000 to $3,000.

A famous special effects commercial from a few seasons back was the one showing a man floating down from the sky and into the driver's seat of a Hertz rent-a-car. Others from the era included washing machines zooming up to ten-foot heights, hands reaching out of washing machines with boxes of detergent, and white knights spreading cleanliness as they rode past the camera.[8]

Jingles

Nothing brings life to a TV commercial more readily or makes it better remembered than a jingle.

The hit tunes tend to come from a small group of writers. Steve Karmen, who wrote "When You Say Budweiser" and "At Beneficial (doot-doot)" among fifteen hundred others, was called by a writer in *New York* in 1979 the "King of the Jingles."

Some jingle writers—like Barry Manilow—move on to write popular songs. Joe Brooks, with jingles to his credit written for Pepsi-Cola, Dr. Pepper, Pan Am, American Airlines, and other advertisers, wrote the Academy Award winner "You Light Up My Life."

Unlike regular songs, jingles are not covered by ASCAP or BMI, so jingle writers ordinarily do not earn royalties. They get a one-time fee for each jingle, a fee that for a national advertiser ranges from $5,000 to $10,000. The singers, though, get residuals, and often earn much more than the writers. No wonder some of the writers try to do their own singing.

Sometimes a new writer-singer beats out the regulars. Ginny Redington did it with her influential "You're the One" for McDonald's. Lots of "you" songs written by other writers for other clients followed, including "You, You Never Looked So Good" for Avon and "You Asked for It; You Got It" for Toyota.[9]

Note the concentration on closeups to show facial expression in this sixty-second spot for United California Bank. This was one of a series starring Sandy Duncan. The agency was Doyle Dane Bernbach, Los Angeles.

VIDEO: Man leaves Sandy's window as Mrs. Grossman approaches.

SANDY: Hello, Mrs. Grossman. How are you today?

MRS. GROSSMAN: Oh my feet are just killing me. I want to make a $100 deposit and then I want to go home and lie down.

SANDY: (not too distinct) I know. Every day about this time my feet...

MRS. GROSSMAN: Oh, my money ...it's gone! I had a $100 bill!

SANDY: Where do you remember having the money last?

MRS. GROSSMAN: I remember, I was in a department store and I was buying pajamas for my grandson. That's him right there.

SANDY: Now you bought the pajamas...

MRS. GROSSMAN: Yes. They have little blue bunnies on them.

SANDY: Did you break the $100 bill to pay?

MRS. GROSSMAN: Oh no, I always charge it.

SANDY: Then you left the department store?

MRS. GROSSMAN: Yes, but I sat down because my feet were killing me.

SANDY: Did you take off your shoes?

MRS. GROSSMAN: Ooooh! (laugh) Sandy, you should be a detective. (laugh)

The best tellers in town. Or your money back.

ANNOUNCER: United California Bank has the best tellers in town. Or your money back.

Jingle singers like to stay off camera so they can perform for various advertisers. A singer who appears on screen for a particular product may lose some believability for another product. One of the most sought-after jingle singers is Linda November, who sang the "meows" for Meow Mix.[10]

An advantage of the jingle in TV advertising is that it can easily move to radio, tying a campaign together.

Some technical aspects

Commercials come mainly in sixty-, thirty-, twenty-, and ten-second lengths. More than 90 percent are thirty seconds long. The popularity of the sixty-second commercial waned as production costs went up and networks quit offering sixty-second slots at special rates.

A short-length commercial is often merely a pruned version of a longer one. Such a commercial is called a "lift."

Local commercials as a rule are longer than network commercials because the time costs less. They may also *seem* longer because they are so often poorly done.

There are three ways to present commercials.

1. *Film.* Film is the most versatile medium for commercials.[11] The film can be made in a studio or, for greater realism, on location. Films made on location cost more than films made in a studio.

An advertiser who cannot afford on-location shooting buys stock film and combines it with studio film.

The size of the film—it's in color, of course—is almost always 35mm. But some commercials are done in 16mm because 16mm film, made with easily maneuvered equipment, provides more realism or a "news" feel. And 16mm films are less polished, which can be an advantage.

But agencies doing commercials that need high visual appeal, as for food and travel accounts, feel that 35mm filming is worth the extra cost.

2. *Tape.* The big advantage of video tape is that it requires no processing. The production team can preview the takes immediately, then make new takes when necessary. The new equipment permits frame-by-frame editing and offers many special effects.

But film is still better for on-location shots and animation. And copies of commercials in film form are less expensive than copies in tape form.

3. *Live action.* You see it in some locally produced commercials; but live action, like tape, is only infrequently used these days for commercials. In the early days of television, it was just about the only way of showing them. Those were the days when, to the embarrassment of advertisers, the appliance door did not open or the dog balked when placed in front of a plate of dog food.

Since late-night talk shows and network news shows are taped earlier in the day, what appears to be a live lead-in is itself taped.

For local commercials, live action often takes the form of a succession of slides or a few flipped hand-lettered signs or an on-camera announcer talking about a product.

Animation

On-location expenses, sound-stage rentals, large crews, equipment, casting, sudden changes in weather—all these send costs for live-action film commercials soaring. And the fact that sixty-second commercials have given way to thirty-second and shorter commercials cuts down on creative possibilities. Howard Sutton, a partner in Tanner/Sutton Studio, New York, producer of animated commercials, makes a case for animation: "Animation has always had certain advantages over the live-action medium, and these advantages seem to be increasing. . . . Animation works very well in compressed formats, and the proliferation of new techniques and art materials offers a great deal of creative freedom. It's no accident that animated commercials display so much more originality than live-action commercials."[12]

". . . the possibilities are endless," says Zander's Animation Parlour in an ad in *Art Direction*. "We have the power to defy all laws of science and rationality by making cups and saucers sing and dance, by making the common cold a living, breathing character, by giving man the strength to literally support the weight of the world on his shoulders."

With so much clutter on TV, a commercial has to stand out, and animation is one sure way to get attention.

Animation often makes use of animals. Kellogg for years has relied on "Tony the Tiger" to put its message across. Another tiger has seen a lot of service with Esso. But animation in advertising involves more than cute cartoon figures. It can bring to life the product itself (showing it in use or being demonstrated), the package it comes in, or the product name or company logo. In animation, these elements swell and twist and change marvelously right before the viewer's eyes.

An estimated five percent of TV commercials involve animation.

For story, song-and-dance, and special-effects commercials, animation can beat live-action film on price. To keep costs down, animators sometimes produce commercials without synchronizing lip movement with body action, without elaborate backgrounds, and with rough, scratchy color rather than the tight, registered color we have come to associate with Walt Disney productions. "The more smooth and flowing and Disneylike, the more expensive, because elaborate action means more complex hand-drawing and cel-by-cel shooting," observed Arthur Bellaire, a TV creative director. "The more limited form naturally costs less, but can still give the feeling of movement."

Some film commercials combine both live human action and animation, a technique Disney introduced in his feature-length movies in the 1930s. And some animation involves puppets rather than cartoon drawings.

You cannot assume that animation is only for the young. It can serve as the ideal medium for explaining complicated or scientific processes to adults as well as children. An enzyme detergent for one of its ads used animation to portray dirt as locks attached to cloth fibers. Then enzymes came on as keys to unlock the locks. And some public-service advertisers find that animation provides the necessary light touch to enhance otherwise dull material. But animation does not rank high in credibility. For that reason agencies tend to use it mostly in advertising for products purchased on impulse.

Planning the commercial

Every detail in a TV commercial has to be just right. Every nuance must be carefully planned.

A former agency employee tells of the care that goes into the "pour" shots in beer commercials. "How the beer looks going down the glass; whether the glass is completely clean and suggests ice-cold beer; how the bubbles look; whether the head on the beer is big enough, but not too big . . . . I remember one pour shot which took 124 takes before the beer looked exactly right."[13] Mort Levin, former copywriter on the Ford account, tells of steps taken to make car commercials effective. If any other cars are in the scene, they are older models of the car being sold, not competitors' cars (unless the ad is a comparison ad). Sound tracks of closing doors are improved with added bass. Station wagon tailgates are closed by youngsters to demonstrate how easily they work. To show a car coming

Open on large beer-hauling semi, traveling up freeway to camera. On the side of truck we see the name "Schludwiller California-Eastern Beer Company." We hear brief music. Cut to inside truck. Inside truck we find Earl Mather, the driver, a man of fading middle age and great wisdom, chewing on a toothpick. Next to him, on the other side of the dangling baby shoes, is his co-pilot and sidekick - a younger, earnest, inquiring fellow named Vern Ogilvy. Vern is puzzled, and speaks

VERN: Earl, how come we're taking this whole load of beer up to Oregon. Don't they have enough beer in Oregon?

EARL: Oh, I don't think it's that, Vern. It's probably just that we got too much beer in California.

Vern puzzles that one over as announcer begins to speak.

ANNCR: Some people think a beer can be better simply

if it comes from someplace else...

Earl spots another sign reading "All Beer Trucks Stop Ahead". Earl is worried.

EARL: Oh-oh...

VERN: Oh-oh...

to a stop, crews shoot it backing, then run the film forward. That way there's no bobbing up and down at the end.

A commercial becomes "an effort to harness attitudes, biases, tastes, life-styles. It seems absurd to ascribe so much to so short a device as a commercial," mused Jeff Greenfield, the writer and political consultant. "But when thousands of dollars go into the planning of every second of what we see and hear, that effort becomes a lot less ludicrous, and a lot more feasible.

"For the most remarkable fact about [TV] advertising is that it *works*. Call it offensive, puerile, insulting to the intelligence, barbarous, intrusive, anti-humanistic, but the damn thing moves the goods."[14]

In a TV commercial, video is more important than audio. The commercial cannot do the job with video alone, however, any more than a photograph, except in the most unusual of circumstances, can do the whole job in a print-medium ad.

Many commercials are planned so that if the volume is turned down

This Blitz-Weinhard commercial shows that you can do a selling job and entertain viewers, too. You see the rough storyboard here. Two truck drivers try to bring a California beer into Oregon, home of Blitz-Weinhard beer, only to be stopped by a beer patrol at the border. Oregonians who have been stopped at California's agricultural inspection stations at the borders could appreciate the analogy. Hal Riney conceived and wrote the commercial; Jerry Andelin art directed. The agency was Ogilvy & Mather, San Francisco. (The frames spread over four pages. Read each page as a unit.)

too low, the viewer will get the message just by looking. Where explanation is needed, type is superimposed over picture. At the same time, the audio is explicit enough so that the message is not lost on the viewer who has ducked into the kitchen to refill his glass or put together a quick snack to help him through the next program.

An attempt is often made to relate the commercial to ads in other media. This contributes to the cumulative value of the advertising. Stills from the commercial may be adapted to magazine, national newspaper, outdoor, and P-O-P (point-of-purchase) advertising.

A thirty-second commercial can handle a maximum of sixty spoken words—two words per second. But it should not be the goal of the writer-designer to completely fill the time with words, or even music. It is sometimes effective to show some of the action in pantomime. A little silence is as useful in television advertising as white space is in print advertising.

A commercial can consist of one scene, with all the action taking place in front of a fixed camera. Or there can be changes of scene—several of

them. Six seconds per scene is considered about right. This means no more than five scenes for a thirty-second commercial.

After working out an idea for a TV commercial, the creator types out a script to indicate audio and video action. The next step is the storyboard, which consists of a series of sketches showing the scenes as visualized by the commercial's creator. Not all the action is shown, of course—only enough so that the sponsor, before putting money into production, can get an idea of what the commercial will look like and what it will say.

The storyboard

At one time Hollywood made its motion pictures through improvisation, the director working from rough notes. With the coming of complicated—and expensive-to-produce—films, the studios insisted on carefully worked out scripts, with scenes, props, and sound effects described in detail and

ANNCR: So if you're looking
for the best in beer,
just remember this.
There's no better beer...

VERN: It was worth a try, Earl...

ANNCR: ...than the beer from
here...

VERN: ...it was worth a try....

As Vern's voice reprises, and
voice and pic grow fainter.
Blitz logo comes on and pull-
back reveals foaming mug of
beer. Super strongly, The
Beer Here. Music up and out.

every camera movement plotted. When animation became popular, the
script took on added importance; it could save hundreds of expensive
drawings. The few rough sketches that became a necessary part of the
animation script were pinned up on a board for review, and the term "storyboard" was born.

The art form was a natural for the TV commercial when it came along.

The storyboard for a TV commercial consists of sets of two frames, the
top frame in each set representing a regular TV screen, the bottom frame
carrying (1) a description of what the screen shows and (2) the words being
spoken, on camera or off, by an announcer or an actor. The number of
sets of frames, as shown on the storyboard, varies from commercial to
commercial and is not necessarily dictated by the length of the commercial.

A storyboard may go through more than one stage, just as a rough
layout for the print media does.

The first stage involves very rough sketches of panels with descriptions

Vern: Hey Earl, how come we're takin' this whole load of beer up to Orygone? Don't they have enough beer in Orygone?
Earl: Oh it ain't that Vern . . . I think it's. . .

probly that we got too much beer in Cali . . . Uh — oh . . .

Inspector: Well now, where you fellas goin' with all that beer?
Vern: . . . ah, here . . . Orygone!
Inspector: Now, you <u>know</u> this is where . . .

we brew Blitz-Weinhard . . . And you <u>know</u> it's brewed entirely natural, <u>without</u> any artificial ingredients . . . Is <u>yours</u>?
Earl: Uh - uh.

Vern: Uh - uh.

Inspector: Well then, why would you fellas be bringin' a whole load of <u>that</u> beer up here to Oregon?

Vern: Earl here says it's probly cause we got too much beer in California!

Announcer: There's no better beer, than the beer from here.
Vern: Earl . . . wanna try Idaho?

and dialogue scribbled in below. At this rough stage, the agency's creative supervisor, the account rep, and someone who knows a lot about TV production go over the storyboard with the copywriter and art director. When the problems have been resolved, the storyboard goes to the art department for a new, more careful rendering. This is the *comprehensive*.

Then the client takes a look. The comp may have to be reworked to incorporate client suggestions or directives. When it is finally ready, duplicate copies are made for the producer, director, cameraman, and others involved in production.

Steven Baker, art director and advertising agency president, thinks the comp itself can be too detailed. "Like everything else," he says, "storyboarding can be carried out too far. Overly accurate boards—unless the television commercial is a rigid graphic venture, such as an animated commercial would be—limit the creativity of the producer just when it could be put to best use."

The presentation to the client includes the look and feel of the unit used to display the storyboard. The presentation can be on a flat board with a

A promotional piece—a photoboard—showing enough stills from Blitz-Weinhard's prize-winning TV commercial to give you a good idea of how it went. The Oregon beer company played to the suspicions that Oregonians feel for their fast-living, resource-consuming neighbors to the south. Oregonians do not want any more immigrants. Some Oregon cars carry the bumper sticker: "Don't Californicate Oregon."

simple flap hanging from above, protecting the artwork from smears. But it can be more elaborate than that. It can be a unit that folds out like an accordion, with one set of frames per panel. It can be a spiral- or plastic-bound book. It can be a filmstrip or even a motion picture like the final.

The script, which accompanies the storyboard, is typed on regular 8½″ × 11″ paper, two columns per page. The column on the left describes the video scenes; the column on the right carries the words spoken by the announcer and actors. This audio material is broken into paragraphs, according to scenes.

". . . Rules for writing copy for this . . . ad medium didn't necessarily carry over from other media," wrote Roger D. Rice, president of the Television Bureau of Advertising, looking back on TV's beginnings. "Top-notch print copywriters, for example, who had no problem adapting to radio, often were stumped by TV's combination of pictures and spoken words. Ad agencies went everywhere looking for new people, hiring such unlikely candidates as recruits from drama schools and unpublished playwrights to build their TV copy departments."[15]

Sometimes one person comes up with the concept, writes the commercial, and designs it. But as in advertising for other media, in most cases the commercial evolves from the creative efforts of several persons.

Designing the storyboard

Among points to keep in mind as you design a storyboard are these:

1. *Relate the video with the audio.* Do not say one thing while you show another. Some agencies feel they must change slightly the spoken word from the words superimposed over the picture, a practice not unlike using a wrong font in a paragraph of otherwise well-printed copy. "He's reading it wrong," is the viewer's reaction.

2. *Let the video carry the weight.* The copy must be secondary in this medium. And among the frames, one frame should stand out as a key frame.

3. *Superimpose type over some of the scenes.* You cannot treat pictures quite so reverently in this medium as in some others. Superimpositions are necessary to take care of the person who turns the volume down at commercial time. They also reinforce what is being shown or said.

4. *Explore fully your camera possibilities.* Allow for changes in both distance and angle for long commercials.

5. *Don't expect too much of your viewer.* Keep the cast of characters small, the number of scenes minimal. Of course, there are occasions when the creator of a commercial wants to impress the viewer with numbers or variety, crowding many rapidly changing scenes into the commercial.

6. *Use mostly closeups.* Avoid detail. Consider this as "coarse-screen" advertising. The horizontal lines that form the picture on the screen are too heavy, too far apart to hold detail that is fragile or far away.

7. *Put the same careful design thinking into each frame that you would put into designing each print-medium ad.* Each frame must be fully designed.

As a storyboard designer, you become artist, director, cameraman, editor—all in one. Words that may be added simply reinforce what the pictures under your direction have to say.

Bear in mind that the pictures you draw in storyboard frames will be strictly from your imagination. The art is not yet available. The sets will be built, cast selected, shooting done after the storyboard is approved. So, more than many other layout jobs, the storyboard calls for truly creative effort.

No matter how carefully you plan the action, you should expect many differences between the storyboard and the actual commercial.

The final commercial—the film—will consist of many, many frames; the storyboard will consist of only a few—from a half-dozen to three dozen, depending upon the length of the commercial and the number of scenes, camera changes, and action changes.

What you present for client approval on a storyboard are *representative* frames: a picture for each scene or action and for each major change of camera position.

You do your designing and drawing in the top frame of each set. The ratio of width to depth is 4:3. A convenient work size is 4″ × 3″. Because the frame represents a TV screen, some designers like to round all four corners.

Working within the frame, you should try to approximate halftone rather than line art. Keep your action—the important details—in the "safety area"—an area slightly smaller than the picture-tube area. Do this to preclude any chance that a part of the message will be missed by the viewer whose set might need some adjusting.

Directly under the "TV screen" frame, separated by a half-inch margin, is the description-and-words frame. Its size is 4″ × 2½″. You can type in the words—or print them in cartoonlike lettering.

A 1″ margin separates each set of frames.

If you do not want to draw boxes for your storyboards, you can buy a Tomkin Telepad with its perforated segments containing video and descriptive boxes surrounded by a gray area. You can also buy black storyboard masks with cutout areas to match the white areas on Tomkin Telepads.

The storyboard precedes the making of a commercial. After the commercial is made, its sponsor may produce a *photoboard* from some of its frames. The photoboard serves as a record and as a promotional piece.

Elements to work with

You can use live actors, animation, puppets, a combination of live actors and animation, superimposition of type over pictures, stop motion, or a split screen with two different actions going on at the same time. And, less expensive, you can use still photos (preferably dull or matte finish) and art pieces. These can be flipped during reading. Or the camera can move from one to the other.

As storyboard designer, you should appreciate costs involved in the building of sets. If you can show your subject in a less expensive setting, do so. Often you can simply hint at the setting, letting a part of a prop do the job. Camera angle can help suggest detail not really there. Crowd scenes can be simulated with noise offstage.

You have long shots, medium shots, medium closeups, closeups, and extreme closeups to consider.

You can zoom in suddenly from a long shot into a closeup, or you can move gradually through the stages.

Keep the subject facing in the same direction through the camera's moving in and out during a scene; otherwise, the viewer will lose continuity, may think a new actor has come on.

Sequence is your most important design consideration. A single frame does not stand by itself. This is "advertising in a series." With occasional exceptions, one picture should flow into another. Transitions are important.

Transitional devices used to change scenes are "opticals." These include (1) *cuts* (the change is abrupt), (2) *dissolves* (one scene fades out as another fades in), and (3) *wipes* (one scene is pushed off while another is pushed on, vertically, horizontally, diagonally, and through geometric shapes).

Long shot, medium shot, medium closeup, closeup, extreme closeup. You can move gradually through the steps, or you can jump suddenly from a long shot to an extreme closeup. But camera angle for most sequences should remain constant; otherwise the viewer might think a new character has been introduced.

Producing the commercial

Commercials are complicated enough to produce so that they require the services of an outside organization specializing in their filming or taping. The agency takes the work through the storyboard stage; then the production house takes over, working at the agency's direction.

The agency may send out copies of the storyboard to several film production houses for bids. Production houses tend to develop reputations for excellence in certain areas, as in animation, humor, special effects, photographic excellence, use of animals, slice-of-life approaches, and so on. Reputation as well as price determines who gets the job.

The production house, once selected, lines up the actors and announcer, finds the costumes, designs the sets, arranges the props, and fixes the lighting. It also picks a director, editor, cameraman, and (to arrange titles and captions shown with the film) a typographer.

The production house may also make the decisions about music. One question to be settled: Will the music be written and performed especially for the commercial, or will it be taken from a bank of music and musical effects?

A commercial may be filmed or taped in one long session. Or the work may be done in several sessions taking weeks and sometimes months. The producer may end up with separate tapes or films—one of the announcer, one of the music, one of the sound effects, several of the actors in their performances. It is the tape or film editor's job to get it all together.

The director is interested primarily in the shooting of the commercial. Typically an agency submits copies of the storyboard to several directors who then bid on the job. The director who gets the job then makes a "shoot board," which helps plan the actual filming. The storyboard does not really indicate staging, lighting, lenses, lengths of shots, camera angles, and so on. These are matters for the director to decide. The director also does the casting, making sure these days to get an acceptable mix of personalities and ethnic types. But the director works always in consultation with the copywriter and art director. Changes occur all through the filming.

A director like Joe Sedelmaier departs from the script and storyboard to put his own stamp on the commercial. The Federal Express fast-talking man was a Sedelmaier commercial. So was Wendy's "Where's the Beef?" commercial. Sedelmaier is responsible for "surreal thirty-second dissertations on the fears of daily life . . . by far, the strongest advertisements on television," as an *Esquire* writer put it.[16]

The director is not involved in the editing—the final stage—when sound mixing and voiceovers take place.[17]

"Over recent years creative people have come to appreciate more and more the contributions of the editor to the success of their commercials," observed Arthur Bellaire. "Alert agency art directors and producers seek out their favorite editors just as they do their favorite directors; and they'll often bid editorial separate from shooting rather than automatically expect the company which shoots the commercial to edit the commercial."[18]

And what does the creator of the commercial do when the director and editor take over? About what the novelist does when the book is made into a picture: observes and advises, nothing more.

Of course there are some people in the advertising business versatile enough, experimental enough to put together the complete package. In nearly every advertising center there are art directors who dabble in copy and photography as well as design and who have created artful commercials for small clients or nonprofit organizations. Under these conditions it is possible to produce a commercial for not much more than a thousand dollars or two. But for a commercial produced in the more conventional manner the cost goes much higher than that.

Costs

Jim Aaby, a copywriter at Wells, Rich, Greene, estimates that it takes $150,000 to produce the average TV commercial for network showing today. Agencies like his spend another $5,000 to produce an "animatic" for each commercial—a rough movie made up of various sketches or photographs and some animation to approximate the look of the final live-action version. The client gets a better idea of the commercial than could be had from an ordinary storyboard.[19]

To produce a commercial costs more, in some cases, than it costs to produce the situation comedy it interrupts. What sends production costs skyrocketing are special effects, exotic settings, and elaborate musical numbers.

But the costs of producing the commercial in most cases represent only a small part of the total cost of television advertising. There is also the matter of network and station costs. A one-time showing of a commercial on a prime-time network show costs $100,000 and more. To appear for thirty seconds on the last episode of M★A★S★H in 1983 cost $400,000. Advertising people wondered if the ceiling had been reached. Some are turning to cable. Close to 40 percent of American homes have cable, making the networks less important than they had been as vehicles for advertising. "The once invincible networks are running scared," one writer observed.[20]

You can't control network or cable costs, but there are many ways to keep production costs down. You can save money, for instance, by confining the shooting to one location and using daylight instead of artificial night lighting and avoiding on-camera sound. Some ideas turn out to be more expensive than others. ". . . if you are going to produce a commercial for Dr. Pepper (as Young & Rubicam, New York, has) that calls for dancers to dance on the floor, the walls and finally the ceiling of a room, be aware that the idea is interesting *and* expensive," said Hooper White, president of Hooper White Co., Barrington, Illinois, a commercials consulting company.[21]

The commercial can be planned using stock footage—that is, film from commercial film libraries which cover every imaginable subject. And concentrating on closeups allows a producer to eliminate some of the costs of staging, setting, props, and extra actors.

Union scales for on- or off-camera performers are high enough that adding one or two can increase greatly the cost of running the commercial. The performers earn a fee each time the commercial runs on a network. In the words of Arthur Bellaire, "As soon as the commercial hits the air, the talent payment meter starts ticking." For local spots, performers get a single fee for each thirteen-week period.

"It has never been proved that the greater the production budget, the greater the commercial's pulling power," Bellaire has pointed out. "More often the reverse is true. I have seen more commercials ruined by money because that money is so often thrown in desperately to try to bolster a weak idea, while a sound idea needs surprisingly little dressing up."[22]

Because it involves so large a total investment, the TV commercial for a major account, like other forms of advertising, is subject to scientifically conducted tests to determine effectiveness. The commercial can be tested before live audiences in special theaters run for the purpose, or it can be tested in actual use, with adjustments in the commercial being made for later showings. One way researchers test a commercial in actual use is to call a sample of TV viewers the next day to see what they remember of it.

Researchers using tools developed by social scientists can determine the answers to such questions as these:

1. What kind of persons see the commercial?
2. Do they understand it?
3. Do they remember it?
4. Does it alter their opinion of the product?
5. Will they buy the product?

While the ultimate goal is to sell the product, service, or idea, the commercial may take as its *immediate* goal the job of simply making the viewer *aware* of what is advertised or providing information about it. It may be the kind of advertising that accepts as its *only* goal, immediate and ultimate, the building of a reputation.

Restrictions on commercials

The restrictions advertisers face from government as well as media groups multiply as the advertiser moves from print to broadcast, because broadcast media, unlike other media, operate under government license. And public pressure against real or imagined advertising abuses focuses on the electronics media, especially television.

The advertiser finds restrictions more intense at the network than at the local-station level. An agency can never be sure of what will be accepted for airing and what will not. Dick Roth, management supervisor

This is a storyboard—a comprehensive rough—for a set of slides to be used by Lamb-Weston to explain company benefits to employees. You see here only a few of the slides, taken from the middle of the program. Designer Frank Farah used Pentel and color markers to make his sketches. He had in mind both photography and cartoon art. Each of the last two panels shown represents more than one slide. The agency: Gary White Advertising, Portland.

25. The plan pays an additional 10% each year, up to 100%, if you have an annual dental examination, and recommended treatment is completed.

26. Some items -- like cosmetic work -- aren't included in the plan.

27. For a complete description of the program, check your handbook. And now's a good time to get started.

28. When it comes to health insurance, we've got you covered . . . in more ways than one. There're three areas: prescription drugs, basic medical and major medical.

29. That's important -- sometimes three separate claims have to be made for you to obtain maximum benefit. To make sure you do, we're ready to help anytime.

30. The Prescription Drug Plan pays 80% of the cost of all prescription drugs and insulin. Some items are excluded: vaccines, vitamins, food supplements, and a few others. They're listed in your handbook.

31. These are a few items covered by basic medical:
$40 per day hospital room and board, up to 70 days. . .
31a. ambulance fees . . .
31b. $5 for each doctor's visit to the hospital . . .

32. $60 for x-ray and lab fees for both accident and illness . . .
32a. and $900 maximum for surgery. But, charges above these amounts are usually covered by major medical.

for Scali, McCabe, Sloves, complained: "They set standards for taste and morality in the ads, and they destroy those standards in their programming!"[23]

The continuity-clearance departments of networks make sure that commercials no longer put glass balls into bowls of soup to make the soup appear to have more diced vegetables than it really has. Nor can commercials put white smocks on actors to make them appear as doctors.

For fear it would offend stutterers, CBS and NBC in 1976 refused to broadcast a dogfood commercial featuring someone who stuttered. The network officials apparently did not recognize the stutterer, Mel Tillis, a highly regarded country-and-western singer, who threatened to file a discrimination complaint with the FCC. "If this isn't discrimination, I don't know what is," he said.

An airline commercial that did not meet network standards a few years ago showed a well-endowed woman leaning into the camera saying: "Now I have two big 747s flying to Atlanta."

The clients themselves are careful about placement of TV advertising. Abbott Laboratories (Selsun Blue, Tronolane, Murine eye drops and ear drops) has set up formal guidelines. It avoids "programs portraying the unlawful or inappropriate use of drugs, excessive or unnecessary violence, or treatment of sex that is judged to be in poor taste." The company studies advance reviews of programs and employs an independent firm "to screen and audit all network programs carrying the company's commercials prior to telecast."[24]

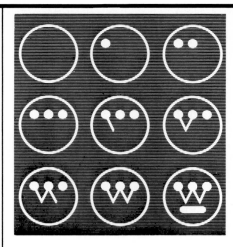

This is how Westinghouse made use of its circle-*W* trademark for TV animation. (Used by permission.)

Writing the television commercial

Writing commercials is more a job for a playwright than for an ordinary prose writer.

The challenge is to overcome viewer annoyance over program intrusion and commercial clutter. The writer can respond by making the commercial either so vociferous it can't be avoided or so interesting or entertaining it can't be ignored. Unfortunately, doing the former is easier than doing the latter. Every community, it seems, must put up with announcers shouting into echo chambers or interrupting themselves after the first couple of sentences with: "Hi. I'm _____." Add to those obnoxious characters the car, furniture, and appliance dealers who take on the announcing duties for their commercials, saving talent fees in the process and establishing themselves as media celebrities of a sort.

As a writer of a television commercial, make your first rough draft a series of quick thumbnail sketches of frames. Think *pictures first.*

The script that you turn over to the person preparing the storyboard would be a sheet of paper divided into descriptions of the scenes at left, labeled "Video," and dialogue and descriptions of sounds at the right, labeled "Audio." Because in most cases you have but thirty seconds to fill, usually a single sheet will do. Still the words are important. You have only about sixty of them to work with in a thirty-second commercial. Each one counts. Even so, you allow some redundancy. You should not be afraid to repeat words or to restate what you stated at the beginning.

The first few seconds are essential. Your lead must immediately enlist the viewer's attention. You do not have time to build to a climax. So you deliver it right away.

Write in a conversational tone if an announcer is speaking. Use brief pieces of dialogue if your commercial is a play.

If you write a series of commercials, make them related. Repeat your theme. Do not attempt to develop more than one theme in a campaign. Strive merely for variations to drive home your single point.

If any advertising writing asks for single-mindedness, it is television writing. You have time for so few words, and what you write must fit perfectly the pictures you show. Although it is an oversimplification to say so, writing a television commercial is like writing a picture caption. Your "caption" can do no more than create a single impression about your product or service.

"Writing copy for television can be demanding and nerve-wracking, but it is never dull," say textbook writers W. Keith Hafer and Gordon E. White. "There is always excitement to every television venture because it is, after all, advertising and show business combined."[25]

Designing the radio commercial

Including a section on radio advertising in a book about design may strike some readers as odd. What is there to say about radio-commercial design other than that you should not include a coupon?

If you accept the broad definition of "design" offered in the introduction, you will see that the word *is* involved in the production of radio commercials. For instance, pauses in radio are the areas of white space in print-medium ads. The various advertising-art-and-design-show annuals are beginning to reproduce the scripts of outstanding radio commercials along with storyboards, posters, trademarks, direct-mail pieces, and print-medium ads.

People tended to write off radio when TV came along in the late 1940s, and radio did suffer from lack of interest for a number of years. But radio came back. By the end of the 1970s it was an important advertising medium. Advertisers turned to it when TV became overcrowded with commercials and too expensive.

Radio has found a new place for itself as a local as opposed to a network medium. It has found a big audience especially among morning people and, of course, among car drivers. It has adapted itself to specific groups of people, forming audiences advertisers can really appreciate. Stations focus on rock-oriented people, disco people, country-music fans, classical-music lovers, news-hungry types, talkers, ethnic groups, and others. FM radio, especially, appeals to specific audiences.

Radio appeals to youth. Ninety-five percent of people 12 years and older listen to radio at least once every week. The audience for nighttime radio is made up mostly of teenagers.[26]

Writing commercials for radio strikes Al Samuelson, a former advertising agency creative director, as a lost art. Too many agencies merely adapt thirty-second TV spots to sixty-second radio spots. Radio, Samuelson said, deserves radio-originated commercials that capitalize on the idea that the medium offers "pictures for the mind." A good radio commercial should force listener participation.

The best national spots for radio these days come from radio houses, not agencies, he says. And most of the spots involve comedy.[27]

"In most agencies, radio gets pretty short shrift," wrote Dave Field of Radioman, Santa Monica. "It can be done so quickly, it's often put off to the last minute. It's a difficult medium for most copywriters, so they don't feel comfortable with it. And they know that when they start looking around for a new job, nobody's going to ask them for their radio tape. So it just doesn't get the attention that television and print do, and the creativity suffers accordingly."[28]

"Think about what your listener is doing at the time your spot goes on the air," advises Ron Armstrong, creative director of Batten Barton Durstine & Osborn, San Francisco. Is the listener alone, with family, at home, or in a car? What is the listener thinking about at that moment?

What works in the morning does not necessarily work in the afternoon or at night. "You may have to write three commercials instead of one, but it will pay off," Armstrong adds.[29]

As in any kind of advertising, in radio advertising you strive to make a single point. You resist the urge to crowd too much into the few seconds allotted to you. Forcing the announcer to speak too rapidly is like using too-small type in a print-medium ad. But sometimes you would want to use a machine-gun delivery of product benefits. A 30-second radio spot can get in about 70 words; a 60-second one can accommodate 150 words. The client's name should be mentioned at least twice.

Writing radio copy is not simply a matter of editing copy written for print. Writing for the ear rather than for the eye imposes restrictions on word choice, sentence length, and sentence construction. The best advice for the radio writer is to write in a conversational tone, using short, declarative sentences and to pay more attention than usual to sentence cadence.

You have to keep numbers—and prices—to a minimum. A retailer must be content to feature one—and certainly no more than three—items per spot.

Much of what you have to say can be said with sound effects. A common practice is to insert sound effects after each sentence. What the copy-

radioman

1418 second street, santa monica, california 90401 (213) 395-4224

```
:60 Toyota     "Sky Writer"

Phone Voice:   Sky writing service.

Toyota Man:    Hi, we'd like to sky write a message for Toyota.

Phone Voice:   Okay, how's it go?

Toyota Man:    The Toyota Corolla 1200 ......

Phone Voice:   The Toyota Corolla 1200 ......

Toyota Man:    .. has the lowest manufacturer's sticker price....

Phone Voice:   .. has the lowest manufacturer's sticker price....

Toyota Man:    .. of any car sold in America.

Phone Voice:   .. of any car sold in America.  Geez, I hope we
               don't have to write this on a windy day.

Toyota Man:    Standard equipment includes ....

Phone Voice:   There's more?  Wait a sec.

Toyota Man:    Electric rear window defogger, reclining bucket
               seats, and front disc brakes.

Phone Voice:   Electric rear - say mister, this is a lot of copy.

Toyota Man:    And we'd like "Toyota Corolla 1200" in italics,
               please, and the words "lowest" and "price" underlined.

Phone Voice:   The guy who does  the underlining is on vacation.

Toyota Man:    Oh really?  Then forget the whole thing and just
               write the jingle.

Phone Voice:   How's it go?

               (:05 second  musical tag)
```

This is the script, in its original form, for a sixty-second radio spot for Toyota. Written by Dave Field of Radioman, Santa Monica, it serves as an excellent example of the visual use of radio. And creator/writer Field considers it "the universal commercial. The concept would work for almost any product or service."

writer does here is much like what a designer does in a rebus ad. (See chapter 5.)

You don't have to say that spring has arrived. You can arrange to have the listener hear birds chirping.

You have an inexhaustible variety of sounds, songs, and voices to draw upon. The commercial can consist of straight talk from an announcer, with or without background sound; it can be a song; it can be an exchange of conversation, an interview, a play.

Humor, provided it is done well and changed often, works better in radio advertising than in any other advertising. Perhaps humor is more necessary in radio advertising. Certainly advertisers have been more willing to use it in radio than elsewhere.

Radio humor often involves a switch on an old joke. You remember the story of the man telling his psychologist what each ink blot reminds him of. So far as he is concerned, each blot is a nude woman. The doctor finally says: "You have a problem." The patient demurs. "Doctor, *you* have the problem. *You're* showing all the naked women." A tire company in a commercial has a man telling his doctor that each blot reminds him of "Schmunks' Tire Company, with all those people standing around smiling—with a car up on a rack, with the owner standing nearby smiling." Finally the doctor says, "You have a problem." The patient answers: "You have the problem. You're showing me all those pictures of Schmunks' tires."

1. Hooper, White, "Has the Tide Run Out on New Wave?" *Advertising Age,* March 7, 1983, p. M-4.

2. Based on observations made by Bruce Kurtz in *Spots* (New York: Arts Communications, 1977), pp. 86–93.

3. Cary Pepper, "Commercial Potential," *American Film,* July-August 1982, p. 13.

4. Peter Ognibene, "TV Advertising for Books," *Publishers Weekly,* April 12, 1976, p. 50.

5. Erik Lacitis, "Long-Playing TV Ad Is a Record Maker," *Seattle Times,* February 4, 1980, p. B2.

6. Bill Abrams, "If Logic in Ads Doesn't Sell, Try a Tug on the Heartstrings," *Wall Street Journal,* April 8, 1982, p. 27.

7. Dan Kelly, "Where Mood Speaks Louder Than Words," *Advertising Age,* August 23, 1982, p. M-2.

8. Noting the limitations of earlier attempts to classify TV commercials, including the attempt in this book, Ibrahim M. Hefzallah and W. Paul Maloney in *Journal of Advertising Research,* August 1979, pp. 57–62, suggested thirteen categories.

9. Louis Gorfain, "Jingle Giants," *New York,* April 23, 1979, pp. 50–53.

10. Robert Masello, "Linda, Queen of the Jingle—and Her Friends," *New York,* April 23, 1979, p. 52.

11. Clio Awards at 30 East 60th St., New York, maintains an archive of more than fifty thousand radio and TV commercials available—at a price—for showing to public gatherings.

12. Howard Sutton, "TV Animation Isn't Just Cartoons," *Advertising Age,* January 31, 1972, p. 51.

13. Quoted by Jeff Greenfield, "Down to the Last Detail," *Columbia Journalism Review,* March/April 1976, p. 17.

14. Ibid.

15. Roger D. Rice, "Baby Medium, Television Grows Up Since 1940s," *Advertising Age,* April 19, 1976, p. 112.

16. Lynn Hirschberg, "When You Absolutely, Positively Want the Best," *Esquire,* August 1983, p. 53.

17. Bruce Kurtz, *Spots* (New York: Arts Communications, 1977), p. 80.

18. Arthur Bellaire, "Making Changes Before 'Stop Print' Stage Prevents Runaway Overages," *Advertising Age,* February 16, 1976, p. 42.

19. Interview with Jim Aaby, New York, May 17, 1983.

20. Bernice Kanner, "The Year of Living Safely," *New York,* May 30, 1983, p. 19.

21. Hooper White, "Cheap or Inexpensive?" *Advertising Age,* August 23, 1982, p. M-26.

22. Arthur Bellaire, "Animation and Closeups Can Save Your TV Spot Dollars," *Advertising Age,* January 11, 1971, p. 70.

23. Quoted by Ted Morgan in "New! Improved! Advertising!" *New York Times Magazine,* January 25, 1976, p. 14.

24. "Abbott Television Advertising Follows Strict Guidelines," *Commitment,* Abbott Laboratories, Fall 1982, p. 7.

25. W. Keith Hafer and Gordon E. White, *Advertising Writing* (St. Paul, Minn.: West Publishing Company, 1977), pp. 133, 135.

26. Figures from *Radio Today* (New York: Arbitron Ratings Company, 1982).

27. Al Samuelson, "The Best Is Begging to Be Heard," *Advertising Age,* April 12, 1982, p. M-6.

28. Letter from Dave Field to the author, March 12, 1976.

29. From a Radio Advertising Bureau sales cassette, April 1976.

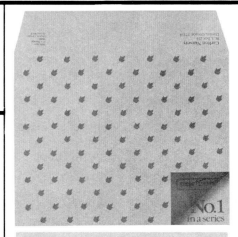

This envelope and folder-broadside are one of a series of mailings going out to contractors, landscape architects, and others needing large trees—specimen trees—to put into place to complete the look of new buildings. Carlton Nursery is a Dayton, Oregon, concern. Joe Erceg was the designer.

One side—the cover side—of a two-color (yellow and black, appropriate to the subject matter) folder inviting rental of Stanley Hydraulic Tools. The silhouette art extends from the front panel to what is the back panel when the unit is folded shut. The agency is Bronson Leigh Weeks.

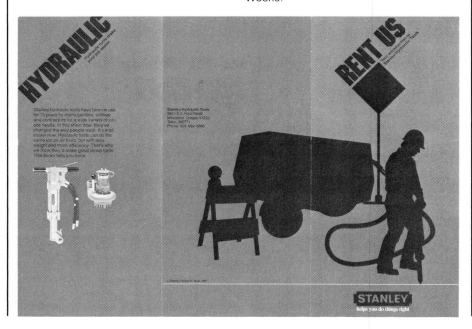

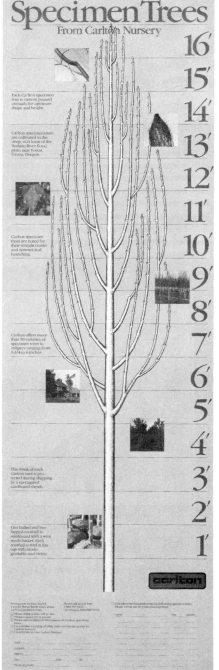

14
Direct-mail advertising

Designers John and Carolyn Percifield, West Lafayette, Indiana, used their creativity to produce a birth announcement. It was a "Designer Genes" tag of the kind one sees attached to designer jeans. The colors were dark blue and silver on white stock, rounded at the corners. The string was dark blue. © 1982, Percifield.

As an advertising medium, direct mail, in dollar volume, ranks just behind newspapers and television.

Direct mail is the universal medium, produced by a vast army of writers and artists, from the most hopeless amateurs to the most polished professionals, and used by every conceivable kind of advertiser. Mail-order businesses rank among the biggest users of direct-mail advertising, and so do magazines, a competing medium that finds direct mail the ideal way to get renewals and new subscriptions. Retailers and small businesses find direct mail useful, as do book clubs, publishers, insurance companies, pharmaceutical companies, and religious and fund-raising organizations.

Direct mail not only accounts for most third-class mail; it also accounts for a healthy chunk of first-class mail.

Everyone gets in on the act, and that accounts for a general low level

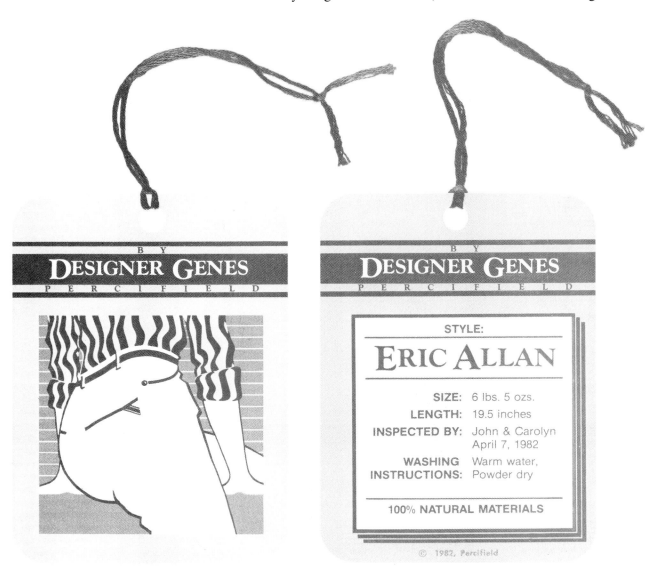

BY
DESIGNER GENES
P E R C I F I E L D

BY
DESIGNER GENES
P E R C I F I E L D

STYLE:
ERIC ALLAN

SIZE: 6 lbs. 5 ozs.
LENGTH: 19.5 inches
INSPECTED BY: John & Carolyn April 7, 1982
WASHING INSTRUCTIONS: Warm water, Powder dry

100% NATURAL MATERIALS

© 1982, Percifield

of design. Direct mail shares with retail advertising the stigma of taste-less, amateurish layout; yet, as in retail advertising, exquisite arrange-ments often emerge from the mass. In fact, some of the best design in advertising today comes in direct-mail form.

Some of the recent upgrading in direct-mail design can be traced to advertising agency interest in the medium. Such advertising usually is not commissionable; but with the development of the straight-fee concept among agencies, J. Walter Thompson Co., Ogilvy & Mather, Young & Rubicam, and McCann-Erickson, among others, have spent considerable sums of their clients' money with this medium.

The Direct Mail/Marketing Association, Inc., 6 East 43rd St., New York, N.Y. 10017 represents persons and organizations producing direct-mail advertising. Among its various services is a library of portfolios showing direct-mail campaigns in seventy-two categories. Its library also maintains files of direct-mail pieces that illustrate the many forms that are possible. DM/MA members pay round-trip postage to make use of the library services. Nonmembers may visit the library at the association's New York headquarters.

Sensitive to public criticism of "junk mail," the association also main-tains a Mail Preference Service (a nice, positive name, that) to remove names from mailing lists. More people want on than off, it turns out.

Up from the "junk mail" designation

There was much talk about "junk mail" in the 1970s, but as the decade came to a close, people were talking more kindly about this form of ad-vertising. It seemed to narrow in on its audience a little better. It carried the kind of information people wanted to have. And in spite of rising paper

The front cover of a four-page folder—a monthly newsletter—published by Suran & Company, certified public accountants, establishes a grid that is carried out on the other three pages. The publication uses a quality tinted stock; the white is printed on. The agency is Bronson Leigh Weeks.

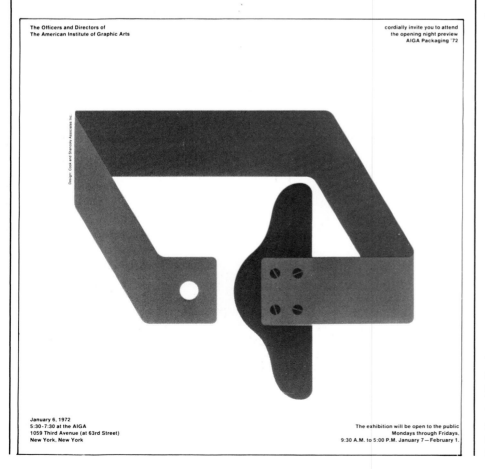

This 9-inch square card, in black and two shades of olive, was used to announce an exhibit of packages sponsored by The American Institute of Graphic Arts. The same design was used for the cover of an AIGA book of winning package designs. Designer: Cook and Shanosky Associates Inc.

The front and back panels on this 8-inch-square, two-fold folder are printed in black on heavy red stock. The rounded corners, the stencil type, and art that suggests the straps and reinforced edges of a film mailer—all help establish this as the program announcement of a Film Classics Society. The client: Incarnate Word College. The designers: Dick McCracken and Bob Welch.

and postal costs, it still was a relatively inexpensive way of reaching a selected audience. Making a case for printed direct-mail pieces, the DM/MA in 1982 said that the average sales call cost the organization making the call about $150, and the average personal sales letter cost close to $7. A printed letter or folder would cost a lot less, sometimes just pennies.

Direct mail became particularly important to people running for office in the 1980s, because it could explain things in great detail and in the most partisan of terms. Richard Parker, a direct-mail consultant to Democrats (and an activist from the 1960s), looks upon the medium as "the underground press of the eighties."[1]

Like other advertisers, direct-mail advertisers try to get their readers

Shown are the front (right) and back covers for a booklet designed by Peter Bradford and published by the League of Women Voters of the United States. Colors used were red and dark gray.

A setting worthy of the occasion.

o restore the Recital Room to its legendary splendor, we summoned the mastercraftsmen. The magnificent stained glass windows, rich oak paneling and the glorious pipe organ have all been beautifully restored.

For smaller meetings and receptions, three charming rooms—The Rousseau Room accommodates 20; the Corot Room, 40; The Miller Room accommodates 80 and can subdivide into two areas.

BARBIZON

East Sixty-Third Street at Lexington Avenue, New York, New York 10021 (212) 838-5700

thought about what you'd really like in a hotel.

In touch with the times.

omething as simple as complimentary coffee and a croissant in the morning in your room. Something as splendid as pot au feu in a restaurant reminiscent of Monet's Dining Room in Giverny. Something as rejuvenating as a day just for yourself in The Spa. This is the new Barbizon.

We've preserved a wonderful landmark and transformed it into a hotel where you'll feel very much at home.

In touch with you.

Detail by detail, we've planned the new Barbizon for you. Intimate guest rooms in subtle pastels. Fresh flowers every day. The morning paper delivered to your room. A concierge, with a computer at his fingertips, to put you in touch with the city's lively arts and entertainment. And we've installed the most advanced security available.

Let the senses rejoice!

The best of New York.

ixty-Third and Lexington. Here you are in the midst of one of New York's most fashionable neighborhoods. All around you is New York: celebrated theaters, restaurants, boutiques and galleries.

The Barbizon puts you temptingly close to Bloomingdale's and your favorite Madison Avenue shops. Close to the auction houses, the Museum of Modern Art and the Metropolitan.

Bring your walking shoes, because we're just a short stroll from Central Park. And convenient to a number of universities, research institutes and medical centers as well as the Decoration and Design Building.

Enjoy the best of New York all around you.

Cuisine Bourgeoise in Monet's Dining Room.

Cuisine as celebration.

e've called our charming little European bar Cafe Barbizon. Blissful for a light breakfast, cold lunch or a late supper. Nibble a pastry over perfect espresso. Or join us for an aperitif any time.

La Maree is a joyous celebration of Cuisine Naturelle. Delicious. Healthful. And beautifully prepared. The best of the sea's own bounty for lunch and dinner. And a breakfast menu that's an inspiration for morning meetings, in a setting that's aglow with sunlight from skylights above.

Monet was as much a master of Cuisine Bourgeoise as he was a master of impressionism. In Monet's Dining Room we've created the atmosphere of his country house in Giverny. Taste the hearty, generous cuisine, so typical of the hospitality of the French countryside.

The Spa. Health. Fitness and Beauty.

ow did we create the quintessential spa? By consulting some of the most respected and innovative names in fitness, health and beauty. They've joined us to offer you the best facilities of any hotel in the city.

Dive into a large refreshing pool. Exercise to music in two aerobic exercise rooms. Work out on our impeccably equipped exercise circuit. Unwind in rock steam rooms. Swiss showers. Swedish and Shiatsu massage. Herbal wraps. The Spa is complete with its own skin and body care salon and hair grooming salon. and Cuisine Santé menu. Guests may enjoy all the Spa activities as a complete daily program or a la carte.

Refresh your body and soul in The Spa.

Meet for a marvelous breakfast in La Maree.

Comfort and Style.

o suit the way we live now, we've opted for comfort and style over opulence. The charming guest rooms and suites with their refreshingly residential flavor will make you feel very much at home.

The carpeting is a soft, rosy terra cotta. Prints by some of our favorite French artists adorn the walls. Even the bedspreads are uniquely Barbizon—a delicate pattern based on traditional provincial designs. There is, of course, HBO in all guest rooms. We've captured some of New York's loveliest views from many of our rooms and suites for you.

Bathrooms are handsomely tiled in warm beiges, complete with makeup lights, magnifying mirrors, wonderful soaps and shampoos and massage showerheads—so you'll feel and look your best.

You see here both sides of a three-fold, eight-panel folder, ''We Thought About What You'd Really Like in a Hotel,'' designed by Milton Glaser for the Barbizon Hotel, New York. The illustrator was Guy Billout. The cover and some of the inside panels use three-dimensional initial letters made from parts of the building. The colors are muted and subtle, and they pick up on colors used in the hotel's interior, which also was designed by Glaser.

---

involved. These advertisers include order cards with punchouts and invite readers to pick one or the other—a "Yes" or a "No"—and attach it somewhere, or slip it into a slot, to register reaction. GEICO (Government Employees Insurance Company) has used "I Accept" and "I Decline" gold-foil stickers on its "Free Auto Rate Quotation Request Form." People who are not interested are not likely to go to the trouble of using such stickers and sending the forms back, but the procedure does make things easier for those who are interested.

Among other GEICO enclosures is an upbeat "Thank You" folder, which assumes that the recipient of the mailing will be interested. The folder ends on this note: ". . . I'll just say thank you again for considering us . . . and congratulations. You're making a wise move."

A form letter introducing all the enclosures starts off with "Dear Big Spender:" And the opening reads like this:

"Please don't take offense at my salutation.

"At least not until I tell you there's no doubt statistically that, if your car is not insured by GEICO, and if you are a good driver, the chances are good you're spending too much on auto insurance."

In a world of ever-changing values and roles, there often emerges a necessity to re-evaluate ourselves, our relationships and our needs. Sometimes this evaluation results in a gradual, logical process of moving smoothly from one stage of life to the next. All too often, however, it becomes a painful period of doubts, uncertainties and insecurities. The individual can be overwhelmed by the whole process of change and may not be able to objectively assess his/her real situation . . . or to determine a positive resolution. At such times, counseling and/ or mediation by a qualified professional may be the solution.

Extensive training in counseling, mediation and education enables Gail Robinson to offer "useful tools" to clients who are seeking solutions to personal situations. In addition to a doctorate in counseling from Oregon State University, she also holds certification by the National Board for Certified Counselors (NCC) and has trained in divorce mediation through the Academy of Family Mediators.

Her professional background includes six years of private counseling/mediation practice in Corvallis and counselor education at OSU, Western Oregon State University, Linfield College and Oregon Health Sciences University. She has been a counselor with WOSC Counseling Center and was also a counselor/mediator with

the Pacific Institute of Child and Family Living, Inc. Prior to that, she taught and counseled for 10 years in the public school systems in Oregon and California. Gail has also served as consultant to the Oregon Department of Education, the Northwest Race Desegregation Center at Portland State University and Old Mill School in Corvallis, a school for handicapped and normally-developing children.

Gail views her clients as basically healthy, competent, caring people who are engaged in activities or behaviors that may be causing pain or distress. Drawing from her own diverse roles as married partner, divorced single parent and step-parent, she is able to relate to clients and communicate with them on a personal level.

Her overall goal is to generate options for her clients, so that they're able to choose the solutions most advantageous to them in working toward the quality of life they want in the future.

Areas of Specialization
• Individual Counseling
• Divorce Mediation
• Children/Adolescent Counseling (juvenile offenders, learning disabled, low achievers, socially delayed)
• Family Counseling and Mediation
• Business/Corporate Counseling and Mediation
Telephone: (503) 757-3564

This two-fold single-color folder was inexpensive to produce; but its design suggests a quiet elegance, appropriate to the client, Gail P. Robinson, Ph.D., N.C.C., who does counseling and mediation. The reverse side carries additional information. Art director: Deborah Kadas; copywriter: Linda Ahlers. The agency: Attenzione!

Direct mail and direct advertising

Some writers prefer the term "direct advertising" to "direct-mail advertising," because not all direct advertising goes through the mails. Some of it is picked up at counters or passed out in the streets. Industry officials like "direct marketing." But this book will use the still-popular term "direct-mail advertising."

Direct-mail advertising is advertising in which advertisers act as their own publishers by (1) producing their own "publications" rather than renting space in existing ones, (2) selecting their prospects, and (3) sending copies of their publication directly to prospects. As a medium of advertising, it is used by mail-order (or direct-marketing) advertisers, but not exclusively by them. *Any* kind of advertiser can use direct mail.

Direct mail has four advantages over other media.

1. *It is selective.* An advertiser can rent or build a mailing list covering the most specialized kind of audience. The advertiser times the material to reach a specialized audience when it is most likely to respond.

Ralph Ginzburg publishes a string of magazines primarily to build lists for direct-mail advertisers. He practically gives away publications like *Moneysworth* and *American Business*. Subscribers' names go on dozens of mailing lists. In 1979 each of the 220,000 subscribers to *American Business* received about 110 sales pitches through the mail from various companies who got the names from Ginzburg's organization.

One of Ginzburg's folders sent to mailing-list brokers described *American Business* subscribers as inherently "scissors-wielding, checkbook-armed, incurably addicted mail-order buyers."[2]

2. *It is personal.* The contents can be made to look like a regular letter. Personalized computer-produced letters that several times in the text show recipients' names and locations have become a major form of direct mail.

A plain wrapper or envelope without an elaborate return address can help maintain privacy.

Even when having to resort to mailing stickers and bulk mailing rates, an advertiser can come up with a personal touch—or what appears to be one. Instead of using "Patron" or "Householder" on its mailing stickers for sale broadsides, Rubenstein's, a furniture store, uses "To our neighbors at" and then the computer-generated address.

3. *It is flexible.* Format possibilities are limited only by the imagination of the designer and, to be realistic, the budget of the advertiser. To promote a supermarket sweepstakes sponsored by Coast Central Credit Union, Eureka, California, Kathleen Gordon-Burke designed an envelope that was really a folded-down kraft-paper sack. It carried several direct-mail pieces giving details. A poster was designed to resemble a large paper bag, complete with band-saw cutting at the top.

All production choices belong to the advertiser. Time-Life Television, to sell a series of "Wild, Wild World of Animals" books, was able, in one of its direct-mail enclosures, to point out to conservation-minded potential customers that "this stationary is made with recycled fibres and recycled water."

4. *It is self-contained.* A direct mailing may contain everything needed to complete a sale. It may contain in addition to the advertising literature an order blank, a pencil to mark it or a cutout of some kind to fit into a "Yes" slot, and a no-postage-necessary envelope to carry the order blank to the seller. Omaha Steaks International, which sells expensive steaks packed in dry ice, found that the use of miniature steak tokens, which had to be punched out and slipped into a slot, increased replies 25 percent.

Shown are some of the covers for small folders issued by Tri-Met, Portland's bus system, to publicize its schedules. Each has its own color and symbol, all part of a nicely coordinated system. The solid-color area is framed in each case by a white border. Note the abstract nature of the art.

The pieces in a multiunit direct mailing are not necessarily design coordinated. There is some value in letting the recipient be overwhelmed by the variety of materials inside the envelope. The mailing becomes a kind of surprise package.

A direct mailing to sell a Time-Life Books series typically comes in an oversize envelope and consists of a four-page letter/folder that appears to be typed; a well printed, full-color broadside; an oversize postage-paid order card; and an "afterthought" note assuring potential buyers that the free-trial offer is for real ("I'm always surprised when people don't take us up on our 15-day free-trial invitation"). In the case of a series of books on home repair and improvement, the afterthought note was "typed" on a ruled yellow tablet sheet.

Direct mail and the designing process

Like the newspaper reporter gathering facts for a story, the direct-mail advertising designer seeks answers to who-what-where-when-why-how questions.

Who is the piece going to? Teachers or business people (to name two broad audiences) might want to file or post it. This would influence size and format. Young people and middle-aged people (to name two broader audiences) may require different art and design approaches.

What is the piece trying to accomplish? If it pleads for funds for a nonprofit organization, would it be wise to use full color on glossy stock?

Where will it be received? If at an office, the designer's job may be to somehow convince a secretary to get it to the boss. A mailing piece going to the home may need a more elaborate envelope, as publishers of classy mail-order books have demonstrated.

When should it be mailed? What other influences are likely to be at work on the recipient at that time?

Why should the recipient be interested? The designer's job is to show why—early in the letter or folder or maybe on the envelope itself.

In cases where the advertiser offers to send more detailed information, the designer might not want to make it too easy for the reader to respond. Let the reader find an envelope and pay the postage.

. . . So the designer's thinking might go before sitting down to work out the design mechanics.

A lot of companies publish corporate-profile booklets to impress customers, investors, and financial analysts. So how does a young company that happens to be the third biggest Northwest-based forest-products industry get *its* booklet noticed? First it distributes it in the usual way; then, for a selected group of executives, it produces a miniature version and "freezes" copies in 2″ × 2″ × 2½″ blocks of clear plastic—perfect paperweights. Byron Ferris is the creator and designer. Thuemmel, Marx & Associates (now Marx, Knoll & Mangels) is the agency. (Photographed by Sand Kam.)

This is a red and black folder designed by Byron Ferris for the Red Wagon, Portland. You see it at the top folded down to fit a no. 10 envelope. Just below you see it with the cover turned back; and here, on an inside panel, is the opening line of type: "The Red Wagon has moved. . . ." At the bottom you see the piece opened out, with the three interior panels showing. Through repeated showings of the wagon, and by changing the viewing angle for each showing, Ferris creates the illusion that it is actually moving.

In direct mail, the advertising must do it all. Ads placed in periodicals and on the air bask in editorial splendor supplied by others. Sprightly features, intriguing photos, hilarious cartoons, high adventure, foot-stomping music. The reader or viewer has already had some satisfaction. The direct-mail piece, by contrast, must start from scratch. It gets help from no one. It makes it on its own.

As the designer of a direct-mail piece, your primary assignment is to get the piece picked up, opened out, and read.

You begin not by drawing thumbnail sketches but by folding and cutting paper. An ordinary two- or three-fold folder may do; an unusual-shaped folder, with varying panel sizes, might be better. Experimentation will tell. A knowledge of paper sizes will help you settle on a form that will cut economically from standard stock with a minimum of waste and when properly folded fit a standard-size envelope.

The first rough will be actual size, with art and copy indicated crudely and without benefit of T-square or triangle. At this stage, the kind of paper is not important, although you will probably use something other than paper from your layout pad, which may be too thin and transparent for folding and for sketching on both sides.

For the comprehensive, to be shown to the client, you will use the actual stock set aside for the printing, or, if it is not immediately available or not suitable as a drawing surface, a good bond, construction, or drawing paper. The comprehensive is not mounted for the client, who will want to hold it to see how big it is, how it folds, how the panels "read."

To facilitate use of your T-square and triangle and your drawing and coloring tools, you should indicate copy and art and letter your headings on flat surfaces, before they are folded. This may mean doing some panels out of their normal order.

You may find it easier to do one side on one sheet of paper, the other side on another sheet, and then paste them together.

If you use pencil or chalks, you will have to use a fixative when you are finished; the comprehensive doubtless will get a good deal of handling.

The designer often plans direct mail as a campaign of related pieces to be mailed at stated intervals over a period of several weeks. A single mailing may consist of an outside envelope, a letter, a folder, an order card or reply form, and a business reply envelope. For these the designer must make decisions involving form, format, paper stock, and printing process.

The Red Wagon has moved....

Letters

The forms of direct-mail advertising are limited only by the inventiveness of the designer. They range from single sheets of paper to three-dimensional objects. To many advertisers, the best form of direct-mail advertising is still the ordinary letter, although it may have to be one that is duplicated instead of hand-typed. It is duplicated in most cases to closely resemble the look of a real letter.

So designers arrange for electronically typed-in names in the middle of the copy and "handwritten" notes and underlines that accompany typed letters. Regular postage stamps rather than postage-meter printings seem to work better, too. Rumor had it that by the late 1970s the industry had available a machine that pastes stamps on envelopes—slightly askew.[3]

If signatures must be printed, Eliot Schein, president of Schein/Blattstein Advertising, suggested printing in blue-black ink to better approximate a real signature. He also stressed the importance of a postscript. "Take full advantage of this device to reiterate your basic selling message, emphasize a benefit, drive home a no-risk guarantee. It also provides the necessary transition to the order form and helps close the sale."[4]

So far as many designers are concerned, the *letterhead* is really what counts on a letter.

Designer Elinor Selame, who has designed countless letterheads, offers this advice: Never start with a blank piece of paper. Instead, have a letter typed, with preferred margins set. This gives you a sort of grid to work against.[5]

Elements to be arranged always include the company name and address, often a phone number, and occasionally a cable address, a description of the company, a slogan, a trademark, some art, and a list of officers. The simpler the letterhead, though, the better. Organizations that insist on listing their officers soon find that when an officer dies or retires or advances, the entire stock of letterheads goes out of date.

Types for most letterheads should be kept small. The name of the firm should be larger than the address or any other element in the design.

Not only is the illustration appropriate for this letterhead for a child-care center (Pine Valley Child Care Inc., Wichita), but so is the "type," which is hand lettered in a style similar to what a child would produce. In its original form, the letterhead comes in two colors: the wagon and handle are red; the legs and type are black. The same illustration/design appears on the envelope, except in a smaller size. Designer and illustrator: Jim Cox of Jim Cox & Associates design firm.

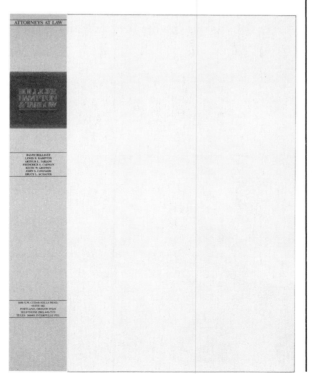

A letterhead for Bolliger Hampton & Tarlow, attorneys at law, utilizes a law-book spine motif. The name is stamped in gold foil on a maroon panel for a leather look. Business cards, labels, etc., carry this same look. The agency is Bronson Leigh Weeks.

(Right)
This family of business stationery was designed by Byron Ferris for the Collaborative Group, a Portland, Oregon, advertising agency. The strong symbol, incorporating a tightfitting *C* and *G*, is used both in outline and solid form.

The Collaborative Group

Marketing Communications

Public Affairs

Studio Building
107 N.W. 5th Avenue
Portland, Oregon 97209
503/226-4553

The Collaborative Group

Studio Building
107 N.W. 5th Avenue
Portland, Oregon 97209
503/226-4553

Marketing Communications

Public Affairs

INVOICE

Client
Description

Date	Description	Commissionable	Non-commissionable	Total

Studio Building   107 N.W. 5th Avenue   Portland, Oregon 97209   503/226-4553

The Collaborative Group

Marketing Communications

Public Affairs

ESTIMATE · PROPOSAL

Account_____   Date_____

Project_____   Budget No._____

This estimate is submitted by The Collaborative Group, as agent for the client and not as a vendor. The costs submitted are based on estimates submitted to The Collaborative Group by artists, craftsmen and vendors, and represent the expectations of this advertising agency. If changes are made by client resulting in an increased cost, the client agrees to pay the cost of such changes plus additional compensation as outlined in this estimate, but it is agreed that The Collaborative Group will use every effort, consistent with good workmanship, to secure the production of the advertising matter within or below the estimate submitted herewith.

Approved by

Date_____

The Collaborative Group

Studio Building
107 N.W. 5th Avenue
Portland, Oregon 97209
503/226-4553

Marketing Communications

Public Affairs

STATEMENT

---

107 N.W. 5th Avenue
Portland, Oregon 97209

A new firm might want to affect a classic style with centered lines of a stately roman type. This might help erase any image of inexperience. As the firm grows larger and more sure of itself or even a bit stilted, it might want to redesign its stationery, using close fitting Helvetica types, for instance, to show that it is up to date and progressive.

A number of firms have moved to colored stock for their letterheads. The color has to be light enough for the typewriter type to be read easily. One problem with colored stock is that the right correction tape or fluid may not be available.

Designing a letterhead is often one part of a total design job, where letterhead, envelopes, business cards and forms, and other units are brought together. Unifying these pieces calls attention to the company as one that is run in an orderly fashion. Such a design program also saves costs because the same typefaces and art pieces are used and the printing is coordinated.

The envelope need not carry all the elements carried on the letterhead. In working on the envelope, the designer should consult postal authorities to determine how much of the envelope's surface can be used.

The design of the envelope often plays a vital role in getting the reader inside. The design may incorporate a headline, as on *Psychology Today*'s often-cited "Do You Close the Bathroom Door Even When You're the Only One at Home?" envelope. The type and design on the envelope often plays down or omits the name of the advertiser.

Bill Jayme, who, with his partner Haikki Ratalahti, created the *Psychology Today* envelope, says that an envelope carrying direct-mail is "the cover of the magazine . . . the sleeve on the record album . . . the dust jacket on the book . . . the display window that lures you into the store. . . . I would estimate that about a third of the time my partner and I spend creating a mailing package goes into conceptualizing the outer envelope."[6]

To get the reader to open an envelope, some advertisers resort to questionable practices, such as simulating the hand-stamping of "Urgent—Return Reply Requested" or making the envelope look as though it comes from a government agency.

Every once in a while you have to update the design of your stationery. Fashions in type change. Design attitudes change. The company wants to keep up. This is not to say that a period piece—art that smacks of the past—has no place in business stationery. It may be that an old, established look is exactly what is needed.

Those firms wanting the finest in letterheads turn to engraving—real engraving. This process allows for what one creator of business stationery calls "the most brilliant results of all the graphic arts processes."[7] But most letterheads are produced by offset lithography.

Thermography—or imitation engraving—is another process for producing letterheads. Like engraving, it makes possible a raised surface on the paper. It works best on delicate or lightface types.

Business cards should probably be in the standard 3½″ × 2″ size so that they can be filed with others, but they need not always be horizontal, as this card for the president of Hidden Valley shows. When you have more than the normal amount of information to convey, you can double the size of the card and fold it down to a 3½″ × 2″ size.

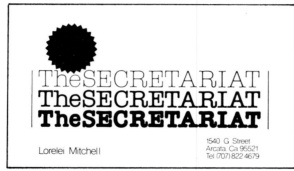

Designer Marian Brady used a notary seal as an art element in this card for a typing service in Arcata, California. (The firm does a lot of legal typing.) The seal could also be a type ball for an IBM typewriter. The firm's name appears in a typewriter face in three boldnesses.

Some firms like blind embossing, another process. It creates a raised surface that is not printed. The blind embossing involves, usually, a symbol of some kind or maybe the name of the company, if it is set bold enough. Small type, like the address and phone number, would appear as regular printing.

Another process, foil-stamping or gold-leaf stamping, adds foil to the printing surface, giving it a rich, shiny look.

Some of the most inventive graphic design can be seen in the letterheads of graphic designers themselves. When the Gilbert Paper Company, Menasha, Wisconsin, introduced its 25 percent cotton Gilbert Writing Bond, it produced some letterheads designed by name designers. Saul Bass, grumbling that "what this world doesn't need is another Saul Bass letterhead," nevertheless came up with one that showed his appropriate and charming trademark, a bassfish with the head of a man (Saul Bass) produced as blind embossing.

Heidi and Robin Rickabaugh are a wife-husband design team who have managed a design that works as a personal letterhead for each partner. The name and address of the firm is printed in the center of the left margin on both sides of the sheet. On one side, the name "Heidi" stands out (above the printing) in blind embossing. On the other, the name "Robin" stands out (below the printing).

Cards and leaflets

Self-mailers (postcards) or inserts to accompany other direct-mail advertising (reply cards) are a form of direct-mail advertising often relegated to standardized or last-minute treatment. They should be handled as if they were small-space ads, which they are; principles of design should apply as they do for any ad.

Like a card, a leaflet is a single sheet, but of lighter weight paper. It can be larger. It can be printed on both sides. It is used usually as an envelope or package insert. It seldom gets enough design attention.

A leaflet is sometimes referred to as a "stuffer."

Folders

A folder is a sheet folded at least once but more commonly two or three times. The folds make for "panels"; each new fold adds two more panels, one for each side of the sheet. So a two-fold folder has six panels, three on one side of the sheet, three on the other. A three-fold folder has eight panels.

The folding is arranged, usually, so that the panels are equal in size. Each panel may be complete in itself in what it says; or the panels may combine to make one large spread when they are opened out.

In a well-designed folder, the message reveals itself logically, in steps, as the panels are opened. The panels can be folded in any number of ways.

These are some common forms of folders. The folded-down size determines the envelope size needed. Some of these pieces can be used as self-mailers, in which case often a staple or paper seal is used to keep them from opening in the mail. Self-mailers need all or part of the panel for addressing purposes. The designer should clear the design with the post office before printing. The accordion folds (fourth and fifth from left) and the gatefold (sixth from left) call for a heavier-than-normal paper stock. For the French fold at the extreme right, popular with producers of inexpensive Christmas cards, a single printing impression will take care of the front and back covers and the inside two-panel spread.

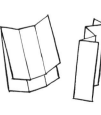

For instance, the piece can open and close like an accordion. The panels in an accordion-fold are folded outward and inward, alternately.

A more serviceable arrangement is the one in which the panels all fold in the same direction. This is called a "roll over" fold. The folder unravels as it is opened, as an ordinary folded business letter does. In designing such a folder, it is necessary to establish for the reader where the front cover (panel 1) is and where the back cover is. In most cases, the designer gives the front cover the display, leaving the back cover blank or nearly blank.

Panel 1's main job is to lure the reader inside. But, where possible, it should also give some hint of what the advertising is about. The sponsor's name ordinarily does not belong on panel 1.

Here is a typical arrangement of panels for a two-fold, six panel folder:

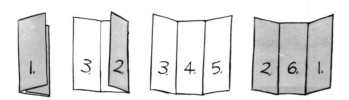

Panel 2 builds interest. It often is heavy on the copy side. If the cover is mostly headline, panel 2 is the subheadline or explanatory blurb. The inside spread (panels 3, 4, and 5), with its collection of facing panels, does the remainder of the advertisement's job. The artist can use artwork here in large sizes, running it across folds to add to its impact without damaging its readability. The inside spread can be handled much like a double-page magazine editorial spread.

Finally, there is the middle panel (panel 6) on the back. This serves as the back cover. If the folder is a self-mailer, it will have to be treated as though it were the face of an envelope. The folder can be designed as a self-mailer or to fit into a no. 10 envelope.

A folder can have vertical or horizontal panels—or square panels, for that matter.

Often an organization puts out a series of direct-mail pieces, using a consistent design approach to unite them. The State Bar of California, for instance, put out a series of "Consumer Rights" folders, using the same kind of title for each: "What Should I Know About Divorce?" "What Should I Know Before I Rent?" "What Should I Know If I Am Arrested?" The art in each case involved a closeup photograph of hands: a hand taking off a ring; a hand offering keys to another hand; hands in handcuffs.[8]

The possibilities for innovations for folders, both in copy and design, are endless. You should file away the many folders that come to you, then study them for ideas.

Broadsides and tabloids

A broadside is a large sheet of paper (17" × 22" is a standard size) folded down to a convenient mailing size. In some cases, as the recipient opens out the broadside, the message builds in intensity until all panels on one side are exposed. Then the full shock or impact is realized. The least used, perhaps, of the direct-mail forms, the broadside fits best a freewheeling, hard-sell client, but a sophisticated client every once in a while, as a change of pace, resorts to the broadside with considerable success.

With a broadside the danger exists that the reader will miss the message on one side. The piece should be designed to encourage the reader to open it all the way. For one of its broadsides, the DeVry Institute of

The cover, in green and black, for a four-page (each page 8½" × 11") folder advertising a book by George A. Hough, 3rd, published by Houghton Mifflin, Boston. The designer sees a connection between the name of the author and the word "THOUGHT" and takes advantage of it with a centered, eight-line headline that spreads over the entire page. The "HOUGH" is in white; the other letters are in black on a green field. A quarter-inch white border surrounds the field and ties in visually with the "HOUGH."

Both sides of an opened out two-fold folder printed on heavy paper stock and distributed to people who might order A. I. Friedman's art supply catalog. The original, designed by Hans Allemann and executed by Toby Moss, appeared in red and black. The return card carrying the mailing label was perforated so that it could be torn out easily. One of the panels was die-cut to allow the double purpose label to be seen.

Technology solved the problem by arranging the folds so that the inside panel-spread was slightly smaller than the outside spread. At the bottom of the inside spread was this notation: "Lift Here."

A tabloid is a half-size newspaper used, for instance, as a sales catalog by retailers. The regular rules for retail advertising layout apply.

Booklets and pamphlets

Synonymity links these terms, but "pamphlet," suggesting political propaganda, belongs mainly to the layman. We will use "booklet." To qualify as a booklet, a direct-mail piece carries eight or more bound pages either saddle stitched (as for the *New Yorker*) or side stapled or sewn (as for *Ladies' Home Journal*). Some booklets with a limited number of pages get by with saddle gluing, a cheaper method of binding.

The printer produces booklet pages in "signatures," a signature being a set of pages printed on a single, large sheet that, after being printed, gets folded down to page size and trimmed. For saddle-stitched booklets, signatures are cradled inside one another; for side-stitched booklets, they are placed side by side.

Signatures come in multiples of 4, 8, 16, 32, and occasionally 64—depending on the size of the press and the paper stock. A sixteen-page booklet could evolve from a single signature—or from two eight-page signatures.

A knowledge of signatures enables you to better plan your double-page spreads and color. Consider color for a moment. Each side of a signature needs a separate impression or printing. One impression takes care of half the pages. These pages are not in numerical order. If, say, on page 2 of a sixteen-page signature you want to use a second color, you might just as well use the same color on pages 3, 6, 7, 10, 11, 14, and 15, but if you want to run the same color on page 4, it will mean an additional printing impression, adding considerably to the cost of the job. In booklet design, planning the signature precedes any other layout step.

In arranging the pages, you should decide on standard margins for the running copy block and see that they remain constant. This is one way to achieve unity for the book. The margin next to the fold, or gutter, is narrowest; the margin increases a bit at the top and more at the outside edge. It is largest at the bottom.

You should consider each double-page spread as a single unit. If art is used, you make one item stand out on each two pages. You join pages together by running pictures or headings across the gutter or by repeating design elements on both pages. Of course a consistency in body type and headings also unifies the pages.

Booklets come in a great variety of shapes and sizes, but the roughly 4″ × 8½″ size that fits into a regular no. 10 business envelope remains a favorite. This unique vertical poses a problem for the designer. The single page is too narrow for many design treatments.

You should consider two kinds of covers: self-covers and separate covers. Page 1 of the first signature acts as the self-cover. The client wanting a separate cover orders an additional four-page "signature," often on a different, heavier paper stock, that is wrapped around the booklet's regular signatures.

Typical booklet jobs include annual reports, employee handbooks, instruction manuals, company histories, and speech reprints.

Catalogs

Catalogs, part of the booklet family, have gained in popularity, as the mail-order business has boomed. There are several reasons for the success of mail order catalogs. In many families both husband and wife are working, so a leisurely afternoon of shopping is out of the question. Besides, shopping trips use precious gasoline. It becomes easier to shop from catalogs. In many cases you can call in your order on a toll-free 800 number. You can pay by charge card. If you send in an order form, you do not even have to fill in your name. You simply peel off the address label that brought the catalog to you and restick the label to the order form.

Buy something from one of these catalogs and you will find yourself almost permanently on the mailing list of that company and of many others who do business by mail. The average American household gets 40 catalogs a year.[9]

About 4,000 mail-order companies in the United States send out a total of 5 billion catalogs a year. One company, L. L. Bean, which specializes in outdoors clothes, distributes about 55 million catalogs a year. The typical L. L. Bean catalog features about 250 items.[10] So well known is this catalog that a parody of it in 1982 and again in 1983 became best sellers in book stores.

Selling by mail is attractive to a retailer because costs are lower. *Advertising Age* says that the profit margin is 6 percent on sales compared to the regular retailer's 3.5 percent profit.

The first catalogs came out in the late nineteenth century. People thumbed through them, and rethumbed, and bought. They became known as "wish books." Many of the current catalogs sell luxury products or novelties. Catalogs are important in industrial, professional, and trade selling as well as consumer selling.

The giants in consumer selling are Sears, Roebuck and Co., Montgomery Ward, J. C. Penney, Alden's, and Spiegel's. Many catalog houses put out several different catalogs each year. Sears put out 43 in 1983.[11]

Crème de la Crème is a cooperative Chicago-based catalog operation that sells pages or spreads to companies not big enough to issue their own catalogs.[12]

In catalog selling, much depends upon the nature and quality of the art. Potential customers cannot feel the merchandise. They can only see it and read about it.

A catalog doesn't have to be stilted. The nationally known Lynchburg Hardware & General Store, Lynchburg, Tennessee, runs folksy, first-person copy blocks under or next to the items being sold through its full-color catalogs. The copy for Jack Daniel Large Rugs says, "I know we call them rugs, but I've got mine framed. I just couldn't imagine wiping my boots on Mr. Jack's face." A note under the copy for the Gallagher "Doc Watson" Guitars built by Don Gallagher ("Don doesn't trust many folks with his guitars") says: "P.S. Just for you, Don, we spelled Gallagher right this year."

The catalog carries the slogan, "All goods worth price charged."

Leichtung, a Cleveland firm selling tools by mail, does not set its prices in type in its full-color catalog. It has an artist draw the prices—and prints them in red ink. This makes them look like sale prices.

In its catalog, Wally Frank Ltd., a Middle Village, New York tobacconist, keeps its information about cigars in front, its information about pipes and pipe tobacco in back. The latter material is printed upside down. To read this material you turn the catalog around so that the back cover becomes the front cover.

The Direct Mail/Marketing Association maintains a Mail Order Action Line that deals with complaints when a customer gets the run-around from a company. But most mail-order houses take returns without questioning them and offer refunds.

Many of the big stores and retailers of luxury items now charge for their catalogs because they are so expensive to produce and the stores want to discourage mere browsing.

Spring

Summer

Autumn

Winter

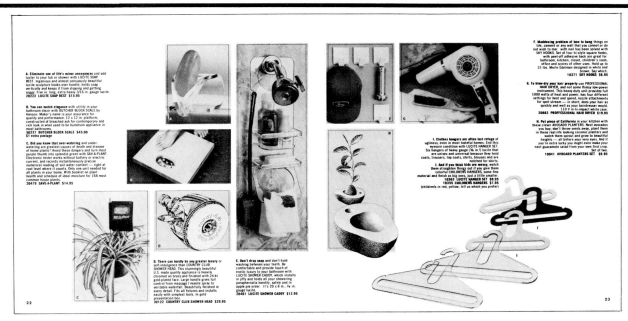

These two pages are typical of the forty-eight pages in a Henniker's catalog. Henniker's is a San Francisco mail-order house specializing in luxury and gift merchandise. The catalog combines photographs with illustrations, and sets off the photographs with thin ruled lines just inside the edges. Descriptions of the items are keyed to the art by letters. Sometimes the item pictured spills out of the rectangular confines of the photograph or illustration. The art is in black, the type in a magenta. The pages are squared, contributing to the feeling of quality. Designer: Sidney Fischer. Copywriter: Gerardo Joffe. Agency: Jomira Advertising.

These four pages from *A Small Treasury of Swedish Food,* a booklet published by SMR, The Swedish Dairy Association, and The Swedish Farmer's Meat Marketing Association, Stockholm, show how a designer can get variety within a grid. In each case, the heading is centered over the middle column, and the sink—the space between the top of the page and the "live copy" area—remains the same. But the size and shape of the cartoon art varies, and so then does the amount of body copy. Anders Gäfvert art directed, Olle Malmberg designed, and Loulou Lindborg wrote the copy. Ted Bates AB was the agency.

Principles of booklet design and retail advertising design, already discussed, apply to catalog design.

Hilary House Publishers, Inc. puts out a yearbook, *DMMP: The Direct Marketing Market Place,* that lists printing services, artists and copywriters, catalog houses, advertising and sales promotion agencies, and other people and organizations connected to the mail-order business.

Company magazines

A booklet issued on a regular basis for public relations and advertising purposes is a company magazine, sometimes called a "house organ." It may serve only the employees; it may cater only to customers, potential customers, and opinion leaders; it may do both. The common size is 8½″ × 11″, although any regular-magazine size is also a company-magazine size. A few company magazines take on a newspaper format.

The laying out of a company magazine is more a job for an editorial than an advertising designer, and although basic principles apply for both, magazine design is different enough from advertising design to be beyond the scope of this book.

Annual reports

A booklet issued once a year to report to stockholders on the financial condition of their company is an annual report. In the mid-1930s the Securities and Exchange Commission made annual reports mandatory for companies owned by stockholders. The content of corporate annual reports is to some extent dictated by the SEC. Certain features must be included. Even type sizes are designated. For instance, footnotes must be run in 10-point type.

In later years the Securities and Exchange Commission further refined the requirements on what corporate annual reports have to include.

Too many annual reports are stilted, self-conscious, and predictable—understandable when you consider SEC directives and the innumerable officers and committees the reports must go through on their way to publication. The sameness in looks and content hurts in that the average shareholder—the reader—holds stock in sixteen different companies, hence sees sixteen reports at about the same time each year.

In the years since the 1930s companies have dressed up their reports, to make them more appealing visually, but have rarely changed the general content. The typical annual report contained—still contains—a letter from the president, some company history, statistics, a financial statement, sales records, production information, and material on company policies and personnel. This is accompanied, usually, by decorative materials and photographs of plant facilities. In the past few years annual reports, like all advertising, have featured members of minority groups in some of their photographs and references to ecology in the copy.

Some annual reports carry features similar to what company magazines would carry. For one of its annual reports the Parker Pen Co. featured a review of its advertising over the years and included many illustrations.

Annual reports are important enough that in some companies executives begin working on them six months before they are published. A company may publish two versions, one for shareholders and a simplified version for employees. The reports are not just handed out or mailed. Gulf & Western, at a cost of $5,000,000, in the late 1970s had its annual report bound into an issue of *Time* magazine.

An annual report does more than tell how a company is doing. It subtly advertises products and even, in some cases, editorializes, not only on the company but also on national affairs. Carrying features and personality sketches, an annual report becomes a sort of magazine.

To tie things together, the editor comes up with a theme, as a school yearbook editor would do. In some cases the annual report enjoys elaborate binding and printing.

The designer of an annual report must keep in mind the purpose of the publication: to give investors and potential investors information to help them make intelligent decisions. In addition, the company expects the publication to build the company's image.

JD Journal, published by Deere & Company, Moline, Illinois, goes out quarterly to 75,000 employees, dealers, retirees, and opinion leaders worldwide. From the standpoint of both its content and design, it is one of the best of the tens of thousands of company magazines. John Gerstner edits, Wayne Burkart art directs, and Tom Sizemore designs.

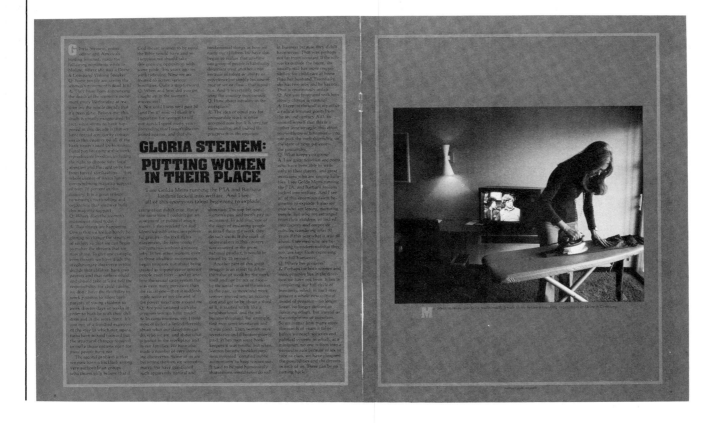

Usually, but not always, the two pages of each magazine spread work together. Not in this case. The "Etcetera . . ." has a very different look from the "Children's Art Contest" page. And with good reason. The "Contest" page is really an "in house" advertisement inviting children to submit pieces of art showing "What My Dad or Mom Does at John Deere." (The page was good enough to inspire imitation by at least one other magazine editor.) Both pages shown here were in full color. From *JD Journal*.

This is a more typical magazine spread in that both pages work together. The art shows that in the right hands a photograph (it's by John Gerstner) can face off the page. That's Gloria Steinem taking time "for a traditional female chore before a speaking engagement at Deere & Company." The touch of irony was appreciated, apparently, by Gerstner, editor of *JD Journal,* and Ms. Steinem herself. The article makes plain that "America's leading feminist" is as strong an advocate for women's rights as she ever was. The caption as well as the article's opening paragraph starts with a large initial letter.

Nonprofit organizations issue annual reports, too. Their efforts are not guided by Securities and Exchange Commission directives, but they have their boards of directors to answer to.

Annual reports are produced usually under the direction of public relations directors or chief financial officers rather than advertising directors. Outside design firms usually handle the graphics.

IBM, with design by Paul Rand, in the 1950s introduced the idea of impressive graphics for annual reports. Litton Industries, with design by Robert Miles Runyan, was another leader. In the 1960s annual reports went "super-glossy," according to Richard A. Lewis, president of Corporate Annual Reports, Inc. They were filled with "elaborately stated concepts and expensive, irrelevant graphics."

It had to come to an end.

Lewis saw the turning point for annual reports occurring in 1969, when the stock market plummeted "and a series of forces were put into play that have altered the content and form of the modern annual report significantly."[13] No more three-printing-processes reports (as General Dynamics produced) or stained-glass covers (as Litton Industries produced).

Pressruns for annual reports go into the tens of thousands—sometimes two or three times the number needed to reach stockholders. The extra copies serve promotional and educational purposes.

For some annual reports, the production and printing costs amount to $3–$5 or more per copy. Yet, "Most companies, I believe, have accepted the fact that the annual report is one of the least expensive forms of corporate communications," Lewis wrote. The cost of an annual report, he observed, "roughly equals one to three spreads of color advertising in *Business Week.* Considering the variety of audiences and the complexity of the message that the annual report must deal with, the cost is really quite reasonable."

James I. Moore, in charge of production for Corporate Annual Reports, Inc., notes these changes in the design of annual reports: adaptability of designer to available paper supplies; more visual restraint; greater

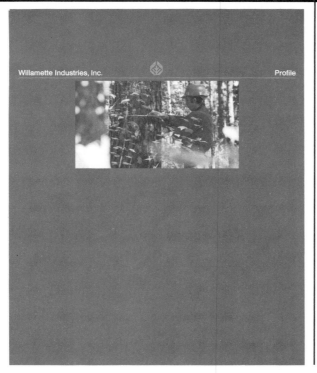

format flexibility; ability of designer to make last-minute changes; and modular design, by which parts of the reports can be used in other publications.

Brochures

A brochure is an *elaborate* booklet, with a cover, often oversize, that may be cut from parchment or an exotic cloth- or leatherlike stock, and inside pages cut from coated or from deckle-edge antique stock. While an or-

Byron Ferris designed this 20-page full-color "profile" booklet for Willamette Industries, Inc. The cover puts a small full-color photograph into an olive field. The sans serif reversed type is small on the page, but big enough to act as a title. The inside spread, like others in the booklet, makes use of "C"-shaped color blocks to unite the pages. The design has a Mondrian feel.

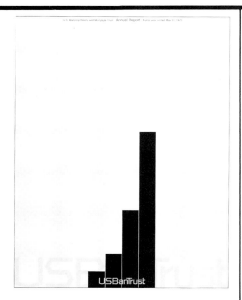

The cover and an inside page of an annual report designed by Byron Ferris for USBanTrust. Note that the graph used as art on the cover is repeated (in a smaller size) and explained on the inside page. The outlined-page format is used throughout. Black and powder blue are the colors. To contrast with the stark look on other pages, the back cover and inside cover are printed in solid blue. There is no type.

dinary booklet costs the client as little as a dime or two a copy, the brochure costs a dollar or much more per copy.

The brochure format fits important prospectuses or sales presentations. Some annual reports are elaborate enough to be considered brochures.

Miscellaneous pieces

What would academicians, textbook writers, and other chronic categorizers do without a "Miscellaneous" heading? How else to describe the kind of direct-mail format that includes calendars, blotters, rulers, balloons, records, and other three-dimensional items sent through the mails with advertising messages?

The mailer can take an unusual shape. It can be completely round. It can have a burned edge. Made from cardboard, it can snap into a box as it is removed from its envelope. Or it can come in the form of a jigsaw puzzle.

Pasted on the mailer, or enclosed with it, can be an endless number of three-dimensional items: aspirin tablet, seeds, ring, Band-Aid, snapshot. The Simpson Logging Company, a Northwest concern, to promote its Seven-Eleven ceiling-high door, once sent to home builders a mailing piece carrying special dice that rolled only to 7 or 11.

Ways to cut costs

The problem often is not how to dress up a direct-mail piece but how to keep its costs down.

Line art made from routine photographs, one ink printed on a colored stock for a two-color effect, stock art and stock photos—these are some ways of getting special effects economically.

The designer may find it possible to use one of the company's advertisements designed for other media. A magazine ad, introduced with appropriate type and art on the cover, could be used intact in the center spread of panels. Or the ad could be cut apart and spread over panels on both sides of the mailer.

Like all advertising, direct mail finds its greatest costs not in production but in *distribution*. More than any other single item, postage bleeds the advertiser; in response, the designer chooses the thinnest and lightest paper consistent with the needs of the job, limits the number of items in the mailing, cuts down on their size, decreases frequency of mailing, goes third class rather than first, and engages in a never-ending effort to update the mailing list to prevent wasted circulation.

The problem of double mailings is always there. Because it may cost more to eliminate the duplication then to simply send extra copies, advertisers try to cover themselves with notes like this: "Please excuse us if you have already received a copy of this mailer. If you have, why don't you pass this copy along to a friend?" A burial organization included this disclaimer on a direct-mail piece: "We sincerely regret if this letter should reach any home where there is illness or sorrow, as this certainly was not intended."[14]

1. Ralph Whitehead, Jr., "Direct Mail: The Underground Press of the '80s," *Columbia Journalism Review,* January/February 1983, p. 44.

2. Jeffrey H. Birnbaum, "After Eros . . . ," *Wall Street Journal,* March 18, 1980, p. 16.

3. "Kind of Crooked," *Time,* July 30, 1979, p. 33.

4. Eliot DeY. Schein, "Twenty Tips," *Folio,* February 1980, p. 77.

5. Elinor Selame, "Simplicity and Other Key Design Considerations for Business Stationery," *Printing Paper* 64, no. 3 (1978), pp. 10, 11.

6. Quoted by John D. Klingel in "Open Me: The Art of the Envelope," *Folio,* March 1983, p. 128.

7. Kimball R. Woodbury, *Printing Paper* 64, no. 3 (1978), p. 14.

8. Interview with Belva Finlay, State Bar of California, San Francisco, September 26, 1983.

9. "Catalogue Cornucopia," *Time,* November 8, 1982, p. 72.

10. "Preppiness Has Bean and Gone," *The Economist,* October 22, 1983, p. 77.

11. Interview with Rodney Nelson, Sears, Roebuck and Co., Los Angeles, October 14, 1983.

12. Bernice Kanner, "Mail Order Mania," *New York,* November 16, 1981, p. 18.

13. Richard A. Lewis, "Gone is the Golden Age," *DA,* Second Quarter 1975, p. 10.

14. David Owen, "Rest in Pieces," *Harper's Magazine,* June 1983, pp. 70, 71.

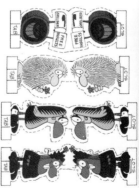

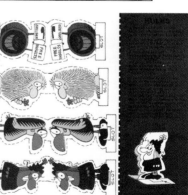

The Tribune Company Syndicate sent out "The Newspaper Game" to newspaper editors to promote its *Broom-Hilda* comic strip by Russell Myers. The game, a 36″ × 24″ poster-playing board and a separate sheet of cards and rules, carries a lot of inside jokes and asides that editors can appreciate. For instance: "All people who can legitimately refer to Katherine Graham as Kay are banned from the game. . . ." From the game board: "Subject of obit calls with a correction. Go back to square one."
© 1983 Tribune Company Syndicate, Inc. (The syndicate adopted a new name in 1984: Tribune Media Services.)

15

Posters and displays

Aside from word-of-mouth advertising, until the fifteenth century the poster and the sign served as the only media through which advertisers could reach their customers. With the coming of printing from movable type, handbills became popular; they were posters made portable. Then with Alois Senefelder's remarkable 1798 discovery of lithography, in Germany, posters took on new life. Drawings could be reproduced as easily as type. Drawings were what posters needed.

Two unlikely figures—widely separated in time, geography, and inclinations—emerge as fathers of modern postermaking. One was the American showman P. T. Barnum, who used sensational sketches to lure people into his shows. The other was the artist Henri de Toulouse-Lautrec, who brought feeling and design to the medium. There is today a little of the Barnum, a little of the Lautrec in the posters dotting our highways.

One of the unique outdoor poster campaigns was conducted by a maker of shaving cream.

The year was 1925. Gas stations and other local establishments for years had drummed up trade by putting signs along the nation's highways. Perhaps, thought Allan Odell, the family business could step up sales by using the same medium. He could put up sets of signs. Five in a set.

They would not have to be big. A short line on each sign would do. At first he tried the hard-sell approach. Sales began to increase at once. But that did not satisfy Odell. Motorists see these signs, he told himself, at remote spots on the highway, perhaps after hours of monotonous driving. Wouldn't they appreciate a touch of rhyme?

They would indeed. It was not long before the catchy Burma-Shave signs—some ironic, some cynical, some absurd, but all of them funny— caught the fancy of nearly everyone, including those ordinarily critical of advertising. Alexander Woollcott said it was as difficult to read just one of those sign sets as it was to eat just one salted peanut.

An example:

IF YOU DON'T KNOW
WHOSE SIGNS THESE ARE
YOU HAVEN'T DRIVEN
VERY FAR
Burma-Shave

They lived as a one-company advertising medium for thirty-five years. And then, when cars traveled too fast for their drivers or riders to take in the more than a dozen words painted in rather small letters, the company phased out its roadside advertising.

Posters and the ecology

Perhaps a growing criticism of advertising that got in the way of highway scenery had something to do with Burma-Shave's decision, too. And with major political candidates announcing they would not use billboards, no wonder the industry grew edgy.

By late 1965 the criticism from ecologists and others resulted in Congress passing President Lyndon Johnson's—and Ladybird Johnson's—highway beautification bill, authorizing a federal-state campaign to landscape major highways, screen or remove junkyards, and push billboards back far enough so they would not interfere with the view. During debate, Senator Warren Magnuson (Democrat, Washington) pointed out that on Route 99 just south of Seattle, Mount Rainier was obscured by a Rainier Beer billboard that showed—a picture of Mount Rainier. The bill warned that lack of compliance in any of the states could result in withholding 10 percent of federal highway funds to those states. Signs on roads not part of the federal-aid highway system were not affected by the law. Nor were signs in commercial and industrial areas. In the form in which it passed, the bill had the support of major segments of the outdoor advertising industry. And one firm, the Stoner System, Des Moines, while the bill was being discussed, had some fun with the junkyards provision. It put up a board reading: "Help Beautify Junkyards. THROW SOMETHING LOVELY AWAY TODAY."

Signs came down in places, but *Newsweek* observed in 1979 that "the program is widely considered a failure, and may soon be abolished." A total of 88,000 signs had been removed by 1979, but 208,000 others remained.

Enforcement of the act had been left to the states, and not all complied. Missouri and New Jersey, to name two states, had done nothing. Georgia had erected 573 new nonconforming signs.[1]

The industry showed signs of healthy recovery in the late 1970s as advertisers turned back to outdoor signs—probably the cheapest of the mass media.

The poster as art

What has bothered the critics has not been the quality of art so much as the intrusion on the landscape. In fact, the art for national outdoor advertising placed by agencies has improved. For one thing, agencies no longer recrop and boil down existing print media ads for outdoor. Outdoor design is not derivative. If anything, the directness and simplicity of outdoor advertising have influenced the look of all other advertising.

Seven rolled up papers in billboard art illustrate the point that the *Los Angeles Times* is an every-day publication. Enough of the logo shows on successive issues to spell out the name.

VERDI'S
LA TRAVIATA
(In Italian)

October 9, 13, 16, 1982
Civic Auditorium 8:00 p.m.

Phone Portland Opera 248~5322 or
Civic Auditorium 248~4496 for tickets

Conducted by Stefan Minde
Directed by Frans Boerlage
Designed by John Wright-Stevens

La Traviata

Deborah Kadas designed this opera
poster in shades of burgundy and slate
gray, centering all of the elements in a
dark frame. The agency was Attenzione!

This is another Deborah Kadas-designed
music poster, done this time in deep
rose and blue-green. The agency was
Attenzione!

As in other areas of graphic arts, Push Pin Studios, New York, with the work of Milton Glaser and Seymour Chwast, has set many of the standards in poster design.

A good deal of the excitement in poster design is to be found in the small-size posters that serve both as advertising and avant garde room hangings. In their homes, apartments, and dorm rooms people display colorful posters promoting travel, concerts, and sports events. People become collectors.

Perhaps the poster with the most impact in the 1960s was one advertising a Jefferson Airplane rock concert in San Francisco. Eager fans removed the posters as rapidly as promoters could put them up. New ones were printed and sold.

There followed a rush by various enterprises to produce and sell nonadvertising posters of every description, many of them political, some of them sick, some of them erotic, some of them psychedelic, some of them pretty and sentimental. And to take advantage of the wave of nostalgia sweeping the country, publishers reprinted posters from the turn of the century, from World War I days, from the 1920s, 1930s, and 1940s.

Spring Mills, Inc., Fort Mill, South Carolina, dug up a couple of its risqué Springmaid sheets ads from the 1940s and 1960s and made them available to nostalgia buffs for $5 the set.

America and other countries had gone through an earlier period with the poster as art—at the end of the nineteenth century, when painters and printmakers became interested. Hayward and Blanche Cirker called this period "The Golden Age of the Poster."[2] Among artists and designers participating then were Aubrey Beardsley, who did posters for theaters and publishers; Will Bradley, art director of *Collier's, Good Housekeeping,*

MIDSUMMER
MUSIC
FESTIVAL
1983

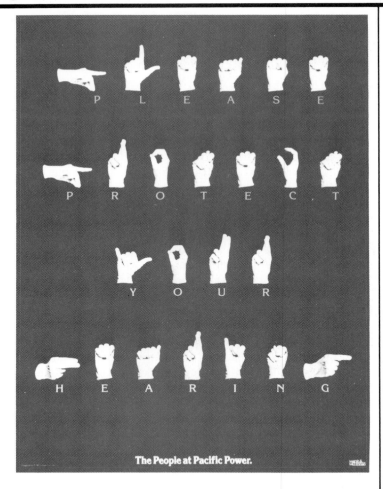

It started out as a routine assignment: come up with a safety poster to encourage workers at Pacific Power & Light's plants to protect their hearing. Larry Oakner and Warren Eakins of Pihas, Schmidt, Westerdahl Company, a Portland, Oregon, advertising agency, came up with the concept shown here: the hands of someone who had lost the ability to hear spelling out the message. Help came from Tom Stewart, who did the photographs; Marsh & McLennan, the insurance safety underwriter; and Mary Ruhl, who gave advice on American Sign Language. The poster won all kinds of national and local awards.

and other magazines; Edward Penfield, art director for *Harper's Magazine* and other magazines; Maxfield Parrish, book and magazine illustrator; and, of course, Toulouse-Lautrec.

Outdoor advertising

You can design a poster in any size or shape, of course. It can go up on a bulletin board, in a store window, on a wall outside—wherever the advertiser can get permission to display it.

The term "outdoor advertising" is reserved for standard-size posters or panels—known as "billboards." The billboard industry—or, to use a term more acceptable to it, the *outdoor advertising* industry—counts about

Frank Nofer builds his letters out of appropriate people, buildings, and artifacts while designing this full-color New York City poster which was used to build confidence in the city during a financial crisis. © Copyright 1975 by Designers Frank Nofer, Inc., Philadelphia.

Some posters are designed to be sold. This Western Graphics Corp. "Pig Out" poster, measuring 21" × 32", is meant for dieters to put on their refrigerator doors. Mary Fish came up with the idea and art directed and designed it. Hugh Barton took the full-color photograph. Gathering together all the goodies and directing the pig to move into them just once, and without disrupting them too much, was the real challenge in this "design" job.

This eye-stopping art was included in a poster for *Squanto,* a play described by its author, Jim Magnuson, as "an epic of the American past replete with pilgrims, Shakespeare, Caliban, Spanish nuns, the ghost of Elizabeth I, and the host of the first Thanksgiving." It was artist Chris Ragus's job to capture all this, which he did by drawing a montage that impresses the viewer at first as merely a portrait. The play was produced at Princeton.

600 operators of standard outdoor advertising facilities who pay rent to some 250,000 property owners for the space occupied by structures erected to display posters.

But standardized outdoor advertising accounts for only a small percentage of the signs and other displays set out along the highways and in the cities. The Outdoor Advertising Association of America, Inc., and the Institute of Outdoor Advertising naturally are sensitive to criticism of outdoor advertising that lumps the standardized posters with less tasteful, nonstandardized roadside posters and signs over which they have no jurisdiction. The Institute of Outdoor Advertising offers Obie Awards each year to the most effective billboards.

The outdoor advertising industry makes a distinction between billboards and "on-premises" signs that identify various businesses and appear on their buildings and properties. Real outdoor advertising is subject to local, state, and federal laws regulating size and placement. Local ordinances also regulate "on-premises" signs.

Outdoor advertising is sometimes referred to now as "out-of-home" advertising. The change has come about because of the posters seen, for instance, inside subway stations and airports. The new term could also be used to include point-of-purchase advertising as well as transit advertising.

The medium lends itself best to reminder advertising to supplement

advertising in other media. But some advertisers use the medium almost exclusively, and some campaigns are kicked off with outdoor advertising. It is a medium for both national and local advertising.

Close to half of the outdoor billboards in this country advertise tobacco products and beverages. Car manufacturers and dealers and food companies are also big users of outdoor advertising. National advertisers who use outdoor advertising use it in geographic areas with people especially receptive to the products.

The national advertising is not designed solely to reach the consumer. Some of it is designed to reach retailers as well, to get them to stock the product. The retailers presumably not only see the promotion but also feel the demand.

At the local level, banks, public utilities, and similar institutions make wide use of the medium. Some businesses set up to serve tourists find outdoor advertising necessary to survivial.

Outdoor advertising sizes

Standardized posters come in these sizes and styles:

1. *The panel poster.* The client can choose the 24-sheet poster, with a copy size of 19'6'' wide by 8'8'' deep; the 30-sheet poster, with a copy size of 21'7'' × 9'7'' (25 percent more display area); or the bleed poster, with a copy size of 22'8'' × 10'5'' (40 percent more display area). The plant operator makes no additional charge for posters occupying the larger areas.

A standard panel designed some years ago by Raymond Loewy to display both 24- and 30-sheet posters, and now bleed posters, measures 24'6'' × 12'3'' at the outside edges. About half of the panels used for standard posters are of the Loewy type. The frame is gray. Inside the frame is a white border or mat (for 24- and 30-sheet posters). Obviously the 30-sheet poster has a narrower white mat than the 24-sheet poster has. The white mat assists in squaring up the sheets and centering the completed poster on the panel.

The terms "24-sheet" and "30-sheet" are misleading. They date to the time when it actually took that many sheets of printed material to fill the board. Now, with larger presses available, the standard panel can be covered with as few as ten sheets. But the terms persist.

2. *The painted bulletin.* Painted bulletins used to come in a variety of sizes, but now the 48' × 14' is pretty much standard. And many "painted"

Christine **BOURDETTE**

Susanna **KUO**

Marie **LYMAN**

Judith **POXON FAWKES**

Carol **TATE**

Alice **VAN LEUNEN**

Judy Lee **VOGLAND**

March 24 to April 18
Art Department,
Fairbanks Hall Gallery
Oregon State
University, Corvallis
Public Reception and
talk: Thursday Evening,
March 27, 7:00-10:00.
Speaker in the Gallery,
8:00: Larry Kirkland

This small poster (13'' × 8½'') done in one color (dark blue) advertised a reception for fibre artists putting on a show at Oregon State University, Corvallis. Marilyn Holsinger designed the poster, which uses a sans serif with strokes rounded at their terminals. The strokes resemble the fibre in the pattern that runs diagonally at the bottom. Holsinger picked up this pattern from one of Dover Publications' public-domain-art books. She converts the white pattern to black for a short distance in order to tie the two parts of the poster together.

bulletins are no longer painted; like regular poster panels, they are printed and posted. The advertiser can buy one such bulletin (in which case it probably *will* be painted) or several. Large, colorful, always lighted, sometimes three-dimensional or with a section extending beyond the set dimensions, with or without a frame, the painted bulletin offers the designer great flexibility in design techniques and construction.

One innovation is to use three-sided vertical panels which can be turned continuously to reveal, alternately, three different pictures.

In 1980 Western Insecticide, Spokane, put up a painted bulletin that dramatized in an unusual way the fact that termites were a problem people should worry about. The sign said, "There Are No Termites in Spokane." Each week for four months the company broke off pieces of the sign, so that at the end it was almost "eaten" away.

3. *The electric spectacular.* It is a huge, complicated, painted display, permanent or near-permanent, making use of moving parts and unusual lighting effects. Perhaps the most famous of the "spectaculars" was the huge Camel sign that blew smoke rings over Times Square for twenty-four years before becoming a victim of progress early in 1966. The R. J. Reynolds Tobacco Company paid a rental fee of nearly $10,000 a month to show various war, TV, and athletic heroes, bigger than life, using the product.

A new outdoor "spectacular" came into being in 1976 in which electronics and computer technology combined to activate thousands of tiny lights. The effect was akin to an animated scoreboard at a sports event. It was possible to program one of these "spectaculars" so that an early morning message could address drivers on their way to work, a midday message could address women heading for supermarkets, and an evening message could address people going out on the town. The developers were Ackerley Communications, Seattle, and American Sign & Indicator Corp., Spokane. (American Sign is known for its on-premises time-and-temperature signs used by banks and savings and loan associations.)

In the early 1980s giant, air-filled, three-dimensional billboards began appearing along the highways. The parts that protrude toward viewers are air bags made of vinyl-coated nylon. An electric fan keeps them puffed up. What protrudes can be, say, a huge beer bottle or a plane.

Solar-activated parts can move on a billboard as the sun moves during the day. Reflective discs vibrate as the sun shines on them. Art can be backlighted. Fiber optics (light-transmitting glass fibers) can illuminate the art.[3]

Locations for outdoor advertisements

Panels are scientifically located to give complete coverage of the market. An advertiser buying standard poster coverage buys a "showing." A 100-showing in a city means that enough boards are contracted for so that by the end of a month everyone in town probably will have seen the ad at least once and probably many times. An outdoor advertising company has a number of 100-showings available in its city. Lesser showings are also

This diagram shows how the three standard poster sizes—24-sheet, 30-sheet, and bleed—fit on a standard panel. (Courtesy the Institute of Outdoor Advertising.)

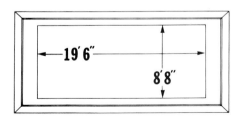
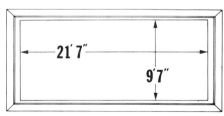
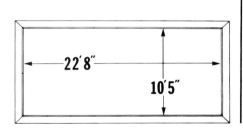

available, and so are showings more intensive than 100-showings. Or a single panel can be rented.

Rent of one panel for a month varies from less than $100 to several thousand dollars. Sometimes an individual contracts for a billboard to impress a spouse or sweetheart with a personal message or just to pull a gag. When Seattle, Washington, was going through a depression because of a slowdown at Boeing, some individuals bought space and said, in effect: "Will the Last Person to Leave Please Turn Off the Lights." Not everybody thought it was funny.

One of the best intersections for outdoor advertising—one of the highest priced—is Wilshire Blvd. and Veteran, in Westwood, Los Angeles. Foster & Kleiser, the outdoor advertising company which owns outlets there, thinks an outlet is worth the price ($9000 a month in 1982) because of the heavy traffic and the quality of the onlookers: professional people and others with high incomes. Several advertisers wait to get the space.[4]

Outdoor advertising production

It takes about two months to put a poster design into production and get it up on boards.

The outdoor advertising "plant operator" can take a job from the beginning, writing and designing the billboard, printing or painting it, putting it up and maintaining it. Or it may be a matter of taking a layout and producing the poster to order. Or it may be a matter of taking already-printed sheets from an advertising agency or printer and seeing that they get the proper display.

When fewer than half a dozen posters are needed, they will probably be hand-painted, even in regular 24- or 30-sheet sizes. An order up to one hundred would call for silk-screen printing. One for more than one hundred would call for offset lithography.

Artwork for hand-printed or silk-screened posters is often "posterized." That is, the gradations in tone are reduced to two or three or four. The tones up close look "patterned," with one quitting abruptly where the other comes on. There are no blends. Just flat colors. Such crisp treatment need not detract from the beauty of the artwork. It is, in fact, quite suited to poster visability.

Here are four in a light-hearted series of outdoor posters establishing the fact that Peoples National Bank of Washington is, indeed, for the people. That it is a member of both the FDIC and the human race is stressed on one of the ads. Chiat/Day Advertising, Seattle, was the agency.

This painted bulletin with a space extension (the thumb sticking up over the top) uses five fingers and a thumb to say, "6 nonstops a day. . . ." The captain's stripes say "airlines." Jerry Box art directed this ad by Chiat/Day Advertising; Roger Livingston wrote the copy.

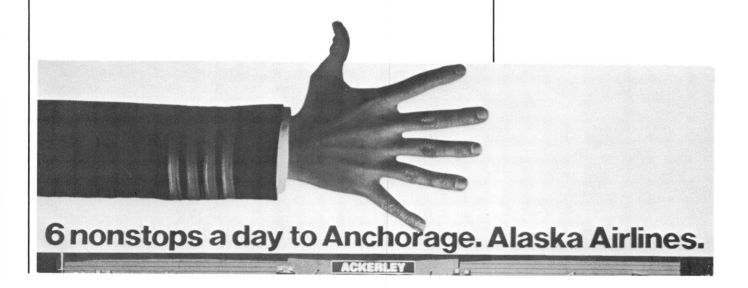

6 nonstops a day to Anchorage. Alaska Airlines.

The poster idea

If it is true for advertising in general, it is all the more true for this kind of advertising: a single theme is all you can develop. A single point made is all you can hope for.

Here are some possible approaches:

1. Make a claim, outright or implied.
2. Offer some news, like the price of a nationally advertised product.
3. Remind the reader to . . .
4. Suggest something different to the reader.
5. Make a comparison. Show your product in association with something already admired.

You can do any of these by jarring the reader, by paraphrasing, by using offbeat humor, through human interest, maybe even through symbolism.

Doing the rough layout or comp

To design a standard poster, start out with thumbnails done in a 2¼: 1 proportion. When you come up with one that looks promising, you work up a rough layout or a comp. At this stage you can work in either a 13½″ × 6″ or an 18″ × 8″ size. The finished art for a printed poster is usually done in a larger size, though not, of course, in actual size.

For painted bulletins the proportions would be roughly 3½: 1. A good comp size would be 26″ × 8″.

The shape is fixed: a horizontal—an *extreme* horizontal if the poster is a painted bulletin. That may limit some things you can do. For instance, you may find it difficult to show a tall building or a full figure standing erect. But the horizontal shape has its advantages. You have an easy time moving the reader from left to right, across the ad. Sequence is no problem.

Outdoor advertising is a medium seen from close up but also from blocks away, at an angle or head-on, in all kinds of weather, under natural light and artificial light, in congested and noncongested areas. The design must do its job under all these conditions.

One designer has described his job as that of "creating a visual scan-

A billboard for the Palm Springs Convention and Visitors Bureau moves in so close that all you see is part of a diving board, the bottom of a pair of legs, and a pleasant sky—enough to say this is a place to vacation. The art nicely illustrates the "Bounce" in the headline. Art directors: Newell Nesheim and Darryl Shimazu; photographer: Walter Swarthout; copywriter: Elain Cossman. The agency was Gumpertz/Bentley/Fried, Los Angeles.

dal." To shock the reader is a necessary function of the billboard. Another designer has described his art as "art of omission." "In poster communication, you can say more by saying less."

You sometimes have trouble at the comp stage seeing the ad in its actual size and in place. Can you be sure your elements are large enough to see? William Miller, art director of General Outdoor Advertising Co., has suggested that the designer step back a distance equal to seventeen times the width of the comp and see if it can be read.

The design of a good billboard is very much like the design of any other advertisement. The same basic principles apply. But you should remember that a billboard differs from other forms of advertising in these two important respects: the audience sees the advertisement while on the move; and the audience sees the advertisement from a distance. It follows that, more than other forms of advertising, the billboard has to be arresting. It also follows that it must be simple, strong, and clear.

Rules for designing billboards

Here are some rules for designing billboards, based in part on advice offered by the Institute of Outdoor Advertising.[5]

1. *Confine the number of elements in the ad to three or, if possible, two or even one.* If you use three elements, they will probably be a photograph or painting of the product either on display or in use, a headline, and some background.

If you show background, keep it uncluttered. And give consideration to the overall silhouette formed by your placement of elements.

2. *Keep the number of words to a minimum of three, four, or five—certainly no more than nine or ten.* The Institute of Outdoor Advertising points out that the poster idea must register within six seconds.

When the *Boston Globe* changed its body type to Brevere, a strong face with a large x-height, it told the story of the change with a billboard. Copywriter Veronica Nash Howard and art director Les Johnson decided the best way to tell the story was in a blown-up version of the new face and without artwork. An award-winning billboard, it shows that the no-more-than-nine-words rule is made to be broken. The agency was Batten Barton Durstine & Osborn.

This is The Globe's new easy-to-read type
Easy to read, isn't it?

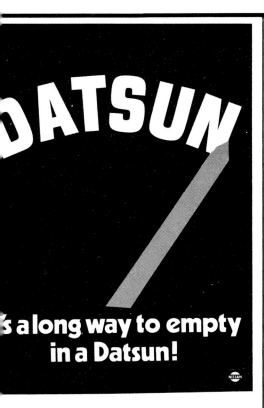

The poster approach—strength, simplicity, legibility—works for print-media ads as well. This is a two-color (black plus red) ad for the newsmagazines prepared by the William Esty Co. (Connie Malalak, art director; Gordon Bushell, copywriter). The car name doubles as a gas-indicator on a car dashboard. The needle (the only red in the ad) is on full, naturally, because the point of the ad is that the Datsun saves gas. This ad offers a real change of pace when viewed in a magazine full of more complicated designs.

3. *Make sure the illustration is big enough.* It is not always necessary to show the product in its entirety. You can move in close, cropping if necessary.

Sometimes you may find that art alone is enough. A bottle of Coke lying in some ice or snow may be all the selling necessary in a summer showing.

The art will almost surely be in full color. To show the product off to advantage, it may be desirable to foreshorten it, exaggerate its perspective, or, to fit the space, show it from a worm's-eye view.

4. *Make sure the art says what the headline says.*

5. *Make sure the type is big and thick enough.* Use a sturdy face in at least a medium and probably bold or ultrabold weight. Consider sans serifs. Legibility is perhaps more important than readability in outdoor advertising.

Beginning designers invariably make the mistake of using letters that are either too spindly or too small in relation to the available space. Or they put them in a color that does not contrast sufficiently with the background.

6. *Organize the elements* so they work together as a single unit.

7. *Use color boldly, in broad strokes.* Cover large areas with flat color. For most jobs choose bright primary colors rather than pastel shades. And choose colors to achieve the greatest possible contrast. Few posters these days go up without color. Black-and-white or full color, the cost for a showing is the same.

8. *Make sure the product is clearly identified.*

Transit advertising

Yet another medium available to advertisers is transit advertising: car cards shown either on the inside or outside of moving vehicles. What other medium can claim "This sign is 26 miles long"?

Inside transit advertising directs itself to a captive audience. It is read by persons who are more often than not bored by their ride. They read the transit ad with a kind of go-ahead-see-if-you-can-amuse-me attitude. That may be a disadvantage. On the other hand, the reader in many cases is riding to the stores. That may be an advantage.

An inside transit ad can contain a pad of coupons or order blanks, allowing any number of viewers to respond.

An inside transit ad is shaped much like a spread in a magazine. It is a spread that does not have to be held to read. But it cannot merely du-

The silhouette the artwork makes can mean a great difference in visibility in outdoor advertising.

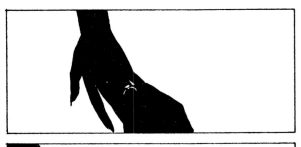

plicate a two-page ad in a magazine. It needs some of the impact of the poster.

The outside transit ad is even more a poster—a poster that moves. It is the reader who often is stationary. In that sense, it is traditional outdoor advertising in reverse. But like any poster, it must say what it says quickly, simply.

The Transit Advertising Association has standardized the sizes of both inside and outside car cards. On the inside the cards may measure 14", 21", 28", 42", or 84" wide by 11" deep. The 28" × 11" size is the most common.

The cards are printed by the advertiser and shipped flat for placement by the medium. When the advertiser buys a *full service,* its card is shown on every vehicle operated by the transportation company. Half and quarter services are also available. The service remains in effect for thirty days, as does a *showing* for outdoor advertising.

Outside car cards, also called "traveling displays," measure 27", 36", or 44" by 21" deep. A 12' × 2' size is also available in some markets.

One advantage of inside-the-car transit advertising is measurement of audience exposure. The fare box is "an auditing system that ranks with the best," as *Advertising Age* has put it. Exposure to outside car cards is almost impossible to measure.

Transit advertising also includes posters and displays in bus, train, and subway stations and in airports.

Transit advertising is particularly effective when it takes advantage of the setting, as in subway advertising that reads: "If you ate Diet Mazola there'd be more room in this car" and "Let the owners of RCA color TVs get off first. They have a better reason to rush home."

Perhaps the biggest user of transit advertising has been the William Wrigley Jr. Company. Other important users include alcoholic beverage, food, tobacco, and pharmaceutical companies. There were indications that the medium was dying in the 1960s, but with increased interest in urban mass transit in the 1970s, the medium began to make a comeback.

Transit advertising faces some special restrictions in that ads appear in or on publicly owned vehicles. The Freedom from Religion Foundation, Madison, Wisconsin, objected to Knights of Columbus advertising, arguing that religious advertising on buses was a violation of the separation of church and state. The foundation followed its objection—fighting fire with fire, as it explained—by placing anti-Bible ads in eighty Madison buses.

Bumper stickers

Bumper stickers—or "bumper snickers," as Paul Harvey calls them—are the individual motorist's answer to transit advertising.

Bumper stickers date to at least the Eisenhower-Stevenson presidential race in 1952. Since then they have advertised all kinds of causes, but the most memorable of the stickers are simply playful. People express their biases and sense of humor through them. *People* magazine estimated that sales of stickers reached 600 million in 1982. One sticker inspires another. Some stickers that were around in the early 1980s:

I've got something money can't buy—poverty.
I'm not as think as you stoned I am.
If you don't like the way I drive, stay off the sidewalk.
Support higher education. Hug a professor.

Related to bumper stickers are license frames that tell the world where people buy their cars; or, if purchased in the stores, tell what happiness

The last four numbers of the phone number spelled out "RAPE." That helped. So did the strong, clear graphics. And outdoor transit was an ideal advertising medium. The client: Rape Reduction Project/City of Seattle. Art director and designer: Hy Yablonka. Writer: Mark Doyle. Agency: Chiat/Day Advertising.

is; or brag about certain worker types being better lovers; or assure us that the drivers of the cars would rather be skiing or performing other sporting acts.

Each of these—stickers and frames—require deft design to crowd a word or two and possibly some decorative element into a small and distorted shape.

Point-of-purchase advertising

The advertisers' one last chance to accost the potential consumer is at the point of purchase. Almost everyone who makes products for sale at the retail level uses the medium. Point-of-purchase advertising has come into increasing favor among advertisers since the advent of self-service stores; P-O-P materials do the job salesmen once did.

P-O-P claims to have a lower CPM than any other medium. Howard Stumpf, president of the Point-of-Purchase Advertising Institute, in 1976 estimated that while print media ads cost several dollars in CPM, P-O-P ads, depending upon which of the many forms you choose, can cost well under a dollar. "A P-O-P sign that you find outside a retail store, which informs passersby of the name and gives the time and temperature, may stay up for fifteen years and deliver a message for less than a penny a thousand," he wrote in *Advertising Age*.

Making the most use of point-of-purchase advertising are the automotive, beverage, food, household goods, personal accessories, and personal products industries. Point-of-purchase advertising serves either as a reminder to buyers, when a product is heavily advertised in another medium, or as a stimulus to impulse buying.

Point-of-purchase advertising dates to the signs used by early tradespeople to identify their various shops. In those days, because people were illiterate, signs featured symbols rather than words. Today we have returned to symbols for many of our signs, especially for our road signs, not because people are illiterate, but because they travel more widely and run into language barriers. Symbols are a universal language. Besides, they can be read more rapidly than words.

One of the most popular store markers of the 1800s was the cigarstore

Indian. He stood as a symbol for tobacco shops because it was the Indian who introduced tobacco to the colonists. Other businesses used for their signs larger-than-life mockups of their products: watches, spectacles, keys, boots. The red-and-white barber pole, still seen, managed to bridge the gap between this century and last.

Neon signs made their debut in the 1920s.

Signs continue to be used both outside and inside stores as well as in store windows. They are one form of point-of-purchase advertising. Another form is the product itself. Another is the container the product comes in. Still another is the carton the containers come in. Sometimes the carton both transports the product and, lid propped up to reveal an advertising message, sells it when it is in the store.

P-O-P comes in an infinite variety. For its annual awards contest, the Point-of-Purchase Advertising Institute has used the following breakdown of "type classifications":

1. Banners
2. Bar and fountain units
3. Bar and fountain tap markers
4. Cash register units
5. Clocks
6. Counter units
7. Dealer loaders
8. Department markers
9. Floor stands
10. Floor stands (poles)
11. On-product units
12. Overheads
13. Portable P-O-P
14. Premium units
15. Prepacks
16. Racks
17. Shelf units
18. Signs
19. Sound
20. Store fixtures
21. Storewides
22. Tags and labels
23. Testers
24. Total programs
25. Wall units
26. Window displays

TANGRAM: The ancient Chinese shapes game from Penguin

This P-O-P poster (16″ × 24″) was also designed by Bernhardt Fudyma Design Group for Penguin. This one is in black and a second color: maroon. The poster advertises a Chinese-shapes game by demonstrating what can be done with the pieces. An Indian chief tells a Chinese person that "You don't have to be Chinese to like TANGRAM." The line is a takeoff of a famous early slogan for a bread advertised in New York. "You don't have to be Jewish to. . . ."

EXCLUSIVELY FROM SCHMID AND THE SATURDAY EVENING POST, THE PERFECT ADDITION TO YOUR COLLECTION.

NORMAN ROCKWELL MUSIC BOXES.

A 9″ × 12″ standup counter card used to sell music boxes produced by Schmid in collaboration with the *Saturday Evening Post*.

A floorstand display for Contac, produced by Color Process Company, Inc. This kind of P-O-P display has the advantage of housing the product and also of offering it for sale.

And, of course, there is a miscellaneous category.

Each of these categories is further subdivided into (1) promotional indoor, (2) permanent indoor, and (3) outdoor P-O-P. And each of these subcategories is subdivided into (a) motion with or without light, (b) illuminated only, and (c) without light or motion P-O-P.

Production in P-O-P involves the designing of materials and the supervision of their manufacture.

It all starts with a few rough sketches. A "blank model" follows. A "blank model" is a rough mockup, showing what the unit will look like—in three dimensions, if it is that kind of P-O-P. If the unit is to hold the product as well as advertise it, the designer will need some engineering ability.

When the client approves the "blank model," the designer does a "mechanical" for use by the printer and manufacturer.

The technical nature of P-O-P materials calls for help from special P-O-P production houses. In fact, advertising agencies have little to do with this advertising medium. Because the work is not commissionable, the house designing and producing P-O-P advertising usually deals directly with the advertiser. Harvey Offenhartz in *Point-of-Purchase Design* recommends the establishment of point-of-purchase agencies that would specialize in this kind of advertising.

To design a P-O-P unit, you should know something about the total advertising program, so that you can design it to fit; you should know what the competitors are using in the way of P-O-P; you should know where the unit or units will be used.

Today the designer of P-O-P materials reckons with motion, odor, sound, lighting, and unique printing methods and materials. Obviously this is a job only for the inventive.

The stores themselves produce P-O-P advertising when they have signs lettered or printed to call attention to their sales, point directions, mark departments, or urge compliance. There is room even here for innovation. A store in New York puts a quiet, neat sign in its window: "Cheer Up. Mark Cross is Having a Sale!" Crouch & Fitzgerald, another New York luggage store, shows this sign dealing with its hours: "Never on Sunday."

Some stores get carried away with their signs. In one of his gag cartoons, *New Yorker* artist J. B. Handelsman showed the inside of an appliance store with signs all over: "Check These Prices! We Must Be NUTS!!" "Why Do We Do It?!? You Never Saw Such a Bunch of Screwballs!" "We're Stark Staring MAD!" A potential customer, pointing to a toaster, says to a frowning clerk: "Across the street, where they make no special claim to emotional instability, this item is a dollar less."

1. "Ladybird's Bill," *Newsweek,* March 5, 1979, p. 18.

2. For a collectioin of full-color reproductions, see their book: Hayward Cirker and Blanche Cirker, *The Golden Age of the Poster* (New York: Dover, 1971).

3. Kenneth Wylie, "What's Good, What's Bad, What's Beautiful," *Advertising Age,* August 8, 1983, p. M-15.

4. Jennifer Pendleton, "Wilshire: Where Past, Future Meet," *Advertising Age,* March 22, 1982, p. M-8.

5. See *The Big Outdoor,* an undated booklet published by the Institute of Outdoor Advertising.

16

Permanence in advertising design

An impossible deadline may proscribe a designer's producing an ad with any real flair, but never mind: after it has had its few days in the magazines and newspapers, the campaign over and another one launched, the ad quietly recedes from consciousness, perhaps not even to yellow as a clipping in the files. Nothing to recall the designer's folly.

But one day someone will ask the designer to design a trademark or other item equally enduring. Years later the trademark will haunt the designer from billboard, check, letterhead, package; the logotype from ads forever inside the paper; the book jacket from counters in bookstores and bookshelves in homes; the record cover from bins in record stores and discount drugstores as well; the package from grocers' shelves.

When design is long-term, the designer comes to grips as never before with the principles of typography, spacing, art and color choices, and symbolism.

From among jobs requiring long-term design, the ordinary *layout artist* handles only a store logotype, and then only rarely and in the small towns; all other long-term design jobs fall in the province of the *graphic designer* or the *art director* capable of executing the finish. In some cases an *industrial designer* becomes involved.

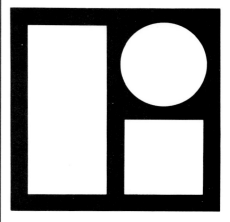

Shown is a beautifully simple trademark made with initials. It is for Litton Industries, Beverly Hills, California.

Trademarks

Used in commerce well before the time of Christ, trademarks developed to serve two divergent needs. One was the artisan's need for adulation. Just as painters signed each canvas, potters or other skilled craftsmen developed individual marks that singled their products out from others, for a competitive advantage. The other need was for identification so that medieval authorities could trace a product to its maker—to punish the artisan if it was inferior or to keep alien products off the market. To the artisan, the trademark was a desirable or undesirable adjunct of trade, depending upon the circumstances. The who's-responsible-for-this? cloud has now largely dissipated, of course; the trademark today is only a badge worn proudly.

Printers' marks. The most discussed and honored of the early trademarks are the marks used by printers of incunabula. Originating with Johann Fust and Peter Schöffer, successors to Johann Gutenberg, the printer's mark from the start was subject to pirating, unprotected as it was by copyright or patent laws. Fust's and Schöffer's obscure-in-meaning but unique insignia on the *Psalterium Latinum,* published at Mainz in 1457, was picked up and used surreptitiously by one printer in 1470 and by some twenty others in the years that followed. Aldus Manutius, the printer-publisher-typographer-scholar of Venice, had a pirating problem with his anchor-and-dolphin symbol, although he acquired some protection from local authorities. This did not stop the counterfeiters outside Italy. Everyone, it seemed, wanted to cash in on the prestige of his Aldine Press. The design was to turn up centuries later as the trademark for that giant American publisher Doubleday & Company, Inc. The Carnegie

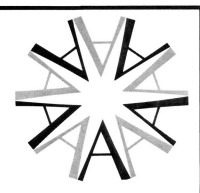

For Artemis, a text and cover paper manufactured by Mohawk Paper Mills, Inc., Cohoes, New York, Leverett Peters designed this attractive insignia. You are looking not at a circle but at a simple ring of *A*s based on a typeface called Optima.

Press, of the Carnegie Institute of Technology (now Carnegie-Mellon University), also has used a dolphin-and-anchor mark that is reminiscent of Aldus's.

The most popular of the early printers' marks was the orb-and-cross, used in various forms until the middle of the sixteenth century, when more elaborate marks came into vogue. The orb-and-cross was a circle with a double-bar cross rising from out of it, suggesting the earth—and faith. (You will find a form of the orb-and-cross surviving on the Nabisco packages of the National Biscuit Company.)

The post-orb-and-cross period was marked by trademarks "so cluttered with ornament that they could be mistaken for book illustrations . . . trapped in a decorative jungle teeming with allegorical elements, mottos and allusive sentences," one art historian has remarked.[1] The first trademark registered in the United States (in the 1800s for a paint company) was that kind of monstrosity. The design of trademarks from then on could go nowhere but up.

Watermarks. Pioneered by eighth-century Chinese, developed by twelfth-century Arabs, used extensively by fifteenth-century German and Italian printers, paper, a substitute for parchment, made printing on a mass scale possible. Like their fellow artisans, papermakers longed to put their mark on their product. Quite by accident they found a way to do this. In the papermaking process, pulp sifts over a wire screen. Somehow a bent piece of wire fell on one of these screens, and as the pulp was pressed against the screen to remove excess water, the imprint, an imperfection in texture, was made. Today watermarks add prestige to some papers, particularly the better-quality rag-content bonds.

Coats of arms. The love of medieval rulers for pomp and pageantry ushered in an era of heraldry. Artists of the Dark Ages kept themselves busy designing coats of arms and crests. "We find in heraldry an unlimited sphere of expression throughout an epoch of more than 1,000 years," wrote Ernst Lehner, an admirer of this ancient art.[2]

Heraldry flourished in the twelfth century to help warriors distinguish between friend and foe. Because suits of armor all look pretty much alike, battle leaders designed crests to identify their own soldiers. The marks appealed to civilians, too, and "coats of arms" became popular with all aristocrats. Today the College of Arms, London, decides which English families are entitled to display coats, but no such agency attempts to police heraldry addicts in America.

Cattle brands. Trademarks have some relationship to cattle brands, which date from the medieval custom of putting family marks on everything a family owned. The early-arriving Spaniards first branded cattle on this continent.

Hobo marks. Over the years hoboes developed a special sign-on-fence language as an aid to their fellow travelers. A drawing of a cat, for instance, meant that "a kind lady lives here." A cross meant that "religious talk gets a free meal."

Present-day trademarks. The Industrial Revolution and the introduction of packaging and brand-name advertising stimulated business's use

Designer Fred Caravetta of Caravetta, Allen, Kimbrough designs his own letters here, with swashes turning into waves, to act as a logo for Norwegian Caribbean Lines.

of identification marks in the nineteenth century. The same old pride in the product of one's hands or one's machines was there, but, more important, the mark was needed to assist customers in picking out a widely advertised product from a shelf crowded with competitors' products. The mark as well as the product was advertised; and, if it was well designed, the mark itself on the package did a point-of-purchase advertising job.

Here is how a few modern trademarks evolved.

In London in the 1800s a curio dealer started selling shell-covered boxes to the tourists. As his business prospered, he took on new products: jewels, mainly, and trinkets of various kinds. Eventually he went international, adding barreled kerosene to his offerings, then oil. Because of the early specialty, the dealer adopted a drawing of a shell as an identification mark for his company—and it stuck. It is today one of the world's best-known trademarks, despite the fact that buyers would not ordinarily associate a seashell with gasoline.

Another well-known trademark is the Prudential Rock of Gibralter. The Rock achieved fame as impregnable to sieges when in 1779–83 the Spaniards failed and failed again to recapture it from the British. It was not until 1896 that the insurance company adopted the Rock as its symbol. But the Rock was still a legend even then. "To associate this known strength with a great financial institution was a happy stroke of advertising skill," one student of trademarks observed. "It is perhaps one of the most effective trademarks ever conceived, as the picture tells the story better than words."[3]

Simon & Schuster, the book publisher, patterned its trademark in 1924 after "The Sower," a painting by Jean François Millet in 1849. The sower represented a source of knowledge, sowing seeds of inspiration with the printed word. Cartoonists like Charles Addams and the late Walt Kelly, in their books for Simon & Schuster, did their own versions for the title pages. "The Sower" on the title page of Jerry Della Femina's book on advertising is shown carrying a briefcase.

Similarly, Alfred A. Knopf has shown various versions of its borzoi, and Random House has shown various versions of its house drawing.

The term *trademark* needs to be further refined.

Ordinary trademarks are any name, symbol, or visual device—or combination of these—used by manufacturers to identify their product or products and distinguish them from other products. A mark used by an organization offering a service (an insurance company, for instance, or an appliance repair company) is called a *service mark*. A mark used by a nonprofit organization is called an *insignia, seal,* or *emblem*. A mark used by a trade association (like the American Plywood Association, for instance) that is interested in promoting a certain kind of product rather than the product of a particular manufacturer is called a *collective mark*. A mark used by a testing company to show that a certain product is of a particular quality is called a *certification mark* (the *Good Housekeeping* "seal of approval" is an example). A rendering in type of hand lettering of the name of the sponsor of an advertisement, with or without a trademark, is called a *logotype* or *logo*[4] or *signature*.

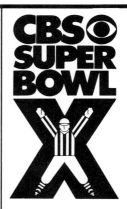

This was the insignia (red for the type, blue for the *X* and figure) used by CBS for station and commercial breaks in the broadcast of the tenth Super Bowl game. Art director/designer: Lou Dorfsman. Artist: Richard Smith.

Max's, a Westport, Connecticut, art supply store, uses a logo that crosses drawing and painting tools to form an "X." James Williams is the designer.

This mark is simplicity itself: the row of books (one seems to have slipped below the shelf) stands for the initials (lowercase) MITP (Massachusetts Institute of Technology Press). Muriel Cooper is the designer. Because the mark always appears with the publisher's name, its oversimplification is no handicap.

These various kinds of marks differ not so much in design as in use.

Students sometimes confuse "trademark" with "trade name." A trade name is simply the name of the product or organization; it *may* be in the form of a trademark, or it may be only a word or words to be spoken or printed, like "Liquid Wrench" (a penetrant that loosens rusted bolts and nuts). As graphic designers, we are concerned with the trade name only insofar as it is lettered, arranged, and illustrated.

These are things trademarks do for their owners:

1. Indicate the origin of the product. Presumably the manufacturer is proud to claim responsibility.

2. Guarantee quality consistency. The trademark tells the prospective buyer that the product is the same as an earlier unit bought and presumably enjoyed.

3. Serve as an advertisement. Simple enough to catch attention, complete enough to tell a story, persuasive enough to move the viewer to action, the trademark is an advertisement in miniature.

The same trademark, though not necessarily in a standard size or rendering, can be used on company stationery, invoices and statements, purchase orders, labels, checks, and all advertising. It can also be used on the product itself and its package and on company trucks and buildings. Because it is so widely used and for so many years, the trademark is a matter of no small concern to a company. It would be reasonable to spend months on its design and testing.

What happens to a trademark can't always be imagined or controlled. For close to a hundred years Procter & Gamble Co. has put a small moon-and-stars symbol—an innocuous symbol—on its packages. In the 1980s some groups and individuals decided the symbol stood for devil worship and so published pamphlets and organized boycotts against P & G products. The company handled as many as 12,000 calls a month from people who had questions about the symbol. It was no laughing matter to P & G, which found it necessary to file libel suits against some of the activists.

Symbols

Trademarks range from the literal to the symbolic. The more symbolic, the more successful. Obviously, when a design is to be looked at again and again, it has a better chance for long life if viewers do not get tired of it. Symbols wear better than words in trademarks. They also say more.

Long before people learned to write, they created symbols as a means of communicating. To warn, to guide, to announce—they built cairns, marked trees, tied knots, piled sticks, scratched drawings on whatever flat surfaces were available to them. People could represent the sun, they found, with a simple circle, the moon with an arc. At first their drawings were literal, then abstract. The circle became a symbol for warmth and life, the arc a symbol for mystery. (Why did the moon change shape? What happened to the moon during daylight hours?)

Designers are free to use long-recognized symbols or to establish ones of their own. Designers know that a symbol can convey two different — even opposite—meanings. "Symbols seem to be neutral," designer George Nelson told a conference of the Art Directors Club of New York. "Symbols look to me like a kind of fly paper, to which various associations get stuck. Then the symbol gets to be a real symbol."[5]

The 1970s saw the gradual shift on U.S. highways to symbol rather than word signs, part of an international program to make highway signs quickly understood by everyone, with no language barriers. An arrow pointing left with a diagonal line through it, for instance, means "No left turn." Such signs had earlier been used widely in Europe.

Sometimes you can improve on an existing symbol—one that is in the public domain. A lightbulb over a character's head in a cartoon means that the character has an idea. The American Association of Advertising Agencies for a booklet on creativity used a lightbulb, by itself, but the lightbulb was different. The bulb was in the shape of a man's head, a sideview, with an eye, nose, mouth, and chin. A lightbulb, a head: you saw them both in the same symbol.

Some of the most common symbols in general use are these:[6]

anchor   hope. This Christian symbol dates to the Apostle Paul, who wrote: "Which hope we have as an anchor of the soul, both sure and stead-fast. . . " (Hebrews 6:19, King James version).

circle   eternity (a circle has no end).

cross   Is there a better-known symbol in all the Western World? The vertical stroke originally represented the oneness of God; the horizontal stroke, earth, on which everything moves on the same plane. Combine the two strokes and you have God and earth in harmony.

crown   honor or glory.

dagger   death. A biologist uses a dagger to say "obscure species."

fish   Christ. The initial letters of "Jesus Christ, God's Son, Saviour" in Greek spell the Greek word for fish.

heart   affection or love.

lion   strength, courage, majesty.

olive branch   peace.

owl   wisdom.

palm   victory.

pine cone   fertility.

rose   beauty.

scythe or sickle   death.

serpent   evil.

skull   death.

star   supremacy.

sun   deity.

swastika   revival and prosperity. "Swastika" is a Sanscrit word meaning "well-being." For American Indians it represented the sun and infinity. Thanks to Hitler, it took on sinister implications.

umbrella   protection. A latter-day symbol, like many others, it is a paradox. An insurance company thinks enough of it to run it in red in all its advertising, but to cartoonists of the twenties it stood for prohibition, and to cartoonists of the thirties and later, because of Neville Chamberlain, who carried one, it has stood for appeasement.

It would be difficult to trace the Smile buttons and the "Have a Nice Day" bumper stickers, so popular in the early 1970s, to Carson/Roberts, the Los Angeles advertising agency that merged with Ogilvy & Mather International. But it is a fact that way back in 1953 the agency introduced this logo, which it used on some of its literature and stationery. It was developed by both Ralph Carson and Jack Roberts, principals in the agency.

What's in a name?

Before the symbol or trademark comes the name. Choosing it can be one of advertising's most important, most creative exercises. The company will be stuck with its name for a long time. Its advertising theme will revolve around it.

Sometimes the name is picked just for its sound. Picture takers still ponder the question: What prompted George Eastman way back in 1888 to call his company Kodak? One explanation is that this name, "as meaningless as a child's first 'goo,' " resulted from Eastman's strange affinity for the letter *K* and his preoccupation with sound effects. "Bitten off by consonants at both ends, it snaps like a 'Kodak' shutter," wrote Isaac E. Lambert.

Sometimes an agency creates a fictitious name to help its client sell the product. Perhaps the name is used as a strawman to knock down, like the imaginary Schludwiller Beer and the California-Eastern Brewing Company set up by Blitz-Weinhard.

Stephen Wm. Snider designed this logo, which has won numerous awards.

PURE VIRGIN WOOL

This symbol-only trademark is helped along by some words below. The Wool Bureau, Inc., authorizes its use in ads promoting products made of wool rather than synthetics.

You have to stay away from real-people names or even names that are associated with real people. A portable toilet manufacturer thought it had the ideal name for its product: Here's Johnny. But Johnny Carson sued and, rightly, won his case against the manufacturer. Most people surely would associate such a name with the introduction to the star of the "Tonight Show."

A name can make all the difference in a product's sales. Take cockroach traps, which are nothing more than glue on paper. A Japanese firm came up with the name Gokiburi Hoy-Hoy ("Hey, hey, cockroaches, come over to my house") for its trap and captured a big part of the market in Japan, where the pests are a real problem. Black Flag in America then introduced Roach Motel, a cigarette-package-size box with the slogan, "Roaches check in, but they don't check out." Sales were impressive. "Saturday Night Live" parodied Roach Motel with a segment on Roach Brothel: "Roaches make out, but they don't get out."[7]

Another pest killer calls itself Snail Jail. A car wax calls itself Rain Dance. A household cleaner calls itself Janitor in a Drum and shows up in an appropriate drum container. A clothing store in California uses this signature: "Yes, Bonds!" giving its name some personality it otherwise would not have. In Cupertino, California, you can browse in A Clean Well Lighted Place for Books, a store that takes its name basically from a Hemingway short story title. A typesetting house in Portland calls itself Irish Setter, presumably because its owner/operator is Irish. The logo shows an Irish Setter dog. An animation company in New York calls itself The Ink Tank.

Fashion Conspiracy sells new styles to young women at discount prices. Beyond Conception sells maternity clothes. A store for large women calls itself Renoir's Lady. Olga makes a bra it calls Secret Hug. It is "An embrace of Lycra lace that softly stretches to fit you in beautiful comfort."

A restaurant in Goleta, California, that features live music calls itself Rhythm & Chews.

Sometimes the cleverness in a name is for insiders only. A used-car dealer calls itself Somewhere West of Laramie, the title of a classic ad that only an advertising major would recognize. J. Brannam, Woolworth's specialty store division, made an acronym out of "just brand names" for its name.

A name can be merely cute, like Cottontails, a line of panties sold in Australia, and Next of Skin T-Shirt Emporium in San Anselmo, California. A correction fluid calls itself Boo Boo Goo.

Some names turn out to be clauses or sentences. Love My Carpet is a carpet cleaner. Some names cause a double take: Courtesy Auto Wreckers, in San Francisco.

In 1983 the Harlem Savings Bank, New York, changed its name to Apple Bank in an attempt to broaden its base. Why "Apple"? One reason, of course, was that New York is the Big Apple. Another reason, as stated

in an Apple Bank ad, was that "Like an apple, we're good for you." A computer company had already successfully used "Apple" as its name.

That so many names of service companies begin with "A" is no accident. Everybody scrambles to be first in Yellow Pages listings. Ace, Acme, and Ajax are so common that cartoonists use them freely, knowing that they cannot be sued.

Even the politicians search for names—names around which to build their campaigns. Starting with Franklin D. Roosevelt in the 1930s, we had the New Deal, which was followed by the Fair Deal, then the New Frontier, the Great Society, and—one that never caught on—the New Foundation. (Can you name the presidents who promoted each of these?)

Some names make enemies. The year 1978 saw the introduction by Yves Saint Laurent of $100-an-ounce Opium perfume to America's affluent, after a year of success in France. And what is such a choice of name if not a celebration of drug taking? Does not the manufacturer or its agency have some kind of responsibility to the public to refrain from glamorizing that kind of activity? The American Coalition Against Opium and Drug Abuse formally objected to the name in 1979 as an insult to Chinese people, but the product was still being pushed in the 1980s. A recent headline bragged: "Never has a perfume evoked such emotion."

And what about names picked with no thought of expansion? Surely Frigidaire for its stoves, Hotpoint and Whirlpool for their refrigerators, and Toastmaster for its power tools have had second thoughts about their choices of names.

The computer has helped many corporations come up with names that are easy to remember, that don't conflict with existing names, that don't carry undesirable meanings in other countries or in other languages. Some trade names come from parts of several names. Dyazide, a drug for high blood pressure, comes from "diuretic," a term for something that reduces fluid in the body, and "hydrochlorothiazide," one of the drug's ingredients.

Sometimes something happens or events change to make a carefully-thought-out name inappropriate. When "gay" became a synonym for "homosexual," a Northwest men's store decided to change from The Gay Blade to simply The Blade. Ayds, an "appetite suppressant candy," faced something of a crisis in 1983 when AIDS (Acquired Immune Deficiency Syndrome) cropped up as a serious disease in the United States.

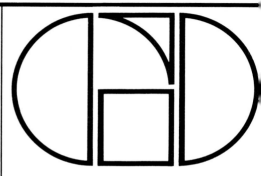

This insignia is for Grosset & Dunlap, Inc., Publishers. Nils A. Shapiro, advertising director for GD, reports it took some seven or eight months to settle on GD's final design, with Alan Wolsky for Associated Advertising & Design, New York, and Louis Sardella for the publisher pooling their design talents.

Designing the trademark

It was a school child responding to a $5 prize contest in 1916 in Suffolk, Virginia, who, inspired by one of Palmer Cox's Brownies, designed the monocled, high-hatted Mr. Peanuts. At one time trademark design could be left to people entering contests. Today too much rests on the design to entrust it to anyone but an experienced designer. Even back then Planters' Peanuts hired a commercial artist to revise the child's entry.

From a design standpoint, a trademark must be:
1. original,
2. legible,
3. stimulating,
4. appropriate to the product,
5. easy to remember.

The trademark can take these forms:
1. symbol,
2. lettering (or initials or numbers),
3. a combination of 1 and 2.

Symbol-only marks. Symbol-only marks come in varying degrees of subtlety, from portraits or drawings of the founder or a deceased U.S. president (living presidents and presidents with living widows are taboo)

"Making a corporate design for your own company is, I believe, one of the most difficult things to do," says Tony van Hasselt, owner of Painting Holidays, New York. "This design evolved from dozens of sketches and almost a month of thinking." Here you see the progression of his thinking, from the "hokey" (van Hasselt's word) suitcase concept to the stylized *ph* incorporating the half-globe, half-artist's pallet. Note the middle stage with the full pallet: a "breakthrough . . . [but] the *h* was not clear."

to stripes of color. No living person can be portrayed without that person's consent, of course; and if the mark is to be registered, a depicting of the flag or a drawing that is "immoral" would not be permitted.

Animals stand near the front of the symbol line. Some of the best known are Mobil Oil Company's put-to-pasture but still-remembered flying red horse (designed by Jim Nash, who also did the smiling Quaker for Quaker Oats); Mack Truck's bulldog; Greyhound's greyhound; Hartford's stag; Borden's Elsie; Camel's camel; and MGM's lion.

The symbol-only trademark is the ultimate in design, but it is the hardest to attach successfully to a product. For almost everyone, a red cross means only one organization; that eye symbol on television (designed by the late William Golding) is seen often enough that there is little danger of its being associated with any network other than CBS. But not all products or organizations lend themselves to trademarks so abstract.

Lettering-only marks. The lettering or typeface trademark can involve made-up words (like "Kodak") or dictionary words, personal names, or geographic names. Initials can take the form of monograms and are easiest to handle when the letters involved are those with symmetrical round or triangular shapes—the *O*s, *V*s, *W*s, and *M*s, particularly.

As the network covering the 1984 Olympics, ABC found that its lowercase initials fit nicely into the familiar five-circles emblem of the games and so created and used a new mark for two weeks.

Combination marks. Combinations of symbols and lettering are the most serviceable and most-often-used trademarks. The layout artist using an already designed trademark as an element to arrange can make a "combination" mark out of a "symbol-only" mark by putting another element—the name set in type—next to the trademark.

Of whatever kind, the mark can fit into a circle, oval, triangle, square, rectangle, diamond, or shield, but often such shapes become intrusive. Some of the best marks form their own silhouette.

Because a trademark might appear in various sizes, the designer should use stroke thicknesses that can take both enlargement and reduction.

The designer picks a typeface for the trademark not so much for the face itself but for how the letters needed will lend themselves to the design. That the name has letters with descenders—letters like *g* and *y*—can influence the choice. "A word with no descenders tends to look more stable. . . . That little descender is a costly thing, too. It takes up more newspaper space [in ads], for example," says Joe Selame of Selame Design, Newton Lower Falls, Massachussetts.[8]

To keep a trademark from becoming dated too soon, you should avoid the following:

1. Unusual typefaces that happen to be popular at the moment. Scripts, for instance, fail to pass the test of time. Romans and well-designed sans serifs are best.

2. Pictures of people in modern dress. The width of the lapel, the length of the dress, the hairstyle—after a few years these will have to be changed if the mark is to do its job. Period costume is something else again; if the company feels it is appropriate to its product now, it likely will be appropriate in the future.

3. Background props that would date the trademark: automobiles, appliances, and the like. Keeping the mark simple would automatically take care of this.

Redesign

"Corporate heraldry," *Time* called it, and noted an increase in it in the 1980s, due partly to reorganizations, mergers, and name changes. One of the most important of the logo designers and redesigners is Lippincott &

Margulies, which by 1982 had created well over 2,000 logos for such companies as Xerox, RCA, and Uniroyal.

"Big Business graphics probably is the only art form in our time that is both uncompromisingly modern and genuinely popular," a writer in *Time* has noted.[9]

It is natural that a trademark should change after years of use. Sometimes the change is gradual, as with Psyche, the White Rock maiden looking at her reflection in the water. Her dress and hairdo from before the turn of the century, when she was adopted, changed with the fashions until she was abandoned. But more often, the trademark change is sudden, because companies get used to their trademarks and do not notice they have become completely outdated. Then it dawns on them.

Not everyone likes what is happening to America's trademarks. One dissenting voice comes from Barbara Knight, a collector of old trademarks. She thinks the trend toward modernizing and even dropping familiar trademarks is robbing the country of a folk art. The old marks, she says in an article written for the American Institute of Graphic Arts, were often "picked up from paintings, comic strips, encyclopedias, children's sketches. Some were concepts; some commissioned or designed; but most just happened, and many companies don't know quite how. Their records don't contain such information."[10]

Writing in the July 17, 1972, issue of *New York,* Tom Wolfe, after his experience as a judge in an American Institute of Graphic Arts awards competition, pondered why abstract logos or trademarks, even though they did not identify as well as, say, Coca-Cola's script or the Alfred A. Knopf borzoi, were popular with corporate executives. He concluded it was because "the conversion of a total-design abstract logo formation somehow makes it possible for the head of the corporation to tell himself: 'I'm modern, up to date, with it, a man of the future. I've *streamlined* this old baby.' Why else would they have their companies pour $30,000, $50,000, $100,000 into the concoction of symbols that any student at Pratt could and would gladly give him for $125 plus a couple of lunches at the Trattoria, or even the Zum Zum? The answer: if the fee doesn't run into five figures, he doesn't feel streamlined. Logos are strictly a vanity industry, and all who enter the field should be merciless cynics if they wish to guarantee satisfaction."[11]

Saul Bass echoed Wolfe's sentiments. Symbols have become sterile, he said; they are cold and too abstract. "I can't think of any corporation that can't use some expression of responsiveness to human needs, and to the society in which it exists."[12]

Despite any great effort on the designer's part to produce a memorable trademark, two conditions beyond design determine the effectiveness of that mark.

One is the extent of its use.

A trademark is not effective or valuable unless it is used widely. A poorly designed trademark fully exploited is more effective than a beautifully designed trademark only half exploited. The main goal of the trademark, after all, is to be recognized.

The other factor is the character of the company behind the mark.

Legal considerations

The Lanham Act of 1946 (known as the Trade-mark Act), which went into effect in 1947, provides the legal basis on the federal level for registering of trademarks and seeking redress when trademark rights are violated.

The U.S. Patent Office houses registration papers on close to three-quarters of a million trademarks, and state agencies have records on many

This is a trademark-pun. The John Deere trademark has changed gradually from clutter in 1876, when it first appeared, to simplicity, keeping up with the times.

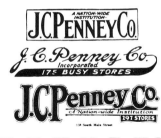

Here are some—but not all—of the changes in the J. C. Penney logo since 1902, when the store was known as The Golden Rule. The most recent version (1971) represents not only a change in typeface but also a change from Penneys back to J. C. Penney. The three initials, without periods, come close to touching, making a sort of ligature. The typeface (Helvetica) is also used for ad headlines.

others. Additional thousands appear on packages and in advertising without benefit of registration.

A small R placed inconspicuously on the mark shows it has been registered. To be registered, the trademark cannot appropriate a common word like "Fresh" or "Big" or "Good," put a graphic fence around it, and expect to keep trespassers away. Before adopting a new trademark, the company will want to check it with its lawyers to make sure it conforms with both federal and state regulations. At the national level, someone will have to check both the Principal Register and the Supplemental Register in the U.S. Patent Office to make sure no other organization is using the mark in substantially the same form.

A well-known trademark occasionally finds itself used by another advertiser, not always to its advantage. To announce an increase in its audience for its news program, Channel 7 in New York, a non-CBS station, ran a full-page ad in *New York* showing the CBS eye slightly closed with a big tear dripping from it. The ad said, "Some of the . . . [new viewers] must have come from Channel 2 [a CBS station]." *Penthouse,* the magazine challenging *Playboy,* has run an altered version of the Playboy bunny in some of its ads directed to media buyers.

The legal implications of using—or even *mis*using—another firm's trademark are not always clear. The designer should do some checking with a lawyer first.

Parker Bros. in the 1980s found that "Monopoly" was too common a name to tie up for a game when a U.S. circuit court of appeals decided that "Anti-Monopoly," a game by another company, was not a trademark infringement.

It is possible to do such a thorough job promoting a trademark (and trade name) that the name becomes generic and falls into public domain, as aspirin did. Companies now know that the best way to protect identity is to use the proper name as an adjective: Bayer Aspirin, DuPont Cellophane, and so on, and to insist on capitalization of the full name in editorial and news columns as well as in all company advertising. Coca-Cola (or Coke) is one of several firms campaigning almost monotonously, but understandably, to get editors and writers to use uppercase when mentioning the product.

It is also possible to lose control of a trademark (and name) by making it descriptive rather than merely suggestive. If some of today's trademarks seem descriptive, it is because they were well established before laws became stringent.

The owner of a trademark ordinarily can hold a name only for one kind of product. As a name, Cadillac is attached to products other than the high-priced automobile, possibly to the chagrin of General Motors. There is *Life* magazine and there was a cigarette with the unlikely same name. Then came Life cereal.

Any kind of description makes for what the lawyers call a "weak" trademark, and a "weak" trademark, to be protected, is likely to involve its owner in litigation. A picture of the product makes for a "weak" trademark, too; other makers of the product can hardly be forced to refrain from picturing their products in their trademarks if they feel such picturing is desirable.

For protection against pilfering, owners of marks used in interstate and international business register their marks with the U.S. Patent Office. Some firms doing only intrastate business register their marks with an appropriate state agency. But the designer looking to other trademarks for "inspiration" should remember that even if the mark is not registered, the courts are likely to decide for the original owner in any suit over ownership.

Corporate identity programs

The 1970s saw a growing movement by companies to establish "corporate identity" programs. More than just the trademark was involved. The typical program modernized and standardized all corporation design—business stationery, advertising, packaging, building and vehicle colors and signs, uniforms, and so on. For some companies, elaborate books were prepared, giving instructions to various branch plants and offices on how and where to use the new symbols and typography. Not only were companies changing these, they were in some cases adopting new names, having been burdened with names inadequate or inappropriate to fields into which they had expanded. U.S. Rubber, to name one corporation, became Uniroyal because rubber products were only part of the business.

Much of the design work appears to be beyond the scope of the firms' advertising agencies. These are jobs for "image consultants" like Lippincott & Margulies, Inc., and Unimark Corp. for Design & Marketing.

One of Dun & Bradstreet's problems, before undertaking a corporate redesign program in 1979, was that people tended to think of it only as an organization engaged in credit reports and ratings. It is much more than that. For instance, it is Corinthian Broadcasting and also Reuben H. Donnelley, printers. The organization changed its name from Dun & Bradstreet Companies, Inc., to The Dun & Bradstreet Corporation, and redesigned its logos to feature in each case one of the companies, like Technical Publishing, with a smaller line, "a company of The Dun & Bradstreet Corporation." Murtha, DeSola, Finsilver, Fiore, Inc. created the design system and logotypes.

One of the most interesting corporate redesign cases involved a TV network and an educational station. In 1975 NBC decided to retire its peacock trademark, which, after seventeen years, had lost its significance. When it was adopted, TV color was a novelty. The magazine [*More*] announced that the bird with the brilliant plumage that unfolded at the start of each color program would be "relegated to the corporate trademark limbo now inhabited by Little Nipper, listening for 'His Master's Voice'— the symbol of NBC's parent company RCA." (But later NBC brought the peacock back in an abstract form for limited use.)

NBC also decided it was time to change its serpentine logo—the one that showed letters drawing themselves right there on the TV screen, the *N* and *B* on top, the *C* taking shape below.

Lippincott & Margulies stepped forward to work out a new design, taking a year or so to research and produce it. The firm settled on the single letter *N,* causing *U&lc.,* a typography publication, to speculate with some amusement: "Did extensive research studies show that the letters 'BC' are outdated since they refer to a period over one thousand nine hundred and seventy-six years ago?" NBC explained that the single-letter design helped separate NBC from the other two television networks. And *N,* besides being the first letter in the corporate initials, was also the only one neither of the other networks had.[13]

This was no ordinary *N.* It was an *N* built from two trapezoids, one red, one blue—an *N* solid enough to allow photography and art effects to evolve inside. The only trouble with it was that another organization, the Nebraska Educational Television Network, had one just like it, except for the color.

Since a big organization must spend hundreds of thousands of dollars in fees and printing costs to switch to a new logo, NBC was, understandably, nervous about the matter after the duplication was called to its attention. There was no question that the Nebraska network's *N* had been

Above: William Korbus's *N* symbol for the Nebraska Educational Television Network—a symbol that preceded NBC's *N* symbol, much to the embarrassment of NBC. Below: The educational network's new symbol, adopted after NBC made an out-of-court settlement for the *N.* Korbus art directed; Michael Buettner designed.

The brouhaha over the new (in 1976) NBC logo and its similarity to the Nebraska Educational Television Network's logo inspired Miami adman Ronald Plotkin and three associates to come up with "The Million Dollar Logo: The Great American Game." The boxed "game" consisted of more than one hundred geometric shapes in three colors that could be assembled into any number of designs. Copy on the box said: "Now YOU can create great logos for national companies and products, local merchants, Dad's business, your firm, family and friends! Now YOU can become a design mogul!" Other copy on the box warned: "Makers of this product are not responsible for the commotion that can result from similar or simultaneous design." Others involved in this rather joyful project were Al Angelo, who did the designing, and Joel Levine and Lyn Plotkin. (Photo courtesy of Ronald Plotkin, Logo Enterprises Inc.)

put into use before NBC unveiled its version. It was not a matter of plagiarism. No one charged that. The duplication was accidental. Two widely separated designers independently arrived at a logical design solution. Even by checking state and federal registers of trademarks a designer cannot be sure that a new mark—or something close to it—is not in use somewhere.

NBC, after its huge investment of time and money, had no choice but to arrange an out-of-court settlement with the Nebraska Educational Television Network: $55,000 in cash and $500,000 worth of new and used television equipment.

The press, which delights in reporting TV embarrassments anyway, had a field day with this story. It had the right ingredient: tiny educational network gets the better of giant corporation. But what caught the reporters' interest most, perhaps, was the disparity between what the educational network paid for its logo (an estimated $100) and what NBC paid (an estimated $750,000).

It was not a fair comparison, though. NBC executives told *Advertising Age* that comparing the educational network's costs to NBC's costs was like comparing apples to oranges. NBC paid for "a whole corporate identification program." Such a program includes elaborate instructions, with layouts and grids, showing exactly how and where the insignia is to be used on stationery, trucks, building walls, and so on. The company gets what Margulies of Lippincott & Margulies calls a "system," not just a logo or trademark.

The cash settlement to the Nebraska Educational Television Network would, among other things, finance the designing of a new logo. A story going around Nebraska had it that Bill Korbus, the NETN staff artist who designed the original *N,* was asked what kind of a new design he would come up with, and he answered: "I was thinking of a sort of eye symbol. . . ."

Logotypes

The logotype is the type or lettering, carried usually at the bottom of the ad, that names the sponsor. Sometimes it incorporates a trademark or insignia into its design. All advertisers use logotypes; it is in retail advertising where logotypes get most prominent display. The retailer refers to the logotype, or logo, as the "signature" or "sig cut."

The principles of design applying to trademarks also apply—or should apply—to logotypes. Yet most logotypes for retailers look as though they were designed not by designers but by show-card writers. The scripts so preferred by fashion houses and some department stores are tight and angular rather than loose and graceful. The gothics of the discount houses and appliance stores are fat and foolish; and to make matters worse, they are tilted, arched, put into perspective, buried in dots and stars and sunbursts and lines of type.

That each logotype has a specific audience to reach and that in many cases the audience is the bargain-basement crowd suspicious of white space and Garamond cannot be denied. One cannot insist that all logotypes look as if they came off the Trajan column of ancient Rome. One can suggest, however, that well-designed, standard types in their normal settings can do anything typographic experiments by tasteless amateurs can do, and without tiring and offending the reader. Ideally, logotypes should be hand lettered by qualified lettering artists who understand letterform; but a perfectly acceptable logotype can be put together by a designer using reproduction proofs of type, doing some cutting and moving around during the pasteup process. Press-on letters are useful, too.

Elements that may be included in the pasteup are the store name, kind of store, address, phone number, hours, and slogan. The big store needs no address in the logotype; the name alone may be the logotype.

Helmut Krone, art director at Doyle Dane Bernbach, does not like logos in ads, especially in brand-name ads. "[A logo] . . . says 'I'm an ad. Please turn the page.' " How does he keep clients from insisting that he include a logo? "There's a way of keeping the bottom of the page so clean and effective that they can't—they don't dare—put a logo in." But he always carefully works the name into the ad so that the reader will know what brand to buy or what store to visit.[14]

Book jackets

To win one $2.50 paperback, 433 *Chicago Tribune* readers once entered a low-key contest run by the "Books Today" columnist to rename "that old misnomer, [the] dust jacket." "Bookini" took the prize, although "outer touter," "lust jacket," "bookbushka," and "puff adder" got strong consideration. Call it what you will, the book jacket is a matter of great concern to today's book publisher.

Its function is primarily to advertise the product and only secondarily to protect it from sun and dust. But so conditioned have book buyers become to this form of advertising that when a jacket is missing or torn, the value of the book diminishes. The bookseller may have to mark down the price and throw the book on the clearance table. In the college bookstore the "text" edition of a book may differ from a more expensive "trade" edition only in that it is without a jacket.

What is there about the jacket that makes it so valuable? Mainly information—about the book's contents and about the author; but also *design*. And pattern, beauty, color. It is less costly to provide all this on a paper jacket than on a cloth cover.

A bonus value of a good jacket was pointed out by a panel of book reviewers at the Trade Book Clinic of the American Institute of Graphic Arts. These people agreed that the design of the book—and this would include the jacket—helps the book-review editor decide whether or not to review the book.

A book jacket designer tries to make five panels—the front, the back, the spine, and two inside flaps—into a unified whole that (1) captures the spirit of the book and (2) convinces the browser to buy. The two inside flaps are the least important panels. Some designers do not even deal with them. They are left to the publisher to make a last-minute sales pitch in a long copy block. Ideally, the flaps would be designed with the covers and spine to make a unified whole.

The back cover of a book jacket usually carries a photograph of the author and an author's blurb. But this Seaview Books back cover repeats the front cover title and author's name and gives the reader a new piece of bleed-all-around art. What happened was this: the publisher could not decide which Rowena Morrill painting it liked best, so it used both of them. "We decided to let the booksellers choose which side to display," said advertising director Morrie Goldfischer.

Shown above is the front cover of Barbara Chase-Riboud's paperback novel *Sally Hemings,* published by Avon (Barbara Bertoli, art director). The book is about a slave woman who, according to the author, was Thomas Jefferson's mistress. That is Jefferson in the locket. This paperback cover art was more revealing than similar art used on the jacket of the hardbound book, which was published by Viking Press.

The most important single panel may well be the spine. Aside from a few best sellers, most books in the stores are stacked or stand front-to-back, on shelf after shelf, so that only their spines show. A readable spine may be a book's only chance.

There is not much, from a design standpoint, that you can do in a space that is half an inch to an inch deep. So you settle for good, clean, colorful, heavy type. You study books on the shelf and try to come up with a combination of type and color that will stand out.

The spine contains three elements: title, author, and publisher (and perhaps the publisher's trademark). For thin books, the type must run sideways; sideways type is more readable on the shelf when it starts at the bottom and runs to the top, but most publishers seem to prefer that the type start at the top. It is not a good idea to be different here, because then the customer would be forced into a contortion to read your particular title. For thicker books, the type can be arranged in normal left-to-right fashion, but in short takes. A condensed type often is required. Word separation is allowed. No matter how the type is arranged on the spine, only last names for the author and publisher need be used.

For the cover of a paperback book dealing humorously with why things go wrong, the publisher allows things to go wrong in the printing—or makes it seem that way. The design pretends that the book was trimmed wrong, and it also runs the words in the title upside down. Price/Stern/Sloan Publishers, Los Angeles, produced the book.

The front cover and spine of a paperback book usually works as a poster, with the back cover being reserved for copy. As ''packages,'' paperback book covers (or back covers) have to put up with universal product codes, which often strike a discordant note. Matt Teppler art directed this handsome cover; Martha Sedgwick did the design. Avon Books was the publisher.

Of course the front cover will get major attention from the designer. For important books, the front cover will be crucial; even for lesser books, once the spine has captured attention, the front cover will take over to develop interest. If a book is to be advertised, the front cover of the jacket is what will be pictured. This means that the colors and tones and sizes must be chosen so that when the jacket is reduced in size for the ad and limited to black and white reproduction, the important elements will be readable.

The publisher will decide what to feature most prominently on the cover—the title or the author's name. If the author has a wide following, the name may call for the largest type—and it may be the largest ele-

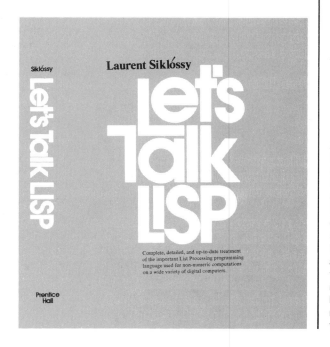

A book jacket does not have to have art to stand out. Type alone, tastefully and even unusually arranged, can do the job. For this jacket (you see only the front cover and the spine) designer Peter Ross for Prentice-Hall uses two colors (black and orange) and, for the title itself, sans serif type doctored and stacked. Note that the bottom of the top *L* serves also as the right half of the cross-bar for the *T* and that the *I* is cut short to make it nestle just above the cross-bar of the lower *L*. The lettering on the spine is more normal because there is less space to play with.

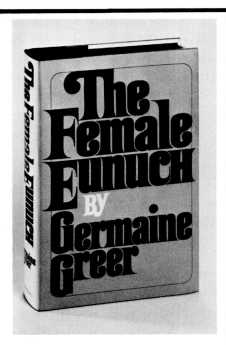

S. Neil Fujita's beautifully drawn and arranged letters are art enough for this book jacket. The book title is in black; the author's name is in purple; the "BY" is reversed in a gold background. The book was published by McGraw-Hill Book Company.

ment—on the cover. If the name is placed above the title, the word "By" is omitted.

Artwork takes a secondary role to type on book jackets. In this regard, book jackets differ from most other forms of print advertising. But the type, carefully chosen or drawn, ingeniously spaced and prominently displayed, *becomes* art for the book jacket. Usually two colors—sometimes more—are used. Only the subsidy publishers—like Exposition and Vantage—seem willing to settle for a single color on the jacket these days. And that is to keep their authors, who must pay the publishing costs, from being overwhelmed by the charges.

Elements that must be included on the front cover are the book's title and the author's full name. Elements that might be added include some identification of the author; the title of another of the author's works; a blurb or some description of the book; some art. The more clutter, the less appeal the cover will have to the sophisticated buyer; and here is a field where customers have a greater degree of sophistication than usual. Of course, some books are not meant for sophisticates; as in all graphic design, the artist will slant the work to the audience.

The back cover is usually reserved for information about the author, perhaps with a picture; or for information on other books offered by the publisher; or for quotes from reviewers who had something good—and promotable—to say about the book. It is not necessary that the front cover/spine/back cover be a wraparound; that is, an art device is not needed to hold all three panels together. Unity can be achieved through judicious use of type and repetition of color.

The inside front flap carries the name of the book again (but in smaller type), a copy block describing the book and the price (in the upper right or lower right corner so it can be clipped off by gift buyers). The inside back flap carries a continuation of the book description and, if it is not carried on the back cover, a rundown on the author. The publisher's name is run on either the inside front or the back flap. If color is used, it is available for the flaps without extra charge (the flaps are printed on the same run with the covers), but it is not a good idea to use it lavishly here; you do not want to diminish your cover impact.

The layout should be done actual size, without margins, in the manner of direct-mail roughs (see chapter 14). The front cover panels are the same size as the book itself; the flaps are usually a little more than half the width of the cover, except for oversize books, for which the flaps are proportionately smaller. The size of the spine panel cannot be determined until a dummy copy of the book is bound; but at the beginning layout stage it can be estimated. For final production, of course, sizes have to be exact; to be off as little as an eighth of an inch could make the spine unreadable or cause some of the cover to disappear into the flap.

Ink color and paper stock are problems to consider at an early stage. A light-colored jacket makes a book look larger than it is; a dark jacket or a jacket with a border around the front cover makes the book look smaller. Books on display in sunny windows end up with faded jackets, particularly if the colors used are pale blues, pale pinks, and mauves. Smooth paper is best for jackets, because rough paper, with its "valleys" that trap dirt, becomes soiled more easily; books put up with an unconscionable amount of pawing during their normal two-year life span in the bookstores. If a coated paper is used, the stock should be polished on only one side; otherwise, the jacket will be slippery against the book. And the grain of the paper should run down the spine, not across it.

The front cover of the jacket is always slightly larger than the page size, to fit the cover board, which, of course, overhangs the pages.

Despite the rules, there is still room for experimentation, for uniqueness. Alexander King's first popular book, *Mine Enemy Grows Older,* came with two jackets, both designed by Ben Feder Inc. The outside jacket, featuring a full-color painting of a hideous character, King, playing a viola that looked shockingly like the back of a nude woman, carried this note: "If this jacket (the author painted it) is too strong for you, take it off. There's a conservative jacket for conservative people underneath." The underneath jacket was of a more standard design: all type, centered, with no illustration.

Some graphic designers specialize in book jackets, doing them on a freelance basis.

He's not known to the general public (who looks at the credit lines on a book jacket?), but among his fellow designers Paul Bacon has earned applause for his covers and jackets of some 4,000 books, including Robin Cook's *Coma,* E. L. Doctorow's *Ragtime,* and Henry Kissinger's *White House Years.* What makes Bacon popular with book publishers' art directors is his versatility (he draws, he designs, he does lettering when he doesn't find the right typeface) and his thorough reading of a book to find appropriate symbolism.

Bacon, who employs an assistant, gets around $1,000 a design, high in the industry but not high when you consider what similar design might bring in other forms of advertising.

With some good training in high school art departments (he didn't go to college) Bacon got his start designing album covers. The book jacket he did for Ira Levin's *Compulsion* brought him his first fame among designers.[15]

Record covers

Designers delight in record album cover design assignments because there is so much freedom there. Once you've accepted the basic square format, you can do almost anything you want. You set out to "mirror the energy of the music contained within the sleeves," as *Art Direction* put it. The images are "arresting and energetic."[16]

Current jackets play around with type so that it is almost unreadable. And great emphasis is placed on reviving old and discredited styles of design. Abstract art is popular.

Student Bruce Adlhoch draws some shadow art and combines it with type from the 1920s to create this simple, strong record album cover for a class assignment. What shows up as white here was really bright red on Adlhoch's original comprehensive.

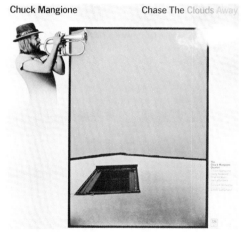

Chuck Mangione   Chase The Clouds Away

Art director Roland Young and designer
Phil Shima have Chuck Mangione
chasing the clouds away, all right—right
across the framed picture and just about
off the page. The gradual fadeaway of
the type at the top right adds to the
appropriate illusion. The reverse side of
this jacket, in full color like the front,
shows the musicians up close. A large
initial letter gets the reader started with
the copy, which was written by Chuck
Mangione. This is an A & M Record.

But Dugald Stermer learned, after studying record jacket design for a
Communication Arts article, that design played only a small part in sales.
He repeated an industry cliché: "If it's in the grooves, it'll sell. If not, you
can wrap it in mink and it'll bomb." Stermer admitted that "I can only
remember a single incident when I was tempted to trade my money for
unknown grooves surrounded by nice art. I resisted the urge, but to give
credit where it was earned, the album in question is called *Chris Darrow,
Artist Proof,* designed by Tony Lane for Fantasy, with art by Darrow
himself."[17]

Yet, Stermer maintains that record jacket design has higher moments
than magazine and book design.

This is a medium in which performers play a major role in design decisions. If the performer is not involved, then a friend is. "It's easy to see
why so many art directors develop tics at the mention of performer control
of covers," Stermer observes. "But it's also clear that this has been responsible for opening up the field to some exciting graphic languages and
techniques."[18]

For regular 12″ records, covers measure 12½″ wide by 12¼″ deep—
essentially a square. The challenge to the designer is to change the width-
depth proportion to a more pleasing vertical or horizontal. The front design almost always makes use of full color. The art is often cropped close
and "posterized."

Elements to be arranged include a picture of the performer, title of the
album, names of the songs, name of the record company, and whatever
additional art may be called for. The designer reserves the right to change
the order of song names so that the type will arrange itself into an interesting silhouette.

That a potential buyer flips through records in a bin means that the
performer's name should go across the top.

The back of the cover used to be a routine matter, but now good design
thinking goes into it, too. To be included on the back are the names of the
album and performer, a copy block describing the record and/or performer, a more detailed listing of the songs, some miscellaneous information, and perhaps some art.

Like any graphic design job, a record cover can utilize gimmicks of one
kind or another. Jackets can include additional compartments, fold into
portrait stands, take on other than square shapes, use exotic paper stock,
carry mirrors or other paste-ons as well as poster inserts. Alice Cooper's
School's Out album yielded a record wrapped in something approximating a woman's undergarment. The Rolling Stones' *Sticky Fingers* album
had a real zipper built into the cover, over an Andy Warhol photograph
of a pair of pants. A clever idea, but the zipper handle pressed against
the records and caused some damage. DJs getting advanced copies complained. Jacket designer Craig Braun told Dugald Stermer: "Then I got
one of my best ideas: Unzip so that the handle would fall over the label.
Nobody cares about scratched labels. I wish I had filmed the scene:
hundreds of ladies . . . unzipping millions of flies."[19]

Pay for jacket art and design ranges from $200 to $700—considerably
less than the artist would get for similar art done for a magazine advertisement. But artists/designers like the work because of the creative possibilities.

Where once the original art for record jackets was discarded or forgotten, in the mid-1970s it caught on with collectors. Some pieces for rock
albums brought as much as $20,000. A new name came into being: Pho-
nographics.

Not all record companies place an emphasis on design. When London
Records dismissed its art director in 1973, it said it was letting the printer
design its jackets. "Perhaps it could save even more money by letting the
man who presses the records select the music," Stermer observed.[20]

In a departure from its usual mailings to doctors, the Texas Pharmacal Co., San Antonio, sent dermatologists samples of Meted® Shampoo and Texacort® Scalp Lotion in a box with graphics showing the intended use for the products. Ralph Grigg was the designer; Sudler & Hennessey, the agency. (Photograph courtesy Texas Pharmacal Company.)

Packages

Not many remember the cracker-barrel days when foods like flour, sugar, and coffee were sold in bulk. Yet, in terms of our years as a nation, packaging is a rather recent phenomenon in the United States. The idea of individual units, wrapped for protection and convenience of handling, gained momentum only in the late part of the last century. One early packager was a St. Paul, Minnesota, grocer who, in looking for a name for an expensive blended syrup he was about to market, thought of his boyhood hero, Abraham Lincoln. "Lincoln" as a name might not be appropriate, but "Log Cabin," almost synonymous with "Lincoln," would work, and with that name, why not shape the can as a log cabin? Another pioneer was the National Biscuit Company, which took its crackers out of the barrel and put them in rather remarkable packages with inner waxpaper wrappings. To dramatize the fact that such wrappers kept the product uniquely dry, the biscuit company adopted as a package symbol a little boy dressed in oilskins.

Among other things, packages extend the life of products, cut shipping costs, and eliminate the need for sales people. "In this era of self-service selling, the package has naturally assumed greater importance, since it must now communicate many of the selling points previously expounded by the sales clerk," James H. Balmos of Container Corporation of America has observed. "It must attract, identify, and denote quality. It must give information, permit the product to be seen [if possible], and make the shopper want to buy it."

As marketing consultant Louis Cheskin sees it, "Advertising must sell the package and the package must sell the product."

Dr. Ernest Dichter, president of the Institute of Motivational Research, thinks that people frequently buy the product for the package itself, rather than for its contents. He refers to the package as "the silent salesman."

Sometimes the package—the product—by itself is enough of an ad. In this full-color, full-page magazine ad you see no headline, really, and no copy block. That the product is transparent is beautifully demonstrated by showing the back of the bottle as well as the front and letting the reader see what is printed on the back of the label. Client: S. C. Johnson and Son, Inc. Agency: Foote, Cone & Belding, Chicago. Art director: Joe Kerr. Copywriter: Dan Mountain.

With the on-shelf tampering of Extra-Strength Tylenol in 1982, the safety and security of packages became an important consideration. The Food and Drug Administration ordered nonprescription drug companies to make their bottles tamper resistant, with the result that new seals and closures made "the old child-resistant caps seem like, well, child's play."[21]

And there is this to consider: the item may not even get on the retailer's shelves unless it is attractively packaged. The head of a supermarket chain said in a talk to members of his trade association: "Our buyers have considered about 6,000 new products during the past year. Less than 5 percent of them were accepted. In every case, attractive packaging influenced the decisions."

"Packages" is a broad enough term to include the plastic, glass, or metal container the product comes in; the paper or cardboard unit that houses the container; the structure that carries a number of the paper or cardboard units. All get some design consideration.

Companies have tried to outdo each other in a rush to make their packages useful, handsome, and unique. But ecologists have attacked the concept of convenience packaging. Some companies have cut back on packages-within-packages, and they have come up with packages that eventually will self-destruct or deteriorate. Some packages carry a circular-arrow insignia sponsored by the American Paper Institute to signify the use of recycled paperboard. In the stores, especially in college towns, clerks are asking customers if they want their purchases placed in sacks.

Package designers face all kinds of criticism and pressure. That packages are wasteful of our resources is only one of the criticisms. Some plastic wrappings are actually harmful to health, it is charged. And the product often does not live up to the promises of the package design. Even the nature of the design—its "commercialism"—irks some buyers. One of the facial tissue companies has put its name and advertising on a wrapper that can be removed and discarded once the product is in the home. That way there is no commercializing in the bedroom or bathroom. And Chiffon has advertised: "Each colorful box . . . gives you more than one color. The top, sides and end panels are different shades of blue, green, pink, yellow and orange. Which means you can match the decor of your bathroom—no matter what your basic colors happen to be."

The production of the package may add considerably to the cost of the product. It is estimated that packaging represents about a third of the price of cosmetics, for instance. A single package design may cost $25,000. It takes many comps and package mockups before a client registers its approval. The Schechter Group created more than 150 designs for Diet Coke before one was chosen.

Once accepted, a package design does not last as long as it did in years past. Companies feel that they have to change their designs often to keep up with the competition.

The big stores frequently change the design on their shopping bags, a form of packaging. The design may change from season to season. Bloomingdale's has half a dozen different shopping bags available at any given time. The bags vary from department to department. The New York-based store pioneered in the design of bags that omit the store name. Fashion-conscious buyers still could easily recognize the store behind the design—". . . the once-ignored shopping bag had been fully recognized for what it was—a form of portable graphic art which, carried incessantly by customers and by those who wished to appear as customers of a particular establishment, resulted in millions of dollars' worth of free advertising."[22]

Most stores charge for their shopping bags to discourage unreasonable requests for them and to help cover, if not fully cover, their costs.

The problems of packaging call for decisions involving the following:

1. *Kind of material for the vessel containing the product.* Legal con-

To design this two-color wine label, Tom Rubick picked a classic roman italic in all caps and put the lines on a slant so that they would form a vertical axis. He also allowed the second big ''C'' to drop below its base line so that the words ''Crystal'' and ''Creek'' could fit closely together. A thick rule and two thin ones provide the only art for this elegantly simple design. Chris Berner co-designed and did the mechanical for Rubick & Funk Graphic Communications.

siderations may be a factor. Is the container sanitary? Will it keep the product safe? Materials available include glass, plastic, metal, and paper. A new packaging technique—aseptics—became popular in the 1980s. Aseptics produce boxes made from thin layers of polyethylene, foil, and paper. The boxes hold liquids and keep them fresh for months without refrigeration. Some come with straws attached. Unfortunately, aseptics can't hold carbonated beverages because pressure from the gas breaks the containers.

2. *Shape and size of the vessel.* Sometimes it can provide a service after the product is consumed. Processed-cheese containers, for instance, become drinking glasses.

3. *Nature of the device for opening and closing the vessel.* Sometimes the convenience of such a device makes a difference in how well the product sells.

4. *Design of the label.* The label can become elaborate, even controversial. In 1982 WHB Manufacturing, Tustin, California, introduced Nude Beer featuring a nude woman on the label. It promised a new label each month. Later it brought out a nude man for female beer drinkers.

5. *Shape and design of the package that may house the vessel.* How well will the package ship and stack?

6. *Design of the package enclosure* (if one is needed).

7. *Design and construction of the carton to ship the packages.*

Package design can originate at the company that manufactures the product, at the company's advertising agency, at the place where packages are manufactured, or at a design studio.

A design firm specializing in packages avoids working for competing products. Often its job is to redesign an existing package, holding onto at least something of the original so as not to lose loyal users.

The challenge is to go far enough to make the package compelling but not so far as to make the buyer uneasy. A detergent box, for example, needs to catch the eye but "it can't be *too* bold, go *too* far," said J. Mac Cato of Cato Johnson Inc., New York design firm. "You can't hype the customer. She'll resent it, be offended, turn off. The important thing is that the package wants to be basically likable."[23]

This is the cover of a 4¼″ × 5½″ four-page tag for Castle Mfg., a Corvallis, Oregon, furniture maker. The printing is in gold on a dark blue stock. Designer: Deborah Kadas. Agency: Attenzione!

This front of an envelope/package is one of many designed by Byron Ferris for Boyd's, a food products company. The colors are red (for tomato) and green-gold (for the harvest of vegetables shown surrounding the cup).

Walter P. Margulies, a principal in Lippincott & Margulies, points out that a good package must both create a mood and do a selling job. This is particularly true for highly competitive products—for household cleaners, for instance, which number more than one hundred. Margulies has high praise for Janitor in a Drum's plastic replica of an industrial drum, calling it "brilliant imagery suggesting factory-style strength and reliability . . . being brought to bear on household chores. Even the ribs of the drum serve as more than design reinforcement, making the container easier to heft and control when pouring."

A number of firms specialize in package design, but advertising agencies design packages, too. Certainly they like to be consulted. Advertising agencies like to become involved in package design not so much for the mechanics of how the package works but for its appearance. "We are creative people," said Robert Taylor, group creative director for J. Walter Thompson Co., "and there are times when we can contribute good ideas to a receptive client. We like to be consulted—not because we want things our way, but because it will help us do a better job advertising the finished product."[24]

As a design problem, a package is unique in that it is three-dimensional. The designer is concerned with the package's ability to sell from any one of its six sides (assuming it is a box rather than a cylinder). Each side must be complete in itself, although the main identification and display are reserved for the side most likely to face out from the dealer's shelf.

Before beginning your design project, you should study a lineup of every competing package in order to determine how to make your package stand out. Because the package must appeal to the customer, cater to the display practices of the dealer, and conform to the facilities and needs of the manufacturer, you must sacrifice some desirable features in order to achieve others.

The package should be designed to be easily recognized in reproductions in ads as well as in competition with other packages on the shelf. The customer should be able to walk right to it and pick it out. On one of the panels there must be included a set of basic instructions for the product's use, even though a leaflet is included inside.

"There is no package design on the market today that is not a compromise between cost and taste, between manufacturing and design opinion, between standards imposed by law and what could be original shapes and dimensions," Raymond Loewy observed.

Perhaps the best-looking packages can be found in the ethical drug business, the same business that produces the handsome direct-mail advertising addressed to doctors. Other good-looking packages can be found in the cosmetics and technical and electronics industries. The worst packages, so far as looks are concerned, come from among those produced by food processors and other consumer-goods companies. But these packages can be handsome, too.

One of the important package-design firms, Landor Associates of San Francisco, is responsible for the design of an estimated 30 percent of the packages in frozen food compartments of grocery stores. The red slash on Sara Lee boxes came from the firm, as well as the star on Armour meats.

"Each design [coming from Landor] is a combination of art and psychology, based partly on instinct, partly on research. The design of the package isn't just a way of grabbing the customer's eye as he wheels his cart down the aisle at the supermarket. It may also be a wordless, instantaneous way of telling the customer something about the product. In Landor's trade, that's called positioning the product," wrote a *San Francisco Chronicle* reporter.[25]

Landor Associates tries to bring an informality to its packages to get away from a large-corporation feel. It puts little floral arrangements on bottles and jars. It produces abstractions of birds. If initials are used, they tend to look like personal monograms. Every firm, every product has a personality, the design firm feels. It is up to the designer to find it and dramatize it.

It is possible, though, to overdesign a package. A too arty look for a tool package, for instance, could hurt sales.

Going after the look of nostalgia is popular among package designers because such a look suggests the past, better times, and lasting quality.

How the sides can be coordinated can best be determined by studying other packages. Some boxes use a wraparound design, each of the four main sides carrying a quarter of the basic design. Correctly fitting four boxes together on the shelves, the dealer can build a sort of poster of them.

Some manufacturers with a varied line of products want a design relationship among their packages; others feel that each product represents a unique problem in packaging, and design unity is not important, or that unity can be maintained by simply repeating the company identification mark.

Color in package design may be the single most important factor. People who have bought a product previously go back to the store to look for a green box or a red can or a bottle with a yellow label.

Primary colors appeal to the less sophisticated, pastels or muted colors to the more sophisticated customers. This consideration must be tempered with a consideration of the appropriateness of color to the product. As a package designer, you would rely on available information about psychological reaction to color. White, for instance, suggests purity; silver or gold suggests richness. The brand that first uses a color puts a claim on it. But it is easy for a newcomer brand to use a similar color and cash in on the goodwill the color has built.

Don E. Forest, a partner in Harte Yamashita & Forest, a Los Angeles design firm, says that designers should also be influenced by what colors the competition is using. Where most breakfast-food packages use white,

Two Neiman-Marcus shopping bags, the one on the left in light olive, orange, black, and white; the one on the right in brown and white. A store with Neiman-Marcus's image is sure enough of itself to confine the store name to a small spot on the sides of the bags. (Photo by the author.)

Which came first: the product or the egg? L'eggs assures us it was the product. The packaging concept, the design of the package, and the name were the inspiration of Roger Ferriter of Lubalin, Smith, & Carnase, Inc., a design firm. The idea was to create packaging as well as a product that would stand out from the more than 600 brands then on the market. The egg is said to be nature's most perfect package. The L'eggs version, made of plastic from an injection molding process, gives the hosiery protection from rough handling and moisture. Shown here is a "boutique," a P-O-P unit that both advertises and sells the product.

yellow, and other light colors, a deep brown box may be the best bet for a new product in that category.[26]

Philip Morris introduced a new brand of cigarette in 1983, Players, and put it in a classy black box. The company took something of a risk in going after young, professional smokers with that kind of a box. Black as a package color is considered by many as too somber. But the unusual box was designed to become something of a status symbol.[27]

On any important package job, you would encourage tests to determine customer reaction to mockups before the package goes into final production. A clean-looking design showing half a dozen cookies arranged tastefully around some type may suggest to customers that the package is only partially filled.

Edward H. Breck of John H. Breck has said: "When a single advertisement misfires, or even if a whole advertising campaign turns out to be wrong, you can simply scrap it and then do something else, but when you commit yourself to a packaging decision, usually the investment is so heavy that the penalty for errors can be tremendously costly."

1. Barnard Rudofsky, "Notes on Early Trademarks and Related Matters," in Egbert Jacobson, ed., *Seven Designers Look at Trademark Design* (Chicago: Paul Theobald, 1952), p. 28.

2. Ernst Lehner, *Symbols, Signs & Signets* (Cleveland: World Publishing Company, 1950), p. 119.

3. Isaac E. Lambert, *The Public Accepts: Stories Behind Famous Trade-Marks, Names and Slogans* (Albuquerque: University of New Mexico Press, 1941), p. 168. Frank Rowsome, Jr. retells some of Lambert's stories in his entertaining *They Laughed When I Sat Down: An Informal History of Advertising in Words and Pictures* (New York: McGraw-Hill, 1959); see chapter 7, "The Trademark Menagerie."

4. The term *logotype* or *logo* also applies to the special lettering or typesetting of the name that goes at the top of page 1 of a newspaper or on the cover of a magazine. *Flag* and *nameplate* are other terms also used in this connection.

5. Elwood Whitney, ed., *Symbology: The Use of Symbols in Visual Communications* (New York: Hastings House, 1960), p. 116.

6. J. E. Cirlot's *A Dictionary of Symbols,* 2d ed. (New York: Philosophical Library, 1972), contains a thorough listing of symbols and their meanings. So does Henry Dreyfuss's *Symbol Sourcebook: An Authoritative Guide to International Graphic Symbols* (New York: McGraw-Hill, 1972).

7. Scot Haller, "Checkout Time at the Roach Motel," *New York,* July 9–16, 1979, p. 71.

8. B. G. Yovovich, "In Search of a New Corporate Label," *Advertising Age,* March 7, 1983, p. M-23.

9. Wolf Von Eckardt, "Heraldry for the Industrial Age," *Time,* October 18, 1982, p. 85.

10. See Barbara Knight, "Trademarks Live!" *Journal of The American Institute of Graphic Arts* 16:2–13.

11. Requoted in *New York,* January 26, 1976, p. 48.

12. John Revett, "Corporate Logos Are His Game, Bass Is His Name," *Advertising Age,* January 8, 1979, p. 38.

13. Joan Kron, "Alphabet Scoop," *New York,* January 26, 1976, p. 48.

14. Gertrude Snyder, "Pro-File: Helmut Krone," *U&lc.,* June 1979, p. 13.

15. Mark Muro, "The Man Who Makes Book Covers," *Boston Globe,* March 12, 1983, pp. 20, 21.

16. "On the Record," *Art Direction,* June 1983, p. 43.

17. Dugald Stermer, "Packaging Sound," *Communication Arts,* January/February 1974, p. 20.

18. Ibid., pp. 25, 26.

19. Ibid., p. 51.

20. Ibid., p. 36.

21. Bernice Kanner, "Wrapping It Up," *New York,* June 6, 1983, p. 12.

22. Maxine Brady, *Bloomingdale's* (New York: Harcourt Brace Jovanovich, 1980), p. 110.

23. Quoted by Walter McQuade, "Packages Bear Up Under a Bundle of Regulations," *Fortune,* May 7, 1979, p. 189.

24. Theodore J. Gage, "Agencies Want Involvement, But Only in Design Process," *Advertising Age,* December 17, 1979, p. S-1.

25. Joan Chatfield-Taylor, "Designing the World Around Us," *San Francisco Chronicle,* July 27, 1979, p. 25.

26. Don E. Forest, "Simple Rules for Success in Package Design," *Adweek,* August 23, 1983, p. 26.

27. "High Hopes in a Black Box," *Newsweek,* August 22, 1983, p. 51.

17

Careers

Although graduation may be months away, it is not too early for you to consider getting your "book" ready, as it is called. What follows applies mainly to job hunting by designers, but much of it is applicable to copywriters as well.

Unless you are applying for work with a small agency, do not pose as a person who can do it all. If you want to be an art director, show mostly design. If you want to be a copywriter, show mostly copy.

"I have observed that people claiming both talents are usually hacks," said Carl K. Hixon, executive vice president of Leo Burnett Co., Chicago, "although in some agencies on technical accounts it seems to work well enough for an account executive to double in writing. You would not find this happening in the majors, however, where competition is so hot that mediocre work and people vanish in a puff of smoke."[1]

But feel free to make the point that you offer *some* versatility. Most important, make sure the agency—or store or newspaper—sees that you are interested in selling, not just in impressing people with your talent.

Your goal is to work full-time as an art director or on your own as a freelancer. As the candidate for an art director's job, you may have to work at first in the production department or in the bullpen doing paste-ups. Then you would move to an assistant art director's position, helping one art director or acting as a general assistant to several.

From art director you could expect to go to a creative director's spot or even a vice president's or president's position. Formerly, only writers

Here are four typical designers (or art directors) as seen by the Neenah Paper Division, Kimberly-Clark Corporation, in a whimsical booklet, *How to be a Successful Designer,* published to call attention to the company's paper grades. The designers are, left to right, The Aging Sophomore ("A true design generalist. Finds much to admire in every style and period—hence has no style of his own."); The Mountain Man ("Carries jobs in his back pack."); Boutique Chic ("Only concerned with 'concepts,' so primary working tools consist of two layout pads and Super Colossal 1,000 Color Set of Magic Markers."); and Continental Urbane ("Empty desk suggests that design is generated by magic and genius, not work, because nothing so mundane ever passes over it."). Illustrator Alex Murawski achieved the stipple effect by laboriously putting in each dot with a Rapidograph pen. Creative concept: Sebstad & Lutrey, Chicago. Art director: Tim Lutrey, Copywriter: Brad Sebstad.

or business people moved into those positions, but the art director's role in advertising is seen as being much more important today. And more is required of the art director.

Where the jobs are

It is a good idea to keep in touch with your professors who, in turn, keep in touch with employers. Local ad clubs are also useful for making contacts. You can also watch the classified ad sections of newspapers and the advertising trade press. Narrowing in on a city, you can check out advertising agencies and art and design studios in the Yellow Pages. The *Standard Directory of Advertising Agencies* lists agencies nationwide.

You can find jobs in advertising with any of the following groups:

1. *Advertising agencies.*

2. *The media, including, especially, newspapers and broadcast stations.* They prepare ads for clients who don't have their own advertising departments or agencies.

3. *Advertisers, even when they have agencies.* Some of what they produce, especially direct mail, may be prepared in-house.

4. *Art and design studios.* As specialists, they work with both agencies and clients.

5. *Book publishers.* Although books themselves need *editorial* rather than advertising design, their jackets, if the books are hardbound, and covers, if they're paperbound, need advertising design. Jackets and covers are really posters.

Because they issue so many books—some 45,000 different titles a year—book publishers depend especially on freelance designers. Each book needs its own feel on the jacket or cover. A staff designer is likely to repeat designs. New ideas need to come from outside.

6. *Printers.* As part of their services, some printers, at a price, offer design, illustrations, and even copy to clients who can't easily get these elsewhere. These services apply mostly to direct-mail advertising.

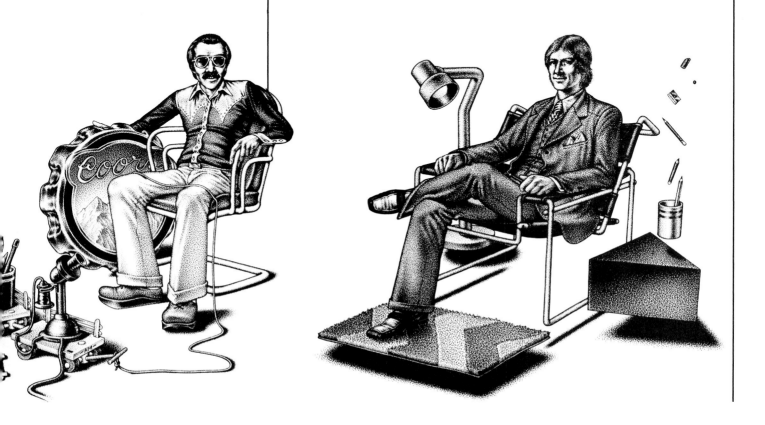

Artist/designer Jean Ening works on a layout. A tabouret at her right holds the tools of design.

Helmut Krone, an art director who became a big name at Doyle Dane Bernbach (and executive vice president), says, "Kids today spend half their lives agonizing over their first move, first job. It doesn't matter; it's how you tackle your work. Stop worrying so much and do *something*."[2]

Jack Summerford, Dallas designer, started out as a layout artist for a department store, "laying out newspaper ads day in and day out. I learned how to use a pencil and how to work fast." Then he worked for an advertising agency, doing tighter layouts and designs as well as mechanicals. His next step was to start his own design studio. He now has two assistants.[3]

Internships

It has become increasingly important in recent years for students to work as summer interns on publications or with agencies or advertising departments before they graduate. Such work not only helps students make important contacts; it also gives them something to put in their resumes. While it is unlikely that an intern working with an art director would create designs right away for major clients, there may be opportunities to do some layouts and pasteups. Just seeing how an agency or studio works is worthwhile.

The nature of the work makes graphic design internships less available than, say, copywriting and production internships. Fewer come into journalism schools and departments. But aggressive and talented students often are able to scout them on their own.

Production entry

A first job for many in advertising is in the production department, where ads, after they are designed, are readied for the printer or the medium to which they are to be sent. Time spent in production will help you become a better—more useful—designer.

A familiarity with production terminology can help you communicate with the printer. The printer's "It can't be done"s will be fewer when it is clear that you understand production. And you will no longer make impossible requests of the printer.

Production experience will help you take advantage of the economies each printing process offers. You will learn to design an advertisement "to fit." When you can't work directly with the printer, as for an ad going into a national magazine, you will consult the appropriate *Standard Rate & Data Service* volume covering that medium and see at once what the mechanical requirements are for the medium. Without an understanding of production, you will not even be able to *read SRDS*.

Production experience will help you prepare materials so they will reproduce at their best. Knowing, for instance, that the halftone process picks up all tones, you will avoid making any marks on photographs, even on the back, for fear they might be picked up as shadows and reproduced as lines or blotches.

With production experience, you will know what kinds of types show up best in the various processes. You will learn, for instance, that some of the Bodoni faces, with their very thin lines contrasting with thicker ones, drop out some of their parts in offset printing, making text matter unreadable. You will learn what types can be reversed in gray areas of photographs.

Appreciating the fact that a printer can hardly be expected to *improve* the quality of a photograph in printing (the printer's cameraman, after all, copies a copy from a negative), you will insist that the starting photograph have enough quality to hold up in copying.

With production experience, you will be infinitely better prepared to handle assignments in direct-mail advertising (discussed in chapter 14). You will make much better use of color in your work (discussed in chapter 10).

And doing pasteups for offset lithography, you will learn more about how printing works.

Knowing computers

David Strong, head of a Seattle-based design studio, says that graphic designers these days have to design ads that communicate. Ads that merely look good won't do.

And when the economy falters, designers must learn to work with less. To keep costs down, they must work faster. "Graphic designers are working in a world that's whirling ever more rapidly. We have to learn to move at that speed."

That means learning to work with a computer. "The computer is going to give us time. . . . I can take a computer and teach it all the facts and figures that I know, and then let it run for 20 minutes by itself. In 20 minutes it will do what would take me hours." And "I might forget something—that's how most of the mistakes in this business are made. The computer doesn't forget."[4]

A computer can help you create charts, graphs, abstract images, illustrations, and animation. It can give a simple drawing an additional dimension and show it from any number of angles. It can also show many design solutions, and you can pick the one that seems to work best. You can design whole pages or complete ads on a computer screen.

The student who understands basic design principles has little trouble applying them to the computer when the time comes to use one.

Preparing the resumé

Like any other job seeker, you will want to prepare a resumé, kept to a single page if possible. Being a designer, your resumé should look better than most others. It can be neatly typed and Xeroxed, but increasingly job seekers are having resumés printed. A printed resumé offers a chance

This is the reception area for a San Francisco agency: Wilton, Coombs & Colnett. The poster at the right was designed for Bay Area Rapid Transit, one of its clients.

for quiet, confident design, based on a grid, perhaps using a few thin ruled lines.

Parallel structure is particularly important. Make sure each heading uses the same grammatical form and that each entry under each heading starts off in the same way. The usual headings are "Personal Details" (optional), "Education," "Work Experience," and "References." You might also want to include "Honors and Awards" after "Work Experience." If you're a "pre-owned car" person rather than a "used-car" person, you might want to change "Work Experience" to "Professional Experience."

Under "Work Experience" include some details about clients and assignments. Leave out nondesign or nonadvertising jobs, or bunch them in a single unit. If you are short on "Work Experience," you could expand the "Education" section to include a description of courses taken in advertising and design and assignments completed.

A number of books tell you how to write resumés and show examples.[5] You might want to keep your resumé distinct from these, but do not make the mistake of making it too clever or cute. Just make it well organized. Your work examples can better show your creativity.

With your resumé should go a cover letter introducing it and elaborating on it, if appropriate. Here is where you offer a paragraph describing your goals. You might also explain why you want to work for the organization. End the letter with a call for some kind of action. Or announce that you will telephone for an interview. Your letter could be a chance to show off a well-designed letterhead.

Maxine Paetro, who hires creative types at Foote, Cone & Belding, told of an offbeat resumé that carried a drawing of a man holding a portfolio. The headline said: "This is an ad for a product that isn't working." The body copy gave the man's name and said that he was looking for his first job. She thought it "effective." But other offbeat resumés have struck her as offensive. One came shaped like a pizza placed with pieces of *real* pizza in a pizza box. It said something about "a slice of life."

Said Paetro: "A tasteful, simple resumé—one that can be scanned

A student's resume, organized to fit a single page, boxed, and printed rather than typed.

Sandi Young's business card, which she designed, uses sign language, "one of the strongest forms of visual communication," to spell out her name. The name is also printed, in red, below. All the other printing is in black. Her letterhead uses the same basic design.

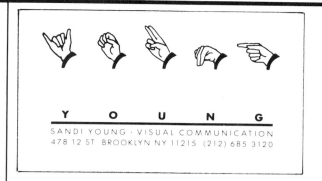

Y O U N G

SANDI YOUNG · VISUAL COMMUNICATION
478 12 ST BROOKLYN NY 11215 (212) 685 3120

quickly, written on, and easily filed, is the best. . . . From where . . . [the job hunter is] sitting, it's mighty tough to judge what's going to be mind-sticking good and what's going to be dumb, tacky or trite. (I've seen about four hundred 'Wanted' poster resumés, for instance.)"[6]

Preparing a portfolio

The beginning designer's chief selling tool is the portfolio. It can be a big zippered case, an attaché case, or a hardboard folder that ties at the top, right, and bottom. The usual size is 14″ × 17″, big enough to show most pieces and small enough to fit under the arm conveniently and open out gracefully on the table of the hiring art director.

What you put into it requires discipline and empathy—discipline to keep the number of pieces to a maximum of twelve to fifteen; empathy to show only pieces that would interest the art director. This would rule out fine-arts pieces that have no commercial application and classroom assignments far removed from anything the art director supervises. What you show in your portfolio would vary from call to call.

You should start building your portfolio while are are still in school, engaging in overkill occasionally for a classroom assignment destined to be included. If you try to produce a lot of pieces especially for your portfolio when you graduate, you will, in your haste, compromise on quality. And you may wander off from reality.

Some job seekers like to create speculative ads for a hiring art director's clients, but this can result in some embarrassments. It is important to know a client's needs before creating the advertising.

The hiring art director likes to see printed pieces. These show that the job seeker knows something about production. The trouble with many printed pieces, though, is that compromises had to be made, more than one person was involved, and the printer made some mistakes. It is not a good idea to point the finger, but you could include your rough layout or comp for a printed piece to show that you were on the right track originally.

How you present your examples makes a difference. Make sure each piece is neat, clean, and protected. Put related pieces together. Figure out an order that builds to something of a climax.

It is a good idea to show a mechanical as well as comps and rough layouts.

Valerie Shaw in the *Los Angeles Times* told of an art school graduate who put her portfolio together as slides, sewed them into a sort of dress, and wore it into the interview with some sort of lighting arrangement underneath. Shaw also told of a copywriter who got an interview with an agency by typing his letter on graph paper and drawing a wavy red line between the typed lines, in the manner of an electrocardiogram. Whenever he mentioned the agency in the letter, or his chances of a job there, he changed the line to fast ups and downs to simulate excitement.

The job interview

In *The Big Time: How Success Really Works in 14 Top Business Careers* (New York: Congdon & Weed, 1983), Glenn Kaplan tells of an advertising copywriter who always wore pinstripe suits when meeting with his client. Once when he was wearing blue jeans at the agency he was called into an emergency meeting with the client, who was apparently pleased with the man's informal dress. "It's good to see you looking like that," the client said. "We were beginning to wonder if you were really creative."

It makes an interesting story, but the truth of the matter is that what a creative person wears in an agency setting does not make much difference to anybody. The ideas for an ad and its execution are what count.

But setting out to find a job, you will want to pay serious attention to what you wear, maybe for the first time in your life.

Art directors tend to dress more informally, even more wildly, than other advertising people, but for a job seeker to come in as a caricature is a mistake. It is better to err on the side of conservative dress. Let the work shown carry the excitement.

Being on time for the interview is important, not only because it shows respect for the hiring art director but also because it establishes the fact that the job applicant is devoted to deadlines. The art director will ask most of the questions; when the questions slow down, the applicant should make an effort to leave. The art director in all probability will want to get back to the drawing board. A half-hour is plenty of time to spend at a first interview.

Follow up your interview with a warm but crisp thank-you letter. If you don't hear from the art director for several weeks, you can send a brief, polite letter of inquiry, maybe including a just-off-the-press sample of your work.

Making the transition

If you thought your design or graphics professor was making too many demands on your time while you were in school, you'll soften your attitude toward school when you are on the outside. There you'll have several jobs going at once, all due yesterday, and right in the middle of one job a client will come in with an entirely new set of instructions.

And designer James Craig has pointed out that "in school, the instructor will accept whatever you do and grade you accordingly. In business, the job is either accepted or it is not. The client is not going to grade your efforts."[7]

What this boils down to is that you should be prepared for a different reception on the outside from what you had in school.

The world of freelancing

As a graphic designer in advertising, you have a choice of working on the staff of an organization or as a freelancer. A staff job offers regular paychecks and a certain amount of security; freelancing offers more excitement but also more frustrations.

As a freelancer, you need a lot of self-discipline, a high degree of self-confidence, and an ability to sell yourself and your work. You need to be able to put yourself in the place of a client or potential client, see and appreciate the design needs, and produce the kind of work that brings the desired results. You need to be able to set prices and keep books.

A freelancer can charge more for a job in advertising than for one used on, say, the editorial side of a magazine, because whatever is paid for the

Jeanine Holly stimulated many phone calls from potential clients and agencies with this folder announcing her services as a freelance copywriter. The copy suggested three tongue-in-cheek advantages she could offer: a money-back guarantee, a freeze on her rates (her "humble contribution to the de-escalation of these depressing, inflationary and inflammatory times"), and a free bottle of Lancers Vin Rosé with any first order for her services ("It makes the bill easier to swallow"). This message was stamped at the bottom: "DIAL 297–1264 NOW! Operators are standing by."

art or design represents but a fraction of the total cost of the ad. Its space in a magazine can run to tens of thousands of dollars, its time on TV to hundreds of thousands.

One answer to the question "What to charge?" might be: whatever the advertiser or agency is willing to pay. Sometimes the employer will mention a figure. "Can you do the job for $250?" In most cases you will set your own rate. It could be by the hour, or it could be by the assignment. Obviously, you will charge less at the beginning because you are less sure of yourself, and you will make more false starts. Furthermore, one of your selling points may be that you are less expensive than established designers, illustrators, or copywriters.

As you become better established, your rates go up.

Whatever you charge, it should be at least as much as a semiskilled working person gets. Twenty dollars an hour for a person with talent is not an unreasonable figure. Pasteup work brings less than design work.

If you must give a price ahead of time, do not underestimate the amount of time involved. And if the job is for a client who demands a lot of your time explaining things and asking for changes, that should be figured in, too.

If you work fast, you might want to avoid hourly rates because you would be working against yourself.

At first you will take any jobs that come along. Eventually you will stay away from jobs that do not pay well enough or that can't be done adequately under the limitations set for them. You will also avoid jobs you don't like doing.

On any one job, you and your client will come to an understanding of what's possible for the price. Often this involves a contract or at least a letter of agreement signed by both of you. You will have to know whether the job calls for camera-ready copy or just a rough or roughs and a comprehensive.

Type and photostatting charges are usually sent directly to the client. If you include them as part of your costs, you would add a 15 percent handling fee.

If selling yourself is distasteful, or if you want to concentrate on what you do best—creating beautiful and useful designs or illustrations—you may want to hire an agent or sales representative. Such an agent usually takes 25 percent of your billings. This compares to the 10 percent taken by literary agents, but what they have to sell are whole books with greater earning potential.

In the beginning you will work out of a studio at home. Then you will rent an outside studio (too many distractions at home and not enough room). Then you will hire a secretary and an assistant or two. You will become a studio head or partner, not just a freelancer.

Working with agencies

A penalty for doing work for an agency is that the agency is always in a hurry. Deadlines are often unreasonable. Charles Saxon, the *New Yorker* cartoonist, does a lot of advertising cartooning but does not like all the rush. Once he questioned an art director about the genuineness of a deadline. "I'm coming in town next Tuesday. Couldn't I bring it in then?"

"Look," said the art director, "if I wanted the job next Tuesday, I would have *called* you next Tuesday!"[8]

Unlike other professionals—freelance writers for magazines, for instance—you work anonymously in advertising. Even as an illustrator you may not be able to sign your work. You ask for high rates in lieu of public recognition for your work.

While the public does not recognize your contribution, the people in advertising do, and often one good piece of work results in other assignments given you by the same advertiser as well as by other advertisers and agencies.

One of the discouraging things about freelancing—and about staff work with an advertiser or agency, for that matter—is subjecting what you do to several layers of critics, many of them uninformed in matters of design and language. To be successful, you will have to master the art of compromise. Sometimes you will decide that your critics are right.

Becoming a specialist

As your career progresses you will, no doubt, begin to specialize. Sometimes the specialty will come about because of an accidental succession of clients. You do a special kind of a job for one; another sees it and requests a similar job.

Sometimes the specialty comes as a result of a talent that leads in a single direction. Adrien Frutiger, a prolific type designer best known for developing a face called Univers, found that in art school he had "a much stronger affinity for abstract designs than for naturalistic or representational ones. And so I discovered that calligraphy and type design are the disciplines in which I can excel."

Frutiger thinks young artists and graphic designers should move into a specialty early: "Focus on one field; our world needs specialists more and more."[9]

Foreign careers

People going to other countries to work in advertising find many adjustments to make. Observed Dick Pruitt, executive creative director for Ogilvy & Mather, Hong Kong, ". . . in a bilingual or 'multi-culture' market, an ad that works for one group can be a disaster if simply back-translated for another." He thinks an "historical weakness" in key Asian markets has been that advertising there has been created by expatriates and the "English headlines are given a literal back-translation by the patient Chinese staff." The result is meaningless advertising.[10]

And if you were to take part in an advertising campaign in Japan, you should know that the attitude of women there about their roles is far different from the attitudes of women in other important countries. In one survey the Japanese Prime Minister's Office on Women's Problems found that 71 percent of Japanese wives believed a woman's place was in the home. In the United States, 34 percent of women accepted this tenet, according to the survey; in Sweden, 13.5 percent.

But the survey also found that in Japanese households nearly 80 percent of the wives controlled budgets—or said they did. That compared to 14.6 percent in the United States.[11]

Working with the client

Designers work differently with their clients. Trusted enough, they don't have to produce tight comprehensives. Jack Summerford shows only loosely executed pencil or marker layouts to his clients.[12]

It's possible to overwhelm the client with choices. Result: indecision and stalemate. And you may find that the one or two fill-out-the-batch roughs are the ones that appeal to the client. They will be the ones you really didn't want to finish. It is better to weed out the designs that don't work well and present only two or three for client selection or approval.

You should be willing, then, to make what changes the client requests. It is the client who is spending the money. Art direction requires com-

DESIGN & CREATIVE SERVICES, INC.
1445 West Rose Suite A, Walla Walla, Washington 99362 509/529-1983

Esprit (ĕ-sprē´), *n.* 1. Spirit, vivacity, sprightly wit. 2. Spirited group of artists, designers and writers offering fresh and professional creative services to clients throughout the Pacific Northwest. 3. Producers of clever, innovative advertisements, brochures, annual reports, etc.
Esprit de corps (ĕ-sprē´ də kôr´), A devotion and common bond of enthusiasm you will develop when you work with Esprit Design on your next creative project.

David Schwantes, launching his new Esprit Design & Creative Services, Inc., at Walla Walla, Washington, sent out this unique announcement card to agencies and printers in the area. His definitions were cleverly tailored to promote the three-person organization. His advice to others starting design studios is to (1) line up an attorney and accountant right away and (2) buy a personal computer with a word processor and business programs.

promises. One of its challenges is to work within what at first appear to be impossible conditions.

And, of course, another challenge is deciding which clients—and which jobs—deserve your attention.

Alexander Woollcott said that "the worst sin of all is to do well that which shouldn't be done at all." Some of the least worthy products get the best design. Like a good lawyer, good design can work for any kind of client.

Designers must constantly make ethical decisions about who to serve and what a design should communicate. As a public service, some designers, without pay, devote after-hours free time to nonprofit clients and causes they can identify with.

Defending design choices

The ability to sell yourself, to exude confidence in your design choices, will do more, perhaps, than anything else to lift you from the ranks of the also-rans to the ranks of the big-name designers. Your confidence develops as your record of successful campaigns grows.

The skeptical client needs reassurance from the designer. The protesting client needs reasons.

In *The Relations Explosion,* William L. Safire discussed that important man in any political campaign, Charlie Regan. "In every headquarters, there is a certain amount of gentle turning down that must be done without offending well meaning volunteers. Horrible campaign songs, meaningless slogans and painful pamphlets are submitted and must be rejected in a way that will not diminish enthusiasm. . . . Strategic delays are necessary." So the campaign manager says, "Sounds great to me, but have you checked it with Charlie Regan?" Or, "I'll give you a firm go-ahead just as soon as Regan gets back." Charlie Regan has a place on the organization charts all right, and there is a sure-enough desk; his raincoat may be draped over a chair or sometimes neatly hung up. But he never seems to get back. When someone calls, he is "down at the printers." The truth is *there is no Charlie Regan.*

" 'The little man who isn't there' is indispensable to any political effort," explained Safire.[13]

Unfortunately, designers have no Charlie Regan. They can't very well put off clients who make what may be unreasonable and impossible suggestions. ("Can you squeeze one more item and price in that blank corner there?" or "Why can't you use some Old English for the headings?") Either designers must defend their layouts or they must make adjustments, however distasteful that may be.

How does one defend an arrangement of elements or a choice of type or art? Is not good layout a matter of taste? When there are disagreements, can designers be sure their tastes are superior to those of the clients?

For each decision made while working on an assignment, the designer formulates a reason for self-assurance if not for client approval. Of course, the rightness and wrongness of the final design *is* a matter of taste, a taste cultivated through hours and then years of observation, study, practice, and experimentation. "It seems to me," said Daniel Berkeley Updike, "that a right taste is cultivated . . . by knowing what has been done in the past and what has been so esteemed that it has lived."

"Your personality shows through in the ads you do," said Amil Gargano, president of the Ally & Gargano agency. "If you're shallow, or dull, or self-indulgent, it shows." Gargano also says that ad makers must be responsive to people. "Don't waste your time in advertising unless you respect people. You can't hide what you are. You're revealed through your work."[14]

When your job is only to supervise the design

In a guest chapter in the first edition of this book, Byron Ferris, a Portland, Oregon, designer, warned that, having mastered the textbook and finished the course in Advertising Layout, the student was not necessarily ready to tackle just any advertising design assignment.

"Indeed," Ferris wrote, ". . . [the student] may himself be able to handle none but the most elementary assignments. As the author has pointed out, the purpose of a course in Advertising Layout offered under other than art school auspices is not so much to train men and women to *do* as to *appreciate* good design.

"Even so, the development of an appreciation of good design is itself a long and involved procedure. A single course in Advertising Layout can be but a beginning. The danger of such a course is that it may build in the student confidence in design judgment not yet justified, not yet tested."

It was Ferris's contention that the ultimate design decisions should remain with the person "most capable of making them—the professional graphic designer or art director."

Ferris was expressing a concern shared by many professional graphic designers. To these men and women it is sometimes better to work with an advertising executive who knows nothing about design and admits it than with one who knows just enough to interfere or who speaks the language but does not understand it.

Ferris's point was well taken.

But there is another side to this. Art directors sometimes allow their enthusiasms to get out of hand. Sid Bernstein once warned against "letting art directors and artists get too far out of their commercial cages." Looking over current ads, he concluded that too many art directors:

1. think that their primary function is to "form a pattern which is pleasing to the eye when observed from a distance of six or eight feet, regardless of its legibility at normal reading distance";

2. fail to use black type on white paper and use, instead, "grey type on oatmeal paper";

3. design coupons too small to fill out.[15]

Bernstein is kidding here to some extent, but his warning is worth considering. The design buyer must realize, too, that among the best salespersons in the advertising business are those who do design work on a freelance basis: the professional graphic designers. Their product is their preferred style, taste, or solution to a communication problem. Their enthusiasm is not always easy to resist. In the face of this enthusiasm, the buyer must continue to consider how well the design performs its job for the advertiser.

Campbell-Ewald, Detroit, dramatizes the variety of its clients in this "company car" drawing by Ron Rae used in an ad in *Advertising Age*. To do the job the illustrator had to let a few products hang outside the car and go to a partial cutaway for others. The pointing lines make this art as much a diagram as a cartoon drawing. The accompanying copy made the point that Campbell-Ewald is "a broad and balanced agency, qualified to perform in a variety of markets."

The inside three panels of a self-promotion folder for Bronson Leigh Weeks, a Portland advertising agency with a reputation for lively design as well as good copy. "Playing it safe is not our style." "The Works" is one of a series, each with its own title.

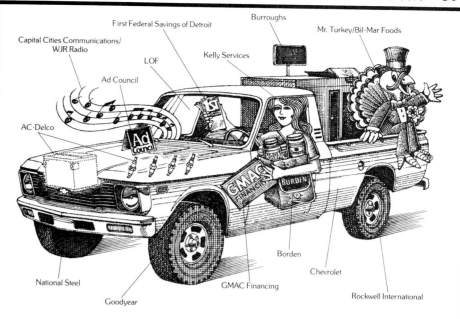

Effective design is hard to prove. A professional designer may win out in an ad manager–designer skirmish, not necessarily because the designer is right, but because the designer is persuasive.

The long-range success of the design-buyer–design-supplier relationship depends upon mutual understanding and cooperation. Design buyers must learn to reject when rejection is necessary but also to defer to sounder judgment than their own, however rare that occasion may be.

1. Carl K. Hixon, *What Every Young Account Executive Should Know About the Creative Function,* Part 1 (New York: American Association of Advertising Agencies, 1979), p. 3.

2. From an ad sponsored by the *Wall Street Journal, Advertising Age,* May 16, 1983, p. 18.

3. "Jack Summerford," *Communication Arts,* September/October 1983, p. 32.

4. Candace Dempsey, "Designers: Don't Miss the Boat!" *Monthly News of the Northwest Advertising Industry,* September 1982, p. 11.

5. Two recent ones are Tom Jackson, *The Perfect Resumé* (New York: Anchor Press/Doubleday, 1981) and J. I. Biegeleisen, *Job Resumés,* revised edition (New York: Putnam Publishing Group, 1982).

6. Maxine Paetro, *How to Put Your Book Together and Get a Job in Advertising* (New York: Executive Communications, 1979), p. 42.

7. James Craig, *Graphic Design Career Guide* (Watson-Guptill, New York, 1983), p. 135.

8. Told by Mort Walker in *Backstage at the Strips* (New York: Mason/Charter, 1975), p. 102.

9. From a page devoted to Adrien Frutiger in James Craig's *Graphic Design Career Guide* (New York: Watson-Guptill, New York, 1983), p. 110.

10. Letter to the author from Dick Pruitt, June 30, 1983.

11. Bruce Roscoe, "Male Dominance Prevails in Japan," *Los Angeles Times,* July 14, 1983, Part V, p. 10.

12. Summerford, p. 32.

13. William L. Safire, *The Relations Explosion* (New York: Macmillan, 1963).

14. "Go, Gargano!" ad sponsored by *Wall Street Journal, Advertising Age,* August 22, 1983, pp. 12, 13.

15. Sid Bernstein, "Keep Them Graphic Artists in Check!" *Advertising Age,* February 27, 1978, p. 16.

Assignments

1. The advertising world

Assignment 1. Search through newspapers and magazines to find examples (one each) of national, retail, mail-order, trade, industrial, professional, and institutional advertising. Evaluate the copy approach and design of each.

Assignment 2. Tom Rubick, designer and teacher, uses this assignment to start off his Advertising Layout classes: From a single issue of your local newspaper, pick out an ad that you think is poorly designed and another that you think is well designed. Bring them to class and be prepared to explain why you feel as you do about the ads.

Pick out ads that are rather large (a quarter-page or more) and are similar in size.

Assignment 3. Clip the following from magazines: a seven-word headline; a block of copy 2″ wide by 3″ deep; a printed photograph 3″ by 4″ (vertical or horizontal); a piece of line art occupying a space no bigger than a 2″ square; and a signature. (Do not waste time hunting for pieces that are the exact size; pick pieces larger than necessary and trim them to size.) Arrange these elements in a rectangle 6″ wide by 9″ deep. Move them around into as many formations as you can; then settle on one.

Seeing how your fellow students solve the same problem, you will be surprised at the variety of arrangements possible even with so many restrictions spelled out.

Assignment 4. For this assignment and others to follow, you might want to skip ahead in the textbook and read chapter 4, "Layout Tools and Techniques."

A square (or rectangle), a triangle, and a circle are the three basic shapes a designer works with. What do they symbolize to you? Create an ad using as *the only art* a filled-in square (or rectangle) with a headline that refers to the art. Do the same for the triangle and the circle. These three ads should be 8½″ × 11″ rough sketches, all for different clients of your choosing, with the art occupying whatever proportion of the space you think is appropriate.

An example of the kind of ad you could come up with: The American Heart Association shows a ¼″ diameter circle with this headline: "A Blood Clot the Size of This Dot Can Cause a Heart Attack."

Assignment 5. Sanity Enterprises, Inc., New York, puts out something called an "Anger Banger," a high-impact absorbent pad in a booklike case. The harried executive simply opens the "book" and pounds away with a fist, easing tension that has built up.

It's not an entirely serious or needed product; at $10 it is probably more a gift item than anything else.

The case is covered with a suedelike material and has the words "Anger Banger" centered on its face.

Design an ad 4¾″ wide by 5″ deep for a magazine like *New York,* using the headline "For Fast Relief, Punch the Pad," and include a coupon (this is mail-order advertising) and some photographic art of your choosing plus a copy block of about 130 words.

At this point in the course your layout can be very rough.

2. The creative process

Assignment 1. Here is an in-class exercise used by Professor Robert M. Anservitz of the University of Georgia School of Journalism to help copywriting students build "adjective banks" and develop "a more incisive awareness of the roles shape, color and texture" play in the identification of objects:

One to three students leave the room; then a relatively common item is brought out and shown to the remaining students. They take three to five minutes to write down descriptions. (The descriptions cannot mention the function of the item.) The instructor then puts the item back out of sight and calls in the students who left the room. Using only descriptions (adjectives or adjective phrases) furnished by their classmates, the returning students individually but simultaneously draw the item at the blackboard. The exercise ends when one of the returning students figures out what the item is.

Assignment 2. Study the several early examples of advertising shown in the opening two chapters and, taking one of them, adopt its basic design and create a new ad that could appear in today's media. Do whatever updating you feel is necessary, but don't lose too much of the early feel. Let your ad wallow in nostalgia.

Your product is Bayer Aspirin, and you have a vertical one-third of an 8½″ × 11″ magazine page available to you. Black only.

Assignment 3. You still see them: those amateurish efforts by local media using the advertising trade press to reach media buyers in national advertising agencies. "You're Only HALF COVERED in Nebraska. . . . Without Lincoln-Hastings-Kearney" says a headline in an ad sponsored by KOLN-TV, Lincoln, and KGIN-TV, Grand Island. Maybe you can guess what the art is. An orchestra conductor without his pants, which apparently he has forgotten to wear.

Take a TV station or newspaper in your hometown and see what you can come up with as an appeal to media buyers who probably know nothing about the medium. What can you say about it that would convince media buyers it is a good medium for the agency's clients? Work up a series of rough sketches of ads. Then narrow in on one and finish it off as well as you can. The ad would appear in *Advertising Age.* You make the space decision.

Assignment 4. Do rough layouts for two different 6″ × 2⅜″ ads (width comes first when measurements are given) for a photography studio about to buy space in the Yellow Pages. Make one ad appeal to a sophisticated audience, the other to an audience likely to be swayed by hard sell. This means you would use two different styles of design.

What will you feature? That is up to you. Assume that the studio does all kinds of work: wedding shots, portraits, passport photos, family and group shots, school pictures, commercial work. You would not have to mention all of these in both ads.

Look at current Yellow Pages ads to see how *not* to do your ad. Probably you should include a photograph with your headline and a small amount of body copy.

Make up a name for the studio.

Indicate to your instructor which one of your two ads works best for the studio and tell why.

Assignment 5. Let us say that your college is feeling the pinch: fewer students are enrolling because there are fewer students out there. The situation is serious because it costs about as much to run a half-empty college as one that is filled. So the college is going to do some advertising.

For a regional magazine or for a regional edition of a national magazine, design three 2¼″ × 9½″ ads—deep, one-column ads—that position your college against the others in your area. Stress its strengths—or at least one of its strengths—and try to recruit some new students: recent or about-to-be-graduated high school students as well as people who have been out of school for a while.

Perhaps you will want to deal with the fact that going to your college will make people more employable in desirable jobs. Or maybe you will want to say that the education will make students better rounded, better able to cope with and enjoy life. Maybe in one of your ads you will want to appeal to college dropouts. You can deal with part-time or full-time possibilities.

Write the headlines and leave room for copy. Design ads (in rough layout form) that in each case make use of some art (whatever you think is appropriate). Let each ad make a different point. Keep them related. Do not use color.

3. Putting it into words

Assignment 1. Gary Anderson, a printmaker and designer, has toyed with the idea of putting out a line of infantwear—in basic black. He would call his line Uncle Gary's Black Baby Clothes.

Assuming a complete line, possibly even including diapers, work out a copy approach—it could be humorous—for upper-middle-class parents (and relatives) and write some copy (any reasonable length) and suggest art. The ad would appear as a full page in magazines.

Assignment 2. Select a nonprofit organization you can identify with and familiarize yourself with it. It can be a religious, educational, health, ecological, trade, or political organization. Pick a cause it espouses and do some research into that cause. Then write an all-copy ad on the subject, making a single major point, and do it without being preachy. End with the notation: "For further information write to . . ." or something similar.

Type out your copy on regular sheets of typing paper, doublespacing it, and keeping it at three or four pages. Doublespace between lines as you would for any copy written for publication. Write the headline and several subheads (headlines within the copy at natural breaks). Do not bother to do a layout for this assignment.

Assignment 3. Professor Willis L. Winter, Jr., as an assignment for his Advertising Copywriting class, asks students to pick out a current ad they greatly admire and write the next ad in the series.

You now have the assignment. Pick an ad that is the current one in a series and study it. Then work up *your* ad, continuing the theme or introducing a new theme. Write both the headline and the copy. Do a quick rough, too, to show what kind of art and design you have in mind. (Your new ad should bear a family resemblance to the existing ad.)

Assignment 4. One of the copywriter's main jobs is to organize material into a logical, easy-to-follow sequence. This would include the writing and arranging of subheads for a direct-mail piece.

Let us say that you are helping put together a folder promoting landscape architecture as a career. The cover carries the not very original title: "So You Want to Be a Landscape Architect!" Good enough, unless you can come up with something better. The inside panel carries the main subtitle "Career Opportunities" and this set of sub-subtitles: "Self-Employed," "Forest Service or BLM," "Teaching," "Architects or Engineers," "Cities and Counties," "Nursery," "College," "Start Early," "High School," and "Experience." Quite a hodgepodge.

See if you can reorder these headings, rewriting some of them, perhaps even dropping some and adding others. Keep the idea of parallel structure in mind.

Then relist them in outline form, showing which should be main subtitles and which should be sub-subtitles. Keep to three levels of importance, including the main title of the folder, which, of course, would be the top level.

Presumably, under each subtitle would be some copy and possibly some art, but you can skip all that. This is simply an exercise in making headings clear.

If possible, consult a landscape architect or a landscape architect major to see if your listing covers all bases.

4. Layout tools and techniques

Assignment 1. Pick out a full-page black-and-white ad from a consumer magazine and a newspaper ad the same size or larger and trace them, taking great care to show graduation of tones. Bear down on the pencil when you trace your headlines, keeping them as near to black as you can. Indicate body copy by ruling parallel lines. If in a copy block you find some boldface type, try

to show this in your tracing. When you have finished, put the originals with your tracings and decide for yourself how close you came to a faithful rendering.

Assignment 2. Do three 2-col. × 8″ and one 4-col. × 15″ ads promoting your local newspaper's classified ads.

The ads will be run at two-day intervals in the sponsoring paper (not in the classified section), small ones first. Use art in each ad. Letter in the headlines; indicate the body type in the usual way. You do not have to write the copy, but your roughs should indicate copy approach.

Points you may want to cover: minimum words accepted in classified, rate per word, deadline for copy. The classified advertising manager is interested in plugging especially the Lost and Found, Houses for Sale, Personals, and Miscellaneous for Sale sections.

Tie your series together so that the reader will see a relationship.

The final ad could be summary in nature. Or you could plan a teaser campaign, using the last ad as the focus.

Your layouts can be very rough. Your client in this case does not need pampering.

Assignment 3. If you had an original painting or a print you were particularly fond of, would this ad convince you that the Eugene Frame Co., with framing as its only business, *has* to be better than the competition? Redesign the ad, making it reflect the fact that this is a quality picture-framing shop. Include the Visa insignia. Indicate body copy by using ruled lines. Keep the ad the size it is here. Use black only.

Assignment 4. The Bettendorf, Iowa, public library, when it was to move to a new building, asked patrons to make a special effort to check out books at the old library and return them to the new. If each of the more than eighteen thousand cardholders checked out 3.4 books, the director figured, all sixty-five thousand books could be moved without having to hire the job done. The library would save an estimated $1000.

Assume that you have drawn the assignment to design a 5½″ × 8½″ sheet, to be printed on one side in a single color, horizontal or vertical, that will be passed out to patrons during the month before the move. The piece would urge patrons to participate and to get other cardholders to participate, too. Rough in the elements your ad would contain. Plan to include one small piece of art.

5. Layout stages and formats

Assignment 1. Although it would be difficult to improve upon Henry Wolf's design for the Olivetti ad shown in this chapter, let us use it as a starting point for an exploration into the possibilities of the various layout formats. He uses a "frame layout" for his ad. Take the basic information from his ad and try doing nine thumbnail roughs—one each for the remaining formats described in the chapter: "Mondrian," "picture-window," "copy-heavy," "circus," "multipanel," "silhouette," "big-type," "rebus," and "alphabet-inspired." Use real headlines, if they suggest themselves to you; otherwise, just scribble down some zigzag lines. These thumbnails can be very rough, and should be black and white.

Do them in a size that would, when blown up to full size, occupy a full page in a magazine like *Time.* Be sure your thumbnails are kept in correct proportions. Make them all the same size and arrange them neatly on one page of your layout pad. You might want to do several of each format and cut out the best ones and paste them down on another sheet. Label each of the thumbnails as to format so your instructor will not have to guess.

Assignment 2. Pick any one of the other thumbnails in this chapter showing various ad formats and, quadrupling the size, do a rather finished rough layout, substituting real words (of your choosing) for the display type and real art (you decide what the ad is to sell) for the crude art shown. Make whatever adjustments you think necessary, but try to capture the feel of the thumbnail.

Assignment 3. You are working for a newspaper's display advertising department, and you are about to pitch a new account: Evergreen Tree Spray Service, Inc. Do a rough layout (or comp, if you wish) for this outfit, on speculation, carrying the following information (it does not have to be worded like this): "In business since 1947. Radio-dispatched trucks. Same-day service in most cases. Modern equipment and methods. Free estimates by phone. Call 313-5005. One-time service or contract-service available. Topping, pruning, trimming, removals, fertilizing, root and leaf feeding, poison oak and poison ivy control, insect and disease control." Maybe you can come up with a good theme and an inviting headline.

The ad will be 6¼″ wide by 8″ deep. You should letter in the headlines and any subheadlines, but you should use ruled lines for the smaller type. Include a logo and any art you think appropriate.

6. Applying the principles of design

Assignment 1. The Virginia Division of Industrial Development paid $50,000 to two nationally known research organizations to make a study of its prime water sites for industry. Now it wants to make the study available to industrial firms who might want to locate in the commonwealth.

It will buy space in *Chemical Week* and other trade journals likely to be read by industrial executives. The ad, in black and white, will occupy two-thirds of a page, or a space 4½″ × 10″. A copywriter offers this headline: "Get a $50,000 Water Study for 20¢" (or whatever a first-class stamp costs at the time you do the assignment).

Do a rough layout to include the headline, about seventy words of copy, a coupon, and a picture of the book containing the study: *Virginia Prime Water Sites for Industry.* Try to put the principles of good design to work.

Assignment 2. Do a 1-col. × 1″ ad for a new correspondence cartoon course. The ad will run in black and white in *Popular Mechanics.*

The school is North American School of Cartooning, P.O. Box 678, your town. The course, written by a "well-known cartoonist," features thirty-six lessons. It stresses today's techniques (other courses are somewhat dated in style) and current markets for car-

toons. It takes a practical approach. But there is no individualized instruction. Purpose of the ad is to get inquiries. The price ($49.95) and other details will be covered in follow-up direct mail, which you are not designing.

See if you can work some kind of cartoon illustration into the ad along with the information you think is vital. You cannot do much, of course, in so small a space. This is the challenge of the assignment.

If you wish, you may do your rough in a larger size, but in proportion to the printed size. Make your rough reasonably comprehensive. Keep your lines and type strong enough to take the reduction.

Assignment 3. The ad for The Colonnade shown in chapter 6 was one of a series of five. Design the other four, making them related to each other in size and appearance. You do not need to stick to the same typeface for the headlines. And you can use Greeking for the headlines if you wish. This is not a copywriting assignment.

The caption for the ad shown tells you what should be featured in each of the remaining ads.

These should be in black and white, and they can be in rough form. But indicate art clearly enough so that you can develop a tie between headlines and art.

Assignment 4. Silhouette Books announced a new line in 1983: a series of romances for "wholesome people who have made a commitment to God." The books were to appear in regular bookstore outlets as well as religious bookstores. Assume that the publisher will be doing advertising in religious magazines to announce the series. Design a full-page ad (no color) for the *Christian Herald* and similar magazines that tells about the series, using an "At Last!" approach. Instead of featuring a particular title, the ad will name and perhaps show several representative titles. (You may make up the book titles, but that exercise would be only incidental to this assignment.)

Feature price; these will be mass-market paperbacks, of course. Come up with a good headline, and indicate copy in the usual way. You need not write the copy.

7. Working with type

Assignment 1. From a type-specimen book pick an old-style roman alphabet, a modern roman alphabet, and a sans serif alphabet in 36-point size and trace the letters (both caps and lower case) and numbers with a sharp pencil. Use the fill-in method, being careful to show how the letter strokes join one another and how serifs fit. Before you begin tracing, draw in some light guidelines.

This exercise, although tedious, will familiarize you with how each of the letters in the major type faces is constructed.

Assignment 2. Take any one of the three original alphabets in assignment 1 and trace the letters to form this headline (all on one line): "It's a Matter of Life and Breath." Use caps and lower case or all lower case. This time you will be making decisions about letter and word spacing.

Assignment 3. Take another of the alphabets and, using it merely as reference, *hand letter* the headline, increasing (by eye) its size to about 60 points and breaking it into three lines.

Assignment 4. A number of packages and book jackets have featured display lettering built of cartoon animals or people, bent and combined, sometimes with props, to spell out words. An example is the lettering on Meow Mix, a cat food.

See what you can do with Wheatreats, a good tasting and nutritious breakfast food (fictitious) in flake form marketed mainly for children. Use happy, healthy looking children to build your all-cap letters. Use single figures when possible, but use two (or more) in combination when necessary. Throw in a prop or two if you have to.

Perhaps you can benefit from seeing how three students handled this assignment. These delightful solutions are by (from the top) Margaret Laine, Cheryl Frederickson, and Bev Fisher. In

constructing your letters, you might want to make the figures heavier and more abstract than these so that they will show up more obviously as letters.

8. Working with art

Assignment 1. Looking through current advertisements in magazines, find examples of six—any six—of the art styles listed in the chapter. Tell why you think the styles are appropriate to the advertisements.

Assignment 2. The campaign booklet mentioned in one of the captions in chapter 3 had a spread (not shown) that said the candidate wanted to "bring the people of Fort Wayne together. . . ." The headline for this spread said, "To Get Fellowship You Need Leadership." The art for the spread showed six representative citizens of Fort Wayne, arms crossed to hold hands with persons on either side. The people, standing erect, smiling, were looking into the camera. The art, bleeding left and right, united the two pages.

Let us assume that you have the assignment of picking models for this shot. Remember, you have room for six persons. What kind of persons would you pick? How many of the six would be male, how many female? Would the division necessarily be three and three? How many of the six would be representatives of minority groups? How many would be from the professional class? How many from the working class?

Make a rough layout showing the people and their manner of dress. A photographer will use your sketch as a guide. The art is to fit into a space 14″ wide by 10″ deep. Leave a little less than half the space for copy.

Assignment 3. Consider the following qualities that could be attached to organizations and see if you come up with an idea for a symbolic picture for each:

well established	sturdy
trustworthy	progressive
vigorous	conservative
prompt	friendly
considerate	fast growing

Sketch out and label your ten symbolic pictures. Do not worry about how well drawn they are. Use stick figures and other shortcuts. If necessary, include descriptions so your instructor will understand your drawings. For this assignment the ideas are much more important than the renderings.

It might help to have a specific organization in mind, such as a bank or utility. Indicate this to your instructor.

You do not have to design any ads. Just draw the symbols.

Assignment 4. Pick out any quote from any book of quotations and come up with an illustration idea. Rough it out. Have in mind either halftone or line art. It may be a photograph or drawing. You will be graded on your concept, not on how well you have drawn your art. But do *design* the art. Consider its composition. Be sure to include the quotation with what you submit to your instructor.

Assignment 5. You're designing an ad for Varig Brazilian Airlines and the Brazilian Tourism Authority to encourage a vacation in Rio and Brazil. You'll point to a low-price airfare and hotel package, and you'll play up the "world famous Copacabana and Ipanema beaches" and the night life in Rio, a city that "gets hotter at night." The ad, in color, will cover two pages in an 8½″ × 11″ travel magazine published in the United States.

You may use any or all of the photos on the next pages (they were taken by Steve Lorton, a magazine editor and writer). You may crop them, if you wish, and of course you can change their sizes. Assume that they are available in both color and black and white. Two of the photos involve dancers at an annual Rio carnival. The third photo shows a woman in Bahia selling street food. Another photo shows an outdoors "dress shop" in Bahia; another shows Bahia boys pausing in their play.

Pick the photo or photos that will work best for you and add others, if you wish. Work out a theme and headlines and include a coupon in your ad for readers who will want to send for further information. You may want to read about Brazil in an encyclopedia before doing your ad.

What you'll turn in to your instructor will be a rough layout.

9. What the designer should know about production

Assignment 1. Find an example of (1) offset lithography, (2) letterpress, (3) gravure, and (4) silk-screen printing. Examine each under a magnifying glass (8-power, if possible), looking especially at the reproduction of the type, and describe the differences in the blackness and crispness of the printing.

Assignment 2. Buy a sheet of press-on or dry-transfer letters in a 24- or 36-point size and, using caps and lower case, set the name of the course you are now taking.

Assignment 3. Take a headline from one 8½″ × 11″ (full page) magazine ad, a piece of art (photo or illustration) from another, a block of copy from another, and a logo from still another and paste them down on an 8½″ × 11″ sheet as though you were preparing camera-ready copy. Be exact in your placement. Neatness counts. While this is an assignment in doing a finished pasteup, and will be graded on that basis, try to create a good design.

10. Working with color

Assignment 1. A few years ago the *Wall Street Journal* reported an upsurge in sales of a product called "Bag Balm," which farmers had used as an ointment for cows with scratched or irritated udders since 1908. The upsurge at first puzzled company officials, because, apparently, the cow population was down from what it had been. It turned out, according to the *WSJ* story, that hippies and other adventurous people were using the product as a cheap and effective treatment for their own minor cuts and scratches. Some doctors had been recommending the product.

In 1983 Charles Kuralt discovered Bag Balm and featured it on his "On the Road" TV show.

Although officially extending the product's market to include human use might involve legal, packaging, and perhaps even manufacturing problems, let us assume, for the sake of this assignment, that the manufacturer has taken care of these matters and intends to capitalize on the new use and to launch an advertising campaign encouraging it. And the campaign will be directed to the middle classes.

Your job is to turn out a full-color, full-page ad for *Family Circle* and similar magazines to announce the "new" product. Let us assume that the company will not change the product itself (including its turpentine smell) or its container (a metal can with a drawing of a cow's udder on the side, as shown in the rough sketch nearby). Let us further assume that the company does not intend to cover up the fact that the product has long been used for animals.

You may want to play the assignment straight. Or you may want to have some fun with it. The client is open minded—so long as the advertising increases the market base.

Work out your theme, write your headline, and decide what you want for art. It will be necessary to show the container (about the size of a three-inch cube, with a lid that lifts off and pushes back on), but if you do not want to show the udder, you can change the viewing angle. Indicate the copy block in the usual way. Do your comp in full color. The container is in magenta, dark green, light green, and white.

Assignment 2. Until the 1960s the Hershey Chocolate Corporation did no national consumer advertising—at least it did none in the United States. Now it does do some. Assume you have drawn the assignment to design a full-page, full-color ad for *Boys' Life* promoting both the plain and almond candy bars. Do a comp. The idea for selling the bars and the appropriateness of the ad to the medium are important parts of this assignment.

Assignment 3. Redesign the black-and-white "Get Cracking" ad reproduced in chapter 5 to make use of a second color (your choice). Double the size of the ad to bring it closer to its original size.

11. Newspaper advertising

Assignment 1. It would be hard to imagine an advertisement more poorly designed than the one on page 379. It ran as a full-page, two-color ad in a newspaper. You may find it instructive as an example of the violation of nearly every rule of good graphic design.

Redesign it. Do a rough layout in full newspaper size, finished enough so that the account can read the headlines, understand the art, and see where the art goes. Hold onto all those elements you think necessary. Use black and any appropriate second color.

Assignment 2. You have your afternoon cut out for you. You are working in the display advertising department of a medium-size newspaper, and you have three ads to knock out before closing time. The ads can be pretty rough. (Your grade will be based partly on the quality and appropriateness of your work and partly on speed. Indicate at the bottom of your roughs how much time you spent on each.)

a. The Organic Terrace, a health food store in your town, is celebrating its first anniversary with a 20 percent markdown on all items in the store. The prices will remain in effect for one week. Do an ad that would occupy about 30 column inches in the local newspaper. (This means the ad can be 2-col. by 15″, 3-col. by 10″, or 4-col. by 7½″.)

Include some art in your rough layout. Indicate where headlines and copy are to go, but do not bother to do any of the writing. Show where the logo and slogan go. The ad will be in black and white.

b. Music City U.S.A., your town, a chain of music stores, is clearing out some floor samples: stereo consoles and component sets, Zenith and Admiral brands, traditional and modern styles.

In an ad occupying roughly 60 column inches (you choose the shape of the ad), announce the clearance and show some sample sets. Play prices big—but use 000s. (Exact figures can be filled in at the last minute.)

Show where headlines and copy go—but do not bother writing them. The logo is an expanded script. Make sure you include a store address. The sale is for three days only.

c. This medium-quality men's store, which happens to bear your last name (_____ 's Men's Wear), has just received a shipment of the new season's suits, sport coats, and slacks. It plans to place a 5-col. × 16″ ad in the local newspaper to sell style and brand rather than low price. (This will not be a "sale" ad.) You decide the items to be featured.

Use a good newsy headline and a little bit of opening copy; leave enough room for a description of each item you feature.

Assignment 3. Do these two newspaper "shop roughs," limiting yourself to twenty minutes for each one:

a. An ad, 40 to 50 column inches, any shape, for Coolside Swimming Pools Co., 156 Whirl Blvd., your city. You are selling all-concrete swimming pools, $4,995, installed, with labor and materials. Easy terms. Make up a headline and dream up a drawing.

b. An ad, 1-col. × 2″, for Chandler Travel Agency, Inc., 1450 Broadway, your city. The client wants to remind local newspaper readers it can handle any travel problem, business or pleasure; and the customer pays nothing more than regular transportation prices.

Assignment 4. Maybe someone will do it someday, but it probably is not a practical idea. Nevertheless it might be interesting to come up with a theme and to design an ad for a new kind of shoe store. (Come up with a name for the store, too.)

It is a store that sells shoes singly, so that people with feet of different sizes can be properly fitted: maybe a 9B for the left foot and a 9½B for the right. If you want to get playful, you could mention that peg-legged people can get by on half of what they'd pay elsewhere. This would also be the preferred store for three-legged people.

People who tend to wear out one shoe before the other (stick-shift drivers who do a lot of clutching with their left foot) might be sold on buying two left-foot shoes to go with one right.

Use a second color in designing your half-page newspaper ad announcing the new store. Mention brand names and competitive prices.

Assignment 5. On the next page you will see some illustrations taken from a single issue of Metro Newspaper Service.

Pick out at least five of the illustrations and put them together in a 6⅝″ wide × 13″ deep ad for a department store conducting a preseason (or postseason, if more appropriate) sale on summer furniture and on patio, backyard, and outdoor accessories.

This is what you must feature in the ad:

a. Redwood picnic table with four benches, cushioned redwood lounge chair and club chair, and table.

b. Wrought-iron love seat, club chair, and table (in white).

c. Redwood-stained wood-frame sandbox with floral-print vinyl canopy (ready to assemble).

d. Folding director's chair with hardwood frame and removable cotton canvas seat and back.

e. Patio seat cushions with floral-print vinyl covers.

f. Backyard screen house with aluminum roof (ready to assemble).

g. Portable, folding grill.

h. Children's gym set with tubular-steel frame.

i. Sand chair (choice of red and white or green and white webbing).

Whether or not they are pictured, all of these items should be mentioned in the ad. You might want to consider putting the non-pictured items into some kind of list, and you can add other items to that list if you wish. All of the items are marked down an average of 20 percent. (You can use 000s for prices; this is only a rough layout.)

Trace your art directly from the book. Note that you have both highlight halftone and line art to indicate. Do not change any of the sizes. But you can rearrange and cluster the pieces to overcome their sameness. Put code numbers for the art out in the margins.

Write a main headline and indicate an opening copy block that introduces the sale. Letter in other headlines and prices, too, and indicate short bits of copy to describe the merchandise. Play up prices.

5917 APR'76 M.P. 39

5810 APR'76 M.P. 35

5920 APR'76 M.P. 39

5806 APR'76
M.P. 35

5813 APR'76 M.P. 35

5915 APR'76 M.P. 39

5921 APR'76 M.P. 37

5918 APR'76 M.P. 39

5812
APR'76 M.P. 36

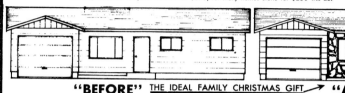
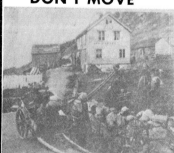

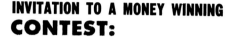

Do not forget to include the name of the store.

Do all of this rather roughly. It is the organization of available material that is important in this assignment, not the rendering.

12. Magazine advertising

Assignment 1. Pick out a brand-name ad in a consumer magazine and pretend it has not run yet. Do an ad for a trade magazine going to dealers likely to handle the product. Tell the dealers about the coming ad campaign and urge them to ready themselves for the demand that will surely follow.

Assignment 2. Pick out a TV commercial or campaign currently showing, but one that, so far as you know, has no magazine advertising follow-up or tie in, and do an appropriate magazine ad. Use a key frame from the commercial, or the theme, or a main character—anything that will extend the effectiveness of the commercial. Your ad—any size—will appear in a consumer magazine of your choosing. Because the commercial is in color, the magazine ad will be in color.

Assignment 3. Take an existing full-page magazine ad and redesign it to fit two other sizes: (1) a one-column ad and (2) a two-page ad. Hold onto the same elements, and keep the same mood. You may enlarge, condense, and rearrange the elements, and, if necessary, you may recrop the art.

Assignment 4. The Patented Products Corp., Danville, Ohio, relies on word-of-mouth advertising to sell its Electric Bedwarmer, an item made from two sheets sewn together with coated copper wire woven into the stitching. It differs from an electric blanket in that it goes under rather than over the sleeper. It is said to give more even heat, to waste less heat because the heat that rises is trapped by a blanket, and to use about half the electricity an electric blanket uses. Like a heating pad, it soothes aches and pains.

It comes in six sizes.

Assume that the company, which sells by mail, is going into magazine advertising. Pick out a magazine you think would be a good medium for this advertiser and design a less than full-page ad for it in black and white. Include a coupon. You will have to figure out a copy approach and write a headline. But do not write the copy. Just indicate copy with the usual ruled lines. In slightly bigger than body-copy type, a line should say that "Prices start at $_____" (make up a figure).

Assignment 5. Until recently, marketing adult diapers for the incontinent has been done through ads likely to be read by doctors and hospital and nursing-home managers. Let's assume that Procter & Gamble Co. wants to sponsor a series of small-space ads for Attends in magazines likely to be read by ordinary people taking care of their aging parents and others who might need the product.

Work up a theme for a series of three 2¼″-wide by 3″-deep ads and design them, incorporating a bit of related art in each. Include a toll-free number for ordering; the packages of diapers will be sent by mail.

13. Broadcast advertising

Assignment 1. Pick one of the photoboards shown in this chapter and do a *storyboard* for it. (What you're doing here is retracing some steps.)

Assignment 2. Do a storyboard for a thirty-second commercial for a new door-to-door cosmetics line called Marimar. The purpose of the commercial is to pave the way for the women who will be calling on housewives in the area.

The products are superior to most others. Some are unique; all are moderately priced.

Heavy schedules are planned in selected cities as sales forces are organized.

The commercial will have a long life and should not be localized. It will be in color, of course.

You earn an automatic *F* if you misspell the name of the client.

Assignment 3. Pick a new, best-selling book, fiction or nonfiction, and assume it is about to go into a paperback edition. Do a storyboard for a thirty-second commercial to be shown in major cities. Keep your production costs down, but do the ad in color.

Assignment 4. Pick out your favorite, if obscure, recording artist, assume that a record company is packaging an LP of the artist's best numbers, and do a sixty-second, hard-sell TV commercial to sell it. It will not be available in stores. Have the viewer send for the album to an address in your home town. Plan to play samples of the music, of course. Crowd a lot into the commercial.

Assignment 5. For some restaurants, takeout orders represent a substantial part of the business. The Red Apple is such a restaurant. One of its most popular dishes is its pasta seafood salad with pasta shells, peas, and crab meat. A one-cup serving with a roll and a sprout salad goes for $2.85. Do a sixty-second radio commercial on this. Mention the fact that the restaurant is known for its light, healthful meals and for its seven soups and seven quiches. It's located in the American Building. Include a phone number in the commercial.

Assignment 6. Using the theme "Shoplifters take everybody's money," the merchants of Philadelphia a few years ago got together to launch what turned out to be a successful ad campaign against shoplifting. Figuring that teenagers account for a large percentage of shoplifting, the merchants directed their campaign largely to that audience.

A good way—perhaps the best way—to reach that audience was through radio. Commercials directed to teenagers mentioned the facts that stealing resulted in higher prices and stealers faced criminal charges if caught. Commercials likely to be heard by parents asked the question: "Was today the day you were going to warn your daughter [or son] about shoplifting?"

It is time to relaunch the campaign—in Philadelphia or whatever big city you are in or near.

Write a sixty-second radio commercial (about 150 words if it is all talk) using any technique you wish. You may pick up the theme from the earlier Philadelphia campaign. Direct your commercial either to teenagers or adults.

14. Direct-mail advertising

Assignment 1. Your client is the imaginary International Insurance Group, which, as a public service, is putting out a series of folders for parents on career opportunities for their youngsters. You have drawn the assignment to design one for the field of advertising.

Do a comprehensive rough of a three-fold folder that will fit a No. 10 business envelope. You should work out a theme and some headings, but you need not write the copy. Doubtless you will want to use subheads to break the copy into readable chunks. You can indicate these with scrambled consonants or sets of *M*s and *W*s. Allow for any halftones and drawings you think are needed.

Plan on using black and a second color throughout.

Paper stock is white offset.

Assignment 2. Pick out some product for which an advertising program involving consumer direct-mail, general-circulation magazine, and dealer trade-magazine advertising would likely be used. Work out a master ad for use in a general-circulation magazine (a column wide by the page-length deep) that could be used in part in the other two media. Do comprehensive roughs of all three ads. Use any direct-mail form you think appropriate. Full color is available for both the general-circulation and the direct-mail ads; use black and white for the trade-journal ad.

The trade-journal ad should have a good deal of the character of the general-circulation ad, because one of the purposes of the trade-journal ad is to remind the dealer of the national advertising program. The direct-mail piece, to be mailed to selected lists, may or may not look like the general-circulation magazine ad. But for economy reasons, you may want to use some of the art from the general-circulation ad.

Assignment 3. In an institutional ad in *Advertising Age,* the

Clinton E. Frank advertising agency coined the name Poppycock, Balderdash & Pshaw to symbolize the competition. Assume that the latter agency has commissioned you to design a new letterhead for its use. Make up the address and other information that should go on the letterhead. Use one or two colors. The agency is flexible on this.

The Plan of Salvation Made Plain to Sinners from the Word of God
By Evangelist John R. Rice

Assignment 4. Redesign this front cover for a religious tract, shown here actual size. It is published by Sword of the Lord Foundation, Murfreesboro, Tennessee. Keep the line art (although not necessarily the black area into which the art extends) and the full wording. You may want to go to regular type instead of hand lettering.

See if you can upgrade the design and make it more contemporary. You have but one ink, but it can be other than black. The foundation used dark blue.

15. Posters and displays
Assignment 1. Do a 24-sheet poster for (a) a political candidate of your choosing or (b) a public cause or crusade that you believe in. If you choose the latter assignment, include the sponsor's name. If the name is part of the message (as in "Give to the Red Cross"), play it up large. Otherwise put it in small type off to one side. Move in close on the art. Use big, thick letters for your type. Apply color generously.

Assignment 2. The Starlight Restaurant in your city is renting a 43' × 10'6'' painted bulletin two miles out on the main highway leading into the city. It will be illuminated. A family-style restaurant, it specializes in steaks and fried chicken at moderate prices. It is open from 8 A.M. to midnight. Closed Mondays.

Design the bulletin, using full colors. If you use artwork, it should be "posterized." Keep the panels within the frame; no extensions.

Assignment 3. The American Bank, with four locations in a medium-size city, is buying a 100-showing of 24-sheet posters. Frankly, it has nothing to promote but the usual services and the fact that it is locally owned.

The purpose of the advertising is to help the bank get its fair share of the business. (Three other banks operate in the area.)

Design the poster. You have no limitation on color.

Assignment 4. The American Cancer Society, the American Lung Association, the American Heart Association, ASH (Action on Smoking and Health), GASP (Group Against Smoking Pollution), and FANS (Fresh Air for Non-smokers) are among organizations fighting cigarette smoking. States and cities are passing legislation and ordinances limiting smoking to designated areas. "Smoking will go the way of spitting," predicts Gordon Wilson of GASP.

Bearing in mind that better-educated people are turning away from smoking and that its appeal these days seems to be mostly to blue-collar classes and to some younger people, work up an outdoor poster that could conceivably be sponsored by one of the antismoking groups. Include a small credit line on the poster.

16. Permanence in advertising design
Assignment 1. Take the words "Car Wash" (caps and lower case, all lower case, all caps—it doesn't make any difference) and make a logo, working a car into it. One solution would be to make a car—a generic car—out of one of the letters.

Assignment 2. On this page you see two different store logos badly in need of redesign. Pick one of them and redesign it. Modernize the look. Include everything that is important, and add an element if you think the logo needs it. If you include the bank cards, bring them up to date. Use no color.

909 S.W. WASHINGTON ST. • 222-3464

Assignment 3. Take the three initials of your name and make a well-designed monogram of them. Include with the initials a piece of art that symbolizes your personality, your intended occupation, or one of your interests; for instance, a sun, a palette, or a ski pole. (Avoid astrological signs.)

Do not let the art overpower the initials. Instead, let it help unite them. Keep it flat, decorative, on the abstract side.

Work in a size big enough so you will not be cramped. But render the monogram boldly enough so that it will reduce to about a one-inch square. Use black only.

You may place the initials and art inside a circle, shield, or other field; or—better—you can let the initials and art stand by themselves. Be sure you end up with a nicely unified whole.

Student Brian P. Wimberly, a music major, shows you how he would handle the assignment.

Assignment 4. Design a record jacket for a C & W instrumental release by Nashville Country Recording Company (fictitious). The artist is Charlie Hatfield (also fictitious), a versatile backup musician who, in this, his first solo LP album, concentrates on the harmonica. A string band accompanies him.

Title of the album is "Mournful Harmonica." Among the numbers is his hit single "I'll Never Get Out of This World Alive," a revival of an old Hank Williams number.

Do a full-color comp.

Assignment 5. From among the thousands of grocery store packages, select one you think needs redesigning—and redesign it.

17. Careers

Assignment 1. Work up a resumé to be used in your hunt for a job in advertising, whether you are applying as a potential designer or art director, copywriter, or other worker. Organize it tightly and use parallel structure. Follow the advice contained in this chapter.

Assignment 2. Do a newspaper ad of approximately 12 column inches (1 column $\times$ 12", 2 columns $\times$ 6", or 3 columns $\times$ 4") announcing the opening in town of your design (or design and copy) studio to serve local advertisers, agencies, and printers. Stress the services you do best and include some art. Design the ad to single out the few readers of the paper who could use your services.

Don't make up facts. Be realistic. If you are short on experience, play up something else in the headline and copy. Concentrate on the quality of your work and, perhaps, on your reasonable fees.

The design of your ad will demonstrate what you can do.

Assignment 3. Design a business card, letterhead, and envelope to use in your new business.

Glossary

Some of the terms appearing here appear also in the glossary for *Publication Design,* a companion volume to this one. Some of those terms carry different meanings here, because advertising usage is not always the same as news/editorial usage.

abstract art   simplified art; art reduced to fundamental parts; art that makes its point with great subtlety. Opposite of realistic or representational art.

accordion fold   a direct-mail piece with panels that fold alternately inward and outward so that the piece opens and closes like an accordion.

account   what the advertising agency or medium calls the advertiser. An agency also refers to the advertiser as a *client.*

account executive   person in the agency in charge of advertising for the account or client. This person may also be called an "account supervisor."

acetate   clear film used for overlays, especially when the artist is preparing art for a color plate.

AD   short for art director.

advertising   communication from an advertiser to a potential buyer in printed, broadcast, or painted form.

advertising agency   organization that prepares and places advertising for various clients.

Advertising Council   nonprofit organization of advertisers, agencies, and media that creates and places public service advertising.

Advertising Review Board   self-regulating organization set up by the advertising industry.

agate line   line of type set in 5½-point type. Also, a unit of measurement. Newspapers sometimes measure ad depths by agate lines: fourteen to a column inch.

agent   business representative for freelance artists of all kinds who offer advertising services.

airbrush   tool that uses compressed air to shoot a spray of watercolor pigment on photographs or artwork. Used for retouching.

align   arrange elements so that they line up with other elements.

all caps   all-capital letters.

animation   in TV commercials, action accomplished through use of cartoon characters or puppets.

annual report   booklet issued each year by an organization to summarize its activities and financial situation.

antique paper   rough-finish, high-quality, often bulky paper.

art   all pictorial matter in an ad: photographs, illustrations, cartoons, charts and graphs, typographic effects.

Art Deco   the look of the 1920s and 1930s: simple line forms, geometric shapes, pastel colors, rainbow motifs.

art director   person in charge of all visual aspects of an ad, including typography.

Art Nouveau   sinuous, decorative, curvy art associated with the turn of the century.

ascenders   portions of letters that rise above the top of the x-height.

asymmetric balance   balance achieved by strategic arrangement of unequal elements in an ad. A heavy item on one side does not require a corresponding element directly across from it. Informal balance.

audio   the part of advertising you can hear, especially in a TV commercial.

availability   time that an advertiser can buy on radio or television.

axis   imaginary line used to align visual elements and relate them.

bait advertising   advertising that lures people into stores for bargains or would-be bargains. Often it is difficult to buy the product advertised.

balance   stability in design; condition in which the various elements on a page or spread are at rest.

bank   see *deck.*

bar chart   art that shows statistics in bars of various lengths.

basis weight   weight of a ream of paper in standard-size sheets. Standard size for book papers is 25″ × 38″.

Bauhaus   school of design in Germany (1919–33). It championed a highly ordered, functional style in architecture and applied arts.

BCU   big closeup, as used in television.

Ben Day   process by which engraver or printer adds pattern or tone to a line reproduction.

billboard   poster panel used in outdoor advertising.

billing   amount of money an agency charges its clients. Includes charges for services rendered plus production and media bills.

binding   that part of a magazine, book, or booklet that holds the pages together.

bird's-eye view   view from above.

black letter   a close-fitting, bold, angular style of type that originated in Germany. Also known as *Old English* and *text.*

bleed   a picture printed to the edge of a sheet (technically, to achieve this effect, the sheet is trimmed after the printing). Used also as a verb.

blind embossing   embossing without printing.

blowup   enlargement. "Blow up" when used as a verb.

blueline   see *Vandyke.*

blurb   copy found on a book jacket, usually extravagant in its praise of the book.

body copy   column of type set in a relatively small size.

body type   type 12 points in size or smaller.

boldface type   heavy, black type.

bond paper   crisp paper used for business stationery, often with rag content.

book   bound publication of forty-eight pages or more, usually with a stiff or heavy cover. Some magazine editors call their publications *books.*

booklet   a publication of between eight and forty-eight bound pages, sometimes with a cover of a slightly heavier stock. Often in a size to fit a No. 10 envelope.

book paper   paper, other than newsprint, used in the printing of books, magazines, and direct mail. Includes many grades and finishes.

border   rule or other art that surrounds an ad and defines its edges. Not all ads need or use borders. Mostly for newspaper ads.

box   design element composed usually of four rules, with type or art inside.

brainstorming   meeting in a group in the hope that members will stimulate each other to create or make discoveries.

bridge   music or sound effect linking two scenes in a commercial.

broadside   direct-mail piece that unfolds to a large sheet about the size of a newspaper page.

brochure   high-quality, expensive direct-mail piece.

brownline   see *Vandyke.*

burnish   smooth down paper letters or pattern sheets so that they will adhere to a pasteup.

business paper   see *trade magazine.*

busy   condition in design in which elements are too numerous for the space and compete with each other for attention.

byline   the author's name set in type, usually over the author's story or article. Ads seldom carry bylines.

calender   polish, as in a finishing step in the making of some paper.

calligraphy   beautiful handwriting.

camera lucida   lens system for tracing and enlarging. Most artists today prefer using a full projector or viewer, such as the Goodkin or Artograph.

camera-ready copy   a pasteup ready to be photographed by the platemaker.

camp   art so bad it is good.

caps and small caps   all capital letters, with the initial letters of words set in larger capitals.

caption   legend accompanying a photograph used as editorial material in a magazine; newspapers use *cutlines*. Advertising photographs usually do not require captions, except in some direct mail.

caricature   drawing that exaggerates or distorts a person's features.

cartoon   humorous drawing, done usually in pen or brush and ink or in washes.

cartouche   fancy border.

casting off   copyfitting.

cathode-ray tube   sophisticated system of phototypesetting making use of a televisionlike tube.

center spread   two facing pages at the center of a saddle-stitched magazine. Elements in an ad can cross the gutter in a center spread without any problems of register.

character   any letter, number, punctuation mark, or space in printed matter.

checking copy   copy of a publication sent to an agency or advertiser for proofing or to prove the ad was actually run as ordered.

chroma   color intensity.

circular   vague term for a direct-mail piece.

circulation   number of copies sold or distributed. Can be accurately measured. *Readership* used in this context refers to the number of people who actually see the publication—a number two to three times higher than circulation in many cases. Readership is harder than circulation to measure.

classified advertising   small-type, usually all-type, small-space ads, sponsored by private individuals as well as companies, arranged by category in one section of the newspaper.

cliché   something used too often, hence boring and no longer effective.

client   see *account*.

clip book   pages of stock art usually on slick paper, ready for photographing by the platemaker.

clip sheet   see *clip book*.

close up   move together.

closeup   picture made with camera so close to subject that only the head and shoulders show.

closing date   deadline for submitting ad to medium if it is to be printed in a specific issue.

coated paper   paper covered with a smoothing agent, making it stiff and, usually, shiny. Good for reproducing photographs.

cold type   type composed by typewriter, paper pasteup, or photographic means rather than metal.

collage   piece of art made by pasting various elements together.

collateral   noncommissionable media used in an advertising campaign.

collating   gathering and arranging printed sheets or signatures into the desired sequence. Usually done by machine.

color separation   negative made from full-color art for use in making one of the plates.

column   section of the text matter (when the text matter is extensive) that runs from the top to the bottom of the copy area. An ad or page can carry more than one column of type.

column inch   area that is one column wide by one inch deep. A column-inch ad in a newspaper can be referred to as a fourteen-line ad. See *agate line*.

column rule   thin line separating columns of type.

combination cut   printing plate made from superimposition of both a line and halftone negative.

comic strip   comic drawing or cartoon that appears in a newspaper on a regular basis; a series of drawn panels. Characters in comic strips have been enlisted for advertising campaigns. And the comic-strip format has been popular with some advertisers, especially those appealing to young audiences.

commercial   advertisement on radio or TV.

commercial art   illustrations, typography, and design used in advertising. Thought to be different from *fine art*, but actually much advertising—or commercial—art ranks with fine art in quality.

commission system   system of payment to an advertising agency: the agency gets 15 percent of what the client spends for time and space with the media. See also *fifteen-and-two*. The system has sometimes come under fire. Another system is for the agency to charge a fee or retainer for its services.

comp   comprehensive layout. Sometimes a preliminary sketch before painting or final illustration is made.

company magazine   see *house organ*.

composition   type that is set. Also, in art or design, the arrangement of elements.

compositor   craftsman who sets type.

comprehensive layout   layout finished to look almost as the printed piece will look.

condensed type   type series with narrow characters.

consumer magazine   advertising person's terminology for *general-circulation magazine*.

continuity   script for a radio or TV commercial.

continuous-tone art   photograph or painting or any piece of art in which tones merge gradually into one another. Requires halftone reproduction.

contrast   quality in design that permits one element to stand out clearly from others.

controlled-circulation publication   publication sent free to interested subscribers. Usually a trade magazine. For benefit of advertisers, the circulation is audited, as it is for paid-circulation publications. Some controlled-circulation publications now call themselves "qualified-circulation" publications.

cool colors   blue and green colors that tend to recede from the viewer. Restful colors.

cooperative advertising   advertising paid for by both the national (brand-name) and the local advertiser. Also, advertising in which several normally competing firms get together to do a common selling job.

copy   written material or text matter for an ad, both before or after it is set in type. Includes the ad's headline. The non-headline part of the copy is called the *copy block*. Also, the pasteup from which the platemaker makes the plate.

copy area   that part of an ad inside the border or margin. Sometimes called "type area."

copy block   text part of an ad; column of copy; all of the copy in an ad except the headline, captions, and logo.

copy chief   head of the copy department of an agency or company.

copyedit   see *copyread*.

copyfit   estimate how much space copy will take when it is set in type.

copy platform   the basic idea for an advertisement or an advertising campaign.

copyread   check the manuscript to correct errors made by the writer.

copyright   protection available to the owner of a manuscript, piece of art, or publication, preventing others from making unfair use of it or profiting from it at the expense of the owner. Most ads are not copyrighted, but publications in which they appear often are. Still, the advertiser, not the publisher, owns the advertising.

copy testing   research into the effectiveness of advertising copy.

copywriting   writing copy for advertisements.

corporate advertising see *institutional advertising*.

corporate identity the look and recognition factor of a corporation; the corporation's image.

cost-per-thousand cost to reach one thousand readers with a full-page ad.

cover stock heavy or thick paper used as covers for magazines or paperback books.

CPM see *cost-per-thousand*.

credit line the photographer's name set in type, usually right next to the picture. Ads on occasion carry credit lines.

crop eliminate unwanted areas in a piece of art, usually by putting marks in the margins to guide the platemaker.

CU closeup shot, as in a TV commercial.

cursor a movable spot of light that appears on a computer display terminal. Controlled by a key on the keyboard, it shows where corrections, insertions, deletions, and other changes can be made in copy.

cut art in plate form, ready to print. For the letterpress process.

cutlines see *caption*.

cut to abruptly change a scene in a TV commercial.

dealer imprint dealer's name and address added onto an already printed advertisement or placed on an advertisement prepared elsewhere.

dealer tie-in manufacturer's advertisement that includes names of dealers.

decal ad, symbol, or sign in the form of a sticker that attaches itself to glass, metal, or other material.

deck portion of a headline, consisting of lines set in the same size and style type.

deckle edge ragged, feathery edge available in some of the quality paper stocks.

deep etch plate used in offset lithography on which the image is slightly recessed.

delete take out.

demographics statistics on a particular market, covering age, sex, education, occupation, and so on.

descenders portions of letters that dip below the baseline of the letters.

design organization; plan and arrangement of visual elements. A broader term than *layout*. Used also as a verb.

designer person who plans and arranges elements in an ad. The art director (an executive) is also often the designer.

"designer's block" temporary suspension of creative facilities.

die-cut hole or other cutout punched into heavy paper. Used also as a verb.

dingbat small typographic decoration.

direct advertising printed advertising other than that appearing in newspapers and periodicals. It comes in many forms, but it does not include posters or point-of-purchase advertising.

direct halftone halftone made by the platemaker photographing the object itself rather than a photograph of the object.

direct-mail advertising direct advertising circulated by mail.

director for a TV commercial, the person immediately in charge of casting, filming, and other details. Works under the producer.

directory advertising advertising in directories such as telephone directories.

display ad local ad in newspaper that makes use of design or random placement of elements of various sizes to attract attention.

display type type larger than 12 points, used for titles in direct mail, headlines for magazine and newspaper ads, and posters. See also *titles*.

dissolve effect of one scene coming into a TV commercial while another goes out. Used also as a verb.

dividers an instrument used to measure distances on a proof or piece of art so that the measurement can be transferred and duplicated.

dolly move camera gradually either in to or back out from the subject, as in a TV commercial.

dot etching correcting color separation negatives by making halftone dots smaller.

double truck newspaper terminology for *spread*.

downstyle style characterized by the use of lower case letters in headlines except for first letters of first words of sentences and for first letters of proper names. Exaggerated downstyle uses no capital letters anywhere.

dropout halftone see *highlight halftone*.

drybrush rendering in which only partially inked brush is pulled across rough-textured paper.

dry-transfer letters see *transfer type*.

DS abbreviation for *dissolve*, as in a TV commercial.

dubbing adding pictures or sound after film or recording is made, as in a commercial.

dummy the pages of a publication in its planning stage, often unbound, with features and pictures crudely sketched or roughly pasted into place.

duotone halftone printed in two inks, one dark (usually black), one lighter (any color).

duplicate plates copies of the original plates prepared for distribution to several publications.

duplicator machine that reproduces a limited number of copies. Large pressruns require regular printing presses.

dust jacket see *jacket*.

ECU extreme closeup, as in a TV commercial.

edit change, manage, or supervise for publication. Also, as a noun, short for *editorial*.

edition part of the pressrun for a particular *issue* of a publication. Space in regional or demographic editions of magazines is available to advertisers at rates less than the rates for an entire issue.

editorial short essay, usually unsigned, stating the stand of the publication on some current event or issue. Also used to designate the nonbusiness side of a publication. Sometimes the advertiser designs the advertising to look like editorial rather than advertising matter.

editorial matter anything appearing in a publication that is not advertising.

electric spectacular outdoor advertisement making extravagant use of electric lights and, in most cases, a form of animation.

electrotype duplicate plate.

element copy, headline, art, rule or box, border, spot of color—anything to be put into an ad.

elliptical dot screen screen that permits a greater range of middle-value grays in halftone reproduction than is possible with a regular dot screen.

em width of capital *M* in any type size. Spacing equal to the *square* of the type size.

emboss print an image on paper and stamp it, too, so that it rises above the surface of the paper.

en width of capital *N* in any type size. Spacing equal to *half the square* of the type size.

English finish smooth finish. English-finish papers are widely used by magazines.

engraving see *photoengraving*.

expanded type type series with wider-than-normal characters.

exploded view an illustration in which parts of an object are separated so that they can be better read.

face style or variation of type.

fact sheet outline of a product's sales points given to or prepared by the advertising copywriter.

fade let a scene in a TV commercial gradually disappear from the screen. Used also as a noun.

family subdivision of a type race.

FCC Federal Communications Commission. A federal agency which licenses broadcast stations.

FDA Food and Drug Administration. A federal agency which regulates advertising of foods, drugs, and cosmetics.

feature play up. As a noun, a quality or characteristic of the ad.

feedback reader's or viewer's expressed response to an advertisement.

felt side best side of a sheet of paper for either printing or drawing. It is the side that, in the manufacturing process, came in contact with felt rollers.

fifteen-and-two standard discount a medium gives an agency for advertising placed. The 15 percent (of the gross bill) is kept by the agency, the 2 percent (of the net bill) is often passed on to the client.

film clip short section of film that can be inserted into a TV commercial.

fine art art created primarily for aesthetic rather than commercial purposes. Art used for advertising is usually referred to as *commercial art.*

fixative clear solution sprayed onto a drawing to keep it from smearing.

flatbed press letterpress press that prints from flat base. Slower than rotary letterpress.

flat color see *spot color.*

FlexForm ad newspaper ad in other than the usual square or rectangle shape.

flop change the facing of a picture. A subject facing left in the original will face right in the printed version. Not a synonym for *reverse.*

flow chart art showing a manufacturing process.

flush left aligned at the left-hand margin.

flush left and right aligned at both the left- and right-hand margins. Justified.

flush right aligned at the right-hand margin.

folder direct-mail piece folded at least once. Of a size, usually, to fit into a No. 10 envelope.

font complete set of type characters of a particular face and size.

foreshorten exaggerate the perspective.

formal balance see *symmetric balance.*

format size, shape, and appearance of an ad or publication.

formula editorial mix of a publication. Of importance to the advertiser in that it determines the audience the advertiser reaches.

foundry type hand-set metal type.

four color full range of colors obtained by printing red, yellow, blue, and black.

fourth cover back cover of a magazine. Most expensive space in the magazine, unless the advertiser can buy the front cover.

frame in film, a single picture from among the many making up the action.

freelancer artist, photographer, designer, or copywriter called in to do specialized jobs for the advertiser.

freeze action action in a TV commercial that stops suddenly, causing actor to appear as though frozen in place.

French fold direct-mail piece printed on one side of a sheet, which is folded into a four-page folder with the blank side of the sheet hidden.

frisket paper that shields part of a drawing or pasteup from ink or exposure. Liquid frisket is also available.

FTC Federal Trade Commission. A federal agency which regulates advertising to some extent.

full color see *four color.*

full position preferred position in a newspaper, next to editorial matter or at the top of a column of ads.

full showing the poster-ad shown on all units in a public transportation system. It can also mean a *100 showing* in outdoor advertising.

"funky" art amateurish, 1930-ish, sometimes outrageous art. Art associated with the underground press and underground, adult, and corner drugstore comic books. Also, art with a polished but primitive charm.

gag cartoon humorous drawing, usually in a single panel, with caption, if there is one, set in type below. Gag cartoonists appearing regularly on magazine editorial pages have occasionally been enlisted by advertisers to help sell products or ideas.

galley tray on which type is assembled and proofed.

galley proof long sheet of paper containing a first printing from a galley—or tray—of type.

ganging up arranging forms in printing so that several different jobs can be printed at the same time on single sheets.

gatefold magazine cover that opens out to two additional pages. Makes possible an ad three pages wide.

gelatin duplicating reproducing a limited number of copies from a gelatin surface. A paper master is used to put the image on the gelatin surface.

general-circulation magazine magazine with popular appeal, usually with a large circulation, usually available on the newsstands. Sometimes called a "slick."

gimmick a sometimes clever, sometimes phony idea or device put into an ad to gain attention or sway the reader.

gingerbread design design with an overabundance of swirls and flourishes; cluttered design.

glossy print photograph with shiny finish. For reproduction purposes, better than a matte-finish print.

golden rectangle classic shape with a width-depth ratio of approximately 3:5 (or 5:3).

gothic term applied to various typefaces that have challenged the traditional. Currently, modern sans serifs.

grain the way cellulose fibers in a sheet of paper line up, giving direction to the paper. You would design a direct-mail piece to fold with the grain, not against it.

grainy dim, distracting pattern in a photograph, lessening its impact and clarity. Like "snow" in a television picture.

graph see *bar chart, line chart,* and *pie chart.* Also, short for "paragraph."

graphic design design of printed material and—stretching the original definition—broadcast material.

gravure method of printing from incised plate. For magazines, a rotary press is involved, hence *rotogravure.*

Greeking making the body copy in a comprehensive layout look like real copy—but copy that cannot be read. You can buy *Greeking* that has been printed on waxed transparent sheets.

grid carefully spaced vertical and horizontal guidelines that define areas in a layout; a plan for designing an ad.

gutter separation of two facing pages.

hairline very thin rule or line.

halftone reproduction process by which the printer gets the effect of continuous tone, as when reproducing a photograph. It is done with dots.

hand lettering lettering done with pen or brush. Used infrequently now that photolettering is available.

head short for *headline.*

heading headline or title.

headline display type in an ad. An ad can be all headline. On the other hand, some ads do not have headlines.

head-on position in outdoor advertising, the placement of an ad so that it directly faces oncoming traffic.

hed short for *head,* which is short for *heading* or *headline.*

hidden offer special offer buried in ad in order to test readership.

high camp see *camp.*

highlight halftone halftone in which some parts have been dropped out to show the white of the paper.

holding power power of a commercial to keep viewer's attention.

hot press paper smooth paper without much "tooth." Used for line drawings.

hot type type made from metal.

house ad advertisement promoting the publication in which it appears.

house agency advertising agency established by advertiser to handle its own advertising. Unlike an advertiser's advertising department, a house agency is a complete unit, often eligible for media discounts.

house organ   publication of an organization or business released regularly for public relations reasons. Usually it does not carry ads. The publication is itself an advertisement doing an institutional job.

house style   style that is peculiar to an agency or that remains the same from ad to ad.

hue   quality in a color that allows us to recognize it—by name. The name of the color.

illustration   drawing or painting. Although a photograph can be used for illustrative purposes, it is not usually called an *illustration*.

illustration board   cardboard or heavy paperboard made for artists, available in various weights and finishes to take various art mediums.

imprint   print local name or material on an already printed piece of advertising. Used also as a noun.

India ink   waterproof drawing ink, usually black.

industrial advertising   advertising designed to reach industry rather than the general public.

industrial designer   designer of products. Packages are sometimes designed by industrial designers, sometimes by graphic designers.

informal balance   see *asymmetric balance.*

initial   first letter of a word at the beginning of advertising copy, set in display size to make it stand out.

insert   advertising page or pages printed elsewhere and mailed to publication for inclusion in an issue or edition. As a verb it means to put into place.

insertion order   authorization from an agency to publish an ad.

inset   art placed inside other art or art surrounded by type.

institutional advertising   advertising designed to create an image or build goodwill rather than sell a product.

intaglio   see *gravure.*

integrated commercial   one that is broadcast as part of the program; not stuck in at a break or tacked on at the beginning or end.

intensity   strength or brilliance of a color.

interabang   combination exclamation mark and question mark. Available in several faces but not widely used. Also spelled "interrobang."

intercut   quick change of the camera from one scene to another in a TV commercial.

intermediate blueprint   detailed sketch giving directions to the producer of a TV commercial.

Intertype   linecasting machine similar to Linotype.

island display   a point-of-purchase display out in the aisle, away from shelves and other displays.

island position   placement of an ad in a publication so that it is entirely surrounded by editorial matter.

issue   all copies of a publication for a particular date. An issue may consist of several *editions.*

italic type   type that slants to the right.

jacket   paper cover that wraps around a book to protect and advertise it.

jingle   musical commercial, especially for radio.

job press   printing press used for small or short-run jobs. Not for periodicals.

justify   align the body type so it forms an even margin on the right and the left.

kerning   in typesetting, arranging a letter so that it fits into another letter's area.

keying   putting a code number or letter on a coupon so when it is mailed in the advertiser will know which of several publications used triggered the response. Also, coding the typewritten copy to show where it fits in the layout.

keyline drawing   drawing done partly in outline to use in making more than one plate for a spot-color job.

kraft paper   heavy, rough, tough paper, usually tan in color.

lap dissolve   in a commercial, the fading of one scene into another; both can be seen for a second or two.

lay out   put visual elements into a pleasing and readable arrangement.

layout   noun form of *lay out.*

lead   (pronounced ledd) put extra space between lines of type.

leaders   (pronounced leeders) dots or dashes used to carry eye across white space usually to a column of numbers.

leading   (pronounced ledding) extra space between lines of type.

leaf   small sheet of paper.

leaflet   small sheet of paper, printed on one or both sides. One of the least pretentious of direct-mail forms.

legibility   quality in type that makes it easy for the reader to recognize individual letters.

letterpress   method of printing from raised surface. The original and still widely used printing process.

letterspace   put extra space between letters. Periodically a popular practice for advertising headlines.

letterspacing   extra spacing between letters.

libel   published defamatory statement or art which injures a person's reputation.

lift   shorter version of a TV commercial.

ligature   two or more joined or overlapped characters on a single piece of type.

light table   table with frosted glass or plastic top with illumination underneath. Used for tracing purposes or for viewing, retouching, and arranging negatives.

linage   amount of advertising space expressed in agate lines: fourteen to the column inch.

line art   in its original form, art without continuous tone, done in black ink on white paper. Also, such art after it is reproduced through *line reproduction.*

linecasting machine   see *Linotype* and *Intertype.*

line chart   art that shows trends in statistics through a line that rises or falls on a grid.

line conversion   continuous-tone art that has been changed to line art. A screen of any one of several patterns is involved.

line reproduction   process by which the printer reproduces a black-and-white drawing.

Linotype   linecasting machine that produces type for letterpress printing or type from which reproduction proofs can be pulled. A trade name.

lip sync   synchronization of an actor's lip movements with sound that is recorded separately.

list broker   agent who rents out lists of potential buyers to direct-mail advertisers.

lithography   originally, process of making prints from grease drawing on stone. See also *offset lithography.*

live action   action in a TV commercial involving real people.

live area   ("live" with a long "i") the interior part of an ad that must be left intact. Area outside of this area can be cropped so ad can run in a magazine with a smaller page size.

local advertising   advertising placed by local retail firms rather than by national manufacturers.

logo   short for *logotype.* The name of the advertiser in art or type form that remains constant from ad to ad. Usually available in more than one size.

long shot   picture taken from far away, as in a TV commercial.

loose art   informally drawn, relaxed art. The impression is that it was done in a hurry.

loss leader   item advertised at a cost below what retailer paid for it. Purpose is to increase store traffic.

lower case   small letters (as opposed to capital letters).

LS   long shot, as in a TV commercial.

Ludlow   machine that casts lines of display-size letters from matrices that have been assembled by hand.

magazine   publication of eight pages or more, usually bound, issued on a regular basis at least twice a year. Also, storage unit for mats for linecasting machine.

mail-order advertising   advertising designed to sell products by mail. Can make use of direct-mail advertising as well as other media of advertising.

make good ad run free by a medium to compensate for significant error made by the medium in content or placement of the original ad.

makeready all the work involved in preparing printing materials and the press for a particular job.

marketing the whole system by which seller and buyer do business. Advertising is one step in the process.

market research research conducted to determine nature and extent of audience for which product is designed.

mass media units of communication: newspapers, magazines, television and radio stations, books, and others.

mat short for *matrix*. Cardboard mold of plate, from which a copy can be made. Also, brass mold from which type can be cast.

matrix see *mat*.

mat service organization that supplies ideas, complete ads, and—most important—mats and proofs of artwork that can be used in ads.

matte combine two scenes into one, as in a TV commercial.

matte finish dull finish.

MCU medium closeup, as in a TV commercial.

measure length of a line or column of type.

mechanical see *camera-ready copy*.

mechanical spacing nonadjusted spacing between letters; opposite of *optical spacing*.

media see *mass media*.

media buyer person in an advertising agency who selects the media and decides the schedule for the clients' ads.

medium singular for media. Also paint, ink, or marking substance used in drawing or painting. In this context, the plural of medium can be "mediums."

medium shot in television, a picture taken not from far away, but not close up either.

merchandising any activity designed to stimulate trade.

mockup facsimile of product or package.

model release signed statement by person authorizing the use of that person's picture in an ad.

modular design highly ordered design, marked by regularity in spacing.

moiré undesirable wavy or checkered pattern resulting when an already screened photograph is photographed through another screen.

Monotype composing machine that casts individual letters. Used for high quality composition.

montage combination of photographs or drawings into a single unit.

mortise a cut made into a picture to make room for type or another picture. Used also as a verb.

motivational research research that attempts to explain why buyers and potential buyers act as they do.

MS medium shot, as in a TV commercial.

mug shot portrait.

Multilith duplicating or printing machine similar to offset lithography presses, but on a small scale. Multilith is a trade name.

national advertising advertising sponsored by manufacturers designed mainly to build interest in specific brands.

"new advertising" advertising characterized by high creativity, understatement, less hyberbole, and in some cases a little humor.

"new journalism" journalism characterized by a highly personal, subjective style. Builds a young audience some advertisers want particularly to reach.

news hole nonadvertising space in a newspaper.

newsprint low-quality paper stock lacking permanence; used by newspapers.

next-to-reading-matter placement of the ad next to editorial matter. Thought to give the ad greater readership.

off-camera not shown, although the voice may be heard, as in a TV commercial.

offset lithography method of printing from flat surface, based on principle that grease and water do not mix. Commercial adaptation of *lithography*.

offset paper book paper made especially for offset presses.

Old English see *black letter*.

100 showing in outdoor advertising, a showing for one month of enough posters to reach the entire market. The number of posters for a 100 showing would vary from city to city.

op art geometric art that capitalizes on optical illusions.

optical any special photographic effect used in a TV commercial.

optical center a point slightly above and to the left of the geometric center.

optical illusion art that plays tricks with the eye; art that can be interpreted in different ways.

optical spacing spacing in typesetting that takes into account the peculiarities of the letters, resulting in a more even look.

optical weight the visual impact a given element makes on the reader.

organization chart art that shows how various people or departments relate to each other. Used occasionally in annual reports.

overlay sheet of transparent plastic placed over a drawing. The overlay contains art or type of its own for a plate that will be coordinated with the original plate.

Ozalid photocopying machine that produces cold-type proofs.

P-O-P point-of-purchase advertising.

page one side of a sheet of paper in a publication.

painted bulletin outdoor poster painted on a panel.

painterly look the look in art that stresses technique, tool, or medium used. The strokes show.

painting illustration made with oil, acrylic, tempera, casein, or watercolor paints. Requires halftone reproduction; if color is to be retained, it requires process color plates.

pan move camera to right or left, as in making a TV commercial.

panel board on which poster is posted. Also, a box, rectangle, page, or other definable unit of display in print-media advertising. Also, a group of persons observed systematically by advertising researcher.

paper stock paper.

parallel structure organization in writing or design that gives equal treatment to each item, making it easy for the reader to comprehend and compare. Each item is introduced with the same phrasing or art device.

passalong readers readers of a publication who did not buy it.

pastel colors soft, weak colors.

pastel drawing drawing made with gray or color chalks.

paste up verb form of *pasteup*.

pasteup see *camera-ready copy*.

pencil drawing drawing made with lead or graphite pencil. Usually requires halftone reproduction.

penetration extent to which a medium or advertisement reaches a market.

perfecting press rotary press that prints on both sides of a sheet or roll of paper in a single operation.

perspective quality in a photograph or illustration that creates the illusion of distance.

photoboard a TV storyboard after the fact, used for promotional purposes when the commercial is actually on the air.

photocomposition composition produced by photographic means.

photoengraving cut or plate made for letterpress printing.

photo essay series of photographs that make a single point. Used mostly on the editorial side.

photolettering display type produced photographically.

Photo-mechanical Transfer copy print. Referred to as a PMT.

photostat photographic copy. Also called *stat*.

phototypesetting body copy set photomechanically or photoelectronically.

pic short for *picture*.

pica   12 points, or one-sixth of an inch.

pictograph   a chart or graph in picture form.

picture   photograph, drawing, or painting.

pie chart   art that shows statistics—usually percentages—as wedges in a pie or circle.

piggyback commercial   commercial run right after another commercial by the same sponsor but promoting a different product.

piggyback type   printed type with no space between lines. Sometimes used for headlines.

pix   plural of *pic*.

plate   piece of metal from which printing is done. See also *cut*.

plug   mention of a product in nonadvertising time, as on a TV program, presumably without the advertiser's having to pay for the mention. Used also as a verb.

point   unit of measurement of type; there are 72 points to an inch.

point-of-purchase advertising   advertising that attempts to do a selling job in or near a retail establishment.

pop art   fine art inspired by comic strips and packages. See also *camp*.

positioning   using advertising to give a product its own personality in the mind of the potential customer; segregating the product from competing products.

posterization   the conversion of continuous-tone art to black-and-white art. Middle grays are dropped; or multiple colors are reduced to a few simple, flat colors.

poster panel   standardized structure on which poster is pasted.

poster plant   local organization that erects and maintains poster panels.

preferred position   desirable place in medium for which advertiser pays a premium rate.

Preprint   ad in a sort of wallpaper design printed in rotogravure in another plant for insertion in a letterpress newspaper.

press-on type   letters printed on transparent paper or thin plastic that can be cut out and pressed into place on a pasteup.

pressrun   total number of copies printed during one printing operation.

printer   craftsman who makes up the forms or operates the presses.

printing   the act of duplicating copies of ads or pages.

process color   the effect of full color achieved through use of color-separation plates; way to reproduce color photographs, paintings, and transparencies.

producer   for a TV commercial, the person put in overall charge after the storyboard has been approved. The producer is not usually connected with the advertising agency.

production   process that readies an ad for publication after copy has been written and ad has been designed. Can also include the typesetting and printing.

production house   for commercials, an organization that takes over after the storyboard (or, in the case of radio, the script) is approved. For point-of-purchase, an organization that designs and supervises the printing of the advertising.

progressive proofs   set of platemaker's proofs of a full-color ad, showing each color plate separately, what happens as each color is added, and finally all four colors in combination.

proofread   check galley proofs against the original copy to correct any mistakes the compositor makes.

prop   item to be placed on a set for a TV commercial to give it authenticity.

proportion   size relationship of one part of the design to the other parts.

psychedelic art   highly decorative art characterized by blobs of improbable colors, swirls, and contorted type and lettering.

publication   product of the printing press, consisting of bound or unbound pages circulated on a regular basis.

public relations advertising   see *institutional advertising*.

publishing   act of producing literature and journalism and making them available to the public. Printing is only one small part of the operation.

pub set   composition supplied by the publication in which the ad is to appear.

race   major category of typefaces.

ragged left   aligned at the right but staggered at the left.

ragged right   aligned at the left but staggered at the right.

rate card   card, folder, or booklet listing various rates for time or space in a medium. It also lists mechanical requirements for ads.

reach   what *readership* is to the print media, *reach* is to television.

readability   quality in type that makes it easy for the reader to move easily from word to word and line to line. In a broader sense, it is the quality in writing and design that makes it easy for the reader to understand the ad.

readership   number of readers of an ad or of a publication. See also *circulation*.

reading notice   ad with the look of editorial matter. It carries little or no display. Its intent often is to make readers forget it is an *advertisement* they are reading.

ream   five hundred sheets of paper.

rear projection   technique that allows actors to be filmed in front of a screen on which is projected a still or moving background.

register   condition in which various printing areas, properly adjusted, print exactly where they are supposed to print. Used also as a verb.

release   see *model release*.

relief   raised printing surface.

render   execute, as in making a drawing.

rep   short for publisher's representative, which is a firm that sells space for publications it represents.

reprint   copy of an ad reprinted after its original appearance in a publication. Often used as a form of direct advertising.

repro   short for *reproduction proof*.

reproduction   a copy.

reproduction proof   a carefully printed proof made from a galley, ready to paste down so it can be photographed.

residuals   payments paid to performers for repeated showings of programs or films in which they play roles.

resize   rearrange and change elements so that the ad can appear in another size.

retail advertising   advertising by retail establishments directed to customers and potential customers.

retouch   strengthen or change a photograph or negative through use of art techniques.

reverse   white letters in a gray, black, or color area. Opposite of *surprint*. Mistakenly used for *flop*. Used also as a verb.

rococo   complicated, crowded, elaborate, overly decorative.

roman type   type designed with thick and thin strokes and serifs. Some printers refer to any type that is standing upright (as opposed to type that slants) as "roman."

ROP   run of paper. Anywhere in the paper, not just on certain pages.

rotary press   in letterpress, a press that prints from plates curved around a cylinder. All offset presses are essentially "rotary," although the term is not generally applied to them.

rotogravure   see *gravure*.

rough   see *rough layout*.

rough layout   more or less crude, preliminary sketch, showing where type and art are to go in the ad.

rout   cut away.

rule   thin line used either horizontally or vertically to separate lines of display type or columns of copy.

runaround   section of text set in narrow, sometimes irregular measure to make room for art.

run in   let the words follow naturally in paragraph form.

saddle stitch   binding made through the spine of a collection of nested signatures.

sans serif type   typeface with strokes of equal or near-equal thickness and without serifs.

saturation   concentrated media coverage.

scale quality in a photograph or illustration that shows size relationships.

scaling working out measurements for art that is being enlarged or reduced to fit a given space.

scene in a commercial, the action and dialogue taking place continuously with the same background.

schedule list of media to be used for an advertising campaign.

schlock vulgar, heavy, tasteless.

scoring crease or partial cut in a piece of cardboard allowing it to be folded easily.

scotch print photographic proof from a plate negative. Used for reproduction purposes.

scratchboard drawing drawing made by scratching knife across a previously inked surface. The English call it a "scraperboard drawing."

screen crosshatched lines on a glass plate used between the camera lens and the film in the halftone process. Also, tint block in a dot pattern. Also, the concentration of dots used in halftone process. The more dots, the finer the screen.

scribing ruling a line by using a special tool to lift a thin layer of emulsion from a negative. Useful for printing forms.

script type that looks like handwriting.

second color one color in addition to black or the basic color.

second cover inside front cover.

self-cover booklet cover made from same paper stock as the inside pages.

self-mailer direct-mail piece that does not need an envelope.

sequence series of related elements or pages arranged in logical order.

series subdivision of a type family.

serifs small finishing strokes of a roman letter found at its terminals.

serigraphy silk-screen printing.

set that unit in a studio that forms the background for the actors in a TV commercial.

set solid set type without leading between lines.

SFX abbreviation for sound effects (because "FX" is pronounced "effects").

shade variation of a color.

shading sheets line or dot pattern printed on transparent paper or thin plastic that can be pressed down or transferred onto original art, creating the illusion of tone. Zipatone is one brand. There are several others.

sheet-fed press press that takes individual sheets of paper rather than rolls of paper.

shelter magazine magazine dealing with homemaking and maintenance.

shop rough very crude rough layout.

side stitch stitch through side of publication to act as its binding.

signature all the pages printed on both sides of a single sheet. The sheet is folded down to page size and trimmed. Signatures usually come in multiples of sixteen pages. A magazine or book is usually made up of several signatures. Also, the name of the advertiser at the bottom of the ad, sometimes called *sig cut*.

silhouette art subject with background removed.

silk-screen printing stencil printing through a silk screen.

silver print photographic print made from the negative used for making a plate.

slab serif type type designed with even-thickness strokes and heavy serifs. Sometimes called "square serif" type.

"slice-of-life" description applied to commercials featuring ordinary people in ordinary situations.

slick magazine magazine printed on slick or glossy paper. Sometimes called simply "slick."

slipcase a display cardboard box open at one end to receive a book or books.

slogan phrase or sentence used regularly in advertising to summarize or sell. Run usually at bottom of the ad, with the logo.

slug line of type produced by linecasting machine. Also, material for spacing between lines, 6 points or thicker.

small caps short for small capitals. Capital letters smaller than the regular capital letters in that point size.

sneak mood music in a TV commercial that comes in almost unnoticed and establishes a mood.

sort what a printer calls a piece of type.

SpectaColor ad printed in rotogravure in another plant for later insertion in a newspaper. Unlike a Preprint ad, a SpectaColor ad has clearly defined margins.

split fountain technique of printing in two colors at one time by using two colors of ink in the press's ink fountain.

split-run publication of two similar ads in a periodical; half the copies contain one of the ads, half contain the other. Used to compare effectiveness of ads.

split screen the picture is divided so that two scenes can be shown at the same time, as involving a couple on the telephone.

spot time segment on TV of sixty seconds or less used as a commercial.

spot color color other than process color. Usually printed as solid areas, in screened tints, or in line.

spot illustration drawing that stands by itself, unrelated to the text, used as a filler or for decorative purposes.

spread two facing pages. "Two-page spread" is redundant but sometimes necessary for clarity.

square serif see *slab serif type.*

SRDS *Standard Rate & Data Service.*

Standard Rate & Data Service series of regularly issued publications that carry production requirements for advertising in the various media: size limitations, plate requirements, and so on.

stat see *photostat.*

station representative to the broadcasting industry what a *publisher's representative* is to the publishing industry.

stereotype plate made from a mat that in turn was made from a photoengraving or from type.

stet proofreader's notation to the typesetter or printer to ignore the change marked on the proof.

stick metal holder into which type or Ludlow mats are placed during hand-setting operation.

stock see *paper stock.*

stock art art created for general use and stored until ordered for a particular job.

stop motion series of pictures in a film in which changes are minor but abrupt, as in the filming of an inanimate object from several angles.

storyboard series of rough sketches of scenes for a TV commercial in its planning stage, along with description of the scenes and wording of the dialogue.

straight matter text matter that is uninterrupted by headings, tables, and so on.

strike-on composition cold-type composition made with a typewriter or typewriterlike machine.

strip-in one negative fitted next to another (but not over it) so the two together can be used to make a single plate. Also used as a verb: "strip in" (two words).

style distinct and consistent approach to art or design as well as to writing.

subhead short headline inside the copy. Also "subhed."

substance weight weight of one thousand sheets of paper in a standard size.

supergraphics huge, colorful letters and typographic art used both to decorate building interiors and exteriors and to identify or give directions.

superimposition a showing of one camera image over another, as in a TV commercial.

surprint black letters over gray area, as over a photograph. Opposite of *reverse.* Used also as verb.

swash caps capital letters in some typefaces with extra flourishes in their strokes, usually in the italic versions.

swatch color sample.

"swipe file" artist's or designer's library of examples done by other artists; used for inspiration.

Swiss design design characterized by clean, simple lines and shapes, highly ordered, with lots of white space; based on a grid system.

symbol picture or abstract graphic device that suggests or stands for a product, service, or idea.

symmetric balance balance achieved by equal weights and matching placement on either side of an imaginary center line.

table list of names, titles, and so on. Particularly used in annual reports.

tabloid newspaper with pages half the usual size; about 11″ × 15″.

tag in a TV commercial, something added, such as an invitation or identification from a local announcer.

take a part of the text matter or, in television, a part of the film or tape. Also in television, a switch from one camera to another.

talent the actors, musicians, and others involved in the making of a TV commercial.

TCU abbreviation for tight closeup, as in a TV commercial.

tear sheet publication page showing the ad.

teaser ad that withholds information, including in some cases the name of the sponsor, until a later ad in the campaign.

technique way of achieving style or effect.

tempera show-card color or poster paint. Unlike watercolor, it is opaque, but it is water-soluble.

text see *body copy.*

text matter see *body copy.*

text type see *black letter.*

theme central idea in an ad or campaign.

third cover inside back cover.

thumbnail very rough preliminary sketch of an ad in miniature.

tight art art done with precision and clarity.

tight shot in a commercial, a frame that shows only the subject, with no distracting background.

tilt move camera up or down, as in making a TV commercial.

tint weaker version of tone or color.

tint block panel of color or tone on which something else may be printed.

tissue rough layout done on thin paper.

tissue overlay thin paper covering over art, copy, or the entire ad. Used as a place for noting corrections or simply as protection for what is underneath.

title crawl effect created by titles in a commercial moving up and out of the picture.

titles type used as superimpositions for TV commercials.

tone darkness of the art or type.

tooth ability of a paper or board to receive a drawing medium.

trade advertising advertising directed to retailers or wholesalers, not to the general public.

trade magazine magazine published for persons in a trade, business, or profession.

trademark symbol which identifies product or organization and which is consciously developed and adopted by that organization.

transfer type letters printed on the underside of transparent paper or thin plastic that can be rubbed off and onto a pasteup.

transparency in photography, a color positive on film rather than paper.

two-color usually black plus one color. But it can mean two separate colors without black.

two-up a printing form in duplicate to permit two copies for each printing, cutting press time in half.

type printed letters and characters. Also, the metal pieces from which the printing is done.

typeface particular style or design of type.

type specimens samples of various typefaces available.

typo typographic error made by the compositor.

typography the type in an ad. Also, the art of designing and using type.

unity design principle that holds that all elements should be related.

upper case capital letters.

value in color, the degree of lightness or darkness.

Vandyke photographic proof from a negative of a page to be printed by the offset process. Sometimes called *brownline* or *blueline.*

Velox photoprint with halftone dot pattern in place of continuous tone, ready for line reproduction.

video visual portion of a TV commercial.

video tape tape for use in broadcasting that contains both audio and video material. Unlike film, it permits immediate playback.

vignette oval-shaped halftone in which background fades away gradually all around.

visual having to do with the eye.

visualization the process by which an artist or designer changes an idea or concept into visual or pictorial form.

VO voiceover.

voiceover sequence in a TV commercial during which an announcer's or actor's voice is heard, but the person is not seen.

VTR video tape recording.

warm colors red and orange colors that tend to project toward the viewer. Stimulating colors.

wash drawing ink drawing shaded with black-and-white watercolor. Requires halftone reproduction.

web-fed press printing press that uses a roll of paper.

weight variation of type that involves the thickness of its strokes: light, medium, bold, ultrabold, and so on.

wf wrong font. Typographic error in which a character from another font is mistakenly used.

whip shot in a TV commercial, fast pan shot which blurs the action on the screen. Also known as "whiz shot," "blur pan," and "swish pan."

white space space in an ad not occupied by type, pictures, or other elements.

wide-angle shot picture made with lens that allows more to be seen at the right and the left than would otherwise be possible.

widow line of type less than the full width of the column.

wild track sound track for a TV commercial added after the filming.

wipe optical effect in a TV commercial in which a blade appears to move across the picture, wiping it clean, while another picture takes its place.

wipe over optical effect in which one picture moves into another, often geometrically.

wire side the poorer side of a sheet of paper. It is the side that rested on a traveling wire screen during the manufacturing process.

woodcut engraving cut in wood. Also, the impression made by such a plate.

worm's-eye view view from low vantage point.

XCU same as ECU.

Xerography inkless printing making use of static electricity.

x-height height of lower case *x* in any typeface. An *x* is used for measuring because its top and bottom rest exactly on the guidelines, if they were drawn.

zinc slang for *photoengraving.*

Zipatone see *shading sheets.*

zip pan see *whip shot.*

zoom a rapid change in camera distance from subject. Used also as a verb.

Bibliography

This bibliography, with a few exceptions, covers volumes published during the past decade. The arrangement follows as closely as possible the organization of material in *The Design of Advertising*. Obviously, any one volume might fit into more than one category, but it is listed only in the category that has the greatest claim on it.

General

Aaker, David A., and Myers, John G. *Advertising Management.* Englewood Cliffs, N.J.: Prentice-Hall, 1982.

Anderson, Robert L., and Barry, Thomas E. *Advertising Management: Text and Cases.* Columbus, Ohio: Charles E. Merrill, 1979.

Atwan, Robert, and others. *Edsels, Luckies and Frigidaires.* New York: Dell Publishing, 1979.

Bay, Stuart, and Thorn, William J. *Visual Persuasion.* New York: Harcourt Brace Jovanovich, 1974.

Bayer, Herbert; Gropius, Ise; and Gropius, Walter, eds. *Bauhaus 1919–1928.* Greenwich, Conn.: New York Graphic Society, 1976.

Benn, Alec. *The 27 Most Common Mistakes in Advertising.* New York: Amacom (American Management Associations), 1978.

Berman, Ronald. *Advertising and Social Change.* Beverly Hills, Calif.: Sage Publications, 1981.

Bernstein, David. *Creative Advertising.* New York: Longman, 1974. (By the director of a London agency.)

Bernstein, Sid. *This Makes Sense to Me.* Chicago: Crain Books, 1976.

Bloomer, Carolyn M. *Principles of Visual Perception.* New York: Van Nostrand Reinhold, 1976.

Bockus, H. William. *Advertising Graphics.* 2d ed. New York: Macmillan, 1974.

Boddewyn, J. J., and Marton, Katherin. *Comparison Advertising: A Worldwide Study.* New York: Hastings House, 1978.

Bolen, William H. *Advertising.* 2d ed. New York: John Wiley & Sons, 1984.

Booth-Clibborn, Edward, and Baroni, Daniele. *The Language of Graphics.* New York: Harry N. Abrams, 1980.

Bovée, Courtland L., and Arens, William F. *Contemporary Advertising.* Homewood, Ill.: Richard D. Irwin, 1982.

Broekhuizen, Richard J. *Graphic Communications.* 2d ed. Bloomington, Ill.: McKnight, 1979.

Brower, Charles. *Me and Other Advertising Geniuses.* Garden City, N.Y.: Doubleday, 1974.

Brozen, Yale, ed. *Advertising and Society.* New York: New York University Press, 1974.

Burke, John D. *Advertising in the Marketplace.* New York: Gregg Division, McGraw-Hill, 1980.

Burton, Philip Ward. *Which Ad Pulled Best?* 4th ed. Chicago: Crain Books, 1981.

Burton, Philip Ward, and Ryan, William D. *Advertising Fundamentals.* 3d ed. Columbus, Ohio: Grid Publishing, 1980.

Burton, Philip Ward, and Sandhusen, Richard L. *Cases in Advertising.* Columbus, Ohio: Grid Publishing, 1981.

Caples, John. *Tested Advertising Methods.* 4th ed. Englewood Cliffs, N.J.: Prentice-Hall, 1975.

————. *How To Make Your Advertising Make Money.* Englewood Cliffs, N.J.: Prentice-Hall, 1983.

Carter, David E. *Best Financial Advertising.* New York: Art Direction Book Co., 1980.

Cleary, David Powers. *Great American Brands.* New York: Fairchild Books, 1981.

Comanor, William S., and Wilson, Thomas A. *Advertising and Market Power.* Cambridge, Mass.: Harvard University Press, 1974.

Cook, Harvey R. *Profitable Advertising Techniques for Small Business.* Fairfield, Calif.: Entrepreneur Press, 1980.

Corkindale, David R., and Kennedy, Sherrel H. *Measuring the Effect of Advertising.* Lexington, Mass.: Lexington Books (D. C. Heath), 1976.

Daniels, Draper. *Giants, Pigmies and Other Advertising People.* Chicago: Crain Books, 1974.

Dean, Sandra Linville. *How to Advertise: A Handbook for the Small Business.* Wilmington, Del.: Enterprise Publishing, 1980.

Dichter, Ernest. *Getting Motivated by Ernest Dichter.* Elmsford, N.Y.: Pergamon Press, 1979.

Dunn, S. Watson, and Barban, Arnold M. *Advertising: Its Role in Modern Marketing.* 5th ed. New York: Dryden Press, 1982.

Dyer, Gillian. *Advertising as Communication.* London: Methuan, 1983.

Ellenthal, Ira. *Selling Smart: How the Magazine Pros Sell Advertising.* New Canaan, Conn.: Folio Magazine, 1982.

Engel, Jack. *Advertising: The Process and Practice.* New York: McGraw-Hill, 1980.

Erté. *Things I Remember.* New York: Quadrangle Books, 1975.

Evans, W. A. *Advertising Today and Tomorrow.* New York: Beekman Publishers, 1974.

Faison, Edmund W. *Advertising: A Behavioral Approach for Managers.* New York: John Wiley, 1980.

Feinman, Jeffrey. *Advertising for a Small Business.* New York: Cornerstone Library, 1980.

Ferber, Robert. *Handbook of Marketing Research.* New York: McGraw-Hill, 1976.

Fochs, Arnold. *Advertising That Won Elections.* Duluth, Minn.: A. J. Publishing Co., 1974.

Fox, Stephen. *The Mirror Makers.* New York: William Morrow & Co., 1984.

Frisby, John. *Seeing: Illusion, Brain and Mind.* New York: Oxford University Press, 1979.

Fryburger, Vernon, ed. *The New World of Advertising.* Chicago: Crain Books, 1975. (Articles from *Advertising Age.*)

Garbett, Thomas F. *Corporate Advertising: The What, the Why, and the How.* New York: McGraw-Hill, 1981.

Gardner, Burleigh. *A Conceptual Framework for Advertising.* Chicago: Crain Books, 1982.

Gardner, Herbert S., Jr. *The Advertising Agency Business.* Chicago: Crain Books, 1977.

Garfunkel, Stanley. *Developing the Advertising Plan: A Practical Guide.* New York: Random House, 1980.

Gilson, Christopher, and Berkman, Harold W. *Advertising: Concepts and Strategies.* New York: Random House, 1980.

Goffman, Erving. *Gender Advertisements.* New York: Harper & Row, 1979.

Greyser, Stephen A. *Cases in Advertising & Communications Management.* 2d ed. Englewood Cliffs, N.J.: Prentice-Hall, 1981.

Groome, Harry C., Jr. *This Is Advertising.* Philadelphia: Ayer Press, 1974.

Harris, Richard Jackson, ed. *Information Processing Research in Advertising.* Hillsdale, N.J.: Lawrence Erlbaum Associates, 1983.

Hart, Norman. *Industrial Advertising and Publicity.* London: Halsted Press, 1978.

Hiesinger, Kathryn B., and Marcus, George H. *Design Since 1945.* New York: Rizzoli, 1983. (Survey of product design.)

Holme, Bryan. *Advertising: Reflections of a Century.* New York: Viking Press, 1982.

Holtje, Herbert F. *Schaum's Outline of Theory and Problems of Advertising.* New York: McGraw-Hill, 1978.

Hopkins, Claude. *Scientific Advertising.* New York: Chelsea House, 1980. (Paperback reprint of a classic.)

Hornsby, Ken. *The Padded Sell: The Secret Life of an Ad Man.* New York: St. Martin's Press, 1980. (Explores the workings of an English ad agency.)

Hornung, Clarence P., and Johnson, Fridolf. *Two Hundred Years of American Graphic Arts: A Pictorial Survey of the Printing Arts and Advertising, Past and Present.* New York: George Braziller, 1975.

Howard, John A., and Hulbert, James. *Advertising and the Public Interest.* Chicago: Crain Books, 1975.

Hyman, Allen, and Johnson, M. Bruce, eds. *Advertising and Free Speech.* Lexington, Mass.: Lexington Books (D. C. Heath), 1977.

Johnson, J. Douglas. *Advertising Today.* Palo Alto, Calif.: Science Research Associates, 1980.

Johnson, Philip M. *How to Maximize Your Advertising Investment.* Boston: CBI Publishing Company, 1980.

Jones, Robert W. *The Business of Advertising.* New York: Longman, 1974.

Jugenheimer, Donald W., and Turk, Peter B. *Advertising Media.* Columbus, Ohio: Grid Publishing, 1979.

Jugenheimer, Donald W., and White, Gordon E. *Basic Advertising.* Columbus, Ohio: Grid Publishing, 1980.

Jussim, Estelle. *Visual Communication and the Graphic Arts.* New York: R. R. Bowker, 1974.

Kaufman, Louis. *Essentials of Advertising.* New York: Harcourt Brace Jovanovich, 1980.

Kennedy, Sherrie H., and Corkindale, David R. *Managing the Advertising Process.* Lexington, Mass.: Lexington Books (D. C. Heath), 1976.

Key, Wilson B. *The Clam-Plate Orgy: And Other Subliminals the Media Use to Manipulate Your Behavior.* Englewood Cliffs, N.J.: Prentice-Hall, 1980.

King, Francis S. *Modern Advertising Skills.* New York: Van Nostrand Reinhold, 1983.

Kleppner, Otto, and others. *Advertising Procedure.* 8th ed. Englewood Cliffs, N.J.: Prentice-Hall, 1983.

Kornfeld, Lewis. *To Catch a Mouse Make a Noise Like a Cheese.* Englewood Cliffs, N.J.: Prentice-Hall, 1983.

Lewis, Herschell. *More Than You Ever Wanted to Know About Mail Order Advertising.* Englewood Cliffs, N.J.: Prentice-Hall, 1983.

Lewis, H. Gordon. *How to Make Your Advertising Twice as Effective at Half the Cost.* Chicago: Nelson-Hall, 1979.

Leymore, Varda Langholz. *Hidden Myth: Structure & Symbolism in Advertising.* New York: Basic Books, 1975.

Lipstein, Benjamin, and McGuire, William J. *Evaluating Advertising: A Bibliography of the Communications Process.* New York: Advertising Research Foundation, 1978.

Lois, George, and Pitts, Bill. *The Art of Advertising: George Lois on Mass Communication.* New York: Harry N. Abrams, 1977.

McGregor, Eric. *Advertising.* New York: International Publications Services, 1974.

Mandell, Maurice I. *Advertising.* 3d ed. Englewood Cliffs, N.J.: Prentice-Hall, 1983.

Millum, Trevor. *Images of Woman: Advertising in Women's Magazines.* Totowa, N.J.: Rowman & Littlefield, 1975. (Covers ads in women's magazines in Great Britain.)

Mitchell, Richard. *Less Than Words Can Say.* Boston: Little, Brown, 1979.

Muller-Brockmann, Josef. *A History of Visual Communication.* New York: Hastings House, 1981.

Naples, Michael J. *Effective Frequency: The Relationship Between Frequency and Advertising Effectiveness.* New York: Association of National Advertisers, 1981.

Neelankavil, James P., and Stridsberg, Albert B. *Advertising Self-Regulation: A Global Perspective.* New York: Hastings House, 1980.

Nicholl, David S. *Advertising.* New York: International Publications Services, 1974.

Nicosia, Francesco M. *Advertising, Management, and Society.* New York: McGraw-Hill, 1974.

Norris, James S. *Advertising.* Reston, Va.: Reston, 1980.

Nylen, David W. *Advertising: Planning, Implementation, and Control.* Cincinnati: South-Western, 1975.

Ogilvy, David. *Ogilvy on Advertising.* New York: Crown, 1983.

O'Toole, John. *The Trouble with Advertising.* New York: Chelsea House, 1981.

Parker, Robert B. *Mature Advertising.* Reading, Mass.: Addison-Wesley, 1980.

Percy, Larry, and Rossiter, John R. *Advertising Strategy: A Communication Theory Approach.* New York: Praeger, 1980.

Pollay, Richard W., ed. *Information Sources in Advertising History.* Westport, Conn.: Greenwood Press, 1979.

Polykoff, Shirley. *Does She . . . Or Doesn't She and How She Did It.* New York: Doubleday, 1975.

Pope, Daniel. *The Making of Modern Advertising.* New York: Basic Books, 1983.

Poppe, Fred C. *The 100 Greatest Corporate and Industrial Ads.* New York: Van Nostrand Reinhold, 1983.

Preston, Ivan L. *The Great American Blow-up: Puffery in Advertising and Selling.* Madison, Wis.: University of Wisconsin Press, 1975.

Pritikin, Robert C. *Christ Was an Ad Man: The Amazing New Testament in Advertising.* San Francisco: Harbor Publishing, 1980.

Quera, Leon. *Advertising Campaigns: Formulation and Tactics.* 2d ed. Columbus, Ohio: Grid Publishing, 1977.

Ramond, Charles. *Advertising Research: The State of the Art.* New York: Association of National Advertisers, 1976.

Rank, Hugh. *The Pitch: How to Analyze Ads.* Park Forest, Ill.: The Counter-Propaganda Press, 1982.

Ray, Michael L. *Advertising and Communication Management.* Englewood Cliffs, N.J.: Prentice-Hall, 1982.

Ries, Al, and Trout, Jack. *Positioning: The Battle for Your Mind.* New York: McGraw-Hill, 1981.

Rohrer, Daniel M. *Mass Media, Freedom of Speech, and Advertising: A Study in Communication.* Dubuque, Iowa: Kendall/Hunt, 1979.

Roman, Kenneth, and Maas, Jane. *How to Advertise.* New York: St. Martin's Press, 1975.

Roskill, Mark, and Carrier, David. *Truth and Falsehood in Visual Images.* Amherst: University of Massachusetts Press, 1983.

Roth, Robert F. *Handbook of International Marketing Communications.* Chicago: Crain Books, 1982.

Runyan, Kenneth E. *Advertising.* 2d ed. Columbus, Ohio: Charles E. Merrill, 1984.

Sackheim, Maxwell. *My First 65 Years in Advertising.* Blue Ridge Summit, Pa.: TAB Books, 1975.

Samuels, Mike, and Samuels, Nancy. *Seeing with the Mind's Eye.* New York: Random House/Book Works, 1975.

Sandage, Charles H., and others. *Advertising: Theory and Practice.* 10th ed. Homewood, Ill.: Richard D. Irwin, 1979.

Schick, Dennis, and Book, Albert C. *Fundamentals of Creative Advertising.* Chicago: Crain Books, 1980.

Schultz, Don E. *Essentials of Creative Advertising.* Chicago: Crain Books, 1981.

Schultz, Don E., and Martin, Dennis. *Strategic Advertising Campaigns.* 2d ed. Chicago: Crain Books, 1984.

Sethi, S. Prakash. *Advocacy Advertising and Large Corporations.* Lexington, Mass.: Lexington Books (D. C. Heath), 1976.

Sissors, Jack Z., and Petray, E. Reynold. *Advertising Media Planning.* Chicago: Crain Books, 1975.

Spero, Robert. *The Duping of the American Voter: Dishonesty and Deception in Presidential Television Advertising.* New York: Lippincott & Crowell, 1980.

Stansfield, Richard H. *Advertising Manager's Handbook.* 2d ed. Chicago: Dartnell, 1982.

Surmanek, Jim. *Media Planning.* Chicago: Crain Books, 1981.

Sutton, Cort. *Advertising Your Way to Success.* Englewood Cliffs, N.J.: Prentice-Hall, 1981.

Switkin, Abraham. *Ads: Design and Make Your Own.* New York: Van Nostrand Reinhold, 1981.

Tolley, B. Stuart. *Advertising and Marketing Research: A New Methodology.* Chicago: Nelson-Hall, 1977.

Ulanoff, Stanley M. *Advertising in America.* New York: Hastings House, 1977.

Urdang, Laurence, ed. *Dictionary of Advertising Terms.* Chicago: Tatham, Laird & Kudner, 1977.

Wademan, Victor. *Risk-Free Advertising: How to Come Close to It.* New York: Wiley-Interscience, 1977.

Walker, Morton. *Advertising and Promoting The Professional Practice.* New York: E. P. Dutton, 1979.

———. *How to Advertise and Promote Your Professional Practice.* New York: Macmillan, 1982.

Weilbacher, William M. *Advertising.* 2d ed. New York: Macmillan, 1984.

Weiss, George. *Plus Business Guide to Effective Advertising.* New York: Metro Associated Services, 1980.

Wheatley, Edward W. *Marketing Professional Services.* Englewood Cliffs, N.J.: Prentice-Hall, 1983.

White, Gordon. *John Caples, Adman.* Chicago: Crain Books, 1978.

White, Roderick. *Advertising: What It Is and How to Do It.* New York: McGraw-Hill, 1981.

Williamson, Judith. *Decoding Advertisements: Ideology and Meaning in Advertising.* Salem, N.H.: Marion Boyars Publishers, 1978.

Winters, Arthur A., and Goodman, Stanley. *Fashion Advertising and Promotion.* 5th ed. New York: Fairchild Books, 1982.

Wright, John S.; Warner, Daniel S.; Winter, Willis L., Jr.; and Zeigler, Sherilyn. *Advertising.* 5th ed. New York: McGraw-Hill, 1982.

Yorke, Malcolm. *Eric Gill: Man of Flesh and Spirit.* New York: Universe Books, 1982.

Advertising Ease. Toronto, Canada: MacLaren Advertising, 1975. (Definitions of advertising terms.)

Ayer Glossary of Advertising and Related Terms. Philadelphia: Ayer Press, 1974.

Controversy Advertising: How Advertisers Present Points of View in Public Affairs. New York: Hastings House, 1977.

Erté at Ninety: The Complete Graphics. New York: E. P. Dutton, 1982.

50 Years of Advertising: 1930–1980. Chicago: Crain Books, 1980.

How It Was in Advertising: 1776–1976. Chicago: Crain Books, 1976. (Reprinting of April 19, 1976 issue of *Advertising Age.*)

Images of Family Life in Magazine Advertising. New York: Holt, Rinehart & Winston, 1981.

Is the Bug Dead? New York: Stewart, Tabori & Chang, 1982. (Reproduction of all the great VW ads.)

Creativity

Amabile, T. M. *The Social Psychology of Creativity.* New York: Springer-Verlag, 1983.

Arieti, Silvano. *Creativity: The Magic Synthesis.* New York: Basic Books, 1976.

Baker, Steven. *Systematic Approach to Advertising Creativity.* New York: McGraw-Hill, 1983. (Paperback edition of 1979 book.)

Buxton, Edward. *Creative People at Work.* New York: Executive Communications (Whirlwind Books, distributor), 1976.

Buzan, Tony. *Use Both Sides of Your Brain.* New York: E. P. Dutton, 1983.

Ceynar, Marvin E., ed. *Creativity in the Communicative Arts: A Selected Bibliography 1960–1970.* Troy, N.Y.: Whitston Publishing, 1975.

Csikszentmihalyi, Mihaly, and Getzels, Jacob W. *The Creative Vision: A Longitudinal Study of Problem Finding in Art.* New York: John Wiley & Sons, 1976.

Edwards, Betty. *Drawing on the Right Side of the Brain: A Course in Enhancing Creativity and Artistic Confidence.* Los Angeles: J. P. Tarcher, 1979.

Edwards, David D. *How to Be More Creative.* San Francisco: Occasional Productions, 251 Parnassus Ave., 94117, 1979.

Ernst, Sandra. *The Creative Style: A Working Text for Advertising Copy and Layout.* Columbus, Ohio: Grid Publishing, 1979.

Garchik, Morton. *Creative Visual Thinking: How to Think Up Ideas Fast.* New York: Art Direction Book Co., 1982.

Gardner, Howard. *Art, Mind, and Brain: A Cognitive Approach to Creativity.* New York: Basic Books, 1982.

Hanks, Kurt, and Belliston, Larry. *Rapid Viz: Techniques for Rapid Visualization of Ideas.* Los Altos, Calif.: William Kaufmann, 1980.

Hixon, Carl K., and Noble, John. *What Every Young Account Representative Should Know About The Creative Function.* New York: American Association of Advertising Agencies, 1979.

Jewler, A. Jerome. *Creative Strategy in Advertising.* Belmont, Calif.: Wadsworth, 1981.

Marstellar, Wm. A. *Creative Management.* Chicago: Crain Books, 1981. (How to deal with creative people.)

May, Rollo. *The Courage to Create.* New York: Liveright Publishing Corp., 1975.

Nordenfalk, Carl. *Creativity and Disease: How Art, Literature and Music Are Influenced by Disease.* Philadelphia, Pa.: George F. Stickley, 1983.

Perkins, D. N. *The Mind's Best Work: A New Psychology of Creative Thinking.* Cambridge, Mass.: Harvard University Press, 1983. (Paperback Edition.)

Rothenberg, Albert. *The Emerging Goddess: The Creative Process in Art, Science, and Other Fields.* Chicago: University of Chicago Press, 1982.

Seeley, J. *High Contrast: Creative Imagemaking for Photographers, Designers and Graphic Artists.* New York: Van Nostrand Reinhold, 1980.

VanGundy, Arthur B. *108 Ways to Get a Bright Idea and Increase Your Creative Potential.* Englewood Cliffs, N.J.: Prentice-Hall, 1983.

Wileman, Ralph E. *Exercises in Visual Thinking.* New York: Hastings House, 1980.

Young, James Webb. *A Technique for Producing Ideas.* New ed. Chicago: Crain Books, 1975.

Zeigler, Sherilyn, and Johnson, J. Douglas. *Creative Strategy and Tactics in Advertising.* Columbus, Ohio: Grid Publishing, 1981.

Copywriting

Burton, Philip Ward. *Advertising Copywriting.* 5th ed. Columbus, Ohio: Grid Publishing, 1983.

Crompton, Alistair. *The Craft of Copywriting.* Rev. Am. ed. Englewood Cliffs, N.J.: Prentice-Hall, 1982.

Gross, Edmund J. *Copy Stimulators.* North Hollywood, Calif.: Halls of Ivy Press, 1975. (A "thesaurus of headlines.")

Hafer, W. Keith, and White, Gordon E. *Advertising Writing.* St. Paul, Minn.: West Publishing, 1977.

Hilliard, Robert L. *Writing for Television and Radio.* 3d ed. New York: Hastings House, 1976. (Includes a chapter on "Announcements and Commercials.")

Lee, Robert, and Misiorowski, Robert. *Script Models: A Handbook for the Media Writer.* New York: Hastings House, 1978. (Style book for radio, TV, and film writers, with material on storyboards.)

Malickson, David L., and Nason, John W. *Advertising—How to Write the Kind that Works.* Rev. ed. New York: Charles Scribner's Sons, 1982.

Milton, Shirley F., and Winters, Arthur A. *The Creative Connection: Advertising Copywriting and Idea Visualization.* New York: Fairchild Books, 1982.

Monnot, Michel. *Selling America: Puns, Language, and Advertising.* Washington, D.C.: University Press of America, 1982.

Norback, Peter, and Norback, Craig. *Great Songs of Madison Avenue.* New York: Quadrangle Books, 1976.

Norins, Hanley. *The Compleat Copywriter.* 2d ed. Melbourne, Florida: R. E. Krieger Publishing, 1980.

Orlick, Peter B. *Broadcast Copywriting.* Boston: Allyn & Bacon, 1978.

Parker, Robert B. *Mature Advertising: A Handbook of Effective Advertising Copy.* Reading, Mass.: Addison-Wesley, 1981.

Rasberry, Leslie. *Computer Age Copyfitting.* New York: Art Direction Book Co., 1982.

Robinson, Sol. *Radio Advertising—How to Sell It and Write It.* Blue Ridge Summit, Pa.: TAB Books, 1974.

Roman, Kenneth, and Maas, Jane. *How to Advertise.* New York: St. Martin's Press, 1976. (Mostly about copy. Written for advertisers.)

Roman, Ken, and Raphaelson, Joel. *How to Write Better.* New York: Ogilvy & Mather, 1978.

Schwab, Victor O. *How to Write a Good Advertisement.* North Hollywood, Calif.: Wilshire Book Co., 1980.

Senger, Frank B. *Advertising Copy and Layout.* Danville, Ill.: Interstate Printers & Publishers, 1979.

Weaver, J. Clark. *Broadcast Copywriting as Process.* New York: Longman, 1984.

Design and layout

Arnold, Edmund. *Arnold's Ancient Axioms.* Chicago: Ragan Report Press, 1978.

Bagley, Stephen. *In Good Shape.* New York: Van Nostrand Reinhold, 1980. (Surveys industrial design of this century.)

Berryman, Gregg. *Notes on Graphic Design and Visual Communication.* Los Altos, Calif.: William Kauffmann, 1979.

Biesele, Igildo G. *Graphic Design Education.* New York: Hastings House, 1981.

Borgman, Harry. *Advertising Layout.* New York: Watson-Guptill, 1983.

Campbell, Alastair. *The Graphic Designer's Handbook.* Philadelphia: Running Press, 1983.

Chadbourne, Bill N. *What Every Editor Should Know About Layout and Typography.* Arlington, Va.: National Composition Association (1730 N. Lynn St., 22209), 1979.

Chwast, Seymour. *Idea's Special Issue of Seymour Chwast.* New York: Museum Books, 1974.

Davis, Alec. *Graphics: Design into Production.* New York: Pitman Publishing Corporation, 1974.

Donahue, Bud. *The Language of Layout.* Englewood Cliffs, N.J.: Prentice-Hall, 1978.

Dorn, Ray. *20 Problems/20 Solutions: The Basic Design Workbook.* Chicago, Ill.: Lawrence Ragan Communications, 407 S. Dearborn St., 60605, 1980.

Gates, David. *Graphic Design Studio Techniques.* New York: Watson-Guptill, 1978.

Gill, Bob. *Forget All the Rules You Ever Learned About Graphic Design. Including the Ones in This Book.* New York: Watson-Guptill, 1981.

Glaser, Milton. *Milton Glaser: Graphic Design.* New York: Overlook Press (Viking), 1973.

Goodchild, Jon, and Henkin, Bill. *By Design: A Graphics Sourcebook of Materials, Equipment and Services.* New York: Quick Fox, 1980.

Hanks, Kurt; Belliston, Larry; and Edwards, Dave. *Design Yourself!* Los Altos, Calif.: William Kaufmann, 1977.

Hartmann, Robert. *Graphics for Designers.* Ames, Iowa: Iowa State University Press, 1979.

Herdeg, Walter. *Graphics/Diagrams: The Graphic Visualization of Abstract Data.* New York: Hastings House, 1975.

Humbert, Claude. *Label Design.* Washington, D.C.: Packaging Design (6400 Goldsboro Road), 1974.

Hurlburt, Allen. *The Grid System.* New York: Van Nostrand Reinhold, 1978.

———. *The Design Concept.* New York: Watson-Guptill, 1981.

Ishioka, Eiko. *Eiko by Eiko.* New York: Callaway Editions, 1983. (Graphic design examples by a famous Japanese art director.)

Jussim, Estelle. *Visual Communication and the Graphic Arts.* New York: R. R. Bowker, 1974.

Karo, Jerzy. *Graphics Design.* New York: Van Nostrand Reinhold, 1975.

Laing, John, ed. *Do It Yourself Graphic Design.* New York: Facts on File, 1984.

Loewy, Raymond. *Industrial Design.* New York: Overlook Press (Viking), 1979.

McConnell, John, ed. *Design and Art Direction.* New York: Hastings House, 1974.

Mayall, W. H. *Principles in Design.* New York: Van Nostrand Reinhold, 1979.

Meggs, Philip. *A History of Graphic Design.* New York: Van Nostrand Reinhold, 1983.

Missingham, Hal. *Design Focus.* New York: Van Nostrand Reinhold, 1978.

Muller-Brockmann, Josef. *The Graphic Designer and His Design Problems.* Rev. ed. New York: Hastings House, 1984.

Munce, Howard. *Graphics Handbook.* New York: Northlight/Van Nostrand Reinhold, 1982.

Nelson, George. *George Nelson on Design.* New York: Whitney Library of Design, 1979.

Pile, John F. *Design: Purpose, Form, and Meaning.* Amherst: University of Massachusetts Press, 1979.

Prohaska, Ray. *A Basic Course in Design.* New York: Van Nostrand Reinhold, 1980.

Schmittel, Wolfgang. *Design/Concept/Realization.* New York: Hastings House, 1976. (Covers design philosophies of six major companies, including Herman Miller and Braun.)

Silver, Gerald A. *Graphic Layout and Design.* Albany, N.Y.: Delmar Publications, 1981.

———. *Mastering Graphics: Design and Production Made Easy.* New York: R. R. Bowker, 1983.

White, Jon. *Graphic Idea Notebook.* New York: Watson-Guptill, 1980.

Print Casebooks 4, Print, Washington, D.C., 1980–81. (Six-volume set showing 266 award-winning design projects. One volume covers annual reports, another shows covers and posters.)

Type and letterform

Baker, Arthur. *Calligraphy.* New York: Dover Publications, 1973.

Biegeleisen, J. I. *Art Directors' Work Book of Type Faces.* Rev. ed. New York: Arco Publishing, 1976.

Cirillo, Bob, and Ahearn, Kevin. *Dry Faces.* New York: Art Direction Book Company, 1978. (Shows one thousand faces available from manufacturers of dry transfer letters.)

Clements, Ben, and Rosenfield, David. *Photographic Composition.* Englewood Cliffs, N.J.: Prentice-Hall, 1974.

Craig, James. *Phototypesetting: A Design Manual.* New York: Watson-Guptill, 1978.

———. *Designing with Type.* Rev. ed. New York: Watson-Guptill, 1980.

Dair, Carl. *Design with Type.* New ed. Buffalo, New York: University of Toronto Press, 1982.

Ernst, Sandra B. *The ABC's of Typography.* New York: Art Direction Book Co., 1978.

Gates, David. *Type.* New York: Watson-Guptill, 1974.

Goines, David Lance. *A Constructed Roman Alphabet.* New York: David R. Godine, 1983.

Haley, Allan. *Phototypography.* New York: Charles Scribner's Sons, 1981.

King, Jean Callan, and Esposito, Tony. *The Designer's Guide to Text Type.* New York: Van Nostrand Reinhold, 1982.

Kleper, Michael L. *Understanding Phototypesetting.* Philadelphia: North American Publishing Co., 1976.

Lawson, Alexander, and Provan, Archie. *Typography for Composition.* Arlington, Va.: National Composition Association (1730 N. Lynn St.), 1976.

Lewis, John. *Typography: Design and Practice.* Rev. ed. New York: Taplinger Publishing, 1978.

Mann, William. *Lettering and Lettering Display.* New York: Van Nostrand Reinhold, 1974.

Menne, Susan. *Teach Yourself to Fit Copy.* Brea, Calif.: Sunrise Communications (Box 1452, 92621), 1980.

Morison, Stanley. *A Tally of Types.* New York: Cambridge University Press, 1973. (Covering types designed by Morison.)

———. *Selected Essays on the History of Letter-forms in Manuscript and Print.* New York: Cambridge University Press, 1982. (Two volumes.)

Ogg, Oscar. *The 26 Letters.* Rev. ed. New York: Van Nostrand Reinhold, 1983.

Rehe, Rolf F. *Typography: How to Make it Most Legible.* Carmel, Ind.: Design Research International (P.O. Box 27, 46032), 1974.

Rosen, Ben. *Type and Typography: The Designer's Notebook.* Rev. ed. New York: Van Nostrand Reinhold, 1976.

Ryder, John. *The Case for Legibility.* New York: Moretus Press, 1979.

Spencer, Herbert. *Pioneers of Modern Typography.* Cambridge, Mass.: MIT Press, 1983. (Paperback edition of 1969 book.)

Torre, Vincent, ed. *A Tribute to William Addison Dwiggins on the Hundredth Anniversary of His Birth.* New York: Inkwell Press, 1983.

Updike, Daniel Berkeley. *Printing Types: Their History, Forms and Use.* New York: Dover Publications, 1980. (Two volumes. Reprint of a classic.)

Walkin, Carol. *Designing with Letters.* New York: Drake Publishers, 1974.

The Type Specimen Book. New York: Van Nostrand Reinhold, 1974. (544 faces, 3,000 sizes.)

Art and photography

Beakley, George C. *Freehand Drawing and Visualization.* Indianapolis: Bobbs-Merrill, 1982.

Borgman, Harry. *Landscape Painting with Markers.* New York: Watson-Guptill, 1977. (The techniques and effects shown can be used to prepare comps and storyboards.)

———. *Drawing in Ink: Drawing for Reproduction.* New York: Watson-Guptill, 1977.

———. *Art & Illustration Techniques.* New York: Watson-Guptill, 1979.

Cardamone, Tom. *Chart and Graph Preparation Skills.* New York: Van Nostrand Reinhold, 1981.

Chamberlain, Betty. *The Artist's Guide to His Market.* Rev. ed. New York: Watson-Guptill, 1975.

Cherry, David. *Preparing Artwork for Reproduction.* New York: Crown Publishers, 1976.

Craven, George M. *Object and Image: An Introduction to Photography.* Englewood Cliffs, N.J.: Prentice-Hall, 1975.

Crawford, Tad. *Legal Guide for the Visual Artist.* New York: Hawthorn, 1977.

Davis, Phil. *Photography.* 3d ed. Dubuque, Iowa: Wm. C. Brown Company Publishers, 1979.

Douglis, Philip N. *Communicating with Pictures.* Chicago: Laurence Ragan Communications (407 S. Dearborn Street, 60605), 1979.

Editors of Eastman Kodak Company. *The Joy of Photography.* Reading, Mass.: Addison-Wesley, 1980.

———. *More Joy of Photography: 100 Techniques for More Creative Photographs.* Boston: Addison-Wesley, 1981.

Edom, Clifton C. *Photojournalism.* 2d ed. Dubuque, Iowa: Wm. C. Brown Company Publishers, 1980.

Evans, Harold. *Pictures on a Page: Photojournalism and Picture Editing.* Belmont, Calif.: Wadsworth Publishing Company, 1979.

Evans, Hilary. *The Art of Picture Research.* London: David & Charles, 1980.

Fincher, Terry. *Creative Techniques in Photojournalism.* New York: Lippincott & Crowell, 1980.

Firpo, Patrick, et al. *Copy Art: The First Complete Guide to the Copy Machine.* New York: Richard Marek Publishers, 1978.

Gray, Bill. *More Studio Tips for Artists and Graphic Designers.* New York: Van Nostrand Reinhold, 1978.

Hammond, Bill. *How to Make Money in Advertising Photography.* Garden City, N.Y.: Amphoto, 1975.

Herdeg, Walter, ed. *Graphis Diagrams: The Graphic Visualization of Abstract Data.* New ed. New York: Hastings House, 1982.

Hinwood, Tony. *Advertising Art: Time- and Money-Saving Tricks of the Trade.* Newton Abbot, England: David & Charles, 1973.

Johnson, Diana L. *Fantastic Illustration and Design in Great Britain, 1850–1930.* Cambridge, Mass.: M.I.T. Press, 1980.

Kemp, Weston D. *Photography for Visual Communicators.* Englewood Cliffs, N.J.: Prentice-Hall, 1973.

Kerns, Robert. *Photojournalism: Photography with a Purpose.* Englewood Cliffs, N.J.: Prentice-Hall, 1980.

Kince, Eli. *Visual Puns in Design.* New York: Watson-Guptill, 1982.

Kobre, Kenneth. *Photojournalism: The Professionals' Approach.* New York: Van Nostrand Reinhold, 1980.

Laliberté, Norman, and Mogelon, Alex. *The Reinhold Book of Art Ideas.* New York: Van Nostrand Reinhold, 1976.

Leymore, Varda Langholz. *Hidden Myth: Structure and Symbolism in Advertising.* New York: Basic Books, 1975.

Lundquist, Par. *Photographics.* New York: Van Nostrand Reinhold, 1972. (Covers ways to posterize photographs.)

McMullan, James. *Revealing Illustrations.* New York: Watson-Guptill, 1981.

Mayer, Ralph. *A Dictionary of Art Terms and Techniques.* New York: Barnes & Noble, 1981.

———. *The Artist's Handbook of Materials and Techniques.* 4th ed. New York: Viking Press, 1981.

Meyer, Susan E. *America's Great Illustrators.* New York: Harry N. Abrams, 1978.

Miller, Ernestine, comp. *The Art of Advertising: Great Commercial Illustrations from The Early Years of Magazines.* New York: St. Martin's Press, 1980.

Munce, Howard, ed. *Illustration in the Third Dimension.* New York: Hastings House, 1978.

Nelson, Norbert N. *Photographing Your Product, for Advertising and Promotion.* New York: Van Nostrand Reinhold, 1970.

Nelson, Roy Paul. *Cartooning.* Chicago: Henry Regnery, 1975. (Devotes some attention to cartoons used in advertising.)

———. *Comic Art and Caricature.* Chicago: Contemporary Books, 1978.

———. *Humorous Illustration and Cartooning: A Guide for Editors, Advertisers, and Artists.* Englewood Cliffs, N.J.: Prentice-Hall, 1984.

Peppin, Brigid. *Dictionary of Book Illustrators 1800–1970.* New York: Arco Publishing, 1980. (Covers twelve hundred artists, with samples of their work.)

Perlman, Bennard B. *F. R. Gruger and His Circle: The Golden Age of American Illustration.* New York: Van Nostrand Reinhold, 1978.

Quick, John. *Artists' and Illustrators' Encyclopedia.* 2d ed. New York: McGraw-Hill, 1977.

Reedy, William A. *Impact—Photography for Advertising.* Rochester, N.Y.: Eastman Kodak Company, 1974.

Rhode, Robert B., and McCall, Floyd H. *Introduction to Photography.* 3d ed. New York: Macmillan, 1976.

Rosen, Marvin J. *Introduction to Photography.* 2d ed. Boston: Houghton Mifflin, 1982.

Rothstein, Arthur. *Photojournalism.* 4th ed. Garden City, N.Y.: Amphoto, 1979.

Salomon, Allyn. *Advertising Photography.* New York: Watson-Guptill, 1982.

Sanders, Norman. *Photographing for Publication.* New York: R. R. Bowker, 1983.

Snyder, John. *Commercial Artists Handbook.* New York: Watson-Guptill, 1973.

Snyder, Norman, ed. *The Photography Catalog: A Sourcebook of the Best Equipment, Materials and Photographic Resources.* New York: Harper & Row, 1976.

Sontag, Susan. *On Photography.* New York: Farrar, Straus & Giroux, 1976.

Swedlund, Charles. *Photography: A Handbook of History, Materials, and Processes.* New York: Holt, Rinehart & Winston, 1981.

Tait, Jack. *Beyond Photography: The Transformed Image.* New York: Hastings House, 1977.

Thompson, Philip, and Davenport, Peter. *The Dictionary of Graphic Images.* New York: St. Martin's Press, 1980.

Wakerman, Elyce. *Air Powered: The Art of the Airbrush.* New York: Random House, 1980.

Wood, Phyllis. *Scientific Illustration: A Guide to Biological, Zoological and Medical Rendering Techniques, Design, Printing and Display.* New York: Van Nostrand Reinhold, 1979.

Art Books, 1950–1979. New York: R. R. Bowker, 1979. (Listing of 37,000 books on fine and applied arts, including design.)

Production and printing

Bockus, William. *Advertising Graphics.* 2d. ed. New York: Macmillan, 1974.

Borowsky, Irvin J. *Handbook for Color Printing.* Philadelphia: North American Publishing Company, 1974.

Cardamone, Tom. *Mechanical Color Separation Skills for the Commercial Artist.* New York: Van Nostrand Reinhold, 1979.

Craig, James. *Production for the Graphic Designer.* New York: Watson-Guptill, 1974.

Craver, John S. *Graph Paper from Your Copier.* Tucson, Ariz.: H P Books, 1980.

Demuney, Jerry, and Meyer, Susan E. *Pasteups and Mechanicals.* New York: Watson-Guptill, 1982.

Dennis, Ervin A., and Jenkins, John D. *Comprehensive Graphic Arts.* Indianapolis, Ind.: Howard W. Sams & Company, 1974.

Field, Janet N., senior ed. *Graphic Arts Manual.* New York: Arno Press, 1980.

Gottschall, Edward M. *Graphic Communication '80s.* Englewood Cliffs, N.J.: Prentice-Hall, 1981. (Covers latest trends in digital/electronic technologies.)

Graham, Walter B. *Complete Guide to Pasteup.* Philadelphia: North American Publishing Company, 1975.

Gross, Edmund J. *How to Do Your Own Pasteup for Printing.* North Hollywood, Calif.: Halls of Ivy Press, 1979.

Jauneau, Roger. *Small Printing Houses and Modern Technology.* Paris: Unesco Press, 1981.

Lasday, Stanley B. *The Handbook for Graphic Communications.* Pittsburgh: Graphic Arts Technical Foundation, 1975.

Latimer, H. C. *Advertising Production.* 3d ed. New York: Hastings House, 1974.

———. *Production Planning and Repro Mechanicals for Offset Printing.* New York: McGraw-Hill, 1981.

Levitan, Eli. *Handbook of Electronic Imaging Techniques.* New York: Van Nostrand Reinhold, 1977.

Mintz, Patricia Barnes. *Dictionary of Graphic Arts Terms.* New York: Van Nostrand Reinhold, 1981.

Moran, James. *Printing in the Twentieth Century: A Penrose Anthology.* New York: Hastings House, 1974.

Munce, Howard. *Graphics Handbook: A Beginner's Guide to Design, Copy Fitting and Printing Procedures.* New York: North Light Publishers (distributed by Van Nostrand Reinhold), 1982.

Sanders, Norman, and Bevington, William. *Graphic Designer's Production Handbook.* New York: Hastings House, 1982.

Schlemmer, Richard M. *Handbook of Advertising Art Production.* 2d ed. Englewood Cliffs, N.J.: Prentice-Hall, 1976.

Seybold, John W. *Fundamentals of Modern Composition.* Media, Pa.: Seybold Publications (Box 44, 19063), 1977.

Silver, Gerald A. *Printing Estimating.* Chicago: American Technical Society, 1973.

———. *Modern Graphic Arts Paste-up.* 2d ed. New York: Van Nostrand Reinhold, 1983.

Simon, Herbert. *Introduction to Printing.* Salem, N.H.: Faber & Faber, 1980.

Spence, William P., and Vequist, David G. *Graphic Reproduction.* Peoria, Ill.: Chas. A. Bennett Co., 1981.

Stevenson, George A. *Graphic Arts Encyclopedia.* 2d ed. New York: McGraw-Hill, 1979.

Turnbull, Arthur T., and Baird, Russell N. *The Graphics of Communications.* 4th ed. New York: Holt, Rinehart & Winston, 1980.

White, William. *Laser Printing.* Madison, N.J.: Carnegie Press, 1983.

Graphic Arts Manual. New York: Musarts Publishing Corp., 1975.

The Lithographers Manual. 5th ed. Pittsburgh: Graphic Arts Technical Foundation, 1975.

Pocket Pal: A Graphic Arts Digest for Printers and Advertising Production Managers. New York: International Paper, published periodically in new editions.

Color

Agogton, G. A. *Color Theory and Its Applications in Art and Design.* New York: Springer-Verlag, 1979.

Ellinger, Richard G. *Color Structure and Design.* New York: Van Nostrand Reinhold, 1980.

Favre, Jean-Paul, and November, Andre. *Color and Communication.* New York: Hastings House, 1979.

Küppers, Harald. *Color: Origins, Systems, Uses.* New York: Van Nostrand Reinhold, 1973.

Sharpe, Deborah T. *The Psychology of Color and Design.* Chicago: Nelson-Hall, 1974.

Halftone Reproduction Guide. Great Neck, N.Y.: Halftone Reproduction Guide (P.O. Box 212), 1975. (More than twelve hundred different effects using two-color printing.)

Retail advertising

Antebi, Michael. *The Nitty Gritty Guide to Co-op Advertising.* Chicago: Crain Books, 1978.

Block, Davida. *A Guide to Effective Real Estate Advertising.* New York: McGraw-Hill, 1981.

Edwards, C. M., Jr., and Liebowitz, Carl R. *Retail Advertising and Sales Promotion.* 4th ed. Englewood Cliffs, N.J.: Prentice-Hall, 1980.

Fochs, Arnold. *The Very Idea: A Collection of Unusual Retail Advertising Ideas.* Duluth, Minn.: A. J. Publishing Co., 1974.

———, ed. *Best Local-Retail Ads 1960–1975.* Duluth, Minn.: A. J. Publishing Co., 1975.

Haight, William. *Retail Advertising.* Morristown, N.J.: General Learning Press, 1976.

Milton, Shirley F. *Advertising for Modern Retailers.* New York: Fairchild Books, 1981.

Ocko, Judy Young. *Retail Advertising Copy: The How, the What, the Why.* Wheaton, Ill.: Dynamo, 1983.

Ocko, Judy Young, and Rosenblum, M. L. *How to Be a Retail Advertising Pro.* Wheaton, Ill.: Dynamo, 1977.

Pegler, Martin M., ed. *Store Windows That Sell.* New York: Art Direction Book Co., 1981.

Rosenblum, M. L. *How to Design Effective Store Advertising.* Rev. ed. Wheaton, Ill.: Dynamo, 1983.

Rosenblum, M. L., and Ocko, Judy Young. *The Secret Ingredients of Good Advertising.* New York: National Retail Merchants, 1974.

Spitzer, Harry, and Schwartz, F. Richard. *Inside Retail Sales Promotion and Advertising.* New York: Harper & Row, 1982.

Watkins, Don. *Newspaper Advertising Handbook.* Columbia, S.C.: Newspaper Book Service, 1980.

———. *Guide to Newspaper Ad Layout.* Wheaton, Ill.: Dynamo, 1983.

Designer's Dictionary: A Handbook of Design Ideas for Retail Display. Lockport, N.Y.: Upson Company, 1974.

Broadcast advertising

Abrahams, Howard P. *Making TV Pay Off: A Retailer's Guide to Television Advertising.* New York: Fairchild Books, 1975.

Arlen, Michael J. *Thirty Seconds.* New York: Farrar, Straus & Giroux, 1980. (About AT&T's "Reach Out and Touch Someone" commercial.)

Baldwin, Huntley. *Creating Effective TV Commercials.* Chicago: Crain Books, 1982.

Bellaire, Arthur. *Controlling Your TV Commercial Costs.* Chicago: Crain Books, 1977.

Bergendorff, Fred L., and others. *Broadcast Advertising & Promotion.* New York: Hastings House, 1983.

Busch, H. Ted, and Landeck, Terry. *The Making of a Television Commercial.* New York: Macmillan, 1981.

Clarke, Beverley. *Graphic Design in Educational Television.* New York: Watson-Guptill, 1974.

Coe, Michelle E. *How to Write for Television.* New York: Crown Publishers, 1980.

Conrad, Jon J. *The TV Commercial: How It Is Made.* New York: Van Nostrand Reinhold, 1983.

Gradus, Ben. *Directing the Television Commercial.* New York: Hastings House, 1981.

Halas, John, and Manvell, Roger. *Computer Animation.* New York: Hastings House, 1974.

Heighton, Elizabeth J., and Cunningham, Don R. *Advertising in the Broadcast Media.* Belmont, Calif: Wadsworth, 1976.

Hurrell, Ron. *Van Nostrand Reinhold Manual of Television Graphics.* New York: Van Nostrand Reinhold, 1974.

Kaatz, Ron. *Cable: An Advertiser's Guide to the Electronic Media.* Chicago: Crain Books, 1983.

Kurtz, Bruce. *Spots: The Popular Art of American Television Commercials.* New York: Arts Communications (14 East 11th St., 10003), 1977.

Lockhart, Ron, and Weissman, Dick. *Audio in Advertising.* New York: Frederick Ungar, 1982.

Murphy, Jonne. *Handbook of Radio Advertising.* Radnor, Pa.: Chilton Book Co., 1980.

Norback, Peter, and Norback, Craig. *Great Songs of Madison Avenue.* New York: Quadrangle Books, 1976.

Price, Jonathan. *The Best Thing on TV: Commercials.* New York: Viking Press, 1978.

Seiden, Hank. *Advertising Pure and Simple.* New York: Amacom, (American Management Associations), 1976. (Mostly about TV commercials.)

White, Hooper. *How to Produce a Television Commercial.* Chicago: Crain Books, 1981.

Woodward, Walt. *An Insider's Guide to Advertising Music: Everything You Must Know for TV and Radio.* New York: Art Direction Book Co., 1982.

Zeigler, Sherilyn K., and Howard, Herbert H. *Broadcast Advertising: A Comprehensive Working Textbook.* Columbus, Ohio: Grid Publishing, 1978.

Direct-mail advertising

Arnold, Edmund C. *The Making of Flyers, Folders, and Brochures.* Chicago: Lawrence Ragan Communications, 1983.

Brann, Christian. *Direct Mail and Direct Response Promotion.* New York: Halstead Press, John Wiley & Sons, 1973.

Hodgson, Richard S. *The Dartnell Direct Mail and Mail Order Handbook.* Chicago: Dartnell Corp., 1977.

Hurlburt, Allen F. *Publication Design.* 2d ed. New York: Van Nostrand Reinhold, 1976.

Jones, Gerre. *How to Prepare Professional Design Brochures.* New York: McGraw-Hill, 1976.

Keller, Mitchell. *The KRC Guide to Direct Mail.* Hartsdale, N.Y.: Public Service Materials Center, 1981.

Kobs, Jim. *Profitable Direct Marketing.* Chicago: Crain Books, 1980.

Lumley, James E. *How to Sell More Real Estate by Using Direct Mail.* 2d ed. New York: Ronald Press, 1982.

Maas, Jane. *Better Brochures, Catalogs and Mailing Pieces.* New York: St. Martin's Press, 1981.

Nash, Edward L. *Direct Marketing.* New York: McGraw-Hill, 1981.

Nelson, Roy Paul. *Publication Design.* 3d ed. Dubuque, Iowa: Wm. C. Brown Company Publishers, 1983.

Reuss, Carol, and Silvis, Donn. *Inside Organizational Communication.* New York: Longman, 1981.

Smith, Cortland Gray. *Magazine Layout: Principles, Patterns, Practices.* Plandome, N.Y.: published by the author, 1973.

Sroge, Maxwell. *Inside the Leading Mail Order Houses.* Colorado Springs, Colo.: Maxwell Sroge Publishing, 1982.

Stone, Bob. *Successful Direct Marketing Methods.* 3d ed. Chicago: Crain Books, 1984.

Sutter, Jan. *Slinging Ink: A Practical Guide to Producing Booklets, Newspapers, and Ephemeral Publications.* Los Altos, Calif.: William Kaufmann, 1982.

White, Jan V. *Designing . . . for Magazines.* New York: R. R. Bowker, 1976.

————. *Editing by Design.* New York: R. R. Bowker, 1974.

Williams, Patrick R. *The Employee Annual Report.* Chicago: Lawrence Ragan Communications, 1983.

The Direct Marketing Executive's Workbook. Rolling Hills Estates, Calif.: Direct Marketing News Digest (708 Silver Spur Road, 90274), 1980.

Fact Book on Direct Response Marketing. New York: Direct Mail/Marketing Assoc., 1979.

Posters and point-of-purchase advertising

Ades, Dawn, et al. *The 20th-Century Poster.* New York: Abbeville Press, 1984.

Berger, Arthur Asa. *Signs in Contemporary Culture.* New York: Longman, 1984.

Gallo, Max. *The Poster in History.* New York: McGraw-Hill, 1974.

Kobal, John. *50 Years of Movie Posters.* New York: Bounty Books, 1976.

Margolin, Victor; Brichta, Ira; and Brichta, Vivian. *The Promise and the Product: 200 Years of American Advertising Posters.* New York: Macmillan, 1979.

Yanker, Gary. *Prop Art: Over 1000 Contemporary Political Posters.* Greenwich, Conn.: New York Graphic Society, 1972.

Trademarks, logotypes, book jackets, record covers, packages

Carter, David D., ed. *The Book of American Trade Marks.* 4 vols. Chicago: Crain Books, 1972–1976.

————. *Designing Corporate Identity Programs for Small Corporations.* New York: Art Direction Book Co., 1982.

Cooper, Al, ed. *World of Logotypes: The Trademark Encyclopedia.* New York: Hastings House, 1976. (Vol. 2 published in 1980.)

Dean, Roger, ed. *The Album Cover Album.* New York: A & W, 1977.

Diamond, Sidney A. *Trademark Problems and How to Avoid Them.* Chicago: Crain Books, 1973.

Dichter, Ernest. *Packaging: The Sixth Sense.* Boston: Cahners Books, 1975.

Dreyfuss, Henry. *Symbol Sourcebook.* New York: McGraw-Hill, 1972. (Eight thousand universal symbols and signs.)

Duncan, Hugh Dalziel. *Symbols in Society.* New York: Oxford University Press, 1974.

Errigo, Angie. *Rock Album Art.* New York: Mayflower Books, 1979.

Herdeg, Walter, ed. *Graphis Record Covers.* New York: Hastings House, 1974.

Kuwayama, Yasaburo. *Trade Marks & Symbols.* 2 vols. New York: Van Nostrand Reinhold, 1973.

Neubauer, Robert S. *Packaging: The Contemporary Media.* New York: Van Nostrand Reinhold, 1973.

Pattison, Polly. *How to Design a Nameplate.* Chicago: Lawrence Ragan Communications, 1982.

Ricci, Franco Maria, and Ferrari, Corinna, eds. *Top Symbols and Trademarks of the World.* 7 vols. Milan, Italy: Deco Press, 1975.

Roth, Laszlo. *Package Design: An Introduction to the Art of Packaging.* Englewood Cliffs, N.J.: Prentice-Hall, 1981.

Sacharow, Stanley. *Packaging Design.* New York: Photographic Book Company, 1982.

Schmittel, Wolfgang. *Process Visual: The Development of Corporate Visibility.* New York: Hastings House, 1978.

Selame, Elinor, and Selame, Joe. *Developing a Corporate Identity: How to Stand Out in the Crowd.* New York: Lebhar-Friedman, 1975.

Smeets, René. *Signs, Symbols & Ornaments.* New York: Van Nostrand Reinhold, 1976.

Stern, Walter. *Stern's Handbook of Package Design.* New York: John Wiley & Sons, 1981.

Thorgerson, Storm; Dean, Roger; and Howells, David; eds. *The Second Volume Album Cover Album.* New York: A & W Visual Library, 1983.

Werkman, Casper J. *Trademarks: Their Creation, Psychology and Perception.* New York: Barnes & Noble, 1974.

White, William W., and Ravenscroft, Byfleet G. *Trademarks Throughout the World.* New York: Boardman, Clark Company, 1973.

Top Symbols & Trademarks of the World. 7 vols. Chicago: Marquis Who's Who, 1975.

Trade Names Directory. 2 vols. Detroit: Gale Research Co., 1976.

Careers

Berryman, Gregg. *Designing Creative Resumés and Portfolios.* Los Altos, Calif.: William Kaufmann, 1984.

Craig, James. *Graphic Design Career Guide.* New York: Watson-Guptill, 1983.

Crawford, Tad, and Kopelman, Arie. *Selling Your Graphic Design and Illustration.* New York: St. Martin's Press, 1981.

Haas, Ken. *How to Get a Job in Advertising.* New York: Art Direction Book Co., 1981.

Holden, Donald. *Art Career Guide.* 4th ed. New York: Watson-Guptill, 1983.

Kirkpatrick, Frank. *How to Get the Right Job in Advertising.* Chicago: Contemporary Books, 1982.

Lewis, William, and Cornelius, Hal. *Career Guide for Sales and Marketing.* New York: Monarch Press, 1983.

Marquand, Ed. *How To Prepare Your Portfolio.* 2d ed. New York: Art Direction Books, 1982.

Montaperto, Nicki. *The Freelancer's Career Book.* New York: Arco Publishing, 1983.

Paetro, Maxine. *How To Put Your Book Together and Get a Job in Advertising.* New York: Executive Communications, 1979.

Winters, Karen. *Your Career in Advertising.* New York: Arco Publishing, 1980.

Zimmerman, Caroline A. *How to Break Into the Media Professions.* Garden City, N.Y.: Doubleday, 1981.

Index